Opening Note

What you are about to read is a deeply personal work and complete expression of its author's exploration of the truth. As a result, we strongly encourage you to explore all of the details and implications of anything you discover or encounter as a result of this work.

Additionally, in accordance with The Mad Duck Coalition's mission of encouraging and providing intellectual stimulation of *all* kinds, we do not—and *cannot*—endorse any of the ideas presented by any member of our flock.

The only things we can—and *do*—endorse are the authorial integrity of the works we publish and the quality of intellectual engagements that they produce and inspire.

The Fate of Analysis

ANALYTIC PHILOSOPHY FROM FREGE TO THE ASH-HEAP OF HISTORY, AND TOWARD A RADICAL KANTIAN PHILOSOPHY OF THE FUTURE

By Robert Hanna

New York

2021 The Mad Duck Coalition ™ First Edition

THE MAD DUCK COALITION, its imprints, and colophones are trademarks of The Mad Duck Coalition, LLC.

For information about our special discounts for libraries, reviews, bookstores, and academic professionals, contact us through our form at thmaduco.org

Copyright © 2021 by Robert Hanna

All rights reserved. No part of this book may be used or reproduced in any form or any manner whatsoever without written permission from the publisher except in the case of brief quotations embodied in critical articles and reviews.

Published in the United States under In The Weeds, an imprint of The Mad Duck Coalition, LLC, New York.

Cover art by Otto Paans

ISBN: 978-1-956389-00-5

Library of Congress Control Number: 2021945765

www.themadduckcoalition.org

Table of Contents

Preface & Acknowledgments i

A Note on References to Kant's and Wittgenstein's Works iii

I. Introduction 1

II. Classical Analytic Philosophy, Frege, Husserl, and Psychologism 7

II.1 What Classical Analytic Philosophy Is: A Potted History, and Two Basic Theses 7
II.2 What Classical Analytic Philosophy Officially Isn't: Its Conflicted Anti-Kantianism 10
II.3 Classical Analytic Philosophy Characterized in Simple, Subtler, and Subtlest Ways ... 10
II.4 Three Kinds of Philosophical Analysis: Decompositional, Transformative, and Conceptual 11
II.5 Frege, the Father of the Founding Trinity of Classical Analytic Philosophy 12
II.6 Frege's Project of (Transformative or Reductive) Analysis 13
II.7 Frege's Dead End 14
II.8 Frege's Semantics of Sense and Reference 15
II.9 Some Biggish Problems for Frege's Semantics 17
II.10 Husserl, Logic, and the Critique of Logical Psychologism 20
    II.10.1 Introduction 20
    II.10.2 What Logical Psychologism is, and Its Three Cardinal Sins 22
    II.10.3 Husserl's Three Basic Arguments Against Logical Psychologism 26
II.10.3a Husserl's Argument Against LP From LP's Modal Reductionism About Logic (MRL) 26
II.10.3b Husserl's Argument Against LP From LP's Epistemic Empiricism About Logic (EEL) 27
II.10.3c Husserl's Argument Against LP From LP's Skeptical Relativism About Logic (SRL) 28
    II.10.4 Has Husserl Begged the Question Against Logical Psychologism? Enter The Logocentric Predicament, and a Husserlian Way Out 30

III. Moore, Phenomenology, Anti-Idealism, and Meinong's World 35

III.1 G.E. Moore, the Second Founding Trinitarian of Classical Analytic Philosophy ... 35
III.2 Brentano on Phenomenology, Mental Phenomena, and Intentionality 36
III.3 Husserl on Phenomenology and Intentionality 41
III.4 Moore and the Nature of Judgment 46
III.5 Moore and the Refutation of Idealism 47
III.6 Meinong's World 48

IV. Russell, Unlimited Logicism, Acquaintance, and Description 55

IV.1 Russell Beyond Brentano, Husserl, Moore, and Meinong 55
IV.2 Russell and Mathematical Logic *versus* Kant 56
IV.3 Russell's Unlimited Logicist Project 57
IV.4 Pursued by Logical Furies: Russell's Paradox Again 57
IV.5 Russell's "Fido"-Fido Theory of Meaning 59
IV.6 Knowledge-by-Acquaintance and Knowledge-by-Description 59

IV.7 Russell's Theory of Descriptions 60
IV.8 Russell's Multiple-Relation Theory of Judgment 62
IV.9 Russellian Analysis, Early Wittgenstein, and Impredicativity Again 63
IV.10 Russell and The Philosophy of Logical Atomism 66

V. Wittgenstein and the *Tractatus* 1: Propositions 1-2.063 69

V.1 A Brief Synopsis of the *Tractatus* 69
V.2 The *Tractatus* in Context 72
V.3 The Basic Structure of the *Tractatus*: A Simple Picture 73
V.4 Tractarian Ontology 73
V.5 Reconstructing Wittgenstein's Reasoning 74
V.6 What *Are* the Objects or Things? 74
V.7 The Role of Logic in Tractarian Ontology 75
V.8 Colorless Objects/Things 75
V.9 Tractarian Ontology, Necessity, and Contingency 75
V.10 Some Initial Worries, and Some Possible Wittgensteinian Counter-Moves 76

VI. Wittgenstein and the *Tractatus* 2: Propositions 2.013-5.55 79

VI.1 What is Logical Space? What is Real Space? 79
VI.2 Atomic Facts *Necessarily Are* in Real Space, But Objects or Things Themselves *Necessarily Aren't* in Real Space 79
VI.3 Logical Space is Essentially More Comprehensive than Real Space 80
VI.4 Why There Can't/Kant Be a Non-Logical World 81
VI.5 A Worry About Wittgenstein's Conception of Logic: *Non*-Classical Logics 82
VI.6 What is a Tractarian Proposition? 83
VI.7 Naming Objects or Things, and Picturing Atomic Facts 84
VI.8 Signs, Symbols, Sense, Truth, and Judgment 88
VI.9 Propositions Again 91
VI.10 Language and Thought 93

VII. Wittgenstein and the *Tractatus* 3: Propositions 4–5.61 95

VII.1 The Logocentric Predicament, Version 3.0: Justifying Deduction 95
VII.2 The Logical Form of Deduction 95
VII.3 Logic Must Take Care of Itself 97
VII.4 Tautologies and Contradictions 97
VII.5 What is Logic? 98
VII.6 Logic is the A Priori Essence of Language 100
VII.7 Logic is the A Priori Essence of Thought 101
VII.8 Logic is the A Priori Essence of the World 102

VIII. Wittgenstein and the Tractatus 4: Propositions 5.62 – 7 105

VIII.1 Tractarian Solipsism and Tractarian Realism 105
VIII.2 Tractarian Solipsism 107
VIII.3 Tractarian Realism 108
VIII.4 What About Mathematics? 110
VIII.5 Is the *Tractatus*'s Point an Ethical One? 111
VIII.6 The Meaning of Life 117
VIII.7 Three Basic Worries About the *Tractatus* 118

VIII.8 Natural Science and the Worry About the Simplicity of the Objects or Things 121
VIII.9 Natural Science and the Worry About the Logical Independence of Atomic Facts
.... 122
VIII.10 Tractarian Mysticism and the Worry About Metaphilosophy: How to Throw
Away the Ladder 122

IX. Carnap, Logical Empiricism, and The Great Divide 125

IX.1 Carnap Before and After the *Tractatus* 125
IX.2 Carnap, The Vienna Circle, and The Elimination of Metaphysics 126
IX.3 The Verifiability Principle and Its Fate 130
IX.4 The Davos Conference and The Great Divide 131

X. Gödel-Incompleteness, Tarski, and Formal Piety: The Death of Classical Logicism in Thirty-One Steps 135

X.1 Two Foxes in The Vienna Circle's Henhouse: Gödel and Tarski 135
X.2 Twenty-Five of the Thirty-One Steps 135
X.3 Tarski's Semantic Conception of Truth 139
X.4 Conclusion: The Last Six Steps 140

XI. Wittgenstein and the *Investigations* 1: Preface, and §§1-27 143

XI.1 From the *Tractatus* to the *Investigations* 143
XI.2 The Thesis That Meaning Is Use 146
XI.3 A Map of the *Investigations* 147
XI.4 The Critique of Pure Reference: What the Builders Did 149

XII. Wittgenstein and the *Investigations* 2: §§28-242 161

XII.1 The Picture Theory, and the Vices of Simplicity and Isomorphism 161
XII.2 Wittgenstein's Argument Against The Picture Theory: A Rational Reconstruction .. 161
XII.3 Understanding and Rule-Following 162
XII.4 Wittgenstein's Rule-Following Paradox: The Basic Rationale 165
XII.5 Wittgenstein's Rule-Following Paradox: A Rational Reconstruction 166
XII.6 Kripkenstein's Rule-Following Paradox: Why Read Kripke Too? 167
XII.7 Kripkenstein's Rule-Following Paradox: A Rational Reconstruction 168
XII.8 How to Solve The Paradox: Wittgenstein's Way and Kripkenstein's Way 169
    XII.8.1 Wittgenstein and The Rule-Following Paradox: A Rational Reconstruction 171
    XII.8.2 Kripkenstein and The Rule-Following Paradox: A Rational Reconstruction 174

XIII. Wittgenstein and the *Investigations* 3: §§242-315 177

XIII.1 What is a Private Language? 177
XIII.2 The Private Language Argument: A Rational Reconstruction 178
XIII.3 Is Wittgenstein a Behaviorist? No. 181
XIII.4 Wittgenstein on Meanings, Sensations, and Human Mindedness: A Rational Reconstruction 183

XIV. Wittgenstein and the *Investigations* 4: §§316-693 and 174ᵉ-232ᵉ 187

XIV.1 Linguistic Phenomenology 187
XIV.2 Two Kinds of Seeing 188
XIV.3 Experiencing the Meaning of a Word 191
XIV.4 The Critique of Logical Analysis, and Logic-As-Grammar 194

XV. Coda: Wittgenstein and Kantianism 199

XV.1 World-Conformity 1: Kant, Transcendental Idealism, and Empirical Realism 201
XV.2 World-Conformity 2: Wittgenstein, Transcendental Solipsism, and Pure Realism 203
XV.3 World-Conformity 3: To Forms of Life 208
XV.4 The Critique of Self-Alienated Philosophy 1: Kant's Critical Metaphilosophy 210
XV.5 The Critique of Self-Alienated Philosophy 2: Wittgensteinian Analysis as Critique 211
XV.6 Wittgenstein, Kant, Scientism, and The Tragic Sense of Life 215

XVI. From Quine to Kripke and Analytic Metaphysics: The Adventures of the Analytic-Synthetic Distinction 217

XVI.1 Two Urban Legends of Post-Empiricism 217
XVI.2 A Very Brief History of The Analytic-Synthetic Distinction 222
XVI.3 Why the Analytic-Synthetic Distinction *Really* Matters 228
XVI.4 Quine's Critique of the Analytic-Synthetic Distinction, and a Meta-Critique 230
XVI.5 Three Dogmas of Post-Quineanism 247
XVI.6 So Much For Quine's Critique and The Three Dogmas 271

XVII. Crisis Management: Husserl's *Crisis*, Post-Classical Analytic Philosophy, and The Ash-Heap of History 273

XVII.1 Husserl's *Crisis* and Our Crisis 273
    XVII.1.1 Introduction 273
    XVII.1.2 The Thematic Structure of the *Crisis* 274
    XVII.1.3 Theme 1: A Husserlian Critique of Science 275
    XVII.1.4 Theme 2: A Teleological Interpretation of European Culture Since the 17th Century, Focused on the History of Modern Philosophy 278
    XVII.1.5 Theme 3: The Core Notion of the Life-World 279
    XVII.1.6 Theme 4: Transcendental Phenomenology 280
    XVII.1.7 Crisis? What Crisis? 283
XVII.2 Formal and Natural Science After 1945, and the Rise of Natural Mechanism . 287
XVII.3 The Emergence of Post-Classical Analytic Philosophy 288
XVII.4 The Two Images Problem and its Consequences 294
XVII.5 The Rise, Fall, and Normalization of Post-Modern Philosophy 295
XVII.6 Why Hasn't Post-Classical Analytic Philosophy Produced Any Important Ideas Since 1985? 297
    XVII.6.1 Analytic Metaphysics as a Copernican Devolution in Philosophy . 301
    XVII.6.2 A Reply to a Possible Objection 307
XVII.7 The Ballad of Donald Kalish and Angela Davis: A Micro-Study 310
    XVII.7.1 Introduction 310
    XVII.7.2 Stage-Setting 310

XVII.7.3 The Ballad 313
XVII.7.4 The Double Life Problem, and The Options 315
XVII.8 Zero for Conduct at The Pittsburgh School: Three Dogmas and Three Radical Kantian Alternatives 316
 XVII.8.1 Introduction 316
 XVII.8.2 PS-Conceptualism and PS-Inferentialism *versus* Strong Non-Conceptualism and Cognitive-Semantics-&-Human-Knowledge-Only-Within-The-Grip-of-The-Given 317
 XVII.8.3 PS-Metaphysical-Quietism *versus* Weak Transcendental Idealism ... 341
 XVII.8.4 Concluding UnPittsburghian Prelude to a Radical Kantian Philosophy of the Future 347

XVIII. Epilogue: The New Poverty of Philosophy and Its Second Copernican Revolution **349**

XVIII.1 Introduction 349
XVIII.2 Wittgenstein's Philosophy of Philosophy Revisited 350
XVIII.3 The New Poverty of Philosophy 354
XVIII.4 How is Philosophy Really Possible Inside the Professional Academy? A Global Metaphilosophical Problem 360
XVIII.5 Philosophy's Second Copernican Revolution, Part 1: The Radical Kantian *Metaphilosophical* Paradigm Shift to Anarcho- or Borderless Philosophy 362
XVIII.6 Philosophy's Second Copernican Revolution, Part 2: The Radical Kantian *Metaphysical* Paradigm Shift to Kantian Neo-Organicism 368
XVIII.7 Conclusion: Analytic Philosophy, The Owl of Minerva, and The Radical Kantian Phoenix of Future Philosophy 377

BIBLIOGRAPHY **379**

Preface & Acknowledgments

This book completes the long arc of a single twenty-year philosophical project, started in 2001 and completed in 2021, including revised versions of materials written at various times during those two decades. As the project evolved into its final form, I decided to combine (i) "quieter-voiced" critical-&-expository material in chapters II to XVI, with (ii) "louder-voiced" critical-&-expository as well as constructive-&-positive material in chapters XVII and XVIII. So, I'll begin with a *caveat lector*: the transition in style and tone between the quieter-voiced material and the louder-voiced material is intended by me to fuse together, and also segue between (i) a comprehensive and critical revisionist study of the history of Analytic philosophy, that's accessible to any philosophically-minded person and can be used in a high-level introductory way by them, (ii) a provocative critique of recent and contemporary post-classical Analytic philosophy and a passionately-felt description of a radical Kantian philosophy of the future.

Because this book has been twenty years in the making, it's humanly impossible to acknowledge everyone who substantially contributed to it and every social institution that significantly supported it. Collectively then, I thank you all most warmly! But in retrospect, a few people and institutions do stand out as special targets of my gratitude: Otto Paans, for his creative assistance with the cover design, several diagrams in the main text, and parts of chapter XVII; Michael Potter; Alex Oliver; Clare Hall Cambridge, for a visiting fellowship in 1998; Fitzwilliam College Cambridge (flanked on one side by the house where Wittgenstein died, and just down the road on the other side from the cemetery where Wittgenstein, Moore, Ramsey, and Anscombe are all buried), for visiting fellowships in 2000, 2001, 2003-2004, and 2006, and a Bye Fellowship in 2008-2009; and the Cambridge Faculty of Philosophy, for invitations to present talks to the Moral Sciences Club in 1994, 2003, and 2008, for the opportunity to supervise and/or lecture part-time in the Faculty during my visiting fellowships, and for a full-time Temporary Lectureship in 2008-2009. Of course, none of those are in any way responsible for the way the project turned out: indeed, in the particular cases of Michael and Alex, they're probably gobsmacked. Nevertheless, in any case, I'm *very* grateful to them both for helping to arrange my visits to Cambridge, and also for their philosophical conversation and friendship when I was living there.

Otherwise, I must also much-more-than-merely-very-gratefully acknowledge the life-companionship, love, and endless patience of my wife, Martha Hanna, our daughter Elizabeth, my parents Alan and Dianne Hanna, and my brothers Douglas and Donald: I love you all too, with all my heart.

A Note on References to Kant's and Wittgenstein's Works

(1) Kant: For convenience, I cite Kant's works infra-textually in parentheses. The citations include both an abbreviation of the English title and also the corresponding volume and page numbers in the standard "Akademie" edition of Kant's works: *Kants gesammelte Schriften*, edited by the Königlich Preussischen (now Deutschen) Akademie der Wissenschaften (Berlin: G. Reimer [now de Gruyter], 1902). For references to the first *Critique*, I follow the common practice of giving page numbers from the A (1781) and B (1787) German editions only. And I occasionally modify the English translations slightly, whenever it seems appropriate to the point I'm making. Here are the relevant abbreviations and English translations:

C: *Immanuel Kant: Correspondence, 1759-99.* Trans. A. Zweig. Cambridge: Cambridge Univ. Press, 1999.

CF: *The Conflict of the Faculties.* Trans. M. Gregor. Lincoln, NE: Univ. of Nebraska Press, 1979.

CPJ: *Critique of the Power of Judgment.* Trans. P. Guyer and E. Matthews. Cambridge: Cambridge Univ. Press, 2000.

CPR: *Critique of Pure Reason.* Trans. P. Guyer and A. Wood. Cambridge: Cambridge Univ. Press, 1997.

CPrR: *Critique of Practical Reason.* Trans. M. Gregor. In I. Kant, *Immanuel Kant: Practical Philosophy.* Cambridge: Cambridge Univ. Press, 1996. Pp. 139-271.

MFNS: *Metaphysical Foundations of Natural Science.* Trans. M. Friedman. Cambridge: Cambridge Univ. Press, 2004.

Prol: *Prolegomena to Any Future Metaphysics.* Trans. G. Hatfield. Cambridge: Cambridge Univ. Press, 2004.

Rel: *Religion within the Boundaries of Mere Reason.* Trans. A. Wood and G. Di Giovanni. In I. Kant, *Immanuel Kant: Religion and Rational Theology.* Cambridge: Cambridge Univ. Press, 1996. Pp. 57-215.

WiE: "An Answer to the Question: 'What is Enlightenment?'" Trans. M. Gregor. In Kant, *Immanuel Kant: Practical Philosophy.* Pp. 17-22.

*(2) **Wittgenstein:*** Again for convenience, I cite Wittgenstein's two major works, *Tractatus Logico-Philosophicus* and *Philosophical Investigations*, infratextually in parentheses. I cite the *Tractatus* by its abbreviated title (*TLP*) and proposition numbers, and the *Investigations* by its abbreviated title (*PI*) and paragraph numbers or English page numbers. Here are the English translations I've used, both of which usefully display the German and English texts in parallel on facing pages:

> TLP: *Tractatus Logico-Philosophicus.* Trans. C.K. Ogden. London: Routledge & Kegan Paul, 1981.

> PI: *Philosophical Investigations.* Trans. G.E.M. Anscombe. New York: Macmillan, 1953.

I. Introduction

> The truly apocalyptic view of the world is that things do not repeat themselves. It isn't absurd, e.g., to believe that the age of science and technology is the beginning of the end for humanity; that the idea of great progress is a delusion, along with the idea that the truth will ultimately be known; that there is nothing good or desirable about scientific knowledge and that mankind, in seeking it, is falling into a trap. It is by no means obvious that this is not how things are. (Wittgenstein, 1980: p.56e)

The online *Philosophical Papers* survey of mainstream professional academic philosophers conducted by David Bourget and David Chalmers in November-December 2009, showed that 81% of the respondents self-identified as belonging to the Analytic tradition.[1] The survey population included professional philosophers from 40 different countries, although principally the USA and the UK. And a few years later, in 2013, Michael Beaney, the editor of *The Oxford Handbook of the History of Analytic Philosophy*, wrote in Whig-historical mode that

> Analytic philosophy is now generally seen as the dominant philosophical tradition in the English-speaking world, and has been so from at least the middle of the last century. Over the last two decades its influence has also been steadily growing in the non-English-speaking world. (Beaney, 2013: p. 3)

In a social-institutional sense, little or nothing has changed in professional philosophy since 2013. Therefore, the Analytic tradition enjoys and exerts intellectual and social-institutional domination, and indeed cultural hegemony, over how philosophy is conceived and practiced in the recent and contemporary professional academy, worldwide.[2]

Shortly after the turn of the millennium, I published a book in which I critically explored some of the deep connections between Immanuel Kant's *Critique of Pure Reason* and the historical and conceptual foundations of the European and Anglo-American tradi-

---

1 See (Bourget and Chalmers, 2014): 2486 out of the 3057 professional philosophers who replied to a question asking them to specify a philosophical tradition to which they belonged, said they belonged to the Analytic tradition. See also Bourget and Chalmers, "What Do Philosophers Believe?" It's significant, I think, that it took five years (i.e., until 2014) for the interpretive follow-up article to be written up and published, and also that the article itself has little or nothing to say beyond summarizing the response data and pointing out various statistical correlations. This in turn strongly suggests that Bourget, Chalmers, and their collaborators at the American Philosophical Association, together with the journal editors, all assume without argument or critical reflection that the Analytic tradition's stranglehold on professional academic philosophy since the 1950s is an obvious, inevitable, and immutable ideological and social-institutional fact, rather like the 2nd Amendment to the US Constitution, advanced capitalism, or the neoliberal nation-State.

2 There was a follow-up PhilPapers survey conducted during October and November 2020, whose results haven't been released yet (as of July 2021); see (Bourget, 2020). But in any case, it seems to me very unlikely that there will be any significant differences between the results of the 2009 survey and those of the 2020 survey.

tion of Analytic philosophy, from Gottlob Frege's 1884 *Foundations of Arithmetic* to W.V.O. Quine's 1951 "Two Dogmas of Empiricism" (Hanna, 2001). More specifically, in that book I argued (i) that Analytic philosophy emerged by virtue of its intellectual struggles with some of the central doctrines of the *Critique of Pure Reason*, (ii) that a careful examination of this foundational debate shows that Kant's doctrines were never refuted but instead, for various reasons, only rejected, and (iii) that ironically enough it's the foundations of *Analytic* philosophy, not the Critical philosophy, that are inherently shaky. In 2006, I followed that up with another book—actually the two books were originally parts of the same 800- or 900-page, single-spaced, monster-manuscript—which extended the same general line of argument, by critically exploring some of the equally deep connections between the Critical philosophy and Analytic philosophy from 1950 to the end of the 20th century (Hanna, 2006a). And in 2008, I published a long essay that began like this:

> Alfred North Whitehead ... quotably wrote in 1929 that "the safest general characterization of the European philosophical tradition is that it consists of a series of footnotes to Plato."[3] The same could be said, perhaps with even greater accuracy, of the twentieth-century Euro-American philosophical tradition and Immanuel Kant. In this sense the twentieth century was the post-Kantian century.
>
> Twentieth-century philosophy in Europe and the USA was dominated by two distinctive and (after 1945) officially opposed traditions: the analytic tradition and the phenomenological tradition. Very simply put, the analytic tradition was all about logic and analyticity, and the phenomenological tradition was all about consciousness and intentionality. Ironically enough however, despite their official Great Divide, both the analytic and the phenomenological traditions were essentially continuous and parallel critical developments from an earlier dominant neo-Kantian tradition. This, by the end of the nineteenth century, had vigorously reasserted the claims of Kant's transcendental idealism against Hegel's absolute idealism and the other major systems of post-Kantian German Idealism, under the unifying slogan "Back to Kant!" So again, ironically enough, both the analytic and phenomenological traditions were alike founded on, and natural outgrowths from, Kant's Critical Philosophy.
>
> By the end of the twentieth century, however—and this time sadly rather than ironically—both the analytic and phenomenological traditions had not only explicitly rejected their own Kantian foundations and roots but also had effectively undermined themselves philosophically, even if by no means institutionally. On the one hand the analytic tradition did so by abandoning its basic methodological conception of analysis as the process of logically decomposing propositions into conceptual or metaphysical "simples" as the necessary preliminary to a logical reconstruction of the same propositions, and by also jettisoning the corresponding idea of a sharp, exhaustive, and significant "analytic-synthetic" distinction. The phenomenological tradition on the other hand abandoned its basic methodolog-

---
3 (Whitehead, 1978: p. 39, footnote in the original).

ical conception of phenomenology as "seeing essences" with a priori certainty under a "transcendental-phenomenological reduction," and also jettisoned the corresponding idea of a "transcendental ego" as the metaphysical ground of consciousness and intentionality.

One way of interpreting these sad facts is to say that just insofar as analytic philosophy and phenomenology alienated themselves from their Kantian origins, they stultified themselves. This is the first unifying thought behind this [essay], and it is a downbeat one. The second unifying thought, which however is contrastively upbeat, is that both the analytic and phenomenological traditions, now in conjunction instead of opposition, could rationally renew themselves in the twenty-first century by critically recovering their Kantian origins and by seriously re-thinking and re-building their foundations in the light of this critical recovery. Or in other words: *Forward to Kant*. (Hanna, 2008b: pp. 149-150)

During the thirteen years since that essay appeared—alongside other projects—I've worked on elaborating and extending those ideas, and writing them up into this book, thereby completing a twenty-year trilogy about the conceptual, epistemic, and metaphysical foundations, history, and fate of Analytic philosophy, all from a Kantian point of view, that began with *Kant and the Foundations of Analytic Philosophy* (2001), and *Kant, Science, and Human Nature* (2006).

More precisely, however, *The Fate of Analysis: Analytic Philosophy From Frege To The Ash-Heap of History*,[4] *And Toward A Radical Kantian Philosophy of The Future*[5] is a comprehensive and critical revisionist history of Analytic philosophy from the 1880s to the present, with special reference (i) to its Kantian provenance, (ii) to the unique, subversive, and indeed revolutionary contributions of Wittgenstein, both early and late, (iii) to illuminating comparisons and contrasts with phenomenology during the period of the intellectual and social-institutional emergence and ascendancy of classical Analytic philosophy, from 1880 to 1950, (iv) to its steady decline and ultimate fall during the period of post-classical Analytic philosophy, from 1950 to the third decade of the 21st century—a dive, crash, and burn that are partially due to its dogmatic obsession with *scientific naturalism* (especially including the sub-doctrines of *scientism* and *natural mechanism*), but also intimately entangled and synchronized with the emergence, triumph, and finally domination and cultural hegemony of academic hyper-professionalism (Schmidt, 2000; Maiese and Hanna, 2019: ch. 4; and Turner, 2019) in the larger context of the neoliberal nation-State, together with what, riffing on Eisenhower's famous phrase, "the military-industrial complex," I've dubbed "the military-industrial-university-digital complex," aka *The Hyper-State* (Hanna, 2021g; Herman and Chomsky, 1988; Mills, 1956);[6] and finally (v) to how, from the ashes of the

---
4 My use of "the ash-heap of history" repurposes Petrarch's and Trotsky's famous/notorious good-riddances to Rome and the Mensheviks respectively.

5 My use of "a philosophy of the future" repurposes the sub-title of Nietzsche's brilliantly edgy 1886 book,*Beyond Good and Evil: Prelude to a Philosophy of the Future*.

6 For an explicit definition of what I mean by *The Hyper-State*, see section XVIII.3 below.

Analytic tradition, a radical Kantian philosophy of the future can and should arise like a phoenix during the next two decades of the 21st century.

Therefore, this book is also a study in *radical metaphilosophy*, with sociopolitical overtones and undertones, and a provocative upshot. In 1981, Richard Rorty wrote:

> In saying that "analytic philosophy" now has only a stylistic and sociological unity, I am not suggesting that analytic philosophy is a bad thing, or is in bad shape. (Rorty, 1982b: p. 217)

Now forty years later, in the 2020s, with 20-20 hindsight and then some, I'm going one or two radical steps beyond Rorty (Hanna, 2020a) by suggesting *and* asserting, not only "that analytic philosophy is … in bad shape," but also that it's "a bad thing." And this is so, **first**, because classical Analytic philosophy was theoretically hobbled by Kurt Gödel's profoundly important first and second incompleteness theorems in the early 1930s, which, when they're taken together with Alfred Tarski's semantic conception of truth in formalized languages,[7] amount to a logico-mathematical 1-2 punch that collectively killed the classical Frege-Whitehead-Russell logicist project for reducing mathematics to logic, **second**, because what remained of classical Analytic philosophy as a serious and substantive philosophical program was in fact effectively brought to an end in the middle of the 20th century by W.V.O. Quine's devastating critique of the analytic-synthetic distinction—indeed, the demise of "the old analysis" was even explicitly noted by J.O. Urmson a decade after the end of World War II (Urmson, 1956), **third**, because of the dogmatic obsession of post-Quinean, post-classical Analytic philosophy with scientific naturalism after 1950, and above all, **fourth**, because of post-classical Analytic philosophy's spiraling descent into academic hyper-professionalism and mind-manacled complicity with the neoliberal nation-state and military-industrial-university-digital complex, aka The Hyper-State, in the late 20th century and the first two decades of the 21st century, *therefore* **fifth**, the 140-year tradition of Analytic philosophy has actually bottomed out and burned up from within, existing now only as a dominant and indeed culturally hegemonic social-institutional husk and Potemkin village inside professional academic philosophy, that most urgently needs to be and ought to be replaced by something essentially different and essentially better—in my opinion, a radical Kantian philosophy of the future, during the next twenty years.

Or in other and fewer words, to update not only the classical slogan of the 19th century neo-Kantians (*Back to Kant!*), but also my back-to-the-future-style Kantian slogan from 2008 (*Forward to Kant!*), I'm hereby issuing a philosophical clarion call for the rest of the 21st century: *Forward and leftward to Kant!*

Finally, in that Kantian connection, here's another *caveat lector*. To be sure, my comprehensive and critical revisionist interpretation of the Analytic tradition and my positive proposal for a philosophy of the future are both Kantian in inspiration. But although I'll sometimes refer to Kant's writings, my view is *neither* intended to be a scholarly interpreta-

---
7 For a compact explication of Tarski's semantic conception of truth, see section X.3 below.

tion of Kant's writings, *nor* is it in any way restricted by the requirement to remain consistent with or defend any of Kant's own doctrines (for example, his alleged noumenal realism, hatred of emotions, moral formalism and rigorism, coercive authoritarian neo-Hobbesian political liberalism, etc.) or his personal prejudices (for example, his alleged racism, sexism, xenophobia, etc.). Thus my overall account and argument are Kantian, but not so *damned* Kantian. This is a spin on Josiah Royce's pithy definition of idealism: "the world and the heavens, and the stars are all *real*, but not so *damned* real" (Royce, 1970: p. 217). In other words, what I'm arguing in *The Fate of Analysis* expresses a creative use of some Kantian ideas that are also independently defensible, and it diverges from either Kant's own writings or orthodox Kantianism *whenever* that's required by attentiveness to manifest reality and/or critical reflection. In view of the social-institutional facts I've called *The Kant Wars*, one element of which is a widespread *anti-Kantian bias* in contemporary philosophy (Hanna, 2020c), it's (unfortunately) necessary to make this point explicitly. So, in order to nail down that point both explicitly and also airtightly, I want to emphasize and re-emphasize from the outset that my overall account and argument are at most only *broadly Kantian*, but above all *radically Kantian*.

II. Classical Analytic Philosophy, Frege, Husserl, and Psychologism

II.1 What Classical Analytic Philosophy Is: A Potted History, and Two Basic Theses

During the period from 1880-1950, especially in Europe and North America, seven fundamental sociocultural or sociopolitical developments collectively provided the larger historical contextual matrix for the emergence and flourishing of classical Analytic philosophy.

First, from 1880 to 1950, humanity experienced radically increasing industrialization and the physical mechanization of production processes, driven by worldwide free-market economics and capitalist speculation.

Second, simultaneously, humanity experienced radically increasing sociopolitical nationalism, imperialism, and militarism, flowing disastrously into the global cataclysm of World War I (Strachan, 2005), the Russian Revolution, the 1918-1919 Influenza pandemic (Kent, 2013), and then the civil wars and other international conflicts in Central, Northern, and Eastern Europe that immediately succeeded the official end of The Great War and stretched into the early 1920s (Gewarth, 2016).

Third, these developments were followed in the mid-to-late 20s and early-to-mid 30s by hyperinflation in Germany, the Stock Market Crash in 1929, the worldwide Depression, and by the rise of fascism and imperialist militarism in Germany, Italy, and Japan. Indeed, the unabsorbed and unresolved sociocultural and sociopolitical fall-out from World War I primed Nazi fascism and its ideological mirror image, Bolshevik communism, alike.

Fourth, at the same time, there were revolutionary advances and transformations in the natural sciences, especially including (i) relativity physics, (ii) quantum mechanics, and (iii) cellular/molecular, evolutionary, and genetic approaches to biology (Kumar, 2010; Mayr, 1985). In particular, the classical Newtonian model of physics was overturned, and biology rejected models of Lamarckian inheritance and vitalism, paving the way for what later would become the Darwinist science of evolutionary development, aka *evo-devo*.

Fifth, simultaneously, and overlapping with these developments in the natural sciences, there were revolutionary advances and transformations in the formal sciences (especially including mathematical logic and pure mathematics) via Alfred North Whitehead's and Bertrand Russell's *Principia Mathematica*, Kurt Gödel's incompleteness theorems,[1] Alan Turing's work on computability and artificial intelligence, the (Alonzo) Church-Turing thesis claiming the necessary equivalence of Turing-computability and recursive functions, L.E.J. Brouwer's work on intuitionist logic and mathematics, David Hilbert's work on formalism and finitism, and Alfred Tarski's semantic conception of truth in formalized

---
[1] For a detailed but informal presentation of Gödel's incompleteness theorems, see ch. X below.

languages,[2] which captures the collective logical upshots of the failure of Whitehead-Russell logicism together with Gödel's profound insights into the incompleteness of mathematical logic and the logical independence of truth and proof.

Sixth, in the 1920s and 30s, there was an emerging set of anti-authoritarian, anti-totalitarian, dignitarian, democratic versions of socialism, for example, the Popular Front in France, Labor parties in the UK, Germany, and the Netherlands, the New Deal in the USA, and "prairie populist" socialism in Canada, as well as various forms of communism that rejected the authoritarian, totalitarian, anti-dignitarian, and anti-democratic models of their Bolshevik counterparts. These movements also expressed a general critique and a vigorous rejection of the alienation, dullness, and monotony inherent in industrial mechanization, advanced capitalism, and the modern division of labor.

And **seventh**, World War II happened from 1939-1945, forming as it were an historical black hole in the middle of the 20th century, indiscriminately and relentlessly absorbing, ending, and/or exploiting massive numbers of human lives and correspondingly massive amounts of intellectual energy, physical material, and sociopolitical energy, all in historically unprecedented ways (Weinberg, 2005). In effect, nothing could escape from the grip of this historical black hole for six years. But at the same time, World War II also created the human, intellectual, and sociopolitical conditions for scientific and technological developments in the decades immediately following the end of the War, especially after 1950. Moreover, these technological advances heavily determined how humanity conceptualized the relationship between the State and society. The idea of "engineering" an entire society and all its citizens gripped humanity, and had immediate and eventually massive philosophical, artistic, scientific, social, and political consequences.

Correspondingly, during the same period from 1880-1950, classical *neo-Kantian philosophy* in Germany and France (Willey, 1978; Köhnke, 1991; Luft and Capeillères, 2010; Beiser, 2014; Crowell, 2017; Heis, 2019; Clarke, 2019), and British *neo-Hegelian philosophy* (Hylton, 1990; Griffin, 1991), carrying over somewhat into the USA—see, for example., T.S. Eliot's Harvard PhD dissertation, "Knowledge and Experience in the Philosophy of F.H. Bradley"[3] and the philosophy of Josiah Royce more generally (Kuklick, 1997)—both came to a more or less bitter end. Slamming the door behind the idealists, and triumphantly (indeed, even triumphalistically) replacing them, and just as often also taking up their vacated university positions, a group of Young Turk *avant-garde* philosophers carrying the banner of the new tradition of classical Analytic philosophy came onto the scene, following on from the work of Gottlob Frege (as it were, the intellectual Father of the founding Trinity of classical Analytic philosophy), but led by G.E. Moore and Bertrand Russell (the other members of the founding Trinity—as it were, the Son and the Holy Ghost—who were,

---

2 For a compact presentation of Tarski's semantic conception of truth, see section X.3 below.

3 Actually, Eliot never bothered to defend his thesis in person, nor did he ever receive his PhD: so much for the attractions of professional academic philosophy. Relatedly, see James's "The Ph.D. Octopus."

appropriately enough, students and Apostles,[4] research fellows, and then lecturers at Trinity College, Cambridge University), by the young Ludwig Wittgenstein, another Trinity College genius and Apostle, by the even younger Frank Ramsey,[5] by The Vienna Circle Logical Empiricists/Positivists (especially Rudolf Carnap, but also including Gödel and Tarski), and by W.V.O. Quine. Moreover, in a sociocultural sense, classical Analytic philosophy also stood in an important elective affinity with the rise of what James C. Scott has aptly called "a high modernist ideology," or *high modernism* for short, which

> is best conceived as a strong, one might even say muscle-bound, version of the self-confidence about scientific and technical progress, the expansion of production, the growing satisfaction of human needs, the mastery of nature (including human nature), and, above all, the rational design of social order commensurate with the scientific understanding of natural laws (Scott, 1998: p. 4),

especially in the applied and fine arts, the formal and natural sciences, and engineering (Janik and Toulmin, 1973; Galison, 1990; The Vienna Circle, 1996; Reisch, 2005; Isaac, 2013). At the same time, the classical Analytic philosophers were also engaged in a serious intellectual competition with *phenomenology*, especially Husserlian transcendental phenomenology (Hanna, 2013b) and Heideggerian existential phenomenology (Friedman, 2000; Hanna, 2008b: 149-150; and also ch. IX below).

Bounded in a nutshell, however, classical Analytic philosophy is founded and grounded on two basic theses: (i) that all necessary truth is *logical truth*, which is the same as *analytic a priori truth*, and that there are no non-logical or non-analytic necessary truths, which I'll call *the thesis of modal monism*, and (ii) that all a priori knowledge is *knowledge of analytic truths* and that this knowledge follows directly from the process of analysis, which I'll call *the thesis of a-priori-knowledge-as-analysis* (Urmson, 1956; Pap, 1972: Hacking, 1975; French et al., 1981; Tugendhat, 1982: esp. part I; Bell and Cooper, 1990; Dummett, 1993; Hanna, 2001; Soames, 2003; Beaney, 2013; Isaac, 2019).

---

[4] That is, they were all members of the Cambridge Apostles, then as now, a highly-selective and highly exclusive Cambridge secret society and discussion group, whose members also include Henry Sidgwick, Whitehead, John Maynard Keynes, Frank Ramsey, and (somewhat fitfully) Wittgenstein. See, e.g., (Levy, 1980).

[5] There's been a recent burst of interest in Ramsey and his work. See, e.g., (Methven, 2015; Potter, 2019; Misak, 2020). For a long time, Ramsey had been mainly known as a co-translator of the *Tractatus* and as a minor figure in classical Analytic philosophy, although, to be sure, during his all-too-brief lifetime, he had already been exceptionally highly regarded by the Cambridge people and The Vienna Circle people alike(see, e.g., Edmonds, 2020: pp. 44, 46, 48, 51-52, 84-85, and 92). But what explains the current Ramsey boom? In my view, it's simply that (i) since the 1980s, Moore's reputation has been significantly downgraded, hence a replacement-genius is needed to fill out the classical "founding Trinity = Frege, Russell, and X" narrative of early Analytic philosophy, (ii) unlike Moore, Russell, and Wittgenstein, Ramsey wasn't importantly influenced by the neo-Kantians, and (iii) the combination of logicism, pragmatism, and scientific naturalism in Ramsey's work also very conveniently fits the tick-the-boxes profile of post-Quinean, late 20th-century/early 21st-century, post-classical Analytic philosophy.

II.2 What Classical Analytic Philosophy Officially Isn't: Its Conflicted Anti-Kantianism

Both of the core ideas of classical Analytic philosophy—the thesis of modal monism, and the thesis of a-priori-knowledge-as-analysis—are officially *anti-Kantian*. For Kant holds (i*) that there are two irreducibly different kinds of necessary a priori truth, namely, *analytically*, conceptually, or logically necessary a priori truths, and non-analytically, non-conceptually, non-logically or *synthetically* necessary a priori truths, which I'll call the thesis of *modal dualism*, and (ii*) that a priori knowledge can be directed to either analytically or synthetically necessary a priori truths, but in either case this knowledge stems essentially from a reflective awareness of just those immanent formal or structural elements of representational content that express the spontaneous transcendental activity of the subject in cognitively synthesizing or mentally processing that content, to which the manifestly real world necessarily conforms, which I'll call the thesis of *a-priori-knowledge-as-self-knowledge-of-transcendental-structure*, as per this famous remark in the B Preface of the first *Critique*:

> reason has insight (*Einsicht*) only into what it itself produces (*hervorbringt*) according to its own design (*Entwurfe*). (CPR Bxiii)

But the rejection of those two theses by the classical Analytic philosophers must also be fully inflected and qualified by the recognition that classical Analytic philosophy is as much an *outgrowth* of Kantian and neo-Kantian philosophy as it's a *critically negative reaction* to it, and also that the development, form, and content of classical (and indeed post-classical) Analytic philosophy are essentially constituted by an ongoing anxiety-of-influence about Kant, together with an ongoing struggle with Kantian ideas and their profound philosophical, scientific, artistic, and sociopolitical impact since the late 18th century: *The Kant Wars* (Hanna, 2020c).

II.3 Classical Analytic Philosophy Characterized in Simple, Subtler, and Subtlest Ways

Given its official anti-Kantianism, a simple characterization of classical Analytic philosophy is that it's what Frege, Moore, Russell, early Wittgenstein, Carnap, and other members or followers of The Vienna Circle (*Wiener Kreis*) did for a living after they officially rejected Kant's and Kantian philosophy. Now a subtler characterization records the fact that, as I mentioned above, classical Analytic philosophy (i) *also* critically superseded British neo-Hegelianism (Hylton, 1990; Griffin, 1991) and (ii) *also* emerged victorious in a direct philosophical competition with phenomenology (Friedman, 2000; Hanna, 2008b). But the subtlest characterization—because it also includes the major contributions of early Wittgenstein, as well as the constitutive historico-philosophical fact of The Kant Wars—is that classical Analytic philosophy is essentially *the rise and fall of the concept of analyticity*.

II.4 Three Kinds of Philosophical Analysis: Decompositional, Transformative, and Conceptual

It's commonplace for those who study the history of classical Analytic philosophy to distinguish between two importantly different types of analysis: (i) *decompositional* analysis, and (ii) *transformative* or *reductive* analysis (Beaney, 2018).[6]

Decompositional analysis is the logical process of (i.1) decomposing analytic propositions (or corresponding facts) into explanatorily or ontologically atomic, primitive, or simple items (for example, concepts, intensions, properties, and relations) that are mind-independently real yet also immediately and infallibly apprehended with self-evidence, and then (i.2) rigorously logically reconstructing those propositions (or facts) by formal deduction from general logical laws and premises that express logical definitional knowledge in terms of the atomic, primitive, or simple constituents. When decompositional analysis picks out atomic, primitive, or simple items that occur at the same semantic or ontological level as the relevant propositions or facts, then it's *non-informative*, and clearly an analytic truth—for example,

Bachelors are unmarried adult males.

But when decompositional analysis provides an explicit representation (aka "the analysans") that picks out simples that occur at a lower and more basic semantic or ontological level than the thing being analyzed (aka "the analysandum"), then it's *informative*, and by no means clearly an analytic truth—for example,

Water is H_2O.

By contrast, *transformative or reductive analysis* is the logical process of

(ii.1) reductively explaining one class of propositions, facts, concepts, intensions, or properties, in terms of a distinct and more basic class of propositions, facts, concepts, intensions, or properties, (ii.2) even if these lower and more basic semantic or ontological items aren't simples. Unlike decompositional analysis, transformative or reductive analysis is *always* informative—for example,

Numbers are nothing but sets of all sets such that their elements can be put into a bijective (= two-way, symmetric) one-to-one correspondence with one another.

---

[6] There's a broad use of the term "philosophical analysis" that means essentially the same thing as *philosophical method* or *philosophical reasoning*. But for the purposes of this book, I'm interested in a narrower use that captures what classical or post-classical Analytic philosophers would typically identify as uniquely characteristic of *their special kind of philosophizing*, in a way that sets them apart from, say, Kantians or neo-Kantians, Hegelians or neo-Hegelians, and existential phenomenologists, and above all from so-called "Continental" philosophers more generally.

Transformative or reductive analysis, if successful, shows that the higher-level items are either *strictly identical to* or *logically strongly supervenient on*[7] some corresponding lower-level items.

But there's also at least one other kind of analysis: *conceptual analysis* (Hanna, 1998a). *Conceptual analysis* is critical, creative reasoning using concepts, when it's specifically addressed to classical or typical philosophical problems. As such, conceptual analysis also includes the logical process of (iii.1) non-contingently *identifying* distinct propositions, facts, concepts, intensions, properties, and relations, and (iii.2) non-contingently *discriminating between* inherently different propositions, facts, concepts, intensions, properties, and relations. Like decompositional analysis, however, the propositions that record the results of conceptual analysis can be either *non-informative*, for example,

> Cats are felines

or

> Cats aren't dogs,

or *informative*, for example,

> Cats are living organisms,

or

> Cats aren't robots.

But in both cases, conceptual analysis is *non-reductive*. As we shall see below, in its post-classical phase after 1950, especially including the work of the later Wittgenstein, Analytic philosophy deploys conceptual analysis *at least as much* as it utilizes decompositional or transformative analysis.

II.5 Frege, the Father of the Founding Trinity of Classical Analytic Philosophy

As I mentioned above, Frege was undoubtedly the Father of the founding Trinity of classical Analytic philosophy (the other members of the Trinity, working at Trinity *Cantabrigiensis*, being Moore and Russell), and this intellectual fatherhood was by virtue of his bold and brilliant attempt to reduce arithmetic to pure logic, whose theorems are all analytic, and thereby demonstrate (i) that Kant was profoundly mistaken in holding that arithmetic truth and knowledge are synthetic a priori, and also (ii) that arithmetic proof is a fully rigorous scientific enterprise (Frege, 1953, 1964, 1972).

---

7 For explicit definitions of strong supervenience, logical strong supervenience, and natural or nomological strong supervenience, see sub-section XVII.8.2 below

According to Frege in his 1884 *Foundations of Arithmetic*, a proposition is analytic if and only if it's either (i) a logical truth, (ii) provable from general laws of logic alone, or (iii) provable from general laws of logic plus what he calls "logical definitions." One problem with this doctrine is that unless general laws of logic are *provable from themselves*, then they do not strictly speaking count as analytic. Another and more serious problem is that the precise semantic and epistemic status of "logical definitions" was never adequately clarified or settled by Frege (Benacerraf, 1981). But the most serious problem is that Frege's set theory contains an apparently insoluble contradiction discovered by Russell in 1901, as a direct consequence of the unrestricted set-formation axiom V in Frege's *Basic Laws of Arithmetic*: namely, *Russell's Paradox*, which says that the set of all sets not members of themselves is a member of itself if and only if it is not a member of itself. I'll say more about that philosophical tragedy in section II.7 below.

In any case, Frege's work is the limited beginning of the project of *logicism*—i.e., the explanatory and ontological reduction of (all or at least some of) mathematics to pure logic—which Whitehead-and-Russell, early Wittgenstein, Carnap, and other members or followers of The Vienna Circle all pursued in the first three decades of the 20th century. Unlimited logicism, for all of mathematics, as pursued by Whitehead and Russell, if it works, provides the first half of modal monism; and the second half of modal monism is provided by the rejection of the very idea of a synthetic a priori proposition. This rejection was the unique contribution of early Wittgenstein and Carnap, via The Vienna Circle and its logical empiricism, aka *logical positivism*, in the third and fourth decades of the 20th century. Indeed, this contribution is so seminal to what we now think of as the mainstream classical Analytic tradition, that it's often overlooked that Frege always explicitly held, *just like Kant*, that geometry is synthetic a priori (Frege, 1953: pp. 101-102, 1971: pp. 22-26). In that important regard, therefore, and also as regards some core features of his epistemology (Sluga, 1980), Frege was always *an unreconstructed neo-Kantian*.

II.6 Frege's Project of (Transformative or Reductive) Analysis

As I also mentioned above, Frege's project of (transformative or reductive) analysis was intended to rigorize our conceptions of arithmetic cognition, arithmetic truth, and arithmetic proofs, by reducing them to purely logical notions. This in turn is a *limited logicism*, since it doesn't include the reduction of *geometry* to pure logic. Pure logic is the science of truth and the a priori necessary rules of how to think and talk, such that one cannot proceed from truth to falsity. Kant, by contrast, had held that not only geometric cognition, truth, and proof, but also *arithmetic* cognition, truth, and proof, all depend on a special kind of a priori insight into our forms of intuition—i.e., our formal or structural representations of space and time—that he calls *pure intuition*. Frege holds that arithmetic expresses analytic truths, *not* synthetic a priori truths. And as I also mentioned above, for Frege, a proposition is analytic if and only if it's either (i) a logical truth, (ii) provable from general laws of logic alone, or (iii) provable from general laws of logic plus what he calls "logical definitions." Otherwise, a proposition is synthetic and depends on principles derived from either "special sciences" (by which Frege apparently means the natural sciences) or sense

13

perception. *Logical definitions* express transformative or reductive analyses, for example, of the concept and/or property of being a number. But here's a problem: are logical definitions in Frege's sense analytic, synthetic, or neither? Frege never tells us, or at least he never tells us *definitively*, hence the very idea of a logical definition remains unclear and indistinct.

II.7 Frege's Dead End

As I *also* also mentioned above, Frege's limited logicist project of analysis ran into a dead end when he attempted to reduce the notion of (or property of being) a number to the logical notion of (or property of being) a class or set, by holding that numbers are nothing but sets of sets whose memberships can be put into one-to-one correspondence (equinumerosity). The problem was that Frege assumed that sets could be formed unrestrictedly by simply describing their membership: that's the notorious Axiom V of *Basic Laws of Arithmetic*, aka "the naïve comprehension axiom." But what about (for example) the set of all sets that aren't members of themselves? Is it a member of itself, or not? Well, necessarily, if it's a member of itself, then it isn't a member of itself, but if it isn't a member of itself, then it's a member of itself: paradox! Russell discovered this paradox in 1901, then promptly informed Frege, who wrote back that "logic totters" (as quoted in Monk, 1996: p. 153). The paradox was a genuine philosophical and personal tragedy for Frege, who never really recovered from its discovery. Russell attempted to get around the paradox in his *Principles of Mathematics*, and then when that didn't work, a few years later, in league with Whitehead, he also attempted to get around it in the first volume of *Principia Mathematica*—but ultimately that didn't work either.

My own view is that Frege and Russell, alike, failed to distinguish between two categorically different ways of forming sets in particular, and infinite totalities more generally, by recursive self-inclusion, aka "impredicativity": (i) one way that *presupposes and is grounded on* the phenomenal structure of space and/or time, which is logically *benign*,[8] and (ii) another way that *transcends and is ungrounded by* the phenomenal structure of space and/or time, which is logically *vicious*. Correspondingly, it's also arguable that the distinction between benign (spatiotemporally grounded) impredicativity and vicious (spatiotemporally ungrounded) impredicativity is a specifically *Kantian* one, anticipated in the "Transcendental Aesthetic" and "Transcendental Dialectic" sections of the first *Critique*. Later, in chapter X, I'll also argue that Kantian benign impredicativity, Georg Cantor's higher-dimensional infinities, and Gödel's incompleteness theorems are *essentially connected with one another*, and that this recognition radically transforms our conception of the foundations of mathematics and logic, towards what I call *formal piety*. And by implication, this recognition also radically transforms our conception of the foundations of philosophy, beyond the end of Analytic philosophy, towards *a radical Kantian philosophy of the future* (Hanna and Paans, 2020; section XVII.9 below; and also ch. XVIII below). But I'm getting ahead of my story. In any case, Frege's limited logicism was a dead letter by

---

8 Another way of putting this is to say that the consistency of Zermelo-Fraenkel set theory, aka ZF, well-ordered set theory with or without the axiom of choice, is secured by our pure intuitional representations of the phenomenal structure of space and/or time.

1903. Nevertheless, *Frege's semantics*, i.e., *his theory of linguistic meaning*, which had been specially designed to subserve the project of his logicism, has lived on and on and on, right up to this morning at 6 a.m.

II.8 Frege's Semantics of Sense and Reference

According to Frege's semantics (Frege, 1979, 1984b, 1984d), linguistic expressions have two different sorts of meaning: *sense* (*Sinn*) and *reference*, aka capital-M "Meaning" (*Bedeutung*). The sense vs. reference/Meaning distinction was introduced to account for a puzzle about true identity statements:

> How can true identity statements be cognitively informative, if what they mean is merely that something is identical to itself?

Frege's solution is that the distinct names in informative true identity statements have *different* senses, but the *same* reference/Meaning. According to Frege, sense is *the mode of givenness (Art des Gegebenseins)* or *mode of presentation*—that is, a description—of the reference/Meaning of an expression, and in turn, the reference/Meaning is *the referent* (if any) of the expression. This leads to an eleven-part general theory of sense and reference/Meaning, as follows.

1. The *sense of a name* (for example, "Frege"[9]) is a complete identifying description (for example, "the philosopher, logician, and mathematician who wrote *The Foundations of Arithmetic*") of an individual object.

2. The *reference/meaning of a name* is the individual object picked out by the sense of that name (for example, Frege himself).

3. The *reference/Meaning of a predicate* (for example, "__ is a logician") is a *concept*, that is, an essentially incomplete entity that's *a function from objects to truth-values*, such that "saturating" its incomplete part, or parts, with an individual object (or several such objects) picked out by a name (or names) and *thereby providing an input* (or inputs) *to the truth-function* (for example, "Frege is a logician") yields one of the two truth-values, The

---
[9] In graduate school, my logic mentor/teacher Ruth Barcan Marcus taught me to be *very* finicky—on pain of logico-semantic death—about the use of quotation marks. The mantra was: (i) we *use* words to *mention things*, and (ii) among the things we can mention, via quotation-marks, are bits of language: (iia) single quotes for *mentioning uninterpreted bits of language*, (iib) double quotes for mentioning *interpreted or meaningful expressions*, (iic) corner quotes for *mentioning formalized expressions in the meta-language*, and (iid) no quotes at all *for the simple or transparent use of language to refer to ordinary non-linguistic things*. So, e.g., "Frege is a philosopher is true," whereas "'Frege' is a philosopher" is not only false but also silly. In this book, I'll continue to heed the distinction between use and mention, but for simplicity's sake, (i) I'll consistently use double-quotes for quoting, scare-quoting, and also mentioning language, whether uninterpreted, interpreted, or meta-linguistic, but (ii) I'll also follow the North American stylistic conventions for (iia) putting punctuation inside quotation-marks and (iib) using single quotes for quoted expressions embedded within quoted expressions.

15

True or The False, as outputs (for example, in this case, of course, The True). Put in terms of classical metaphysics, Fregean concepts are best understood as *properties* and *relations*, i.e., one-place and many-place *universals*, with the important qualification that for Frege, concepts are essentially *abstract, incomplete* entities, whereas classical metaphysicians generally think of universals as essentially *abstract, complete* entities, as opposed to *concrete, complete* entities, aka "individuals," in space and/or time.

4. What's *the sense of a predicate*? Frege doesn't explicitly say, but presumably, just as the concept is an essentially abstract, incomplete entity, then correspondingly the sense of the predicate is an essentially *abstract, incomplete sense*, perhaps something like a *rule* specifying the operation of a given concept, insofar as it maps from objects to truth-values. In that way, there could be different senses for different predicates (say, the sense expressed by the predicate-expression "__ is an oculist" and the sense expressed by the predicate-expression "__ is an eye doctor"), each of which picks out the same concept.

5. Relatedly, what's *the sense or reference/Meaning of function-terms* in mathematics?, and what's *the sense or reference/Meaning of logical constants* in natural or ordinary language and in formal logic (for example, "if," "and," "if and only if," "or," "not," "all," "some," etc.)? Again Frege doesn't explicitly say, but I think that we can also plausibly speculate that for him *all* functions and whatever it is that the logical constants refer to, are essentially abstract, incomplete *entities*, and that correspondingly the senses of the terms that refer to functions or to whatever it is that logical constants refer to are essentially abstract, incomplete *senses*, perhaps something like rules specifying the operations of the corresponding functions and logical constants.

6. The *sense of an indicative sentence* (for example, "Frege is a philosopher") is a *proposition* or *thought*, that is, a logically-structured description of a truth-value (for example, The True).

7. The *referent/Meaning of an indicative sentence* is its *truth-value*, The True or The False.

8. Truth-values are *what is shared by all sentences that are true of the world or false of the world*, hence they can be intersubstituted without going from truth to falsity or from falsity to truth, yet they can also differ in sense.

9. More precisely, however, what *are* The True and The False? I think it's best to think of them as *total states of the world*. The True is *how everything in the world actually has to be, such that any given proposition or thought about it is correct*. And The False is every *other* total state of the world, i.e., the *non-actual possibilities*. So interpreted, Frege would be a *modal actualist* who accounts for all non-actual possibilities in terms of propositional falsity relative to the actual world.

10. Frege's theory of reference/Meaning is based on *his theory of functions and objects*. *Functions* are systematic mappings from something (i.e., arguments of the function) to something else (i.e., values of the function). The total set of arguments is the *domain* of the function and the total set of values is the *range* of the function. Functions can map from objects to objects, for example,

$x + 2 = y$,

or from objects to truth-values, for example,

x is a philosopher,

or

x is taller than y.

Concepts for Frege are therefore *functions from objects to truth-values*. The collection of objects that map to the truth-value True is *the value-range, aka extension, of the concept*. And in turn Frege identified *classes or sets* (of unordered or ordered objects) with *the value-ranges, or extensions, of concepts*.

11. There are four basic Fregean principles about sense and reference/Meaning, as follows:

P1 Sense-Determines-Reference: The sense of an expression uniquely determines its reference/Meaning.

P2 Compositionality 1: The sense of a complex expression is a function of the senses of its parts.

P3 Compositionality 2: The reference/Meaning of a complex expression is a function of the references/Meanings of its parts.

P4 The Context Principle: Words have sense and reference/Meaning only in the context of whole sentences, propositions, or thoughts.

II.9 Some Biggish Problems for Frege's Semantics

One biggish problem for Frege"s semantics is "empty names," aka "non-referring names." According to **P1 Sense-Determines-Reference**, the senses of names are supposed to uniquely determine their reference, yet some names clearly don't refer to anything that exists in the actual world, for example, "Mr. Pickwick." Moreover, the occurrence of an empty or non-referring name in a sentence will guarantee that the whole sentence does non't have a truth-value, since according to **P3 Compositionality 2**, the incomplete sense of the whole sentence will fail to deliver a compound reference/Meaning for that whole sentence, if any of its component expressions fails to deliver a referent/Meaning for that component expression. So such sentences, it seems, can't be accounted for by pure logic in Frege's sense, which includes a *strong principle of bivalence*:

> Necessarily, every proposition or thought is either true or false, not neither (aka "truth-value gaps"), and not both (aka "truth-value gluts").

(A moderate principle of bivalence would hold that necessarily, every proposition or thought is either true or false, or neither, but not both—thereby allowing for truth-value *gaps*, but not for truth-value *gluts*. And a weak principle of bivalence would hold that necessarily, not every proposition or thought is both true and false, and every proposition or thought is either true, false, neither, or both [provided that the logic is also *paraconsistent*]—thereby allowing for truth-value gaps and truth-value gluts alike, but not for universal glut-ishness, aka *explosion*, aka *logical chaos*.)

Corresponding to the problem of empty or non-referring names are two sub-problems.

First, how can we ever determine in advance of actual language–use, which names are going to be empty and which are going to be non-empty? Frege simply *stipulated* that all names will have reference/Meaning for the purposes of logical analysis—so, all names will be non-empty—but that seems just to dodge the deeper worry and also avoid facing up to the problem of the semantics of fiction. In at least one place, in his unpublished 1897 *Logic* (1979: 130), Frege did briefly discuss fictional names and fictional sentences, and said that they respectively expressed "mock senses" and "mock propositions" or "mock thoughts." But that seems obviously insufficient, since isn't the following sentence obviously and non-mock-ishly true?:

> In Charles Dickens's picaresque novel *Pickwick Papers*, Mr. Pickwick is a jolly, rotund man who has many amusing adventures.

Or would Frege have held that such sentences also have "mock truth-values"? But if so, then *what in Kant's name* might *those* be?

Second, how are we to construe the truth of negative existential claims?, for example,

> Mr. Pickwick doesn't exist.

If the occurrence of an empty or non-referring name in a sentence guarantees that the whole sentence *doesn't* have a truth-value, then the truth of this sentence cannot be explained by Frege's theory.

Another biggish problem for Frege's semantics is figuring out *Frege's triadic ontology and his platonism*. According to these doctrines, all senses, all functions (including, of course, concepts), all classes or sets (i.e., the value-ranges or extensions of concepts), and all universal and necessary truths, are neither mental nor physical, but instead exist in a "third realm," outside of time and space, that's nevertheless cognitively accessible to all rational cognizers. The "first realm" is *the mental or psychological world*, and the "second realm" is *the physical world*, so that as an ontological triadist Frege seems to be working with a classical Cartesian mental-physical dualism as an ontological starting place, and then adding one more ontological category that's *neither* mental (temporal but not spatial) *nor* physical (spatiotemporal). Earlier in the 19th century, the Bohemian (as opposed to bohemian) priest, logician, and philosopher Bernard Bolzano had already postulated something similar to the inhabitants of Frege's third realm, which Bolzano called the "representation in itself" (*Vorstellung an sich*) or the "objective representation" (*objektive Vorstellung*) (Bolzano, 1972; Hanna, 2011). And an immediate predecessor and partial contemporary of Frege's, Hermann Lotze, held that in addition to the class of mental entities and the class of physical entities, there's also a third class of entities, including contents of mental representations, as well as universal and necessary a priori truths, all possessing "validity" (*Gültigkeit*) (Lotze, 1888). Generalizing, we might say then that the population of Frege's third realm includes *semantic contents* (i.e., senses of all kinds), *functions, properties, and relations* (especially all kinds of "concepts" in Frege's sense), *logical constants*, and other abstract entities like *logical laws* and *logical truths*. Nevertheless, The True and The False don't seem to fit comfortably into *either* the first realm, *or* the second realm, *or* the third realm.

Moreover, according to Frege, in order to understand a word or sentence we must cognitively "grasp" (*greifen*) its sense. Notice that the term for "concept" in German is *Begriff*. So, presumably, if we follow the clue of German etymology, a concept is the cognitively "graspable" sub-part of the complete sense of a sentence that corresponds to its predicate-expression. Indeed, *the sense of the predicate* corresponds to what Kant and many or even most other post-Kantian philosophers, for example, Husserl, would call a "concept." But for Frege, the concept is *the reference/Meaning of the predicate*, and *not* its sense. Thus, what Kant and many or even most post-Kantian philosophers call a "concept" is *not* what Frege calls a "concept," even though for Frege cognitively "grasping" the sense of a predicate is essentially the same as what Kant and many or even most post-Kantian philosophers call *conceptualization*, or *understanding a concept*. So it's both philosophically unfortunate and also consistently confusing that Frege *didn't* call his concepts "properties," "relations," or "one-place and many-place universals," for example. In any case, a belief or judgment is the assertion of a sentence that expresses a proposition or thought, which we and others thereby "grasp" and understand, so that we and others can "advance" in thinking from the sense of the sentence to the reference/Meaning of that sentence, i.e., to its truth-value. But precisely *how* do we cognitively "grasp" senses, if our thinking is mental and therefore in time, and even if, as many materialists or physicalists hold, our minds are identical or otherwise reducible to or anyhow strongly supervenient[10] on our brains, and our brains are physical and exist in space, *yet senses exist in the third realm?*

This is of course a classical problem for any platonic epistemology, more recently and famously re-formulated by Paul Benacerraf as the following dilemma about mathematical truth and knowledge: *on the one hand*, we're committed to a standard, Tarskian realistic semantics[11] of mathematical truth, according to which such truths and their component referring expressions stand for entities and states of affairs to which these truths refer and correspond; but *on the other hand*, our prima facie best epistemology, which connects knowers causally or at least directly with the objects they know, can't make any sense of our engagement with the abstract entities and states of affairs picked out by mathematical truths (Benacerraf, 1972).

There are, of course, various *destructive* solutions to the Benacerraf dilemma that involve either rejecting our standard Tarskian realistic semantics, or rejecting our prima facie best epistemology, or both. Nevertheless, I think that there's at least one *constructive* solution that accepts *both* our standard Tarskian realistic semantics *and also* our prima facie epistemology, then refines and reformulates the theory of abstract mathematical entities as a *structuralist* theory, and is broadly Kantian in inspiration (Hanna, 2015a: chs. 6-8). But since the Analytic tradition, whether classical or post-classical, is officially anti-Kantian from the get-go, its card-carrying members are unlikely to pay any attention whatsoever to any Kantian solution to the Benacerraf dilemma or to any other fundamental philosophical problem, much less seriously consider it, much less actually adopt such a solution. Indeed, this huge and philosophically crippling anti-Kantian blindspot is a vocational disease of Analytic philosophy—leaving aside Wittgenstein, both early and late, whose work is significantly influenced by Kant's and neo-Kantian philosophy (see chapter XV below)—that I'll look at more closely in chapters XVI and XVII below. In any case, without some serious broadly and radically Kantian help, Frege's triadic ontology and platonic epistemology remain forever impaled on the horns of the Benacerraf dilemma.

II.10 Husserl, Logic, and the Critique of Logical Psychologism

II.10.1 Introduction

According to Edmund Husserl in his 1901 philosophical blockbuster, the *Prolegomena to Pure Logic,* which constitutes the preliminary rational foundation for—and also the entire first volume of—his equally blockbuster-ly book *Logical Investigations*, pure logic is the a priori theoretical, nomological science of "demonstration" (*LI* 1, 57).[12] For him, demonstra-

---
10 For explicit definitions of strong supervenience, logical strong supervenience, and natural or nomological strong supervenience, see sub-section XVII.8.2 below

11 For a compact explication of Tarski's semantic conception of truth and realistic semantics see section X.3 below.

12 For convenience, in the rest of this section I'll use internal citations of Husserl's *Logical Investigations*. They'll include an abbreviation of the English title, volume number, and page number. The English edition used is (Husserl, 1970). I generally follow the English translation, but also have occasionally modified it where appropriate.

tion includes both *consequence* and *provability*. *Consequence* is the defining property of all and only formally valid arguments, i.e., arguments that cannot lead from true premises to false conclusions. And provability, aka completeness, is the property of a logical system such that, for every truth of logic in that system, there is, at least in principle, a rigorous step-by-step logically valid procedure demonstrating its validity according to strictly universal, ideal, and necessary logical laws. In this way, the laws of pure logic completely determine its internal structure. Moreover, these laws and these proofs are all knowable a priori, with self-evident insight (*LI* 1, 196). So not only is pure logic independent of any other theoretical science, in that it requires no other science in order to ground its core notion of demonstration, it also provides both epistemic and semantic foundations for every other theoretical science, as well as every practical discipline or "technology." To the extent that pure logic is the foundation of every other theoretical science, it's the "theory of science," or *Wissenschaftlehre* in Bolzano's sense of that term (*LI* 1, 60), the "science which deals with the ideal essence of science as such" (*LI* 1, 236), and thus *the science of science*.

Logical Psychologism, or henceforth for convenience, "LP," is a particularly strong version of the denial that pure logic is an independent and absolutely foundational science. LP was a widely held view in the second half of the 19th century that grew out of the neo-Kantian and neo-Hegelian traditions alike, and it's also closely associated with the origins of empirical psychology as an autonomous discipline (Kusch, 1995). Husserl's arguments against LP in chapters 1-8 of the *Prologemena*, often referred to simply as Husserl's "refutation" of LP, constitute one of the most famous and broadly influential critical set-pieces in 20th century philosophy, comparable in these respects to W.V.O. Quine's famous attack on the analytic-synthetic distinction in "Two Dogmas of Empiricism," published almost exactly fifty years after the *Prolegomena*.

In this connection, it's surely by no means a historical or philosophical accident that the original working title of another one of Quine's famous and closely-related essays from the same period was "Epistemology Naturalized: Or, the Case for Psychologism" (Kusch, 1995: p. 11). By the 1950s, psychologism was making a serious comeback in *epistemology*, if not in the philosophy of logic. But radically unlike Quine's five seminal essays— "Truth by Convention" (1936), "Two Dogmas of Empiricism" (1951), "Carnap and Logical Truth" (1963), "Epistemology Naturalized" (1969), and Quine, "Ontological Relativity" (1969)—all of which are still widely read, studied, and taught in contemporary Anglo-American and European Analytic-philosophy-oriented departments of philosophy, Husserl's *Prolegomena* nowadays is rarely read or studied, and even more rarely taught.

Insofar as the debate between LP and anti-psychologism is still an issue, moreover, it's *Frege's* logico-philosophical writings that Analytic philosophers take to be the seminal texts on anti-psychologism. It's obvious that Husserl's conception of pure logic shares much with Frege's conception of pure logic in his 1879 *Begriffsschrift* and other manuscripts he was working on in the 1880s and 90s (Frege, 1979), even allowing for differences in the formal details of their logical theories. It's also obvious that Husserl's critique of LP shares much with Frege's critique of LP in his 1884 *Foundations of Arithmetic* and the Forward of his

21

1893 *Basic Laws of Arithmetic*, and that there's a direct, important, influential relationship between Frege's devastating 1894 review of Husserl's *Philosophy of Arithmetic* (Frege, 1984c), and Husserl's lengthy and passionate defense of his conception of pure logic against LP. Indeed, this is all explicitly conceded by Husserl in the second half of an unintentionally ironic footnote that's buried away almost exactly in the middle of the *Prolegomena* (*LI* 1, 179, n.**):

> Cf. also G. Frege's stimulating work, *Die Grundlagen der Arithmetik* (1884), p. vi f. I need hardly say that I no longer approve of my own fundamental criticism of Frege's antipsychologistic position set forth in my *Philosophie der Arithmetik* I, pp. 124-32. I may here take the opportunity, in relation to all of the discussions of these Prolegomena, to refer to the Preface of Frege's later work, *Die Grundgesetze der Arithmetik*, vol. 1 (Jena, 1893)

Whatever the precise nature of Frege's influence on Husserl himself, and whatever the contemporary status of Frege's anti-psychologistic writings, Husserl's arguments against LP in chapters 3-8 of the *Prolegomena* are independently philosophically interesting, and in fact they had a massively greater intellectual and professional impact on the development of German and European philosophy in the first half of the 20th century than Frege's arguments did (Kusch, 1995: chs. 1, 3-4). Moreover, and perhaps most importantly, as we'll see in section II.13 below, one of the deepest problems in the philosophy of logic arises directly from Husserl's arguments against LP. Correspondingly, Husserl's two-part response to this deep problem offers a prima facie compelling line of argument to which contemporary philosophers of logic and philosophical logicians should pay close attention.

II.10.2 What Logical Psychologism is, and Its Three Cardinal Sins

According to Husserl, LP is the thesis that

> the essential theoretical foundations of logic lie in psychology, in whose field those propositions belong—as far as their theoretical content is concerned—which give logic its specific character (*Gepräge*). (*LI* 1, 90)

In this way, LP is the thesis that logic is *reducible* to empirical psychology in the strong, dual (i.e., explanatory and ontological) sense that (i) a complete knowledge of the empirical, natural facts and causal laws with which empirical psychology deals would yield a *complete a priori knowledge* of the existence and specific character of logic, and

(ii) the empirical, natural facts and causal laws with which empirical psychology deals *strictly determine* the existence and specific character of logic (Hanna, 2006c: ch. 1). Or in other words, according to LP, logic is *nothing over and above* empirical psychology, i.e., logic is *logically strongly supervenient on*[13] empirical psychology. This does not entail that empirical psychologists of logic are, in and of themselves, logicians, but instead only

---
13 For explicit definitions of strong supervenience, logical strong supervenience, and natural or nomological strong supervenience, see sub-section XVII.8.2 below

that whatever it is that logicians know about logic can in principle be known by empirical psychologists wholly and solely by virtue of their knowing all the empirical, natural facts and causal laws that are relevant to logical thinking.

Husserl's presentation of LP proceeds by means of a lengthy and sometimes repetitive critical exposition of the views of the leading 19th century exponents of LP, including Mill, Bain, Spencer, Wundt, Sigwart, Erdmann, Lange, Lipps, Mach, and Avenarius. As against the "psychologicists," Husserl explicitly aligns himself with Leibniz, Kant, Herbart, Bolzano, Lotze, and (somewhat more covertly, as I noted above) Frege. In the crucial case of Kant, however, there is some apparent equivocation, when in a footnote Husserl asserts that "even transcendental psychology *also* is psychology" (*LI* 1, 122, n.1). This apparent equivocation on Husserl's part can perhaps be explained away by distinguishing between *Kant's* theory of logic, which is explicitly and strongly anti-psychologistic (Hanna, 2001: 71-76, 2021f), and some *neo-Kantian* theories of logic, which are arguably psychologistic. If this is correct, then Husserl is not really equivocating; instead, he is attributing psychologism to the mere followers, aka "epigones," of Kant, but not to Kant himself, who would on the contrary be historically and rhetorically aligned with Husserl's own anti-psychologism. Quite apart from the historical and rhetorical *vehicle* of Husserl's critique of LP, however, its underlying *content* and *structure* involve, **first**, a pair-wise contrastive characterization of LP's conception of logic over and against Husserl's own conception of pure logic, and then **second**, a set of critical arguments showing how LP either fails by external rational standards or internally refutes itself.

The pair-wise contrastive characterization of logic according to LP versus pure logic according to Husserl, can be summarized as follows:

Logic according to LP is:	*Pure Logic according to Husserl is:*
contingent	necessary
based on particulars	based on real universals
based on empirical facts	based on non-empirical essences
concretely real	abstractly ideal
governed by causal laws	governed by strictly universal laws
conditional	unconditional
belief-based	truth-based
based on relativized, subjective truth	based on absolute, objective truth
known by sense experience	known by self-evident insight
a posteriori	a priori
empirical	non-empirical
instrumentally normative	categorically normative

It should be especially noticed that the items on the left-hand side all differ from the corresponding items on the right hand side not in *degree* but rather in *kind*. In each pairing, some extra *non-natural or ideal* property has been added by Husserl to the right-hand item of that pair in order to distinguish it in kind from the corresponding item on the left-hand side. The extra properties attributed by Husserl to pure logic are "non-natural" or "ideal" in two senses. **First**, none of the extra properties is to be found in the physical, spatiotemporal world. **Second**, none of the extra properties is knowable by experiential, experimental methods. So according to Husserl, pure logic is uniquely characterizable in terms of a set of special non-natural or ideal kinds to which LP has no ontological access (since LP has access only to the physical, spatiotemporal world) or explanatory access (since LP has access only to concepts and beliefs that are generated by experiential, experimental methods).

This catalogue of sharply opposed conceptions of logic is then strategically exploited by Husserl in his three basic charges against LP—as it were, the three "cardinal sins" of LP.

Husserl's **first** basic charge against LP is that LP is committed to what I'll call *Modal Reductionism about Logic* or MRL, which says logical laws and logical truths are explanatorily reducible to merely causal laws and merely contingent, probabilistic truths:

> The task of psychology is to investigate the laws governing the real connections of mental events with one another, as well as with related mental dispositions and corresponding events in the bodily organismSuch connections are causal. The task of logic is quite different. It does not inquire into the causal origins or consequences of intellectual activities, but into their truth-content. (*LI* 1, 93-94)

> Laws of thought, as causal laws governing acts of knowledge in their mental interweaving, could only be stated in the form of probabilities. (*LI* 1, 101)

Logical laws according to Husserl are *necessary* rules, and logical truth according to Husserl is *necessary* truth. On the classical Leibnizian account, a rule or proposition is logically necessary if and only if it's true in every "possible world," i.e., in every total set of "compossible" or essentially mutually consistent substances, insofar as this compossibility is completely envisioned by God. Sometimes this Leibnizian, or theocentric, type of logical necessity is also called *metaphysical necessity*. By contrast, according to the Kantian account, a rule or proposition is logically necessary if and only if it's "strictly universal" and also "analytic," that is: (i) it's true in a complete class of humanly conceivable variants on the actual experienced world, (ii) there's no humanly conceivable variant on the actual experienced world that's an admissible counterexample to it, and (iii) its denial entails a contradiction (Hanna, 2001: chs. 3, 5). Sometimes this Kantian, or anthropocentric, type of logical necessity is also called *conceptual necessity*.

Otherwise put now, and regardless of whether the necessity is construed as metaphysical necessity (Leibnizian or theocentric logical necessity) or as conceptual necessity

(Kantian or anthropocentric logical necessity), logical laws and logical truths, as necessary, are always *absolutely* or *unrestrictedly* true. By sharp contrast, merely causal laws and merely probabilistic laws are inherently *restricted* by brute facts about the actual world. As Hume pointed out, there's no absolute guarantee that any causal law, no matter how *generally* it holds in the actual world of sensory experiences, will *always* hold. And mere probabilities, no matter how probable, are always less than 1. So Husserl's first basic charge against LP, or MRL, says that by explanatorily reducing logical laws and logical truths to merely causal laws and merely contingent, probabilistic truths, LP radically restricts the *scope* of pure logical truth.

Husserl's **second** basic charge against LP is that it's committed to what I'll call *Epistemic Empiricism about Logic* or EEL, which says that logical knowledge is explanatorily reducible to merely a posteriori knowledge:

> [According to LP] no natural laws can be known *a priori*, nor established by sheer insight. The only way in which a natural law can be established and justified, is by induction from the singular facts of experience. (*LI* 1, 99)

> On this basis [of LP], no assertion could be *certainly* judged correct, since probabilities, taken as the standard of all certainty, must impress a merely probabilistic stamp on all knowledge. (*LI* 1, 101)

Logical knowledge according to Husserl is *a priori knowledge* and also *certain knowledge*. A priori knowledge, in turn, is belief that's sufficiently justified by evidence which is underdetermined by all sets and sorts of sensory experiences, possibly also including evidence that includes no sensory experience whatsoever and is rationally "pure." Certain knowledge is *indubitable belief*, i.e., belief that's not open to refutation by actual or possible counterexamples, and more particularly, it's not open to refutation by sensory experiences or factual statistics. So Husserl's second basic charge against LP, or EEL, says that LP radically underestimates the epistemic force of pure logical knowledge.

Husserl's **third** basic charge against LP is that it's committed to what I'll call *Skeptical Relativism about Logic*, or SRL, which says that logical laws, logical necessary truth, and logical knowledge are explanatorily reducible to either individually-held beliefs (individual relativism) or species-specific beliefs (specific relativism):

> In order to criticize psychologism we have ... to discuss the concept of *subjectivism* or *relativism*, which is also part of the above-mentioned [skeptical] theory. One of its original forms is caught in the Protagorean formula: "man is the measure of all things," provided this last is interpreted as saying "The individual man is the measure of all truth." For each man that is true which seems to *him* true, one thing to one man and the opposite to another, if that is how he sees it. We can therefore opt for the formula "All truth (and knowledge) is relative"—relative to the contingently judging subject. If, however, instead of such a subject, we make

> some contingent *species* of judging beings the pivot of our relations, we achieve a new form of relativism. Man as *such* is then the measure of all truth. Every judgment whose roots are to be found in what is *specific* to man, in the constitutive laws of man as species—is a true judgment, for us human beings. To the extent that such judgments belong to the form of common human subjectivity, the term "subjectivism" is in place here too (in talk of the subject as the ultimate source of knowledge, etc.). It is best to employ the term "relativism," and to distinguish *individual* from *specific* relativism. The restriction of the latter to the human species, stamps it as *anthropologism*. (*LI* 1, 138)

Relativism—or more precisely, *cognitive* relativism, which is about theoretical beliefs and truth, as opposed to *moral* relativism, which is about ethical beliefs and principles of conduct—says that truth is determined by belief or opinion. In turn, there are two distinct types of cognitive relativism. On the one hand, *individual* cognitive relativism says that truth is determined by individual beliefs or opinions (= subjective truth). And on the other hand, *specific* cognitive relativism or *anthropologism* says that truth is determined by beliefs or opinions that are either the result of human agreement (= truth by mutual contract, or truth by social convention) or are innately biologically specified in all human beings (= truth by instinct). According to Husserl, logical truth is *objective* truth, hence *mind-independent* truth, hence truth that is inherently resistant to determination by any merely subjective, contractual, social-conventional, or biological facts. So Husserl's third basic charge against LP, or SRL, says that LP implies a mistaken and indeed ultimately skeptical theory of the determination of truth.

II.10.3 Husserl's Three Basic Arguments Against Logical Psychologism

Corresponding respectively to the three "cardinal sins" of LP, Husserl develops three basic arguments against it. It's possible to spell out Husserl's arguments in step-by-step detail (Hanna, 1993b; Kusch, 1995: ch. 3). But for our purposes here, it's necessary only to cite Husserl's formulations of the arguments, describe their general form, and then offer a brief exposition of Husserl's underlying rationale for each argument.

II.10.3a Husserl's Argument Against LP From LP's Modal Reductionism About Logic (MRL)

Here's what Husserl says about MRL:

> [According to LP] logical laws, must accordingly, without exception rank as mere probabilities. Nothing, however, seems plainer than that the laws of "pure logic" all have *a priori* validity. (*LI* 1, 99)

> The psychologistic logicians ignore the fundamental, essential, never-to-be bridged gulf between ideal and real laws, between normative and causal regulation, between logical and real necessity, between logical and real grounds. No

conceivable gradation could mediate between the ideal and the real. (*LI* 1, 104)

Here's the general form of Husserl's anti-MRL argument:

> 1. LP entails MRL.
>
> 2. MRL is inconsistent with the existence and specifically *modal* character of pure logic—in particular, MRL is inconsistent with the *absolute necessity* of pure logical laws and pure logical truths.
>
> 3. Therefore, LP is false.

And here's the underlying rationale for Husserl's anti-MRL argument:

> 1. Given Husserl's characterization of the modal character of pure logic, it follows that pure logical laws and pure logical truths are absolutely or unrestrictedly true, regardless of whether this absolute truth is construed, Leibniz-wise, as metaphysical necessity, or else construed, Kant-wise, as conceptual necessity.
>
> 2. Now, if LP is correct, then MRL is correct, and then logical laws and logical truths are non-absolutely or restrictedly true precisely because they're *restricted to the actual world*.
>
> 3. But logical laws and logical truths are absolutely or unrestrictedly true.
>
> 4. So LP must be false.

II.10.3b Husserl's Argument Against LP From LP's Epistemic Empiricism About Logic (EEL)

Here's what Husserl says about EEL:

> [The laws of pure logic] are established and justified, not by induction, but by apodeictic inner self-evidence. Insight justifies no mere probabilities of their holding, but their holding or truth itself. (*LI* 1, 99)

> The justified possibility of [the exact factual sciences] becomes the absurdity of [pure logic]. We have insight into, not merely the probability, but the truth of logical laws. Against the truth that is itself grasped with insight, the strongest psychologistic argument cannot prevail; probability cannot wrestle with truth, nor surmise with insight. (*LI* 1, 100)

> How plausible the ready suggestions of psychologistic reflection sound. Logical laws are laws for validation, proofs. What are validations but peculiar human

trains of thought, in which, in normal circumstances, the finally emergent judgments seem endowed with a necessarily consequential character. This character is itself a mental one, a peculiar mode of mindedness and no more.... How could anything beyond empirical generalities result in such circumstances? Where has psychology yielded more? We reply: Psychology certainly does not yield more, and cannot for this reason yield the apodeictically evident and so metempirical and absolutely exact laws which form the core of all logic. (*LI* 1,100-101)

Here's the general form of Husserl's anti-EEL argument:

1. LP entails EEL.

2. EEL is inconsistent with the existence and specifically *epistemic* character of pure logic—in particular, EEL is inconsistent with the self-evident insights of pure logical knowledge, which are both a priori and certain.

3. Therefore, LP is false.

And here's the underlying rationale for Husserl's anti-EEL argument:

1. Given Husserl's characterization of the epistemic character of pure logic, it follows that logical beliefs are sufficiently justified by self-evident insights, i.e., rational intuitions.

2. Self-evident insights, or rational intuitions, are a priori or non-empirical, and even if not strictly infallible (in the sense that their rejection entails a contradiction), then at least certain and indubitable.

3. Now, if LP is correct, then EEL is correct, and then even sufficiently justified logical beliefs are all a posteriori or empirical, fallible, and dubitable.

4. But sufficiently justified logical beliefs are a priori and certain or indubitable.

5. So LP must be false.

II.10.3c Husserl's Argument Against LP From LP's Skeptical Relativism About Logic (SRL)

Here's what Husserl says about SRL:

> [The individual relativist] will naturally reply: My theory expresses my standpoint, what is true for me, and need be true for no one else. Even the subjective fact of his thinking he will treat as true for himself and not as true in itself.... The content of such assertions rejects what is part of the sense or content of

every assertion and what accordingly cannot be significantly separated from any assertion. (*LI*, 1, 139)

Specific relativism makes the assertion: Anything is true for a given species of judging beings that, by their constitution and laws of thought, must count as true. This doctrine is absurd. For it is part of its sense that the same proposition or content of judgment can be true for a subject of the same species…, but may be false for another subject of a differently constituted species. The same content of judgment cannot, however, be both true and false: this follows from the mere sense of "true" and "false." If the relativist gives these words their appropriate meaning, this thesis is in conflict with its own sense…. "Truth for this or that species," e.g., for the human species, is, as here meant, an absurd mode of speech. It can no doubt be used in good sense, but then it means something wholly different, i.e., the circle of truths to which man as such has access. What is true absolutely, intrinsically true: truth is one and the same, whether men or non-men, angels or gods apprehend it. Logical laws speak of this ideal unity, set over against the real multiplicity of races, individuals, and experiences, and it is of this ideal unity that we all speak when we are not confused by relativism. (*LI* 1, 140)

Here's the general form of Husserl's anti-SRL argument:

1. LP entails SRL.

2. SRL is self-refuting, given the fact of the existence and specifically *alethic* (i.e., truth-based) character of pure logic—in particular, SRL is inconsistent with the objectivity of the truths of pure logic.

3. Therefore, LP is false.

And here's the underlying rationale for Husserl's anti-SRL argument:

1. Given Husserl's characterization of the alethic character of pure logic, it follows that logical truth is objective, or mind-independent, and inherently resistant to determination by merely subjective, contractual, conventional, or biological facts.

2. Now if LP is correct, then SRL is correct, and then truth is either individually relativized or specifically relativized.

3. Suppose that truth is individually relativized.

4. Then whatever anyone believes or opines is true, is true.

5. This includes the person who believes or opines that LP is false.

6. So if truth is individually relativized, then LP is both true (relative to the defender of LP) and false (relative to the critic of LP) and thus self-contradictory.

7. Suppose, alternatively, that truth is specifically relativized.

8. Then there can be other communities, or other species, that say radically different and opposing things about the nature of truth.

9. This is the possibility of conceptual, semantic, and theoretical *incommensurability*.

10. But given the possibility of conceptual, semantic, and theoretical incommensurability, it follows that these other communities or other species are really talking about something *other than* what we mean by "truth"—instead, they're really talking about *schmuth*, or whatever.

11. But *truth*, after all, is objective or mind-independent.

12. So if truth is specifically relativized, then these other communities or other species are not actually disagreeing with us about truth, since they're talking about something other than truth.

13. To summarize: If LP is correct, then SRL is correct, and if SRL is correct, then it's either self-contradictory or talking about something other than truth.

14. So LP must be false.

II.10.4 Has Husserl Begged the Question Against Logical Psychologism? Enter The Logocentric Predicament, and a Husserlian Way Out

It should be very clear from sub-section II.10.3 that Husserl's three basic arguments against LP all have the *same* general form, and that they all directly invoke non-natural or ideal facts about the specific character of pure logic, whether modal, epistemic, or alethic. But it can be objected that Husserl only ever *asserts* that pure logic exists and also has the several non-natural or ideal specific characters he attributes to it, and that he never actually *justifies* this assertion. In this way, on the face of it, Husserl seems to have merely begged the question against LP.[14]

But *has* he? It's equally clear that Husserl would reply to this charge by saying that he has *not* begged the question against LP. Instead, and on the contrary, what he's done is to show *that* and also *precisely how* the existence and specific character of pure logic is covertly presupposed and used, even by the defenders of LP:

---
[14] The question-begging objection was first made in 1901 by Paul Natorp, in (Natorp, 1977). In that connection, see also (Kusch, 1995: ch. 4; Hanna, 2006c: ch. 1).

> Logic ... can as little rest on psychology as on any other science; since each science is only a science in virtue of its harmony with logical rules, it presupposes the validity of these rules. It would therefore be circular to try to give logic a first foundation in psychology. (*LI* 1, 95)

In this way, since LP is a theory, it falls under logical constraints, for example, laws of logical consistency, laws of logical consequence, and the inferential justification of its theses and beliefs. So LP covertly *invokes* pure logic, just as every other theory and every science explicitly or implicitly invokes pure logic.

But given this line of argument, as Husserl himself anticipates, the defenders of LP have one last arrow in their quiver, and its arrowhead is a very sharp one indeed:

> The opposition will reply: That this argument cannot be right, is shown by the fact that it would prove the impossibility of all logic. Since logic itself must proceed logically, it would itself commit the same circle, would itself have to establish the validity of rules that it presupposes. (*LI* 1, 95)

In other words, the defenders of LP will retreat to the charge that in his showing pure logic to be what is covertly presupposed and used by the defenders of LP, Husserl has himself run up against one of the deepest problems in the philosophy of logic, namely, *the explanatory and justificatory circularity of logic*—or what the Harvard logician H.M. Sheffer later very aptly called the "logocentric predicament":

> The attempt to formulate the foundations of logic is rendered arduous by a ... "logocentric" predicament. In order to give an account of logic, we must presuppose and employ logic. (Sheffer, 1926: p. 228)

A specific version of The Logocentric Predicament is Lewis Carroll's famous skeptical argument, published in *Mind* six years before *Logical Investigations* appeared in 1901—an article Husserl might have read, or at least have read *about*—which says that any attempt to generate the total list of premises required to deduce the conclusion of a valid argument leads to a vicious regress (Carroll, 1895). But for our purposes here, The Logocentric Predicament is just this:

> How can pure logic in Husserl's sense ever be explained or justified, if every explanation or justification whatsoever both presupposes and uses pure logic in Husserl's sense?

Correspondingly, how can Husserl respond to The Logocentric Predicament? One possible way out would be for Husserl just to concede that pure logic is explanatorily and justificationally *groundless*, in the manner of the famous mock-logician invented by Carroll, Tweedledee:

> If it was so, it might be; and if it were so, it would be; but as it isn't, it ain't. That's logic. (Carroll, 1988: p. 61)

But then Husserl would have no *rational* defense against LP and no *rational* response to The Logocentric Predicament. And it would clearly be self-stultifying for Husserl to defend anti-psychologism and then to respond to The Logocentric Predicament by lapsing into a *non-rational*, or as it were *fideist*, approach to the foundations of pure logic, which by Husserl's own reckoning—not to mention by a historical and rhetorical appeal to the authority of Kant's theory of logic—is supposed to provide categorically normative laws of *rationality*. It made good sense for Kant to claim in the B edition Preface to the *Critique of Pure Reason* that in order to make room for moral faith in our freedom of the will, he had to "deny" or limit our scientific knowledge—especially our scientific knowledge of natural causal laws, which (apparently) entails universal natural determinism; but it would make no sense for Husserl to say that in order to make room for pure logic, he had to deny rationality.

Husserl's actual strategy of response to The Logocentric Predicament has two parts.

First, he distinguishes carefully between reasoning *according* to logical rules, and reasoning *from* logical rules:

> Let us, however, consider more closely what such a circle would consist in. Could it mean that psychology presupposes the validity of logical laws? Here one must notice the equivocation in the notion of "presupposing." That a science presupposes the validity of certain rules may mean that they serve as premises in its proofs: it may also mean that they are rules in accordance with which the science must proceed in order to be a science at all. Both are confounded in our argument for which reasoning *according* to logical rules, and reasoning *from* logical rules, count as identical. There would be a circle only if the reasoning were *from* such rules. But, as many an artist works without the slightest knowledge of aesthetics, so an investigation may construct proofs without ever having recourse to logic. Logical laws cannot therefore have been premises in such proofs. And what is true of single proofs is likewise true of whole sciences. (*LI* 1, 95)

Husserl is saying that it's only if one mistakenly confuses reasoning *according* to logical rules and reasoning *from* logical rules that one will also cite those logical rules as *axiomatic premises* in one's argument, and thereby encounter the circularity problem. But logical rules can be perfectly legitimately *used* in proofs without also *citing or mentioning* them as premises in those very proofs. Indeed, the very idea of *natural deduction systems*, later discovered by Gerhard Gentzen, is based on this fact (Gentzen, 1969). Furthermore, that Husserlian observation seems to be *precisely* the right reply to make to Carroll's vicious regress version of the Predicament (Hanna, 2006c: pp, 55-59).

But I think that Husserl is also making an even deeper point than this one. His deeper point is that it is not only possible but necessary, given our commitment to human rationality, to conceive of the laws of pure logic as *supreme constructive categorically normative logical meta-principles*, telling us how we unconditionally ought to go about constructing all possible lower-order logical principles or rules, all possible lower-order logical proofs, all possible lower-order logical systems, all possible lower-order formal scientific principles or rules, all possible lower-order formal scientific proofs, and all possible lower-order formal sciences themselves. It's to be particularly emphasized that this does *not* mean that the lower-order sciences are supposed to be *deduced* from these supreme meta-principles, construed as axiomatic premises. Instead, and on the contrary, the lower-order sciences are all simply *constructed and operated according to* these supreme constructive categorically normative meta-principles. This deeper point, in turn, leads directly to the second step of Husserl's response to The Predicament.

Second, then, Husserl explicitly addresses the issue of how to characterize the explanatory and justificatory status of pure logic, when we assume we must always reason according to (i.e., not *from*) the laws of pure logic conceived as supreme constructive (i.e., not *deductive*) categorically normative (i.e., not instrumental, causal, or merely descriptive) meta-principles (i.e., not *lower-order* principles) that tell us how we unconditionally ought to construct first-order formal sciences, including all first-order logical systems. Here's what he says:

> [The unifying aim or purpose of pure logic] is the ideal of a pervasive, all-embracing rationality. If all matters of fact obey laws, there must be some minimum set of laws, of the highest generality....[15] These "basic laws" are, accordingly, laws of supreme coverage and efficacy, whose knowledge yields the maximum of insight in some field, which permits the explanation of all that is in any way explicable in that field.... This goal or principle of maximum rationality we recognize with insight to be the supreme goal of the rational sciences. It is self-evident that it would be better for us to know laws more general than those which, at a given time, we already possess, for such laws would lead us back to grounds deeper and more embracing. Plainly, however, our principle is no mere biological principle, or principle of thought-economy: it is a purely *ideal* principle, an eminently *normative* one.... The ideal drift of logical thinking is as such towards rationality. (*LI* 1, 208)

In other words, Husserl is arguing that insofar as we must always reason *according to* pure logic, and insofar as the laws of pure logic are conceived as supreme constructive categorically normative meta-principles for constructing all lower-order formal sciences, then it follows that pure logic is the necessary a priori condition of the possibility of any explanation or justification whatsoever, in the sense that it is innately constitutive of *human rationality*.

---
15 In this elided passage, Husserl seems to be asserting precisely what he himself had earlier rejected in his response to the circularity objection—namely, that the laws of pure logic are themselves axiomatic premises in deductive proofs. But charitably interpreted, this must be a mere slip. Like Homer, even Husserl nods.

This argument assumes, as a "transcendental fact," that we are rational human animals, and that as a consequence our manifest capacity for generating and using pure logic in the cognitive or practical construction of any explanation or justification whatsoever belongs innately to our cognitive and practical rational human nature. Correspondingly, the very idea of "logically alien" rational human thinking is synthetic a priori impossible (Conant, 1991). Therefore, pure logic exists and also has the specific character attributed to it by Husserl. In turn, from this "transcendental argument from rationality," it would also directly follow that Husserl's arguments against LP are sound.

    Whether or not one ultimately accepts a Husserl-style transcendental rationalist solution to The Logocentric Predicament (Hanna, 2006c: chs. 3, 7), and whether or not one ultimately accepts Husserl's correspondingly robust reinforcement of his arguments against LP, which might otherwise seem to be question-begging, nevertheless Husserl's response to The Logocentric Predicament is at least prima facie compelling, and therefore represents a philosophically significant advance beyond Frege's anti-psychologism—even if it reverts to some Kantian ideas that are *streng verboten* according to the official ideology of classical Analytic philosophy.

III. Moore, Phenomenology, Anti-Idealism, and Meinong's World

III.1 G.E. Moore, the Second Founding Trinitarian of Classical Analytic Philosophy

G.E. Moore was the second member of the founding Trinity of classical Analytic philosophy, principally by virtue of (i) his inventing and promulgating *philosophical analysis* in the full-strength sense that includes decompositional analysis, transformative or reductive analysis, and conceptual analysis alike, and (ii) his doctrine of *platonic atomism*, which says that everything in the world is built out of mind-independent, abstract *concepts* (i.e., non-spatiotemporal one-place properties or many-place properties) standing in a multiplicity of external relations to one another, that are also cognitively accessible by mental acts of direct acquaintance—paradigmatically, rational insight or intuition (Baldwin, 1990: chs. I-II). Paradoxically, however, Moore invented and promulgated philosophical analysis not so much by writing about it, as instead by *living it*, that is, by virtue of his relentlessly deploying the methods of decompositional analysis and conceptual analysis (Moore, 1952; Langford, 1952), especially in his early philosophical writings, including *Principia Ethica* (Moore, 1903) and the essays later collected in his *Philosophical Studies* (Moore, 1922), and by the powerful influence of his charismatic, passionate philosophical personality on Russell and Wittgenstein (Levy, 1980).

This personal influence naturally faded with time, and now, 120 years later (but especially since the 1980s), Moore's philosophical reputation has been steadily downgraded[1] to the point at which it's now an open question amongst contemporary post-classical Analytic philosophers whether Moore was truly a "great philosopher" or not (Baldwin, 2020). But here's one way of answering that open question. By *a brilliant philosopher*, I mean a philosopher who manifests great intellectual creativity, insight, and originality, opens up a new way of looking at a large domain of concepts, facts, phenomena, theories, and/or other information, and *would have* significant impact and influence if their views *were to be* widely disseminated and adopted. And by *an important philosopher*, I mean a brilliant philosopher whose views are actually widely disseminated and adopted, hence a brilliant philosopher with *actual significant impact and influence*. Granting that line of thinking, then whether or not Moore counts as "great," or indeed as a "philosophical genius" in the specifically Cambridge-ian sense of that term (which nowadays apparently uncontroversially applies only to Russell, Wittgenstein, and Ramsey), nevertheless Moore was most certainly *an important philosopher*.

Moore began his philosophical career as a psychologistic neo-Kantian, and wrote his fellowship dissertation on Kant, under the direction of the equally neo-Kantian and Brentano-inspired philosophical psychologist James Ward (Ward, 1911), who'd been Moore's undergraduate supervisor and mentor at Trinity College. But like other young philosophers with minds of their own—and, ironically enough, quite like the early Husserl in relation to Brentano—Moore vigorously rejected the teachings of his teacher. Moore's

---
[1] Whereas, by an almost exactly inverse proportion, Ramsey's philosophical reputation has been steadily upgraded: see, e.g., (Methven, 2015; Potter, 2019; Misak, 2020).

specific act of iconoclastic rebellion against his mentor Ward was to develop, in his Trinity fellowship dissertation, a sharply anti-psychologistic, anti-idealistic, and radically realistic critique of Kant's theory of judgment (Hanna, 2017d). In the same dissertation, Moore also developed an equally sharply anti-psychologistic and radically realistic (and in particular, moral-intuitionist) extension of Kant's ethics, although in this respect Moore's views importantly paralleled Brentano's views in his 1902 *Origin of Our Knowledge of Right and Wrong*, as Moore explicitly pointed out in the preface to *Principia Ethica* (Moore, 1903: pp. x-xi).

Moore's iconoclastic critique of Kant's theory of judgment and its corresponding idealistic metaphysics was later published in his remarkable papers "The Nature of Judgment" (1899) and "The Refutation of Idealism" (1903), which together spell out the basics of platonic atomism. And in the same year as "Refutation," Moore also published his Brentano-inspired, rational-intuitionistic, radical extension of Kant's ethics in *Principia Ethica*. I'll get back to Moore's iconoclastic critique of Kant's idealistic theory of judgment later in this chapter; but before that, let's have a look at what Brentano and his student Husserl were up to, philosophically speaking, insofar as they discovered or invented *phenomenology*.

III.2 Brentano on Phenomenology, Mental Phenomena, and Intentionality

Phenomenology, according to its founder Brentano, in his *Psychology from an Empirical Standpoint* (1874), is "descriptive psychology," and descriptive psychology is the a posteriori science of "mental phenomena" or "inner phenomena" (Brentano, 1995: pp. 3-73, 2002: pp. 51-54):

> We must consider only mental phenomena in the sense of real states as the proper objects of psychology. And it is in reference only to these phenomena that we say that psychology is the science of mental phenomena. (Brentano, 1995: p. 100)

> 1. By [descriptive psychology] I understand the analysing description of our phenomena. 2. By phenomena, however, [I understand] that which is perceived by us, in fact, what is perceived by us in the strict sense of the word. 3. This, for example, is not the case for the external world.... 5. Something can be a phenomenon, however, without being a thing in itself, such as, for example, what is presented as such, or what is desired as such. 6. One is telling the truth if one says that phenomena are objects of inner perception, even though the term "inner" is actually superfluous. All phenomena are to be called inner because they all belong to one reality, be it as constituents or as correlates. (Brentano, 2002: p. 51)

This account clearly and contrastively refers back to Kant's "Paralogisms of Pure Reason" in the first *Critique*, where Kant thoroughly criticizes *rational* psychology, flowing from the Cartesian and Leibnizian-Wolffian traditions, which fallaciously concludes that the mind is a simple substantial immortal Cartesian soul or Leibnizian-Wolffian monad, or a subjective thing-in-itself, by starting with the true premise that the rational human mind is self-conscious and synthetically unified (*CPR* 341-405/B399-432). In other words, rational psychology is the inherently problematic a priori science of mental *noumena*, whereas descriptive psychology in Brentano's sense is the empirically well-grounded a posteriori science of mental or inner *phenomena*. In this way, Brentano's technical term "phenomenology" is obviously derived proximally from the Kantian technical term "phenomenon" and also more remotely from the Greek word *phainomenon*. Collectively, those earlier terms mean *whatever veridically appears (or really manifests itself) to a rational human conscious sensory subject, in inner sense or outer sense.*

Brentano also distinguishes between descriptive psychology or phenomenology and what he calls "genetic psychology":

> By calling the description of phenomena descriptive psychology one particularly emphasizes the contemplation of psychical realities. Genetic psychology is then added to it as the second part of psychology.... Physiology has to intervene forcefully in the latter, whereas descriptive psychology is relatively independent of it. (Brentano, 2002: p. 51)

In Brentano's terminology, genetic psychology is *physiological* psychology, or *naturalistic* psychology: namely, psychology whose object is the discovery of causal natural laws underlying mental phenomena. Phenomenology, by sharp contrast, according to Brentano, yields necessary, infallible, non-empirical truths about mental phenomena.

Hence phenomenology, as "empirical" descriptive psychology in Brentano's sense, is not an *empiricist* psychology, but in fact a thoroughly *aprioristic* philosophical psychology, metaphysically grounded on the notion of a "mental phenomenon," that specifically consists in a certain threefold denial of *rational* (Cartesian and Leibnizian-Wolffian) psychology, *naturalistic* psychology, and also merely *empiricistic* psychology alike.

Brentano presents five different characterizations of mental phenomena, which I'll briefly spell out one-by-one.

Characterization 1: **In terms of mental acts of *Vorstellung*.**

According to Brentano's first characterization, mental phenomena are mental acts in which something is directly "presented" to a conscious sensory subject:

> Every idea or presentation which we acquire either through sense perception or imagination is an example of a mental phenomenon. By presentation I do not mean that which is presented, but rather the act of presentation. Thus, hearing a sound, seeing a colored object, feeling warmth or cold, as well as similar states of imagination are examples of what I mean by this term. I also mean by it the thinking of a general concept. ... Furthermore, every judgment, every recollection, every expectation, every inference, every conviction or opinion, every doubt, is a mental phenomenon. Also to be included under this term is every emotion: joy,

sorrow, fear, hope, courage, despair, anger, love, hate, desire, act of will, intention, astonishment, admiration, contempt, etc. (Brentano, 1995: pp. 78-79)

The term *Vorstellung*, here translated by Rancurello at al. as "presentation," was *also* used as a technical term by Kant, but is usually, and I also think far more accurately, translated by the English term "representation." The verb *vorstellen* means "to place something *X* (stellen) before (vor) a conscious subject." In either Kant's or Brentano's usage of *Vorstellung*, there is no implication whatsoever that anything *mediates* or *intervenes* between the conscious subject and what is represented by that subject, or presented to that subject. Hence *Vorstellungen* or representations in either the Kantian or Brentanian sense are *not* to be understood as "ideas" in the sense in which *indirect realists* use that notion. Thus Kant, Brentano, and, correspondingly, all other phenomenologists in the Kant-Brentano tradition of the metaphysics of intentionality, are *direct realists*, where "direct realism" is the view that nothing gets between—whether by mediation or intervention—cognizing subjects and the (in some sense or another) existing objects of their cognition. Or in other words, direct realism says that *cognition is acquaintive and relational*.

Characterization 2: **In terms of the distinction between mental phenomena and physical phenomena.**

According to Brentano's second characterization, the distinction between mental phenomena and *physical* phenomena, mental phenomena are either *Vorstellungen* or any phenomenon that is based on a *Vorstellung* (for example, a judgment, or an emotion):

[T]he term "mental phenomena" applies to presentations as well as to all the phenomena that are based on presentations. (Brentano, 1995: p. 80)

Acts of *Vorstellung* are said to be mental acts in which an object *appears* to a conscious sensory subject: "[a]s we use the verb "to present," "to be presented" means the same as "to appear" (Brentano, 1995: 81). *Physical* phenomena, by contrast, are passive, externally-generated sense data:

Examples of physical phenomena, on the other hand, are a color, a figure, a landscape which I see, a chord which I hear, warmth, cold, odor which I sense; as well as similar images which appears in the imagination. (Brentano, 1995: pp. 79-80)

Characterization 3: **In terms of intentionality.**

According to Brentano's third characterization, mental phenomena are mental acts in which an intentional object is immanently contained, i.e., *acts of intentionality*, and these are essentially different from physical phenomena:

Every mental phenomenon is characterized by what the Scholastics of the Middle Ages called the intentional (or mental) in-existence of an object, and what we might call, though not wholly unambiguously, reference to a content, direction toward an object (which is not to be understood here as meaning a thing), or immanent objectivity. Every mental phenomenon includes something as object within itself, although they do not all do so in the same way. In presentation something is presented, in judgment something is affirmed or denied, in love loved, in hate hated, in desire desired, and so-on. This intentional in-existence is characteristic exclusively of mental phenomena. No physical phenomenon exhibits anything like it. We can, therefore, define mental phenomena by saying that they are those phenomena which contain an object intentionally within themselves. (Brentano, 1995: pp. 88-89)

It's to be particularly emphasized that in-existence is *immanent containment*, not *non*-existence.

Characterization 4: **In terms of inner perception.**

According to Brentano's fourth characterization, mental phenomena occur in inner consciousness and are perceived only in inner consciousness, which is immediate, infallible, self-evident, and solipsistic:

> Another characteristic which all mental phenomena have in common is the fact that they are only perceived in inner consciousness, while in the case of physical phenomena only external perception is possible.... Besides the fact that it has a special object, inner perception possesses another distinguishing characteristic: its immediate, infallible, self-evidence. (Brentano, 1995: p. 91)

> [I]t is obvious that no mental phenomenon is perceived by more than one individual. (Brentano, 1995: p. 92)

Furthermore, *only* inner perception is immediate, infallible, and self-evident; by contrast, external perception is inferential, fallible, and dubitable:

> Of all the types of cognition of the objects of experience, inner perception alone possesses this characteristic.... Moreover, inner perception is not merely the only kind of perception which is immediately evident: it is really the only perception in the strict sense of that word. As we have seen, the phenomena of so-called external perception cannot be proved true and real even by means of indirect demonstration.... Therefore, strictly speaking, so-called external perception is not perception. (Brentano, 1995: p. 91)

Moreover, only mental phenomena *really exist*. By contrast, physical phenomena have a merely phenomenal and intentional existence:

> We said that mental phenomena are those phenomena which alone can be per-

ceived in the strict sense of that word. We could just as well say that they are those phenomena which alone possess real existence as well as intentional existence. Knowledge, joy, and desire really exist. Color, sound, and warmth have only a phenomenal and intentional existence. (Brentano, 1995: p. 92)

Characterization 5: **In terms of the unity of the mental.**

And according to Brentano's fifth characterization, mental phenomena are not simple items, yet they always appear to us as a unity or whole, while physical phenomena may appear as disconnected or as a mere aggregate:

Mental phenomena, which we perceive, in spite of their multiplicity, *always* appear to us *as a unity*, while physical phenomena, which we perceive at the same time, do not always appear in the same way as parts of one single phenomenon. (Brentano, 1995: p. 98)

Finally, Brentano explicitly holds that the *primary* characterization of mental phenomena—that is, the most philosophically informative characterization—is *in terms of intentionality*, hence, according to *Characterization 3*:

that feature which best characterizes mental phenomena is undoubtedly their intentional in-existence. (Brentano, 1995: p. 98)

So it should be obvious by now that philosophically there's a great deal going on in Brentano's five different characterizations of mental phenomena. But for my purposes, here are five crucial points about those characterizations. **First,** Brentano's mental phenomena are essentially the same as the contents of what Kant earlier called "inner sense," and what William James later called "the stream of consciousness" or "stream of thought" (James, 1950: vol. 1, ch. ix). **Second,** mental phenomena are occurrent apparent facts about the human activity of consciously representing objects, which Brentano (explicitly following the Scholastics) dubbed *intentionality*. But despite Brentano's use of the Scholastic *term* "intentionality," it's clear that *the very idea of intentionality* is fundamentally derived from Kant's cognitive semantics (Hanna, 2013b: section II). According to Brentano, intentionality is a necessary and sufficient condition of mental phenomena (Brentano, 1995: pp. 88-91). Conversely, the presence of mental phenomena before the mind is a necessary and sufficient condition of intentionality. Therefore the very idea of intentionality in Brentano's sense is necessarily equivalent with Kant's doctrine of *inner sense* and his corresponding doctrine of *specifically subjective phenomena*. **Third,** another necessary and sufficient condition of mental phenomena is *inner perception*, which is an immediate, infallible, self-evident knowledge about intentional facts (Brentano, 1995: p. 91). Brentano's notion of inner perception in turn corresponds to what Kant called "empirical apperception" (*CPR* B132), with the crucial difference that unlike Brentano, Kant does not suppose that empirical apperception is either immediate (because for Kant it's always mediated by concepts), infallible (because for Kant it's merely contingent cognition), or certain (because for Kant it's merely empirical cognition). **Fourth,** according to Brentano, every act of intentionality—every mental phenomenon—has an intentional object or "immanent objectivity." Intentional objects in turn have the ontological property of "in-existence" or *existence-in*, which means that their being necessarily depends on the being of the act of intentionality itself. So for Brentano the act of intentionality literally *contains* its intentional objects as intrinsic contents. Consequently, an intentional object in Brentano's sense *cannot* also exist outside the mind, as a thing-in-itself or noumenon. An intentional object in Brentano's sense is therefore necessarily equivalent to Kant's notion of *an appearance of inner sense*, i.e., a *specifically subjective appearance* (Brentano, 1995: p. 81). **Fifth** and finally, when an intentional object is represented spatially or by means of what Kant called "outer sense," whether or not it is represented as actually extended in space (as, for example, in the case of the visual experience of color, which sometimes is directed proximally to phosphenes—the tiny phenomenal fireworks you experience when you close your eyes and press your fingers on your eyelids—and not distally to colored surfaces), then it's what Brentano calls a "physical phenomenon" (Brentano, 1995: pp. 83-85).

Brentano's notion of *phenomenology* is therefore, with one crucial qualification, the same as Kant's notion of *empirical psychology*, with its exclusive focus on the specifically subjective appearances of inner sense. Correspondingly, Brentano's phenomenology, when considered metaphysically, is clearly a version of *subjective or phenomenal idealism*, according to which the world we cognize is nothing but a structured complex of specifically subjective appearances in consciously-experienced time, but not in real space. The one crucial qualification here is that whereas for Kant, empirical psychology can never be a genuine science—that is, an a priori discipline whose basic claims are necessarily true, law-governed, and known with certainty—due to the non-mathematizable and idiosyncratically subjective character of its subject-matter (*MFNS* 4: 470-471), by contrast for Brentano, phenomenology is a genuine empirical science founded on first-person epistemic self-evidence and certainty.

This lingering Cartesian assumption in Brentano's phenomenology, namely, that there's a "privileged access" to mental phenomena—implying, in effect, their intrinsic non-relationality, logical privacy, infallibility, ineffability, and immediate apprehensibility, and therefore, in effect, implying that mental phenomena are nothing but *phenomenal qualia* (Dennett, 2002)—has fundamental significance for the phenomenological tradition and for the classical Analytic tradition alike. For in addition to Brentano's subjective or phenomenal idealism, to the extent that an assumption of privileged access is also retained by him, it further entails that phenomenology after Brentano, and equally early Analytic philosophy, via Brentano's influence on Moore, and as a direct consequence, on the Moorean-Russellian notion of a *sense datum*, are always teetering on the edge of Cartesian ontological dualism.

III.3 Husserl on Phenomenology and Intentionality

Phenomenology, as Husserl understood it in 1900 in the first edition of the *Logical Investi-*

gations, is an elaboration of "descriptive psychology" in Brentano's sense.[2] More precisely, phenomenology, as Husserl initially understood it, is the first-person, introspective, non-reductive philosophical psychology of consciousness and intentionality, as opposed to the natural science of empirical psychology (*LI* V, §7). As a specifically *philosophical* psychology, its basic claims, if true, are non-logically or synthetically necessarily true and a priori.

As Husserl points out in Investigation V, "consciousness" (*Bewußtsein*) is *subjective experience*, where the notion of "experience" includes both (i) *Erlebnis*, i.e., "lived experience" or *phenomenal awareness,* and (ii) *Erfahrung* in Kant's sense, i.e., "objective experience" or *intentionality* that is directed towards either cognizable objects ("thick" objects, empirical states of affairs) or merely thinkable objects ("thin" objects, noumena). In turn, every conscious intentional mental item *M* has four individually necessary and jointly individuating features: (i) *M* is a mental *act* (*psychischerAkt*) with its own "immanent content" or "act-matter" and its own specific character (i.e., phenomenal character) (*LI* V, §§11, 14, 20), (ii) *M*'s mental act falls under a specific intentional *act-type* or "act-quality," e.g., perceiving, imagining, remembering, asserting, doubting, etc. (*LI* V, §20), (iii) *M*'s mental act has an intentional *objective reference* (*objektive Bezeihung*) which at the very least has ontic status or "being" (*Sein*) and perhaps also actual existence or "reality" (*Wirklichkeit*), although this object need not necessarily have reality—hence intentional objects can include fictional objects, impossible objects, abstract objects, ideal objects, etc. (*LI* V, §§11, 17, 20), and (iv) *M* has an intentional *meaning content* or "semantic essence" (*bedeutungsmässige Wesen*), which presents its target in a certain specific way, where this meaning content is either *propositional* or *referential* (*LI* V, §§21, 31-36).

It's crucial to note that this general phenomenological analysis holds *both* for the intentionality of judgment and belief, which presupposes pure formal logic and necessarily requires the existence of natural language and the intentional subject's linguistic competence, *and also* for the intentionality of perception and other modes of sensory cognition such as imagination and memory, which do not presuppose pure formal logic or necessarily require the existence of natural language or linguistic competence. Thus in the *Logical Investigations* Husserl introduced an importantly new idea about intentionality that was a significant advance over Brentano's doctrine: namely, a sharp and explicit tripartite distinction between (i) the subjectively conscious "lived experience" (*Erlebnis*) or "act" (*Akt*) of intentionality, (ii) the objectively existing and intersubjectively shareable logical or semantic "content" (*Inhalt*) of intentionality, and (iii) the mind-independent "objective reference" (*objektive Beziehung*) of intentionality. More precisely, Husserl showed how, while each of these is an intrinsic feature of every intentional mental act, state, or process, each component can nevertheless vary logically independently of the other.

In the same period, Frege also systematically developed essentially the same distinction between what he called (i*) the subjective "idea" (*Vorstellung*) or attitudinal

---

[2] In this section, for convenience, I'll cite Husserl's 1901 *Logical Investigations* by means of (i) parenthetical internal references that include an abbreviation of the title, the investigation number, and the section number, and (ii) some specific page references to the second (1913) edition.

"coloration" (*Farbung*), (ii*) "sense" (*Sinn*), and (iii*) "reference" or "Meaning" (*Bedeutung*). Nevertheless, if the truth be told, both Husserl *and* Frege were merely recurring to *Kant's* tripartite distinction, made explicitly in and throughout the first *Critique*, between (i**) the psychological *Form* and *Materie* (i.e., the representational character and phenomenal character) of inner sense, that is, its subjectively experienced attitudes, desires, feelings, sensations, and images, (ii**) the *Inhalt* or mental content of concepts or judgments, that is, their descriptive or propositional sense or meaning, and (iii*) the *Beziehung* of intuitions or the *Umfang* of concepts, that is, their singular objective reference or their general objective reference (i.e., their *comprehension* or *extension*—what Russell later called "denotation").

There is, however, a fundamental meta-philosophical tension in *Logical Investigations*. This tension is that Brentano's phenomenology, as a descendant of Kant's empirical psychology of inner sense, is at bottom factual and empirical, while Husserl's phenomenology is irreducibly modal, non-empirical, and non-logical. Husserl's response to this tension is to reinterpret Brentano's notion of self-evident inner perception as a priori *insight* (*Einsicht*) or a priori *self-evidence* (*Evidenz*).[3] So for Husserl, phenomenology has an a priori foundation, and its basic truths are synthetically necessary and a priori. It may then seem that Husserl is back safely in the Kantian fold of *transcendental* psychology. Nevertheless, there's another problem. Brentano's phenomenology has no rational soul as a subjective foundation, but instead only a functional unity of human intentional activities, and Husserl had explicitly adopted this conception of the phenomenological ego in the first or 1901 edition of *Logical Investigations*:

> I must frankly confess, however, that I am quite unable to find this ego, this primitive, necessary centre of relations [to the contents of experience]. (*LI* V, §8, 549)

But by the time of the second or 1913 edition, Husserl explicitly realized that this would not suffice for an epistemic foundation of his apriorist version of phenomenology, and that he had to upgrade to a higher-order ego:

> I have since managed to find [this ego], i.e., have learnt not to be led astray from a pure grasp of the given through corrupt forms of the ego-metaphysic. (LI V, §8, 549, n. 1)

In other words, Husserl managed to find a Kant-style *transcendental ego* in order to ground his theory of intentionality.

According to Husserl in his *Idea of Phenomenology* (1907), *Ideas I* (1913), and *Cartesian Meditations* (1931), finding a transcendental ego requires a special philosophical effort, or more precisely a series of such efforts. Recall that the function of a transcendental ego for Husserl is to ground his a priori rationalist phenomenological epistemology. And a transcendental ego in the Kantian sense isn't a Cartesian mental substance, but instead an

---
3 This is made clear in the second edition version of the Introduction to vol. 2 of the *Logical Investigations*, published in 1913.

innately specified spontaneous non-empirical generative cognitive capacity for self-consciousness. So the nature of a transcendental ego must be such that the act of self-conscious reflection suffices for the knowledge of the propositional content of intentionality. This in turn requires (i) that this propositional content be guaranteed to be true, and (ii) that this content be grasped by the thinking subject with self-evidence. And *that* in turn requires (i*) that this propositional content be materially identical with the truth-making object of the proposition (let's call this *the material identity condition*), and (ii*) that the form of this propositional content be immediately and infallibly apprehended by the thinking subject (let's call this *the apprehension condition*).

Now Husserl secures condition (i*), i.e., the material identity condition, by means of what he calls "the transcendental-phenomenological reduction." This treats the mental content of intentionality (now dubbed the *noema*, as opposed to the *noesis*, which is the intentional act) as *identical to* the objective reference of intentionality, and is therefore broadly equivalent to Kant's breathtaking fusion of transcendental idealism and empirical realism. But there's a subtle difference. Whereas Kant had argued for both his transcendental idealism and also his empirical realism, alike, via his thesis of the transcendental ideality of space and time, as explicated and defended in the Transcendental Aesthetic of the first *Critique*, Husserl takes a different route, which he rather unhelpfully calls by the Greek term *epoché*, and only slightly more helpfully calls "abstention" (*Enthaltung*), "bracketing" (*Einklammerung*), and "putting out of play" (*außer spiel zu setzen*).

The basic idea goes back to Brentano's idea of an intentional *Vorstellung* of an object and to Husserl's own corresponding notion of a "mere presentation (*Präsentation*)" in *Logical Investigations V*: it is one thing to represent an object or state-of-affairs *as actually existing*, and another thing altogether to represent it merely *as possibly not existing*. Given Cartesian skeptical doubts, the object possibly does not exist. Assuming that this possibility obtains in a relevant relation to the actual world, then all that remains for the thinking subject of intentionality is the *content* of intentionality which represents the object in a certain way. So this content itself becomes the new or *indirect* object of intentionality. Frege discusses essentially the same idea under the rubric of the "indirect reference" of meaningful expressions in "opaque" contexts—that is, ordinary referring expressions falling within the scope of certain psychological verbs followed by propositional complements, such as "believes that" or "wonders whether," and so-on—although without the Cartesian and Kantian metaphysical backdrops assumed by Husserl. What the parallel with Frege shows is that transcendental idealism and empirical realism do not automatically *follow* from the transcendental-phenomenological reduction, but must in fact be a further metaphysical hypothesis added by Husserl in order to guarantee the truth of the propositional content to which the truth-making object has been "reduced."

Correspondingly, Husserl secures condition (ii*), i.e., the apprehension condition, by means of what he calls "seeing essences" (*Wesensschau, Wesenserschauung*) and "eidetic intuition." Despite the obvious allusion to the Platonic *eidos* however, seeing essences isn't supposed by Husserl to be Platonic insight, or a mysterious infallible grasp of mind-independent, non-spatiotemporal, causally inert, universal, ideal objects; nor is it supposed to be Cartesian insight, i.e., the infallible, certain, clear and distinct awareness of innate ideas.

Instead, it's in effect *Kantian* insight or *Einsicht*, which is a reflective awareness of just those formal elements of representational content that express the spontaneous transcendental activity of the subject in synthesizing that content: "reason has insight only into what it itself produces according to its own design" (*CPR* Bxiii). So Kantian insight is a special form of *self*-knowledge. The crucial point of contrast with Husserl's eidetic insight, however, is Kant's fallibilistic thesis that insight yields at best only a subjective sufficiency of belief or "conviction" (*Überzeugung*), but not, in and of itself, objective "certainty" (*Gewißheit*) (*CPR* A820-822/B848-850). The world must independently contribute a "given" element, the manifold of sensory content, in order for knowledge to be possible (*CPR* B145). Husserl, by sharp contrast, takes eidetic insight to be infallible and certain, which again shows his troublesome tendency to run together Kantian transcendental idealism/empirical realism, which is explicitly anti-Cartesian, and Cartesian indirect realist epistemology, which entails a corresponding Cartesian metaphysics of ontological dualism (Kolakowski, 1987). Descartes's indirect realist epistemology is forever haunted by skepticism, and his ontological dualism of mental substance (whose essence is *thinking*) *vs.* physical substance (whose essence is *extension*) is forever haunted by the unintelligibility of mind-body interconnection and causal interaction. Indeed, in order to avoid being haunted by skepticism and unintelligibility, Husserl's *Cartesian Meditations* should have been called *Kantian Reflections*.

Let me now try to make this critical point more clearly, using Husserl's distinction between *noesis* and *noema*. For the transcendental-phenomenological Husserl, the *noesis* is the intentional act, as self-evidently grasped from the standpoint of the phenomenological reduction, and the *noema* is the mental content of intentionality, as self-evidently grasped from the standpoint of the phenomenological reduction. The pure transcendental ego is the metaphysical ground of all noetic acts and noematic syntheses. The intentional object, correspondingly, is the object specifically *as* prescribed by the "core" or objective essence of the noematic content. Therefore, the intentional object *is identical to* the "core" or objective essence of intentional content. Now there is one and only one object, the intentional object, whether taken from the standpoint of the natural attitude or from the transcendental standpoint. This doctrine, in turn, is essentially the same as Kant's *strong transcendental idealism*, according to *The Two Aspect Theory*, which says that the real empirical object, which is *identical with* the well-formed content of judgments of experience, is such that it can be both *regarded or taken* as phenomenal or "for us," and also *regarded or taken* as noumenal or "in-itself" (see, for example, *CPR* Bxxvii). But even leaving aside any reasonable worries one might have about The Two Aspect Theory (Hanna, 2001: pp. 108-109, 2006a: pp. 422-423), there's a much more serious worry about Husserl's transcendental phenomenology: Does this mean that necessarily, all the contents of intentionality (i.e., all the noemata) and also all the real intentional objects go out of existence whenever *we* go out of existence? As far as I can see, *Yes*. So Husserl's transcendental-phenomenological theory of intentionality entails strong transcendental idealism, which, I think, is objectively false (Hanna, 2006a: ch. 6, 2015a: section 7.3).

III.4 Moore and the Nature of Judgment

During the first two decades of the 20_{th} century, Husserl and G.E. Moore were both direct philosophical descendants of Brentano, and therefore were both traveling along the same philosophical highway, even despite their driving in different lanes, by virtue of their belonging to different emerging early 20_{th} century philosophical traditions—transcendental phenomenology and early classical Analytic philosophy—right up to the fork in the highway when they decisively branched apart. Husserlian phenomenology took the Kantian branch, and Moorean analysis took the anti-Kantian branch. Thus although Moore's ostensible target in "The Nature of Judgment" is the British neo-Hegelian F.H.Bradley's theory of judgment in his *Principles of Logic* (1883), the real target is Kant, and more specifically Kant's theory of judgment in the *Critique of Pure Reason* (Hanna, 2001: pp. 55-56).

Moore's basic objection is that Bradley's (read: Kant's) theory of judgment involves a psychologistic confusion between two senses of the "content" of a cognition: (i) *content* as that which literally belongs to the phenomenally conscious mental act of cognizing (= the psychologically immanent content, or intentional act-content), and (ii) *content* as that which the mental act is directed at, or "about" (= the psychologically transcendent content, or objective intentional content). The communicable meaning and truth-or-falsity of the judgment belong strictly to objective intentional content. According to Moore, the Bradley-Kant theory of judgment assimilates the objective intentional content of judgment—that is, the proposition—to the act-content of judging. This is what, in the Preface to *Principia Ethica*, Moore glosses as

> the fundamental contradiction of modern Epistemology—the contradiction involved in both distinguishing and identifying the *object* and the *act* of Thought, "truth" itself and its supposed *criterion*. (Moore, 1903: p. xx)

Given this "contradiction," the communicable meaning and the truth-or-falsity of cognition are both reduced to the point of view of a single phenomenally conscious subject. The dual unpalatable consequences of that double reduction are (i) that meaning becomes unshareably private (semantic solipsism) and (ii) that truth turns into mere personal belief (individual cognitive relativism).

For Moore himself by contrast, judgments are essentially truth-bearing or falsity-bearing connections of mind-independent platonic universals called "concepts." So concepts are decidedly not, as they were for Kant, simple or complex unities of mental content under the analytic and synthetic unities of self-consciousness. Nor do Moorean concepts and judgments relate to objects in the world, as concepts and judgments alike had for Kant, via directly referential, singular, existential, non-conceptual sensory mental representations, or intuitions (*Anschauungen*). On the contrary and in explicit rejection of Kant's theory of judgment, for Moore complex concepts and judgments alike are mind-independent logically unified semantic complexes built up by external relations out of simple concepts grasped by direct platonic insight. But not only that: according to Moore, *the world* itself is nothing but a relational nexus of abstract simple (one-place) or complex (many-place) concepts (i.e., properties), insofar as they enter into true propositions, and are cognitively accessible by mental acts of direct acquaintance, and, as I mentioned above, this thesis constitutes Moore's platonic atomism. No wonder then that, as his fellow Cambridge Apostle and philosophical sparring partner, the logician and economist John Maynard Keynes, later wryly reported, Moore once had a nightmare in which he could not distinguish propositions from tables (Keynes, 1949: p. 94).[4]

III.5 Moore and the Refutation of Idealism

Moore's "Refutation of Idealism" and his corresponding Aristotelian Society paper "Kant's Idealism" (1904) are even more explicitly anti-Kantian. Here Moore ingeniously doubly assimilates Kant's transcendental idealism to Brentano and to Berkeley by interpreting Kantian appearances as sensory intentional objects that "in-exist" and are nothing but immanent contents of phenomenal consciousness. This of course completely overlooks Kant's crucial distinction between inner sense and outer sense, not to mention his equally crucial doctrine of empirical realism, and his "Refutation of Idealism" (*CPR* B274-279). And not altogether coincidentally, it also ushered in another hundred years of phenomenalistic interpretations of Kant's theory of appearances.[5]

By vivid contrast to Kant's supposed phenomenalism however, Moore's radical realism is the thesis that every object exists as the external relatum of the intentionality of a sheer transparent subjective consciousness. But this implies, in an odd reversal of Brentano's doctrine of mental phenomena—whereby intentional objects reduce to "immanent objectivities"—that all intentional contents are now external intentional objects, and that therefore there will be as many mind-independently real objects as there are fine-grained differences between intentional contents. So Moore uses the transparency of consciousness to escape what I'll dub "Brentano's Box"—i.e., the domain of narrowly ideal phenomenal content enclosed within the individual intentional act—only to lose himself in a looking-glass world of unrestrictedly many real intentional objects, one for each and every distinct act of thought—presumably even including the six impossible things that Lewis Carroll's White Queen boasted of believing before breakfast (Carroll, 1988: p. 92). Carroll, of course, was really Arthur Dodgson, an Oxford philosophical logician and semi-contemporary of Moore and Russell, and the author of *Alice's Adventures in Wonderland* (1865), *Through the Looking Glass, and What Alice Found There* (1871), "What the Tortoise Said to Achilles" (1895), and *Symbolic Logic* (1896).

---

4 As I mentioned above, the Cambridge Apostles were (and still are) a highly-selective and highly-exclusive Cambridge secret society and discussion group. See also (Levy, 1980).

5 Phenomenalistic, subjective idealist interpretations of Kant's idealism have been around, and possibly even predominant, from at least the time of the Christian Garve-Johann Feder review of the first *Critique* in 1782. For influential mid-to-late 20th century versions, see, e.g., (Strawson, 1966; Van Cleve, 1999). Most of the many changes made by Kant in the B edition of 1787 were directed specifically against this profoundly mistaken—or at the very least, highly philosophically uncharitable—interpretation; nevertheless, 234 years later, it's still part of the standard-issue kit of Kant-scholarship orthodoxy and anti-Kantianism alike: see (Hanna, 2020c).

III.6 Meinong's World

In any case, Brentano's student, the radical ontologist Alexius Meinong, had also broken out of Brentano's Box, then passed through precisely the same ontological looking-glass as Moore, and created his Theory of Objects (Meinong, 1960; 1983). More precisely, Meinong held three prima facie plausible and radically realistic principles to the effect that (i) intentional consciousness is the directedness (*Gerichtetsein*) of mind to objects, (ii) for every act of conscious intentionality there is a corresponding object (this is of course highly reminiscent of Plato's Parmenidean Principle in the *Parmenides*, to the effect that Thought and Being are One), and (iii) every object has an ontological status—that is, a being (*Sein*) or an existence (*Existenz*)—of some definite kind, whether this is concrete reality (*Realität, Wirklichkeit*), abstract subsistence (*Sosein*), or hyper-abstract "indifference-to-being" or generic ontic status (*Aussersein*).

In holding these principles, Meinong was heavily influenced by Brentano, yet clearly also by Kant's striking remark in the first *Critique* that

> once I have pure concepts of the understanding, then I can also think up objects that are perhaps impossible, or perhaps possible in themselves but cannot be given in any experience since in the connection of their concepts something may be given that yet necessarily belongs to the condition of a possible experience (the concept of a spirit), or perhaps pure concepts of the understanding will be extended further (*weiter ausgedehnet*) than experience can grasp (the concept of God). (*CPR* A96)

Kantian objects that can be thought even though they're impossible are also what he calls "objects in general," especially including "positive" *noumena*, aka "things-in-themselves," i.e., humanly transcendent objects such that, if they actually existed, would be non-spatiotemporal, non-sensible, self-subsistent, and also constituted by non-relational properties. In other words, Kantian positive noumena or things-in-themselves are a generalization of Leibniz's *monads*. "Positive" noumena or things-in-themselves (for example, God) should also be distinguished from merely "negative" noumena, namely, any *non-empirical* object whatsoever (for example, numbers). Positive noumena or things-in-themselves are *also* negative noumena (in that they're non-empirical), but not every negative noumenon is also non-spatiotemporal, non-sensible, self-subsistent, and also constituted by non-relational properties (for example again, numbers), hence not every negative noumenon is also a positive noumenon or thing-in-itself. Thus "indifference-to-being" is just Meinong's way of talking about Kant's realm of "objects in general," i.e., positively or negatively noumenal or transcendent objects, including but not restricted to things-in-themselves.

But although he's clearly been influenced by Kant's conception of noumena, Meinong isn't a Kantian *Critical* philosopher, and therefore he doesn't restrict cognition or intentionality to the objects of actual or possible human experience. As a consequence, his Parmenidean-sounding, Kant-inspired, and Brentano-inspired principles jointly yield an *awful* lot of objects, and correspondingly an *awful* lot of definite kinds of being or existence. For not only are there the concretely or empirically real objects we perceive through the senses, but also: the abstract or ideal objects we imagine or fantasize about, remember, and reason logically about; all the universal objects, like Redness, Hotness, and Goodness; all the logical objects, like Negation, Conjunction, and Disjunction; all the unreal objects we encounter in fiction and pretence of all sorts, like Hamlet, Humpty Dumpty, and The Man in the Moon; all the "subjective objects" of conscious introspection, self- knowledge, and philosophical psychology; also all the negative facts, like the fact that 7+5 does not = 11, the fact that Donald Trump is not a compassionate man, and the fact that Hamlet does not actually exist (even if Hamlet does indeed have some *other* definite sort of being or existence, as we'll see later in this section); also all the unreal objects that are still consistently thinkable or possible, like golden mountains, the present King of France, and God; and finally, most troublingly of all, there are also all those weirdly unreal objects we can somehow think about that are *not* consistently thinkable, or more plainly put, are analytically, conceptually, and logically *im*possible, like round squares.

So here we are now, thinking about the round square. By Meinong's three principles, the round square must have *some* definite sort of being or existence, even if it cannot have either concrete reality or abstract subsistence. And in fact for Meinong the round square has only an "indifference to-being" or *Aussersein*. But no matter how fine you slice your ontological categories, it remains the case that a round square is square, hence not round, hence both round and not round. Similarly, the round square is round, hence not square, hence both square and not square. So for Meinong, the round square both (i) has *some or another* kind of being, in order to be an object of conscious intentionality, and yet also, (ii) by virtue of its violating the universal law of non-contradiction, it's utterly analytically, conceptually, or logically impossible. Curiouser and curiouser!

Here, now, is Meinong's radical ontology in more detail. Like Brentano, Meinong starts his version of phenomenology from the primitive fact of intentionality, and its basic two-part intentional act/intentional object metaphysical framework. Like early Moore, Meinong is a radical realist. And like early Russell (1973b, 1995: ch. V), Meinong is deeply interested in the logic and ontology of intentionality. Unlike Husserl and Frege, however, Meinong has no theory of *content* or *meaning* or *sense*, apart from the basic two-part intentional act/intentional object metaphysical framework. Nor does Meinong seem to be interested in the third basic element of intentionality for Brentano, *inner consciousness*. Meinong is primarily interested in *intentional ontology*, not in philosophical semantics or philosophical psychology. This is what he calls "The Theory of Objects" or *Gegenstandtheorie*. The semantics of intentionality and the psychology of intentionality are not strictly speaking *excluded* by The Theory of Objects. Nevertheless, they are derivative theories for Meinong, in the sense that for him intentional ontology or The Theory of Objects is *metaphysically prior* and *justificationally prior* to philosophical semantics and psychology, although at the same time it's Brentanian descriptive psychology or phenomenology that originally leads, in the order of discovery, to The Theory of Objects. Why did Meinong, a student of Brentano the phenomenologist, become a radical realist? My historico-philosophical hypothesis is

The Fate of Analysis

that Meinong clearly recognized that Brentano's theory of intentionality entails subjective idealism or phenomenalism, and sought to avoid this unhappy outcome by turning that theory of intentionality into an intentional ontology or theory of objects.

Ontology, in general, is the theory of "what there is," i.e., of the different categories and kinds of beings, and their essential relationships to one another. Correspondingly, Meinong's basic ontology consists of *objects* (individuals) and *objectives* (states of affairs). In turn, the objects can be either existing (i.e., real/actual) or non-existing (i.e., non-real/non-actual), and the objectives or states of affairs can be either actual/real or non-actual/non-real. This leads to the "four-boxes ontology" I call *Meinong's World*:

Box 1: Existing, i.e., actual/real objects	**Box 2:** Actual/real states of affairs
Box 4: Non-existing, i.e., non-actual/non-real objects	**Box 3:** Non-actual/non-real states of affairs

And here are the basic logical and ontological relationships between the four boxes in Meinong's World. Everything in **Box 1** (for example, the real living philosopher Socrates) necessarily also goes into **Box 2** (for example, given that Socrates exists, i.e., is actual/real, then necessarily, it's an actual/real state of affairs that Socrates exists, i.e., is actual/real). Everything in **Box 1** (for example, Socrates) can go into **Box 3** (for example, it's a non-actual/non-real state of affairs that Socrates is an insurance salesman), but not everything in **Box 1** necessarily goes into **Box 4** (for example, Socrates isn't necessarily not an insurance salesman). Nothing in **Box 1** (for example, Socrates, who exists, i.e., is actual/real) can ever go into **Box 3** (i.e., the domain of things that don't exist, i.e., aren't actual/real), for example, universals, numbers, contingently non-existing objects like Pegasus, the winged horse, and necessarily non-existing, i.e., necessarily non-actual/non-real, objects like the round square). Everything in **Box 3** (for example, the round square) necessarily also goes into **Box 4** (for example, it's necessarily a non-actual/non-real state of affairs that the round square exists, i.e., is actual/real). Everything in **Box 3** (for example, the round square) can go into **Box 2** (for example, it's an actual/real state of affairs that the round square doesn't exist, i.e., isn't actual/real), but not everything in **Box 3** necessarily goes into **Box 1** (for example, Pegasus doesn't necessarily not exist, i.e., Pegasus isn't necessarily non-actual/non-real). And nothing in **Box 3** (for example, the round square, which necessarily doesn't exist, i.e., necessarily isn't actual/real) can ever go into **Box 1** (i.e., the domain of things that do exist, i.e., are actual/real).

Folded into Meinong's four-boxes ontology, are also Meinong's five basic ontological categories, as follows: (i) *Existenz* or *Wirklicheit* = existence or actuality/reality, (ii) *Sein* = being, (iii) *Sosein* = being such-and-such = subsistence = the being of objectives or states of affairs, (iv) *Nichtsein* = non-existence or non-being, and (v) *Aussersein* = indifference-to-being, or generic ontic status, corresponding to Kant's category of "objects in general," which includes all "positive" noumena, aka "things in themselves," as well as all "negative" noumena, i.e., non-empirical objects. In turn, Meinong's Theory of Objects has five basic ontological principles, as follows:

50

Principle I: Every intentional object whatsoever has generic ontic status.

Principle II: Every well-formed, meaningful linguistic expression stands for an object.

Principle III: If a whole complex object has an ontic status of a specific kind, then each of its parts has an ontic status of that specific kind too.

Principle IV: *Sosein* or subsistence is independent from *Sein* or being.

Principle V: Every object whatsoever is essentially "indifferent" to being or *Sein* in the sense that every object whatsoever has generic ontic status, although at least one of its two being-objectives—i.e., its being or non-being—subsists.

In view of the direct connection between Meinong's notion of *Aussersein* and Kant's notion of "objects in general," it's especially illuminating to relate Meinong's intentional ontology to Kant's distinction between phenomenal and noumenal objects. For Kant, all and only phenomena would necessarily go into **Box 1**, and all noumena—whether "positive" noumena, i.e., "things-in-themselves," or "negative" noumena, i.e., any non-empirical object—would necessarily go into **Box 3**. For example, the real living philosopher Socrates, as a real empirical person, would necessarily go into **Box 1**; God, as a "positive" noumenon, would necessarily go into **Box 3**; and the number 7, as a "negative" noumenon, would also go into **Box 3**. More generally for Kant, all empirically real objects, as truly cognized or cognizable (in the narrow sense of "cognition" or *Erkenntnis*) objects, hence "thick" objects of experience, would necessarily go into **Box 1**; whereas all merely thinkable objects, or "thin" objects, i.e., "objects in general," including all "positive" and "negative" noumena, as well as both analytically or logically impossible objects like the round square and also synthetic a priori impossible objects like cats that grow on trees, would necessarily go into **Box 3**.

In this connection, there are two "intolerably" hard problems for Meinong's Theory of Objects, both explicitly noted by Russell in "On Denoting" and also *notoriously* so noted, in that these problems are sometimes supposed by post-classical Analytic philosophers to demonstrate conclusively the silliness of Meinong, and by association, the silliness of phenomenological ontology—and by another stretch, and above all, the *essential* silliness of all so-called "Continental" philosophy:

> It is contended [by Meinong], for example, that the existent present King of France exists, and also does not exist; that the round square is round and also not round, etc. But this is intolerable; and if any theory can be found to avoid this result, it is surely to be preferred. (Russell, 1971b: p. 45)

But as we'll see, Russell's two hard problems for Meinong are actually solvable, and therefore the latter's views are eminently non-silly and tolerable, even if radical.

Russell's Intolerably Hard Problem I. The Puzzle of Negative Existentials.

According to Russell, if Meinong is right, then somehow both of the following contradictory sentences are true:

1. The existent present king of France does not exist.

2. The existent present king of France exists.

For Meinong *himself*, however, sentence 1 means that *it's true that the individual object that's the present king of France is not among the existing or actual/real objects*. And for Meinong himself, sentence 2 means that *it's true that the individual object that's the present king of France has generic ontic status*. Hence, his response to this supposedly intolerably hard Russellian problem is to distinguish carefully between (i) the ontological category of an individual object's existence or actuality/reality, which in the four-boxes ontology is equivalent to an object's being placed (or not being placed, in the case of non-existence or non-actuality/non-reality) in **Box 1**, and (ii) *generic ontic status*, which, according to Principle I, every intentional object whatsoever has, even impossible ones. There's no paradox whatsoever if the individual object that's the present king of France has a generic ontic status, but *isn't* placed in **Box 1**: on the contrary, the individual object that's the present king of France, which is a contingently non-existing, i.e., contingently non-actual/non-real object, is simply placed in **Box 3**, not in **Box 1**. In turn, the individual object that's the present king of France can visit **Box 2** as a proper part of the actual/real state of affairs of the individual object that's the present king of France's not existing, i.e., not being actual/real, and also the individual object that's the present king of France necessarily visits **Box 3** as a proper part of the non-actual/non-real state of affairs of the individual object that's the present king of France's existing, i.e., being actual/real. So Meinong can *easily* solve *that* Russellian hard problem.

Russell's Intolerably Hard Problem II: The Puzzle of Logically Impossible Objects.

But if things looked bad for Meinong's encounter with the present King of France, they're apparently even worse when it comes to the round square, and analytically, conceptually, or logically impossible objects more generally. That's because of this line of reasoning:

1. The round square is square. (premise: by analyticity.)

2. The round square is round. (premise: by analyticity.)

3. Whatever is round is not square. (premise: by analyticity.)

4. Therefore, the round square is not square. (By 2, 3, & hypothetical syllogism)

> 5. Therefore, the round square is both square and not square. (By 1, 4, & conjunction introduction)

So the very idea of a round square entails an analytic, conceptual, or logical contradiction.

In this way, Meinong was prepared to admit that the Law of Non-Contradiction does not hold for *all* objects or states of affairs. So according to him there are *some true contradictions* and also some *inherently logically and analytically, conceptually, or logically impossible objects*. This doctrine is called *dialetheism*. The main problem with unqualified dialetheism is the logical fact that every statement whatsoever, *and* its denial, can be proved from a true contradiction. This is the logical phenomenon known as *Explosion*. Contrastively, however, dialetheic *paraconsistent* logics systematically rule out Explosion. In a well-known article, Graham Priest rhetorically asks "what is so bad about contradictions?" (Priest, 1998). The Kantian answer to Priest's rhetorical question is:

> "You're so right! In fact, there's nothing wrong with analytic, conceptual, or logical contradictions, as a species of necessary falsehoods, given that we already fully admit them into our valid and sound reductio proofs, provided that the background logic is paraconsistent, and therefore provided that Explosion is absolutely ruled out of court."

But a world in which explosion is *allowed* to exist is logically chaotic and anti-rational. Such a world is just the sort of world that Lewis Carroll's outrageous misologist or logic-hater, the White Queen, would have dictated in *Through the Looking Glass*:

> Alice laughed. "There's no use trying," she said: One ca'n't believe impossible things." "I daresay you haven't had much practice," said the Queen. "When I was your age, I always did it for half-an-hour a day. Why, sometimes I believed as many as six impossible things before breakfast!"(Carroll, 1988: pp. 91-92, non-standard spelling of "can't" as "ca'n't" in the original)

Now Carnap famously said in *The Logical Syntax of Language*:

> *In logic there are no morals.* Everyone is at liberty to build up his own logic, i.e., his own form of language, as he wishes. (Carnap, 1937: p. 52)

And that was bad enough. But Meinong's theory of intentionality is seemingly saying, in an *über*-Carnapian way:

> *In logic everything can go all pear-shaped.* Everyone is at liberty to contradict himself, i.e., to put analytically, conceptually, or logically impossible objects into **Box 3**, whenever he wishes.

In other words, without paraconsistency, Meinong's **Box 3** would be *Logical Pandora's Box*, and to that extent, Meinong's World would be *Logical Hell*: and that's utterly rationally unacceptable.

But I also think it's exceptionally rationally *uncharitable* to think that Meinong would *not* have explicitly or implicitly defended paraconsistency, as per the following Carnap-like slogan:

In logic we recognize true contradictions, but pull back at the edge of the abyss.

That is: everyone is at liberty to contradict himself, i.e., to put analytically, conceptually, or logically impossible individual objects into **Box 3**, in order to study the fascinating consequences of "self-conscious dialetheism" (Priest, 2002: p. 7), but *only* insofar as they're *also* prepared to rule out Explosion.

Therefore, if charitably-interpreted Meinongianism is "intolerable," then so is Carnap's logical pluralism, and so is Priest's dialetheic paraconsistency, and so is non-classical logic more generally. In effect, then, Russell is saying that all advances in logical theory after *Principia Mathematica* are *streng verboten*. But that's absurd; therefore, by *reductio*, it's *Russell* who's being essentially silly, by virtue of his arbitrarily shutting down progress in logical theory, *not* Meinong.

IV. Russell, Unlimited Logicism, Acquaintance, and Description

IV.1 Russell Beyond Brentano, Husserl, Moore, and Meinong

Whatever his actual level of philosophical essential silliness or non-silliness, Russell's self-set great task, as the third founding Trinitarian of classical Analytic philosophy, was to follow Moore and Meinong out of Brentano's Box and Husserl's transcendental phenomenology, cross over with the two Mighty Ms into the weird world of intentional objects behind the ontological looking glass, armed only with his logician's "feeling for reality," and *then* to bring them all back alive, safe, and sane:

> In such theories [as Meinong's], it seems to me, there is a failure of that feeling for reality which ought to be preserved even in the most abstract studies. Logic, I should maintain, must no more admit a unicorn than zoology can; for logic is concerned with the real world just as truly as zoology, though with its most abstract and general features. (Russell, 1993: p. 169)

Like Moore, Russell began his philosophical career, **first**, as a neo-Hegelian, and then, a few years later, **second**, as a psychologistic neo-Kantian, in a treatise on the nature of geometry, *An Essay on the Foundations of Geometry* (1897), which was based on Russell's Trinity fellowship dissertation, just as Moore's early essays were based on his own Trinity fellowship dissertation, and then finally **third**, following Moore's anti-Kantian turn, as an anti-psychologistic, logicistic, radically realistic, anti-Kantian Analytic philosopher.

The basic point of Russell's *Essay on the Foundations of Geometry* is to determine what could be preserved of Kant's Euclid-oriented theories of space and geometry after the discovery and development of *non*-Euclidean geometries. Again like Moore, Russell had been supervised by Ward, but also and above all by Whitehead, who discovered and nurtured Russell's logical and mathematical brilliance. At the same time, there was also a significant neo-Hegelian element in Russell's early thought, inspired by his close study of Bradley's *Logic* and discussions with yet another Trinity man and fellow Apostle, the imposingly-named Scottish neo-Hegelian metaphysician John McTaggart Ellis McTaggart (Hylton, 1990: part I; and Griffin, 1991).

Despite being a close friend of Russell, Moore wrote a sternly critical review of the *Essay* that was comparable in its both its philosophical content and also its impact on Russell to Frege's review of Husserl's *Philosophy of Arithmetic*, in that it accused Russell of committing the "Kantian fallacy" of grounding a priori modal claims on psychological facts (Moore, 1899). Moore's "friendly" criticism seems to have almost instantly liberated Russell from his neo-Hegelian and neo-Kantian beliefs. At the same time, however, he retained a serious philosophical interest in Husserl's early phenomenology as worked out in his 1900 *Logical Investigations*, construed as a robustly anti-psychologistic and realistic doctrine. Indeed, Russell took a copy of the second (1913) edition of *Logical Investigations* with him to prison in 1918 for the purposes of re-reading and reviewing it, and more generally, as Andreas Vrahimis puts it,

> [Russell] seems to have thought highly of the book, which he would later praise as being "a monumental work" which he sees as part of "a revolt against German idealism.... from a severely technical standpoint" and which he places alongside the work of Frege, Moore, and himself. (Vrahimis, 2015: p. 94)

Russell's encounter with early Husserl's anti-psychologism and phenomenological realism, combined with the close, critical study of Meinong's writings, and with Moore's powerful philosophical influence, led him (i.e., Russell) to a radically realistic Moorean see-through epistemology, and to a correspondingly rich looking-glass ontology of concrete and abstract real individuals—although as we have seen, he also prudently deployed his logician's "feeling for reality" and stopped short of accepting the being or existence, in any sense, of Meinongian impossibilia (Russell, 1993: pp. 169-170). One might well wonder, of course, why accepting the being or existence of Redness, Hotness, Goodness, Negation, Conjunction, and Disjunction is perfectly acceptable for Russell, whereas postulating unicorns, Hamlet, and round squares is rationally abominable. By what criterion does the logician's "feeling for reality" justifiably distinguish between the *good* Meinongian objects and the *bad* ones? We'll come back to that dangerous thought again shortly.

IV.2 Russell and Mathematical Logic *versus* Kant

In any case, powered by strong shots of Meinong-&-Moore, with a twist of early Husserl, Russell's titanically brilliant, restless, and indeed obsessive intellect (Monk, 1996: part I) was now focused exclusively on the logical foundations of mathematics, and deeply engaged with the works of George Boole, Frege, and the Italian logician Giuseppe Peano. By 1903 Russell had produced the fairly massive *Principles of Mathematics*, and then by 1910, in collaboration with Whitehead, the even more massive first volume of *Principia Mathematica*. Above all however, on the collective basis of his intellectual encounters with the works of Kant, Bradley, Boole, Frege, Peano, Whitehead, Meinong, & Moore, Russell developed a fundamental conception of *mathematical logic*.

Mathematical logic, as Russell understood it, is the non-psychological, universal, necessary, and a priori science of deductive consequence, expressed in a bivalent propositional and polyadic predicate calculus with identity as well as quantification over an infinity of individuals, properties, and various kinds of functions. Mathematical logic in this heavy-duty sense has some correspondingly heavy-duty metaphysical implications. But most importantly for our purposes here, Russell's logic expresses the direct avoidance of Kant's appeal to pure intuition in the constitution of mathematical propositions and reasoning:

> [T]he Kantian view . . . asserted that mathematical reasoning is not strictly formal, but always uses intuitions, *i.e.* the *à priori* knowledge of space and time. Thanks to the progress of Symbolic Logic, especially as treated by Professor

Peano, this part of the Kantian philosophy is now capable of a final and irrevocable refutation. (Russell, 1996: p. 4)

The result of all these influences, together with Russell's manic creative intellectual drive in the period from 1900 to 1913 (when he had a head-on collision with a Wittgensteinian juggernaut—of which, more below), was a critical refinement of Moore's conception of philosophical analysis, involving a radically realistic, platonistic, atomistic, and above all *logicistic* realism, according to which (i) not merely arithmetic, but literally *all* of pure mathematics, including algebra, geometry, etc., explanatorily and ontologically reduces to mathematical logic, which is the full-strength thesis of *unlimited logicism* (for more details, see directly below), (ii) propositions literally contain both the simple concrete particulars (instantaneous sense-data) and also the simple abstract universals (properties or relations) that populate the mind-independently real world (Russell, 1981), (iii) propositions also literally contain the logical constants (Negation, Conjunction, Disjunction, etc.) that express the purely logical form of propositions, and (iv) not only the simple concrete particulars and the simple abstract universals, but also the logical constants are known directly and individually by cognitive acts of self-evident and infallible acquaintance (Russell, 1995: ch. V).

IV.3 Russell's Unlimited Logicist Project

As I just mentioned, Russell not only shared Frege's view that arithmetic is explanatorily and ontologically reducible to logic, but also outdid Frege by holding that literally *all* parts of pure mathematics, especially including geometry, are reducible to logic. Unlike Frege, Russell didn't think of logic as the science of the most general laws of truth but instead as the maximally general science of deductive consequence, or of drawing conclusions from premises in a necessarily truth-preserving way. Russell wasn't as concerned as Frege was with finding true premises, much less with finding necessarily true premises: it's the idea of *necessary truth-preservation with respect to any subject-matter* that matters for him, so the basic premises might in principle turn out to be false or purely suppositional.

The crucial point is that Russell's mathematical logic, unlike other sciences, does *not* contain a body of fundamental general truths or axioms. On the contrary, for mathematical logic, any axioms you postulate don't really matter, and the theorems derived from those axioms also don't really matter: what matters are the essentially logical relations between the axioms you happen to choose and the theorems you deductively derive. Or in other words, for Russell mathematical logic doesn't "say" or "state" anything about the world: rather it only expresses *a set of special relations between propositions* that, in turn, "say" or "state" things about the world.

IV.4 Pursued by Logical Furies: Russell's Paradox Again

As I've already noted more than once, A Funny Thing Happened To Russell On The Way to Unlimited Logicism. Like Frege, Russell had hoped to reduce numbers to classes or sets of equinumerous sets; but he was bedevilled by the discovery of his paradox of classes or sets, which persistently pursued his work in mathematical logic like a swarm of avenging logical Furies. Sets are uniquely determined by their membership, and the membership of a set is specified by a conceptual description of what will count as a member of that set. Some sets aren't members of themselves: for example, the set of all dogs isn't a dog, so it isn't a member of itself. Other sets, by contrast, *are* members of themselves: for example, the set of all non-dogs is a non-dog, so it *is* a member of itself. This distinction then allows the formation of a set *K* whose membership is specified by the conceptual description that it contains all and only those sets that aren't members of themselves. Russell's paradox then follows immediately if one asks about the logical status of *K*: is *K* part of its own membership, or not? Obviously, *K* is a member of itself if and only if *K* is not member of itself: paradox! This in turn exemplifies a general point about paradoxes, namely that they express propositions that are not merely contradictory (both true and false) but in fact *hyper*-contradictory (true if and only if false).

Having discovered the set-theoretic paradox, and having also promptly informed Frege about it, to the latter's tragic dismay, Russell then adopted a series of strategies to try to avoid it, including (i) the proto-eliminativist so-called *no-class theory*: there are no real classes or sets but instead only propositional functions, i.e., mappings from objects to propositions (Russell, 1996: pp. 79-80), (ii) the proto-stipulationist *vicious circle principle*: no totality of things can be constructed such that it increases its size only by including itself, aka "impredicativity" (Whitehead and Russell, 1962: pp. 37-38, and (iii) the proto-structuralist *theory of types*: there's a hierarchy of propositional functions such that the collections of objects formed by a given propositional function always occurs one level lower than that function and therefore cannot belong to that collection (Russell, 1971c; Whitehead and Russell, 1962: pp. 37-65). The problem with (i), i.e., the no-class theory, is that it *hand-waves the problem away* and begs the question at issue, by merely banishing the problematic entities, classes or sets, into the realm of philosophical bad dreams. The problem with (ii), i.e., the vicious circle principle, is that it *engages in logical overkill* and also begs the question at issue, by merely banishing all logical constructions of the same general form (i.e., impredicativity) as the specific ones that lead to paradox, into the same realm of philosophical bad dreams. And the problem with (iii), i.e., the theory of types, is that it's formally possible to construct an exact analogue of the paradox of classes or sets *by using Russellian propositions* (Potter, 2000: ch. 5, esp. section 5.5). So, sadly, after all that work, Russell never actually solved the set-theoretic paradox.

Russell was also much exercised by a similar, yet also interestingly different, paradox in the foundations of the theory of meaning: *reflexivity* or *self-reference* can also lead to paradox whenever there is a sentence that says of itself that it's false, for example—

The only indented and italicized sentence on page 58 of this book is false.

Let's call this sentence "BERTIE." What is BERTIE's logical status? Or more precisely, is BERTIE true or false? If BERTIE is true, then BERTIE is false; but if BERTIE is false then BERTIE is true; so BERTIE is a sentence that is true if and only if it is false: so, in short,

BERTIE is a hyper-contradiction or paradox, although a logical Fury of a slightly different color than Russell's set-theoretic paradox and others formally like it. This differently-colored logical Fury and others formally like it are usually called *semantic paradoxes*. Russell's informal solution to the semantic paradoxes—mentioned, for example, in Russell's Introduction to the first English translation of Wittgenstein's *Tractatus* in 1922—is to postulate a hierarchy of languages, each of which contains the "semantic predicates" (for example, "is true," "is false," "refers to,", etc.) of the language directly beneath it in the hierarchy, so that a sentence can never literally say of itself that it's true or false. This is known as *the meta-linguistic solution* to the semantic paradoxes, because a language L^1 that refers to a given target language L (sometimes also called "the object language") is said to be a "meta-language" of L. This basic strategy for avoiding the semantic paradoxes, together with a "semantic conception of truth," was later famously and formally developed by the brilliant Polish logician, mathematician, semanticist, and Vienna Circle-associated philosopher Alfred Tarski (Tarski, 1943, 1956). In sections X.1 and X. 3 below, I'll highlight the special role of Tarski's meta-linguistic strategy and his semantic conception of truth, in tandem with Gödel's incompleteness theorems, in bringing about the death of the classical logicist project.

IV.5 Russell's "Fido"-Fido Theory of Meaning

Russell held what's sometimes called a *"Fido"-Fido*, aka "purely referential," theory of meaning, which is that the meaning of a term is *just the object for which it stands* or *to which it refers* (Russell, 1973c, 1981, 1992, 1995: chs. V-XVIII). Thus "Fido" *means* Fido. More generally, for Russell (i) proper names such as "Ludwig" mean an individual object or thing, (ii) general terms such as "philosopher" mean universals, for example, the concept or property of being a philosopher, and (iii) logical words such as "is," "and," "or," "not," "if…. then," "if and only if," "all," "some," etc., all mean logical objects of some sort, for example, Copula, Conjunction, Disjunction, Negation, Conditionalization, Biconditionalization, Universal Quantification, Particular Quantification, etc.

Since Russell's "Fido"-Fido theory of meaning is *one-factor*, it follows that he rejected Frege's *two-factor* theory, and therefore that he also rejected Frege's basic distinction between sense and reference/Meaning. Indeed, one of the most contorted and puzzling passages in all of classical Analytic philosophy occurs in Russell's "On Denoting"—itself supposedly a paradigm of philosophical analysis—when Russell attempts to criticize Frege's theory of sense and reference by reformulating it as a very confused version of his own "Fido"-Fido theory (Russell, 1971b: pp. 49-50). This unintentionally farcical passage, which nowadays reads like an early version of that *bête noire* of post-modern philosophy, "Sokal's Hoax" (Sokal, 1996; and also section XVII.5 below) is generally known as *The Gray's Elegy Argument*.

IV.6 Knowledge-by-Acquaintance and Knowledge-by-Description

Early Russell's theory of knowledge was heavily influenced by Kant's theory of cognition (*Erkenntnis*) and in particular by Kant's basic and categorical distinction between (i) intuitions (*Anschauungen*) and (ii) concepts (*Begriffe*) (Hanna, 2001: sections 1.3, 4.3-4.4). Kant's notion of intuition, in turn, Russell understood in the very broad sense of the notion of a "presentation of an object," as developed by Meinong. Like Kant, Russell distinguishes sharply between two basic types of cognition: (i) knowledge-by-description, or knowledge that's mediated by the ascription of identifying properties (including relational properties) to the objects of cognition, and (ii) knowledge-by-acquaintance, or direct and unmediated infallible awareness of the object of cognition. But whereas Kant had held that all of our meaningful cognition contains an intuitional component, Russell holds a fairly narrow view of the scope of acquaintance: we can be acquainted with abstract n-place universals in rational intuition, and with concrete sense data in sense perception, and that's it. Thus Russell holds that *most* of our knowledge is by-description only. At the same time, however, Russell also holds that a subject cannot understand a sentence or a word unless that subject is acquainted with every one of its meaningful parts (I'll call this *Russell's principle of acquaintance for linguistic understanding*), which, when taken along with the "Fido"-Fido theory of meaning, implies that a subject cannot understand the meaning of a sentence (i.e., a *proposition*) unless that subject is acquainted with each of the things the several words of that sentence stand for.

IV.7 Russell's Theory of Descriptions

Russell's principle of acquaintance for linguistic understanding directly implies that in the case of propositions that include *only* descriptive elements—i.e., definite descriptions, or phrases of the form "The F" (for example, "The present king of France"), and indefinite descriptions, or phrases of the forms "an F," "some Fs," or "all Fs"—we must be acquainted (i) with all the universals picked out by general terms such as "present king of France" and also (ii) with all the logical objects picked out by logical words such as "the," "a," "some," and "all," in order to understand those phrases. In most cases, however, we are *not* also acquainted with the objects that are described by those definite or indefinite descriptions, so our knowledge of those objects is *purely* descriptive or identificational in character. This point, in turn, is closely connected with one of Russell's leading contributions to classical Analytic philosophy: his idea that there's a sharp difference between (i) the *grammatical form*, aka "natural or ordinary language syntax," aka "surface grammar," of a proposition, and (ii) the underlying *logical form*, aka "logical syntax," aka "depth grammar," of that proposition, and that fundamental logico-philosophical confusions arise when we fail to heed this distinction. If we put all of this together, the result is Russell's celebrated *theory of descriptions* (Ostertag, 1998; Russell, 1971b, 1981, 1993: pp. 167-180, 1995: ch. V; Whitehead and Russell, 1962: pp. 0-32, 66-71, 173-175).

The primary example of definite descriptions is terms in natural or ordinary language that *appear* to be names and thus to stand for particular things, but actually aren't names, because they in fact mean parts of general propositions. Hence they're *incomplete symbols*, aka "syncategorematic terms," that have meaning only in the context of larger complexes of symbols, and not on their own. Symbols that have meaning on their own, such as "Russell," "logician," or "Russell is a logician" are *complete symbols*, aka "categorematic terms." For example, in the meaningful sentence (hence a complete symbol and categorematic term)

> PKF: The present King of France is bald

the definite description "The present king of France" might seem to be a name. But if it's a meaningful name, then it stands for an object that doesn't exist, of which it's impossible to decide whether it's bald or not. So sentence PKF seems to have no definite truth-value. Russell's analysis of sentence PKF is that

> The present king of France is bald

actually means the same as

> There is one and only one present king of France and he is bald

which is false if there are no present kings of France, or if there's more than one present king of France, or if there's one and only one present king of France and he's not bald, and true otherwise. So definite descriptions of the form "the F" aren't names at all, and in fact are incomplete symbols or syncategorematic terms belonging to larger propositional complexes, that mean the same as "there exists an F and only one F," which, in standard logical symbols is

$$(\exists x) [Fx \& (y) (Fy \to y = x)]$$

Translating sentence PKF using this model, we get

$$(\exists x) \{[PKFx \& (y) (PKFy \to y = x)] \& Bx\}$$

Here we can see that the symbol

$$(\exists x) [PKFx \& (y) (PKFy \to y = x)]$$

occurs meaningfully only within the larger propositional complex that translates sentence PKF, hence it's an incomplete symbol or syncategorematic term.

This analysis can also be extended to most of the names in natural language, since it's true that for most names, for example, "Socrates," we're not actually immediately or presently acquainted with the bearers of those names, and yet we also know what those names mean. Impressed by that fact, Russell then proposed that most ordinary names are *disguised definite descriptions*. It didn't occur to him that there might instead be effective cognitive, causal, and/or social mechanisms *for extending the scope of acquaintance beyond immediacy and the present moment*, and that therefore most ordinary names are actually *directly referential terms*, and *not* disguised definite descriptions (Hanna, 1993a; 1997).

IV.8 Russell's Multiple-Relation Theory of Judgment[1]

According to Kant, propositions are the truth-value-bearing representational contents of judgments. And according to Frege, propositions are the senses expressed by those complete meaningful indicative sentences that have a truth-value as their reference/Meaning. But according to Russell, a proposition is nothing but the "complex" consisting of the class or set of things with which we are acquainted when we understand a sentence. This implies, for instance, that for Russell, in the case of the sentence

> Wittgenstein is shorter than Frege

the proposition expressed by that sentence *literally contains* Wittgenstein, Frege, and the "shorter than" relation. This striking view, in turn, is intimately connected with Moore's and Russell's radically realist "revolt against idealism": if all propositions are literally composed of real mind-independent things, then semantic facts are mind-independent facts, and cannot be ideal or mind-dependent.

One problem with this radically realistic view of the proposition, however, is *the problem of the unity of the proposition*: what accounts for the ordered character of the elements in the proposition, such that they go together in such a way as to constitute something that is definitely true or false? Given the set of three propositional elements (Wittgenstein, Frege, shorter than), what makes it the case that the proposition composed of those elements says *that Wittgenstein is shorter than Frege*, instead of saying *that Frege is shorter than Wittgenstein*, or even, for example, *that Shorter-Than freges Wittgenstein*? Moreover, if whatever it is that establishes the unity of the proposition, by relating all the elements to one another in a certain way (let's call that "the relating relation"), is *itself* another object, hence a *fourth* object, then yet another *fifth* object is required to relate all three original objects and the relating relation to one another, and so-on and so forth viciously *ad infinitum*. This is sometimes called *Bradley's Regress*, after the British neo-Hegelian F.H. Bradley, who used it to argue, by *reductio*, for absolute idealism, via the *necessary internality of all relations to absolute wholes*.

In any case, Russell's answer to the unity problem is that the mind of the person making a judgment relates the several parts of the proposition to one another by multiply acquainting herself with those objects in a certain order, thereby stopping the threatened regress right then and there. So a judgment is essentially *a psychological relation between a judging subject and the things in the world that constitute the elements of the proposition*. Then the proposition is true if and only if the things do indeed stand in just that ordered relation to each other in the actual world, and false if and only if they don't stand in just that relation. The judgment thus "corresponds" to reality *by means of the judging subject's act of psychologically identifying its propositional constituents and their relations, with real-world objects and their relations*. The obvious problem with this proposed solution to the unity-of-the-proposition problem is that it entails *solipsistic psychologism* at the level of judg-

---
[1] See, e.g., (Russell, 1973c, 1981, 1992, 1995: chs. V-XIII).

ment, since the underlying structure of the proposition, and therefore its overall meaning and truth, then depend wholly on the mental acts and choices of individual judgers . How ironic—not to mention revolting—that the Moorean/Russellian "revolt against idealism" would ultimately end up in psychologism and solipsism.

IV.9 Russellian Analysis, Early Wittgenstein, and Impredicativity Again

In autobiographical retrospect, Russell explicitly identified his conception of philosophical analysis with his complete rejection of Kant's metaphysics and epistemology:

> Ever since I abandoned the philosophy of Kant . . . I have sought solutions of philosophical problems by means of analysis; and I remain firmly persuaded . . . that only by analysing is progress possible. (Russell, 1959: pp. 14-15)

But that tells only *part* of the story about Russellian analysis. In fact Russell's program of philosophical analysis had fundamentally collapsed by 1914, mainly as the result of his tumultuous personal and philosophical encounters with his erstwhile student and then collaborator Wittgenstein, in 1912 and 1913:

> [Wittgenstein] had a kind of purity which I have never known equalled except by G. E. Moore.... He used to come to see me every evening at midnight, and pace up and down my room like a wild beast for three hours in agitated silence. Once I said to him: —Are you thinking about logic or about your sins? "Both," he replied, and continued his pacing. I did not like to suggest that it was time for bed, as it seemed probable both to him and me that on leaving me he would commit suicide. (Russell, 1975: p. 330)

From 1912 to 1914 Wittgenstein was ostensibly Russell's research student, working with him on the philosophy of logic and the logical foundations of mathematics, and supposedly becoming Russell's philosophical successor. But the student, who was as personally difficult as he was philosophically brilliant, soon very helpfully pointed out to his teacher the irreversible philosophical errors in his work-in-progress, *Theory of Knowledge* (Eames, 1992: pp. xiv-xx). The fundamental error was Russell's crypto-Meinongian idea that the logical constants, the vehicles of logical form, are themselves logical *objects* of some sort, belonging to the proposition in the same way that simple concrete particulars and simple abstract universals belong to the proposition. But how can the logical form of a proposition, its intrinsic form or *structure*, also be one of the contents or *constituents* of the very same proposition? The problem is that if the logical form or structure of a proposition is also treated as one of the propositional constituents, then there will necessarily be a logical and ontological vicious infinite regress whereby new *higher-order* structures are endlessly or unrestrictedly generated in order to bind *lower-order* structures to the other basic or zero-level constituents of the proposition.

Nowadays logicians and set theorists call this sort of logico-ontological regress *impredicativity*, and as I've noted in section II.7 above, at least *some* cases of impredicativity are vicious—even if some other cases are benign. But as Heidegger might have put it with essentially the same explanatory force, the philosophical error of confusing logical form or propositional structure with logical objects or propositional constituents is confusing *Being* with *beings*. This fundamental distinction is what Heidegger calls "ontological difference" (Heidegger, 1962: Introduction, 1984: pp. 150-154). Or as Kant might have put it with even greater explanatory force, vicious impredicativity is the logically chaotic result of confusing *transcendental logical conditions for the possibility of judging or thinking objects* with *judgeable or thinkable objects themselves*. So vicious impredicativity is what happens when you confuse *the transcendental* with *the empirical*.

Impredicativity, whether benign or vicious, is implicit in *Cantor's theorem*, discovered by Georg Cantor, which says that for any set *A*, the set of all its subsets (i.e., its power set), has a greater cardinality (i.e., counting-number-osity) than *A* itself, when the theorem is applied to infinite sets, and *Cantor's paradox*, which says that there's no greatest cardinal number and hence no set of all cardinal numbers, on pain of contradiction (Hallett, 1984). But it exploded onto the logico-mathematical scene with Russell's stunning discovery of the paradox of classes or sets produced by Frege's notorious axiom V in the *Basic Laws of Arithmetic*. As I mentioned above, axiom V is a principle for unrestrictedly generating classes from the extensions of *concepts*, which in turn are functions from objects to truth-values. Russell exploited axiom V in order to yield the class of all classes not members of themselves, which in turn is necessarily a member of itself if and only if it's not a member of itself. And as I also mentioned above, this isn't only a contradiction, it's a *hyper*-contradiction. From a mere contradiction you can always infer the falsity of one or more of the premises from which that contradiction is logically validly derived. But a hyper-contradiction, or paradox, is a contradiction such that the premises from which that contradiction is logically validly derived, are *themselves* contradictory and therefore necessarily false. So all the propositions essentially involved in that chain of reasoning are equally true and false, hence "truth value gluts," and necessarily, true if and only if they are false. Thus there is literally, logically, no way out. This is what Kant called an *antinomy*, and as he stressed in the "Dialectic of Pure Reason" section in the first *Critique*, an antinomy is always a complete philosophical disaster.

For Frege and Russell alike, indeed, the discovery of the paradox was an unmitigated *personal* and philosophical disaster. Frege was stopped dead in his tracks, tragically writing to Russell in 1902, as I mentioned above, that "logic totters," and that

> your discovery of the contradiction has surprised me beyond words, and I should like to say, thunderstruck. (As quoted in Monk, 1996: 153)

Sadly, Frege remained thunderstruck and never did groundbreaking work on the logical foundations of mathematics again. Even the much younger Russell, then at the very peak of his amazing logical powers and philosophical self-confidence, was flummoxed for several months (Monk, 1996: 142-199).

To be sure, as I mentioned in section IV.5, Russell-the-philosophical-juggernaut eventually produced several putative solutions for the paradox, including the no-class theory (which eliminates classes in favor of propositional functions), the vicious circle principle (which bans all impredicativity), and the Theory of Types (which systematically organizes classes and their memberships into logically benign distinct levels in a well-ordered hierarchy). But it was all to no avail, and the general problem of vicious impredicativity, of which Russell's paradox was only a particularly nasty instance, ultimately blew Russell's early philosophy apart. So much for the reliability of his logician's "feeling for reality"! In any case, Wittgenstein's relentless criticism changed Russell's philosophical life, and he (Russell) abandoned his book-in-progress, *Theory of Knowledge*, shortly thereafter:

> I wrote a lot of stuff about Theory of Knowledge, which Wittgenstein criticised with the greatest severity.... His criticism ... was an event of first-rate importance in my life, and affected everything I have done since. I saw he was right, and I saw that I could not hope ever again to do fundamental work in philosophy. My impulse was shattered, like a wave dashed to pieces against a breakwater.... I *had* to produce lectures for America, but I took a metaphysical subject although I was and am convinced that all fundamental work in philosophy is logical. My reason was that Wittgenstein persuaded me that what wanted doing in logic was too difficult for me. So there was really no vital satisfaction of my philosophical impulse in that work, and philosophy lost its hold on me. That was due to Wittgenstein more than to the war. (Russell, 1975: 282)

Despite having his fundamental philosophical impulse shattered to pieces against a breakwater, Russell nevertheless promptly sat down and wrote *Our Knowledge of the External World* (1914) for his Lowell Lectures at Harvard. This was characteristically Russellian, and as Ray Monk notes, "rarely can Russell have passed a day in his long lifetime... without writing, in one form or another, two or three thousand words" (Mink, 1996: p. xvii). But leaving aside Russell's characteristic self-dramatization and his amazing logocentric and logographic libido, the two simple facts of the matter are that Wittgenstein had seriously challenged four fundamental elements of Russell's seminal conception of analysis, and that Russell had no effective reply to Wittgenstein's challenges.

We'll recall that Russell's notion of analysis in the period from 1900 to 1913 was logicistic, platonistic, radically realistic, and grounded epistemically on a series of self-evident infallible acquaintances with the simple concrete or abstract constituents of propositions and also with the logical constants, the vehicles of logical form. The **first** problem with this notion is that Russell never provides an adequate explanation of how a human mind in real time and space can be directly related to causally inert non-spatio-temporal universals (the problem of *non-empirical knowledge*). A **second** problem, already previewed, is how propositions construed as ordered complexes of individuals, properties, and relations, along with logical constants such as *all, some, and, or, not*, and *if-then*, can ever be formally or materially unified into coherent, semantically unambiguous truth-bearers (the problem of *the unity of the proposition*). A **third** problem, also already previewed, is that the notion of a direct self-evident infallible acquaintance with logical constants, as if they were regular objects and propositional constituents alongside real individuals, properties, and relations, also leads to vicious impredicativity (the problem of *the nature of the logical constant*). And a **fourth** and final problem is that Russell never adequately clarifies the nature or status of logical necessity, and in particular whether logical truths are analytic a priori, synthetic a priori, or something else (the problem of *the nature of necessity*).

To be sure, all four problems had already been handled by Kant by means of his transcendental idealism: (i) non-empirical knowledge is based on transcendental reflection or self-knowledge, (ii) the unity of the proposition is based on the transcendental unity of apperception, (iii) logical constants are nothing but universal a priori or transcendental functions of thought, corresponding to higher-order pure concepts of the understanding, and (iv) logical necessity is irreducibly analytic necessity, not synthetic necessity. But it was precisely the Kantian approach that Russell was completely rejecting. So these possible solutions to his problems were already ruled out, and as a consequence Russell's fundamental philosophical impulse, like a wave against a Wittgenstein-constructed breakwater, was literally dashed to pieces—or more precisely, into logical atoms.

IV.10 Russell and The Philosophy of Logical Atomism

Russell's philosophy of *logical atomism*—which says that all meaningful propositions and real worldly objects are relationally composed of logically and ontologically independent simples according to logically sound and non-impredicative recursive principles—was Russell's considered view after his decisive encounter with Wittgenstein in the period immediately preceding The Great War, together with his critical reflections on that encounter during and after the War.

As World War I unfolded, Russell and Wittgenstein were personally and politically divided by the international hostilities. Russell very bravely professed pacifism and anarcho-socialism, in a nation hell-bent on smashing the Germans and protecting the rest of the world from the cultural and spiritual depredations of The Hun, and was imprisoned by the British government and lost his Trinity fellowship—a bellicose and by now personally- and philosophically-alienated McTaggart working hard to bring about Russell's excommunication by Cambridge—for his troubles. Wittgenstein went back to Austria, fought bravely on the German side on the Eastern Front, and was imprisoned by the Allies in Italy after the German surrender for *his* troubles. Back in England however, by the end of The Great War, Russell had completely capitulated to Wittgenstein's conception of philosophical analysis. He officially recorded the details of this conversion in his long essay, "The Philosophy of Logical Atomism":

> The following is the text of a course of eight lectures delivered in Gordon Square London, in the first months of 1918, which are very largely concerned with explaining certain ideas which I learned from my friend and former pupil, Ludwig

Wittgenstein. I have had no opportunity of knowing his views since August, 1914, and I do not even know whether he is alive or dead. (Russell, 1971d: p. 177)

Wittgenstein was indeed alive, if not altogether well, having seen frontline action on the Eastern Front and then later imprisoned at Como, Italy—where he read and carefully studied the *Critique of Pure Reason* for the first time, in 1918 (Monk, 1990: p. 158)—but in any case working relentlessly, in the midst of the conflagration and tragedy of World War I, on his masterpiece, and the only book published by him during his lifetime, the *Tractatus Logico-Philosophicus* (Wittgenstein, 1981).

V. Wittgenstein and the *Tractatus* 1: Propositions 1-2.063

V.1 A Brief Synopsis of the *Tractatus*

The "certain ideas" that Russell referred to in the Preface of the "Logical Atomism" essay, were worked out by Wittgenstein in a much-reworked series of notes and journal entries on philosophical logic written from 1912 or 1913 to 1918, and finally published in journal format in 1921 (in German) and as a book in 1922 (in an English translation by C.K. Ogden, assisted by Ramsey, who had translated it into English while still in high school), as the *Tractatus*. Its full English title (in Latin, obviously) was very cleverly suggested by Moore (a former classicist), and clearly plays a riff on the title of Spinoza's *Tractatus Theologico-Politicus*, therefore strongly suggesting both logico-philosophical iconoclasm, as well as Spinoza's rational mysticism, according to which personal enlightenment or wisdom is being able to see the world *sub specie aeternitatis*.

Indeed, Wittgenstein's "logico-philosophical treatise" (*Logisch-philosophische Abhandlung*) presents a radically new and revolutionary conception of philosophical analysis, according to which (i) metaphysics reduces to the propositions of logic, including both the truth-functional tautologies and also the logico-philosophical truths of the *Tractatus* itself, (ii) facts reduce to logically-structured complexes of ontologically neutral "objects," which can variously play the structural roles of both particulars and universals (including both properties and relations), (iii) factual propositions are nothing but linguistic facts that "picture" other facts according to one-to-one isomorphic correspondence relations, (iv) all non-factual propositions are either (iva) "senseless" (*sinnlos*) truth-functional tautologies expressing nothing but the formal meanings and deductive implications of the logical constants, or (ivb) the logico-philosophical propositions of the *Tractatus* itself, or (ivc) "nonsensical" (*unsinnig*) pseudo-propositions that violate logico-syntactic rules and logico-semantic categories, especially including all the synthetic a priori claims of traditional metaphysics, (v) the logical constants do not represent facts or refer to objects of any sort (*TLP* 4.0312), but instead merely "display" (*darstellen*) the a priori logical "scaffolding of the world" (*TLP* 6.124), which is also "the limits of my language" (*TLP* 5.6), and can only be "shown" or non- propositionally indicated, not "said" or propositionally described, (vi) the logical form of the world is therefore "transcendental" (*TLP* 6.13), and finally (vii) the logical form of the world reduces to the language-using metaphysical subject or ego, who or which is not in any way part of the world but in fact solipsistically identical to the world itself.

Looking more closely now at theses (v), (vi), and (vii), we can clearly see that Wittgenstein's icon-smashing "transcendental" conception of analysis is radically ontologically ascetic, since everything logically reduces to one simple thing: the language-using metaphysical subject or ego. Indeed, it's by means of considering theses (v) and (vi) that we can recognize the surprising and often-overlooked but quite indisputable fact that the *Tractatus* is every bit as much a *neo-Kantian idealistic metaphysical treatise* directly inspired by Schopenhauer's *World as Will and Representation* (1819/1844/1859), and thereby indirectly inspired by Kant's *Critique of Pure Reason*, as it is a *logico-philosophical treatise* inspired by Frege's *Begriffsschrift* and

The Fate of Analysis

Whitehead's and Russell's *Principia*. As I mentioned at the end of the immediately preceding chapter, Wittgenstein first read and carefully studied the first *Critique* in 1918 (Monk, 1990: p. 158). And he later told G. H. von Wright that "he had read Schopenhauer's *Die Welt als Wille und Vorstellung* in his youth and that his first philosophy was Schopenhauerian epistemological idealism" (Von Wright, 1984: p. 6). The Schopenhauerian influence is also fully explicit in Wittgenstein's *Notebooks 1914-1916* (Brockhaus, 1991). Indeed, in 1920 Wittgenstein told Frege that there are "deep grounds for idealism" (*tiefen Gründe des Idealismus*) (Monk, 1990: pp. 190, 605). And in 1931 Wittgenstein wrote that "Boltzmann, Hertz, Schopenhauer, Frege, Russell, Kraus, Loos, Weininger, Spengler, [and] Sraffa have influenced me" (Wittgenstein, 1980: p. 19^e, underlining added). So whereas the Moore-powered Russell *abandoned* or *rejected* Kant's epistemology and metaphysics, Wittgenstein instead *assimilated* or *sublimated* them. And from this standpoint, we can see that the *Tractatus* is fundamentally an essay in *transcendental logic*:

> The limit of language is shown by its being impossible to describe the fact which corresponds to (is the translation of) a sentence, without simply repeating the sentence. (This has to do with the Kantian solution of the problem of philosophy.) (Wittgenstein, 1980, p. 10^e).

The *Tractatus* ends with the strangely moving proposition, "Whereof one cannot speak, thereof one must be silent / *Wovon man nicht sprechen kann, darüber muss man schweigen* (*TLP* 7)—a proposition that, not altogether coincidentally, is also the single repeated lyric of a bizarrely beautiful song by the bizarrely brilliant Finnish composer and performer M.A. Numminen (2021). What on earth does this proposition mean? One possible interpretation, now known as *the resolute reading*, is that proposition 7 is saying that the *Tractatus* itself—except for the Preface and proposition 7, that is—is logically and philosophically worthless nonsense (Diamond, 1991). So according to the resolute reading, the *Tractatus* is the self-conscious *reductio* of classical metaphysics. But on the contrary, the resolute reading, in effect, confuses the *Tractatus* with Carroll's *Through the Looking Glass*. Both, to be sure, are wonderful books written by brilliant philosophical logicians—but two radically different kinds of book.

More precisely, for Wittgenstein, to say that a proposition is "nonsense" is *only* to say *that it literally does not picture an atomic fact*, and also *that the proposition is not a contingent* (i.e., non-tautological, non-contradictory) *truth-function of propositions that picture atomic facts*. This exhausts the domain of what can be "said" in the strict sense. According to Wittgenstein, by this criterion many seemingly sensible, supposedly intelligible, putatively important philosophical propositions and their contraries alike (for example, "God exists," "God doesn't exist," "human freedom exists," "human freedom doesn't exist," "the human soul is immortal," "the human soul isn't immortal," etc.) are all shown to be in fact nonsensical, in roughly Carroll's sense of a proposition's being logically absurd and worthless, end-of-story, even if charmingly amusing in a children's book. Such strings of words do not, properly speaking, belong to any well-ordered logical or natural language. Correspondingly, in the later *Philosophical Investigations* Wittgenstein says that

> [w]hen we say "Every word in language signifies something" we have so far said

nothing whatever; unless we have explained exactly what distinction we want to make. (It might be, of course, that we wanted to distinguish the words of language ... from words "without meaning" (*ohne Bedeutung*) such as occur in Lewis Carroll's poems, or words like 'Lilliburlero' in songs.) (*PI* §13)

But according to Wittgenstein in the *Tractatus*, it's also the case that many fully intelligible and deeply logically important, or as Kant would have said, "thinkable," propositions are classified as nonsense by this criterion, along with some other deeply aesthetically or ethically important propositions that silently *show* things rather than strictly *saying* them. The logical, aesthetic, and ethical relevance and value of these propositions is *not* affected by their shown to be being non-factual, non-scientific, and thus in one sense "nonsensical" propositions. On the contrary, their logical, aesthetic, or ethical relevance and value is *magnified* and *preserved* precisely because these propositions *cannot* be reductively analyzed in the manner of scientifically meaningful or factual propositions. In this special sense, the *nonsensicality* of a given proposition is equivalent to its *logical irreducibility* and its *axiological integrity*.

Thus the resolute reading of the *Tractatus* neither distinguishes between the various crucially different ways in which propositions can be non-factual, nor takes the fundamental saying vs. showing contrast sufficiently seriously. The main point of the *Tractatus* is that there are many *crucially different* kinds of nonsense. And certain kinds of nonsense are radically more logically, aesthetically, or ethically *important* than factual meaning itself. So to collapse the several kinds of nonsense into a single flattened-out logically absurd and worthless kind, full stop, is just to miss that main point. But most crucially of all, against an explicitly Kantian and Schopenhauerian backdrop, the resolute reading can be neatly avoided, because proposition 7 is then instead, in effect, saying (i) that traditional metaphysics has been destroyed by the philosophical logic of the *Tractatus* just as Kant's first *Critique* had destroyed traditional metaphysics, (ii) that the logico-philosophical propositions of the *Tractatus* itself *would have* counted as absurdly nonsensical in Lewis Carroll's sense because they're neither factual propositions nor truth-functional logical truths, *were it not for* a much deeper fact, namely, (iii) that these Tractarian propositions are *self-manifesting transcendental truths in the Kantian sense* about the nature of logic, and therefore have the basic function of constituting a logical stairway or "ladder" (*Leiter*) to axiological heaven, aka "God," aka "the highest good," between the factual natural sciences and aesthetics or ethics, and finally (v) that ethics consists in the mystical feeling that the world can be viewed *sub specie aeternitatis* and in decisive, action-guiding, world-changing noncognitive volitions (*TLP* 6.4 - 6.522), not propositional thoughts.

So at the end of the *Tractatus* Wittgenstein logically transcends scientific knowledge in order to reach the *ethical* standpoint in a Kantian, and also a Spinozan, Pascalian, Kierkegaardian, and more generally *Existentialist* sense.[1] And this is precisely why, in 1918—again,

---

[1] Existentialists hold that philosophy begins and ends with the irreducible facts of human consciousness, human freedom, and the creative, passionate, lifelong human pursuit of authenticity and meaning or purpose, in a world in which God (or any transcendent source of meaning or purpose) either does not exist or else has infinitely receded from intervention in human life and from human understanding. See, e.g., (Barnes, 1959; Solomon, 1974; Crowell, 2012).

shortly after he'd read and carefully studied the *Critique of Pure Reason* for the first time (Monk, 1990: p. 158)—Wittgenstein told the journal editor Ludwig von Ficker that "the [*Tractatus*]'s point is an ethical one" (as quoted in Brockhaus, 1991: p. 296). Kant makes essentially the same radical move in the B edition Preface to the first *Critique*: "I had to deny [scientific] **knowledge** (*Wissen*) in order to make room for [moral] **faith** (*Glaube*)" (*CPR* Bxxx, boldfacing in the original). Moral faith in the Kantian/Wittgensteinian sense is when we stop cognitively generating all those scientific *words*, achieve some degree of purity of heart, and silently perform ethical *deeds*. (In this connection, we'll recall Goethe's famous line from *Faust* 1, "In the beginning was the Deed," itself adapting the Bible's famous line from the Book of John 1 ("In the beginning was the Word.")

V.2 The *Tractatus* in Context

As Wittgenstein stresses in the Preface, he "makes no claim to novelty in points of detail" and does not care whether he is borrowing ideas from other philosophers, especially Frege and Russell. Moreover, it's obvious from the 1914-1916 notebooks that Wittgenstein was also heavily influenced by Schopenhauer, and thus by neo-Kantian philosophy. He'd read and carefully studied the first *Critique* in 1918 (Monk, 1990: p. 158), and, as we've seen a few paragraphs above, he explicitly told Von Wright that "he had read Schopenhauer's *Die Welt als Wille und Vorstellung* in his youth and that his first philosophy was a Schopenhauerian epistemological idealism" (Von Wright, 1984: p. 6). And we've also seen that in 1920 Wittgenstein told Frege that there are "deep grounds for idealism" (Monk, 1990: pp. 190, 605). However, Von Wright also says that

> I know nothing about how this interest was related to [Wittgenstein's] interest in logic and the philosophy of mathematics, except that I remember his saying that it was Frege's conceptual realism which made him abandon his earlier idealistic views. (Von Wright, 1984: p. 6)

In view of the self-admitted fact that Von Wright "knows nothing about how" Wittgenstein's idealism is related to his interest in logic and the philosophy of mathematics, then is Von Wright likely to be correct that in the *Tractatus* Wittgenstein actually *abandons* his earlier neo-Kantian idealism in light of his reading of Frege? Or is it instead the case that Wittgenstein merely *reformulates his earlier neo-Kantian idealism* in light of his reading of Frege? My proposal is that it's the latter.

So I can now motivate a general interpretation of the *Tractatus* by situating it in its historico-philosophical context. More precisely, according to this interpretation, (i) Wittgenstein accepts the basic metaphysical and epistemological framework of Kant's transcendental idealism and his theory of cognition but rejects Kant's *modal dualism* of analytic vs. synthetic a priori necessary truths and replaces it with a *modal monism* of logically necessary truths, (ii) Wittgenstein accepts Schopenhauer's neo-Kantian reduction of both the noumenally real epistemic subject and also the noumenally real epistemic object (or "thing-in-itself") of Kant's transcendental idealism, to *the will*, i.e., to *the metaphysical subject*, (iii) Wittgenstein accepts the basic project of logical analysis as implicit in Fregean logicism, but rejects Frege's fundamental appeal to set theory, (iv) Wittgenstein accepts the Frege-Russell idea that logic is "first philosophy," but rejects both of their conceptions of logic: for Wittgenstein, logic is neither the science of laws of truth nor the absolutely general science of deduction; instead, *logic is transcendental* in Kant's sense, (v) Wittgenstein accepts Frege's semantics of sense and reference/Meaning—that is, he accepts what Von Wright calls "Frege's conceptual realism"—but rejects Frege's platonist ontology of the "third realm" and also rejects Russell's one-factor or "Fido"-Fido theory of meaning, except for names, and finally, (vi) Wittgenstein accepts Russell's distinction between knowledge-by-description and knowledge-by-acquaintance, Russell's theory of descriptions, and also Russell's radically simple correspondence theory of truth, but he rejects Russell's multiple-relation theory of judgment.

V.3 The Basic Structure of the *Tractatus*: A Simple Picture

Here's a simple diagram or picture of the basic structure of the Tractatus, as divided into an "upper" or essence level (roughly, a transcendental level), and a "lower" or natural/ordinary level (roughly, an empirical level). And poised between the upper (essence or transcendental) and lower (natural/ordinary or empirical) levels, equally participating in both, is the subject who uses language to represent its world, the world of facts, not objects or things. To read the diagram correctly, start in the middle with the unboldfaced sentence running from left to right, then either look upwards towards the corresponding essence level, or downwards towards the corresponding natural/ordinary level:

ESSENCE LEVEL

metaphysical subject	logic	**form/structure:** *logical space (+/- real space, time, and color)* **matter/substance:** *objects or things*
the subject uses language	to represent	the world = the facts
psychological subject	thought = private language natural/ordinary language	**natural/ordinary world**

NATURAL/ORDINARY LEVEL

Figure 1. A simple picture of the basic structure of the Tractatus

V.4 Tractarian Ontology

The *Tractatus* opens with a series of ontological assertions: (i) the world (*Welt*) or reality (*Wirklichkeit*) is the totality of facts (*Tatsachen*), not objects or things, (ii) facts can be either atomic facts (*Sachverhalten*) or else molecular facts, and all the atomic facts are modally independent of one another (i.e., only contingently related to one another), (iii) atomic facts can be either positive (existent) or negative (non-existent), (iv) positive or negative atomic facts are states of affairs (*Sachlagen*), made up of possible combinations of objects or things, which in turn are simple entities, knowable by acquaintance, and (v) all the possible combinations of objects or things in atomic facts (va) are built into the very nature of the objects or things themselves, as their "internal qualities," and (vb) are necessarily governed by logic, which specifies the "logical forms" of objects or things (real space, time, and color), *therefore* (vi) the objects or things are the matter or "substance" of the world, and the world's overall form or structure is "logical space."

V.5 Reconstructing Wittgenstein's Reasoning

How can we make sense of all this? My proposal is that we reconstruct Wittgenstein's reasoning as follows:

> 1. Let's suppose that philosophy is possible only as logical analysis, and that there really is such a thing as logical analysis: then what *must* be the case?

> 2. Answer: "Every statement about complexes can be analyzed into a statement about their constituent parts, and into those propositions which completely describe the complexes" (*TLP* 2.0201).

> 3. Now what, in turn, *must* be the case if 2. is true?

> 4. Answer: the world must be ultimately made up of simple objects or things that compose the substance or substrate of the world, which in turn are combined into complexes (the facts), and all the objects together with all the facts or complexes into which they constitutively enter, must exhaust the nature of reality, and logical analysis must be the correct description of this reality.

V.6 What *Are* the Objects or Things?

All we really know about the objects or things is that they must be able to combine with one another in order to make up all the facts, and in particular they must able to combine with each other in order to make up all the *atomic* facts. Therefore, although the objects or things are "simple" in that they're primitive and not further decomposable, nevertheless they're not undifferentiated and without distinct natures. On the contrary, the objects or things are necessarily internally articulated, which is to say that they must have both "internal qualities" that specify precisely how they can combine or fail to combine with one another, and also general "logical forms" that govern these combinations. Wittgenstein says that these general logical forms include real (as opposed to purely logical) space, time, and color. This directly implies that all atomic facts must be spatiotemporal and phenomenal in character, and that *simply as a matter of logic,* two different colors cannot occur in one and the same place and time. So *simply as a matter of logic*, nothing can be everywhere red and somewhere green, or everywhere green and somewhere red, at one and the same time. So, whatever the objects or things are, they're presented to the language-using subject *only via the spatiotemporal sensibly manifest or phenomenal facts and their necessary logical forms*.

V.7 The Role of Logic in Tractarian Ontology

Now something that Wittgenstein isn't telling us here is that, while logic inherently *governs* the objects and their combinations into atomic facts, logic isn't specifically *about* the atomic facts. Rather, logic is specifically *about* the relations of truth-dependency between atomic facts that constitute the *molecular* facts. For example, the fact that P is an *atomic* fact, and the fact that Q is another *atomic* fact, but the fact that if *P* then *Q*, is a *molecular* fact.

V.8 Colorless Objects/Things

Wittgenstein says that the objects or things are "colorless": but why? This is because although we can be directly acquainted with them, nevertheless nothing can be fully cognized until the objects or things are combined into facts. In other words, although there *must* be objects/things, in principle *we cannot know what they are* "in themselves": rather we can fully cognize objects/things *only insofar as they appear to us as constituents of facts*. So we must remain consistently agnostic about the inner nature of the objects. We know *that* they subsist, and *that* they must be combined into the facts, but not *what* they are in themselves. This of course is a deeply Kantian point: due to the inherent limitations of our innately specified cognitive capacities, and our "human, all-too-human" nature, we *cannot* know things-in-themselves, and we *can* know only *objects of experience*, namely, the sensibly manifest or phenomenal facts that correspond to true *judgments of experience*.

Moreover, again as per Kant, we *do* know something a priori about the general shape or form of objects or things, namely that they *must* conform to the general shape or form of statements or propositions. Thus, as we'll discover later, there are basic or atomic propositions that correlate with the basic or atomic facts, and there are one-to-one correspondences between the parts of the atomic propositions and the parts of the atomic facts. In particular, the subjects and predicates of simple sentences stand for objects or things of different sorts: Fregean *individuals*, and Fregean *concepts* (i.e., one-place or many-place universals, i.e., properties and relations).

V.9 Tractarian Ontology, Necessity, and Contingency

According to Wittgenstein, objects, facts, the world, and logical space stand in various relations of necessity or contingency. This is captured by two fundamental theses. **First**, the natures of the objects or things necessarily determine all the possible combinations of objects into atomic facts. But **second**, all atomic facts are modally and indeed logically independent of one another, which is to say that they are only *contingently* related to one another. That is, for Wittgenstein, precisely how the objects in any *one* atomic fact stand in relation to one another cannot necessarily dictate how the objects in any *other* atomic fact stand in relation to one another. This naturally prompts the question: why?

The answer is three-part. **First**, if atomic facts necessarily depended on one another, then the meaning or truth of an atomic proposition about a single fact would depend on the meaning or truth of another proposition about another fact, ad infinitum, which would entail a coherence or holistic theory of truth or meaning (*TLP* 2.0211-2.0212), in which case the correspondence theory of truth would have to be false, which is absurd because the correspondence theory for Wittgenstein is a necessary condition of the possibility of logical analysis. **Second**, if atomic facts necessarily depended on one another, then necessary connections between them could not be merely logical in character, since logic applies only to the relations between molecular facts, and there would then have to be non-logically necessary truths, which is absurd, because for Wittgenstein modal monism is a necessary condition of the possibility of logical analysis. And **third**, although logic does not determine the exact configuration of objects, it's a necessary condition of the configurations of objects and it frames all facts: so from the standpoint of logic, just *how* the individual facts are determined is an open question, yet at the same time necessarily, every fact is determined according to an a priori repertoire of logical forms (*TLP* 2.013-2.0131).

V.10 Some Initial Worries, and Some Possible Wittgensteinian Counter-Moves

Here are some initial worries about Tractarian ontology that we'll need to keep in mind as we move forward, critically and hermeneutically, through the book.

(Worry 1) Are the simple objects *absolute* simples, or are they simple only relative to *a given natural or ordinary subject who is doing the analyzing*? If it's the latter, then logical analysis is egocentrically private, cannot be shared, and does not generalize: in short, solipsistic psychologism. [One possible counter-move that Wittgenstein could make here is to stress that the subject or ego of analysis is a *metaphysical* or *transcendental* subject or ego, not a *psychological* or *empirical* subject or ego.]

(Worry 2) What about the modal independence of atomic facts: is this correct? If point A is red (positive atomic fact 1), then isn't it *necessarily not the case* that point A is green (negative atomic fact 2)? And if point A is brighter than point B (positive atomic fact 1), and point B is brighter than point C (positive atomic fact 2), then isn't it *necessarily the case* that point A is brighter than point C (positive atomic fact 3)? [One possible counter-move that Wittgenstein could make here is to deny that facts like these are really *atomic*, and assert that instead they're really *molecular*.]

(Worry 3) Let's say that a *transcendental argument* has the following form:

1. Assume the truth of a factual proposition P.

2. Then find a non-trivial, fundamental a priori presupposition of P, APP.

3. Then, from the truth of P, conclude that, necessarily and a priori APP, and that APP is a (or the) condition of the real possibility of the fact that P.

Since the *Tractatus* has the general form of a transcendental argument from the fact of logical analysis, then it's still possible to reject the initial assumption: that is, it's still possible to reject the assumption *that there really is such a thing as logical analysis*. But how can this be shown by Wittgenstein, without simply begging the question? [One possible counter-move that Wittgenstein could make here is to connect, in a metaphysically substantive way, logical analysis with the nature of the exact sciences (i.e., mathematics and the basic natural sciences, for example, physics and chemistry): that is, he could claim that logical analysis is itself a non-trivial, fundamental a priori presupposition of the exact sciences, which uncontroversially *do* exist.]

VI. Wittgenstein and the *Tractatus* 2: Propositions 2.013-5.55

VI.1 What is Logical Space? What is Real Space?

According to the *Tractatus*, all actual or possible facts, whether positive or negative, and whether atomic or complex, occur within a unique "logical space" that's a non-trivial, fundamental a priori presupposition of, but not a strictly sufficient condition of, those facts (*TLP* 2.013). This space is "logical" precisely because *it's the way that logic manifests itself in the world*, namely, *as the immanent logical structure of all actual or possible facts*. What supplies the other condition, that, together with logical space, is strictly sufficient for the facts, is the domain of objects. This other condition is relatively independent of logic, and in that sense it's simply "given" to the representing subject. Hence logic is before the "How" (i.e., the actual or possible facts), but not before the "What" (i.e., the substance of the world, the objects or things) (*TLP* 5.552). Furthermore, one of the three basic logical forms of objects is what, in order to distinguish it from logical space, I'll call *real space* (*TLP* 2.0233). Since one of the other basic forms is color, this implies *that real space is sensibly manifest or phenomenal space*. This, in turn, guarantees that all atomic facts are facts *about* spatiotemporal sensibly manifest or phenomenal objects.

Do these two points together imply either (i) that the objects or things themselves are spatiotemporal sensibly manifest or phenomenal objects?, or (ii) that logical space is identical to real space? The answer is *no* in both cases.

VI.2 Atomic Facts *Necessarily Are* in Real Space, But Objects or Things Themselves *Necessarily Aren't* in Real Space

As regards (i), objects or things are inherently "colorless" and do not acquire any "material properties" until they're combined in atomic facts (*TLP* 2.0231). Empirical reality is *limited* by the totality of objects (*TLP* 5.5561), but empirical reality is not merely a *collection* of objects. In other words, the objects or things necessarily *determine* all the facts and occur *in* all the facts, but also, necessarily, subsist at an ontological level that's *below* the facts. It's crucial to note that this point strongly militates *against* the Russellian logical atomist and The Vienna Circle-style logical empiricist/positivist reading of the *Tractatus*, according to which the objects or things are sense data or sensory experiences/sensory events of some sort. More emphatically put: the Tractarian Wittgenstein is *a logicistic neo-Kantian*, and *not* a logical atomist or logical empiricist/positivist.

Closely connected with this point is Wittgenstein's striking idea that the mere occurrence of a set of objects in a fact, even the mere occurrence of the objects *in a certain order*, does not in and of itself determine precisely *which* fact it is: the very same set of objects in the very same order might in fact give rise to two distinct facts, as in the case of The Necker Cube (*TLP* 5.5423). What's going on in the case of The Necker Cube is that two distinct orientations of the same perceiving subject are possible, relative to the same spatial figure: the two aspects of The Necker Cube are in fact *enantiomorphic* or right-handed/

left-handed mirror images of one another. So they're what Kant calls *incongruent counterparts*. This is possible only in an *orientable space* with *intrinsic right-hand and left-hand directions*. Hence the occurrence of the two facts requires not merely the objects or things as constituents, and not merely their occurrence in a certain order, but also the non-trivial, fundamental a priori presupposition of a spatial framework of representation that's contributed by the representing subject or ego.

Kant, of course, made this very point in the Transcendental Aesthetic section of the *Critique of Pure Reason*. And in the Tractarian framework, this crucial Kantian point also generalizes. Every actual or possible fact expresses not only the objects or things and relations between them but also the a priori formal representational contributions of a representing subject or ego: therefore, all facts are partially determined by our forms of representation. The crucial difference is that whereas Kant takes this representational contribution to be *purely intuitional*, hence *essentially non-conceptual, non-discursive, non-logical*, and *non-propositional* in character, Wittgenstein takes it to be purely *logical, conceptual, discursive, propositional*, and *linguistic* in character. So *pure logic* and the conceptual, discursive, propositional parts of *language* for Wittgenstein play essentially the same representational role that Kant's *pure forms of spatial and temporal intuition* play in the Transcendental Aesthetic. Substituting either Fregean/Russellian pure logic or the conceptual, discursive, propositional parts of language for pure intuition, in turn, is a *classical neo-Kantian* move, especially characteristic of early 20th century members of the *Marburg School*, for example, Ernst Cassirer (Friedman, 2000: chs. 6-7).

In this way, for Wittgenstein, whereas the objects or things and their internal qualities are *the ontological inputs* to the constitution of facts, the facts themselves are *the ontological outputs* of the objects or things, together with the a priori structure of logical space and the logical activities of the representing subject or ego. Objects or things are "nothing for us," no matter what they might be in themselves, *until and just insofar as* they occur in such facts.

Moreover, it would be a big mistake to think of the contribution of the representing subject or ego to facts as a passive template that could somehow be detached from the representing subject or ego, and then separately isolated and analyzed, like "spatial spectacles" (*TLP* 4.0412). The problem here is one of vicious infinite regress: isolating a spatial template would involve placing it in a still more comprehensive, or larger, space and then spatially comparing it to what was seen *through* the spectacles. So the active contribution of the representing subject or ego to the facts cannot itself be represented *as* a fact: it's a non-trivial, fundamental, non-empirical presupposition of representing the facts, and therefore immanent in the act of linguistic and conceptual, discursive, propositional factual representation itself.

VI.3 Logical Space is Essentially More Comprehensive than Real Space

Whereas all atomic facts occur in real—i.e., sensibly manifest or phenomenal—space, nevertheless not all facts are atomic. Over and above *the simple or atomic facts*, each of which is modally independent of all the others, are *the complex or molecular facts*, which are connected by various logical relations, including negation, conjunction, disjunction, conditionalization, etc. Wittgenstein's view is that all of these relations are *truth-functional* in Frege's sense: that is, they express systematic mappings from truth-values to truth-values. For example, the conjunction sign "and" (or "&," or whatever) expresses the 2-place truth-function which maps from T and T to T, but otherwise maps to F for all other combinations of T and F. Some of these mappings always yield truth and thus correspond to logical tautologies (for example, any proposition of the form "(P & Q) → P"); some of these mappings always yield falsity and thus correspond to logical impossibilities or contradictions (for example, any proposition of the form "P & not-P"); and some of these mappings are sometimes true and sometimes false and thus correspond to contingent propositions (for example, "P & Q") (*TLP* 4.46).

Now the scope of logic is essentially more comprehensive than the scope of geometry; correspondingly, logical space is essentially more comprehensive than real space. In real space, which is a three-dimensional, egocentrically-centered, orientable space, it's *geometrically or spatially impossible* for the right and left hands to coincide, i.e., to be congruent, even despite the fact that they're one-to-one mirror-reflected counterparts (aka *enantiomorphs*). But Wittgenstein further holds that it's *logically possible* for there to be perfect congruence of the right and left hands in a four-dimensional egocentrically-centered space (*TLP* 6.36111). So what's geometrically or spatially impossible can still be logically possible. Not only that, but physical possibility is even narrower than geometric or spatial possibility, since some geometrically or spatially possible atomic facts (for example, synchronous necessarily coordinated movements of enantiomorphs) violate the laws of relativity physics, a phenomenon that shows up as one of the paradoxes of quantum mechanics, *nonlocality*. Only the *actual* world necessarily obeys the laws of logic, geometry, *and* physics.

VI.4 Why There Can't/Kant Be a Non-Logical World

No fact in the world, whether atomic or complex, falls outside logic. The atomic facts are constrained by the logical forms of space, time, and color; and the complex facts are constrained by the internal structure of classical logic. For our purposes here, "classical logic" is *Principia Mathematica*-style bivalent (two-valued) propositional and predicate calculus with identity and quantification over objects (first-order logic), as well as quantification over Fregean concepts or properties/relations and functions (second-order logic), but *without* set theory. That's why logic is "not a theory but a reflection of the world" and, in a specifically Kantian sense, "transcendental" (*TLP* 6.13): the world, as the result of our linguistic representations of facts, non-trivially, fundamentally presupposes, and hence is necessarily constrained by, the a priori essence of language, i.e., classical logic.

In this way, the world in logical space is necessarily a *logical world* (*TLP* 3.031-3.032), just as every figure in real manifest or phenomenal space necessarily obeys the laws of geometry (*TLP* 3.0321). Therefore, it's impossible to represent in language anything that violates the laws of logic, just as it's impossible to represent spatially anything that violates the laws of geometry. This *doesn't* however mean there can't be contradictory propositions in logic: such propositions, to be sure, cannot represent any facts in logical space, but are fully within the scope of logic: otherwise, *reductio* arguments would not be logically valid.

The non-logical is therefore not *the contradictory*, but rather that which falls, in one way or another, altogether outside the "bipolar" notions of truth and falsity, aka "bivalence," hence *the non-bivalent*. Some examples of the non-logical or non-bivalent would be (i) unacceptably nonsensical pseudo-propositions that involve *sortal incorrectness* or *incoherence of semantic categories*, for example, "Colorless green ideas sleep furiously" or "Quadruplicity drinks procrastination," (ii) propositions that have no truth-value at all, whether T or F, for example, "All of John's children are girls," when John in fact has no children, aka *truth-value gaps*, (iii) propositions that are both true *and* false, for example, Liar sentences, aka *truth-value gluts*, and (iv) propositions that have a value *other than* T or F, for example, "The nth digit in the decimal expansion of pi is an even number," if you are a constructivist or intuitionist in mathematics, aka *non-classical* values.

VI.5 A Worry About Wittgenstein's Conception of Logic: *Non***-Classical Logics**

One of the most striking developments in logical theory since the *Tractatus* is the discovery or invention of *non-classical logics*: either (i) logics that are *conservative extensions* of classical logic, in the sense that they entail no violations of the basic syntactic or semantic principles of classical logic—for example, normal modal logic, as per the systems described in C.I. Lewis's *Survey of Symbolic Logic* (1918) or Carnap's *Meaning and Necessity* (1956)—or (ii) logics that *non-conservatively deviate from* classical logic, aka *deviant logics*, in the sense that they do entail violations of at least some of the basic syntactic or semantic principles of classical logic (for example, dialetheic logic, intuitionist logic, fuzzy logic, etc.) (Haack, 1996; Priest, 2001). Some deviant logics allow truth-value gaps, and/or truth-value gluts, and/or non-classical values, and/or reject the universal law of non-contradiction and/or the universal law of excluded middle. So the non-classical logic worry about Wittgenstein's conception of logic is that it's scientifically *needlessly narrow* and *retrograde*: that is, he's wrongly assumed that classical logic is *The One True Logic*.

The non-classical logic worry, in turn, is precisely analogous to Fregean, Russellian, and Vienna Circle-style worries about Kant's scientifically needlessly narrow and retrograde commitments to "Aristotelian," aka *monadic* (i.e., sentential and one-place predicate) logic, Euclidean geometry, and Newtonian physics. Moreover, the non-classical logic worry *also* has the interesting and ironic twist that Frege, Russell, and virtually all the members of The Vienna Circle—with the sole exception of early Carnap, who explicitly held in *Logical Syntax of Language* that "in logic there are no morals" (Carnap, 1937: p. 52)—are, along with the Tractarian Wittgenstein, *are no less guilty than Kant of scientifically needless narrowness and retrogression*. So why don't contemporary post-classical Analytic philosophers bitterly complain about the scientific narrowness and retrograde character of Fregean, Russellian, and most Vienna Circle-style *conceptions of logic*, just as they bitterly complain about the scientific narrowness and retrograde character of Kant's *conceptions of the formal and natural sciences*? Do you suppose that it might have *something* to do with their vocational anti-Kantianism?

In any case, one possible response open to Wittgenstein here would be to allow for a plurality of syntactically and semantically different classical and non-classical languages and logics, which would also in effect fully *relativize* his Tractarian metaphysics. But this seems to violate the Marburg-style logicistic neo-Kantian spirit of the *Tractatus*, which requires a single unified and universal *transcendental* logic. Another possible response open to Wittgenstein that's closer to the spirit of the *Tractatus* itself, and therefore also smoothly consistent with the Marburg-style logicistic neo-Kantian idea of a single unified and universal transcendental logic, I think, would be to retreat from classical logic to an a priori *Ur*-logic or *proto*-logic that's weaker than classical logic, but still *consistent with* classical logic, and also *preserved in* all non-classical logics, whether conservative extensions or deviant logics. Such an priori Ur-logic or proto-logic would contain, for example, *the weak or minimal principle of non-contradiction*:

> It's not the case that every proposition (sentence, statement, etc.) is both true and false. (Putnam, 1983; Hanna, 2006: ch. 2)

VI.6 What is a Tractarian Proposition?

From the standpoint of philosophical logic in general, and leaving aside subtleties about whether propositions are essentially the same as or different from interpreted sentences and/or statements, etc., a proposition is (i) *the semantic content* of a judgment (assertion, belief, etc.), i.e., "what it says," and (ii) *the essential truth-bearer* for specifically logical and more generally theoretically rational and scientific purposes, i.e., whatever has a classical truth-value (T or F) inherently. But apart from that, there are *many* saliently different theories of the nature of propositions, not only prior to Kant, but also and especially in the wake of Kant's theory of judgment (Hanna, 2017d) and throughout the classical and post-classical Analytic traditions (McGrath and Frank, 2018).

According to Kant, propositions are complex mental representations, systematically built up out of intuitions and concepts, intrinsically governed by logical forms and laws, unified under the a priori formal constraint that necessarily, every proposition is assertible by some or another self-conscious thinking subject,[1] that in turn constitute mind-dependent empirical or non-empirical states of affairs insofar as they are well-formed, intersubjectively sharable, and based on the actual givenness of objects to human sensibility. According to Frege, propositions are the complex senses of indicative sentences and the objects of assertions or judgments, systematically composed under maximally general logical laws, that are

---
[1] This claim must not be confused with the substantially different claim that necessarily, there's a noumenal self-conscious thinking subject who/which asserts every proposition—that would be a "quantifier shift fallacy" used in service of a wrongheaded noumenal metaphysics, and a prime example of what Kant calls a "paralogism of pure reason" (*CPR* A341-405/B399-432).

about The True and The False. And according to Russell, propositions are ontic complexes built of objects of different types—individuals, one-place properties, many-place properties or relations, logical constants, etc.—to which judging subjects are multiply psychologically related in a certain order. The Tractarian theory of propositions draws eclectically from all of these sources, but also depends crucially on Wittgenstein's theory of *facts*: namely, states of affairs built up out of Tractarian objects, logical forms of objects, classical logic, and the active contribution of the representing and language-using subject or ego. For Wittgenstein, then, a proposition is a linguistic fact, presupposing logic, that's directly correlated by a thinking and language-using subject with another (usually non-linguistic) fact in order to cognize that fact, such that the first (linguistic) fact "pictures" the other fact and thereby significantly represents that fact.

Since logic is transcendental and since language mirrors the world, then necessarily for every actual or possible fact there's also a correlated "picturing" proposition, and necessarily for every proposition there is also a correlated "pictured" fact. Moreover, necessarily for every actual fact (= what's positively the case) there's a true proposition, and necessarily for every merely possible fact (= what's negatively the case) there's a false proposition. This directly implies (i) that necessarily for every positive or negative atomic fact there's a correlated true or false atomic proposition, directly related by negation to its bipolar/bivalent logical opposite, and (ii) that necessarily for every complex or molecular fact there's a correlated complex or molecular proposition that's a truth-function of atomic propositions. It should be noted that for Wittgenstein falsity is the logical complement of truth (i.e., it applies to everything in the world other that is other than what is actually the case), and negation is a logical operation that reverses the truth-value of any proposition to which it is applied. So if a proposition P is true, then it follows logically that not-P is false, and that not-not-P is true. But if P is true, it doesn't follow that we can determine a unique proposition not-P = Q that's false, for not-P merely tells us that the whole world is actually other than it would have been if (contrary to actual fact) P had been the case.

VI.7 Naming Objects or Things, and Picturing Atomic Facts

Because the world bottoms out in atomic facts (remember, objects or things are the *substance* or *substrate* of the world, not the world itself), and since language and logic both mirror the world, then the set of all propositions bottoms out in atomic propositions. Atomic propositions are linguistic sequences of names of objects, occurring in a certain fixed order, as used by a talking and thinking subject. Names are the simple or undecomposable atoms of propositions, just as objects or things are the simple or undecomposable bits of substantial/substrate-level reality. Considered apart from its use, the linguistic sequence of names of objects or things is a propositional "sign," and *the propositional sign is itself a fact in the world*. Each name has its meaning by directly picking out an object, and the proposition "pictures" the world by having each of its names correlated one-to-one with an object, and also by exemplifying an isomorphism relation—i.e., a *sameness-of-structure* relation—between the configuration of names in the propositional sign, and a corresponding configuration of the objects picked out by the names. Picturing is thus an isomorphism between a linguistic fact (the propositional sign) and another fact in the world.

In this way, each atomic proposition is itself a *linguistic diagram, model,* or *picture* of a positive or negative atomic fact. For example, the (let's assume it's) true propositional symbol

Frege is taller than Wittgenstein

linguistically depicts the real-world relation of relative height between Frege and Wittgenstein. What the proposition and the fact share in common—i.e., the same structure—is called *the form of representation*. One crucial thing to note here is that the atomic propositional symbol

Frege is taller than Wittgenstein

which can be formally symbolized as, for example,

T^2fw

and which depicts the positive atomic fact that Frege is taller than Witt, contains not just *two* but *three* names: (i) "T^2xy," (ii) "f," and (iii) "w." In other words, strange as it may seem, "T^2xy" names an object or thing! More precisely, "T^2xy," or (in English), "x is taller than y," *names a dyadic relation*. More generally, the class of Tractarian objects includes individuals, properties (aka one-place universals), and n-adic relations (aka many-place universals), and every meaningful expression in the atomic proposition, whether a proper name or a predicate, is a Tractarian name. So

Frege is a philosopher

which can be formally symbolized as

P^1f

contains *two* names, namely, "P^1x" or "x is a philosopher," a name that refers to the property (one-place universal) of being a philosopher, and "f" or "Frege," a name that refers to Frege.

This in turn enables us to construct a highly simplified—aka "toy"—model of Wittgenstein's Tractarian theory of picturing in atomic propositions, that I'll call *the-balls-&-hooks-&-hangers model*. It's, as it were, a system of *Tractarian Christmas tree ornaments*; and we do know "that Wittgenstein knew [Dickens's] *A Christmas Carol* practically by heart" (Monk, 1990: p. 569): so here it is. Think of individual Tractarian objects or things as decorative balls connected to hangers by means of hooks. The decorative pattern on each ball indicates its internal qualities, i.e., its individual essence or nature. For each ball

The Fate of Analysis

there must be one hook, and hooks occur only on hangers. But hangers are *also* Tractarian objects or things. And each hanger can have either one hook or more than one hook. Now think of a 1-hook hanger as a property/1-place universal, and think of a many-hook hanger as an n-adic relation/many-place universal. Then for each of the n names in a proposition there are n-1 balls, each of which (in my Tractarian Christmas tree ornament model) is an individual object or thing named by that name. And for each 1-place predicate or relational predicate in one of these propositions, we have in (in my Tractarian Christmas tree ornament model) an n-1 hooked hanger which is either a property/1- place universal or else an n-adic relation/many-placed universal, named by that predicate.

Consider, for example,

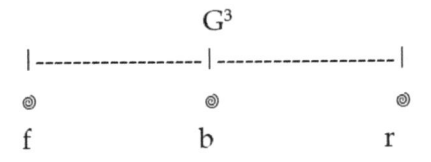

$$G^3$$
|------------------|------------------|
◎ ◎ ◎
f b r

Frege gives the beer bottle to Russell.

This propositional symbol is formally symbolized as "G^3fbr." The three individual names are "f" or (in English) "Frege," "b" or (in English) "the beer bottle"—i.e., a definite description—and "r" or (in English) "Russell"; and the fourth name of the triadic relation/3-place universal is "G^3xyz" or (in English) "x gives y to z." Here's another example:

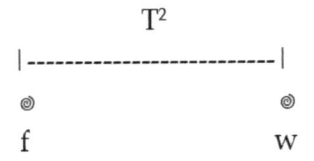

$$T^2$$
|--------------------------|
◎ ◎
f w

Frege is taller than Wittgenstein.

This propositional symbol is formally symbolized as "T^2fw." The two individual names are "f" or (in English) "Frege" and "w" or (in English) "Wittgenstein"; and the third name of the dyadic relation/2-place universal is "T^2xy," or (in English) "x is taller than y." And finally, for the lower bound, or bottom level, case of facts, i.e., facts constructed out of an individual and a property/1-place universal, here's the third and last example:

$$P^1$$
| ---------------
◎
f

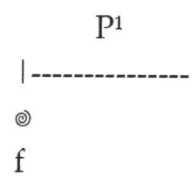

Frege is a philosopher.

This sentence is formally symbolized as "P^1f." The individual name is "f" or (in English) "Frege"; and the name of the property/1-place universal is "P^1x" or (in English) "x is a philosopher."

One important point that's clearly made by the Tractarian Christmas tree ornaments model is that *Tractarian objects or things are not homogeneous in ontological character*. Some of them (the decorative balls) are what Frege would have called *saturated* entities, essentially complete individual objects or things, aka *particulars*, whereas others (the hangers) are what Frege would have called *unsaturated* entities, essentially incomplete non-individual objects or things, aka *universals*. In the third example, for example, they're one-place Fregean *concepts*, that is, one-place functions from objects to truth-values, i.e., properties/one-place universals.

Frege postulated a radical ontological difference between individual objects and functions, and this got him into unresolvable paradoxical difficulties. In particular, the concept *horse* is not a concept! And that's because "the concept *horse*" is a meaningful name (a definite description, to be precise) and therefore must pick out an *essentially complete individual (saturated) object or thing*; but concepts are functions, hence they're *essentially incomplete non-individual (unsaturated) objects or things*. Wittgenstein deftly gets around this problem by allowing in *not only* essentially complete (saturated) individual objects or things (decorative balls), *but also* essentially incomplete (unsaturated) non-individual objects or things (n-hook hangers), as *bona fide* Tractarian objects or things.

The other especially important point about the Tractarian Christmas tree ornaments model is that it's now quite easy to see how atomic propositions picture facts, and don't merely *sequentially name* objects or things, that is, they don't merely *make lists* of objects or things. In other words, atomic propositions not only represent objects or things, but also depict *specifically how objects of one type go together with other objects of another type in order to form structured atomic facts*: so, as it were, they also depict *specifically how the system of balls-&-hooks-&-hangers works*. This requires, in effect, that the user of language must always *project* in a certain way *from* the several names making up the propositional sign *onto* the configuration of objects. Otherwise it would be impossible to explain why

> Frege is taller than Wittgenstein

is a propositional sign, whereas

> Frege Russell Wittgenstein

isn't a propositional sign. To grasp precisely *how* the propositional sign is to be projected onto the correlated objects or things by the user of the sentence, is to grasp *the sense* of that proposition.

VI.8 Signs, Symbols, Sense, Truth, and Judgment

Signs are perceptible, real parts of language—i.e., words—and more specifically signs are *types* of words, and only derivatively *tokens* of words. The type-token distinction for letters can be easily grasped by asking yourself:

> How many letters are there in the word "aardvark"?

If you say "8" then you're counting letters as *tokens*, but if you say "5" then you're counting letters as *types*. Symbols, by contrast to signs, are signs with a meaning, whether this meaning is a sense (*Sinn*) or a reference/Meaning (*Bedeutung*).

In natural or ordinary language, it's of course possible to have two or more different signs with the same meaning (synonymy), and it's of course also possible that one sign has two or more different meanings (ambiguity). And it's also possible for signs to lack a meaning altogether, for example, empty names like "Mr. Nemo" or sortally incorrect predicates like "is a procrastination-drinking cloud of quadruplicity." Hence two or more different signs can express the same symbol, the same sign can express different symbols, and some signs don't express symbols. Ambiguity or semantic emptiness can lead to confusion, unsoundness in arguments, contradiction, or even paradox. In a logically *perspicuous* language, however, aka a logically *ideal* language, every sign has a meaning, and each sign has one and only one meaning.

It's crucial to recognize that signs do not have a meaning on their own: *they have to be correctly used*. Otherwise put, signs without a use are semantically *dead*. In order to be meaningful and get a semantic *life*, they must be *vivified* by a correct use of those signs. More precisely, signs acquire a meaning *only* by being correctly used by some talking and thinking subject or ego, in the larger context of propositions. Not just any old "mess of words" (*Wörtergemisch*) (*TLP* 3.141), or word-salad, will count as a propositional sign however: on the contrary, only sequences that obey *logico-grammatical formation rules*, aka *rules of logical syntax*, will be allowed to come to life as propositional signs. For example,

> Is and but not or doggy if spittoon Frege

and

> Sweetly the sweetly Wittgenstein whereas whisky

are *not* propositional signs and therefore it is *streng verboten* to admit them into the semiotic land of the living, no matter how logographically amusing or poetically pleasant they might be (to me, anyhow).

It should be noted that there are two different kinds of logico-grammatical formation constraints, hence two distinct levels of the logical syntax of language. The **first** sort of constraint has merely to do with the ordering of names in atomic propositions, and of names together with logical constants in molecular propositions.

"Frege is a philosopher" is a well-ordered propositional sign, but "Sweetly the sweetly Wittgenstein whereas whisky" isn't. Such violations are nowadays called cases of *ill-formedness* and constitute logico-grammatical *nonsense*. The **second** sort of constraint has to do with the *logical types* of names, and correspondingly with the *logical forms* of objects correlated with those names (for example, real space, time, and color). Importantly, violations of these rules can emerge even when the sequence of names obeys rules of well-ordering, for example:

> Frege is nothing but a colorless green idea that's always sleeping furiously when it should instead be thinking and writing about the foundations of logic and mathematics.

> Frege and quadruplicity both drink procrastination not wisely but too well.

These violations are nowadays called *sortal incorrectness*, and are logico-grammatical nonsense of a higher order than mere syntactical ill-formedness.

Such violations are also of great philosophical import for Wittgenstein, because according to him, virtually all philosophical errors consist in some or another kind of logico-philosophical sortal incorrectness. Correspondingly, one profound difficulty about sortally incorrect nonsense is that it may superficially *seem* acceptable. For example, according to Wittgenstein, the following well-formed sequences,

> Two is a number

> Frege is identical to Frege

> Tully is identical to Cicero

and

> Frege judges (asserts, believes, etc.) P

are all *subtle* cases of logico-philosophical sortal incorrectness, even though in fact they seemed perfectly sortally correct to Frege and Russell. Among other things, this means that while our linguistic well-formedness intuitions are a generally reliable basis for theorizing about natural language syntax—as Noam Chomsky later pointed out (1986)— by contrast our logico-philosophical sortal correctness intuitions are *not* generally reliable. So the formation of propositional signs with a sense is necessarily constrained by a set of logico-grammatical rules, some of which, at the very least, aren't self-evident, and might even be profoundly hidden from us due to fundamental philosophical confusions. In any case, the essence of sense is the picturing relation as it occurs in atomic propositions. And every complex sense of a complex or molecular proposition is systematically inherited from the senses of its constituent atomic propositions.

But what's the "sense" of sense? That is, what's *the meaning or rational purpose* of sense? The sense of sense is to convey true or false information about facts. An atomic proposition is true if and only if the fact that it pictures is a positive or actual fact, and otherwise it's false. And a molecular proposition is true if and only if the truth-function of its component atomic propositions assigns it the truth-value T or true; and otherwise it's F or false. Wittgenstein's theory of truth for atomic propositions can be regarded as *the purest version of the correspondence theory of truth*, since from the user's grasp of the structure of the propositional sign it's possible literally *to read off* the structure of its correlated fact. Moreover, Wittgenstein's theory avoids the fundamental problem for the traditional correspondence theory of truth: that the cognizer is required to recognize and then justify or validate the similarity between sign and object or thing, which then requires a vicious regress of higher-order correspondence relations, recognitions, and justifications/validations. According to Wittgenstein's correspondence theory, the isomorphism between propositional symbol and fact *is built right into the sense of the proposition*: then truth is merely the question of whether that fact actually exists or not, which is external to the representing subject or ego.

This brings us to the way in which Wittgenstein's theory of truth is a highly realistic theory of truth, aka *a semantic conception of truth* in Tarski's sense (Tarski, 1949, 1956).[2] Wittgenstein's theory introduces no representational intermediary between language and truth-making fact, hence it is fully immediate or direct: the correct use of the sentence maps the representing subject onto the fact, then that fact either actually exists or not, and *that's it*. It should be noted in this connection that the very idea of *realism* has at least three importantly different senses that are not always carefully distinguished: (i) mind-independence of the facts (*metaphysical realism*), (ii) objective knowability of the facts (*epistemic realism*), and (iii) direct or unmediated representation of the facts (*semantic realism*). As a Marburg-style logicistic neo-Kantian theory, Wittgenstein's theory of truth *isn't* realistic in sense (i), but it *is* realistic in senses (ii) and (iii), and *especially* in sense (iii). This point comes forward in two ways.

First, Wittgenstein's picture theory of meaning entails a *truth-maker semantics*. That is, positive and negative facts are themselves the worldly *truth-makers* and *falsity-mak-*

---
2 For a compact presentation of Tarski's semantic conception of truth, section X.3 below.

ers of atomic propositions, and senses of atomic propositions are intrinsically bound up with the bipolarity of the proposition, i.e., its classical truth or classical falsity. Given a sense of an atomic proposition, it completely divides the world into the atomic fact it pictures, its truth-maker, and everything else other than that atomic fact, its falsity maker.

Second, Wittgenstein's picture theory of meaning entails a *transparency theory of judgment* (assertion, belief, etc.). That is, for Wittgenstein the judger's use of language is nothing but a transparent *cognitive conduit* to the facts. How does this work? What I'll call *primitive sense* or *primary sense* is how an atomic propositional sign in ordinary language or thought is used by a talking and thinking subject or ego as a symbol to picture an atomic fact with a view to truth. According to Wittgenstein's theory, then, there's no need to add an act of judgment (assertion, belief, etc.) to account for picturing, because when a propositional sign is used in the correct way, it just *is* a judgment (assertion, belief, etc.). Correspondingly, (i) the correct use of a propositional sign and (ii) propositional activity in ordinary language (judgment, assertion, belief, etc.) or in thinking, *are the very same thing*. So, for Wittgenstein, to say that I judge (assert, believe, etc.) P, is only to say:

"P" says P

or

"P" has a sense.

No psychological verbs are required, and in fact the explicit addition of psychological verbs produces logico-philosophical sortal incorrectness or unacceptable higher-level syntactic nonsense, rather like those somewhat bumptious bumper-stickers that say, "If you can read this, thank a teacher," whereas they *should* simply say, "Thank a teacher."

VI.9 Propositions Again

Tractarian propositions, as we've seen, are at once (i) the semantic contents of judgments (assertions, beliefs, etc.), (ii) bipolar essential truth-bearers, (iii) logical pictures of atomic facts, and (iv) vehicles of sense. But propositions have several other crucial features as well.

First, *propositions are the proper objects of logical analysis*, in that they're essentially decomposable into their simple symbols, or names, and the way in which those names are configured into a propositional structure. Each proposition has a unique complete decomposition (*TLP* 3.25), and logical "elucidation" is the activity of decomposing a proposition uniquely into its simple constituent symbols (*TLP* 3.263).

Second, in the reverse direction, *propositions are essentially compositional*, in that each propositional symbol is a function of its component simple symbols or expressions. This compositionality of the proposition entails what Chomskyans call the "creative" or "productive" aspect of language: namely, that an infinitely large number of new propositions can

The Fate of Analysis

be constructed from a finite set of simple symbols plus rules for construction (*TLP* 4.03). Also anticipating Chomsky's psycholinguistics (Chomsky, 1965, 1966, 1980, Wittgenstein regards our human compositional capacity for language as an innate endowment (*TLP* 4.002).

Third, *propositions are essentially generalizable*, in that each meaningful part of the proposition can be replaced by a variable while other parts are held constant, thus producing a class of propositions of that form. For example, the proposition

> Frege is taller than Wittgenstein

can be generalized as

> x is taller than Wittgenstein

and then there will be a class of propositions determined by substituting different individual constants for the variable "x." Or it could be generalized as

> Frege is taller than y

or

> Frege bears R to Wittgenstein

or

> x bears R to Wittgenstein

or

> x bears R to y

and so-on. The absolutely general form of a proposition is the propositional variable "P," which simply means *such and such is the case* (*TLP* 4.5).

Fourth, *propositions are the primary or primitive units of meaning*, in that all other symbols, including names (*TLP* 3.3), have meaning (i.e., either sense or reference/Meaning) only in the context of whole propositions. This, of course, is Frege's *context principle* (see section II.8 above).

Fifth, *propositions are semantically self-intimating*, in that they convey sense and are the vehicles of sense, but propositional senses cannot described or named: they can only be shown (*TLP* 4.022).

What's *showing*? I think that the best overall characterization of "showing" is that it covers *all* the basic types of linguistic meaning *other than* describing facts, which is what Wittgenstein calls "saying." So showing includes, at the very least, (i) *intensional* discourse, i.e., discourse about meanings, (ii) *reflexive* discourse, i.e., self-referring discourse, (iii) *speech-act-expressing* discourse, i.e., discourse that communicates different types of language-use, for example, imperatives, questions, subjunctives, etc., (iv) *emotive* discourse, for example, discourse expressing approval or disapproval, (v) *non-literal* discourse, for example, jokes or metaphors, and, crucially, (vi) *transcendental* discourse, i.e., *logico-philosophical* discourse, i.e., Tractarian discourse. Notice, moreover, that in this non-descriptive, non-fact-stating respect, even (vii) *directly referential* discourse, i.e., naming objects or things, is *also* a kind of showing. So whereas *saying* is a rather narrowly constrained and defined, and also—except for those who prefer "the icy slopes of logic"—a somewhat boring and quotidian sort of thing, nevertheless *showing*, like love according to the kitschy movie and novel,[3] *is a many-splendored thing.*

Sixth, *propositions are semantically non-reflexive*, in that they cannot be about themselves (*TLP* 3.332). Correspondingly, *functions* also cannot contain themselves as arguments (*TLP* 3.333). Together, these two forms of Tractarian irreflexivity automatically rule out the possibility of the Liar paradox and other semantic paradoxes, as well as the set-theoretic paradoxes.

Seventh, *propositions are essentially first-order*, in that when we take the fifth and sixth features of propositions together, it follows that although complex or molecular propositions are possible, *no higher-order propositions are logically possible*. That is: there are no senses of senses (hence no hierarchy of senses), and there are no propositions about propositions (hence no hierarchy of propositions). Wittgenstein's implicit rationale here seems to be that such hierarchies are in themselves anti-rational and lead to vicious impredicativity. On the other hand, however, by logically banning senses of senses and propositions about propositions, at least prima facie, he puts his own *Tractarian* discourse in jeopardy. For how can the author of the *Logisch-philosophische Abhandlung* meaningfully talk about propositions? As I've indicated already, the correct Tractarian answer is that such strictly speaking nonsensical discourse is *transcendental showing*, not *saying*. This Tractarian metaphilosophical insight, like so many others, is simply overlooked by the "resolute" reading of the *Tractatus*. Though this be nonsense, yet there is Marburg-style logicistic neo-Kantian method in't.

VI.10 Language and Thought

Language as a whole is the totality of propositions (*TLP* 4.01). Among other things, this tells us that in the context of the *Tractatus*, Wittgenstein is providing *a logico-philosophical theory of language* only insofar as language is *an information-carrying means or medium*, i.e., only insofar as it's a means or medium for *saying*, and not insofar as it's a means or medium for

---
3 I mean of course the 1955 film, *Love is a Many-Splendored Thing*, directed by Henry King and starring William Holden and Jennifer Jones, and the same-named best-selling 1952 novel by Han Suyin.

showing. In the context of the *Tractatus*, language as a means or medium for showing is only *shown*, not said. (In the context of the *Philosophical Investigations*, by contrast, language as a means or medium for showing is *not only* shown, *but also* said: but that's another story for later in this book.) Moreover, the totality of true propositions is complete natural science (*TLP* 4.11). Among other things, *this* tells us that Wittgenstein is treating positive atomic facts or the truth-makers as ultimately reducible to the natural facts (= explanatory and ontological naturalism).

Language, however, is not merely the set of *outer* or *public* inscriptions or utterances or texts: it also includes *any* proposition-constructing activity, whether *inner* or *outer*. This is what Wittgenstein calls "thought" or "thinking" (*TLP* 3.1-3.11). I take it that by "thinking," Wittgenstein means *rational human thinking*, which naturally occurs via inner speech or outer speech. So *all thinking is essentially linguistic in character*. This has two important consequences. **First**, all thinking, whether or not accompanied by utterance, *occurs in a private language of thought*. Thinking is *inner propositional activity*. **Second**, natural language and cognition are both essentially conceptual, discursive, and propositional and thought-based in character, even though they may not appear to be such. The surface structure of either inner or outer natural language (its psychological syntax or surface grammar) thoroughly disguises its real structure (its depth grammar or logical syntax) (*TLP* 4.002). *Only* logical analysis can reveal this underlying structure. But this logical analysis should *not* be regarded as a *reform* of language (i.e., a prescriptive depth grammar, or prescriptive logical syntax); on the contrary, everything in natural language is logico-grammatically *perfectly in order, just as it is* (*TLP* 5.5563).

In this respect, Wittgenstein's approach to logical analysis is sharply different from that of The Vienna Circle logical empiricist/positivists, who were explicitly logico-grammatical prescriptivists and reformers—for example, Carnap took a strong interest in the Esperanto movement (Edmonds, 2020: p. 49). On the contrary, for Wittgenstein, logical analysis is there merely to clarify what we already *implicitly* fully understand. In any case, almost all of our propositional thinking is in fact "tacit" or *non-self-conscious* cognizing. It's only philosophers of logic, language, and thought who can adequately recover the nature of this nonconscious cognizing. But this recovery is not psychological in character (*TLP* 4.1121): instead it's the result of *transcendental reflection* in the Marburg-style logicistic neo-Kantian sense (*TLP* 6.13).

VII. Wittgenstein and the *Tractatus* 3: Propositions 4–5.61

VII.1 The Logocentric Predicament, Version 3.0: Justifying Deduction

As I mentioned in section II.1 above, one fundamental problem in the philosophy of logic is what Harry M. Sheffer (inventor of the Sheffer stroke function) aptly called "the logocentric predicament": in order to explain or justify logic, logic must already be presupposed and used, hence logic is inexplicable, unjustifiable, and rationally groundless (Sheffer, 1926: p. 228). In fact, The Logocentric Predicament has several interestingly different specific sub-versions, including Lewis Carroll's famous "What-the-Tortoise-Said-to-Achilles" syllogistic regress problem (Carroll, 1895), and Quine's equally famous argument against the conventionalist theory of logical truth (Quine, 1976c). And there's also a specific sub-version 3.0, as it were, called *the problem of justifying deduction*:

> 1. Logical deduction can be justified either deductively or non-deductively.
>
> 2. A deductive justification of logical deduction is circular.
>
> 3. A non-deductive justification of logical deduction (for example, an inductive, intuitive, holistic, pragmatic, etc., justification) is insufficient.
>
> 4. Therefore, logical deduction is unjustifiable, i.e., deduction is rationally groundless. (Hanna, 2006c: ch. 3)

In his pre-Tractarian 1913 "Notes on Logic," Wittgenstein saw this problem clearly:

> Deductions only proceed according to the laws of deduction but these laws cannot justify deduction. (Wittgenstein, 1979b: p. 93^e)

Indeed, one illuminating way of construing Wittgenstein's Tractarian theory of the nature of logic is that it's essentially an extended attempt to solve the problem of justifying deduction, as a crucial sub-species of the fully *general* problem of The Logocentric Predicament (Hanna, 2006c: ch. 3).

VII.2 The Logical Form of Deduction

I've already looked briefly at one part of Wittgenstein's theory of the logical form of propositions: the idea that there are as many ways of generalizing propositions as there are ways of abstracting out names as variables and holding the other propositional elements fixed (*TLP* 3.31-3.317). The general form of a proposition is the limit case of abstraction in which all names are replaced by variables, and the proposition itself is considered as a single variable (*TLP* 4.5). A deduction, by contrast to a single proposition in isolation, is a sequence of propositions that are related by "laws of inference," such that the last proposition in the sequence (the conclusion) is a logical consequence of the other propositions in the sequence (the premises), according to those laws. Wittgenstein's idea is that the conclusion of every such deduction is "internally related" to the complex proposition that's the true conjunction of all its premises, and thereby "contained" in that complex proposition (*TLP* 5.131). Another way of putting this is to say that, in deduction, the conditions under which all the premises are true will suffice for the truth of the conclusion (*TLP* 5.11, 5.123-5.124). But the most perspicuous way of putting this is to say that the logical *structure* of the complex proposition that's the true conjunction of all the premises guarantees the truth of the conclusion (*TLP* 5.13).

What's going on here? Figuring that out involves our getting a handle on Wittgenstein's general theory of the logical form of propositions. This has four basic parts. **First**, all propositions can be reduced to logical operations on atomic or elementary propositions (*TLP* 5.21-5.3). **Second**, all logical operations on propositions and also all logical relations between propositions (represented by the logical constants) are exclusively *truth-functional operations* and *truth-functional relations* (*TLP* 4.3-4.45, 5). **Third**, the truth definition of the universal quantifier is that it's an extended conjunction of all the atomic propositions generated by replacing the individual variables by individual constants (= the logical product), and the truth definition of the existential quantifier is that it is an extended disjunction of all the atomic propositions generated by replacing the individual variables by individual constants (= the logical sum) (*TLP* 5.521-5.524). **Fourth** and finally, all truth-functional relations between propositions can be reduced to the single Sheffer stroke function, aka *continuous negation*:

$$(P|Q) \equiv (\sim P \ \& \sim Q) \text{ [or alternatively: } (\sim P \ v \sim Q)]$$

For example, using the classical De Morgan equivalences relating negation, conjunction, and disjunction, i.e.,

$$(P \ \& \ Q) \equiv (\sim P \ v \sim Q)$$

$$(P \ v \ Q) \equiv (\sim P \ \& \sim Q)$$

and also the equivalence between the conditional, and negation, disjunction, and conjunction, i.e.,

$$(P \rightarrow Q) \equiv (\sim P \ v \ Q)$$

$$(P \rightarrow Q) \equiv \sim (P \ \& \sim Q)$$

it's easy enough to see informally how every truth-functional relation can be expressed as a function of the Sheffer stroke, for example,

$$[P|(Q|Q)] \equiv (P \rightarrow Q).$$

Now, this four-part theory of logical form entails that every valid deduction can be represented by a truth-table showing that for every assignment of truth-values to the atomic propositions of the premises, their true conjunction will suffice to guarantee the truth of the conclusion. So Wittgenstein's over-arching thesis here is that because logical deductions are fully guaranteed by the internal truth-functional structure of complex propositions, then "laws of inference" are in fact unnecessary, and deduction is thereby *internally justified a priori* (*TLP* 5.132-5.133). This, in turn, provides a uniquely Tractarian solution to the specific sub-version 3.0 of The Logocentric Predicament, i.e., the problem of justifying deduction. For Wittgenstein, the justification of deduction is *self-intimating* or *self-manifesting*—in effect, logically strongly supervenient[1]—on the truth-functional connections underlying the deductive structure of the valid argument. The error in the original problem of justifying deduction was the implicit assumption that the justification had to be logically *said*: on the contrary, it's logically *shown*.

VII.3 Logic Must Take Care of Itself

This solution to the problem of justifying deduction is closely related to another striking Tractarian doctrine, namely, that logic is explanatorily self-contained (*TLP* 5.473). This can also be construed as a solution to the *general* logocentric predicament. That is: in a certain sense, it's impossible to make mistakes in logic, hence logic is self-justifying, because if we have indeed already cognitively constructed a logic, then this logic is perfectly in order *just as it is* (*TLP* 5.475). "Self-evidence" (self-intimation, self-manifestation, etc.) is thus entirely internal to the process of cognitively constructing a logic (*TLP* 5.4731).

VII.4 Tautologies and Contradictions

All propositions are either atomic (elementary) or molecular (complex). But the total class of all atomic and molecular propositions can be cross-classified into two disjoint classes: (i) contingent (sometimes true and sometimes false) *versus* (ii) necessary (always true or always false). Propositions that are always true are *tautologies*, and they can be *shown* to be tautologous by constructing their truth-tables, which come out "T" (for "true") under every line of their main connective. Tautologies are also called "propositions of logic," because they're true by virtue of their logical form alone. But there are no "primitive propositions of logic": every tautology is equally primitive (*TLP* 6.1271). Propositions that are always false are *contradictions*, and similarly to tautologies, mutatis mutandis, they can be *shown* to be contradictory by constructing their truth-tables, which come out "F" (for "false") under every line of their main connective. There's also a deep connection between valid deductions and tautologies: for every valid deduction there's a tautology in *modus ponens* form, consisting of a conditional proposition containing each of the premises as distinct conjuncts in one big conjunction as its antecedent, and the conclusion as its consequent (*TLP* 6.1264-6.1265). What this means is that the tautologies logically encode and "give" all the valid deductions of logic, thereby yielding the entire theory of deduction via the theory

---
1 For explicit definitions of strong supervenience, logical strong supervenience, and natural or nomological strong supervenience, see sub-section XVII.8.2 below.

of tautologies (*TLP* 6.124-6.127). Proof is only of merely psychological relevance, to help us recognize tautologies, but not in any way necessary for logic itself (*TLP* 6.1262).

Wittgenstein is explicitly and fully committed to the thesis that *the logical constants do not represent anything* (*TLP* 4.0312, 4.441, 5.4), sharply unlike Russell, who, as we saw, thought that they represented abstract objects of a peculiar kind, and correspondingly encountered the problem of the unity of the proposition and Bradley's Regress, which he (Russell) could avoid only by recourse to psychologism. But for Wittgenstein, *the logical relations between propositions cannot be represented*, and in particular *the logically necessary relations between the parts of tautologies or contradictions cannot be represented*: so the problem of the unity of the proposition and Bradley's Regress are dissolved from the get-go.

Since tautologies *cover all* of logical space (like a whiteout) and since contradictions *fail to cover any part* of logical space (like a blackout), they cannot picture atomic facts, and cannot represent complex facts. As a consequence, tautologies and contradictions are "senseless" in that they "say" nothing (*TLP* 4.461), and do not provide logical pictures of reality (*TLP* 4.462). But all the same, they're also not *unacceptably nonsensical* (*TLP* 4.4611), although strictly speaking they *are* nonsensical, in that they are *other* than what conveys a sense. So Wittgenstein is implicitly using a distinction between (i) logically *unacceptable* nonsense, and (ii) logically *acceptable* nonsense. This distinction is crucial for understanding the *Tractatus*, since it will turn out that *what can only be shown, and not said, with respect to logic* is equivalent with *logically acceptable nonsense*. For our present purposes, then, tautology and contradiction are logically acceptable nonsense, and thus *only showable, and not sayable, with respect to logic*.

VII.5 What is Logic?

According to the *Tractatus*, what's logic? In earlier sections of this chapter, I looked at one part of Wittgenstein's answer to this question: logic is how we make propositional forms and deduction *manifest*; and logic must also "take care of itself," in that it justifies deduction internally via tautologies. But Wittgenstein *also* wants to connect the nature of logic directly with the nature of language, the nature of thought, and the nature of the world, as per the following propositions:

> 3.221 Objects I can only *name*. Signs represent them. I can only speak *of* them. I cannot *assert them*.
>
> A proposition can only say *how* a thing is, not *what* it is.
>
> 5.471 The general form of the proposition is the essence of the proposition.
>
> 5.4711 To give the essence of the proposition means to give the essence of all description, therefore the essence of the world.

5.4731 Self-evidence, of which Russell has said so much, can only be discarded in logic by language itself preventing every logical mistake. That logic is a priori consists in the fact that we *cannot* think illogically.

5.552 The "experience" which we need to understand logic is not that such and such is the case, but that something *is*; but that is *no* experience.

Logic *precedes* every experience—that something *is* so. It is before the How, not before the What.

5.5521 And if this were not the case, how could we apply logic? We could say: if there were a logic, even if there no world, how then could there be a logic, since there is a world?

5.6 *The limits of my language* mean the limits of my world.

5.61 Logic fills the world: the limits of the world are also its limits.

We cannot therefore say in logic: This and this there is in the world, that there is not.

For that would apparently presuppose that we exclude certain possibilities, and this cannot be the case since otherwise logic must get outside the limits of the world: that is, if it could consider these limits from the other side also.

What we cannot think, that we cannot think: we cannot therefore *say* what we cannot think.

6.12 The fact that the propositions of logic are tautologies *shows* the formal—logical—properties of language, of the world.

6.124 The logical propositions describe the scaffolding of the world, or rather they exhibit (*stellen ... dar*) it. They "treat" of nothing. They presuppose that names have Meaning, and that elementary propositions have sense. And this is their connexion with the world. It is clear that it must show something about the world that certain combinations of symbols—which essentially have a definite character—are tautologies.

Herein lies the decisive point. We said that in the symbols which we use something is arbitrary, something not. In logic only the latter expresses: but this means that in logic it is not *we* who express, by means of signs, what we want, but in logic the nature of the essentially necessary signs speaks for itself. That is to say, if we know the logical syntax of any sign language, then all the propositions of logic are already given.

6.13 Logic is not a theory but a reflexion of the world. Logic is transcendental.

Obviously, these propositions are not self-explanatory. But three basic theses emerge from them:

1. Logic is the a priori essence of language.

2. Logic is the a priori essence of thought.

3. Logic is the a priori essence of the world.

For my purposes in this book, to say that something is "a priori" is to say *that its truth, meaning, or justification is necessarily underdetermined by* (that is, neither identical with nor necessarily determined by, aka strongly supervenient on[2]) *any and all sensory experiences and/or contingent empirical facts*. And to say that something X is "essential" is to say *that X is metaphysically necessary and metaphysically sufficient for something else, Y, so that X is Y's nature, X grounds Y, and Y flows from X*. But apart from that, what do these theses actually mean? Does Wittgenstein have any arguments for them? And quite apart from what Wittgenstein actually argues, are there any good reasons to think that his theses are true? Let's consider the three of them in turn.

VII.6 Logic is the A Priori Essence of Language

This thesis means that logic captures the underlying semantic and syntactic structure of any actual or possible natural or ordinary language. Nothing will count as a language unless it satisfies logical constraints and anything that meets all logical constraints is at least a possible language. Otherwise put, logic tells us *how to construct a language*. Obviously, "language" here means a totality of propositions or rational-information-bearing signs, and *not* signs insofar as they are or might be used for other purposes. So Wittgenstein's thesis is that logic captures the underlying semantic and syntactic structure of any actual or possible natural or ordinary rational-information-bearing language.

In turn, we can distinguish between two distinct Tractarian arguments for this thesis.

The **first** argument starts from logical analysis as an actual given fact, and then regressively concludes to the thesis that the logic presupposed by logical analysis must take the precise form that Wittgenstein spells out in the *Tractatus*: bivalent truth-functional propositional and polyadic first-order and second-order predicate logic, with identity, but not set theory (i.e., what I'm calling classical logic). One critical question we could raise here is whether logical analysis in Wittgenstein's sense actually exists. Another critical question is whether, even on the assumption that logical analysis is or must be precisely

---
[2] For explicit definitions of strong supervenience, logical strong supervenience, and natural or nomological strong supervenience, see sub-section XVII.8.2 below.

as Wittgenstein assumes it to be, it still follows that logic *must* be of this precise form. For example, even if logical analysis in Wittgenstein's sense actually exists or must be, as such, then must logic also be *classical*?

And the **second** argument abstracts away from the specific existence of logical analysis and starts instead from the assumption that, as an actual given fact, there are natural or ordinary rational-information-bearing languages, and then concludes to the claim that *some* logic or another must be the a priori essence of all such languages: *some* logic or another must tell us how to construct and understand any natural or ordinary language. Otherwise, what accounts for the unity of language across all the many different natural or ordinary languages? Notice that even if the first argument fails, the second argument might still be sound.

VII.7 Logic is the A Priori Essence of Thought

This second thesis assumes the premise that all thought or thinking is a form of language-use, and that it's specifically *a mental language,* aka a *lingua mentis.* The idea here is that the mental language is not merely *contingently* private, but instead *inherently* private, i.e., *necessarily and sufficiently* private, i.e., *logically* private, i.e., *solipsistic.* So the thesis that logic is the a priori essence of thought means that logic captures the underlying semantic and syntactic structure of any actual or possible *lingua mentis,* namely, any actual or possible logically private or solipsistic language. The general picture here is that all language is first constructed by us internally, and then secondly externally, but always by means of logic. Not only does each of us possesses both an inner, mental language—as it were, *mentalese*[3]—and also at least one outer, natural or ordinary language—say, English, German, or whatever—but also the former is more basic than the latter. Notice that Wittgenstein's thesis here isn't that our logical construction of language always or even usually occurs *consciously* or *self-consciously*: indeed it can and apparently does occur mostly *unconsciously* or at least *unself-consciously*.

As in the case of the first thesis (namely, that logic is the a priori essence of language), we can also distinguish two different sorts of arguments for the second thesis (namely, that logic is the a priori essence of thought).

The **first** argument assumes that thought or thinking is essentially *propositional* activity, proceeds as a first step to the intermediate conclusion that thinking must be nothing but inner discourse in a logically private or solipsistic language, and then proceeds as a second step from language to logic as per the first thesis. Obviously, the second step of the argument will be subject to the same criticism as the first thesis. One critical question about the intermediate conclusion contained in the first step of the argument, moreover, is whether we have good reason to believe that thought or thinking is essentially propositional activity. Another critical question is whether, even on the assumption that thought

---
[3] For a highly influential post-classical Analytic version of this idea, refracted through Chomskyan psycholinguistics, see (Fodor, 1975).

or thinking *is* essentially propositional activity, it then must be nothing but inner discourse in a logically private or solipsistic language: why can't thoughts be shared, as Kant, Frege, and Husserl all held?

And the **second** argument abstracts away from the notion of a logically private or solipsistic language and argues from the assumption that thought or thinking is essentially propositional activity, as a first step, to the intermediate conclusion that *thought must be sufficiently like a public natural or ordinary language* in order to account for the construction of a public language by means of thought, then argues, as a second step, from language to logic, again as in the case of the first thesis. Again, obviously the second step of the argument will be subject to the same criticism as the first thesis. It should be noted, however, that even if the assumption that thought is essentially propositional activity is false, the intermediate conclusion, that thought must be sufficiently like a public natural or ordinary language in order to account for the construction of such a language by means of thought, could still be true. In other words, thought could also be importantly *non*-conceptual, *non*-discursive, *non*-propositional activity (Hanna and Paans, 2021), provided that every public natural or ordinary language is also importantly *non*-conceptual, *non*-discursive, and *non*-propositional in nature. Indeed, as we'll see in chapters XI to XIV below, the later Wittgenstein's work in general, and the *Philosophical Investigations* in particular, thoroughly explore that philosophical gambit.

VII.8 Logic is the A Priori Essence of the World

At least on the face of it, this third thesis is the hardest one to understand: logic and the world seem to essentially different from one another, so how can logic be the essence of the world? Wittgenstein's answer is that since language enters directly into the constitution of the world, along with the objects, and since the essence of language is logic, it follows that logic enters directly into the constitution of the world. Otherwise put: since logic captures the underlying semantic and syntactic structure of language, and since the world of facts, given by the objects, is constructed by the language-using subject or ego, then it follows that the structure of the world is essentially semantic and syntactic, and that logic captures that structure. Thus Wittgenstein holds that logic is the a priori essence of the world, precisely because he's a linguistic and Marburg-style logicistic neo-Kantian transcendental idealist. Correspondingly, in a neo-Kantian way, Wittgenstein is saying the world of facts is *nothing but* a structured totality of *phenomena* (i.e., mind-dependent entities) constructed by a talking and thinking subject or ego via language and logic, given by the objects, and *not* a totality of *things-in-themselves* (wholly mind-independent entities, constituted by their non-relational essences), and the structure of that totality directly reflects the innate constructive capacities of the subject or ego. But what's his actual argument for this thesis?

One possibility is that he's arguing that this thesis is *the unique a priori presupposition of the fact that logical analysis actually exists*. This is then a *transcendental argument* in the Kantian/Marburg-style logicistic neo-Kantian sense. Another possibility is that Wittgenstein is arguing that this thesis is *the best overall explanation of logic, language, and the world, considered as given data or facts.* This is then an "inference-to-the-best-explanation," aka IBE, argument. Put this way, as an IBE argument, and leaving aside for a moment the possibility that Wittgenstein is arguing transcedentally, one could then ask this hard question: are there any other *better* overall explanations of the existence of logical analysis? If not, then the Tractarian hypothesis stands until further critical notice.

VIII. Wittgenstein and the Tractatus 4: Propositions 5.62 – 7

VIII.1 Tractarian Solipsism and Tractarian Realism

One of the initially most puzzling features of the *Tractatus* is its background metaphysics of "solipsism" and "realism." I've scare-quoted these terms because Wittgenstein develops these notions in ways significantly different from, although still related to, their uses in the idealistic and realistic traditions to which the *Tractatus* belongs. As I've asserted, Wittgenstein's *idealism* should be situated within the historico-philosophical context of Kant's transcendental idealism in the *Critique of Pure Reason*, Schopenhauer's neo-Kantian idealistic monism in the *The World as Will and Representation*, and above all within the context of the logicistic neo-Kantianism of the early 20th century phase of the Marburg neo-Kantian tradition, especially Cassirer. But on the other hand, Wittgenstein's *realism* should be placed within the context of Frege's platonism, Moore's platonic atomism, and early Russell's theory of acquaintance. Correspondingly, here are the most relevant texts from the *Tractatus* and the *Notebooks*:

> 5.61 .... What we cannot think, that we cannot think: we cannot therefore say what we cannot think.
>
> 5.62 This remark provides a key to the question, to what extent solipsism is a truth.
>
> In fact what solipsism *means,* is quite correct, only it cannot be *said*, but it shows itself.
>
> That the world is *my* world shows itself in the fact that the limits of language (*the* language, which I understand) means the limits of *my* world.
>
> 5.621 The world and life are one.
>
> 5.63 I am my world. (The microcosm.)
>
> 5.631 The thinking, presenting subject: there is no such thing.
>
> If I wrote a book, *The world as I found it,* I should also have therein to include a report on my body, and report which parts were subordinate to my will, and which were not, etc.,
>
> This then would be a method of isolating the subject, or rather of showing that in an important sense there is no subject; that is to say, of it alone in this book mention could *not* be made.
>
> 5.632 The subject does not belong to the world but it is a limit of the world.

5.633 Where *in* the world is a metaphysical subject to be found?

You say that this case is altogether like that of the eye and the field of sight. But you do *not* really see the eye.

And from nothing *in the field of sight* can it be concluded that it is seen from an eye.

5.634 This is connected with the fact that no part of our experience is also a priori.

Everything we see could also be otherwise.

Everything we can describe at all could also be otherwise.

There is no order of things a priori.

5.64 Here we see that solipsism strictly carried out coincides with pure realism.

The I in solipsism shrinks to an extensionless point and there remains the reality co-ordinated with it.

5.641 There is therefore really a sense in which in philosophy we can talk of a non-psychological I.

The I occurs in philosophy through the fact that "the world is my world."

The philosophical I is not the man, not the human body or the human soul of which psychology treats, but the metaphysical subject, the limit—not a part of the world.

6.373 The world is independent of my will.

6.43 If good or bad willing changes the world, it can only change the limits of the world, not the facts; not the things that can be expressed in language.

In brief, the world must thereby become quite another. It must so to speak wax or wane as a whole.

The world of the happy is quite another than that of the unhappy.

6.431 As in death, too, the world does not change, but ceases.

6.4311 Death is not an event of life. Death is not lived through.

If by eternity is understood not endless temporal duration but timelessness, then he lives eternally who lives in the present.

Our life is endless in the way that our visual field is without limit.

***

What has history to do with me? Mine is the first and only world. I want to report how *I* found the world.

What others in the world have told me about the world is a very small and incidental part of my experience of the world.

I have to judge the world, to measure things.

The philosophical I is not the human being, not the human body or the human soul with the psychological properties, but the metaphysical subject, the boundary (not a part) of the world.

The human body, however, my body in particular, is a part of the world among others, among beasts, plants, stones, etc., etc. (Wittgenstein, 1979a: p. 82ᵉ)

This is the way I have travelled: Idealism singles men out from the world as unique, solipsism singles me alone out, and at last I see that I too belong with the rest of the world, and so on the one side *nothing* is left over, and on the other side, as unique, *the world*. In this way idealism leads to realism if it is strictly thought out.

17.10.16

And in this sense I can also speak of a will that is common to the whole world. But this will is in higher sense *my* will.

As my representation is in the world, in the same way my will is the world-will. (Wittgenstein, 1979a: p. 85e)

VIII.2 Tractarian Solipsism

As the texts from the *Notebooks 1914-1916* (Wittgenstein, 1979a) clearly show, Tractarian solipsism is an especially strong version of metaphysical idealism. Metaphysical idealism says that all things are necessarily mind-dependent, in the sense that mind is a necessary condition of the existence and specific character of those things. Solipsism then says that all things are necessarily dependent *on my mind alone*. So in this way, according to Wittgenstein, I am my world (*TLP* 5.63) and the world is *my* world (*TLP* 5.641). What reasons does

The Fate of Analysis

he have for holding that the subject is identical to its world—which on the face of it would seem to imply, by the symmetry of identity, that it's as true to say that the subject belongs to the world as that the world belongs to the subject—yet also holding, in a stronger and asymmetric sense, that the subject possesses the world but not the converse?

I think that this follows directly from the premise that the world of facts is constructed by the language-using subject or ego, given the objects or things as an independent constraint. In other words, since (i) the world of facts, in order to be constituted, requires the dual inputs of the language-using subject or ego together with the objects or things, and since (ii) language is a logically private or solipsistic language of thought, it follows that (iii) the limits of my language are the limits of the world, and also that the world is necessarily dependent on my mind alone.

Strikingly, Wittgenstein's solipsism has two somewhat distinct dimensions: (i) a solipsism of the *representing* subject or ego, and (ii) a solipsism of the *willing* subject or ego. Wittgenstein's solipsism of the representing subject or ego says that all worldly facts are necessarily dependent on my mind alone in the sense that linguistic form (and its a priori essence, logical form) enters directly into the constitution of every fact, and language itself is constructed by the individual subject or ego. Wittgenstein's solipsism of the will, by contrast, says that the specific internal nature of the objects is necessarily dependent on my attitudes, desires, and volitions (willing). The world of facts is independent of my will, but the *limits* of the world, which are partially constituted by the specific internal nature of the objects, are necessarily dependent on my will. Now the world and my life are the same thing. Therefore, the world can "wax or wane as a whole," depending on my acts of willing, just as all the events of my life depend on my will. They do not, however, depend on my will in the sense that I can actually change any facts—I cannot—but in the sense that I can control the personal meaning or *value* of those facts. My will determines how I value the world and my life, which in turn partially determines the "substance" of the world by partially determining the nature of the objects. In this way, the world of the happy person, for example, is essentially distinct from the world of the unhappy person.

Here we can see that although the constitution of the facts is dual, with language on the one side, and the objects or things on the other, the metaphysical subject or ego ultimately grounds both of the dual inputs by acting both as the language-user and also as the determiner of the specific character of the objects. So the solipsistic metaphysics of the *Tractatus* is also a form of idealistic monism. I'll come back to the will's independence from the facts, which is the basis of a fundamental fact-value dichotomy in the *Tractatus*, when I discuss Wittgenstein's views on aesthetics, ethics, and the meaning of life, in section VIII.4 below.

VIII.3 Tractarian Realism

Now back to the dependence of the world on the individual representing subject. Wittgenstein wants to claim that his solipsism, when properly understood, is in fact a "pure realism."

How can this be the case when the metaphysics of the *Tractatus* is explicitly idealistic? In answering this question, what we must remember is that classical realism is the conjunction of three somewhat distinct theses: (i) mind-independence of the facts (*metaphysical realism*), (ii) objective knowability of the facts (*epistemic realism*), and (iii) direct or unmediated representation of the facts (*semantic realism*). These are distinct, because although they are all logically and conceptually consistent with each other, it is also possible to hold any one of the theses while denying the other two. For example, a Cartesian skeptic could hold (i) while denying both (ii) and (iii). A Russellian logical atomist or Carnapian logical constructivist could hold (i) and (iii) while denying (ii). And a platonic realist or a scientific realist could hold (i) and (ii) while denying (iii). Wittgenstein, by sharp contrast, as a Marburg-style logicistic neo-Kantian who's *also* a Russellian acquaintance theorist, denies (i) while holding both (ii) and (iii). We can know the facts and objects or things, and also represent them *directly*.

The direct accessibility of a fact or object/thing to semantic representation means that nothing—whether another faculty of the mind, an idea or mental image, a Fregean sense, a platonic universal—intervenes or mediates between the representing subject or ego and what she represents. So Wittgenstein's Tractarian realism says that nothing intervenes or mediates between our correct use of language, on the one hand, and the facts and objects/things we thereby represent, on the other. We represent facts directly through the correct use of complete propositional symbols, and we represent objects or things directly through the correct use of names. Then *we know the facts* if and only if our judgments are true.

This doesn't, however, in and of itself, tell us how solipsism *leads to* pure realism. Here Wittgenstein wants to say that his solipsism is not a solipsism of the *psychologically individual subject or ego* (an "empirical subject or ego" in the Kantian sense), who's individuated by his/her/their body and his/her/their own personal history, but rather a solipsism of the individual subject or ego considered only as *an anonymous representer and language-user* (a "transcendental subject or ego" in the Kantian sense). This anonymous (transcendental) subject or ego is an "extensionless point" precisely because it functions *only* as the means of representing the world through language. Here Wittgenstein uses the striking analogy of the visual field and the eye: the seeing eye is the necessary vehicle or means of vision, but it is not itself *part of* the visual field or its contents; rather the seeing eye is *presupposed by* the visual field and its contents. Similarly, the world contains all facts, including facts about my psychologically individual (empirical) subject or ego; but when *all* of these facts have been recorded, there is still something left over, namely, the representing and language-using (transcendental) subject or ego as such, which is contentless, yet presupposed by all the facts. Then when we consider the world of facts from the standpoint of that contentless representing and language-using (transcendental) subject or ego, we recognize that this entire world (my world, my life) *is directly presented to me and also fully knowable by me precisely insofar as I represent it via true judgments*.

VIII.4 What About Mathematics?

Now, what about mathematics? Immediately after writing that "logic is transcendental" (*TLP* 6.13), Wittgenstein also writes these propositions:

6.2 Mathematics is a logical method.

The propositions of mathematics are equations, and therefore pseudo-propositions.

6.21 Mathematical propositions express no thoughts.

6.22 The logic of the world which the propositions of logic show in tautologies, mathematics shows in equations.

6.233 To the question whether we need intuition for the solution of mathematical problems it must be answered that language itself here supplied the necessary intuition.

6.234 Mathematics is a method of logic.

6.2341 The essence (*Das Wesentliche*) of mathematical method is working with equations.

On this method depends the fact that every proposition of mathematics must be self-evident.

Thus mathematics belongs to logic, and like logical truths, mathematical truths are senseless ("express no thoughts"). But strictly speaking, the truths of mathematics are *not* themselves tautologies, precisely because instead they're *equations*, with an identity or "equals" sign connecting their objectual elements instead of a logical operator or logical constant. Moreover, the identity or "equals" sign *shows* but does *not* say anything, and in that sense they're only "pseudo-propositions."

By means of the showing function of the identity or equals sign, mathematics also shows "the logic of the world" via those equations, and those equations are "self-evident": hence, just like logic, *mathematics is transcendental*. The key to understanding Wittgenstein's line of thinking here is the claim that instead of holding, like Kant himself, that mathematics requires intuition (*Anschauung*), which would make mathematics synthetic a priori, we should hold that "language itself ... supplies the necessary intuition." Similarly, the later Marburg neo-Kantians, for example Cassirer, also did away with Kant's thesis that mathematics needs intuition, and (in effect) asserted *conceptualism* about the nature of mental representation (see section XVII.8 below). So, *via language*, mathematics becomes a methodological part of logic, which entails logicism, and this again displays Wittgenstein's Marburg-style logicistic neo-Kantianism. But even so, as we'll see later in chapter X, the assimilation of mathematical truth to logical truth doesn't jibe with Gödel's incompleteness theorems and Tarski's semantic conception of truth, and indeed it's outright inconsistent with them.

VIII.5 Is the *Tractatus*'s Point an Ethical One?

In 1919, in a letter to Ludwig von Ficker, editor of the journal *Der Brenner*, Wittgenstein glossed the *Tractatus* as follows:

> The book's point is an ethical one. I once meant to include in the preface a sentence which is not in fact there but which I will write out for you here, because it will perhaps be a key to my work for you. What I meant to write then, was this: My work consists of two parts; the one presented here plus all that I have *not* written. And it is precisely this second part which is the important one. My book draws limits to the sphere of the ethical from the inside as it were, and I am convinced that this is the ONLY *rigorous* way of drawing these limits. In short, I believe that where *many* others today are just *gassing*, I have managed in my book to put everything firmly in place by being silent about it. (As quoted in Brockhaus, 1991: 296)

This letter has often been dismissed by commentators as an intentionally misleading attempt by Wittgenstein to get a non-philosopher interested in publishing the *Tractatus*. And it's true that at the time, Wittgenstein was having difficulties getting the *Tractatus* published. Even so, I think that it would be a big mistake *not* to take these remarks seriously, as a self-commentary on the following propositions about aesthetics, ethics, and the meaning of life in the *Tractatus* and the *Notebooks*:

> 5.621 The world and life are one.

> 6.37 A necessity for one thing to happen because another has happened does not exist. There is only *logical* necessity.

> 6.373 The world is independent of my will.

> Even if everything we wished were to happen, this would only be, so to speak, a favour of fate, for there is no *logical* connection between will and world, which would guarantee this, and the assumed physical connection itself we could not again will.

> 6.4 All propositions are of equal value.

> The sense of the world (*Sinn der Welt*) must lie outside the world. In the world everything is as it is and happens as it does happen. *In* it there is no value--and if there were, it would be of no value.

> If there is a value which is of value, it must lie outside all happening and being-so. For all happening and being-so is accidental.

What makes it non-accidental cannot lie *in* the world, for otherwise this would again be accidental.

It must lie outside the world.

Hence also there are no ethical propositions.

Propositions cannot express anything higher.

6.421 It is clear that ethics cannot be expressed.

Ethics is transcendental.

(Ethics and aesthetics are one.)

6.423 Of the will as the subject of the ethical we cannot speak.

And the will as a phenomenon is only of interest to psychology.

6.43 If good or bad willing changes the world, it can only change the limits of the world, not the facts; not the things that can be expressed in language.

In brief, the world must thereby become quite another. It must so to speak wax or wane as a whole.

The world of the happy is a quite another than that of the unhappy.

6.431 So too at death the world does not change, but ceases.

6.4311 Death is not an event of life. Death is not lived through.

If by eternity is understood not endless temporal duration but timelessness, then he lives eternally who lives in the present.

Our life is endless in the way that our visual field is without limit.

6.4312 The temporal immortality of the human soul, that is to say, its eternal survival after death, is not only in no way guaranteed, but this assumption in the first place will not do for us what we always tried to make it do. Is a riddle solved by the fact that I survive forever? Is this eternal life not as enigmatic as our present one? The solution to the riddle of life in space and time lies *outside* space and time.

(It is not problems of natural science which have to be solved.)

6.432 *How* the world is, is completely indifferent for what is higher. God does not reveal himself *in* the world.

6.5 For an answer which cannot be expressed, the question too cannot be expressed.

The *riddle* does not exist.

If a question can be put at all, then it *can* also be answered.

6.52 We feel that even when all *possible* scientific questions have been answered, the problems of life have still not been touched at all. Of course there is then no question left, and just this is the answer.

6.521 The solution to the problem of life is seen in the vanishing of this problem.

(Is this not the reason why those who have found after a long period of doubt that the sense of life [*Sinn des Lebens*] became clear, could not say wherein this sense consisted?)

6.522 There is indeed the inexpressible. This *shows* itself; it is the mystical.

7 Whereof one cannot speak, thereof one must silent.

***

21.7.16

What really is the situation of the human will? I will call "will" first and foremost the bearer of good and evil. (Wittgenstein, 1979a: p. 76e)

Let us imagine a man who could use none of his limbs and hence could, in the ordinary sense, not exercise his *will*. He could, however, think and *want* and communicate his thoughts to someone else. He could therefore do good or evil through the other man.

Then it is clear that ethics would have validity for him, too, and that he in the *ethical sense* is the bearer of a *will*. (Wittgenstein, 1979a: pp. 76e-77e)

The World and Life are one.

Physiological life is not of course "Life." And neither is psychological life. Life is the world.

Ethics does not treat of the world. Ethics must be a condition of the world, like logic.

Ethics and aesthetics are one. (Wittgenstein, 1979a: p. 77e)

It seems one can't say anything more than: Live happily!

The world of the happy is a different world from that of the unhappy. The world of the happy is *a happy world.*

I keep on coming back to this! simply the happy life is good, the unhappy bad. If I now ask myself: but why should I live *happily*, then this of itself seems to me to be a tautological question; the happy life seems to be justified, of itself, it seems that it *is* the only right life.

But this is really in some sense deeply mysterious! It is clear that ethics cannot be expressed!

What is the objective mark of the happy, harmonious life? Here it is again clear that there cannot be any such mark, that can be described.

This mark cannot be a physical one but only a metaphysical one, a transcendental one. (Wittgenstein, 1979a: p. 78e)

Ethics is transcendental. How things stand, is God. God, is how things stand.

Only from the consciousness of the uniqueness of my life arises religion ... and art.

2.8.16

And this consciousness is life itself.

Can there be any ethics if there is no living being but myself? If ethics is supposed to be something fundamental, there can.

If I am right, then it is not sufficient for the ethical judgment that a world is given. Then the world in itself is neither good nor evil.

Good and evil enter only through the subject. And the subject is not part of the world, but a boundary of the world.

As the subject is not a part of the world but a presupposition of its existence, so good and evil which are predicates of the subject, are not properties in the world.

(Wittgenstein, 1979a: p. 79e)

For Wittgenstein, then, willing (wanting, preferring, choosing, etc.) and feeling (including emotional attitudes and the passions) are essentially the same. That's one reason why ethics and aesthetics are one. And another reason is that for Wittgenstein neither aesthetics nor ethics has a conceptual, discursive, propositional, fact-representing, or logical component. More generally, the metaphysical subject or ego has two essentially different capacities: (i) an intellectual, conceptual, discursive/linguistic, propositional, fact-representing, thinking, and logical capacity, and (ii) a non-intellectual, non-conceptual, non-discursive/linguistic, non-propositional, non-fact-representing, feeling, willing, and ethical capacity. But although these intellectual and non-intellectual capacities are exercised with respect to the same set of objects (the world of facts, or life), their contents are wholly divergent. So Wittgenstein's ethics is thoroughly *non-conceptualist*, *non-discursivist/linguisticist*, *non-propositionalist*, and *non-intellectualist* (again, see section XVII.8 below).

Moreover, the world of facts is modally independent of feeling and willing, and cannot be changed by the will. That is: what's nowadays called "mental causation," whereby a mental event is a sufficient cause of some physical event, is impossible, because all connections between facts in space and time (as per Hume) are either logically necessary or logically contingent, never *non-logically* (i.e., synthetically) *necessary*:

5.135 In no way can an inference be made from the existence of one state of affairs to the existence of another entirely different from it.

5.136 There is no causal nexus which justifies such an inference.

5.1361 The events of the future *cannot* be inferred from those of the present.

Superstition is the belief in the causal nexus.

But all value, all good and evil, inheres in the will of the metaphysical subject or ego. This means that Wittgenstein is positing a radically sharp fact-value dichotomy: (i) the world as represented through propositions, language, and science is wholly factual and logically-governed, but without any value, (ii) whereas the will has fundamental value, (iii) yet the value-properties of the will are not properties that can be represented conceptually, discursively/linguistically, or propositionally, (iv) because although my will is always directed towards my own life, which (given solipsism) is the same as my world, (v) those value-properties attach only to the metaphysical subject or ego, which is not *part* of the world, but instead *a fundamental, unique a priori presupposition* of the world's existence and specific character.

This radical fact *vs.* value (or its capacity-based equivalent: intellectual *vs.* non-intellectual) dichotomy has two crucial consequences.

The **first** is that natural science (the totality of contingent truths about the world of facts) and logic are absolutely *value-neutral*. So even if the world were to be completely described by the natural sciences and all of its logical truths made manifest, the problem of the *value* of rational human life in general, and the value of *the subject's oe ego's* life in particular, hence *the meaning of life*, would not have been touched. This problem of the value of (the subject's or ego's) life, and of the meaning of life, which is the basic problem of aesthetics and ethics, consists precisely in how the subject or ego is to be good and/or happy, and natural science and logic have nothing to do with it.

And **second**, the aesthetic and ethical problem or the problem of the value of (the subject's or ego's) life, and of the meaning of life, i.e., how I am to be good and/or happy, is radically unlike any scientific problem that can be propositionally formulated and then (at least in principle) solved. Indeed, Wittgenstein suggests that the fundamental *barrier* to solving the problem of the value of (the subject's or ego's) life is to treat the issue of my goodness or my happiness *as if it were sort of natural-scientific problem to which factual answers could be given*. On the contrary, it's only when I'm able to realize fully that the problem of the value of (the subject's or ego's) life *isn't* a problem in the factual or natural-scientific sense, and that there simply *is* no such problem of the value of (the subject's or ego's) life in this sense, can my will be converted into a possible bearer of goodness and/or happiness.

In other words, just like Kant, Wittgenstein "had to deny [scientific] **knowledge** (*Wissen*) in order to make room for [moral] **faith** (*Glauben*)" (*CPR* Bxxx, boldfacing in the original). In *Religion Within the Boundaries of Mere Reason*, Kant calls this conversion a "revolution of the heart" and a "revolution of the will," namely, a fundamentally life-changing *Gestalt*-shift in a person's "attitude" or "disposition" (*Gesinnung*) towards himself/herself/themselves and the world:

> If by a single and unalterable decision a human being reverses the supreme ground of his actions by which he was an evil human being (and thereby puts on a "new man"), he is, to this extent, by principle and attitude of mind, a subject receptive to the good; but he is a human being only in incessant laboring and becoming, i.e., he can hope … to find himself upon the good (though narrow) path of constant *progress* from bad to better. For him who penetrates to the intelligible ground of the heart (the ground of all the maxims of the power of choice/sensible will) …[1] this is the same as actually being a good human being … and to this extent the change can be considered a revolution. (*Rel* 6: 48)

---

[1] In this text I've elided references to God. This isn't because I think that the notion of God is unimportant in Kant's conception of practical rationality and moral agency—on the contrary, it's of fundamental importance—but only because Kant's moral theology is exceptionally subtle, even by Kantian standards. Hence discussing it here would only add needless complexity and length to the present account. In any case, I discuss Kant's moral theology in detail in Hanna, "If God's Existence is Unprovable, Then is Everything Permitted? Kant, Radical Agnosticism, and Morality." But for an alternative account of the same material, see (Chignell, 2013, 2015).

According to Wittgenstein, how does such a radical conversion happen? There are two parts to this.

First, we realize that the world of facts, and its a priori essence, logic, are in themselves valueless. This is closely connected to recognizing the senselessness of the propositions of the *Tractatus* and "throwing away the ladder" in proposition 6.54, about which I'll have more to say later in this chapter.

And **second**, because we cannot change or in any way affect the facts *in* the world, we must instead *change our volitional stance towards the world as a whole*. This, in turn, can determine a radically different world. On the metaphysical side, Wittgenstein is saying here that the willing subject or ego can jointly re-constitute the objects or things and its own language alike, and thus bring about the existence of a distinct world of facts, which again cannot themselves be changed or affected by our will. This is my will conceived as the "world-will," aka what I called Wittgenstein's "solipsism of the willing subject or ego." But on the first-personal side, Wittgenstein is saying that to change the world and my own life is not to change any facts whatsoever, but instead fundamentally to change the internal configuration of my will so that it becomes internally coherent or harmonious (goodness, happiness) rather than internally incoherent or discordant (badness, unhappiness). Or in other words, to change the world and my own life is *not* to change any facts whatsoever, but rather to carry out a complete personal transformation, by conversion to some essentially new set of values or commitments. The similarity of this line of thinking to Existentialist themes (Barnes, 1959; Solomon, 1974; Crowell, 2012) in, for example, the works of Augustine, Pascal, Kierkegaard, Schopenhauer, Dostoevsky, Nietzsche, Kafka, and early Heidegger (and we know that Wittgenstein had read, or at least read about, all of these), as well as the post-1945 works of Camus, De Beauvoir, and Sartre, should be obvious.

VIII.6 The Meaning of Life

The *Tractatus* is a book about logic, meaning, and mind (i.e., transcendental subjectivity). But there are several importantly different kinds of meaning.

A central kind of meaning discussed in the *Tractatus* is *discursive* or *linguistic*, and in particular *conceptual* and *propositional*. This is meaning as referring (naming) or as describing (saying), and the content of such meaning is either (i) the Fregean reference/Meaning (*Bedeutung*) of names, predicates, and sentences (namely, objects or things, and atomic facts or states of affairs), or the sense (*Sinn*) of propositional signs (namely, how the propositional sign, as correctly used by the language-using subject or ego, pictures facts). Many readers of the *Tractatus* think that this kind of meaning exhausts or at least fully circumscribes the content of Wittgenstein's theory of meaning

Nevertheless, there's another sharply different kind of meaning in the *Tractatus*, namely "the sense of the world" (*Sinn der Welt*) mentioned in proposition 6.41 and "the sense of life" (*Sinn des Lebens*) mentioned in proposition 6.521. This is the same as the value of (the subject's or ego's) life, aka the meaning of life, which in turn is the same as the goodness/badness or happiness/unhappiness of my will. It has two fundamental features. **First**, the sense, value, or meaning of (the subject's or ego's) life is not *in* the world, but rather is strictly *transcendental* to the world (i.e., a fundamental, unique a priori presupposition of the world) in a way strictly analogous to logic's relation to the world, precisely because the sense/value/meaning of life is a property of the metaphysical subject or ego, not a property of the facts, hence not a property of the objects or things towards which the will is directed. And **second**, the sense, value, or meaning of (the subject's or ego's) life, although it is unsayable and transcendental, is a genuine kind of sense, value, or meaning: indeed it is *the fundamental and most authentic kind of sense, value, or meaning*. And that's why the point of the *Tractatus* "is an ethical one."

Otherwise put, the point of the *Tractatus* is to get us to recognize the essential irrelevance of the world of facts, propositions, and logic (or what Schopenhauer called "the world as representation"), and to transcend *that* merely factual-logical sort of sense or meaning, in order to encounter the sense, meaning, or value of (the subject's or ego's) life. So *this* is the basic respect in which the propositions of the *Tractatus* are "senseless": they are *intrinsically valueless*, and irrelevant to my goodness and/or happiness. Still otherwise put, the point of the *Tractatus* is to move the reader from semantics, logic, mathematics, and natural science, to Wittgensteinian ethics: or, roughly speaking, from the metaphysics of Russellian logical atomism and/or Carnapian logical empiricism/ positivism, to what Miguel de Unamuno aptly calls "the tragic sense of life" (Unamuno, 2005), i.e., to Existentialism. In this respect, the *Tractatus* is *not* ultimately a logico-philosophical treatise, but instead ultimately a trigger for personal conversion or transformation, comparable to Augustine's *Confessions*; and the logico-philosophical part is only the disposable means—a "ladder" that must be kicked away—to that end. Those who correctly understand the *Tractatus* cannot remain personally unchanged and unmoved by it. Or at least, that was Wittgenstein's core authorial and philosophical intention.

VIII.7 Three Basic Worries About the *Tractatus*

It's philosophically commonplace to raise three basic worries about the *Tractatus*.

The **first** basic worry is that Wittgenstein offers no sufficient justification for his claim that the atomic facts in the world must be composed of absolutely or metaphysically simple objects (*TLP* 2.02). Here it's important, however, to remember that simplicity does not imply that the objects or things don't have internal properties or internal complexity—they *do* (*TLP* 2.01231, 2.0233-2.02231)—but only that the objects are explanatorily and ontologically basic, hence undecomposable into more objects. So even granting that, why couldn't the objects or things be *complex*, nevertheless *still* undecomposable, for example, if their elements are essentially complementary or "entangled," like physical particles in quantum-mechanical relationships? And why couldn't the objects or things be only *relatively* simple—say, relative to each logical analyst, or relative to each user of the language, or relative to each context of utterance, etc.? Let's call this *the worry about the simplicity of the objects or things*.

One possible response that Wittgenstein could make to this worry is just to insist that the metaphysical subject or ego is a *transcendental* and *anonymous* subject or ego, not an individual psychological subject (*TLP* 5.641). Then the objects are simple, *relative to a single transcendental subject or ego, and to a single language*. But that response still doesn't answer the worry about simplicity, since metaphysical complexity and *relative* simplicity are perfectly conceptually consistent with one another.

The **second** basic worry is that there appear to be clear counterexamples to Wittgenstein's thesis that the atomic facts are logically independent of one another. If point A is red (positive atomic fact 1), then isn't it *necessarily not the case* that point A is green (negative atomic fact 2)? And if point A is brighter than point B (positive atomic fact 1), and point B is brighter than point C (positive atomic fact 2), then isn't it *necessarily the case* that point A is brighter than point C? Let's call this *the worry about the logical independence of atomic facts*.

One possible response that Wittgenstein could make to this worry is just to insist that *if* these facts are indeed logically dependent on one another, then that shows *only* that they are complex facts, not atomic or elementary facts, and that the proposition, "This point in the visual field is simultaneously both red and green" is actually a logical contradiction, as per the following propositions:

> 6.375 As there is only a *logical* necessity, so there is only a *logical* possibility.

> 6.3751 For two colours ... to be at one place in the visual field, is impossible, logically impossible, for it is excluded by the logical structure of colour.

> Let us consider how this contradiction presents itself in physics. Somewhat as follows: That a particle cannot at the same time have two velocities, *i.e.*, that at the same time it cannot be in two places, *i.e.*, that particles in different places at the same time cannot be identical.

> (It is clear that the logical product of two elementary propositions can neither be a tautology nor a contradiction. The assertion that a point in the visual field has two different colours at the same time, is a contradiction.)

But that response is still open to the objection that *whenever* some example of an elementary proposition is given by Wittgenstein, yet another "red-green"-style counterexample can be constructed that apparently shows that atomic facts are not modally independent of one another—and if at *that* point, Wittgenstein again claims that this shows *only* that these facts are complex, not atomic, then surely he's merely begging the question.

And the **third** basic worry is that Wittgenstein's conception of philosophy is ultimately *nihilistic* or *radically skeptical*, in the sense that he rejects all or at least virtually all of traditional philosophy (for example, all of classical metaphysics) as unacceptable nonsense

(*TLP* 4.003), but at the same time he also has no positive or metaphysical conception of philosophy to offer in its place, and in fact claims that all his own philosophical claims in the *Tractatus* ("my propositions") are nonsense (*TLP* 6.54). Let's call this *the worry about metaphilosophy*.

> One possible response that Wittgenstein could make to the worry about metaphilosophy is to claim that on his view philosophy is simply the *activity* of logical analysis, not a positive theory; hence merely because it's not a positive philosophical theory in the classical sense of being a super-science, it doesn't follow that it's in any way nihilistic or excessively skeptical:
>
>> 4.112 The object of philosophy is the logical clarification of thoughts. A philosophical work consists essentially of elucidations.
>>
>> The result of philosophy is not a number of "philosophical propositions," but to make propositions clear.
>>
>> Philosophy should make clear and delimit sharply the thoughts which otherwise are, as it were, opaque and blurred.

Nowadays, this is called *metaphysical quietism* (Macarthur, 2017; and section XVII.8 below), and it's also closely related to the "resolute" reading of the *Tractatus*. But that response is still open to the objection that this approach to philosophy is wholly parasitic on the natural sciences, and that at the end of the day, it's in fact only an opening to various updated versions of Locke's "underlaborer" conception of philosophy, aka *scientism*, as per the following propositions:

> 4.11 The totality of true propositions is the total natural science (or the totality of the natural sciences).
>
> Philosophy limits the disputable sphere of natural science.
>
> It should limit the thinkable and thereby the unthinkable.
>
> It should limit the unthinkable from within through the thinkable.
>
> 6.53 The right method of philosophy would be this. To say nothing except what can be said, i.e., the propositions of natural science, i.e., something that has nothing to do with philosophy: and then always, when someone else wished to say something metaphysical, to demonstrate to him that he had given no meaning to certain signs in his propositions. This method would be unsatisfying to the other—he would not have the feeling that we were teaching him philosophy—but it would be the only strictly correct method.

So, can Wittgenstein offer defensible counter-replies to these worries and counter-worries? My claim is that he *can*, if we look more closely at his conceptions of natural science and the mystical.

VIII.8 Natural Science and the Worry About the Simplicity of the Objects or Things

Wittgenstein's conception of the natural sciences provides a defensible counter-response to the worry and counter-worry about the simplicity of the objects. The crucial point here is that his approach to natural science is explicitly *conventionalist*. That is, Wittgenstein's idea is that every basic natural science—for example, Newtonian mechanics—is nothing but a "form of description," aka a "conceptual scheme," aka a "conceptual framework," that, like the imposition of a grid or mesh or network on an otherwise shapeless field of coloured content, determines or structures that content in a way that's consistent with logic but not automatically entailed by logic. And this is what the following propositions say:

> 6.341 To the different networks correspond different systems of describing the world.
>
> Mechanics determine a form of description by saying: All propositions in the description of the world must be obtained in a given way from a number of given propositions--the mechanical axioms. It thus provides the bricks for building the edifice of science and says: Whatever building thou wouldst erect, thou shalt construct it in some manner with these bricks and these bricks alone....
>
> 6.342 And now we see the relative position of logic and mechanics. (We could construct the framework out of figures of different kinds, as out of triangles and hexagons together.) That a picture like that instanced above can be described by a network of a given form asserts *nothing* about the picture. (For this holds of every picture of this kind.) But *this* does characterize the picture, the fact, namely, that it can be *completely* described by a definite net of *definite* fineness.
>
> So too the fact that it can be described by Newtonian mechanics asserts nothing about the world; but *this* asserts something, namely, that it can be described in that particular way in which as a matter of fact it can be described. The fact, too, that it can be described more simply by one system of mechanics than by another says something about the world.
>
> 6.343 Mechanics is an attempt to construct according to a single plan all *true* propositions which we need for the description of the world.
>
> 6.3431 Through their whole logical apparatus the physical laws still speak of the objects of the world.

Hence, for Wittgenstein, the simplicity of the objects or things is always relative to a scientific form of description (conceptual scheme, conceptual framework); yet such schemes guarantee an absolute or metaphysical simplicity only *internally* to those schemes. So, the metaphysical simplicity of the objects, in any given scientific scheme, is simply a requirement of the atomistic, microphysical conception of the world that inherently belongs to the contemporary natural sciences.

At this point, if the objector is going to insist that objects can *still* be metaphysically complex, then they're going to have to do so in the face of, and against the grain of, the natural sciences as they're currently constituted.

VIII.9 Natural Science and the Worry About the Logical Independence of Atomic Facts

Wittgenstein's conception of natural science also provides a counter-response to the worry and counter-worry about the logical independence of the atomic facts. The crucial point triple here is (i) that not only that atomic facts are indeed all logically independent, but also (ii) that the laws of natural science are logically necessary only within or internally to scientific forms of description (conceptual schemes, conceptual frameworks), and furtheremore (iii) that natural-scientific laws are merely logically contingent when considered outside such schemes (*TLP* 6.35, 6.37, 6.375). So, in other words, Wittgenstein can hold that there will always be *scientifically lawlike* connections between atomic facts *within* a given scientific form of description, and that these will be logically necessary *internally to* that form of description, even though, when considered *apart from* or *outside* that form of description, the facts are themselves logically independent and the laws are logically contingent. This strongly anticipates Carnap's arguments in supplements A and B of *Meaning and Necessity*: "Empiricism, Semantics, and Ontology" and "Meaning Postulates" (Carnap, 1956b, 1956c).

VIII.10 Tractarian Mysticism and the Worry About Metaphilosophy: How to Throw Away the Ladder

Finally, Wittgenstein's conception of the natural sciences also provides a counter-response to the worry and counter-worry about metaphilosophy. The crucial point here is that for Wittgenstein, philosophy is *not* in any way a natural science or somehow reducible to, or parasitic upon, the natural sciences, hence it cannot *say* anything about the world, but instead can only *show* things about the world. This is the upshot of the following propositions:

> 4.111 Philosophy is not one of the natural sciences.
>
> (The word "philosophy" must mean something which stands above or below, but not beside the natural sciences.)
>
> 6.432 *How* the world is, is completely indifferent, for what is higher. God does not reveal himself in the world.

> Not *how* the world is, is the mystical, but *that* it is.
>
> The contemplation of the world sub specie aeterni is its contemplation as a limited whole.
>
> The feeling of the world as a limited whole is the mystical feeling.
>
> 6.522 There is indeed the inexpressible. This *shows* itself; it is the mystical.

In other words, Wittgenstein is saying that the positive content of metaphysics in his sense is ultimately wholly aesthetic (and thus also wholly ethical) in character. It consists in grasping the world as a limited whole—as limited by logic, language, and the transcendental subject or ego—via a profound contemplative feeling that marvels at the contingent fact of the existence of the world, just as Spinoza had insisted, "under a species of eternity." Thus philosophy, properly understood, is indeed *not* some sort of super-science; but that *doesn't* mean that it's nihilistic or excessively skeptical, or indeed any sort of "metaphysical quietism." On the contrary, it's an essentially non-conceptual, non-discursive/linguistic. non-propositional, and non-intellectual way of appreciating the transcendental features of the world:

> 6.54 My propositions are elucidatory is this way: he who understands me finally recognizes them as senseless, when he has climbed out through them, on them, over them. (He must so to speak throw away the ladder, after he has climbed up on it.)
>
> He must surmount these propositions; then he sees the world rightly.
>
> 7 Whereof one cannot speak, thereof one must be silent.

To this extent, the meta-philosophy of the *Tractatus* is very much a return to Aristotle's idea that philosophy begins in wonder, (as I mentioned just above) to Spinoza's idea that philosophy is an attempt to grasp the world *sub specie aeternitatis*, and to Kant's notion of *reverence*:

> [T]wo things fill the mind with ever new and increasing admiration and reverence (*Ehrfurcht*), the more often and more steadily one reflects on them: *the starry heavens above me and the moral law within me*. I do not need to search for them and merely conjecture them as though they were veiled in obscurity or in the transcendent region beyond my horizon; I see them before me and connect them immediately with the consciousness of my existence. (*CPrR* 5: 161-162)

The *Tractatus*, therefore, is profoundly opposed to scientific naturalism. Hence it's also profoundly *ironic* that the *Tractatus* became the secular Bible of logical empiricism/positivism, and thereby, via Carnap, Quine, and Wilfrid Sellars, the founding text of scientific naturalism. For it then follows that all (classical or post-classical) Analytic philosophy after 1921 is based on a *mis-reading* of the *Tractatus*.

IX. Carnap, Logical Empiricism, and The Great Divide

IX.1 Carnap Before and After the *Tractatus*

Wittgenstein gave up philosophy for roughly ten years after the publication of the *Tractatus*. At the same time, during Wittgenstein's "silent decade"—interestingly comparable to and contrastible with Kant's own "silent decade" between the early 1770s and the early 1780s—Carnap was discovering his own philosophical voice. Falling into what will by now no doubt seem like a familiar pattern, and indeed very like Russell, Carnap started his philosophical career as a neo-Kantian philosopher of the foundations of geometry:

> I studied Kant's philosophy with Bruno Bauch in Jena. In his seminar, the *Critique of Pure Reason* was discussed in detail for an entire year. I was strongly impressed by Kant's conception that the geometrical structure of space is determined by our forms of intuition. The after-effects of this influence were still noticeable in the chapter on the space of intuition in my dissertation, *Der Raum* [published in 1922].... Knowledge of intuitive space I regarded at the time, under the influence of Kant and the neo-Kantians, especially Natorp and Cassirer, as based on 'pure intuition,' and independent of contingent experience. (Carnap, 1963: pp. 4, 12)

In this connection, it's not irrelevant that Bauch was virulently anti-semitic and eventually a Nazi (Sluga, 1993: esp. ch. 4), whereas Carnap was an anti-fascist, a universalist, an egalitarian, and at least while he still lived in Europe, also a radical socialist; and it's also not irrelevant that Carnap was importantly influenced by another of his teachers, Herman Nohl, a student of Dilthey (Nelson, 2018). So seems to me quite possible that Carnap's sharp moral, political, and sociocultural disagreements with Bauch also primed his officially anti-Kantian and anti-neo-Kantian turn by the late 1920s and early 30s (Friedman, 2000: esp. ch. 5).

In any case, Carnap's progress away from Kant's metaphysics and neo-Kantianism more generally, followed the by-now familiar dual pattern for classical Analytic philosophers of (i) treating post-Kantian developments in the formal and natural sciences as refutations of basic Kantian theses, and (ii) replacing transcendental idealism with philosophical logic. By the early 1930s, Carnap had been heavily influenced by the Theory of Relativity and by the close study of Frege's writings, along with the Russell's and Whitehead's *Principia*, Russell's *Our Knowledge of the External World*, and above all, by the *Tractatus*. Carnap's intellectual ferment was expressed in two important books, *The Logical Structure of the World* (*Logische Aufbau der Welt*) (1928), and *The Logical Syntax of Language* (1934). The *Aufbau* played a crucial variation on Russell's platonistic conception of philosophical analysis by turning it into *constructive empiricism*, which can be glossed as follows:

> The natural world as a whole is the object of analysis. But the simples out of which the world is logically constructed are not noumenally mind-independent substances, but instead nothing but subjective streams of experience and a single fundamental relation, *the recollection of similarity*.

The Fate of Analysis

Correspondingly, *Logical Syntax* converts Wittgenstein's Marburg-style logicistic neo-Kantian transcendental and activist conception of analysis into *logico-linguistic conventionalism*, which can be glossed this way:

> There is no One True Logic, just as there is no One True Natural Language, but instead there as many distinct logical languages as there are formal symbolic calculi constructed on the models of the *Begriffsschrift* and *Principia*, plus distinct axiom-systems, or distinct sets of logical constants, or distinct notions of logical consequence; and the choice of precisely which logical language is to be adopted as the basis of the exact sciences is purely a pragmatic matter (whether voluntaristic or social) having nothing to do with logic itself.

The overall result is that Kant's *transcendental turn* from the apparent or manifestly world to a set of a priori world-structures that are (according, at least, to the strong versions of Kant's transcendental idealism) imposed on phenomenal appearances by our innate spontaneous cognitive capacities, is replaced by Carnap with *the linguistic turn* (Rorty, 1967a, 1967b) from the apparent world to a set of a priori world-structures that are imposed on those phenomenal appearances by the syntax and semantics of our logical and natural languages.

Needless to say, however, even *after* the linguistic turn, the strategy of imposing a priori logico-linguistic structures on phenomenal appearances remains basically a neo-Kantian and thereby (arguably, again depending on your interpretation of Kant's metaphysics) also a Kantian move (Richardson, 1998). Indeed, the very same Carnapian empiricist/positivist fusion of pure logic and epistemological neo-Kantianism is vividly evident in C.I. Lewis's *Mind and the World Order* (1929) and Nelson Goodman's *The Structure of Appearance* (1951/1966).

IX.2 Carnap, The Vienna Circle, and The Elimination of Metaphysics

In any case, Carnap's *Aufbau* and *Logical Syntax*, together with the basic writings of Frege, Russell, and early Wittgenstein, and also Moritz Schlick's *General Theory of Knowledge* (1925), became the philosophical *Ur*-texts of The Vienna Circle (Passmore, 1967; Waismann, 1979; Friedman, 1999; Edmonds, 2020) which flourished throughout most of the 1930s, until the coming-to-power of the Nazis in Germany caused the diaspora of its core membership to England and the USA. The political leanings of the inner circle of the Circle were anti-fascist, universalist, egalitarian, radical socialist, and indeed Communist. So staying in Austro-Germany would have most certainly meant their cultural and intellectual deaths, and very probably their actual deaths too. Indeed, Schlick was murdered by a pro-Nazi student (although, it appears, mainly for personal reasons) in 1936 (Edmonds, 2020: esp. ch. 15).

As I've mentioned several times, The Circle philosophically professed logical empiricism/logical positivism, which is essentially the fusion of Carnap's constructive empiricism and logical conventionalism, plus the explicit rejection of Kant's notion of the synthetic a priori. More precisely, according to Carnap, (i) synthetic a priori propositions are meaningless, and (ii) all and only analytic propositions and empirical propositions are meaningful. Even more specifically, here's how Carnap argues for this two-part thesis, step-by-step, in his enormously influential 1932 essay, "The Elimination of Metaphysics through Logical Analysis of Language" (Carnap, 1959).

Step 1. Carnap's basic claim is that every statement of metaphysics is entirely meaningless or nonsensical; indeed, every metaphysical statement is a *pseudo-statement*.

Step 2. There are two kinds of pseudo-statements; more specifically, a sentence is a pseudo-statement if and only if either (2.i) it contains meaningless words, or (2.ii) it violates rules of syntax.

Step 3. A word W is meaningful if and only if W is applicable to "the given" in sense experience, and has a set of determinate conditions under which it is thereby applicable, which in turn is necessarily equivalent with saying that the whole sentence S which contains W is itself meaningful.

Step 4. A non-logical sentence S is meaningful if and only if (4i) S has well-formed *grammatical* syntax, (4ii) S has well-formed *logical* or *semantic* syntax, which is the same as to say it's *sortally correct*,[1] and (4iii) S is *verifiable*, which is the same as to say that it's made true or false by application to the given in sense experience, which in turn implies that its component words have determinate application-conditions.

Step 5. Metaphysical words—for example, "God" or "Being"—are meaningless because either (5i) they have no determinate application-conditions, or (5ii) the whole sentence that contains it is meaningless.

Step 6. Metaphysical statements generally violate rules of either grammatical or logical/semantic syntax—for example, Heidegger's notorious statement, "The nothing nihilates" (*das Nichts nichtet*) in his equally notorious 1929 essay, "What is Metaphysics?" (Heidegger, 1977: p. 105).

Step 7. More generally, all metaphysicians, like Heidegger, explicitly reject logic and natural science as sources of fundamental philosophical insight.

Step 8. All metaphysics, especially Heidegger's, is meaningless by one or another, or all, of the three criteria of meaningfulness, i.e., (8i) grammatical well-formedness of sentences, (8ii) sortal correctness of sentences, and (8iii) verifiability, which entails determinate application-conditions for component words.

---

[1] In view of Husserl's commitment to the existence and meaningfulness of synthetic a priori propositions, it's ironic (i) that Carnap studied briefly with Husserl, (ii) that the theory of sortal correctness conditions was created or discovered by Husserl in *Logical Investigations*, so in all likelihood Carnap originally learned about it *from* Husserl, and (iii) that the axioms of that sortal-correctness theory are all synthetic a priori. See, e.g., (Hanna, 1984).

The Fate of Analysis

Step 9. As another example of the logico-semantic emptiness of metaphysics, Descartes's famous Cogito argument is logically invalid: "I think" entails only "something exists that thinks." Correspondingly, here's an instructive critical side-comment. Carnap claims that the logical form of The Cogito is as follows:

1. "a" means me, myself, I (by definition)

2. "Fx" means "x thinks" (by definition)

3. Fa (premise)

4. (∃x) Fx (by existential generalization)

5. Therefore, "(∃x) Fx," which means "something exists that thinks," is a logical consequence of "Fa," which means "I think"

But on the contrary, I think that it's far more plausibly arguable that the correct logical form of Descartes's Cogito is as follows:

1. "a" means me, myself, I (by definition)

2. "Fx" mean "x thinks" (by definition)

3. Fa (premise)

4. "x=x" means "x is identical to itself" (by definition)

5. Every substitution instance of "x=x" is necessarily true (principle of identity)

6. Therefore, "a=a" is necessarily true (by substitution from 5.)

7. (∃x) x=a (by existential generalization from 6.)

8. A necessary truth is a logical consequence of every set of premises, including the empty set, because (8a) necessary truths are true in every set of circumstances, hence (8b) no matter what the set of premises, there's no possible set of circumstances such that the premises are true and the conclusion false (lemma, by the definitions of "logical consequence" and "necessary truth")

9. Therefore, "(∃x) x=a," which means "I exist," is a logical consequence of "Fa," which means "I think" (by 3., 7., & the lemma proved in 8.)

And this argument *is* logically valid and sound. But most importantly, it also shows us that for Carnap and the other classical Analytic philosophers who subscribe to

Principia Mathematica-style logic, the astounding ontological fact of something's existing and indeed my existing, instead of there being nothing at all, *is a necessary truth of predicate logic with identity, hence analytically necessary and a priori*—which seems highly questionable: isn't logically possible that nothing ever existed or exists? At most, the necessity of identity is synthetically necessary and a priori. More generally, *mathematical logic is not metaphysically innocent*. Correspondingly, the highly instructive conclusion to draw from this, is that correct insight into the underlying logical form of propositions and arguments expressed in natural language, and into their ontological implications, is *not* immediately self-evident, even to leading classical Analytic philosophers, like Carnap and those other logical empiricists/positivists who self-consciously undertake the destruction of metaphysics via "the logical analysis of language," precisely because these same philosophers have *not* undertaken a metaphysical critique of mathematical logic.

Step 10. Leaving aside Descartes, a great many pseudo-statements are encountered in the writings of Heidegger and Hegel.

Step 11. By sharp contrast, there are two and only two kinds of meaningful statement: (11i) logical truths (analytic statements), and (11ii) verifiable statements.

Step 12. Therefore, a sentence S is meaningful if and only if S is either analytic or verifiable.

Step 13. By this criterion of meaningfulness, all metaphysics is meaningless: so what were all those metaphysicians really doing, and what were all those treatises in metaphysics really about?

Step 14. The answer is that they were simply expressions of attitudes towards life; but this sort of activity is done much more effectively by writers like Nietzsche (who thereby, presumably, doesn't count as a "philosopher" but instead as an *anti*-philosopher), especially musicians and poets: hence metaphysicians are merely *failed artists*.

Step 15. Moreover, by this criterion of meaningfulness, all normative-claims and value-claims more generally (especially including ethical claims) are also meaningless.

Step 16. What, then, is left over for philosophy to do if metaphysics and all normative-claims and value-claims more generally (especially including ethical claims) are meaningless?

Step 17. The answer to this burning question is that philosophers can engage in *either* logical analysis (meta-logic) *or* scientific philosophy/philosophy of science, and *that's it*: in short, henceforth *philosophy is nothing but an underlaborer of the formal and natural sciences*.

IX.3 The Verifiability Principle and Its Fate

According to Carnap and also to the ill-fated Schlick, the official founder and leader of The Circle, synthetic a priori propositions are meaningless because they are *neither* tautological logical truths or falsehoods (analytic propositions) *nor* verifiable empirical truths or faleshoods, and analyticity and verifiability exhaust the possible sources of cognitive significance (Schlick, 1949).[2] The Carnap-Schlick attack on the synthetic a priori, plus constructive empiricism, plus logico-linguistic conventionalism, plus the general semantic thesis that all and only meaningful propositions are either analytic propositions or else verifiable empirical propositions (*The Verifiability Principle*, aka The VP), were all crisply formulated and beautifully written up for English-speaking philosophers in A.J. Ayer's *Language, Truth, and Logic* (1936).

It's a notorious and serious problem for Ayer in particular, however, and for The Vienna Circle more generally, that The VP itself is neither an analytic proposition nor a factual proposition. Looked at with a wide-angle lens, the problem of the logico-semantic status of The VP is merely a special case of Wittgenstein's earlier worry about the logico-semantic status of his Tractarian logico-philosophical propositions. The standard purported solution to this problem is to say that The VP is a meta-linguistic or meta-logical proposition, hence The VP is nothing but a further bit of language and logic that also happens to be about language and logic. Unfortunately, however, that move in turn only invokes an even more general and intractable worry, which we have already encountered in Husserl's critique of psychologism, the *Tractatus*, and elsewhere, about the logico-semantic status of meta-languages and meta-logics: namely, *The Logocentric Predicament*, which says that since any attempt to explain or justify logic must itself already presuppose and use some or all of the very logical principles and concepts that it aims to explain or justify, then logic is inexplicable and unjustifiable, i.e., rationally groundless.

From the critical vantage point of this book, one obvious way out of the problem about the status of The VP would be to return to Kantian modal dualism and say that The VP is non-logically necessary and a priori, i.e., synthetic a priori. But of course this violates the official logical empiricist/positivist ban on the synthetic a priori. So the problem of the status of The Verifiability Principle leaves logical empiricism/positivism between a rock (a close encounter with the seemingly insoluble logocentric predicament) and a hard place (being forced to accept the already-rejected Kantian notion of the synthetic a priori).

That's bad enough. But as I've already anticipated, and as we'll see in detail in chapter XVI, the ultimate death-blow to logical empiricism/positivism came from *inside* The Vienna Circle—from Carnap's protégé, Quine, himself a member of the Circle in the early 30s—and his ruthless logico-semantic destruction of the logical empiricists'/positivists' version of the analytic-synthetic distinction.

---

2 As Donald Davison observes in passing in his (1999), the Feigl-Sellars collection in which Schlick's essay appeared was the bible of young Analytic philosophers trained in the 1950s.

IX.4 The Davos Conference and The Great Divide

In Davos, Switzerland, from 17 March to 6 April 1929, an "International University Course," sponsored by the Swiss, French, and German governments, brought together the leading neo-Kantian Ernst Cassirer, the middle-aged and already famous author of the multi-volume *Philosophy of Symbolic Forms* (1925, 1927, 1929), and the soon-to-be leading existential phenomenologist Martin Heidegger, the young but already famous author of *Being and Time* (1927), in an official and more or less explicit attempt to bring about a philosophical reconciliation between Marburg-style logicistic (and also exact-science-oriented) neo-Kantianism and existential phenomenology. The soon-to-be leading logical empiricist/positivist Carnap was there too, along with many other professors and students from across Europe. Significantly, Cassirer's version of neo-Kantianism was *not only* logicistic and oriented towards mathematics and the natural sciences, but *also* neo-Hegelian and historicist, and later had an important impact on American philosophy when Cassirer taught at Yale during the Nazi period. So there were significant social and political overtones and undertones at Davos too: Cassirer was a Jewish liberal democrat, Heidegger was soon to be a Nazi, and Carnap was a radical socialist. Yet a good time was had by all: "It appears that the Davos encounter itself took place in atmosphere of extraordinarily friendly collegiality" (Friedman, 2000: p. 5).

The key sessions at Davos were two lecture series by Cassirer and Heidegger, followed by a public disputation between them. Significantly and strikingly, both the lectures and the disputation dealt with the question of how to interpret the *Critique of Pure Reason* correctly (Cassirer, 1967, 1981; Heidegger, 1990). In other words, the crucial Davos conference was all about Kant and the neo-Kantian origins of existential phenomenology. Now for this reason it can be argued, and indeed has been argued by Michael Friedman (2000: esp. ch. 9), that the Davos conference was emblematic of the death-by-mitosis of the neo-Kantian tradition, during the 1930s, into two fundamentally distinct and irreconcilable philosophical traditions: the classical Analytic tradition (whose paradigm case was logical empiricism/positivism), and the phenomenological tradition (whose paradigm case was existential phenomenology). According to this historical reconstruction, the basic disagreements between classical Analytic philosophy and (either transcendental or existential) phenomenology were latent in the period 1900-1930, during which—as we've seen above—Moore, Russell, and Carnap all started their philosophical careers as neo-Kantians, but went on to reject neo-Kantianism and Kant by means of foundational work in mathematical logic, and taking onboard the latest developments in mathematics and physics, and then correspondingly worked out various new logically-driven conceptions of a priori analysis. And then, so the story goes, the latent eventually became manifest, and the post-Kantian phenomenological mainstream consisting of Brentano, Husserl, and Heidegger was officially Greatly Divided from the post-Kantian classical Analytical mainstream consisting of Frege, Moore, Russell, early Wittgenstein, and Carnap-and-The-Vienna-Circle. And the essential difference between them was split by *Meinong's World*, the stomping grounds of Meinong, half-Analytic ontologist and half-phenomenologist, like some misbegotten inmate of the island of Dr Moreau, *The Island of Lost Souls* ("half-man, half-beast!"). In any case, according to this story, classical Analytic philosophy and (either transcendental or existential) phenomenology decisively broke up because the phenomenologists rejected the Frege-Russell conception of pure logic—especially Heidegger, the notorious logic-hater, exact-science-hater, and Nazi—as it were, *Hitlegger*.[3] But Meinong and his nether World also provided a particularly egregious case of (as I've sardonically noted) a half-Analytic ontologist, half-phenomenologist madman, who explicitly rejects the universal law of non-contradiction—thereby implicitly endorsing *dialetheism*, a dark logical sin whose name could not be spoken and that could not come out of the closet again until Graham Priest had defended dialetheism in the late 1980s (Priest, 1987), and thereby brought neo-Hegelianism, like a wolf, back onto the scene dressed in post-classical Analytic sheep's clothing, under the not-so-very-scary sounding label "non-classical logic." All the while, contrariwise, supposedly, the classical Analytic philosophers had very rightly and virtuously affirmed pure logic in its classical versions *only*. And never the twain shall meet.

But although this makes a conveniently neat interpretation of The Great Divide, it's at least arguably not quite true to the historico-philosophical facts. The highly cordial atmosphere at Davos was no polite put-on. Obviously, there were some important differences and disagreements between logical empiricism/positivism and phenomenology (especially existential phenomenology). Nevertheless, Heidegger took Carnap very seriously as a philosopher well into the 1930s; and conversely Carnap also took Heidegger very seriously as a philosopher during the 1920s and well into the 30s (Friedman, 2000: ch. 2).

So too, relevantly: so did Wittgenstein, who had an explicit and strong philosophical sympathy for existentialism from his Tractarian period onwards, and who told The Vienna Circle in 1929 that

> I can readily think what Heidegger means by Being and Dread. Man has the impulse to run up against the limits of language. (Wittgenstein, 1978: 80)

In any case, and for his part, Heidegger was every bit as dismissive of traditional metaphysics as Carnap was (Carnap, 1959, 1967b; Heidegger, 1977). And while it's quite true that Heidegger sharply criticized the Fregean and Russellian mathmatical logic of the *Begriffsschrift* and *Principia Mathematica*, so too did Carnap; after all, that's the main point of *Logical Syntax of Language*. Furthermore, objectively considered, Heidegger's existential phenomenology is not essentially *more* different from or opposed to mathematical logic, or logical empiricism/positivism for that matter, than is Dewey's pragmatism, which despite its radical critical philosophical and metaphilosophical implications (Rorty, 1982; Baghramian and Marchetti, 2019), cohabited very comfortably with mainstream Analytic philosophy in the USA after 1945. Nor, objectively speaking, is Heidegger's existential phenomenology essentially *more* different from or opposed to either mathematical logic, or logical empiricism/ positivism, than is Wittgenstein's later philosophy as expressed in the *Investigations*, which despite its equally radical critical philosophical and metaphilosophical implications (Hacker, 1996: ch. 5)—which I'll explore in chapters XI to XV be-

---
3 Thanks to Addison Ellis for this abusive epithet—ironically intended, of course.

low—*also* cohabited very comfortably with post-classical Analytic philosophy in the USA and England after 1945, until the mid-1980s, when a hypertrophied version of The Great Divide nudged the philosophy of the later Wittgenstein into the enemy camp of so-called "Continental philosophy." So it manifestly appears that The Great Divide between Analytic philosophy and phenomenology *didn't* actually happen in the 1920s and 1930s. And it also manifestly appears that The Divide *isn't* the consequence of any fundamental philosophical disagreements between classical Analytic philosophers and phenomenologists (even existential phenomenologists) about pure logic. In fact, as I mentioned in section IV.1, Russell thought highly of Husserl's *Logical Investigations* and not only strongly endorsed early Husserl's anti-psychologism and realism, but also explicitly placed early Husserl's phenomenology in the classical *Analytic* tradition. So on the contrary, it manifestly appears that The Divide happened almost entirely after 1945, and that it was the joint result of the three following factors.

First, there was the sharply divisive cultural politics of anti-fascism and anti-Communism in Anglo-American countries after World War II: (i) Heidegger publicly and notoriously supported the Nazis in the mid-thirties, and never explicitly repudiated his fascist sympathies (Sluga, 1993: esp. chs. 1, 10), (ii) Vienna Circle exiles in the USA were understandably very eager to avoid being persecuted during the McCarthy Communist-trials era for their pre-war radical-socialist and Communist sympathies, so were generally playing it safe (Carnap, however, being a notable exception[4]) by, at the very least, not rocking the boat, and, all-too-frequently, not only actively accommodating McCarthyism during the early Cold War (McCumber, 2001, 2016), but also, along with their colleagues and students, actively accommodating *the military-industrial complex* throughout the entire Cold War era (Reisch, 2005; Isaac, 2013) and (iii) the leading French existential phenomenologists Jean-Paul Sartre and Maurice Merleau-Ponty were both closely politically associated with the radical Left (Judt, 1992).

Second, there was the sharply divisive struggle for control of the major Anglo-American philosophy departments after World War II: given the aging and retirement of the leading historically-trained philosophers, neo-Kantians, neo-Hegelians, and pragmatists, it was going to be *either* the Analytic philosophers *or* the phenomenologists who took over, but not both—indeed, the Analytic philosophers won that battle, hands down, and controlled all the leading philosophy departments by the end of the 1950s (Wilshire, 2002: chs. 1-4; Katzav and Vaesen, 2017).

And **third**, there was the sharply divisive debate about the cultural-political significance and philosophical implications of *the formal and natural sciences* after World War II: (i) taking his cue from Heidegger's *Being and Time*, but also reflecting on the worsening cultural-political situation in Europe, Husserl had seriously criticized the epistemological and metaphysical foundations of the exact sciences in his *Crisis of European Sciences* (see section XVII.1 below) and then (ii) taking his cue directly from Husserl, Merleau-Ponty

---
4 Carnap refused to sign a McCarthyist oath of allegiance that was required of all faculty at UCLA; see also (Carnap, 1963: pp. 81-84).

further deepened and developed this critique in his brilliant 1945 book, *Phenomenology of Perception*.

At the same time, however, it's also quite true that a number of important intellectual, sociocultural, and political developments flowing from *World War I*—for example, significant anti-Kantian trends in Anglo-American philosophy, the demise of the classical neo-Kantian tradition, and of course the all-consuming rise of the Nazis and fascism in Germany—fused together during the 1920s and 30s to provide something like "the condition of the possibility" of The Divide after 1945. So although The Great Divide wasn't by any means *determined* philosophically—on the contrary, classical Analytic philosophy and phenomenology are essentially mutually coherent, although with some minor domestic disagreements—The Divide was nevertheless heavily mind-shaped by the sociocultural and political forces and consequences of the two World Wars, especially including the McCarthy era and the Cold War (Simons, 2010; Vrahimis, 2015; Hanna, 2020c; Hanna and Paans, 2020). In other words, I'm proposing that although The Great Divide between Analytic philosophy and phenomenology (especially existential phenomenology) *is* real enough, nevertheless it didn't happen until after 1945, and it was essentially the result of *sociocultural and political factors*, together with one serious and substantive philosophical disagreement, namely, *about the metaphysical foundations and epistemic status of the formal and natural sciences*. But by the 1930s, and leaving aside for the time being the natural sciences, what actually *was* the status of the formal sciences? Enter Gödel and Tarski.

X. Gödel-Incompleteness, Tarski, and Formal Piety: The Death of Classical Logicism in Thirty-One Steps

X.1 Two Foxes in The Vienna Circle's Henhouse: Gödel and Tarski

What follows in this chapter is an informal presentation, in 31 steps, of Kurt Gödel's brilliant, famous, and philosophically devastating argument for the incompleteness of mathematical logic (Göedel, 1931), where "mathematical logic" is understood as per Whitehead's and Russell's *Principia Mathematica*, and essentially similar systems, together with some concluding remarks on the larger philosophical significance of Gödel-incompleteness for classical Analytic philosophy in particular and the Analytic tradition more generally.

Moreover, Gödel's devastating impact on Analytic philosophy was super-charged by the logico-mathematical work of a close contemporary and, in effect, accomplice: Tarski. He and Tarski were both core members of The Vienna Circle (Edmonds, 2020), but they were also two very dangerous foxes indeed to let into The Circle's logico-linguistic henhouse.[1] For they discovered that the attempt to map the definition of truth directly into the language of any logical system, other formalized system, or formalized theory (or even any natural language) that's rich enough to contain either the Peano axioms for arithmetic (Gödel) or its own bivalent truth-predicate (Tarski), entails paradoxes, thereby killing classical logicism. To be sure, Tarski's irreflexivity result and his semantic conception of truth are brilliant generalizations of and responses to Gödel-incompleteness, and as it were the *coup de grâce* for classical logicism; but Gödel's two incompleteness theorems are the *Ur*-results that jointly brought about the original mortal wound.

X.2 Twenty-Five of the Thirty-One Steps

Step 1. As we've seen in earlier chapters, *logicism* is—or more precisely, was—the logical, mathematical, and philosophical project of explanatorily and ontologically reducing mathematics to logic. And as we've also seen in earlier chapters, logicism was closely, and indeed essentially, associated with the emergence, rise, and fall of classical Analytic philosophy from 1880 to 1950. More generally, it's a necessary condition of carrying out the logicist reduction of mathematics to logic in the classical Frege (for arithmetic only) and Whitehead-&-Russell (for all of mathematics) sense that every true mathematical sentence be provable within a *Principia*-style logical system.

Step 2. In the late 19th century, Frege had attempted this logicist reduction for arithmetic in *Basic Laws of Arithmetic*. And in Whitehead's and Russell's *Principia Math-*

---

[1] This was only obliquely recognized by other members of The Circle, and usually dismissively and tendentiously formulated by them as "Gödel's platonism" or "Tarski's metaphysics." Indeed, and relatedly, during the 1970s and 80s an entire cottage industry arose within post-classical Analytic philosophy whose primary aim was to boil the philosophical nutrients out of Tarski's semantic conception of truth for the purposes of post-Quinean scientific naturalist consumption. See, e.g., (Field, 1972; Davidson, 1984).

135

ematica, they present a system of mathematical logic that was supposed to be the logical vehicle for doing this for all of mathematics: it's a classical bivalent quantified (over individuals and functions) polyadic (many-place) predicate logic. But Gödel-incompleteness *killed* the logicist project in its classical Fregean and/or Whiteheadian-&-Russellian versions, alike, and thereby *put a serious kink* in the project of classical Analytic philosophy.

Step 3. Intriguingly, and significantly, Gödel's argument uses an extremely surprising mathematical discovery (or invention) made by Cantor: *the diagonalization argument* for the existence of *transfinite numbers*, i.e., *non-denumerable infinities*, i.e., infinite sets that *cannot* be put into a 1-1 correspondence with the infinite set of natural numbers (Cantor, 1891). How did Cantor do this? Let's assume that the set of natural numbers (i.e., 1, 2, 3...) is infinite: then a set of numbers is *denumerably infinite* if and only if it can be put into a 1-1 correspondence with the set of natural numbers. It turns out that the whole numbers (0, 1, 2, 3 ...) and *also* the integers (the whole numbers and their negative mirror) and also the rational numbers (integers plus all repeating and terminating decimals), and *also* all sets of numbers based on basic (primitive recursive) mathematical operations over the rationals, all have the same *cardinality* (counting-number-osity) as the natural numbers, because they can be paired 1-1 with the natural numbers. Basically, Cantor created a method for displaying a top-down vertical list of all the number sequences in the system of positive rational numbers (and since the negative numbers are just a mirror of the positive ones, they don't differ except in their being marked as negative). Then he constructed or "drew" a diagonal line across the list. Since, by hypothesis, a complete list contains *all* the rationals, and there are infinitely many rationals, then the infinite number picked out by the diagonal *isn't* on the list, hence its cardinality is *non*-denumerable but still infinite, aka transfinite. Moreover, because the list is a two-dimensional array, and since the constructed diagonal line that runs across it systematically picks out a number that is *not* displayed within the two-dimensional space of the array, then it in effect *represents a third and higher spatial dimension* over and above the two-dimensional array. So, in effect, transfinite numbers *are higher-dimensional numbers*.

Step 4. Now, the systemwide logical property of *consistency* says that a system contains no contradictions, where a contradiction is a sentence that's the conjunction of a sentence and its negation. Contradictions are logically necessarily false, i.e., false in every logically possible world. Classically, the appearance of a contradiction in any logical system is A Very Bad Thing,[2] because, starting with a contradiction as your sole premise, *you can prove any sentence whatsoever*, no matter how false (or silly for that matter). This systemwide logical property of contradictions is rightly called *explosion*.

Step 5. The systemwide logical property of *soundness* says that all the *theorems* (provable sentences) of a system are *true sentences* of that system.

---

[2] Actually, as we've already seen in passing in my discussion of Meinong, some post-classical Analytic philosophers think that contradictions aren't such a very bad thing after all, and are correspondingly prepared to admit contradictions, including paradoxes, into (non-classical, "deviant") systems. See, e.g., (Priest, 1987, 1998). It's worth noting again, however, that even those wild-&-crazy, contradiction-loving, deviant logicians (aka dialetheists) still want systematically to rule out *Explosion*, a systematic ruling-out that's called *paraconsistency*. Explosion is Hell.

Step 6. And the systemwide logical property of *completeness* says that all the true sentences of a system are theorems (provable sentences) of that system.

Step 7. Next, assume the normatively strict direct relevance of those three systemwide logical properties. Against that theoretical backdrop, how does one go about demonstrating Gödel-incompleteness?

Step 8. Starting with a *Principia*-style system of mathematical logic, add to it the basic axioms of (Peano) arithmetic, namely: (i) 0 is a number, (ii) the successor of any number is a number, (iii) no two numbers have the same successor, (iv) 0 is not the successor of any number, and (v) any property which belongs to 0, and also to the successor of every number which has the property, belongs to all the numbers, taken together with the primitive recursive functions over the natural numbers—the successor function, addition, multiplication, exponentiation, etc.

Step 9. Then, assume that the enriched system is consistent, sound, and complete.

Step 10. Because the enriched system represents arithmetic via the Peano axioms and the primitive recursive functions, there will be a denumerably infinite number of true sentences in the system.

Step 11. Gödel created a way to number each of the (true or false) sentences in such an enriched system, aka their *Gödel-numbers*, so because the enriched system is assumed to be sound, there will be a denumerably infinite number of provably true sentences, each of which has its own Gödel number. In effect, its Gödel-number says "I am provable, I am true." This might remind you of Descartes's "I am, I exist," which, necessarily, is true whenever you think it or say it (Descartes, 1984: p. 17), and the fact of necessarily self-guaranteeing self-reference is essentially the same. So in effect, then, Gödel *mapped the definition of truth into the system itself*.

Step 12. Then, using each provably true sentence's Gödel number, we create a top-down denumerably infinite vertical list of *all* the provably true sentences.

Step 13. Then, we use Cantor's diagonalization method to show that there is at least one provably true sentence that is *not* on that list.

Step 14. Since, by hypothesis, we've already created a denumerably infinite list of *all* the provably true sentences, such a sentence must be *unprovable*. Moreover, in effect, by virtue of its non-denumerable or transfinite Gödel number, that sentence *says* of itself that it's unprovable.

Step 15. But if it's unprovable, then, since we're assuming completeness, that sentence also has to be false, by *modus tollens* (every true sentence is provable, but if it's not provable, then it's not true, i.e., it's false).

Step 16. But if it's false that it's unprovable, then the sentence has to be provable.

Step 17. So the sentence is both provable and unprovable: *contradiction!* But even worse than that, necessarily, that sentence is provable if and only if it's not provable: *paradox!*

Step 18. Since we've shown that the system contains not only an unprovable sentence, but also a contradiction (indeed a paradox), therefore the system is inconsistent (indeed *hyper*-inconsistent), which, from the standpoint of classical logic, is a Very Bad Thing.

Step 19. Now we face a super-hard systemwide choice: consistency or completeness? In order to retain the consistency of the system, as per classical logic, we have to give up its completeness (i.e., we have to give up the property that all true sentences are provable).

Step 20. Thus, every *Principia*-style system enriched by the axioms of Peano arithmetic and the primitive recursive functions, insofar as it's consistent, contains true but unprovable sentences, and *therefore it's incomplete*. That's Gödel's *first* incompleteness theorem.

Step 21. And in this way, the project of classical logicism *also* fails, because in order to retain consistency in enriched *Principia*-style systems, we have to give up completeness, and therefore *not all true sentences of mathematics are provable*, hence mathematics is *not* explanatorily reducible to logic.

Step 22. Now, we've reached this conclusion by assuming that provability is sufficient for truth (soundness), and by showing that every provably true sentence in an enriched *Principia*-style system can be listed by using its Gödel number, which as we saw above, in effect *says* that it's true, hence in effect mapping the definition of truth *into* the system itself.

Step 23. But as we've also seen, mapping truth *into* the system in this way leads to *inconsistency*, on the assumption of its completeness.

Step 24. Hence, in order to show that any such enriched *Principia*-style system is *consistent*, on the assumption of its incompleteness, we have to define truth *outside* that system, i.e., *the consistency of the system cannot be demonstrated inside the system itself*. And that's Gödel's *second* incompleteness theorem.[3]

Step 25. Given all that, since it's a necessary condition of carrying out the logicist reduction of mathematics to logic in the classical Fregean and/or Whiteheadian-&-Russel-

---
3 Several of the ideas in this presentation of Gödel-incompleteness, especially including the crucial role played by Cantor's diagonalization method, were inspired by reading Saul Feferman's and Jörgen Veisdal's compact and informative presentations of the incompleteness theorems (Feferman, 2006; Veisdal, 2020).

lian sense that every true mathematical sentence be provable within a *Principia*-style logical system, then the project of classical logicism is *kaput*.

X.3 Tarski's Semantic Conception of Truth

Steps 13-17 in the unfolding of Gödel-incompleteness jointly present a version of the notorious *Liar Paradox*, i.e., the sentence that says of itself that it's false: so if it's true then it's false, and if it's false then it's true, hence necessarily, it's true if and only if it's false. Once upon a time, there was a Cretan who said that all Cretans are liars: was he telling the truth or not? If he was, then he wasn't, but if he wasn't, then he was. Interestingly, you can get out of *this* (apparent) paradox just *by denying that there ever was or will be such a silly Cretan*. But the Liar Paradox isn't contingently solvable in this way: it's about meaningful sentences that predicate falsity of themselves, not about *the users of those sentences*.

Tarski's semantic conception of truth in formalized languages (1949, 1956) flows naturally from these insights about the Liar. Any formal (or indeed any natural) language that's rich enough to contain various devices of self-reference and its own bivalent truth-predicate permits the construction of Liar-sentences of the form

This very sentence is false

or

The only indented and italicized sentence on page 139 in this book is false

and so-on. Every such sentence is, necessarily, true if and only if it's false. Or in other words, *mapping the definition of truth for a given language L, into L itself, entails instances of the Liar Paradox*. Therefore, the bivalent truth-predicate for any given language L, and correspondingly L's truth-definition, must occur in a "higher" and distinct language *that refers to L*, i.e., in a *meta-language* L^1 that defines truth-in-L.

Now according to Tarski, what is the definition of truth? In view of Gödel-incompleteness, the definition of truth cannot be *logical* or proof-theoretic, since mapping the definition of truth into any formal language rich enough to contain the Peano axioms for arithmetic, entails paradox. Tarski's idea is then that the definition of truth must instead be *semantic* or model-theoretic. In turn, he provides three versions of the semantic or model-theoretic definition of truth: (i) an informal explication of the nature of truth, (ii) a formal definition of truth for any language L whatsoever, and (iii) a material definition of truth in any given language L.

Here's Tarski's informal explication of the nature of truth:

a true sentence is one which says that the state of affairs is so and so, and the state-of-affairs indeed is so and so.

He then says, by way of qualification:

> From the point of view of formal correctness, clarity, and freedom from ambiguity of the expressions occurring in it, the above formulation leaves much to be desired. Nevertheless its intuitive meaning and general intention seem to be quite clear and intelligible.(Tarski, 1956: p. 155, italics in the original)

The formal definition of truth for any language L whatsoever then directly corresponds to this informal explication, by means of the device of *disquotation*, i.e., removing the flanking quotation-marks, which creates what is generally known as *the Tarski-schema*, aka the *T-Schema*, aka *Convention-T*:

"S" is true if and only if S

where "S" is any indicative or statement-making sentence, and S is the actual state of affairs picked out by "S." Any indicative or statement-making sentence "S" in L, or any translation of "S" into any other language L*, can be slotted into the Tarski-schema and disquoted.

Tarski then defines a relation of *satisfaction* between (i) ordered sequences of objects in the domain of discourse (i.e., the world W, i.e., the model M) and (ii) referring terms, n-place predicates, and complete indicative or statement-making sentences, such that the former saturate or validate the latter, i.e., such that S. Then he defines truth in terms of satisfaction. That is, "S" is true if and only if it's satisfied by any ordered sequence of objects in the domain (the world W or the model M) that corresponds to "S,"[4] i.e., if and only if S. The material definition of truth in any a given language L flows naturally from the informal explication of the nature of truth and the formal definition of truth, by systematically substituting every indicative or statement-making sentence in L into the Tarski-schema, and then collecting all the true ones, according to the criterion of truth-as-satisfaction, into a complete list of the true sentences of L.

X.4 Conclusion: The Last Six Steps

I'll conclude with six remarks on the larger philosophical significance of Gödel-incompleteness for the Analytic tradition.

Step 26. By *piety* in the specifically scientific and/or philosophical sense, I mean the rational acceptance of certain facts as basic or primitive, such that any further attempt to explain or justify those facts in terms of something else would invoke *those very facts*, and therefore lead to self-undermining circularity. For example, in order to explain or justify

---
[4] Actually, Tarski's explicit, formal definition of truth-as-satisfaction calls for the referring terms, predicates, and complete sentences to be satisfied by *all* ordered sequences of objects in the domain (the world W or the model M), but that's a technical refinement we can dispense with for the purposes of this compact presentation. In any case, it seems to me likely that by means of that refinement, Tarski was trying to capture Frege's idea of The True: see section II.8 above.

logic, logic must also be presupposed and used, hence any attempt to explain or justify logic in terms of something else already presupposes logic, and is self-undermining-ly (if that's a word) circular. More generally, then, logic cannot itself be explained or justified *except in terms of itself*, and therefore logic is both inexplicable and unjustifiable, i.e., rationally groundless. That predicament, as we've seen several times already, is what Sheffer called *The Logocentric Predicament*:

> The attempt to formulate the foundations of logic is rendered arduous by a … "logocentric" predicament. In order to give an account of logic, we must presuppose and employ logic. (Sheffer, 1926: p. 228)

Step 27. Now, one approach to The Logocentric Predicament is simply to *accept* that circularity; as the later Wittgenstein says of other similar predicaments in *Philosophical Investigations*:

> If I have exhausted the [explanations or] justifications I have reached bedrock, and my spade is turned. Then I am inclined to say: "This is simply what I do." (*PI*, §217)

In other words, Wittgenstein is saying, we've reached *a basic or primitive starting point of explanation or justification*, and we simply rationally accept that; moreover, to ask for *further* explanations and justifications would lead to self-undermining circularity. In turn, this acceptance can also be regarded, Kant-wise, as picking out a *transcendental* fact (Hanna, 2006c: ch. 3)

Step 28. By *formal* piety, then, I mean the rational acceptance of certain *formal-logical* facts as basic/primitive—and arguably transcendental—starting points for *formal-logical* explanations and/or justifications. Correspondingly, I think that Gödel's incompleteness theorems brilliantly manifest formal piety, in that (i) they rationally accept *incompleteness* as a basic/primitive fact about any enriched *Principia*-style system, *so that acceptance is built into our concepts of mathematics and logic themselves*, and (ii) they rationally accept *truth* as a basic/primitive fact about any enriched *Principia*-style system, a fact that is *never to be (completely) captured by provability*, and that *must be defined and known outside any such system*. More generally, Cantor's mathematics of transfinite or "transcendental" numbers, which *bears witness to higher-dimensional infinities*, Gödel's incompleteness theorems, which *bear witness to the inherently non-logical character of mathematical truth*, and Tarski's semantic conception of truth, which *bears witness to Gödel-incompleteness, the Liar Paradox, and the semantic irreflexivity of truth*—all brilliantly manifest formal piety.

Step 29. In view of the incompleteness theorems, Gödel held that logically undecidable and unprovable truths of mathematics would have to be known directly *by mathematical intuition* (Tait, 2010). In turn, I think that one of those logically undecidable and unprovable truths of mathematics must be Cantor's thesis that there exist non-denumerably infinite, aka transfinite, aka transcendental, numbers, since diagonalization requires what

Kant calls *spatial intuition (Anschauung)* (CPR A19-49/B33-73) and *therefore diagonalization isn't strictly logical.*

Step 30. If so, then Gödel-incompleteness, *since it presupposes Cantorian diagonalization*, would require spatial intuition in the Kantian sense; therefore, against the backdrop of Kant's or Kantian philosophy, this would also entail *that mathematics is synthetic a priori, not analytic* (Hanna, 2001: ch. 5, 2006a: ch. 6).

Step 31. And one last remark, by way of a coda: I also think that *contemporary physics* manifests a precise natural-scientific analogue of Gödel-incompleteness, that the right scientific and philosophical attitude to take towards this fact is a precise natural-scientific analogue of Gödelian formal piety, namely *natural piety*, and also that *fixing* this incompletness, via a moderate version of The Anthropic Principle, entails a suitably weak version of Kantian transcendental idealism. But that's another philosophical story for another day, and perhaps also another book (Hanna, 2021a; 2021c; 2021d; 2021e). For my purposes here, the deeply important take-away point is that *if* formal piety is required for logic and mathematics, and *if* natural piety is also required for physics, *then* the doctrine of *scientific naturalism* to which the post-classical Analytic tradition is fully committed, is *false*. I'll have more to say about that in chapters XVII and XVIII below.

XI. Wittgenstein and the *Investigations* 1: Preface, and §§1-27

XI.1 From the *Tractatus* to the *Investigations*

Russell's "Philosophy of Logical Atomism" was published in 1918; but the *Tractatus* brought a definitive closure to the project of logical atomism only three years later, in 1921, by pushing the Frege-Russell philosophical project of decompositional and transformative logical analysis to its limits and beyond. Or at least, this is how Wittgstenstein himself came to regard the *Tractatus* by the time of his 1953 *Philosophical Investigations*. Indeed, in the Preface of the *Investigations* the later Wittgenstein explicitly rejects and radically re-thinks his own Tractarian conception of logical analysis:

> Four years ago [i..e, in 1941—the Preface was written in 1945] I had occasion to re-read my first book (the *Tractatus Logico-Philosophicus*) and to explain its ideas to someone. It suddenly seemed to me that I should publish these old thoughts and the new ones together: that the latter could be seen in the right light only by contrast with and against the background of my old way of thinking. For since beginning to occupy myself with philosophy again, sixteen years ago [i.e., in 1929], I have been forced to recognize grave mistakes in what I wrote in that first book. (*PI x^e*)[1]

It would be quite false and misleading, however, to say that there are no continuities between the *Tractatus* and the *Investigations*. On the contrary, not only is almost every doctrine of the latter is anticipated somewhere in the former, but also the basic topics of both books are the same: logic, meaning, and mind. Furthermore, both books take philosophy to be nothing more and nothing less than "critique of language," and this ultimately determines a single Kantian/neo-Kantian line of argument running right through them both. Indeed, just as the *Tractatus* is arguably a brilliantly original variation on Marburg-style logicistic neo-Kantianism, so too the *Investigations* is arguably a brilliantly original variation on *Baden/Southwest-style human-science-oriented and value-theory-oriented* neo-Kantianism (Willey, 1978; Köhnke, 1991; Luft and Capeillères, 2010; Beiser, 2014; Crowell, 2017; Heis, 2019; Clarke, 2019). So the fundamental link between the two works is a pair of brilliantly original variations on neo-Kantianism.

Nevertheless, as we've just seen, there is also a very definite sense in which the *Investigations* is intended by Wittgenstein to be the antithesis of the *Tractatus*. Whereas the *Tractatus* had proposed an essentialist a priori reduction of logic, meaning, and even the world itself to solipsistic transcendental mind, the *Investigations* fully sinks logic, meaning, and mind into the everyday actions and practices of natural-language-using human animals in their commonsense or ordinary world. The basic results of this radical move are (i) that under the slogan that *logic is grammar*, the pure classical logic of propositions is replaced by a strongly non-classical logic of natural language, that's at once (ia) intuitionistic (i.e., it entails the rejection of the universal law of excluded middle), (ib) non-bivalent (i.e.,

---
[1] See also, e.g., (Hacker, 1996: ch. 5).

it permits vagueness in its predicates), and (ic) non-monotonic (i.e., it permits multiple logically distinct conclusions), and dialetheic (i.e., it permits "truth-value gluts," namely, some sentences that are both true and false, and thereby entails a rejection of the universal law of non-contradiction), (ii) that under the slogan *meaning is use* the nature of linguistic meaning becomes fully embedded in human action and human life, (iv) that under the rubric of *language games*, the scope of meaning is radically widened to include direct and indirect speech-acts (implicature), indexicality or context-dependency, emotive expression, metaphor, and more generally linguistic actions of all sorts, (v) that under the slogan I'll frame as *human behavior is human mindedness*, the Cartesian and Schopenhauerian solipsistic mind of the Tractatus becomes the living form of essentially embodied human comportment, and (vi) that under the slogan "what has to be accepted, the given, is—so one could say, forms of life" (*PI* §226ᵉ), Tractarian essentialism and Tractarian solipsistic idealism are sharply criticized and replaced by an anthropocentric metaphysics of the commonsensical or the ordinary, according to which essences and structures are all manifestly real ("nothing is hidden"), although normally unrecognized by us because of conceptual confusions unselfconsciously transmitted by our natural or ordinary language.

Correspondingly, in the *Investigations* there's also a radical turn in Wittgenstein's conception of philosophy, from *logical analysis* or the "logical clarification of thoughts" (*TLP* 4.112) to *logical psychoanalysis* or "a battle against the bewitchment of our intelligence by means of language" (*PI* §109). The most obvious historical parallels here are with Freudian psychoanalysis, and more remotely, Kant's Transcendental Dialectic in the second half of the first *Critique*. One crucial quasi-technical notion in this connection is that of a philosophical "picture," that is, a simple philosophical analogy, diagram, image, metaphor, model, stereotype, template, etc., that's unselfconsciously transmitted by our language and therefore presupposed by us without argument, which narrowly constrains and limits our thinking:

> One thinks that one is tracing the outline of the thing's nature over and over again, and one is merely tracing around the frame through which we look at it.... A *picture* held us captive. And we could not get outside it, for it lay in our language and language seemed to repeat it to us inexorably. (*PI* §§114-115)

Such pictures typically lead to antinomies or paradoxes, and, more generally, to insoluble "problems of philosophy,": "the mind-body problem," the "free will problem," the problem of universals," "the problem of skepticism," and so-on.

These radical methodological features of the *Investigations* are perfectly reflected in its title (specifically *not* a treatise or systematic work), its organization (a series of numbered remarks without any attempt at dividing them into topics or sections, without headings, etc.), its argument-style (entirely non-linear and dialectical, with thought-experiments, epigrammatic pronouncements, constant use of metaphors, jokes, etc.), and its prose style (highly conversational and elliptical—notice, for example, the constant use of dashes, also of quotation-marks to indicate different voices and interlocutors, etc). This, in turn, raises a more fundamental point about philosophical explanations in the *Investigations*. In the *Tractatus*, the explanation of some fact or phenomenon typically took the form of a systematic decomposition to simple entities plus classical logic. The crucial features there are the idea of deeper and more basic levels of reality, and classical logic as a priori, universal, and essential for thought, linguistic meaning, and the world. In the *Investigations*, by sharp contrast, explanations always appeal to factors at the same level as what's being explained, and logic is neither classical nor essentially separate from the original phenomenon of meaningful natural or ordinary language itself: that is, this logic is *essentially embedded in meaningful natural or ordinary language*, which is why Wittgenstein calls it "grammar." Against that backdrop then, the philosophical explanation for the fact that meaning is use is twofold: **first**, that language is essentially embedded in basic human linguistic practices called *language-games*, and **second**, that language-games in turn are essentially embedded in actual historical networks of human activity and human culture called *forms of life*. And that's where philosophical explanation *stops*.

One crucial consequence of this is that for Wittgenstein in the *Investigations*, meaningful natural or ordinary language is ultimately a kind of *human action*, indeed the characteristic kind of human action. Adapting Goethe's line from *Faust* 1 ("In the beginning was the Deed"), which itself adapts the line from the Bible's Book of John 1 ("In the beginning was the Word"), we can then say that for the later Wittgenstein, *meaningful words are human deeds*:

> Words are deeds [*Taten*]. (Wittgenstein, 1980: p. 46^e)

> In this way, I should like to say the words "Oh, *let* him come!" are charged with my desire. And words can be wrung from us, —like a cry. Words can be *hard* to say: such, for example, as are used to effect a renunciation, or to confess a weakness. (Words are also deeds [*Taten*].) (*PI* §546)

Human animals essentially are linguistic agents, and the use of language is essentially the mastery of a skill (*PI* §20). In turn, this opens up the very idea of meaning to every conceivable role that language can play in human activity (see *PI* §23). It also opens up the possibility that some actions are essentially linguistic, for example, giving commands, promising, or legal actions. In the two decades immediately following the publication of the *Investigations*, J.L. Austin, John Searle, and others then developed this idea into the scientific-seeming theory of *speech acts*, according to which there's a finite, generative set of universal a priori rules that strictly govern our ability to use words, especially including our ability *to utter* φ (for example, "I do") *and thereby* ψ (for example, thereby marry someone), that is, our ability to make *performative utterances* (Austin, 1962; Searle, 1969). But Wittgenstein never intended the thesis that meaningful words are human deeds to become the foundation of a science, whether in philosophy or theoretical linguistics.

Correspondingly, unlike the *Tractatus*, the *Investigations* is emphatically not a *treatise*, that is, it's *not* a systematic scientific work written down as a linear philosophical text governed by the deductive canons of classical logic. Still, even in non-classical logic there are *arguments*. So I do think that we can reconstruct Wittgenstein's argument for the meaning-is-use thesis as a two-step line of non-classical reasoning: **first**, one displays the inadequacies of the classical theories of meaning (dialectical criticism), and then **second**, one asserts the thesis that meaning is use as the best overall explanation of the phenomenon of meaning (inference to the best explanation). He carries this out by considering simpler languages and simpler language practices than our own, which in his terminology is to say that he carries it out by considering "language games" in a second sense of that term, and in particular by considering the "Augustinian" language games in *PI* §§1-21.

XI.2 The Thesis That Meaning Is Use

In the *Tractatus*, the only admissible sort of linguistic meaning (aka "saying") is the *sense* of propositions, and there are four different sorts of meaning belonging to the sense of propositions: (i) the meaning of a name (whether a singular term or a general term) is nothing but the referent or bearer of the name, i.e., an object (*Referentialism*), (ii) the meaning of a sentence is nothing but either (iia) an isomorphic picture of an atomic fact, or else (iib) a truth-functional compounding of such sentences (aka, the Picture Theory—see also section VI.8 above), (ii) the meaning of any linguistic sign is nothing but a rule for manipulating or operating with that sign in a logical or mathematical calculus, or other non-formalized language- system (*Rule-Based Semantics*), and (iii) the meaning of a name, sentence, or other linguistic sign is nothing but a conscious mental representation (or "idea") in the mind of an individual speaker of a language (*Semantic Solipsism*). By sharp contrast to all of these, in the *Investigations*, Wittgenstein wants to defend the thesis that the meaning of any part of language is its *use*.

Here the concept of use covers two slightly distinct but intimately related sub-notions: (i) *semantic function*, according to which the meaning of a word is its specific role (i.e., a specific rule-governed normative pattern of operations) in a living human language, and (ii) *semantic application*, according to which the meaning of a word is determined by how it is applied by individual human speakers, in communities of speakers, in actual speech contexts. With respect to the semantic function of words, Wittgenstein is saying that any meaningful part of a language is essentially a "tool" that can be used correctly or incorrectly in the context of a larger totality of linguistic equipment or technology (see *PI* §11). In this connection, then, and more generally, it's crucial to note Wittgenstein's appeal to rules (functions, ways of organizing information contents or actions), norms (ideals or standards), and totalities of signs (holism). Correspondingly, with respect to the semantic application of words, Wittgenstein is saying that any meaningful part of language requires both context-dependency (indexicality) and communities of human speakers (anthropocentric communitarianism). So, combining these two ideas, Wittgstenstein's overarching thesis in the *Investigations,* to the effect that linguistic meaning is use, is the thesis that the meaning of a word is its specific role in a living human language *together with* how it is applied by individual human speakers in communities of human speakers in actual contexts. Or, to sloganize: *meaning is the career of words in human action*. It's very important to emphasize *both* of these factors and not merely the application factor, because the latter alone gives the false impression of an extreme empiricism and relativism about meaning. But meaning for Wittgenstein in the *Investigations*, although it certainly has strong empiricist and relativist components, isn't reducible to either of these.

What resists such reduction are the *rule-governedness, normativity, holism, indexicality*, and *anthropocentric communitarianism* of meaning. Of course, what's then very tricky is how to *explain* these irreducible factors. Here's a proposal: I think we can reconstruct Wittgenstein's non-classical arguments in the *Investigations* for the thesis that meaning is use just by asking ourselves: what are the implications and critical limitations of the four classical theories of meaning (i.e., Referentialism, the Picture Theory, the Rule-Based Semantics, and Semantic Solipsism)? The thesis that meaning is use will then be established in and through dialectical criticism (involving both deconstruction and also destruction) of the classical theories. The primitive language games are supposed to make this directly evident to us—in, as it were, philosophical "living pictures," or *dioramas*— at least as far as Referentialism and the Picture Theory are concerned. Later in the *Investigations*, Wittgenstein offers separate arguments against Rule-Based Semantics (i.e., *The Rule Following Paradox*) and Semantic Solipsism (i.e., *The Private Language Argument*). At the same time, the failures of the classical theories indirectly and cumulatively point up the several basic elements of the thesis that meaning is use. Then, on Wittgenstein's behalf, we can conclude that the thesis that meaning is use is the best overall explanation of all the meaning-phenomena.

XI.3 A Map of the *Investigations*

In the Preface to the *Investigations*, Wittgenstein beautifully describes the non-linear, non-Tractarian, non-classical logical structure of his book:

> The thoughts that I publish in what follows are the precipitate of philosophical investigations which have occupied me for the last sixteen years. They concern many subjects: the concepts of meaning, of understanding, of a proposition, of logic, the foundations of mathematics, states of consciousness, and other things.… It was my intention at first to bring all this together in a book whose structure I pictured differently at different times. But the essential thing was that the thoughts should proceed from one subject to another in a natural order and without breaks. After several unsuccessful attempts to weld my results together into such a whole, I realized that I should never succeed. The best that I could write would never be more than philosophical remarks; my thoughts were soon crippled if I tried to force them on in any single direction against their natural inclination.—And this was, of course, connected with the very nature of the investigation. For this compels us to travel over a wide field of thought criss-cross in every direction.— The philosophical remarks in this book are, as it were, a number of sketches of landscapes which were made in the course of these long and involved journeyings. The same or almost the same points were always being

approached afresh from different directions, and new sketches made. Very many of these were badly drawn or uncharacteristic, marked by all the defects of a weak draughtsman. And when they were rejected a number of tolerable ones were left, which now had to be arranged and sometimes cut down, so that if you looked at them you could get a picture of the landscape. Thus this book is really only an album. (*PI*, ix^e)

Thus, the logical structure of the *Investigations* is analagous to the topological and dynamic structure of a real-world landscape filled with living organisms: it cannot be digitally computed and recursively generated, like a decidable theorem in classical truth-functional logic or the monadic fragment of first-order classical predicate logic. But at the same time, it's not in any way *amorphous*. On the contrary, it's replete with rich logical structure of a non-computable, unprovable, and non-classical kind. Moreover, its non-classical logical structure can still be *mapped*.

In light of that fact, and more explicitly now, I want to say that the basic argument-structure of the *Investigations* has seven distinct non-classical logical parts or "regions," as follows.

First (region 1), the main thesis of the book is that *linguistic meaning is use*, where the concept of *use* is the conjunction of the sub-concepts of (i) *word-function*, or the normatively rule-governed role of words in the whole language, and (ii) *word-application*, or the actual deployment of words by the linguistic acts of individual users, in communities, in context.

Second (region 2), the fact of linguistic use is then held to be explained by two more primitive facts: (i) language-games, or basic human linguistic practices, and (ii) forms of life, or actual living human beings in their actual human communities and their historically-embedded social practices, considered as unified normatively rule- governed bearers of meaning and purpose.

Third (region 3), the use theory is then indirectly demonstrated by rejecting four inadequate semantic theories: (i) Referentialism or "Fido"-Fido Semantics, (ii) The Picture Theory, (iii) Rule-Based Semantics, and (iv) Solipsistic Semantics. Referentialism says that the meaning of a word is nothing but its reference. *Pure* Referentialism says that all names are proper names, and that the meaning of every basic proper name in a basic proposition (whether a basic singular term or a basic general term—aka a "concept-word") is nothing but the referent or bearer of the name, i.e., an absolutely simple individual concrete object or a definite abstract concept or universal. Correspondingly, Wittgenstein's rejection of Pure Referentialism primarily appeals to critical arguments based on negative existential propositions and family resemblance concepts. The Picture Theory says that the meaning of a sentence is nothing but how it isomorphically models an atomic fact or else truth-functional compoundings of such sentences. Correspondingly, Wittgenstein's rejection of the Picture Theory primarily appeals to an argument against absolute simples from the impossibility of unique decompositions of macrophysical objects. And Rule-Based Semantics says that the meaning of any linguistic sign is nothing but a rule for manipulating or operating with that sign in a logical or mathematical calculus, or other non-formalized language-system. Correspondingly, Wittgenstein's rejection of Rule-Based Semantics primarily appeals to the Rule Following Paradox. Finally, Solipsistic Semantics says that the meaning of a name, sentence, or other linguistic sign is nothing but a conscious mental representation or "idea" in the mind of an individual speaker of a language. And correspondingly, Wittgenstein's rejection of Solipsistic Semantics primarily appeals to The Private Language Argument.

Fourth (region 4), the rejections of the four inadequate semantic theories then lead correspondingly to five positive Wittgensteinian theses about meaning: (i) The meaning of a singular term is a partial function—or a specific contingently-determined set of mappings or "routes"—from language-games employing singular terms and forms of life onto individual objects, and each of these "routes" is literally part of the meaning itself, (ii) concepts, the meanings of predicate expressions, are family-resemblance networks, (iii) propositions are pictures of facts *only* internally to propositional language games and under a relativized ontology of object-samples, (iv) rule-following is externally normatively justified by communal rule-following practices to which the rule-follower belongs non-cognitively by an "agreement" or *Übereinstimmung* with other participants in that language-game, which in turn supervenes on the deeper fact that human speakers are necessarily practically and vitally embedded in some or another form of life, and (v) semantic anti-individualism and semantic externalism both hold for sensation-language.

Fifth (region 5), the two positive sub-theses under thesis (v) then conjointly lead to a further four positive theses about the mind: (v.1) the token privacy of sensations, (v.2) essential embodiment, (v.3) sensation personalism, and (v.4) an activist phenomenology of mental states and processes.

Sixth (region 6), these four theses, in turn, conjointly lead to the linguistic phenomenology of *seeing* (or visual experience), which also has four theses: (i) there is a basic distinction between *direct seeing* (seeing-this) and *interpretive seeing* (seeing-as), (ii) interpretive seeing requires direct seeing, (iii) interpretive seeing requires conceptual abilities, and (iv) the phenomenon of aspect-blindness entails that direct seeing can occur without any sort of interpretive seeing, hence direct seeing is *essentially non-conceptual*.

Seventh (region 7), and finally, these four theses are then extended to the linguistic phenomenology of *experiencing the meaning of a word*, which completes the whole account by returning full-circle to the meaning-is-use thesis and demonstrating some further positive theses about the concept of use.

XI.4 The Critique of Pure Reference: What the Builders Did

Let's now visit regions 1 and 2, and a part of region 3. As I mentioned above, Referentialism holds that all words are names, and that the meaning of a name is nothing but the referent or bearer of that name. Referentialism, as its name obviously implies, identifies linguistic meaning with reference. Thus according to Referentialism, and its "Fido"-Fido semantics, the word "Fido" means Fido and the word "dog" means the concept DOG. Furthermore, as I also mentioned above, according to Pure Referentialism, all names are proper names, and the meaning of every basic proper name in a basic proposition—whether a basic singular term or a basic general term, i.e., a concept-word—is nothing but the referent or bearer of the name: an absolutely simple individual concrete object or a definite abstract concept or universal.

In turn, according to Wittgenstein, there are two main problems with Pure Referentialism. **First**, identifying meaning with reference to individual objects in the case of singular terms doesn't account for systematic variations in the use-based meanings of ostensive terms having the same referent (*PI* §§28-38). And **second**, identifying meaning with reference in the case of general terms fails because there are no uniquely identifiable concepts or universals (*PI* §§66-71, and 75-78). What follows now is a three-step, 1-2-3, style rational reconstruction of Wittgenstein's opening argument against Pure Referentialism in the first twenty or so sections of the *Investigations*, as a paradigmatic case study in how he argues for the thesis that meaning- is-use. In turn, the meaning-is-use thesis is to be understood, as I've said, as the thesis that meaning is the career of words in human action, with its two distinct sub-notions of semantic function and semantic application, taken together with the five non-empiricistic and non-relativistic facts about meaning. For each of the three steps in the reconstruction I'll provide a detailed critical commentary on that step's rationale and implications.

Step 1. Referentialism holds that all words are names, and that the meaning of any word is nothing but the object it names. And according to Pure Referentialism, all names are proper names, and every basic proper name in a basic proposition (whether a basic singular term or a basic general term) is nothing but the referent or bearer of the name, an absolutely simple individual concrete object or a definite abstract concept or universal.

Commentary on **Step 1**. Referentialism as a philosophical thesis goes at least as far back as Plato's *Theaetetus*. Indeed, Wittgenstein explicitly quotes the *Theaetetus* in §46, in support of the particular version of Referentialism he's focusing on:

> What lies behind the idea that names really signify simples? Socrates says in the *Theatetus*: "If I make no mistake, I have heard some people say this: there is no definition of the primary elements—so to speak—out of which we we and everything else are composed; for everything that exists in its own right can only be *named*, no other determination is possible, neither that it *is* nor that it *is not*.... But what exists in its own right has to be ... named without any other determination. In consequence it is impossible to give an account of any primary element; for it, nothing is possible but the bare name; its name is all it has. But just as what consists of these primary elements is itself complex, so the names of the elements become descriptive language by being compounded together. For

the essence of speech is the composition of names." Both Russell's "individuals" and my "objects" (*Tractatus Logico-Philosophicus*) were such primary elements. (*PI* §46, 21ᶜ)

This particular version of Referentialism thus includes two sub-theses to the effect that (i) the basic referring terms in basic propositions are all proper names (as opposed to, say, definite descriptions), including both basic singular terms in grammatical or logical subject position and also basic general terms or concept-words in grammatical or logical predicate position, and (ii) the objects for which these basic singular terms and basic general terms stand are absolutely simple concrete individuals and definite abstract concepts or universals. But not all Referentialists are as semantically puristic as Plato's Socrates was in the *Theaetetus*. So this raises the critical question of whether *every* possible version of Referentialism need be committed to the thesis that the basic referring terms in basic proposition are all *proper* names. Indeed, it seems clear that a less puristic Referentialist might instead take the basic referring terms in basic propositions to be *demonstratives* or some other kind of essential indexical (Perry, 1979; Evans, 1982; Kaplan, 1989; Hanna, 1993a; Hanna, 1997). It also raises the critical question of whether every possible version of Referentialism need be committed to the puristic thesis that the objects for the basic singular terms stand are absolutely simple concrete individuals and that the objects for which the basic general terms stand are definite abstract universals. Indeed, it seems that a Referentialist might instead hold that the objects picked out by basic singular terms are only *relatively* simple concrete individuals, that is, simple relative to some particular way of humanly conceptualizing a decomposition of a complex perceivable object, and that the objects for which basic general terms stand are just *human concepts* in all their varying degrees of vagueness and variety.

I've been calling the special version of Referentialism that's committed to the puristic thesis that the basic referring terms are *proper* names (including both basic singular terms and basic general terms, concept-words), and also to the further two-part purist thesis that the simple concrete individual objects for which basic singular terms stand are *absolute* simples and that the objects for which basic general terms stand are *definite abstract* concepts or universals, "Pure Referentialism." This is a crucial interpretive move. For it's Pure Referentialism, and not Referentialism *as such*, that's the philosophical target of Wittgenstein's deconstructive critique of Referentialism in the *Investigations*. Moreover, the bull's-eye of the philosophical target of Pure Referentialism is not in fact the semantics of names proposed by Plato's Socrates in the *Theaetetus*, but instead a double bull's-eye consisting of *Russell's* semantics of names circa 1912 and *early Wittgenstein's* semantics of names in the *Tractatus*.

Russell's semantics of names circa 1912, in turn, depends heavily on two doctrines that we've looked at already: (i) the *multiple relation* theory of judgment, which says that a proposition is nothing but an ordered set of absolute simples, definite abstract concepts or universals, and abstract logical constants organized by the mind of a subject who stands in multiple acquaintance relations to these objects in the act of judging, and (ii) the cognitive distinction between *knowledge by acquaintance* and *knowledge by description*. Here's the core of what Russell says about these doctrines.

> When we judge that Charles I died on the scaffold, we have before us not one object but several objects, namely, Charles I, dying, and the scaffold. Similarly, when we judge that Charles I died in his bed, we have before us the the objects Charles I, dying, and his bed. These objects are not fictions: they are just as good as the objects of the true judgment. We therefore escape the necessity of admitting objective falsehoods, or of admitting that in judging falsely we have nothing before the mind. Thus in this view judgment is a relation of the mind to several other terms: when these other terms have *inter se* a "corresponding" relation, the judgment is true; when not, it is false. (Russell, 1973c: p. 153)

> Knowledge of things, when it is of the kind we call knowledge by *acquaintance*, is essentially simpler than knowledge of truths, and logically independent of knowledge of truths, though it would be rash to assume that human beings ever, in fact, have acquaintance with things without knowing some truth about them.

> Knowledge of things by *description*, on the contrary, always involves ... some knowledge of truths as its source or ground.... We shall say that we have acquaintance with anything of which we are directly aware, without the intermediary of any process of inference or any knowledge of truths. (Russell, 1995: p. 46)

> All our knowledge, both knowledge of things and knowledge of truths, rests upon acquaintance as its foundation. It is therefore important to consider what kinds of things there are with which we have acquaintance.... We have acquaintance in sensation with the data of the outer senses, and in introspection with the data of what may be called the inner sense—thoughts, feelings, desires, etc.; we have acquaintance in memory with things what have been data either of the outer senses or inner sense... In addition to our acquaintance with particular existing things, we also have acquaintance with what we shall call *universals*, that is to say, general ideas, such as *whiteness, diversity, brotherhood*, and so on. Every complete sentence must contain at least one word which stands for a universal, since all verbs have a meaning which is universal... [We must] guard against the supposition that whatever we can be acquainted with must be something particular and existent. Awareness of universals is called *conceiving*, and a universal of which we are aware is called a *concept*. (Russell, 1995: pp. 48-52)

In the *Tractatus* Wittgenstein explicitly rejects Russell's multiple relation theory of judgment because it's psychologistic (*TLP* 4.1121), and also because he (Wittgenstein, that is) denies that logical constants stand for *any sort of object*—"my fundamental thought is that the 'logical constants' do not stand for something (*nicht vertreten*)" (*TLP* 4.0312). But in the *Tractatus* he also explicitly *accepts* Russell's distinction between knowledge by acquaintance and knowledge by description (in German, the distinction between *Kennen* and *Beschreibung*). As a consequence of explicitly accepting Russell's acquaintance-description distinction, in the *Tractatus* Wittgenstein also explicitly accepts Pure Referentialism. Here are the relevant texts:

> If I know (*kenne*) an object, then I also know (*kennen*) all the possibilities of its occurrence in atomic facts. (*TLP* 2.0123)

> In order to know (*kennen*) an object, I must know (*kennen*) not its external but all its internal qualities. (*TLP* 2.01231)

> States of affairs can be described (*beschreiben*), but not *named*. (Names resemble points; propositions resemble arrows, they have sense.) (*TLP* 3.144)

> The simple signs employed in propositions are called names. (*TLP* 3.202)

> The name means (*bedeutet*) the object, The object is its meaning (*Bedeutung*). (*TLP* 3.203)

> In the proposition the name stands for (*vertritt*) the object. (*TLP* 3.22)

> Objects I can only *name*. Signs stand for (*vertreten*) them. I can only speak *of* them. I cannot *assert them*. A proposition can only say *how* a thing is, not *what* it is. (*TLP* 3.2221)

> Reality must be completely described (*beschreiben*) by the proposition.

> A proposition is a description (*Beschreibung*) of a fact. (*TLP* 4.023)

Now, in the *Investigations* Wittgenstein wants to establish the meaning-is-use thesis. He therefore rejects the distinction that "the author of the *Tractatus Logico-Philosophicus*" had accepted between acquaintance and description. Nevertheless the human *act* of acquaintance, in the form of a demonstration-act of ostensive pointing, plays an important yet subsidiary role in the concept of meaning-as-use. For as we have seen, Wittgenstein argues that although *generally* the meaning of a word is its use, *sometimes* the meaning of a name is explained by pointing to its bearer. This two-part claim is what he wants to prove in two steps, **first** by means of his deconstructive critique of the philosophical living picture of Pure Referentialism that is etched into the Augustinian theory of language, and then **second** by appealing to the meaning-is-use thesis as the best overall explanation of all the relevant linguistic facts.

Step 2. The Augustinian language game of the Builders in *PI* §§2, 6, and 8, is a living picture or diorama of a Pure Referentialist language.

The Fate of Analysis

Commentary on **Step 2**. The *Investigations* begins with a text from Augustine's *Confessions*, I, 8:

> When they (my elders) named some object , and some accordingly moved towards something, I saw this and I grasped that the thing was called by the sound they uttered when they meant to point it out. Their intention was shewn by their bodily movements, as it were the natural language of all peoples: the expression of the face, the play of the eyes, the movement of other parts of the body, and the tone of voice which expresses our state of mind in seeking, having, rejecting, or avoiding something. Thus, as I heard words repeatedly used in their proper places in various sentences, I gradually learnt to understand what objects they signified; and after I had trained my mouth to form these signs, I used them to express my own desires. (*PI* n.1)

In order to understand Wittgenstein's use of this text from the *Confessions*, we must recall that the notion of a "language game" in this particular context means "the idea of a language more primitive than ours" (*PI* §2). As the self-appointed Grand Inquisitor of his own earlier Pure Referentialist conception of meaning in the *Tractatus*, Wittgenstein is deeply interested in *the Augustinian language game* in particular, precisely because "that [Pure Referentialist] philosophical concept of meaning has its place in a primitive idea of the way language functions" (*PI* §2). Here's what Wittgenstein says about the Augustinian language game:

> Let us imagine a language for which the description given by Augustine is right. The language is meant to serve for communication between a builder A and an assistant B. A is building with building stones : there are blocks, pillars, slabs, and beams. B has to pass the stones, and that in the order in which A needs them. For this purpose they use a language consisting of the words "block," "pillar," "slab," and "beam." A calls them out; —B brings the stone which he has learnt to bring at such-and-such a call. —Conceive this as a complete language game. (*PI* §2)

> We could even imagine that the language of §2 was the *whole* language of A and B; even the whole language of a tribe. The children are brought up to perform *these* actions, to use *these* words as they do, and to react in *this* way to the words of others. (*PI* §6)

> We can also think of the whole process of using words in [§2] as one of those games by means of which children learn their native language. I will call these games "language-games" and will sometimes speak of a primitive language as a language-game. And the processes of naming the stones and of repeating words after someone might also be called language-games. Think of much of the use of words in games like ring-a-ring-a-roses. I shall also call the whole, consisting of language and the actions (*Tätigkeiten*) into which it is woven, the "language-game." (*PI* §7)

> Let us now look at an expansion of language [§2]. Besides the four words "block," "pillar," etc., let it contain a series of words used as the shopkeeper in [§1] used the numerals [to stand for finite cardinal numbers and counting out groups of objects] (it can be the series of letters of the alphabet); further, let there be two words, which may as well as be "there" and "this" (because this roughly indicates their purpose), that are used in connexion with a pointing gesture; and finally a number of colour samples. A gives an order like: "d—slab—there." At the same time he shews the assistant a colour sample, and when he says "there" he points to a place on the building site. From the stock of slabs B takes one for each letter of the alphabet up to "d," of the same colour as the sample, and brings them to to the place indicated by A. —On other occasions A gives the order "this—there." At 'this' he points to a building stone. And so on. (*PI* §8)

Wittgenstein never does tell us what the Builders are building. But it's not too fanciful, and indeed it even makes very good instructive philosophical sense, to imagine that the Builders described in §§2, 6, and 8 are trying to build either the Tower of Babel, as described in Genesis 11: 1-9—

> And the LORD came down to see the city and the tower, which the children of men builded. And the LORD said, Behold, the people is one, and they have all one language; and this they begin to do: and now nothing will be restrained from them, which they have imagined to do. Go to, let us go down, and there confound their language, that they may not understand one another's speech. So the LORD scattered them abroad from thence upon the face of all the earth: and they left off to build the city. Therefore is the name of it called Babel; because the LORD did there confound the language of all the earth: and from thence did the LORD scatter them abroad upon the face of all the earth.

—or perhaps the wall upon which Humpty Dumpty sat in *Through the Looking Glass*:

> "Don't stand chattering to yourself like that," Humpty Dumpty said, looking at her for the first time, "but tell me your name and your business."
>
> "My name is Alice, but—"
>
> "It's a stupid name enough!" Humpty Dumpty interrupted impatiently. "What does it mean?"
>
> "*Must* a name mean something?" Alice asked doubtfully.
>
> "Of course it must," Humpty Dumpty said with a short laugh: "my name means the shape I am—and a good handsome shape it is, too. With a name like yours, you might be any shape, almost." (Carroll, 1988: pp. 105-106)

It makes sense that the Builders are trying to build the Tower of Babel. This is because we can think of the logical atomists, including both the author of the *Tractatus* and Russell circa 1912, as attempting to build a logico-semantic tower, called *the Ideal Language*, all the way up to Platonic heaven. But this project led inevitably to a logico-semantic Great Fall into the irreducible and sometimes almost incommensurable plurality of different natural languages and language games scattered abroad upon the face of all the earth. The ultimately abandoned, half-built tower of logical atomism—and here we can think of the amazing painting by Breugel the Elder, "The Tower of Babel" (c. 1563)—is then rightly called *Babel*. But it also makes sense that the Builders are trying to build Humpty Dumpty's wall.

This is because, at least as Lewis Carroll presents that bumptious egghead H.D., he's quite explicitly a Pure Referentialist who holds that his own proper name uniquely means his own shape, and that he can use his own name to point directly to his shape.

Whatever the possible subterranean philosophical influences of the Book of Genesis and *Through the Looking Glass* on the *Investigations*, however, Wittgenstein's own explicit two-part gloss on the text from Augustine's *Confessions* says this:

> These words, it seems to me, give us a particular picture of the essence of human language. It is this: the individual words in language name objects—sentences are combinations of such names. —In this picture of language we find the roots of the following idea: Every word has a meaning (*Bedeutung*). This meaning is correlated with the word. It is the object for which the word stands.
>
> Augustine does not speak of there being any difference between kinds of word. If you describe the learning of language in this way you are, I believe, thinking primarily of nouns like 'table', 'chair', 'bread', and of people's names, and only secondarily of the names of certain actions and properties; and of the remaining kinds of word as something that will take care of itself. (*PI* §1).

So the Augustinian language game is a diorama of Pure Referentialism. But why did Wittgenstein use the passage from *Confessions* as his opening text, and not other very similar passages from the *Theaetetus* or, indeed, from *Through the Looking Glass*? One obvious answer is that in addition to being a Pure Referentialist *avant la lettre*, Augustine also strongly anticipates Cartesian epistemology and metaphysics of mind, not to mention Husserl's semantic phenomenology in the *Logical Investigations I*, chapter 1, section 10, provocatively entitled "Expressions in Solitary Life," as well as Carnap's equally provocative notion of "methodological solipsism" in *The Logical Structure of the World*. Augustine's *Confessions*, in short, strongly anticipates *semantic solipsism*. Augustine tellingly says this about his confessions:

> Why then does it matter to me whether men should hear what I have to confess, as though it were they who were to cure all the evil that is in me? They are an

inquisitive race, always anxious to pry into other men's lives, but never ready to correct their own. Why do they wish to hear from me what sort of man I am, though they will not listen to you when you tell them what they are? When they hear me speak about myself, how do they know I am telling the truth, since no one *knows a man"s thoughts, except the man's own spirit that is within him*? (Augustine, 1961: X, 3, p. 208)

Augustine's *Cartesian* semantic solipsism, in turn, captures the core of Wittgenstein's own *transcendental* semantic solipsism in the *Tractatus*, which I discussed in chapter VIII above. And in the early stages of his critical discussion of the Augustinian theory of language in the *Investigations*, Wittgenstein directly addresses Cartesian and transcendental semantic solipsism alike:

If you do not keep the multiplicity of language-games in view, you will perhaps be inclined to ask questions like: "What is a question?" –Is it the statement that I do not know such-and-such, or the statement that I wish the other person would tell me ....? Or is it the description of my mental state of uncertainty? –And is the cry "Help!" such a description? ... The significance of such possibilities of transformation, for example of turning all sentences into sentences beginning "I think" or "I believe" (and thus, as it were, into descriptions of *my* inner life) will become clearer in another place. (Solipsism.) (*PI* §24)

Of course, what he means here by saying that things "will become clearer in another place" is The Private Language Argument (Hacker, 1972, 1986; Kripke, 1982; Pears, 1987: vol. 2, chs. 13-15).

Step 3. It's manifest that not everything that is language has meaning in this way (*PI* §3), if only because the referring terms of the Builders' language also function as orders (*PI* §18). In fact, it's massively more correct to think of words as tools embedded in language-games and in forms of life, and as playing any number of roles relative to different games and forms of life, than to think of them as playing a single de-contextualized semantic role in the language, such as naming objects (*PI* §§19-23, 26-27).

Commentary on **Step 3.** This last step in the opening three-step argument is the philosophically seminal one, insofar as it presents Wittgenstein's thesis that meaning-is-use. As far as *establishing* the meaning-is-use thesis, however, the crucial move here is to get us to see how Pure Referentialism turns out to be either (i) a completely tautologous and trivial thesis, or else (ii) a significant thesis that's clearly false.

With regard to option (i), Pure Referentialism's being either tautologous or trivial, Wittgenstein says:

When we say: "Every word in language signifies (*bezeichnet*) something" we have so far said *nothing* whatever; unless we have explained exactly *what* distinction

157

we want to make. (It might be, of course, that we wanted to distinguish the words of language (8) from words "without meaning" such as occur in Lewis Carroll's poems, or words like "Lilliburlero" in songs. (*PI* §13)

In other words, there are as many different uses of meaningful language as there are different kinds of human intentional action, and the only *real* point of asserting a thesis like Pure Referentialism would be to distinguish meaningful language in general from nonsense. This is not to say, however, that nonsense cannot have its *own* uses or career in human action—as, for example, in Carroll's *The Walrus and the Carpenter* (Carroll, 1988: pp. 65-71)—but instead just that this specifically nonsensical kind of linguistic career is distinct from that of meaningful words. The human career of nonsensical language is distinguished fundamentally from the human career of natural or ordinary language by the manifest *playfulness* of nonsense as opposed to the manifest *everday seriousness* of natural or ordinary language, despite the deep fact that both are language *games* embedded in *forms of life*, or normatively rule-governed episodes in the total career of words in human action. So ultimately the difference in language use lies in different human act-intentions, as also of course do all real differences in meanings. If Pure Referentialism is taken in this way, then it simply re-states the meaning-is-use thesis.

But if, on the other hand—now exploring the option (ii) I mentioned above—Pure Referentialism is taken to stand for the substantive three-part thesis that all words are proper names, that the meaning of word is nothing but the object it names, and that every basic proper name in a basic proposition (whether a basic singular term or a basic general term or concept-word) denotes either an absolutely simple individual concrete object or a definite abstract concept or universal, then it is simply false, by the following argument, which leads us deeper into the *Investigations*, and well beyond the simple constructions of the Builders:

1. In a Pure Referentialist semantics, there are two distinct types of basic proper names: basic singular terms and basic general terms or concept-words.

2. Absolutely simple individual concrete objects are assigned to basic singular terms, and definite abstract concepts or universals are assigned to basic general terms.

3. Absolutely simple individual concrete objects are assigned to basic singular terms by ostension (*PI* §6).

4. Singular reference is then best understood as ostensively attaching a name-label to an absolutely simple individual thing, i.e., by dubbing it (*PI* §37).

5. But every ostension is open to many distinct possible interpretations (*PI* §§28-38), and only actual use will uniquely fix an interpretation.

6. Moreover, if the meaning of a basic singular term were just the bearer of the name, then whenever the bearer was destroyed, the meaning would be destroyed, which is absurd because it would make true negative existentials with singular terms into nonsense (*PI* §40).

7. But true negative existentials containing singular terms, such as "Moses did not exist," are in fact perfectly meaningful, although such sentences do also allow of irreducibly different meanings, depending on their use (*PI* §79).

8. Furthermore, there are no such things as absolutely simple individual concrete objects, because every object we can perceive is complex in various ways, and allows of no unique decomposition into ultimate simple parts (*PI* §§46-64).

9. So Pure Referentialism about basic singular terms is false, and the thesis that meaning-is-use is the best overall explanation of how even basic singular terms have meaning.

10. Pure Referentialism as applied to basic general terms requires that every concept-word stand for a definite abstract concept or universal.

11. But not all concept-words, as actually used, mean definite abstract concepts or universals: on the contrary, at least some of them mean only family resemblances or clusters of partially overlapping human concepts, at least some of which have blurred or vague boundaries—see, e.g., the concept GAME (*PI* §§66-71).

12. Only the actual use of the general term will adequately disambiguate its meaning as a concept-word. Indeed there are no analytic definitions of general terms, only our actual patterns of application of them (*PI* §§75-78).

13. So Pure Referentialism about general terms is false, and the thesis that meaning-is-use is the best overall explanation of how even basic general terms have meaning.

14. Therefore, Pure Referentialism more generally is false, and the thesis that meaning-is-use is the best overall explanation of how words have meaning.

It then follows from **Step 1**, **Step 2**, and **Step 3** that the meaning-is-use thesis is true, including the important qualification that sometimes the human act of ostending an object that bears a name also explains the meaning of that name. And in this way, the Augustinian theory of language leads directly from Referentialism to human action.

XII. Wittgenstein and the *Investigations* 2: §§28-242

XII.1 The Picture Theory, and the Vices of Simplicity and Isomorphism

Now let's venture further into region 3. The Picture Theory identifies the meaning of a sentence with how sentences are either isomorphic models of atomic facts or else truth-functional compoundings of these. According to Wittgenstein, just like Pure Referentialism, there are also two basic problems with The Picture Theory. **First,** The Picture Theory is committed to the existence of absolutely simple objects, but there's no sufficient reason to think that there are anything but only relatively simple objects, relativized to language games. This in turn raises the important issue of the role of "samples" in language games. And **second,** The Picture Theory is committed to an isomorphism between propositional structures and the structure of facts, but there's no way to establish the existence of such an isomorphism short of either some sort of mysterious externally pre-established harmony or else transcendental idealism. This raises the equally important issue of semantic realism vs. anti-realism.

XII.2 Wittgenstein's Argument Against The Picture Theory: A Rational Reconstruction

1. The Picture Theory says that the meaning of a sentence is nothing but how sentences isomorphically model atomic facts or else truth-functional compoundings of such sentences.

2. Atomic facts, in turn, are composed of configurations of absolutely simple objects in isomorphic correspondence with the parts of the atomic proposition, which is a configuration of "real names" (Frege's *Eigennamen*).

3. So The Picture Theory presupposes that "real names" in atomic propositions stand for absolutely simple objects (*PI* §39).

4. In this respect, Russell's early semantics, the *Tractatus*, and Plato's *Theaetetus* have all captured the same basic idea (*PI* §46).

5. But what's an absolutely simple object? An obvious proposal is that an absolutely simple object, unlike complex objects, cannot be broken down into its constituent parts.

6. The problem here, however, is that complex, macroscopic objects apparently have no unique decomposition into simple parts (*PI* §47).

7. And if we try to imagine a primitive language game that models the Tractarian version of The Picture Theory, we find the same lack of unique decomposition into simple parts (*PI* §48).

> 8. So there are no absolutely simple objects, and The Picture Theory is therefore false.
>
> 9. But the language game of using factual propositions implies the constant semantic availability of simple objects of some sort, even across the difference between existence and non-existence (*PI* §§50, 55).

(This claim can also be usefully compared and contrasted with Meinong's theory of objects, and his corresponding notion of *Aussersein* or "indifference-to-being," which, in turn, has a conceptual-historical foundation in Kant's theory of positive noumena, aka things-in-themselves: see section III.6 above.)

> 10. Contrary to the picture theory, then, it seems to be a much better overall explanation of the semantic of factual propositions to say that the "simple" objects are in fact systems of paradigms or samples—hence only *relatively* simple objects—that belong strictly to the "instruments" or technology of the particular language-game (say, of factual propositions about colours) that's in play (*PI* §§50-51).
>
> 11. Therefore, even though the picture theory is false, relativizing simple objects to language-games gives a better overall explanation of the semantics of factual propositions, hence use is the best overall explanation of how sentences have meaning.
>
> 12. This conclusion, however, implies the relativization of the ontology of atomic facts to language games (*PI* §§59-60), which also undermines the semantic realism of The Picture Theory.

XII.3 Understanding and Rule-Following

Now we'll venture even further into region 3. As a lead-up to The Rule Following Paradox and its solution, Wittgenstein wants to establish two theses that he'll be able to use in that argument. The first thesis (**Thesis 1**) follows from considerations concerning propositions and understanding, and the second thesis (**Thesis 2**) follows from considerations concerning understanding and reading. In the text of the *Investigations* itself, these arguments run seamlessly together; but for my purposes it's useful to provide a rational reconstruction of them in two distinct chunks I'll call *prolegomena*.

First Prolegomenon to The Rule-Following Paradox: Propositions and Understanding

> In the *Tractatus*, it was assumed that concept of a proposition expressed the *essence* of the proposition: necessarily and sufficiently, all propositions describe facts ("this is how things are"), and every proposition is bipolar ("a proposition is whatever can be true or false") (*PI* §§134, 136). So, necessarily, a part of language is a proposition if and only if it satisfies these basic conditions. This dictum, however, also pre-reflectively invokes a bad (i.e., false, misleading, and mind-enslaving) philosophical picture about the inherent

systematicity of language, a picture according to which propositions are hypostatized, substantial, platonic (i.e., non-spatiotemporal, abstract, non-causal) entities floating around listlessly in Frege's Third Realm. On the contrary, it's essentially more enlightening to say simply that there's a language-game about propositions and a proposition is automatically whatever is determined by the use of signs in that game (*PI* §137). But since you can always automatically either add as a prefix the phrase "This is how things are:" or add as a suffix the phrase "is true," to any proposition whatsoever, it seems that, necessarily, any part of language is a proposition if and only if it satisfies this condition (*PI* §137).

Similarly, it seems that any part of language has meaning if and only if it satisfies the sense of a sentence that I understand; and in this connection, we'll also recall Frege's famous remark: "only in a proposition have … words really a meaning" (Frege, 1953: §60, p. 71), i.e., a word has meaning only in the context of a whole proposition, aka The Context Principle—see section II.8 above. And understanding, it also seems, is "grasping" the meaning of a word or other expression in a "flash." But if a flash-grasping understanding of words is possible, then this contradicts the thesis that the meaning of a word is its use (*PI* §138).

So what *is* understanding a word? Understanding a word is *neither* a picture that comes before my mind when I hear a word, *nor* it a picture plus a method of projection from the picture, because (i) the same mental picture/projection method can be correlated with different applications of the word (*PI* §§139-140), and (ii) the same application can occur without the occurrence of that particular mental picture or projection method (*PI* §141). As an example, let's consider understanding how to complete a series by writing down signs representing the natural numbers (*PI* §§140-148). Here understanding a word is neither a state of consciousness nor a mental process because (i) mental states have temporal duration, whereas understanding does not (*PI* §59e), and (ii) to hold that understanding is a mental process is to confuse the characteristic *accompaniments* of understanding—which can vary widely across contexts—with understanding itself (*PI* §§149-152).

This argument requires two implicit premises in order to be valid. The **first** implicit premise says that mental pictures, rules of projection, states of consciousness, and mental processes exhaust the possible inner determinants of understanding. And the **second** implicit premise says that the determinants of understanding are either inner or outer, and not both. Therefore, since understanding is after all determined by *something*, it can only be determined by something *outer*: by the manifest or behavioral mastery of a linguistic technique (*PI* §150), and by the "particular circumstances," or context, of displaying that mastery (*PI* §§154-155). (**Thesis 1**)

Second Prolegomenon to The Rule-Following Paradox: Understanding and Reading

Let's consider now a simplified form of mastery of a linguistic technique that doesn't itself involve understanding: namely, *reading*, where this is specifically the activity of rendering out loud what's written or printed, writing from dictation, writing out something printed, following a score, etc. (*PI* §156). There's no single set of necessary and sufficient conditions (a definition or criterion) for mastery of this linguistic technique. Consider, for example, self-consciously attentive reading, human "reading machines," beginning readers, etc. (*PI* §§156-158). We're tempted to say that the criterion for reading is the conscious act of reading (*PI* §159), but even if the conscious act of reading were lacking—imagine a "reading- zombie"—it's at least conceivable that such a creature might still count as a reader (*PI* §160).

This raises an absolutely crucial point that I want to flag now for later discussion: Wittgenstein is implicitly presupposing and deploying a fundamental distinction between (i) *conceptual or logical* possibility, and (ii) *real or metaphysical* possibility. Roughly speaking, something is conceptually or logically possible if and only if it's consistent with the basic principles or laws of classical logic, conservatively extended to include a theory of fine-grained concepts. By contrast, something is really or metaphysically possible if and only if it's consistent with the basic principles or laws of classical logic *together with* a theory of fine-grained concepts, *together with* the basic principles or laws of mathematics, *together with* the formal structures of manifestly real spacetime, and *together with* the basic principles or laws of non-equilibrium thermodynamics, especially including those governing organismic life, all of them *indexed to the actual world*. In short, real or metaphysical possibility not only picks out a *more* restricted class of possible worlds than conceptual or logical possibility does, but also picks out a *less* restricted class than natural or physical possibility does, which is further constrained to what satisfies the Conservation Laws, together with The 2nd Law of Thermodynamics, i.e., equilibrium thermodynamics. Then, for example, molecule-for-molecule, behaviorally identical, but also non-conscious and mechanistic duplicates of human "all-too-human" creatures like us, aka zombies, are *conceptually or logically* possible, but not *really or metaphysically* possible, since creatures like us are living organisms, not natural mechanisms, and consciousness is a form of organismic life. A detailed theory of all that is another philosophical story for another day (Hanna and Maiese, 2009): the absolutely crucial point for the purposes of this book is that the later Wittgenstein is implicitly fully onboard with this fundamental distinction.

So consciousness is not the criterion of mastery. What then about "deriving the reproduction from the original" as a criterion of mastery of this linguistic technique? The problem with this is that even if someone never sticks to a single method of derivation, we can still plausibly call him a reader (*PI* §163). Hence there's no single sort of mastery of a technique: even for reading, there's a *family* of criteria for what counts as reading (*PI* §164), and there's no single specific marker of what will count as a genuine reading (*PI* §§165-168), because reading can, at least in principle, always occur without any such single specific marker. Even if there is no single specific marker, however, it's still true that reading always involves some sort of causal influence between the letters and the reading (*PI* §169). More generally, in all cases of reading I let myself be guided by the letters (*PI* §170). Therefore, mastery of a linguistic technique always involves "being guided" by the linguistic basis of the technique. This could also be equivalently described as the subjective experience of having the sound of the word "intimated" to me by the letters, such that there's a manifest *unity* between word and sound (*PI* §171). (**Thesis 2.**)

Notice, moreover, that this subjective experience of having the sound of the word intimated to me by the letters is clearly *a mode of consciousness*, i.e., this is *a phenomenological structure of reading*, which is smoothly consistent with Wittgenstein's earlier claim that reading-zombies are conceptually or logically *possible*, *only if* he's also committed to the view that reading-zombies are really or metaphysically *impossible*.

XII.4 Wittgenstein's Rule-Following Paradox: The Basic Rationale

In the fairly massive Wittgenstein-literature in mainstream post-classical Analytic philosophy from the 1950s through the 1980s and even into the 90s, the central parts of *Investigations* are generally known as *the rule following considerations*, because they're mainly given over to, first, developing, and then, second, resolving, a deep skeptical worry about the notion of following a rule: *The Rule-Following Paradox*.

The basic rationale behind The Rule-Following Paradox has three elements.

First, The Rule Following Paradox exposes a fatal flaw in Rule-Based Semantics, according to which the meaning of a linguistic sign is nothing but a rule for manipulating or operating with that sign in some logical or mathematical calculus, or other non-formal language-system. This in turn exposes a fatal flaw in any *function-based, compositional* theory of meaning, according to which the meaning of a complex expression is nothing but a function of the meanings of its simple parts, since such functions are taken to provide rules for computing the meaning of any expression in the language-system, no matter how long and complex, thus explaining how infinitely large languages (whether natural or artificial, for example, arithmetic) are learnable by finite cognizers like us from finite informational and behavioral inputs.

Second, the notion of following a rule is essential to Wittgenstein's own positive conception of linguistic understanding as manifest, public mastery of linguistic techniques in context. But, in view of later Wittgenstein's conception of philosophy as the active achievement of clarity by stating descriptive truisms in the right way, the correct characterization of rule-following can emerge and be philosophically illuminating only indirectly, by revealing the inadequacy and incoherence of various characterizations of rule-following that are overdetermined by bad philosophical pictures.

Third, the leading *in*adequate characterization of rule-following is also a version of Solipsistic Semantics—according to which the meaning of a name, sentence, or other linguistic sign is nothing but conscious mental representation or idea in the mind of some individual speaker. Hence the rejection of *that* particular inadequate characterization is *also* a crucial part of Wittgenstein's critique of Solipsistic Semantics.

That is, the rejection of that particular inadequate conception of rule-following is also a crucial part of The Private Language Argument.

XII.5 Wittgenstein's Rule-Following Paradox: A Rational Reconstruction

1. The Rule Following Paradox begins with an implicit premise: We assume that the meaning of any linguistic sign is nothing but a rule for operating with that sign in some logical or mathematical calculus, or other non-formal language-system (i.e., Rule-Based Semantics).

2. Therefore, understanding the meaning of any linguistic sign S is being able to follow the rule for operating with S, i.e., being "guided" by the rule for S (*PI* §§ 172-184).

3. Every rule is expressible as a function-sign which determines a systematic mapping from inputs, or arguments of the function, to outputs, or values of the function (*PI* §§143-146, 151, 185).

4. Moreover, the meaning of that function-sign—hence the complete set of its systematic mappings—is understood by grasping the rule in a flash (*PI* §§186-197).

5. But every function-sign can be multiply differently interpreted, such that although the interpretations yield the same mappings to outputs/values for all existing inputs/arguments, they diverge on some future inputs (*PI* §185).

6. And since every interpretation is in turn expressible as a higher-order function sign, then each interpretation itself stands in need of further interpretation, which itself in turn can be multiply differently interpreted, ad infinitum (*PI* §198).

7. So anything the speaker does with S can, on some interpretation or another, be in accordance with the rule (*PI* §201).

8. Correspondingly, anything the speaker does with S can, on some interpretation or another, be also in conflict with the rule (*PI* § 201).

9. So the speaker's actions, no matter what they are, neither accord with the rule nor conflict with the rule (*PI* § 201).

10. Therefore, it's impossible for a speaker to follow a rule.

11. Therefore, it's impossible for a speaker to understand the meaning of an expression.

12. Therefore, Rule-Based Semantics is false, by *reductio*.

So much for Rule-Based Semantics. But here's an important complication for

Wittgenstein's Rule Following Paradox. Even if Rule-Based Semantics is outright rejected by the argument I just spelled out, there's still a serious leftover problem, precisely because Wittgenstein *himself* is committed to a version of step 2. in the argument:

> understanding the meaning of any linguistic sign S is being able to follow the rule for operating with S, i.e., being "guided" by the rule for S.

This commitment is determined by Wittgenstein's antecedent commitment to **Thesis 1** and **Thesis 2**, which, as we saw in section XI.3, followed respectively from the prolegomena on *understanding* and *reading* that prefaced "the rule-following considerations." So The Rule-Following Paradox requires a more adequate and deeper solution.

XII.6 Kripkenstein's Rule-Following Paradox: Why Read Kripke Too?

In the early 1980s, Saul Kripke worked out a creative interpretation of the *Investigations* that quickly took on a philosophical life of its own, not only in the secondary mainstream Analytic literature on Wittgenstein, but also in the primary mainstream Analytic literature on "the rule-following considerations" (Kripke, 1982). Kripke's interpretation focuses on The Rule-Following Paradox and its solution in *Investigations* §§134-242. In a two-cell nutshell, he argues (i) that the sequence of paragraphs form §§134-242 constitutes the essence of The Private Language Argument, which on the contrary other commentators have almost always placed in *PI* §§243-315, and (ii) that "the rule-following considerations" introduce a radically new form of philosophical skepticism that should be taken every bit as as seriously as (iia) Cartesian evil-demon dream skepticism in the *Meditations on First* Philosophy, and (iib) Hume's skepticism about induction and the concept of necessity in the *Treatise* and *Enquiry concerning Human Understanding*.[1]

The upshot of this highly influential interpretation is, strictly speaking, *neither* Wittgstenstein's own argument, *nor* Kripke's own argument, but instead a philosophical hybrid commonly known as "Kripkenstein's Argument." Whatever its merits as a faithful interpretation of the *Investigations*, or as a piece of original philosophy in its own right, Kripkenstein's Argument is nevertheless a paradigmatic example of how post-classical Analytic philosophy had become a self-propelled, self-replicating professional academic engine by the mid-1980s. Moreover, the influence of Kripkenstein's Argument in post-classical Analytic philosophy steadily grew in inverse proportion to the influence of the *Investigations* itself in post-classical Analytic philosophy, which had fallen off drastically by the beginning of the 21st century. Indeed, by then, it was not uncommon to hear mainstream post-classical Analytic philosophers, especially those working in Analytic metaphysics (see sections XVII.3 and XVII.6 below), dismiss the *Investigations* in particular and the later Wittgenstein's work more generally, as pseudo-profound exercises in so-called "Continental philosophy." So

---

1 Kripke also explicitly and relevantly compares and contrasts his interpretation of Wittgenstein's Rule- Following Paradox with Quine's famous "indeterminacy of translation" and "inscrutability of reference" arguments about the nature of meaning in *Word and Object*, and Goodman's equally famous "grue" paradox about the nature of induction in (Goodman, 1983).

Kripkenstein's Argument is well worth looking at, not only for its own sake, but also for the light it indirectly casts on the fate of Analysis.

XII.7 Kripkenstein's Rule-Following Paradox: A Rational Reconstruction

1. Consider any meaningful use of language but more specifically any meaningful mathematical use of language and in particular our everyday use of the word "plus" and the symbol "+."

2. It's a given fact that by means of my external symbolic representation and internal mental representation of the arithmetic addition-function, aka the plus function, I *grasp* the rule for addition.

3. Although I've computed only finitely many sums in the past, the rule for addition also determines my answer for the indefinitely many sums that I've never considered.

4. Indeed, the arithmetic addition-function corresponding to the rule for addition determines a complete collection of infinitely many values/outputs for infinitely many arguments/inputs to the plus function.

5. Suppose, however, that I compute "68+57" for the first time.

6. I'm confident that the correct answer is "125," and it's true that the plus function when applied to the inputs 68 and 57 yield 125 as the output, and also true that "plus," as I intended to use it in the past, denoted an arithmetic addition-function, that, when applied to the numbers I called "68" and "57," yields the value 125.

7. But now a "bizarre skeptic" challenges my answer on the following grounds: that I might just as easily have intended (and indeed might just as easily now be intending) to use "plus" such that the correct answer is in fact "5" and the correct value of the function I intended is 5!

8. That's because in the past I computed only finitely many sums and by hypothesis had never encountered "68+57" (and let's also assume, for simplicity's sake, that I had always referred only to natural numbers less than 57), and it's therefore really possible that the rule I followed (and am following) corresponded in fact to the function *quus*:

If either x or y is less than 57, then x quus y = x + y, but if either x or y is greater than or equal to 57, then x quus y = 5.

9. So the rule-following skeptic claims that it's really possible that I'm misinterpreting my own previous (and present) usage: more specifically, the skeptic

claims that for all I know, by "plus" or "+" I always meant (and am currently meaning) quus, *not* plus.

10. Now any adequate reply to the rule following skeptic must satisfy two conditions: (10i) it must give an account of what fact it is about my mental state that constitutes my meaning plus, not quus, and (10ii) it must show how I'm normatively rationally justified in giving the answer "125" to "68+57," that is, it must show that I *should* give the answer "125."

11. But there's *no mental fact about me*, whether it is an occurrent mental representation such as a mental image, or an image together with a projection that interprets it, a mental disposition, a mental state or process, or even a unique phenomenal *quale* uniformly associated with my use of "plus" and "+," that uniquely determines what I meant (and currently mean) by the use of those symbols, and therefore there is no mental fact about me that determines that I meant (and currently mean) plus and not quus, precisely because the existence of each of those mental facts can be interpreted consistently with the hypothesis that I actually meant (and am currently meaning) quus and not plus, or that (mutatis mutandis) I am "quounting" and not counting, etc.

12. Indeed there's no mental fact about me that determines that I meant (and am currently meaning) *any definite function whatsoever* by "plus" or "+."

13. So I might have meant (and currently mean) nothing definite at all!, and not even *God* could tell, by inspecting my mental facts, whether I'm following the rule for plus or quus.

14. Therefore, I have no normative, rational justification for my claim that the correct answer to "68+57" is "125" and that the corresponding value of the function is 125.

XII.8 How to Solve The Paradox: Wittgenstein's Way and Kripkenstein's Way

There are two crucial differences between Wittgenstein's Rule-Following Paradox and Kripkenstein's Rule-Following Paradox.

The **first** difference is that Wittgenstein's version directly concerns *cognitive semantics* and is aimed against Rule-Based Semantics, whereas Kripkenstein's version directly concerns the *epistemology* of normative justification and is aimed against at Solipsistic Semantics. To be sure, Wittgenstei"s version and Kripkenstein's version agree about the idea that The Private Language Argument substantially depends on the results of The Rule Following Paradox, so they converge on a substantive issue in the philosophy of mind. But the fact remains that Kripkeinstein's Rule-Following Paradox mainly concerns the epistemology of rule-following and *not* rule-theoretic approaches to cognitive semantics.

The **second** and even more important difference arises from the fact that Wittgenstein's version of The Rule-Following Paradox takes essentially the form of a non-classical logical paradox about the very idea of a rule, just as the Liar is a classical logical paradox about the very idea of truth under the special parameter of self-reference, or as Russell's Paradox is a classical logical paradox about the very idea of a logical collection or set under the special parameter of impredicativity. By sharp contrast however, Kripkenstein is essentially concerned with *skepticism* about normative rational justification, not with logical paradoxes, whereas Wittgenstein himself doesn't seem to have had this primarily in mind.

Crucial as it is, this second difference might have a largely historico-contextual and social-institutional origin. Epistemological and skepticism-oriented readings of Wittgenstein were very much in the air in the Harvard Department of Philosophy in the late 1960s, 70s and early 80s, and are directly reflected in influential work in language-oriented epistemology from that period by Stanley Cavell, Thompson Clarke, and Barry Stroud (Stroud, 1968; Clarke, 1972; Cavell, 1979; Stroud, 1984). Perhaps not too surprisingly at this point in the book, upon a closer examination, we'll see that this Harvardian epistemological activity was as much influenced by *neo-Kantianism* as it was *Wittgenstein*-influenced (Stroud, 1968). No doubt this followed on more or less directly from C.I. Lewis's epistemological neo-Kantianism in the first half of the century—see, especially, his 1929 *Mind and the World-Order*—together with Quine's skeptical attack on the analytic-synthetic distinction, and Peter Strawson's transcendentalist response to Quine (see chapter XVI below). Not entirely coincidentally, moreover, Kripke himself did a BA in mathematics at Harvard from 1958-1962, and was subsequently both a Junior Fellow in the Harvard Society of Fellows and also taught in the Harvard Department of Philosophy, until he moved to Rockefeller University in 1967. So, no doubt, Kripke's epistemological reading of Wittgenstein was heavily primed by the neo-Kantian social-institutional mind-shaping processes that were characteristic of the Harvard Department of that era.[2]

In any case, Kripkenstein wants to insist that any solution to the Rule-Following Paradox can therefore only be a *skeptical* solution that respects the skeptical result, as opposed to a *straight* solution that accepts the constraints in 10. and also shows that—contrary to 11. and 12.—there is some mental fact about me which determines that I meant plus and not quus, and that I therefore have a normative mentalistic justification (i.e., a good reason directly citing the relevant mental fact) that the correct answer to "68+57" is "125" and that the corresponding value is of the function is 125. We'll look more closely at Kripkenstein's skeptical solution shortly, but just to anticipate now, it consists in claiming (i) that I do indeed mean plus and not quus without *any* inner justification or reasons and thus follow the rule "blindly" (see *PI* §219), and (ii) that no rule can be obeyed only "privately" (see *PI* §202): on the contrary rules are followed by individual speakers only in the context of social practices (language-games and forms of life) and are legitimated *non-cognitively* solely in terms of those social practices alone, so *this is simply what I do* (*PI* §217), because this is simply what *we* do. As we'll see, this conclusion brings Kripkenstein's skeptical solution to

---

2 On social-institutional mind-shaping in general, see (Maiese and Hanna, 2019; and on social-institutional mind shaping in post-classical Analytic philosophy in particular, see chs. XVII and XVIII below.

The Rule-Following Paradox very close to Hume's skeptical solution to his own skepticism about causation and induction, and also to Goodman's skeptical solution to the "new riddle of induction" (Goodman, 1983). Goodman's solution, like Kripkenstein's, is broadly speaking Marburg-style neo-Kantian, in that they both convert what are essentially cognitive-semantic or hermeneutic issues, into epistemological issues. Wittgenstein himself, by an important contrast, proposes a cognitive-semantic and/or hermeneutic solution that's essentially either straight Kantian or Southwest/Baden-style neo-Kantian, neither Humean nor Goodmanian, and more generally not Marburg-style neo-Kantian.

XII.8.1 Wittgenstein and The Rule-Following Paradox: A Rational Reconstruction

1. We start with the following assumptions, justified by earlier arguments:

(1i) that linguistic understanding actually occurs, (1ii) that all linguistic understanding is determined by something outer, not by something inner, and involves manifest, public mastery of a linguistic technique, together with the particular circumstances or context of displaying that mastery, (1iii) that manifest, public mastery of a linguistic technique always involves "being guided" by the linguistic basis of the technique (as, for example, in reading), (1iv) that understanding the meaning of any linguistic sign S is being able to follow the rule for using S, i.e., being guided by S, (1v) that every rule is expressible as a function-sign determining a systematic mapping from inputs (arguments to the function) to outputs (values of the function), (1vi) that the meaning of a function-sign is understood by grasping the rule in a flash (i.e., mentally and instantaneously), (1vii) that a function-sign is given a meaning by virtue of assigning an interpretation to the function-sign, which in turn is itself expressible as a higher-order function-sign, and (1viii) that all such function-signs can be multiply differently interpreted.

2. From these assumptions, it follows that

> [n]o course of action could be determined by a rule because every course of action can be determined by the rule.... [I]f everything can be made out to accord with the rule, then it can also be made out to conflict with it. And so there would be neither accord nor conflict here (*PI* § 201),

or in other words: rule-following is impossible.

3. Therefore, rule-following both actually occurs and also is impossible, which of course is self-evidently paradoxical.

4. Here's an implicit premise drawn from classical logic: given a contradictory conclusion, at least one of its premises must be false.

5. In particular, it's false that a function-sign is given a meaning by virtue of assigning an interpretation to the function-sign, which in turn is itself expressible as a higher-order function-sign:

> It can be seen that there is a misunderstanding here from the mere fact that in the course of our argument we gave one interpretation after another; as if each one contented us for a moment, until we thought of yet another standing behind it.
>
> What this shows is that there is a way of grasping a rule which *is not an interpretation*, but which is exhibited in what we call "obeying the rule" and "going against it" in particular cases. (*PI* §201)

6. In other words, assumption (1vii) above is false, and must be replaced by the new thesis that how a rule is given a meaning is fully displayed by *the speaker"s actual acts of obeying the rule or going against the rule*.

7. Given the truth of 6., it's also false that the meaning of a function-sign is understood by grasping the rule in a flash (i.e., mentally and instantaneously):

> And hence "obeying a rule" is a practice. And to *think* one is obeying a rule is not to obey a rule. Hence it is not possible to obey a rule "privately": otherwise thinking one was obeying the rule would be the same thing as obeying it. (*PI* §202)

8. In other words, assumption (1vi) above is also false, and must be replaced by the new thesis that the speaker's actual acts of obeying the rule or going against the rule are *practices*, or essentially *social* enterprises of manifest, public mastery of a linguistic technique, together with the particular circumstances or context of displaying that mastery.

9. The practice of following a particular rule is a normative activity involving both some type of imperative constraint on the rule-follower and also training in the linguistic techniques involved in the practice:

> Following a rule is analogous to obeying an order. We are trained to do so: we react to an order in a certain way. (*PI* §206)

10. But rule following is *not* a practice that also requires *my* giving reasons for acting in the way I do, hence it does not require *my* providing an *internal* justification:

> How can he *know* how he is to continue a pattern by himself—whatever instructions you give him?—Well, how do I know?—If that means "Have

> I reasons?" the answer is: my reasons will soon give out. And then I shall act, without reasons. (*PI* § 211)

11. On the contrary, the practice of following a particular rule itself *externally* justifies what I do, insofar as I merely *agree and engage non-conceptually* in that practice:

> "How am I to obey a rule?" —If this is not a question about causes, then it is about the justification for my following the rule in the way I do. If I have exhausted the justifications I reach bedrock, and my spade is turned. Then I am inclined to say: "This is simply what I do." (*PI* §217)
>
> "All the steps are really already taken" means: I no longer have any choice. The rule, once stamped with a particular meaning, traces the lines along which it is to be followed through the whole of space. —But if something of this sort were really the case, how would it help?
>
> No; my description only made sense if it was to be understood symbolically. —I should have said: *This is how it strikes me.*
>
> When I obey the rule I do not choose.
>
> I follow the rule *blindly*. (*Ich folge der Regel* **blind**, emphasis in the original, *PI* §219)

(Here we should recall, emphasize, and re-emphasize Kant's dictum that "intuitions without concepts are blind" [*Anschauungen ohne Begriffe sind blind*, *CPR* A51/B75]. In either a straight Kantian or Southwest/Baden-style neo-Kantian context, "blind" activity is *non-conceptual activity*. [Hanna, 2016b].)

12. This external justification and my "blind," aka non-conceptual, activity also provides the basis for my projecting the rule infinitely into the future:

> Whence comes the idea that the beginning of a series is a visible section of rails invisibly laid to infinity? Well, we might imagine rails instead of a rule. And infinitely long rails correspond to the unlimited application of the rule. (*PI* §218)

13. My following a rule therefore depends on my "blindly," aka non-conceptually, entering into an agreement with (and here we are to think comparatively and contrastively about the very idea of a *social contract*) and also an engagement with the other people who belong to the same practice:

The Fate of Analysis

> The word "agreement" ("*Übereinstimmung*") and the word "rule" ("*Regel*") are related to one another, they are cousins. If I teach anyone the use of the one word, he learns the use of the other with it. (*PI* §224)

14. But this blind/non-conceptual agreement-&-engagement does *not* imply a non-truth-conditional theory of truth: on the contrary, truth is still correspondence to the facts and the blind/non-conceptual agreement and engagment consists in the more basic sharing of a language [-game] and of a form of life:

> —So you are saying that human agreement decides what is true and what is false?—It is what human beings *say* that is true and false; and they agree in the *language* they use. That is not agreement in opinions but in form of life. (*PI* §241)

In other words: Wittgenstein is not only a *radical externalist* about justification and understanding (both as to their semantic content and their representational vehicles), but also an *internal realist* about truth, and above all a *non-conceptualist* about agreement and engagment in rational human practices. This fundamentally blind/non-conceptual agreement and engagement in language-games and forms of life, in turn, is given essentially in the activity of *making judgments*:

> If language is to be a means of communication there must be agreement not only in definitions but also (queer as this may sound) in judgments. This seems to abolish logic, but does not do so. (*PI* §242)

So the fundamentally blind/non-conceptual agreement and engagement that's in play both in language-games and also in forms of life *consists in our intersubjectively shared capacity for judgment*. Judgment is essentially a conceptual activity, but *also* grounded non-conceptually. In this way, Wittgenstein's own solution to The Rule-Following Paradox, bounded in a nutshell, is that we can follow rules "blindly," aka non-conceptually, just because talking and reasoning human animals like us are nothing more and nothing less than *judging animals*.

XII.8.2 Kripkenstein and The Rule-Following Paradox: A Rational Reconstruction

1. By virtue of The Rule Following Paradox, Wittgenstein is committed to a radical skepticism about the determination of future linguistic usage by the past contents of my mind.

2. This is fundamentally analogous to Hume's skepticism about the determination of the future by the past, where we understand this skepticism both *inferentially* (skepticism about induction) and also *causally* (skepticism about natural necessity).

3. The Rule Following Paradox can therefore be resolved only by a "skeptical solution" which accepts not only (3i) that there is no mental fact about me that

determines whether I am following the rule for plus or the rule for quus, but also (3ii) that I have no internal justification for my claim that the correct answer to "68+57" is "125," and then looks purely descriptively at the actual circumstances under which I can be correctly said to be following plus rather than quus and in which it can be asserted that the correct answer to "68+57" should be "125."

4. If we consider a single individual in isolation, then although it's an empirical fact that the individual does assert confidently, or at least has the disposition to assert confidently, that the correct answer to "68+57" is "125," nevertheless, by step (3ii), there's no internal justification for this assertion.

5. But if we take into account the fact that the individual is in a community, then the philosophical picture radically changes and we must adopt *an assertibility-conditions semantics* (according to which a statement is true if and only if it is legitimately assertible) and *reject a truth-conditional semantics* (according to which a statement is true if and only if it corresponds to the facts).

6. The empirical fact of our successful rule-following practices (see step 4.) depends essentially on the further brute empirical fact that we agree with one another in responses like "What is 68+57?"

7. Hence the relevant assertibility-condition for the answer "125" is simply whether the individual's response agrees with everyone else's response to the same question, and this external judgment is determined just by observing the individual's behavior and surrounding circumstances.

8. This solution to The Rule-Following Paradox, in turn, is fundamentally analogous to Hume's claim to have shown that the only way to make sense of a causal relation between two phenomenal events is simply to subsume it under a customary or habitual regularity of constant conjunctions of instances of the relevant event-types.

9. Therefore, the Wittgensteinian thesis that there is no private language is necessarily equivalent to the Wittgensteinian thesis that there is no private rule-following.

Whatever our respective critical takes on the soundness of Wittgenstein's and Kripkenstein's solutions to The Rule-Following Paradox, we can at the very least clearly and distinctly recognize that Kripkenstein is *not* Wittgenstein.

XIII. Wittgenstein and the *Investigations* 3: §§242-315

XIII.1 What is a Private Language?

Finally, we've arrived at, as it were, the headwater or source of the philosophical Congo River—the "heart of darkness"—in region 3. All rationally charitable readers of the *Investigations* agree that one of its central and principal achievements is The Private Language Argument: Wittgenstein's demonstration of the impossibility of (or: the incoherence of the concept of) a private language. But unfortunately very few readers, even the most rationally charitable ones, agree either (i) about what precisely a "private language" is, or (ii) about what The Private Language Argument actually is. Obviously, however, since no progress can be made on the second question unless the first question has been adequately answered, then that's where we'll start.

First and foremost, a private language is a *solipsistic language* in the sense that it is a language whose *meanings* are nothing but mental representations (or "ideas") in the mind of an individual speaking subject. A solipsistic language of this sort is such that *only one person can understand it, because its meanings or semantic contents are determined wholly and solely by what is inside that person's head* (or alternatively: *inside that person's Cartesian soul*, if you're a substance dualist). I'll call any language that's solipsistic in this way *a language that's solipsistic with respect to its semantic content*. But unfortunately, even the notion of a language that's solipsistic with respect to its semantic content is ambiguous, because there are at least two disjointly different classes of subjective mental representations that might be identified with meanings: (i) *sensations* (i.e., phenomenal qualia or phenomenally conscious mental states) of various kinds, all of which *lack* representational content, and (ii) other mental items (i.e., other sorts of mental states, mental processes, mental images, mentalistic terms for direct reference, aka "intuitions," *Anschauungen*, mentalistic concepts, aka *Begriffe*, rule-following impressions, memories, anticipations, desires, emotions, etc.), of various kinds, generally called *cognitions*, all of which *contain* representational content. As a consequence, there are at least two different kinds of language that are solipsistic with respect to their semantic contents: (i) *sensation languages*, i.e., solipsistic languages in which words have meaning by standing for an individual speaker's sensations, and (ii) *cognition languages*, i.e., solipsistic languages in which words have meaning by standing for an individual speaker's cognitions. And in fact, Wittgenstein wants to argue against the possibility of *both* sensation languages *and* cognition languages.

In a **second** way, however, a private language can *also* be a solipsistic language in the quite different sense of a "mental language" or *lingua mentis*, that is, a language whose *words* (types and tokens alike) are nothing but mental representations in the mind of an individual speaking subject. A solipsistic language of this sort is such that only one person can understand it, because its *grammatically-structured signs or symbols* are determined wholly and solely by what is inside the head (or Cartesian soul) of a single speaking subject. I'll call languages of this sort *languages that are solipsistic with respect to their syntactic vehicles*.

From the standpoint of clearly understanding The Private Language Argument, the unfortunate thing about private languages that are solipsistic with respect to their syntactic vehicles is that they *aren't* necessarily equivalent with private languages that are that are solipsistic with respect to their semantic contents. And that's because of the following two facts. **First**, it's possible for there to be languages that *are* solipsistic with respect to their *semantic contents*, but also are *not* solipsistic with respect to their *syntactic vehicles*. These languages would include sensation languages that are also public natural languages. For example, according to phenomenalists (say, the early logical empiricists/positivists), the ordinary English sensation-word 'pain' would mean *this painy sensation now*. And **second**, it's possible for there to be private languages that *are* solipsistic with respect to their *syntactic vehicles*, but also are *not* solipsistic with respect to their *semantic contents*. These languages would include any mental language or *lingua mentis* that has a direct translation into a public natural language. For example, my mental word "##" could mean the same as "beetle" in English.

And if this were not already bad enough, there are *also* private languages that are actually public with respect to their semantic vehicles, but *trivially solipsistic with respect to their syntactic vehicles*. Consider, for example, Robinson Crusoe's monologues on his island before encountering Friday, or the text of Lewis Carroll's *Jabberwocky* before he actually showed it to anyone else (or perhaps even before he actually wrote it down).

Now, what's the point of drawing all these careful distinctions? The answer is that the private languages that are the target of The Private Language Argument are *just these*:

> All and only languages that are solipsistic with respect with their semantic contents, *whether or not* they're also solipsistic with respect to their syntactic vehicles, including all sensation languages and all cognition languages.

And this excludes *many* languages that are solipsistic with respect to their syntactic vehicles, as well as *most* languages that are trivially solipsistic with respect to their syntactic vehicles.

XIII.2 The Private Language Argument: A Rational Reconstruction

> 1. Let's consider the possibility of languages that are solipsistic with respect to their semantic contents (as opposed to languages that are solipsistic with respect to their syntactic vehicles, whether trivially or not), and, more specifically, consider the possibility of *sensation languages*:
>
>> But we could also imagine a language in which a person could write down or give vocal expression to his inner experiences—his feelings, moods, and the rest—for his private use? —Well, can't we do so in our ordinary language? —But that is not what I mean. The individual words of this language are to refer to what can only be known to the

person speaking; to his immediate private sensations. So another person cannot understand the language. (*PI* §243)

2. Now such sensation languages are solipsistic with respect to their semantic contents *by virtue of the fact* that the sensations for which the words stand are knowable by the individual speaker alone:

> In what sense are my sensations *private*? —Well, only I can know whether I am really in pain; another person can only surmise it. (*PI* §246)

3. And if sensations are to be knowable *in any way* by the individual speaker, then it must also be possible for the speaker to identify and re-identify her sensations over time and across individual persons:

> "Another person can't have my pains." —Which are *my* pains? What counts as a criterion of identity here? Consider what makes it possible in the case of physical objects to speak of "two exactly the same," for example, to say "This chair is not the one you saw here yesterday, but is exactly the same as it." In so far as it makes *sense* to say that my pain is the same as his, it is also possible for us both to have the same pain. (*PI* §253)

4. If, however, sensations are knowable by the individual speaker alone, then that speaker's identification and re-identification of those sensations over time will lack any criteria for correctness:

> Let us imagine the following case. I want to keep a diary about the recurrence of a certain sensation. To this end I associate it with the sign "E" and write this sign in a calendar for every day on which I have the sensation. —I will remark first of all that a definition of the sign cannot be formulated. —But I can still give myself a kind of ostensive definition. —How? Can I point to the sensation? Not in the ordinary sense. But I speak, or write the sign down, and at the same time I concentrate my attention on the sensation—and so, as it were, point to it inwardly.—But what is this ceremony for? for that is all it seems to be! A definition surely serves to establish the meaning of a sign. —Well, that is done precisely by the concentration of my attention; for in this way I impress on myself the connection between the sign and the sensation. —But "I impress it on myself" can only mean: this process brings it about that I remember the connection *right* in the future. But in the present case I have no criterion of correctness. One would like to say: whatever is going to seem right to me is right. And that only means that here we can't talk about "right." (*PI* §258)

5. Moreover, if an individual speaker's identification and re-identification of sensations over time lack any criteria of correctness, then it's also possible for everyone to *believe* that they are sharing the same sensation, yet still *have* different sensations:

> The essential thing about private experience is really not that each person possesses his own exemplar, but that nobody knows whether other people also have *this* or something else. The assumption would thus be possible—though unverifiable—that one section of mankind had one sensation of red and another section another. (*PI* §272)

6. And if it's possible for everyone to believe that they're sharing the same sensation yet still have different sensations, then it's also possible for everyone to have *no* sensations at all, in which case it's impossible to determine whether the sensation-word has any meaning at all:

> If I say of myself that it is only from my own case that I know what the word "pain" means—must not I say the same thing of other people too? And how can I generalize the *one* case so irresponsibly? Now someone tells me that *he* knows what pain is only from his own case! —Suppose that everyone had a box with something in it: call it a "beetle." No one can look into anyone else's box, and everyone says that he knows what a beetle is only by looking at *his* beetle. —Here it would be quite possible for everyone to have something different in his box. One might even imagine such a thing constantly changing. —But suppose the word "beetle" had a use in these people's language? —If so it would not be used as the name of a thing. The thing in the box has no place in the language-game at all; not even as a *something*; for the box might even be empty. —No, one can "divide through" by the thing in the box; it cancels out, whatever it is. (*PI* §293)

7. Therefore, sensation languages are impossible.

8. And by a simple generalization of the same argument, cognition languages—especially those in which words have meaning by standing for *rule-following impressions*—are also impossible:

> And to *think* one is obeying a rule is not to obey a rule. Hence it is not possible to obey a rule "privately": otherwise thinking one was obeying a rule would be the same thing as obeying it. (*PI* §202)

> Are the rules of the private language *impressions* of rules?—The balance on which impressions are weighed is not the *impression* of a balance. (*PI* §259)

9. Therefore private languages are impossible, and it follows that linguistic meanings or semantic contents are *not* determined wholly and solely by what is inside individual speakers' heads (or their Cartesian souls).

The conclusion clearly states Wittgenstein's *anti-individualism about semantic content*. So, otherwise put, The Private Language Argument is ultimately an argument for *externalism about semantic content*—namely, the thesis that linguistic meanings or semantic contents are determined at least partially by what is outside individual speakers' heads (or Cartesian souls). And The Private Language Argument *also* indirectly shows that Wittgenstein is a radical syntactic vehicle externalist. For it's not signs per se, and especially not signs in a mental language or *lingua mentis*, but instead only *public uses of signs by judging animals like us*, that have linguistic meaning or semantic content.

XIII.3 Is Wittgenstein a Behaviorist? No.

We're now in the clear again, out of the abysmal heart of darkness (the horror!, the horror!), and exploring region 4. As we've just seen, The Private Language argument, if sound, shows that private languages—i.e., languages that are solipsistic with respect to their semantic content, i.e., languages such that their meanings or semantic contents are determined wholly and solely by what is inside an individual speaker's head (or Cartesian soul)—are impossible. So linguistic meanings or semantic contents are determined at least partially by what's outside the speaker's head (or Cartesian soul), and externalism about semantic content is true.

Perhaps even more controversially, however, Wittgenstein also believes that he can advance from this negative conclusion to a positive doctrine about the nature of mental states, and in particular about the nature of sensations, i.e., states of phenomenal consciousness. One outstanding interpretive question about this positive doctrine is whether it's form of *metaphysical behaviorism*.

Behaviorism, as we currently understand that view, is a doctrine in the philosophy of mind that emerged from The Vienna Circle and logical empiricism/ positivism and quickly dominated mid-20th century scientific psychology, via Carl Hempel's 1935 essay, "The Logical Analysis of Psychology," and B.F. Skinner's 1953 book, *Science and Human Behavior* (Block, 1980). Metaphysical behaviorism says that *mental properties are identical to behavioral properties*, where behavioral properties are second-order physical properties consisting in either (i) a set of occurrent causal mappings from stimulus inputs to living organisms, to response outputs from those organisms, i.e., various natural or unlearned bodily movements, orientations, positionings, or sounds—and this is "animal behavior" in the broadest possible sense, or (ii) a set of dispositions to animal behavior. By contrast, *methodological* behaviorism says that scientific psychology should be conducted as if mental properties are identical to behavioral properties. And *semantic* behaviorism says that the linguistic meanings or semantics contents of mentalistic terms are nothing but rules for verifying or falsifying judgments about animal behavior.[1] The logical empiricists/positivists and Skinnerians were metaphysical, methodological, *and* semantic behaviorists.

One basic problem with metaphysical and semantic behaviorism alike, as Hilary Putnam pointed out in 1961, is that it's a priori conceivable and therefore conceptually or logically possible that there's a race of humanoids who have completely suppressed natural human pain-behavior and yet still feel pain, aka "super-spartans" (Putnam, 195c). Correspondingly, it's also a priori conceivable and therefore conceptually or logically possible that there's a race of humanoids who have fully developed natural human pain-behaviors and yet completely lack pain experiences accompanying those behaviors, aka "super-fakers." Indeed, the truth of metaphysical behaviorism is a priori conceivably and logically consistent with a world in which all human beings lack all phenomenal consciousness whatsoever. So for all that metaphysical behaviorism tells us, we might be *zombies* in the philosophical sense, i.e., perfect microphysical and behavioral duplicates of us as we actually are, only *without* our "human, all-too-human" inner lives—all the lights are on, but no one is ever home. If so, then metaphysical behaviorism cannot possibly be correct. For as David Chalmers famously pointed out in the mid-1990s, if zombies are conceptually or logically possible, then not only is it the case that mental properties *aren't* identical with physical properties, but also mental properties *don't* logically supervene on physical properties, and therefore the human mind *cannot* be reductively explained in terms of behavioral properties (Chalmers, 1996).

In any case, my own view is that Wittgenstein is *neither* a metaphysical behaviorist, *nor* a methodological behaviorist, *nor* a semantic behaviorist. Indeed, Wittgenstein's views are essentially closer to the views expressed in Gilbert Ryle's brilliant 1949 book, *The Concept of Mind*, where Ryle is at pains explicitly to repudiate behaviorism in the logical empiricist/positivist sense (Ryle, 1963: pp. 308-311). Sadly, however, Ryle seriously muddles matters of real philosophical importance by also writing that "the general trend of this book will undoubtedly, and harmlessly, be stigmatized as 'behaviourist'" (Ryle, 1963: p. 308). — Well, not so *very* harmlessly: that's a little like saying that "the general trend of my arbitrarily violent actions last Thursday resulting in X's death will undoubtedly, and harmlessly, be stigmatized as 'murder.'" Even more sadly, those matters are even more muddled by the fact that several different German terms, including *Benehmen, Handlungsweise,* and *Treiben,* were used by Wittgenstein is this connection, but are all translated without differentiation by Anscombe as "behaviour."

Leaving aside Ryle and Anscombe now, my view is that in the *Investigations* what Wittgenstein was *actually* talking about, when he talked about "human mind" is nothing more and nothing less than *a special, unified set of human capacities, dispositions, and powers, all of which are not only essentially embodied, manifest, and public, but also have an irreducibly inner, first-person, phenomenally conscious aspect.* If so, then as a matter of real or metaphysical necessity, wherever human mind is, it's *no zombies allowed.* Or in other

---

[1] See, e.g., (Kim, 1998: ch. 2). What I'm calling "metaphysical behaviorism" Kim calls "ontological behaviorism," and what I'm calling "semantic behaviorism" Kim calls "logical behaviorism."

words, Wittgenstein's view in the *Investigations* is that the essentially embodied, manifest, public character of human mind is really or metaphysically necessarily connected with, the non-logically-strongly-supervenient[2] existence and fine-grained character of human phenomenal consciousness. In order to distinguish "human mind," in this philosophically rich and uniquely Wittgensteinian sense, from "human behavior," in the philosophically stale, flat, and unprofitable behaviorist sense, let's call it *human mindedness*. Correspondingly, I'll call Wittgenstein's view *the human mindedness theory*. So let's see in more detail, now, how the human mindedness theory plays out. This brings us into region 5.

XIII.4 Wittgenstein on Meanings, Sensations, and Human Mindedness: A Rational Reconstruction

> 1. One basic result of The Private Language Argument is that sensation-languages are impossible—which is to say that languages containing sensation-words that are solipsistic with respect to semantic content are impossible.

> 2. From this result it follows that the meanings of sensation-words are *not* determined wholly and solely by what is inside individual speakers' heads (or Cartesian souls).

> 3. Implicit premise: The meanings of words are determined *either* by what is inside the heads (or Cartesian souls) of individual speakers *or* by what is outside the heads (or Cartesian souls) of individual speakers, and there are no other alternatives.

> 4. So the meanings of sensation-words are determined *at least partially* by what is outside the heads (or Cartesian souls) of individual speakers.

> 5. Sensation-words refer to private sensory experiences; but sensations are "private" only in the truistic, ordinary sense that *only the living human person who actually has a particular token of a sensation-type, actually "has" that particular token sensation as an inner aspect of their essentially embodied, manifest, public human existence*:

>> Other people cannot be said to learn of my sensations *only* from my behavior (*Benehmen*),--for *I* cannot be said to learn of them. I *have* them. (*PI* §246)

>> The proposition "Sensations are private" is comparable to: "One plays patience by oneself." (*PI* §248)

---

[2] For explicit definitions of strong supervenience, logical strong supervenience, and natural or nomological strong supervenience, see sub-section XVII.8.2 below.

6. The truistic, ordinary "privacy" of sensations, however, is fully consistent with the thesis that the meaning of a sensation-word is at least *partially* determined by the natural human bodily expressions of sensation, for example, grimacing or wincing when in pain, clutching the affected spot, and so-on:

> How do words *refer* to sensations? ... Here is one possibility: words are connected with the primitive, the natural expressions of the sensation and used in their place. A child has hurt himself and cries; and then adults talk to him and teach him exclamations and, later, sentences. They teach the child new pain-behavior (*Schmerzbenehmen*). "So you are saying that the word 'pain' really means crying?" —On the contrary, the verbal expression of pain replaces (*ersetzt*) crying and does not describe it. (*PI* §244)

> *How* do I use words to stand for my sensations? —As we ordinarily do? Then are my words for sensations tied up with my natural expressions of sensation? In that case my language is not a "private" one. Someone else might understand it as well as I. (*PI* §256)

> An "inner process" stands in need of outer criteria. (*PI* §580)

> The human body is the best picture of the human soul. (*PI* p. 178^e)

7. If 4., 5., and 6. are all true, then a necessary condition of having a sensation *is being the kind of creature that has the capacity to engage in the natural human bodily expressions of sensation*—i.e., living human beings and any other creatures there might be that comport themselves like living human beings:

> "But doesn't what you say come to this: that there is no pain, for example, without pain-behavior (*Schmerzbenehmen*)?" –It comes to this: only of a living human being and what resembles (behaves like) a living human being can one say: it has sensations; it sees; is blind; hears; is deaf; is conscious or unconscious. (*PI* §281)

> Only of what behaves (*was sich benimmt*) like a human being can one say that it *has* pains. (*PI* §283)

8. This thesis, however, does *not* imply that the subject of sensation is the human body as such, or any of its proper parts: instead, the subject of sensation is the *whole individual living human being, or living human person*, and this is immediately manifest and public in our ordinary ascriptions of sensations to others:

> But isn't absurd to say of a *body* that it has pain? —And why does one feel an absurdity here? In what sense is it true that that my hand does

not feel pain, but I in my my hand? What sort of issue is: Is it the *body* that feels pain? —How is it to be decided? What makes it plausible that it is *not* the body? —Well, something like this: if someone has a pain in his hand, then the hand does not say so (unless it writes it) and one does not comfort the hand, but the sufferer; one looks into his face. (*PI* §286)

If one has to imagine the pain of someone else's pain on the model of one's own, this is none too easy a thing to do: for I have to imagine pain which I *do not feel* on the model of pain which I *do feel*. That is, what I have to do is not simply to make a transition in imagination from one place of pain to another. As, from pain in the hand to pain in the arm. For I am not to imagine that I feel pain in some region of his body. (Which would also be possible.) Pain-behavior (*Schmerzbenehmen*) can point to a painful place—but the subject of pain is the person who gives it expression. (*PI* §302)

"I believe that he is suffering." —Do I also *believe* that he isn't an automaton?

It would go against the grain to use the word ["believe," i.e., *glaube*] in both connections. (Or is it like this: I believe that he is suffering, but am certain that he is not an automaton. Nonsense!) ….

"I believe that he is not an automaton," just like that, so far makes no sense. My attitude towards him is an attitude towards a soul. I am not of the *opinion* that he has a soul. (*PI* p. 178ᵉ)

9. And in turn, the fact that the subject of sensation is the whole living human being, or living human person, and not merely the human animal body of that person, also implies that sensation is *not* identical to "sensation-behavior" in the behaviorists' sense: for conceivably and in principle, pain-behaviors can be expressed by human persons without the corresponding pain-sensations, as per "super-fakers."

10. More generally however, mental states or mental processes are *activities of the whole living human being or living human person* that must also exist as "inner states" or "inner processes," along with their behavior.

11. So it's a synthetically (aka really or metaphysically) a priori necessarily false that there could be *human behavioral sensation-automata*, that is, *zombies* in the philosophical sense:

"But you will surely admit that there is a difference between pain-behavior accompanied by pain and pain-behavior without any pain?"

> Admit it? What greater difference could there be? "And yet you again and again reach the conclusion that the sensation is itself a *nothing*." —Not at all. It is not a *something*, but not a *nothing* either! The conclusion [of The Private Language Argument] was only that a nothing could serve just as well as a something about which nothing could be said. We have only rejected the grammar [of the private language of sensation] which tries to force itself on us here. (*PI* §304)

> "But surely you cannot deny that, for example, in remembering, an inner process takes place." —What gives the impression that we want to deny anything? (*PI* §305)

> Why should I deny that there is a mental process? But "There has just taken place in me the mental process of remembering ...," means nothing more than: "I have just remembered...." To deny the mental process would mean to deny the remembering; to deny that anyone ever remembers anything. (*PI* §306)

In this way, Wittgenstein's thesis that sensations in particular, and mental states and processes more generally, are activities of the whole human person, requiring at least the capacity to behave, and *allowing for* the conceptual or logical possibility of human sensation-behavior without corresponding sensations of that type, *but also denying* the real or metaphysical possibility of human sensation-behavior automata (i.e., zombies), is *not* a form of metaphysical behaviorism. More generally, however, metaphysical behaviorism is a reductive materialist or physicalist identity thesis (which also implies a corresponding logical supervenience thesis[3]) that's essentially based on a "grammatical fiction," i.e., a bad philosophical picture:

> "Are you not really a behaviorist in disguise? Aren't you at bottom really saying that everything except human behavior is a fiction?" —If I do speak of a fiction, then it is of a *grammatical fiction*. (*PI* §307)

So Wittgenstein *isn't* a metaphysical behaviorist. Sharply on the contrary, he's *a phenomenologist of human mindedness*. (For more on Wittgenstein as a phenomenologist, see the next chapter.) Therefore, what he's saying about sensations is nothing more and nothing less than this:

> necessarily, if X is a living human being or living human person, and X has a sensation, *then that sensation occurs only in and through the living human body of that living human being or living human human person, which in turn includes an irreducibly inner, first-person phenomenally conscious, aspect.*

---

[3] For explicit definitions of strong supervenience, logical strong supervenience, and natural or nomological strong supervenience, see sub-section XVII.8.2 below.

XIV. Wittgenstein and the *Investigations* 4: §§316-693 and 174ᵉ-232ᵉ

XIV.1 Linguistic Phenomenology

Now, finally, we can explore regions 6 and 7. The later Wittgenstein, I've claimed, is a phenomenologist of human mindedness: that's his brilliantly original view in the philosophy of mind. Correspondingly, his brilliantly original methodology in the philosophy of mind is, I think, most accurately described as *linguistic phenomenology*. In this sense, his methodology is importantly a reversion to the basic themes of the early phenomenological tradition—especially Husserl's *Logical Investigations*—yet *without* the solipsistic idealism that afflicts both the *Tractatus* and Husserl's transcendental phenomenology alike, and also *without* Husserl's lingering Cartesianism. Indeed, there are profound metaphysical and methodological parallels between Wittgenstein's linguistic phenomenology of human mindedness in the *Investigations* and Merleau-Ponty's *Phenomenology of Perception*. This, in turn, metaphilosophically means that the later Wittgenstein is every bit as much an (existential) phenomenologist as he is an Analytic philosopher, thereby performatively refuting the post-World War II hegemonic philosophical dogma that there not only *is* but also *must be* a Great Divide between Analytic philosophy and (existential) phenomenology. One easy way of witnessing this performative refutation is simply to recognize that that Wittgenstein's philosophical writing style is not only highly *literary-poetic*, but also highly *logico-analytical*, in a brilliantly integrated way that implicitly shatters another post-World War II hegemonic philosophical dogma to the effect that never the stylistic twain of Analytic and so-called "Continental" philosophy shall meet.[1] Indeed, in this stylistic regard, the *Investigations* strongly recalls Pascal's *Pensées*. In any case, as we've just seen, Wittgenstein's phenomenology of human mindedness theory fully avoids the reductive metaphysical, methodological, and semantic behaviorism of the logical empiricists/positivists and the Skinnerians.

Correspondingly, Wittgenstein's methodology of linguistic phenomenology flows from The Private Language Argument, which entails that (i) the meanings of sensation-words are neither wholly nor solely determined by what is inside individual speakers' heads (or Cartesian souls), i.e., **thesis 1: semantic anti-individualism for sensation language**. Assuming then that the meanings of words are determined either by what is inside the heads (or Cartesian souls) of individual speakers or by what is outside the heads (or Cartesian souls) of individual speakers, and that there are no other alternatives, it follows directly that (ii) the meanings of sensation-words are determined at least partially by what is outside the heads (or Cartesian souls) of individual speakers, i.e., **thesis 2: semantic externalism for sensation language**. This is in turn becomes the basis of a positive claim about the meaning

---

[1] See, e.g., (Vrahimis, 2019). Interestingly, Vrahimis doesn't explicitly mention that the *Investigations* is (just as, indeed, the *Tractatus* is, although in a modernist literary-poetic mode) an obvious counterexample to the dogma that Analytic philosophers must write in a logico-analytical style, whereas so-called "Continental" philosophers must write in a literary-poetic style—although it's pretty much implied by his approvingly citing one of Wittgenstein's remarks in *Culture and Value*, in note 14.

of sensation-words: (iii) the meaning of a sensation-word is at least partially determined by types of human bodily comportment, which function in particular contexts as criteria for the application of sensation-words, i.e., **thesis 3: bodily comportment and sensation language**. On the basis of these three claims, Wittgenstein then asserts four other positive theses about the nature of the human mind: (iv) sensation-words refer to private sensory experiences, but sensations are "private" only in the truistic, ordinary sense that only the living human person who actually has a particular token of a sensation-type, actually "has" that particular token sensation as an inner aspect of their essentially embodied, manifest, public human existence, i.e., **thesis 4: the token privacy of sensations**, (v) a necessary condition of X's having a token sensation is X's being essentially the kind of creature that has the capacity to express sensation-behavior only in and through its entire living organismic body: human beings and other animals constituted like human beings, i.e., **thesis 5: essential embodiment** (Hanna and Maiese, 2009: esp. chs. 1-2), (vi) the subject of a token sensation is the whole individual living human person, i.e., **thesis 6: sensation personalism**, and finally (vii) mental states and mental processes are inner activities of the whole living human person and its outer activities, and not any sort of static objects or things that could exist in the absence of such activities of the whole living human person, i.e., **thesis 7: the activist phenomenology of mental states and processes**.

XIV.2 Two Kinds of Seeing

In light of **theses 3, 4,** and **7**, Wittgenstein is able to conduct a robust phenomenological investigation of various types of inner mental states and mental processes, just by describing various uses of sensation language, hence he not only espouses but also actually engages in *linguistic phenomenology*. In particular, he undertakes the linguistic phenomenology of visual perception, and argues for the following four-part conclusion: (i) that there are two irreducibly and indeed categorically different kinds of seeing: (ia) *direct* seeing (aka "seeing-this"), and (ib) *interpretive* seeing (aka "seeing-as"), (ii) that interpretive seeing requires direct seeing, (iii) that interpretive seeing requires high-grade, self-conscious or reflective—and more specifically, conceptual, propositional, and logical—aka *intellectual*—cognitive capacities, whereas direct seeing does not, and (iv) that direct seeing can occur in the absence of interpretive seeing.

More explicitly now, here's a rational reconstruction of Wittgenstein's argument for these four claims.

> 1. It's one kind of phenomenon of visual experience to see *this* directly, and *another* distinct, and indeed categorically different, kind of phenomenon of visual experience to see this *as* having a certain visual aspect:
>
> > Two uses of the word "see." The one: "What do you see there?" – "I see *this*" (and then a description, a drawing, a copy). The other: "I see a likeness between these two faces"—let the man I tell this to be seeing the faces as clearly as I do myself. The importance of this is the

categorical difference between the two "objects" of sight. The one man might make an accurate drawing of the two faces, and the other notice in the drawing the likeness which the former did not see. I contemplate a face, and then suddenly notice its likeness to another. I *see* that it has not changed; and yet I see it differently. I call this experience "noticing an aspect." (*PI* p. 193ᵉ)

2. Interpretive seeing requires direct seeing:

> The description of the immediate experience, i.e., of the visual experience, by means of an interpretation—is an indirect description. "I see the figure as a box" means: I have a particular visual experience which I have found that I always have when I interpret the figure as a box or when I look at a box. But if it meant this I ought to know it. I ought to be able to refer to the experience directly, and not only indirectly. (*PI* pp. 193ᵉ-194ᵉ)

3. Interpretive seeing requires high-grade, self-conscious or reflective—and more specifically, conceptual, propositional, and logical—aka *intellectual*, cognitive capacities, including sub-capacities for (3i) multiple interpretations of the same direct visual object, for example, the "ambiguous figures" at *PI* pp. 193ᵉ and 200ᵉ), (3ii) multistability as between different aspects of the same direct visual object, for example, the figures at *PI* pp. 194ᵉ, 203ᵉ, and 207ᵉ—and also The Necker Cube at *TLP* 5.5423, (3iii) introduction of three dimensionality into 2D visual objects, for example, the figure at *PI* 203ᵉ and The Necker Cube again at *TLP* 5.5423), and (3iv) organizations of directly-seen shapes into pictorial representations, for example, Wittgenstein's sketch at *PI* p. 194ᵉ of the classical Jastrow diagram of the ambiguous duck-rabbit figure.

> You could imagine the following illustration appearing in several places in a book, a text book for instance. In the relevant text something different is in question every time: here a glass cube, there an inverted open box, there a wire frame of that shape, there three boards forming a solid angle. Each time the text supplies the interpretation of the illustration. But we can also *see* the illustration now as one thing now as another. –So we interpret it, and *see* it as we *interpret* it. (*PI* p. 193ᵉ)

> I shall call the following figure, derived from Jastrow, the duck-rabbit. It can be seen as a rabbit's head or as a duck's. And I must distinguish between the "continuous seeing" of an aspect and the "dawning" of an aspect. (*PI* p. 194ᵉ)

> The change of aspect. "But surely you would say that the picture is altogether different now!" But what is different: my impression? my point

of view? –Can I say? I *describe* the alteration like a perception; quite as if the object had altered before my eyes. (*PI* p . 195ᵉ)

"Seeing as …." is not part of perception. And for that reason it is like seeing and again not like…. If you are looking at the object, you need not think of it; but if you are having the visual experience expressed by the exclamation ["a rabbit!"], you are also *thinking* of what you see. Hence the flashing of an aspect on us seems half visual experience, half thought. (*PI* p. 197ᵉ)

How does one tell that human beings *see* three-dimensionally? …. The only thing that is natural to us is to represent what we see three-dimensionally; special practice and training are needed for two-dimensional representation whether in drawing or words. (The queerness of children's drawings.) (*PI* p. 198ᵉ)

Hold the drawing of a face upside down and you can't recognize the expression of the face. Perhaps you can see that it is smiling, but not exactly what *kind* of smile it is. You cannot imitate the smile or describe it more exactly. (*PI* p. 198ᵉ)

Of course we can say: There are certain things which fall equally under the concept "picture-rabbit" and under the concept "picture duck." And a picture, a drawing, is such a thing. –But the *impression* is not simultaneously of a picture- duck and a picture rabbit. (*PI* p. 199ᵉ)

Take as an example the aspects of a triangle. This triangle can be seen as a triangular hole, as a geometrical drawing; as standing on its base; as hanging from its apex; as a mountain, as a wedge, as an arrow or a pointer, as an overturned object which is meant to stand on the shorter side of the right-angle, as a half- parallelogram, and as various other things. (*PI* p. 200ᵉ)

Certain drawings are always seen as flat figures, and others three- dimensionally…. And then it seems queer that with some drawings our impression should be a flat thing, and with some a three-dimensional thing. One asks oneself "Where is this going to end?" (*PI* p. 202ᵉ)

"Is it a *genuine* visual experience?" The question is: in what sense is it one? Here is it difficult to see that what is at issue is the fixing of concepts. A *concept* forces itself on one. (This is what you must not forget.) (*PI* p204ᵉ)

The aspects of the triangle: it is as if an image came into contact, and for a time remained in contact, with the visual impression. In this, however, these aspects differ from the concave and convex aspects of the step (for example). And also from the aspects of the figure (which I shall call a "double cross")as a white cross on a black ground and a black cross on a white ground. You must remember that the descriptions of the elternating aspects are of a different kind in each case. (*PI* p. 207ᵉ)

4. But it's also possible for perceivers to *lack* certain abilities under one another of the sub-capacities for seeing aspects, and thereby to have "aspect-blindness" in that respect. Therefore, direct seeing can occur in the absence of interpretive seeing:

> The question now arises: Could there be human beings lacking in the capacity to see something as *something*—and what would that be like? What sort of consequences would it have? .... We will call it "aspect-blindness"—and will next consider what might be meant by this. (A conceptual investigation.) (*PI* p. 213ᵉ)

> The [humans who are] "aspect-blind" will have an altogether different relationship to pictures from ours. (Anomalies of *this* kind are easy for us to imagine.) Aspect blindness will be *akin* to the lack of a "musical ear." (*PI* p. 214ᵉ)

Although Wittgenstein doesn't explicitly say this, it also seems very easy to imagine creatures who are capable of direct seeing but also are either characteristically or else *constitutionally* aspect-blind, for example, infant humans and various kinds of non-human animals. This, in turn, strongly suggests that the distinction between the irreducibly and indeed categorically different capacities for direct seeing and interpretive seeing in normal adult humans is, in turn, a specific instance of two irreducible and indeed categorically different kinds of basic human cognitive capacities: (i) essentially *non*-conceptual capacities and (ii) essentially *conceptual* capacities, such that (ii) is asymmetrically grounded on (i), (i) *is* shared with human infants and non-human animals, aka "babes" and "beasts," and (ii) *isn't* shared with babes and beasts. Or in other words, the later Wittgenstein is a strong non-conceptualist *avant la lettre* (Bermúdez and Cahen, 2020; Dretske, 1969; Evans, 1982: esp. p. 150; Gunther, 2003; Hanna, 1993a, 1997, 2005, 2008a, 2015a: ch. 2, 2021b; McDowell, 1994; O'Shea, 2019; Speaks, 2005; Schulting, 2016; and section XVII.8.2 below).

XIV.3 Experiencing the Meaning of a Word

We've just seen that Wittgenstein's linguistic phenomenology of visual perception yields four substantive results: (i) that there are two irreducibly and categorically different kinds of seeing: (ia) *direct* seeing (aka "seeing-this," aka "essentially non-conceptual seeing"), and (ib) *interpretive* seeing (aka "seeing-as," aka "essentially conceptual seeing"), (ii) that interpretive seeing requires direct seeing, (iii) that interpretive seeing requires high-grade, self-conscious or reflective—and more specifically, conceptual, propositional, and logical—aka *intellectual*—cognitive capacities, whereas direct seeing does not, and (iv) that direct seeing can occur in the absence of interpretive seeing. In the final phase of the *Investigations*, Wittgenstein extends these four claims to the linguistic phenomenology of *experiencing the meaning of a word*. This fascinating investigation then completes the whole argument of the *Investigations* by returning us full-circle to the meaning-is-use thesis and by demonstrating some further positive theses about the concept of use.

Here's a rational reconstruction of that final phase of argumentation:

1. Just as there's a linguistic phenomenology of seeing, so too there's an analogously structured linguistic phenomenology of experiencing the meaning of a word:

> The importance of this concept [of aspect blindness] lies in the connection between the concepts of "seeing an aspect" and "experiencing the meaning of a word." For we want to ask "What would you be missing if you did not *experience* the meaning of a word?" What would you be missing if you did not understand the request to pronounce the word "till" and to mean it as a verb, —or if you did not feel that a word lost its meaning and became a mere sound if it was repeated ten times over? (*PI* p. 214^e) [See substantive result (iv) directly above.]

> When I pronounce this word while reading with expression it is completely filled with meaning. –"How can this be, if meaning is the use of the word?" Well, what I said was intended figuratively. Not that I chose the figure: it forced itself on me. (*PI* p. 215^e) [See substantive result (i) directly above.]

> "But what is this queer experience?" –Of course it is not queerer than any other; it simply differs in kind from those experiences which we regard as the most fundamental ones, our sense impressions for instance. (*PI* p. 215^e) [See substantive result (ii) directly above.]

> You can say the word "March" to yourself and mean it at one time as an imperative at another as the name of a month. And now say "March!"— and then "March *no further!*" —Does the *same* experience accompany the word both times—are you sure? (*PI* p. 215^e) [See substantive result (iii) directly above]

2. But the phenomenology of experiencing the meaning of a word also saliently *differs from* the phenomenology of seeing, in that words can be sometimes used "transparently," that is, *without* any special experience of meaning:

> If a sensitive ear shows me, when I am playing this game [with "March"], that I have now *this* now *that* experience of the word—doesn't it also show me that often I do not have any experience of it in the course of talking? —For the fact that I also mean it, intend it, now like *this* now like *that*, and maybe also say so later is, of course, not in question. (*PI* pp. 215ᵉ-216ᵉ)

3. Therefore *the meaning of a word*—i.e., its use, which necessarily involves both its function and its application—is not the same as *experiencing the meaning of a word*:

> Someone tells me: "Wait for me by the bank." Question: Did you, as you were saying the word, mean this bank? –This question is of the same kind as "Did you intend to say such-and-such to him on your way to meet him?" It refers to a definite time (the time of walking, as the former question refers to the time of speaking)—but not to an *experience* during that time. Meaning is as little an experience as intending. (*PI* pp. 216ᵉ–217ᵉ)

> Meaning is not a process which accompanies a word. For no *process* could have the consequences of meaning. (*PI* p. 217ᵉ)

> "At that word we both thought of him." Let us assume that each of us said the same words to himself—and how can it mean MORE that that?—But wouldn't even those words contain only a *germ*? The must surely belong to a language and to a context, in order really to be the expression of the thought *of* that man. If God had looked into our minds he would not have been able to see there whom we were speaking of. (*PI* pp. 217ᵉ)

4. Nevertheless the speaker's possession of a *human cognitive capacity* for experiencing the meaning of a word is at least a necessary (although not a sufficient) condition of using a word meaningfully:

Experiencing a meaning and experiencing a mental image. "In both cases," we should like to say, "we are experiencing something, only something different. A different content is proffered—is present—to consciousness." –What is the content of imagining? The answer is a picture or a description. And what is the content of the experience of meaning? I don't know what I am supposed to say to this.—If there is any sense in the above remark, it is that the two concepts are related like "red" and "blue" [i.e., two determinates under the same determinable concept *conscious experience*]; and that is wrong. (*PI* pp. 175ᵉ-176ᵉ)

The importance of this concept [of aspect blindness] lies in the connection between the concepts of "seeing an aspect" and "experiencing the meaning of a word." For we want to ask "What would you be missing if you did not *experience* the meaning of a word?" What would you be missing if you did not understand the request to pronounce the word "till" and to mean it as a verb, —or if you did not feel that a word lost its meaning and became a mere sound if it was repeated ten times over? (*PI* p. 214ᵉ)

"Talking" (whether out loud or silently) and "thinking" are not concepts of the same kind; even though they are in closest connection. (*PI* p. 217ᵉ)

XIV.4 The Critique of Logical Analysis, and Logic-As-Grammar

We're now in a position to return explicitly to the main theme of *The Fate of Analysis*—the philosophically chequered but (after 1950) social-institutionally dominant and indeed (since the mid-1980s) hegemonic career of Analytic philosophy from Frege to this morning at 6am, and the spiralling descent of recent and contemporary post-classical Analytic philosophy into the ash-heap of history—from the later Wittgenstein's standpoint, i.e., under a later-Wittgensteinian *aspect*. Later Wittgenstein is, as it were, the supposedly mainstream classical Analytic *duck* who spontaneously flips over into being an *anti*-Analytic, existential-phenomenological, and Southwest/Baden-style neo-Kantian *trans*-Analytic *rabbit*: for further elaboration of that (in effect, second Copernican) revolutionary thought, see chapters XV and XVIII below. But in the present context, I want to focus on how this *metaphilosophical multistability* manifests itself in his philosophically liberating proposal that logic is really nothing but grammar.

Here's a rational reconstruction of that emancipatory line of thinking.

1. Frege, Russell, and the author of the *Tractatus* all hold the thesis that logic is something "sublime": universal, a priori, necessary, and essential to everything in the empirical world, as well as essential to language, propositions, and thought (*PI* §§ 89, 90, 92, 97).

2. Furthermore, logic is required to carry out a complete decompositional analysis of our forms of language, propositions, and thoughts, which reveals their "hidden" and "simple" structures and constituents, that is, their decomposable essences (*PI* §§91-92).

3. This in turn implies that language, propositions, thought, and the world all *possess* decomposable essences (*PI* §§ 93-96).

4. But in fact, (4i) every sentence in our language is in order just as it is, (4ii) vagueness (via the pervasive family resemblance nature of all concepts) is a *constitutive* feature of meaning, (4iii) language is essentially a spatiotemporal phenomenon, not something abstract, and (4iv) the essence of language, proposition, thought, and the world is something that "already lies open to view and that becomes surveyable by a rearrangement" (*PI*§§92, 98-100, 108-109).

5. So neither language, nor propositions, nor thought, nor the world have hidden decomposable essences, and therefore the thesis that logic is sublime is false.

6. Furthermore the thesis that logic is sublime turns out to be only a methodological assumption we have unintentionally imposed upon the phenomena, indeed nothing but an artifact of an idealized bad philosophical "picture" that lay hidden in our language and held us captive (*PI* §§101-108, and 110-115).

7. On the contrary, however,

> the philosophy of logic speaks of sentences and words in exactly the sense in which we speak of them in ordinary life when we say, e.g., "Here is a Chinese sentence," or "No, that only looks like writing; it is actually an ornament' and so on." (*PI* §108)

That is: we can regard logic as purely descriptive or re-descriptive, *not* essentialist and a priorist; and in this way, "what *we* do is to bring words back from their metaphysical use to their everyday use" by asking "is the word ever actually used in this way in the language which is its original home" (*PI* §116).

8. Therefore, we should assert the thesis that logic is really nothing but grammar, which

> sheds light on our problem by clearing misunderstandings away. Misunderstandings concerning the use of words, caused, among other things by certain analogies between the forms of expression in different regions of language .... [and] some of them can be removed by substituting one form of expression for another; this may be called an "analysis" of our forms of expression, for the process is sometimes like one of taking things apart. (PI § 90)

And for an explicit example of this, see the discussion of negation at PI §§547-557.

9. Furthermore, the goal of logic or grammar is to produce a "perspicuous representation" of language, propositions, thought, human mindedness, and the world, which produces "that understanding which consists in 'seeing connections'" (*PI* §122).

10. Therefore, logic *isn't* sublime, and logical analysis as logical-decompositional analysis is *impossible*, but on the contrary logic-as-grammar is *really possible*, and grammar in this sense is the descriptive logic of our language games, as embedded in our forms of life. And to the extent that logic as a theory of valid reasoning still exists in logic-as-grammar, this logic is *strongly non-classical* (Haack, 1996; Priest, 2001).

If Wittgenstein's argument against the sublimity of logic is sound, *then logical analysis is impossible*, and the classical Analytic tradition has collapsed. So then what, more precisely, does philosophical analysis become for Wittgenstein after the collapse of logical analysis, and in effect, the collapse of classical Analytic philosophy? We'll need to approach the answer to this question in two stages.

First, later Wittgenstein's conception of philosophical analysis in fact shares some fundamental features in common with his activist conception of analyis in the *Tractatus*. But this new activist conception of analysis is now *minus the sublimity of logic*, that is to say, minus the comprehensive *noumenal* bad philosophical picture of logic, language, thought, human mindedness, and the world that would justify the logical-decompositional theory of analysis. Here are some relevant texts describing this new form of philosophical analysis:

> Philosophy is a battle against the bewitchment of our intelligence by means of language. (*PI* §109)

> The results of philosophy are the uncovering of one or another piece of plain nonsense and of bumps that the understanding has got by running its head up against the limits of language. (*PI* §119)

> A philosophical problem has the form: "I don't know my way about." (*PI* §123)

> Philosophy may in no way interfere with the actual use of language; it can in the end only describe it. For it cannot give it any foundation either. It leaves everything as it is. (*PI* §124)

> The civil status of a contradiction, or its status in civil life: there is the philosophical problem. (*PI* §125)

> Philosophy simply puts everything before us, and neither explains nor deduces anything. —Since everything lies open to view, there is nothing to explain. For what is hidden, for example, is of no interest to us. One might give the name "philosophy" to what is possible *before* all new discoveries and inventions. (*PI* §126)

> The work of the philosopher consists in assembling reminders for a particular purpose. (*PI* §127)

> If one tried to advance *theses* in philosophy, it would never be possible to question them, because everyone would agree to them. (*PI* §128)

> It is not our aim to refine or complete the system of rules for the use of words in unheard-of ways. For the clarity that we are aiming at is indeed *complete*

clarity. But that simply means that the philosophical problems should *completely* disappear. The real discovery is one that makes me capable of stopping doing philosophy when I want to.

—The one that gives philosophy peace, so that it is no longer tormented by questions which bring *itself* into question.... There is not *a* philosophical method, though there are indeed methods, like different therapies. *(PI* §133)

We are not analysing a phenomenon (e.g. thought) but a concept (e.g. that of thinking), and therefore the use of a word. *(PI* §383)

In philosophy we do not draw conclusions. "But it must be like this!" is not a philosophical proposition. Philosophy only states what everyone admits. *(PI* §599)

I'll call this *dialectical conceptual analysis*, where, as in Kant's sense of the term, "dialectical" means *about or concerning the logical critique of metaphysical illusion in philosophy, as a form of rational self-knowledge* (CPR A61-62/B85-86, A293-298/B349-354). The main idea is that by deploying a strongly non-classical logic, the later Wittgensteinian philosophical analyst or logical grammarian (i) displays and diagnoses the dialectical structure of philosophical problems, (ii) describes, unpacks, compares, and contrasts the concepts implicit in our various ordinary uses of language and states truisms about them, and then (iii) it simply *stops doing philosophy*: i.e., it simply *stops doing (classical or post-classical) Analytic philosophy*.

Second, the other crucial thing about Wittgenstein's later conception of philosophical analysis is that it's is fundamentally desire-based, emotive, normative, and practical (aka "non-cognitive"). According to this non-cognitivist view, philosophical analysis is neither a formal or natural science, nor indeed in any sense a source of factual knowledge, but instead essentially a self-conscious and deliberate practice—hence we can truly call it "doing philosophy," a phrase that unfortunately nowadays has become a trite cliché. But its original, emancipatory, and indeed revolutionary later-Wittgensteinian meaning is that the aim of the practice of doing philosophy is seeing crosswise conceptual connections, but *not* decompositional conceptual connections (except in highly restricted contexts), and thereby finally achieving perspicuous insight into what already is completely there already in front of us: human beings and their linguistic activities in their human world, that is, *forms of human life*:

> So you are saying that human agreement decides what is true and what is false?— It is what human beings *say* that is true and false; and they agree in the *language* they use. That is not agreement in opinions but in form of life. *(PI* §241)

This linguistic agreement in form of life, in turn, is given essentially in the activity of making judgments:

> If language is to be a means of communication there must be agreement not only in definitions but also (queer as this may sound) in judgments. This seems to abolish logic, but does not do so. (*PI* §242)

In other words: our linguistic agreement in form of life *consists in our shared human capacity for logical and practical rationality.*

Now, as the Wittgensteinian duck of classical Analytic philosophy spontaneously flips over into the Wittgensteinian rabbit of anti-Analytic and trans-Analytic philosophy, what is to be done? Here's the post-classical Analytic philosopher Donald Davidson's apt formulation of the fundamental connection between primary reasons and human agency:

> In the light of a primary reason, an action is revealed as coherent with certain traits, long- or short-termed, of the agent, and the agent is shown in his role of Rational Animal. (Davidson, 1963: p. 690)

In the light of this, we can say that the new and revolutionary aim of philosophical analysis for the later Wittgenstein is, by linguistic-phenomenological means, to achieve insight into the nature of a humanly-minded linguistic agent in their role as a Judging Animal. Or even more specifically put: in the inherently emotively-, normatively- and practically-oriented Kantian, existential-phenomenological, and Southwest/Baden-style neo-Kantian tradition of philosophical logic to which Wittgenstein's later philosophy belongs, *Rational Human Minded Animals* are nothing more and nothing less than *Talking Animals*, who in turn are nothing more and nothing less than *Judging Animals* (Hanna, 2017d).

XV. Coda: Wittgenstein and Kantianism

> The limit of language is shown by its being impossible to describe the fact which corresponds to (is the translation of) a sentence, without simply repeating the sentence. (This has to do with the Kantian solution of the problem of philosophy.) (Wittgenstein, 1980: p. 10^e)

> May God grant the philosopher insight into what lies in front of everyone's eyes. (Wittgenstein, 1980: p. 63^e)

In musicological terminology, a "coda" is a concluding passage that briefly recapitulates the basic structure of the whole piece of music that it concludes. In this chapter, I'll do that philosophically for my close, critical readings of Wittgenstein's *Tractatus* and *Investigations* in relation to Kantianism.

During the 1970s, Peter Hacker and Bernard Williams argued that Wittgenstein was a Kantian transcendental idealist (Hacker, 1972; Williams, 1981). In the 1980s, Hacker officially rescinded this interpretation (Hacker, 1986: pp. ix, 206-214); and Williams in any case regarded Wittgenstein's transcendental idealism as a philosophical mistake. And ever since, there's been a lively debate about Wittgenstein's Kantianism, anti-Kantianism, or non-Kantianism. In my opinion, however, this particular line of Wittgenstein-interpretation and debate was a *dead letter* from the start: for if I'm correct, then Hacker and Williams adopted a false, or at least needlessly uncharitable, conception of Kant's transcendental idealism in particular and also of his Critical philosophy more generally, from the get-go—hence the gambit of interpreting Wittgenstein as a transcendental idealist or Critical philosopher in *that* sense was bound to lead to "obscurity and contradictions" (*Dunkelheit und Widersprüche*) (*CPR* Aviii). But if we revolutionize the way we think about Kant, we can, correspondingly, revolutionize the way we think about Wittgenstein in the light of Kant's transcendental idealism and the Critical philosophy; and that, in turn, can revolutionize the way we think about Analytic philosophy, both classical and post-classical (see also chapter XVIII below).

No one doubts that throughout his philosophical writings, Wittgenstein saw a fundamental connection between language and human life. But if I'm correct, then not only is Wittgenstein's conception of human language is essentially the same as Kant's Critical conception of human rationality, but also Wittgenstein and Kant are jointly engaged in the self-same philosophical project of what Jonathan Lear aptly dubs *transcendental anthropology* (Lear 1982, 1986; Lear and Stroud, 1984). What's transcendental anthropology? The short-and-sweet answer is that it's a way of doing philosophy which tells us (i) how the veridically apparent or manifestly real world *must be*, in order to conform to the innately specified forms and structures of the basic cognitive and practical capacities of rational human animals, (ii) how rational human animals *must choose, act, and try to live*, in order to conform to the highest norms, rules, and standards they legislate for themselves, and also, tragically, almost inevitably fail to meet, and (iii) how philosophy *must not be*, because otherwise it will inevitably, and tragically, fall into logical antinomy, radical skepticism, and cognitive/practical self-alienation.

In view of (ii) and (iii), we can clearly see how transcendental anthropology is also an intimate fellow-traveler with Existentialism and/or existential phenomenology (Barnes, 1959; Solomon, 1974; Crowell, 2012)—as expressed, for example, in Augustine's *Confessions* or Pascal's *Pensées* (which Kant would have known), and in Kierkegaard's *Fear and Trembling* or Dostoevsky's *Brothers Karamazov* (which Wittgenstein knew), early Heidegger's *Being and Time* (which Wittgenstein knew), and Merleau-Ponty's *Phenomenology of Perception*—and shares with Existentialism and existential phenomenology a radically metaphysically anthropocentric, meta-philosophically critical, morally-charged, and ultimately *tragic* sense of human life (Cavell, 1979: esp. parts 1-2; Bearn, 1997; Unamuno, 2005). Otherwise put, transcendental anthropology is *the philosophy of the rational human condition*. Moreover, as I noted earlier in section XI.1, just as the *Tractatus* is arguably, in effect, a brilliantly original variation on Marburg-style, logicistic neo-Kantianism, so too later Wittgenstein's transcendental anthropology in the *Investigations* and *On Certainty* is arguably, in effect, a brilliantly original variation on Southwest/Baden-style human-science-oriented and value-theory-oriented neo-Kantianism.

Lear's critical judgment on the later Wittgenstein's transcendental anthropology is that it's ultimately a failure, due to an incoherence between the prima-facie-opposed "transcendental" (i.e., non-empirical) and "anthropological" (i.e., empirical) levels of reflection (Lear, 1986: esp. pp. 283-293). As will become evident in the course of this chapter, however, my critical judgment is just the reverse. I think that Lear failed to understand Kant's transcendental idealism in the right way, and also failed to take into proper account the existential dimensions in Kant's and Wittgenstein's philosophical thinking.

If I'm correct, then that's the "big picture" into which we can fit Wittgenstein, Kant, and the Existentialists/existential phenomenologists alike. But the specific purpose of this chapter, as a coda to my close readings of the *Tractatus* and the *Investigations* in chapters V-VIII and X-XIII respectively, is to explore two central themes in the philosophy of early and later Wittgenstein alike, as deeply motivated by Kant and also importantly inflected by existential/existential-phenomenological insights: (i) how the veridically apparent, aka manifestly real,[1] world *necessarily conforms to human mind and life,* and (ii) the critique of *self-alienated philosophy*, paradigmatically represented by classical Analytic philosophy as Wittgenstein knew it first-hand, but also and especially by post-classical Analytic philosophy as it was saliently emerging after World War II up to the time of Wittgenstein's death in 1951, and already beginning to assert and secure its 70-years-plus social-institutional domination of Anglo-American professional academic philosophy, right up to 6am this morning.

---

[1] On the crucial distinction between (i) authentic, *veridical* appearances, which are intersubjectively objective (the totality of which make up the manifestly real world) and (ii) mere, *falsidical* appearances, which are purely subjective and idiosyncratic (e.g., illusions, hallucinations, etc.), see (Hanna, 2017d).

XV.1 World-Conformity 1: Kant, Transcendental Idealism, and Empirical Realism

According to Kant, a mental representation is *transcendental* when it is either part of, or derived from, our non-empirical (hence a priori) innately specified spontaneous cognitive capacities (*CPR* A11/B25, *Prol* 4: 373n.). Then Kant's transcendental idealism (TI) can be formulated as a two-part philosophical equation:

TI = (i) Representational Transcendentalism + (ii) Cognitive Idealism.

What do these terms mean? Here's what. (i) *Representational Transcendentalism*: Necessarily, all the forms or structures of rational human cognition are generated a priori by the empirically-triggered, yet stimulus-underdetermined, activities of our innately specified spontaneous cognitive capacities (i.e. cognitive competences, cognitive faculties, cognitive powers). (ii) *Cognitive Idealism*: Necessarily, all the proper objects of rational human cognition are sensory appearances or phenomena (i.e. mind-dependent, spatiotemporal, directly perceivable, veridically apparent or manifestly real objects) and never things-in-themselves or noumena in the positive sense (i.e. mind-independent, non-sensible, non-spatiotemporal, real essences constituted by intrinsic non-relational properties) (*CPR* A369, *Prol* 4: 293-94, 375). Now (i) + (ii) also = Kant's "Copernican revolution" in metaphysics (*CPR* Bxvi), which I will rationally reconstruct as (iii) *The Conformity Thesis*: It's not the case that rational human minds passively conform to the objects they cognize, as in classical rationalism and classical empiricism. On the contrary, necessarily, all the proper objects of rational human cognition conform to—i.e., they have the same form or structure as, or are isomorphic to—the forms or structures that are non-empirically generated by our innately specified spontaneous cognitive capacities. So necessarily the essential forms or structures of the veridically apparent or manifestly real world we cognize are mind-dependent. In this way, all versions of Kant's TI hold that the veridically apparent or manifestly real world we cognize conforms to the non-empirical forms or structures of our innately specified cognitive capacities in some modally robust sense.

Correspondingly, many Kantians are committed to what I call *strong transcendental idealism* (STI), which says (i) that things-in-themselves (aka *noumena* in the positive sense, or "really-real" things, i.e. things as they could exist in a "lonely" way, altogether independently of rational human minds or anything else, by virtue of their intrinsic non-relational properties) really exist and cause our perceptions, although rational human cognizers only ever perceive mere, "falsidical" (i.e., the contrary of "veridical") appearances, i.e., subjective phenomena, (ii) that rational human cognizers actually impose the non-empirical forms or structures of their innate cognitive capacities onto the apparent or manifest world they cognize—i.e. necessarily, all the essential forms or structures of the proper objects of human cognition are literally type-identical to the a priori forms or structures that are non-empirically generated by our innately specified spontaneous cognitive capacities, and (iii) that necessarily, if all rational human cognizers went out of existence, then so would the merely, falsidically apparent or subjective world they cognize.

But some other Kantians (especially including me, as someone whose view is both broadly and also radically Kantian) think that Kant's STI is objectively false and are committed instead only to the objective truth of what I call *weak or counterfactual transcendental idealism* (WCTI), which says (i) that things-in-themselves are logically possible, but at the same time it is knowably unknowable and unprovable whether things-in-themselves exist or not, hence for the purposes of an adequate anthropocentric or "human-faced" metaphysics, epistemology, and ethics, they can be ignored (*radical agnosticism and methodological eliminativism about things-in-themselves*) (Hanna, 2017c), (ii) necessarily, all the proper objects of rational human cognition have the same forms or structures as—i.e., they are isomorphic to—the forms or structures that are non-empirically generated by our innately-specified spontaneous cognitive capacities, but at the same time those apparent or manifest worldly forms or structures are not literally type-identical to those a priori cognitive forms or structures (*the isomorphism-without-type-identity thesis*), (iii) it's a necessary condition of the existence of the veridically apparent or manifestly real world that if some rational human animals *were* to exist in that world, then they *would* veridically cognize that world, via either essentially non-conceptual (i.e. intuitional) content or conceptual content, at least to some extent (*the counterfactual cognizability thesis*), and (iv) the veridically apparent or manifestly real world has at some earlier times existed without any rational human animals to cognize it veridically, and could exist even if no rational human animals ever existed to cognize it veridically, even though some rational human animals now do actually exist in that world—for example, I (R.H.) now actually exist in the veridically apparent, manifestly real world—who do in fact cognize it veridically, at least to some extent (*the existential thesis*). Otherwise put, Kant's WCTI says that, necessarily, the veridically apparent or manifestly real world we really cognize is pre-formatted for our cognition—but it exists *outside* our heads, not *inside* our heads.

Whether one accepts STI or (as I think, the correct view) WCTI, it remains importantly true that Kant's TI is sharply distinct from Berkeley's *subjective or phenomenal idealism* and also from Cartesian *skeptical idealism*. TI entails that necessarily some directly knowable material things actually exist outside my conscious states (i.e. inner sense) in space; in other words, it entails the falsity of both Berkeleyan subjective or phenomenal idealism and Cartesian skeptical idealism alike, and also the truth of empirical realism:

> [The empirical realist] grants to matter, as appearance, a reality which need not be inferred, but is immediately perceived [*unmittelbar wahrgenommen*]. (*CPR* A371)

> Every outer perception ... immediately proves [*beweiset unmittelbar*] something real in space, or rather is itself the real; to that extent, empirical realism is beyond doubt, i.e., to our outer intuitions there corresponds something real in space. (*CPR* A375)

And this empirical realism is in fact the explicit two-part conclusion of Kant's "Refutation of Idealism":

The consciousness of my existence is at the same time [*zugleich*] an immediate consciousness of the existence of other things outside me. (*CPR* B276)

XV.2 World-Conformity 2: Wittgenstein, Transcendental Solipsism, and Pure Realism

As we saw in chapters V-VIII above, Wittgenstein's *Tractatus* offers a radically new conception of philosophical analysis, according to which (i) metaphysics reduces to the propositions of logic, including both the truth-functional tautologies and also the logico-philosophical truths of the *Tractatus* itself, (ii) facts reduce to logically-structured complexes of ontologically neutral "objects," which can variously play the structural roles of both particulars and universals (including both properties and relations), (iii) factual propositions are nothing but linguistic facts that "picture" other facts according to one-to-one isomorphic correspondence relations, (iv) all non-factual propositions are either (iva) "senseless" (*sinnlos*) truth-functional tautologies expressing nothing but the formal meanings and deductive implications of the logical constants, or (ivb) the logico-philosophical propositions of the *Tractatus* itself, or (ivc) "nonsensical" (*unsinnig*) pseudo-propositions that violate logico-syntactic rules and logico-semantic categories, especially including all the synthetic a priori claims of traditional metaphysics, (v) the logical constants do not represent facts or refer to objects of any sort (*TLP* 4.0312), but instead merely "display" (*darstellen*) the a priori logical "scaffolding of the world" (*TLP* 6.124), which is also "the limits of my language" (*TLP* 5.6), and can only be "shown" or non- propositionally indicated, not "said" or propositionally described, (vi) the logical form of the world is therefore "transcendental"—

6.13 Logic is not a theory but a reflexion of the world.

Logic is transcendental.

—and finally (vii) the logical form of the world reduces to the language-using metaphysical subject or ego, who or which is not in any way part of the world but in fact solipsistically identical to the world itself:

5.63 I am my world. (The microcosm.)

5.632 The subject does not belong to the world but it is a limit of the world.

Looking at theses (v), (vi), and (vii), we can clearly see that Wittgenstein's radically new conception of philosophical logic is correspondingly radically ontologically ascetic, since everything logically reduces to one simple thing: the language-using metaphysical subject or ego. Indeed, it's by means of theses (v) and (vi) that Wittgenstein directly expresses the surprising and often-overlooked but quite indisputable fact, as I've noted several times, that the *Tractatus* is every bit as much a neo-Kantian idealistic metaphysical treatise inspired by Schopenhauer's neo-Kantian *World as Will and Representation* (Brockhaus, 1991), and, at least implicitly, belonging to the Marburg-style logicistic neo-Kantian tradition, as it is a logico-philosophical treatise inspired by Frege's *Begriffsschrift*, Frege's critique of psychologism, Moore's and Russell's revolt against idealism, and Russell's and Whitehead's *Principia Mathematica*.

Now, let's recapitulate the reasons for holding this view.

We know that Wittgenstein first carefully read and studied *The Critique of Pure Reason* along with Ludwig Hänsel in 1918 (Monk, 1990: p. 158), three years before the publication of the *Tractatus*. I don't think that Wittgenstein's reading of the first *Critique* in 1918 directly or substantially influenced the *Tractatus* itself, since in fact virtually no changes were made to the manuscript of the *Tractatus* between 1918 and its publication in 1921 (Potter, 2009). But as I've argued in earlier chapters I do think that Wittgenstein's early philosophy is essentially the result of his indirect engagement with Kant's Critical philosophy, via Schopenhauer, prior to 1918, and also that Wittgenstein's later philosophy is essentially, although mostly implicitly and without fanfare, the result of Wittgenstein's direct engagement with Kant's Critical philosophy after 1918. So whereas Moore and Russell explicitly abandoned and rejected Kant's Critical epistemology and metaphysics, Wittgenstein, both early and late, creatively absorbed and sublimated them.

From this standpoint, again, we can see that the *Tractatus* is basically an essay in transcendental logic—hence a certain kind of neo-Kantian logicism—in the Marburg-style logicistic neo-Kantian sense. As Wittgenstein stresses in the Preface of the *Tractatus*, he "makes no claim to novelty in points of detail" and doesn't care whether he is borrowing ideas from other philosophers, especially Frege and Russell. It's also very clear from the *Notebooks 1914-16*, that Wittgenstein was heavily influenced by Schopenhauer. Indeed, as I mentioned in section V.1, (i) Wittgenstein told von Wright that "he had read Schopenhauer's *Die Welt als Wille und Vorstellung* in his youth and that his first philosophy was a Schopenhauerian epistemological idealism" (Von Wright, 1984: p. 6), (ii) in 1920, Wittgenstein wrote to Frege about "deep grounds for idealism" (*tiefen Gründe des Idealismus*) (Monk, 1990: pp. 190, 605), and (iii) in 1931, Wittgenstein wrote that "Boltzmann, Hertz, Schopenhauer, Frege, Russell, Kraus, Loos, Weininger, Spengler, [and] Sraffa have influenced me" (Wittgenstein, 1980: p. 19e, underlining added). It's notable that Kant's name does not appear on this list. But as the first epigraph of this chapter shows, in 1931 Wittgenstein also saw a fundamental parallel between his own work and "the Kantian solution to the problem of philosophy."

More precisely: if I'm correct, then (1) in the *Tractatus* Wittgenstein accepts the basic framework of Kant's transcendental idealism/empirical realism and theory of cognition, and in particular Wittgenstein accepts a version of strong transcendental idealism or STI, but rejects Kant's "modal dualism" of analytic and synthetic a priori necessary truths and opts for a "modal monism" of logically necessary truths, (2) in the *Tractatus* Wittgenstein accepts Schopenhauer's reduction of both the noumenal metaphysical subject and the noumenal metaphysical object (or thing-in-itself) of Kant's transcendental idealism, to the will, (3) in the *Tractatus* Wittgenstein accepts the Frege-Russell idea that logic is first philosophy, but rejects both of their conceptions of logic: for Wittgenstein, logic is neither the science of laws of truth nor the absolutely general science of deduction; instead,

XV. Coda: Wittgenstein and Kantianism

for Wittgenstein, logic is transcendental in the Kantian sense, hence, again, Wittgenstein's view is a specifically neo-Kantian version of logicism, implicitly and unofficially, even if not explicitly and officially, very much in the tradition of contemporary Marburg-style logicistic neo-Kantians like Ernst Cassirer:

> Light on Kant's question "How is pure mathematics possible?" through the theory of tautologies. (Wittgenstein, 1979a: p. 15^e)

As we saw in chapter VIII above, one of the initially most puzzling features of the *Tractatus* is its background metaphysics of *solipsism* and *pure realism*:

> 5.64 Here we see that solipsism strictly carried out coincides with pure realism. The I in solipsism shrinks to an extensionless point and there remains the reality co-ordinated with it.

> 5.641 There is therefore really a sense in which in philosophy we can talk of a non-psychological I.

> The I occurs in philosophy through the fact that "the world is my world."

> The philosophical I is not the man, not the human body or the human soul of which psychology treats, but the metaphysical subject, the limit—not a part of the world.

These propositions compactly express Wittgenstein's creative absorption and sublimation of Kant's transcendental idealism, in the specific sense of strong transcendental idealism or STI, and also Kant's empirical realism, in the first *Critique*. In the *Notebooks, 1914-1916*, Wittgenstein even more explicitly presents this line of thinking:

> This is the way I have travelled: Idealism singles men out from the world as unique, solipsism singles me alone out, and at last I see that I too belong with the rest of the world, and so on the one side *nothing* is left over, and on the other side, as unique, *the world*. In this way idealism leads to realism if it is strictly thought out. (Wittgenstein, 1979a: p. 85^e)

Now, the role-players of the specific ontological and epistemic roles of things-in-themselves or noumena in STI are Wittgenstein's *objects* (*TLP* 2.014-2.0232). Correspondingly, the role-players of the specific ontological and epistemic roles of empirically real appearances, aka "objects of experience," in STI are Wittgenstein's atomic facts (*TLP* 1-2.11). So in these ways, according to Wittgenstein, *I* am my world (*TLP* 5.63) and the world is *my* world (*TLP* 5.641), the subject does not belong to the world but is a limit of the world (*TLP* 5.631-5.632), and the metaphysical subject is a non-psychological ego (*TLP* 5.633, 5.641).

What basic reasons does Wittgenstein have for holding this specifically Schopenhauerian, Marburg-style, logicistic neo-Kantian, and solipsistic version of Kant's STI? The answer is that these basic reasons follow directly from (i) the Tractarian thesis that the world of facts is constructed by the language-using subject, together with (ii) the Tractarian thesis that the objects, or Wittgensteinian things-in-themselves, are given as an independent constraint on language and thought, together with (iii) the Tractarian thesis that language is fundamentally a language of thought. In short, Wittgenstein's specifically Schopenhauerian, Marburg-style logicistic neo-Kantian, and solipsistic version of Kant's STI in the *Tractatus* is *linguistic STI* (LSTI):

> 5.6 *The limits of my language* mean the limits of my world.

Strikingly, Wittgenstein's transcendental solipsism, i.e. his LSTI, has two importantly distinct although fully complementary dimensions: (i) a transcendental solipsism/LSTI of the representing subject, and (ii) a transcendental solipsism/LSTI of the willing subject. Or, as he puts it:

> 6.373 The world is independent of my will.
>
> 6.43 If good or bad willing changes the world, it can only change the limits of the world, not the facts; not the things that can be expressed in language.
>
> In brief, the world must thereby become quite another. It must wax or wane as a whole.
>
> The world of the happy man is a different one from that of the unhappy man.

Wittgenstein's transcendental solipsism/LSTI of *the representing subject* says that all worldly facts are metaphysically dependent on my mind in the double sense (i) that linguistic form (and its a priori essence, logical form) enters directly into the constitution of every fact, and (ii) that language itself is constructed by the individual subject. But Wittgenstein's solipsism/LSTI of *the willing subject*, by sharp contrast, says that the specific internal nature of the objects is metaphysically dependent on my attitudes, desires, and volitions—on my willing. The world of facts is independent of my will, but the form and limits of the world, i.e., the global a priori structure of the world, which is partially constituted by the specific internal nature of the objects, is dependent on my will. Now, the world and my life are the same thing (*TLP* 5.621-5.63). Thus the world can "wax or wane" as a whole, depending on my acts of willing, just as all the events of my life depend on my will. They do not, however, depend on my will in the sense that I can actually change any facts—I cannot—but in the sense that I can control the personal meaning or *value* of those facts, which is bound up essentially with the world's global structure. So my will determines how I value the world and my life, which in turn partially determines the "substance" of the world by partially determining the nature of the objects, and thereby partially determining the global a priori structure of the world. In this way, the world of the happy person, say, is metaphysically distinct from the world of the unhappy person. Here we can see that

XV. Coda: Wittgenstein and Kantianism

although the constitution of the facts is dual (with language on the one side, and the objects on the other), the metaphysical subject ultimately grounds both of the dual inputs by acting both as the language-user and also as the partial determiner of the specific character of the objects and of the world's global a priori structure, i.e., of its transcendental structure. In that sense, whether I live in "the world of the happy," or not, is solely up to me, and something for which I am alone fully responsible, no matter what the natural facts may be. This is obviously a doctrine that Wittgenstein shares with the Existentialists/existential phenomenologists, and this elective affinity shows up again in his later reflections on Christianity and Kierkegaard (Wittgenstein, 1980: p. 53^e).

This existential up-to-me-ness of world-structuring, in turn, is directly reflected in the dependence of the world on the individual representing subject. Wittgenstein wants to argue that his transcendental solipsism/LSTI, when properly understood, is in fact a "pure realism." In order to make sense of this, we must remember that the classical philosophical thesis of realism, when formulated from a Kantian point of view, comes in two very different versions: (i) *noumenal realism*, which says that things in the world have an essentially mind-independent existence and nature—i.e., they are things-in-themselves, and (ii) *empirical realism*, which says that things in the apparent or manifest world are directly knowable by means of veridical human cognition, at least to some extent. Classical rationalists and classical empiricists hold (i)—with sharply different degrees of epistemic confidence about the knowability of things-in-themselves, to be sure—and reject (ii). By sharp contrast, both Kant and Wittgenstein hold (ii) and firmly reject any version of (i), and also hold that in order to be an empirical realist/pure realist, one must also be a transcendental idealist/transcendental solipsist.

More precisely, Wittgenstein's pure realism is that nothing mediates between our correct use of language and the facts we thereby know: we cognize facts directly through the correct use of complete propositional symbols, and we cognize objects directly through the correct use of names. Then, provided that our judgments are true, we know the facts directly. This does not, however, in and of itself tell us how transcendental solipsism/LSTI leads to pure realism. Here Wittgenstein wants to say that his transcendental solipsism/LSTI isn't a solipsism/LSTI of the psychologically individual subject, who is individuated by their body and their own personal history, but rather a solipsism/LSTI of the individual subject considered as an anonymous or generic representer and language-user. This anonymous or generic subject is an "extensionless point," precisely because they function only as the means of representing the world. Here Wittgenstein uses the striking analogy of the visual field and the eye: the seeing eye is the necessary vehicle or means of vision, but it is not itself part of the visual field or its contents; rather the seeing eye is presupposed by the visual field and its contents. Similarly, the world contains all the facts, including the facts about my psychologically individual subject. But when all of these facts have been recorded, there's still something left over, namely, the anonymous or generic representing language-using subject as such, which/who is contentless, yet presupposed by all the facts. Then when we consider the world of facts from the standpoint of that anonymous or generic representing language-using subject as such, we recognize that this entire world (my world, my life, the totality of facts) is directly presented to me and also fully knowable by me just insofar as I linguistically represent it.

XV.3 World-Conformity 3: To Forms of Life

For Wittgenstein in *Philosophical Investigations*, and also throughout his later philosophy, including, for example, the writings published as *On Certainty*, language is ultimately a kind of rational human action, indeed the fundamental kind of rational human action. As I mentioned in section XI.1, adapting Goethe's line from *Faust* 1 ("In the beginning was the Deed"[2]), which itself adapts the biblical line from the Book of John 1 ("In the beginning was the Word"), we can then say that for the later Wittgenstein meaningful utterances just *are* human deeds, and that language-practices made up of meaningful words, aka "language-games," just *are* living collections of human deeds:

> Words are deeds [*Taten*].(Wittgenstein, 1980: p. 46ᵉ)

> In this way, I should like to say the words "Oh, *let* him come!" are charged with my desire. And words can be wrung from us, —like a cry. Words can be *hard* to say: such, for example, as are used to effect a renunciation, or to confess a weakness. (Words are also deeds [*Taten*].) (*PI* §546)

Rational human minded animals essentially are linguistic agents, and our use of language is essentially the mastery of a skill (*PI* §20). In turn, this opens up the very idea of meaning to every conceivable role that language can play in rational humanl minded animal activity (*PI* §23).

Granting that, what I want to propose now is that although in the *Investigations*, via the private language argument (*PI* §§243-315), the later Wittgenstein clearly, explicitly, and specifically rejects the solipsism of LSTI in the *Tractatus*, he never rejects and in fact permanently continues to hold onto the transcendental idealism of LSTI—only, in later writings, he does so in a communitarian or social-practical version that's essentially equivalent to Kant's weak or counterfactual transcendental idealism, WCTI, and, even if only implicitly and unofficially, is very much in the tradition of Southwest/Baden-style human-science-oriented and value-theory-oriented neo-Kantianism. The basic connection here relies on the notion of rational human minded animal life, i.e., the individual and social biological, conscious/sensory, self-conscious, cognitive, affective/emotional, and active/practical life of language-using creatures like us. Now Kant essentially identifies rational human *mind* and rational human *life*:

> Life is the subjective condition of all our possible experience. (*Prol* 4: 335)

> The mind for itself is entirely life (the principle of life itself). (*CPJ* 5: 278)

---

[2] Wittgenstein explicitly quotes this, e.g., in his (1972: §402, p. 51ᵉ).

XV. Coda: Wittgenstein and Kantianism

In the *Tractatus*, exactly the same essential identification is made, in two explicit steps and an implicit conclusion: (i) the world is identical to life, (ii) I am my world, (iii) therefore, I am life:

> 5.621 The world and life are one.
>
> 5.63 I am my world. (The microcosm.)

In the *Investigations*, this two-part essential identification between rational human mind and life is extended to a four-part essential identification that includes the intentional activity of judging and also the social language-using practices—language-games—in which rational human mind, life, and judging are ineluctably embedded:

> The term "language-game" is meant to bring into prominence the fact that the *speaking* of a language is part of an activity [*Tätigkeit*], or a form of life [*Lebensform*]. (*PI* §23)
>
> So you are saying that human agreement decides what is true and what is false?— It is what human beings *say* that is true and false; and they agree in the *language* they use.
>
> That is not agreement in opinions but in form of life. (*PI* §241)
>
> If language is to be a means of communication there must be agreement not only in definitions but also (queer as this may sound) in judgments. This seems to abolish logic, but does not do so. (*PI* §242)

And in *On Certainty*, the fourfold essential identification of rational human minded animality, life, judging, and language-games is extended to an explicit acknowledgment of the cognitive-practical apriority and certainty that naturally flow from our membership in language-games:

> We just *can't* investigate everything, and for that reason we are forced to rest content with assumption. If I want the door to turn, the hinges must stay put. My *life* consists in my being content to accept many things. (Wittgenstein, 1972: §§343-344, p. 44ᵉ)
>
> You must bear in mind that the language-game is so to say something unpredictable. I mean: it is not based on grounds [...]. It is there—like our life. (Wittgenstein, 1972: §559, p. 73ᵉ).

If rational human minded animality, life, judging, and language-games are all essentially the same, and if these naturally yield cognitive-practical apriority and certainty for the members of language-games, then it follows that the a priori forms and structures of rational human minded animals' minds are essentially the same as the a priori forms and structures of life, judging, and language-using. And if the manifestly real world necessarily conforms to the former, as **The Conformity Thesis** requires, then it necessarily conforms to the latter too. So the manifestly real world in which we live, move, and have our being necessarily conforms to our *forms of life*: "[w]hat has to be accepted, the given, is—so one could say, *forms of life*" (PI 226^e).

XV.4 The Critique of Self-Alienated Philosophy 1: Kant's Critical Metaphilosophy

The 1781 or A edition of the *Critique of Pure Reason* doesn't include a motto. But the 1787 or B edition includes a Latin quotation from the preface of Francis Bacon's *Great Instauration* of 1620. Now, given that the word "instauration" means "restoration" or "renewal," the point of the B edition's Motto, then, is just to establish the following analogy:

> As *The Great Instauration* is to scholastic metaphysics, so the *Critique of Pure Reason* is to classical rationalist metaphysics, including its Cartesian, Spinozan, Leibnizian, and (especially) Wolffian versions.

Both are proposing a restorative, renewing, and indeed revolutionary anthropocentric turn in philosophy.

But Kant's revolutionary turn goes well beyond Bacon's, and has three sources: (i) the self-annihilating character of classical rationalist metaphysics, demonstrated by the antinomy of pure reason, evident in the fact that contradictory claims seem to be equally supported by metaphysical reasoning; this demonstrated the need for a critique of pure reason, discovered by Kant in 1766, and beautifully captured by the first few sentences of the A edition Preface:

> Human reason has this peculiar fate in one species of its cognitions which it cannot dismiss, since they are given to it as problems by the very nature of reason itself, but which it also cannot answer, since they transcend every capacity of human reason [...]. The battlefield of these endless controversies is called **metaphysics** (*CPR* Avii-viii, boldfacing in the original),

(ii) Hume's skeptical empiricism about the content, truth, and justification of human cognition, especially as applied to the classical rationalist metaphysical concepts of causation and causal necessity, remembered by Kant in 1771 or 1772, and (iii) Kant's own revolutionary idealistic thesis about the necessary conformity of the ontic structure of space and time to the mentalistic structure of rational human sensible cognition, discovered and formulated by him between what he himself called his "year of great light," 1769, and 1772. These three philosophical sources combined to produce the three-part critical metaphilosophy of the *Critique of Pure Reason*, which is, **first,** the rejection of classical rationalist metaphysics, **second,** the rejection of the equal and opposite destructive and self-alienating radical skepticism which follows from the self-annihilating character of classical rationalist metaphysical reasoning, and **third**, the revolutionary replacement of classical rationalist metaphysics by a new, inherently anthropocentric, and *mitigated* kind of rationalist metaphysics: transcendental idealism.

XV.5 The Critique of Self-Alienated Philosophy 2: Wittgensteinian Analysis as Critique

According to what I'll call *the logico-decompositional conception of analysis* (see also section II.4 above), which—together with transformative or reductive analysis—is a necessary and indeed dominant element in the conception of analysis found in the writings of Frege, Moore, Russell, and early Wittgensteinfrom the 1880s to the mid-1920s—i.e., classical Analytic philosophy prior to Vienna Circle logical empiricism/positivism—philosophical analysis is the process of logically decomposing propositions into conceptual or metaphysical simples which are mind-independently real yet immediately and infallibly apprehended with self-evidence, and then rigorously logically reconstructing those propositions by formal deduction from general logical laws and premises that express logical definitional knowledge in terms of the simple constituents (Hanna, 2007). But in the *Investigations*, as we've seen in section XI.4 above, the later Wittgenstein's devastating critique of the semantic and logical doctrines of his own earlier philosophical self in the *Tractatus* motivates a radically wider and more open-textured conception of philosophical analysis. At the same time, his self-critique of Tractarian solipsism—The Private Language Argument—further radicalizes his conception of philosophical analysis by rejecting several of the fundamental assumptions of classical rationalist Cartesian epistemology and metaphysics that had been explicitly or implicitly retained by Frege, Moore, Russell, and "the author of the *Tractatus Logico-Philosophicus*" (*PI* §23). Indeed, Wittgenstein's radical transformation of philosophical analysis goes significantly and seriously beyond the analytic tradition, and also returns us full-circle to Kantian transcendental Critical metaphilosophy.

In the *Tractatus*, Wittgenstein importantly extends the Frege-Moore-Russell conception of logico-decompositional analysis. According to the Tractarian account, the proper targets of this analysis are propositions. Tractarian logico-decompositional analysis then consists in completely and uniquely decomposing propositional symbols into their constituent simple symbols, whether names of objects or logical constants (*TLP* 3.23-3.261). Objects are known by direct cognitive acquaintance (*TLP* 2.0123-2.01231), and logical constants are known "transcendentally," i.e., by means of a priori showing (*TLP* 4.12-4.1213). Every proposition has a unique and complete decomposition (*TLP* 3.25). The way in which those names are configured into a propositional structure is made manifest through the process of analysis itself. Tractarian logico-decompositional analysis is thus essentially a series of logical "elucidations" (*Erläuterungen*). Indeed, Tractarian logico-decompositional analysis is essentially the *activity* (*Tätigkeit*) but not the *theory* (*Lehre*) of decomposing a proposition into its simple constituent symbols (*TLP* 4.112).

More precisely, the activist Tractarian conception of logico-decompositional analysis has two basic parts, and correspondingly two basic aims.

First, the activity of logico-decompositional analysis is a "critique of language" (*TLP* 4.0031) in that it displays the fact that most propositions and questions that have been written about philosophical matters are not false but nonsensical (*unsinnig*) (*TLP* 4.003), recognizes that truths of logic are tautologous and non-pictorial, hence "say nothing" (*sagen nichts*) (*TLP* 6.11), then asserts as fully significant only the propositions of natural science (*TLP* 6.53), then recognizes its own propositions as nonsensical, and finally ends in mystical silence (*TLP* 6.54). Thus the first basic aim of Tractarian logico-decompositional analysis is to articulate the difference between sense (factual meaningfulness) and nonsense. Here we must remember that "nonsense" for early Wittgenstein is literally *what is other than sense*, i.e., everything of a cognitive or semantic nature that is other than what is described or pictured or 'said' by atomic propositions. So "nonsense" can be either sheer absurdity, or *meaninglessness*, for example,, Lewis Carroll's *Jabberwocky*, or else it can be *illuminatingly what is other than sense* in some other non-atomic-fact-representing, but still logically, semantically, aesthetically, or ethically important way.

Second, the activity of logico-decompositional analysis is the process of logically clarifying thoughts, consisting in a series of propositional elucidations which "make clear and delimit sharply the thoughts which otherwise are [...] opaque and blurred" (*TLP* 4.112). In this way, the second basic aim of Tractarian logical analysis is to reveal the deep or *logico*-grammatical structure of natural language and thought, as opposed to its merely surface or *psychologico*-grammatical structure. In order to reveal the deep structure of language, Tractarian philosophers must construct and study symbolic logical systems like those developed in Frege's *Begriffsschrift* and Whitehead's and Russell's *Principia Mathematica*. Such symbolic systems are "ideal" in the sense that the syntax of a *Begriffsschrift*-type notational system itself displays, encodes, or mirrors the deep structure of natural language and thought, and thereby also the deep structure of the world of facts that language and thought represent. Even so, Tractarian logico-decompositional analysis does not aim at the *prescriptive reform* of natural language or thought. On the contrary, everything in natural language and thought is perfectly in order, just as it is (*TLP* 5.5563).

In the *Investigations*, there's a radical turn in Wittgenstein's conception of philosophy from his activist logico-deccompositional analysis, or the "logical clarification of thoughts" (*TLP* 4.112), to what I'll call *the critique of pure logic*, or CPL, which says that logic is nothing "sublime" but instead is really nothing but grammar.

Here's a rational reconstruction of CPL, very much along the lines of section XII.5 above:

1. Frege, Moore, Russell, the author of the *Tractatus*, Carnap, the members of The Vienna Circle, and other classical Analytic philosophers, all explicitly or implicitly hold the thesis that logic is something "sublime": universal, a priori, necessary, and noumenally essential (*PI* §89).

2. Furthermore, logic is required to carry out any complete or partial decom-

positional analysis of our forms of language, propositions, and thoughts, which reveals their "hidden," "simple" structures and constituents, that is, their decomposable essences (*PI* §§91-6).

3. But in fact, (3i) every sentence in our language is in order just as it is. (3ii) vagueness is a partially constitutive feature of linguistic meaning, (3iii) language is essentially a spatiotemporal phenomenon, not something abstract, and (3iv) the essence of language, propositions, thought, and the world is something that "already lies open to view and that becomes surveyable by a rearrangement" (*PI* §92, and §§98-100, 108-109).

4. So neither language, nor propositions, nor thought, nor the world have hidden decomposable noumenal essences, and therefore the thesis that logic is sublime is false.

5. Furthermore the thesis that logic is sublime turns out to be only a methodological assumption we have unintentionally imposed upon the phenomena, indeed nothing but an artifact of an idealized bad philosophical "picture" that lay hidden in our language and held us captive (*PI* §§101-8, 110-15).

6. Now,

> the philosophy of logic speaks of sentences and words in exactly the sense in which we speak of them in ordinary life when we say, e.g., "Here is a Chinese sentence," or "No, that only looks like writing; it is actually an ornament" and so on. (*PI* §108)

That is: we can regard logic as purely descriptive, not noumenally essential; and "what *we* do is to bring words back from their metaphysical use to their everyday use" by asking "is the word ever actually used in this way in the language which is its original home" (*PI* §116).

7. Therefore, we should adopt the thesis that logic is really nothing but "grammar," the latter

> shedding light on our problem by clearing misunderstandings away .... misunderstandings concerning the use of words, caused, among other things by certain analogies between the forms of expression in different regions of language.... [And] some of them can be removed by substituting one form of expression for another; this may be called an "analysis" of our forms of expression, for the process is sometimes like one of taking things apart. (*PI* §90)

8. Furthermore, the goal of logic-as-grammar is to produce a "perspicuous representation" of language, propositions, thought, and the world, which produces "that understanding which consists in 'seeing connections'" (*PI* §122).

9. So logic isn't sublime, and logical-decompositional analysis is impossible, but logic-as-grammar is really possible, and grammar in this sense is the descriptive logic of our language-games, i.e., what represents a priori forms of life, which are transcendentally embedded in our communal practices.

10. Therefore, to the extent that logic as a theory of valid reasoning still exists in the form of logic-as-grammar, this logic is fully transcendental in the Kantian and also Tractarian sense.

Now, let's suppose that CPL is sound. What does philosophical analysis become after the collapse of the sublimity of logic? Here are the three essential texts:

> The work of the philosopher consists in assembling reminders for a particular purpose. (*PI* §127)

> If one tried to advance *theses* in philosophy, it would never be possible to question them, because everyone would agree to them. (*PI* §128)

> It is not our aim to refine or complete the system of rules for the use of words in unheard-of ways. For the clarity that we are aiming at is indeed *complete* clarity. But that simply means that the philosophical problems should *completely* disappear. The real discovery is one that makes me capable of stopping doing philosophy when I want to. –The one that gives philosophy peace, so that it is no longer tormented by questions which bring *itself* into question [...]. There is not *a* philosophical method, though there are indeed methods, like different therapies. (*PI* §133)

And here is the two-part answer to that leading question.

First, later Wittgenstein's conception of philosophical analysis in fact shares some fundamental features in common with his activist logico-decompositional conception of analysis in the *Tractatus*. But this activist logico-decompositional conception of logical analysis is now minus the "sublimity" or "noumenal essentialism" of logic, that is to say, minus the comprehensive noumenal essentialist metaphysical picture of logic, language, thought, and the world that would justify the logical-decompositional theory of analysis, but still accepting the transcendental character of logic, now understood to be logic-as-grammar. Logic *isn't* sublime, but logic *is* transcendental, even in the *Investigations*. In short, the later Wittgenstein's radical turn in philosophical analysis towards logic-as-grammar is simply a radical *re*-turn to Kant's Critical meta-philosophy, that is, a radical return to transcendental logic understood as transcendental dialectic, which is the meta-philosophical critique of metaphysical illusion in philosophy, as a form of rational self-knowledge (*CPR* A61-2/B85-

6, A293-8/B349-54). The main idea is that, as a logical grammarian, one (i) displays and diagnoses the dialectical structure of philosophical problems, i.e., displays and diagnoses "the civil status of a contradiction, or its status in civil life" (*PI* §125), (ii) describes, unpacks, compares, and contrasts the concepts implicit in our various ordinary uses of language and states a priori truisms about them (*PI* §§123-6), and then (iii) stops doing (professional academic Analytic) philosophy when one wants to, in order to change one's life, or the direction of one's life, and in order to achieve "insight into what lies in front of everyone's eyes" (*PI* §133).

Second, and as a direct consequence of the **first** part, the other crucial thing about later Wittgenstein's conception of philosophical analysis is that it is fundamentally *non-cognitive*, that is, fundamentally desire-based, emotive, normative, and practical. On this view, philosophical analysis is neither a natural science nor a mere source of factual knowledge but rather essentially a self-conscious and deliberative activity—that of "doing philosophy." In turn, doing philosophy means achieving perspicuous insight into what already is completely there in front of us: rational human animals and their language, fully embedded in their apparent or manifest world, intentionally acting according to the normatively guiding a priori structures of their living, shared social practices, i.e. according to the forms of rational human life (*PI* §241). In the light of this, we can now also say that the aim of philosophical analysis for the later Wittgenstein is precisely to achieve a Kant-style Critical insight into what lies before everyone's eyes, i.e., into the cognitive and practical capacities of creatures like us, and into the nature of our veridically apparent or manifestly real world.

XV.6 Wittgenstein, Kant, Scientism, and The Tragic Sense of Life

As Quine (Hylton, 2007: esp. chs. 9, 12), Hans Reichenbach (1951), and Wilfrid Sellars so clearly saw in the 1950s, after the successive downfalls of classical logicism and logical empiricism/positivism during the first half of the twentieth century, and thus the downfall of classical Analytic philosophy, then post-classical Analytic philosophy became, essentially, a series of minor variations on the theme of *scientific philosophy*:

> In the dimension of describing and explaining the world, science is the measure of all things, of what is that it is, and of what is not that it is not. (Sellars, 1963b: p. 173)

This is philosophy in Sellars's *scientific image* (Sellars, 1963c). But later Wittgenstein, following Kant's lead and also (at least implicitly and unofficially) the lead of the Southwest/Baden school of human-science-oriented and value-theory-oriented neo-Kantianism, and also channelling Existentialism and/or existential phenomenology, radically challenges and rejects this essentially *scientistic* conception of philosophy:

> I had to deny [scientific] **knowledge** [*Wissen*] in order to make room for [moral] **faith** [*Glauben*]. (*CPR* Bxxix-xxx, boldfacing in the original)

> It was true to say that our considerations could not be scientific ones [*wissenschaft-

> lich]. It was not of any possible interest to us to find out empirically "that, contrary to our preconceived ideas, it is possible think such-and-such"—whatever that may mean [...]. And we may not advance any kind of theory [...]. We must do away with all *explanation*, and description alone must take its place. These are, of course, not empirical problems; they are solved, rather, by looking into the workings of our language, and that in such a way as to make us recognize those workings: *in spite of* an urge to misunderstand them. The problems are solved, not by giving new information, but by arranging what we have always known. (*PI* §109)

In this way, transcendental anthropology as practiced by Kant, the Existentialists and/or existential phenomenologists, the Southwest/Baden-style neo-Kantians, and by Wittgenstein, doesn't *either* seek a humanly impossible, absolutely justifying, pure rational insight into things-in-themselves, *or* draw Pyrrhonian skeptical conclusions from our inevitable and tragic failure to achieve a godlike "intellectual intuition" of ourselves and the world (*CPR* B72), *or* fall into scientism. For all three of these latter philosophical projects, whether dogmatically rationalistic, destructively skeptical, or reductively naturalistic, are equally inherently self-alienating and "inauthentic" in the existentialists'/existential phenomenologists' sense. Indeed, it's significant that even when, in the second edition of *Insight and Illusion*, Hacker officially rescinds his earlier Kant-oriented interpretation of Wittgenstein in the first edition (1972), he still admits that

> more than any other philosophers, Kant and Wittgenstein were concerned with the nature of philosophy itself and sought to curb its metaphysical pretensions by clarifying its status and circumscribing what one may rationally hope for in philosophical investigation. Both saw philosophical and metaphysical *pretensions of reason* as at least a large part of the subject, and the eradication of such illusions as a major goal of their work. (Hacker, 1986: p. 207)

Otherwise put, with the tragic sense of life as their philosophical sensorium, Kant, the Existentialists and/or existential phenomenologists, the Southest/Baden-style neo-Kantians, and Wittgenstein all fully recognize that we must renounce every variety of *the bad faith of reason* in order to make room for an authentic, autonomous, rational humanl minded animal life. And fundamentally appealing to this authentic, autonomous, rational human minded animal life, in turn, is nothing more and nothing less than an anthropocentric rationalist version of Kierkegaard's "knighthood of faith," as it were, *the knighthood of rational faith*, whereby you can radically change your life, or change the direction of your life. And that's the deepest lesson of transcendental anthropology. Moreover and finally, it's a lesson that, when it's properly understood and reflected-upon, thereby also decisively demonstrates to us that the later Wittgenstein's philosophy is not only an *anti*-Analytic philosophy but also a *trans*-Analytic philosophy, at once effectively *subverting* and equally effectively *transcending* the Analytic tradition as Wittgenstein knew it by 1950, the last full year of his life, a philosophical tradition on the very cusp of passing over from its classical and *heroic* (although philosophically failed) phase, into its post-classical and *epigone* (although social-institutionally triumphant) phase.

XVI. From Quine to Kripke and Analytic Metaphysics: The Adventures of the Analytic-Synthetic Distinction

In his 1951 philosophical juggernaut, "Two Dogmas of Empiricism," W.V.O. Quine informally characterized the first dogma of what he called "modern empiricism," i.e., logical empiricism/positivism, as

> a belief in some fundamental cleavage between truths which are *analytic*, or grounded in meanings independently of matters of fact, and truths which are *synthetic*, or grounded in fact. (Quine, 1961b: p. 20)

Then he went on (i) to reject the analytic-synthetic distinction *in this specifically logical empiricist/positivist sense*, on the grounds that it couldn't be reductively explained in other terms, and then (ii) to propose the elimination of *the very idea* of an analytic-synthetic distinction:

> for all its a priori reasonableness, a boundary between analytic and synthetic statements simply has not been drawn. That there is such a distinction at all is an unempirical dogma of empiricists, a metaphysical article of faith. (Quine, 1961b: p. 37)

So take *that!*, not only Vienna Circle logical empiricism/positivism, but also Kant and the Kantians, and any other benighted philosophical soul who might consider taking seriously *any* analytic-synthetic distinction whatsoever.

XVI.1 Two Urban Legends of Post-Empiricism

Without a doubt, the greatest urban legend of post-logical empiricist/positivist philosophy, and more generally of post-classical Analytic philosophy, is the belief that Quine refuted and eliminated the analytic-synthetic distinction, especially including Kant's or any other Kantian version of the distinction, in "Two Dogmas of Empiricism" in 1951. This is indeed a *mere* legend, however, for five reasons.

First, Quine's critique of the analytic-synthetic distinction was actually a cumulative argument that included at least three other important texts in addition to "Two Dogmas," spread out over three decades from 1935 to 1965—namely, "Truth by Convention" (1935), *Word and Object* (1960), and "Carnap and Logical Truth" (1963).[1]

---

[1] Actually, the publishing history of "Carnap and Logical Truth" (Quine, 1976b) is somewhat complicated. It was originally written in 1954 for the Library of Living Philosophers volume on Carnap, which eventually appeared in 1963. But parts of the 1954 paper appeared in 1956 (in Italian) and in 1957 (in English); and a complete English version also appeared in *Synthese* in 1960.

Second, and more importantly, Quine's argument in "Two Dogmas" seriously mischaracterizes Kant's or any Kantian theory of the analytic-synthetic distinction by falsely assimilating them to Frege's and Carnap's theories,[2] hence, in effect, by falsely assimilating them to the logical empiricist/positivist conception of the analytic-synthetic distinction, and by assuming without argument that the very idea of the synthetic a priori (including the notion of synthetic necessity and also the notion of synthetic a priori knowledge) is unintelligible. So Quine never even *rejected* Kant's or any Kantian version of the analytic-synthetic distinction itself, much less *refuted* it.

Third, and very importantly, as I'll argue in detail later in this chapter, Quine's critical arguments against the analytic-synthetic distinction, especially including Kant's or any Kantian version of the distinction, are all demonstrably *unsound*, even despite their undeniable fame and powerful influence.

Fourth, and equally importantly, as a part of his eliminative strategy Quine introduced a deflationary or *ersatz* version of the analytic-synthetic distinction that effectively converts what was originally, for Kant and other Kantians, a *cognitive-semantic* distinction, into a merely *epistemic-pragmatic* distinction. More precisely, having mistakenly rejected the *original* Kantian analytic-synthetic distinction—i.e., the distinction between (i) necessary truth in virtue of conceptual content, such that this content is always taken together with some things in the manifestly real world beyond conceptual content, although never in virtue of those worldly things alone, and (ii) necessary or contingent truth in virtue of things in the manifestly real world beyond conceptual content, as represented by essentially non-conceptual content, such that this content is always taken together with some conceptual content, although never in virtue of that content alone—Quine then strategically replaced it with a very different distinction. That distinction was between (i*) asserted statements or beliefs that stubbornly resist recalcitrant experience and can be acquired

---

[2] In "Carnap and Logical Truth," however, Quine accurately points up the most important difference between Kant's theory of analyticity, Frege's theory, and Carnap's theory:

> Altogether, the contrasts between elementary logic and set theory are so fundamental that one might well limit the word "logic" to the former..., and speak of set theory as mathematics in a sense exclusive of logic. To adopt this course is merely to deprive "ε" of the status of a logical word. Frege's derivation of arithmetic would then cease to count as a derivation from logic; for he used set theory. At any rate we should be prepared to find that [Carnap's] linguistic doctrine of logical truths holds for elementary logic and fails for set theory, or vice versa. Kant's readiness to see logic as analytic and arithmetic as synthetic, in particular, is not superseded by Frege's work (as Frege supposed), if "logic" be taken as elementary logic. And for Kant logic certainly did not include set theory. (Quine, 1976b: p. 111)

In fact, Kant's pure general logic is closest in structure to *monadic* logic (i.e., classical sentential logic plus quantification into one-place predicates only), although it also includes quantification over first-order predicates or concepts for the purposes of representing analytic containment-, identity- and/or exclusion-relations. So unlike Frege and Carnap alike, Kant would have regarded both elementary logic (which includes identity and multiple quantification into relational predicates) and also set theory as *synthetic*, not analytic. See (Hanna, 2017d, 2021f).

without experiential evidence and inquiry, aka "armchair beliefs," aka "the a priori," and (ii*) asserted statements or beliefs that are flexibly sensitive to recalcitrant experience and cannot be acquired without experiential evidence and inquiry, aka "experimental beliefs," aka "the a posteriori."[3]

By a strange historical twist, this Quinean deflationary or ersatz epistemic-pragmatic version of the original Kantian analytic-synthetic distinction has become, in effect, *the standard version of the analytic-synthetic distinction in the post-classical Analytic traditio* (Boghossian, 1996). So, ironically enough, Quine not only mistakenly rejected and falsely purported to eliminate the analytic-synthetic distinction, especially including Kant's original version or any other Kantian version of the analytic-synthetic distinction, as he, Quine, originally understood it in "Two Dogmas"—namely, as the "modern empiricist," aka logical empiricist/positivist, conception of the analytic-synthetic distinction—but he also created another and different distinction. This new Quinean distinction, however, even despite its being highly influential in post-classical Analytic philosophy, is significantly less intelligible and defensible than the original Kantian distinction, as I'll argue later.

In this connection, it's directly relevant to note that the 2009 Bourget-and-Chalmers *PhilPapers* survey of 3226 mainstream professional academic philosophers—and here we'll remember from the Introduction that 81% of those who said they belonged to a philosophical tradition, explicitly self-identified as Analytic philosophers—showed (i) that 71% of the respondents accepted the existence of a priori knowledge, and also (ii) that 65% accepted the analytic-synthetic distinction (Bourget and Chalmers, 2009; 2014). In his editorial comments on the results, posted online, Bourget wrote that he was surprised by the high rate of acceptance of the analytic-synthetic distinction, and Chalmers wrote in reply that

> [a]s for the analytic/synthetic distinction, it's worth noting that quite a few people said "yes" while also noting in the comments that they don't think the distinction does important philosophical work. (Bourget and Chalmers, 2009)

All that seems correct to me. So in other words, although most recent and contemporary post-classical Analytic philosophers believe in the existence of a priori knowledge and also believe in the analytic-synthetic distinction, nevertheless many of those same philosophers *also* believe that the analytic-synthetic distinction itself doesn't do any important or serious philosophical work, even if they do continue to think that the notion of apriority does some important and serious philosophical work in epistemology and semantics. This especially includes Chalmers himself, and other proponents of "The Canberra Plan"—for example, David Lewis and Frank Jackson—in contemporary Analytic metaphysics, under the rubrics of "a priori entailments" and "a priori intensions" (Braddon-Mitchell and Nola, 2008: esp. Introduction). I'll explore some possible reasons for this (to me, frankly, bizarre) philosophical "disconnect" between the analytic-synthetic distinction and the a priori-a posteriori distinction later in the chapter.

---
[3] For a more explicit formulation, and critique, of Quine's distinction between apriority and aposteriority, see (Hanna, 2015a: section 7.2).

Fifth, and most importantly of all, no one has yet explained how either classical or post-classical Analytic philosophy themselves can really be possible without adequate theories of (i) conceptual analysis, (ii) analyticity, (iii) how to ground an intelligible and defensible distinction between (iiia) logically, conceptually, weakly metaphysically, or *analytically* necessary truths, i.e., truths about the kind of necessity that flows from the nature of concepts, and (iiib) non-logically, essentially non-conceptually, strongly metaphysically, or *synthetically* necessary truths (Chalmers, 1996: pp. 136-138; Fine, 1994, 1995, 2005b; Hanna and Maiese, 2009: section 7.4; Kripke, 1980, 1993), i.e., truths about the kind of necessity that flows from the nature of things in the veridically apparent or manifestly real world, as represented by essentially non-conceptual content, (iv) a priori knowledge of logical truths and conceptual truths, (v) a priori knowledge of non-logically, essentially non-conceptually, strongly metaphysically, or synthetically necessary truths, especially including mathematical truths, and finally (vi) the nature and status of logic. So if Quine refuted and eliminated the analytic-synthetic distinction, especially including Kant's and any other Kantian version of it, then in effect he refuted post-classical Analytic philosophy too. But obviously Quine didn't refute post-classical Analytic philosophy: on the contrary, he substantially helped to prolong its social-institutional life for at least another seventy years. Therefore, he didn't refute the analytic-synthetic distinction, especially including Kant's or any other Kantian version of the distinction, either.

Equally without a doubt, the second greatest urban legend of post-logical empiricism/positivism and post-classical Analytic philosophy more generally, is that the analytic-synthetic distinction does not matter anyway. To many or even most recent and contemporary post-classical Analytic philosophers, the analytic-synthetic distinction seems almost unbearably technical, tedious, and trivial. Nothing more quickly produces a grimace or nauseated look than to say "the analytic-synthetic distinction" out loud, without irony, in polite philosophical conversation with post-classical Analytic philosophers. But on the contrary, it seems clear to me that if the analytic-synthetic distinction were either unintelligible or indefensible, then the very idea of a semantic content would go down. And then, like so many dominoes, the very ideas of belief, cognition, thought, understanding, justification, knowledge, intentionality, and human rationality—whether cognitive rationality or practical rationality—would all go down too, since all these notions inherently involve and basically presuppose the notion of semantic content. More precisely, I'll soon present what I call *A Transcendental Argument for the Existence of a Robust Analytic-Synthetic Distinction, From the Very Idea of a Semantic Content*.

To be as clear as possible, here's what I mean by the notion of a transcendental argument. An *argument* is a set of sentences or statements Γ (and possibly Γ = the null set of sentences or statements), i.e., the premises, such that a sentence or statement S (which may or may not be a member of Γ), i.e., the conclusion, is held to follow validly or soundly from Γ. Then an argument is a *transcendental argument* if and only if (i) some version of transcendental idealism is assumed to be true,[4] i.e., weak or counterfactual transcendental idealism, and (ii) that argument advances from a sentence or statement S, taken as a single premise, to an a priori necessary presupposition *APNP* of S—i.e., "*a* condition of the possibility" of S—taken as a single conclusion, as follows:

1. S

2. S presupposes *APNP*

3. Therefore, *APNP*.

Furthermore, by the notion of "a robust analytic-synthetic distinction," I mean a version of the analytic-synthetic distinction that explanatorily includes and fully preserves an essential difference between (i) analytic truths, which are inherently necessary and a priori, and (ii) synthetic truths, with the possibility also being explicitly left open of explanatorily including and fully preserving another essential difference between (iia) synthetic necessary and a priori truths, and (iib) synthetic contingent and a posteriori truths. Now for the argument itself.

A Transcendental Argument for the Existence of a Robust Analytic-Synthetic Distinction, From the Very Idea of a Semantic Content

1. Belief, cognition, thought, understanding, justification, knowledge, intentionality, and human rationality more generally, all inherently involve and a priori presuppose *standard* notions of reference, truth or falsity, and logical consequence, for example, as defined by Tarski, all of which are *semantic content notions*.

2. Therefore, the very ideas of belief, cognition, thought, understanding, justification, knowledge, intentionality, and human rationality more generally all inherently involve and a priori presuppose the very idea of a semantic content.

3. Every semantic content is an intension of some sort, which inherently correlates with an actual or possible extension of some sort.

---

[4] In his (1968), Barry Stroud famously and trend-settingly argued that the soundness of transcendental arguments presupposes the truth of either verificationism or transcendental idealism. In my opinion, that's correct. For the purposes of argument, let us then assume that verificationism is false, and leave it aside. That leaves just the claim that the soundness of transcendental arguments presupposes transcendental idealism. But only if transcendental idealism is false, is this actually an objection to transcendental arguments. And the version of transcendental idealism that Stroud considered was in fact old-school, Oxford-style, conceptualist *strong* transcendental idealism (i.e., the phenomenalist, subjective idealist interpretation), which I completely agree is false. But if transcendental arguments are in fact supported by an arguably true version of transcendental idealism, i.e., a non-conceptualist, manifest realist, weak or counterfactual version of transcendental idealism, then Stroud's objection is perfectly harmless. In defense of the latter version of TI, see (Hanna, 2015a: section 7.3). And for a good survey of Stroud's papers and the Stroud-driven debate about transcendental arguments, (Stern, 2019: section 3).

4. The very idea of a difference between intension and extension inherently includes the distinction between (4i) normative intensional facts, including semantic facts about accurate reference, semantic facts about the truth of sentences or statements, and semantic facts about the validity or soundness of arguments, in what Sellars aptly calls the "logical space of reasons" on the one hand, and (4ii) *non-normative natural facts*, including natural facts about natural objects, natural facts about natural properties, natural facts about natural states of affairs, and natural facts about natural relations between natural objects, natural properties, and natural states of affairs, in what Sellars calls the "natural space of facts," on the other hand (Sellars, 1963b: p. 169, and more generally, §17 and §36; McDowell, 1994, 2009a).[5]

5. Only analytic a priori statements can truly pick out normative intensional facts such as (5i) the fact that "*a*" accurately refers to *a* if and only if "*a*" actually refers to *a* and never refers to anything else, (5ii) the fact that "*S*" is true if and only if *S*, (5iii) the fact that "*Q*" is a valid consequence of "*P*" if and only if there is no possible set of circumstances such that "*P*" is true and "*Q*" is false, and (5iv) the fact that "*Q*" is a sound consequence of "*P*" if and only if "*Q*" is a valid consequence of "*P*," and "*P*" is true, and only synthetic a posteriori statements can truly pick out non-normative natural facts.

6. Therefore, the very idea of a semantic content inherently involves and a priori presupposes a robust analytic-synthetic distinction.

In other words, how could there be intelligible and defensible notions of belief, cognition, thought, understanding, justification, knowledge, intentionality, and human rationality more generally, without the correlative notions of belief-content, cognitive content, and thought-content? The connection between the former and the latter is that the latter are all priori necessary presuppositions of the former, and in turn the latter all a priori presuppose a robust analytic-synthetic distinction. So in this way, the rejection or elimination of the analytic-synthetic distinction entails the rejection or elimination of the very idea of *human rationality*.

XVI.2 A Very Brief History of The Analytic-Synthetic Distinction

For the vast majority of Analytic philosophers, whether classical or post-classical, the analytic-synthetic distinction is merely an updated version of *Hume's Fork*, which in turn is the two-pronged epistemic and cognitive-semantic distinction between (i) trivial, merely stipulative, necessary, and a priori "relations of ideas," and (ii) substantive, empirical, con-

---

[5] It's important to note in this connection that whereas Sellars and McDowell (at least in *Mind and World* [1994]) are both strong conceptualists who hold that normative intensional/semantic facts flow from conceptual content and conceptual capacities alone, on the contrary, strong or essentialist non-conceptualism insists that normative intensional/ semantic facts flow not only from conceptual content and capacities but also from essentially non-conceptual content and capacities. See (Hanna, 2015a: ch. 2) and also section XVII.8 below.

tingent, and a posteriori "matters of fact." (Hume, 1977: p. 15). But in fact *Kant's* original analytic-synthetic distinction was a *three-pronged pitchfork* designed for philosophical digging in the real earth of the veridically apparent or manifestly real world. What I mean is that it's a threefold epistemic and cognitive-semantic distinction between (i) conceptually, logically, or "weakly metaphysically necessary" analytic a priori truths, (ii) non-logically, essentially non-conceptually, or "strongly metaphysically necessary" synthetic a priori truths, and (iii) contingent synthetic a posteriori truths (*CPR* A6-10/B10-24). In this way, the original Kantian analytic-synthetic distinction is nothing more and nothing less than the categorically sharp contrast between (i) necessary truth in virtue of conceptual content, such that this content is always taken together with some things in the veridically apparent or manifestly real world beyond conceptual content, although its truth is never in virtue of those worldly things alone, and (ii) necessary or contingent truth in virtue of things in the veridically apparent or manifestly real world beyond conceptual content, as represented by essentially non-conceptual content, such that this content is always taken together with some conceptual content, although its truth is never in virtue of conceptual content alone.

To be sure, there were anticipations of the original Kantian analytic-synthetic distinction in the writings of Locke, Hume, and Leibniz (Proust, 1989: pp. 3-39). But since Kant is the official creator or discoverer of the original analytic-synthetic distinction—in the sense that he was the first to use that terminology, and the first to make it an absolutely central feature of his logic, semantics, epistemology, metaphysics, and ethics—then the question naturally arises: How did Kant's Pitchfork turn into Hume's Fork? Here's a much-simplified, blow-by-blow version of that deeply important historico-philosophical story, some of which will already be somewhat familiar to us from earlier chapters.

In the 19th century and at the turn of the 20th, Bernard Bolzano, Hermann Lotze, Frege, and early Husserl claimed to have purified Kant's original tripartite analytic-synthetic distinction of its vitiating idealism and psychologism (Bolzano, 1972; Frege, 1979; Husserl, 1970a; Hanna, 2006c: ch. 1, 2011c; Lotze, 1888; and also sections II.10 to II.13 above), and then Frege tried to reduce arithmetic truths to logically analytic truths by deriving them a priori from general logical laws together with something he called "logical definitions" (Benacerraf, 1981; Coffa, 1991; Frege, 1953; and Proust, 1989: pp. 49-163; and sections II.5 to II.9 above).

At the *fin de siècle* and during the first decade of the 20th century, Moore and Russell attacked neo-Hegelian philosophy and Kant's transcendental idealism, and asserted *platonic atomism*, according to which concepts and other universals are the primitive, ultimate constituents of propositions and reality alike, and can be known directly and self-evidently by acts or states of cognitive acquaintance (Baldwin, 1990: chs. 1-2; Hanna, 2001: ch. 1; Hylton, 1990: parts I and II; Moore, 1993a; Russell, 1995; and ch. III above).

In the 1920s and 30s, building on Wittgenstein's theory of logic and meaning in the *Tractatus*, Carnap and the other logical empiricists/positivists rejected the very idea of the synthetic a priori, and adopted the conventionalist theory of analyticity (Carnap, 1937;

Coffa, 1991: chs. 9-17; Friedman, 1999: chs. 7-9; Proust, 1989: pp. 165-240; and chapters V to VIII above).

Also in the 1930s, in "Truth by Convention," Quine argued that the conventionalist theory of analyticity fails because its definition of logical truth or analyticity covertly presupposes and uses non-conventional classical logic.

Carnap responded to Quine in 1947 in *Meaning and Necessity* (Carnap, 1956a).

In 1951, in "Two Dogmas," Quine explicitly rejected the analytic-synthetic distinction as it was understood in "modern empiricism," i.e., in logical empiricism/positivism, and proposed the elimination of the very idea of any analytic-synthetic distinction.

Carnap responded to Quine again in "Meaning Postulates" and "Meaning and Synonymy in Natural Languages" in 1954 (Carnap, 1956c, 1956d).

Quine responded to Carnap in *Word and Object* (which, ironically enough, is dedicated to "RUDOLPH CARNAP, Teacher and Friend") in 1960, and then again in "Carnap and Logical Truth" in 1963, and at the same time Quine strategically introduced the deflationary, ersatz, or epistemic-pragmatic version of the analytic-synthetic distinction between armchair beliefs, aka "the a priori," and experimental beliefs, aka "the a posteriori."

H.P. Grice and P.F. Strawson criticized Quine in "In Defense of a Dogma" (Grice and Strawson, 1956).

Strawson alone criticized Quine in "Propositions, Concepts, and Logical Truths" (Strawson, 1957).

Arthur Pap criticized Quine and defended the analytic-synthetic distinction at length in *Semantics and Necessary Truth* (Pap, 1958).

And then Jerrold Katz criticized Quine in "Some Remarks on Quine on Analyticity" (Katz, 1967).

Nevertheless, all this important philosophical work was in vain, and *made no noticeable difference whatsoever*. By the end of the 1960s it had become conventional wisdom that Quine had not only actually *refuted* the analytic-synthetic distinction, but also *eliminated* the very idea of any analytic-synthetic distinction, and not merely *rejected* them. Indeed, by the early 1990s, Tyler Burge could write this with a confident expectation of general agreement:

> No clear reasonable support has been devised for a distinction between truths that depend for their truth on meaning alone and truths that depend for their truth on meaning together with (perhaps necessary) features of their subject

matter. (Burge, 1992)

Then what happened after that? Sadly, things went from bad to worse for Kant's Pitchfork.

In the 1960s, 70s, and 80s, Kripke and Putnam, assisted by Keith Donnellan, rejected the very idea of a necessary equivalence between necessity and apriority by arguing for the existence of *necessary a posteriori statements* such as

(WH) Water is H_2O

(GE) Gold is the element with atomic number 79

(CT) Cicero is Tully

and

(HP) Hesperus is Phosphorus

and also *contingent a priori statements* such as

(SM) Stick S is one meter long at t_0 [According to Kripke]

(CA) Cats are animals [According to Putnam, but not Kripke]

(WL) Water is a liquid [According to Putnam, but not Kripke]

and

(WM) Whales are mammals [According to Donnellan, but not Kripke].[6]

At the same time Donnellan, Gareth Evans, David Kaplan, Kripke, Ruth Barcan Marcus, and John Perry collectively developed *Direct Reference Semantics*, also known at the time as "The New Theory of Reference" (Donnellan, 1966; Evans, 1982; Kaplan, 1978, 1989; Kripke, 1980, 1993; Marcus, 1978; Perry, 1979). Direct Reference Semantics explicitly includes ostensive dubbings, causal-historical chains of name-use, division of linguistic labor, contexts of utterance, and perceptual demonstration acts as "meta-semantic" reference-determining mechanisms. All of this, in turn, entails that the linguistic knowledge—including knowledge of the referent itself, as well as knowledge of the operating rules of the language—possessed by a competent user of directly referential terms, is minimal and often a posteriori.

---

6 (Donnellan, 1962; Kripke, 1980, 1990, 1993; Putnam, 1975b, 1975d, 1979, 1996.) Kripke defends the necessity of "Cats are animals" but not its analyticity, and presumably would say the same thing about "Whales are mammals"; see (Kripke, 1980: pp. 122-126).

Moreover, in *Demonstratives* (1989), Kaplan also argued for the existence of *analytic contingent statements* in the logic of indexicals, for example,

(KAP) I am here now.

In turn, "I am here now" is of course strongly reminiscent of Descartes's famous proposition in *Meditations* 2:

> So after considering everything very thoroughly, I must finally conclude that this proposition, *I am, I exist*, is necessarily true whenever it is put forward by me or conceived in my mind. (Descartes, 1984: p. 17)

Descartes's famous proposition then seemingly yields another analytic contingent statement that Katz very usefully dubs "The *Existo*":

(EXISTO) I am, I exist. (Katz, 1986: chs. 7-9, 11-12)

And as if things were not already bad enough for Kant's Pitchfork, in the 1980s and 90s, Graham Priest developed and defended the notion of radically non-classical or "deviant" dialetheic paraconsistent logics, as we saw in section VI.5 above. In such logics, contradictions can occur as theorems, and some propositions, sentences, or statements—known as "truth value gluts" or "true contradictions"—are assigned both the truth-value T and also the truth-value F, although contradictions are not permitted to "explode" and entail any proposition, sentence, or statement whatsoever (Priest, 1987, 1998). But in any case, it began to look as if even the seemingly self-evident universally necessary and analytic a priori law of non-contradiction could not hold up under critical scrutiny.

Then in the 1990s, some mildly non-conformist post-classical Analytic philosophers like John McDowell and the later Putnam began to wonder what was left of the "Analytic" in "Analytic philosophy," what it was all coming to, and whether it really was the end of the world as they knew it (McDowell, 1994; Putnam, 1990a, 1994, 1999).

Other fully conformist post-classical Analytic philosophers just shrugged their shoulders, however, took their cue from the reductive, scientistic sides of Quine's and Sellars's work, and became scientific naturalists, and/or proponents of "Experimental Philosophy," aka X-Phi, in the tradition of Hume and Mill (Alexander, 2012; Appiah, 2008; Horvath and Grundmann, 2012; Knobe and Nichols, 2008).

But at the same time, some other leading Analytic philosophers—particularly including David Lewis at Princeton and other Lewis-influenced philosophers, for example, Chalmers, Jackson, Ted Sider, and Williamson, at the Australian National University, Cornell, New York University, and Oxford, respectively, by Kripke, and by Kit Fine—created what I'll call a *Copernican Devolution in philosophy* (see section XVII.6.1 below)—by going back behind the historical Kant to pre-Kantian *noumenal* metaphysics for guidance and inspiration (Chalmers, 2001, 2004; Chalmers and Jackson, 2001; Fine, 2005a; Kripke, 1980; Lewis, 1986; Sider, 2011; Williamson, 2013). They call this "Analytic metaphysics," a strategic label that nicely hides its epistemically and metaphysically naïve, pre-Kantian origins:

> The central theme of [*Writing the Book of the World*] is: realism about structure. The world has a distinguished structure, a privileged description. For a representation to be fully successful, truth is not enough; the representation must also use the right concepts, so that its conceptual structure matches reality's structure. There is an objectively correct way to "write the book of the world." ... I connect structure to fundamentality. The joint-carving notions are the fundamental notions; a fact is fundamental when it is stated in joint-carving terms. A central task of metaphysics has always been to discern the ultimate or fundamental reality underlying the appearances. I think of this task as the investigation of reality's structure. (Sider, 2011: p. vii)

Three cheers for things-in-themselves!, and three more cheers for being able to know them without any skeptical worries! In any case, Analytic metaphysics unabashedly includes metaphysically robust versions of Leibniz's conception of possible worlds, Meinongian ontology, Frege's sense-reference distinction, scientific essentialism, and/or Aristotelian essentialism. Moreover, and for my purposes in this chapter, most importantly, Analytic metaphysics self-professedly employs a rigorously "analytic" methodology. Yet at the same time it has also avoided and still avoids discussing the analytic-synthetic distinction with remarkable tenacity, even despite its using the notions of "a priori intensions," "a priori entailments," and more generally a priori conceptual and modal-logical thinking, with remarkable liberality.

Even so, under the towering mushroom cloud of Quine's critique, and since the late 1940s, at least nine important attempts have been made to reconsider, re-evaluate, re-interpret, re-criticize, or re-defend the analytic-synthetic distinction: (i) Carnap's *Meaning and Necessity* in 1947, (ii) Grice's and Strawson's "In Defense of a Dogma" in 1956, (iii) Pap's *Semantics and Necessary Truth* in 1958, (iv) Paul Boghossian's "Analyticity Reconsidered" in 1996, (v) Katz's "The New Intensionalism" in 1992, and then five years later, (vi) his "Analyticity, Necessity, and the Epistemology of Semantics," in 1997, (vii) Timothy Williamson's *The Philosophy of Philosophy* in 2007, (viii) Gillian Russell's *Truth in Virtue of Meaning* in 2008, and finally (ix) Cory Juhl's and Eric Loomis's *Analyticity* in 2010. As I noted above in commenting on the critical responses to Quine up through the mid-60s, all this important philosophical work was in vain and made no noticeable difference whatsoever. And *that's the way we live now* until, inevitably, post-classical Analytic philosophy goes down into the ash-heap of history—just as its social-institutional predecessor, neo-Kantian philosophy, did in the late 1920s and early 30s, almost exactly a century ago.

XVI.3 Why the Analytic-Synthetic Distinction *Really* Matters

Leaving aside the conventional wisdom of recent and contemporary post-classical Analytic philosophy, however, it seems to me that there at least six very good reasons why the analytic-synthetic distinction is not just philosophically important, but also *really* matters.

First, if the analytic-synthetic distinction is intelligible and defensible, then an adequate theory of it provides an explanation of (i) necessary truth and a priori knowledge, and (ii) contingent truth and a posteriori knowledge.

Second, if the analytic-synthetic distinction is intelligible and defensible, and you are also a Kantian, and especially if your view (like mine) is broadly and radically Kantian, then an adequate theory of it provides explanations of (ia) analytically necessary truth and a priori knowledge of it, (ib) synthetically necessary truth and a priori knowledge of it, and (iia) synthetically contingent truth and a posteriori knowledge of it. In short, it provides an explanation of Kant's Pitchfork.

Third, if the analytic-synthetic distinction is intelligible and defensible, then an adequate theory of it provides explanations of (ia1) logical analytically necessary truth and a priori logical knowledge of it, (ia2) conceptual analytically necessary truth and a priori conceptual knowledge of it, hence also an explanation of (ia3) the nature and status of logic, and (ib1) non-logically, essentially non-conceptually, strongly metaphysically or synthetically necessary truth, whether a priori knowable or a posteriori knowable.

Fourth, if the analytic-synthetic distinction is intelligible and defensible, then it provides a foundation for classical Analytic philosophy as conceived by Frege, Moore, Russell, early Wittgenstein, and Carnap.

Fifth, if the analytic-synthetic distinction were either unintelligible or indefensible, then it's very difficult to see how recent and contemporary Analytic metaphysics would be possible, since it requires, at the very least, explanations of (ia1), (ia2), (ia3), and (ib1).

Sixth and finally, if the analytic-synthetic distinction were either unintelligible or indefensible, then the very ideas of (ia1), (ia2), (ia3), and (ib1) would all go down, and as I argued above, then the very idea of a *semantic content* would also go down, and correspondingly, domino-style, the very ideas of belief, cognition, thought, understanding, justification, knowledge, intentionality, and human rationality more generally would all go down too, since all these inherently involve and a priori presuppose the very idea of semantic content. Or in other words, if the analytic-synthetic distinction were either unintelligible or indefensible, then what I call *postmodernist anti-rational nihilist skepticism*, aka PARNS, would be true.

But quite frankly, if PARNS were true, then I'd rather be dead. Or to put it more precisely and less bombastically: If PARNS were true, then there would be no rational human animals or real human persons whatsoever, so I wouldn't actually exist, and you, the sentient, sapient reader of this sentence, wouldn't actually exist either.

Luckily, as Descartes pointed out, we exist and, necessarily, we can also know that we exist, given that we think (Descartes, 1984: p. 17). Even more to the point, I think that it's simply impossible to see how one could ever formulate, defend, or establish PARNS without also presupposing categorically normative human cognitive and practical rationality in the form of logical reasoning and moral justification according to (at least) minimal principles of consistency, validity, soundness, and consistent universalizability. This presupposition, in turn, self-undermines postmodernist anti-rational nihilist skepticism. I'm vividly reminded here of the Nihilist thugs in the cult-favorite Coen brothers' 1998 movie *The Big Lebowski*, who loudly complain that it's *not fair* that The Dude has lied to them. In point of fact, only a rational human animal or human person could ever doubt or attempt to refute rationality, or morally justify doing so. Or in other and plainer words, PARNS is cognitive suicide by logico-rational and moral self-stultification (Bonjour, 1998: esp. chs. 1, 3, 4; Hanna, 2006c: ch. 7).

My overall conclusion so far, then, is that in order to make a broadly and radically Kantian philosophy of the future really and truly possible after post-classical Analytic philosophy goes down into the ash-heap of history, and more generally in order to save the world as we know it from being taken over by self-conscious, explicit or unwitting, implicit defenders of PARNS, an intelligible and defensible version of the analytic-synthetic distinction is now absolutely required. In other words, we have no rational choice but to bring about *the return of the analytic-synthetic distinction.*

Furthermore, and in defence of Kant's Pitchfork, I also want to reject and refute what I will call *The Ultimate Dogma of Empiricism*, which says that

> There's one and only one basic kind of necessity, and thus one and only one basic kind of necessary truth (= *modal monism*).

This is because, on the contrary, I believe that there are two essentially different and basic kinds of necessity—namely, (i) the kind of necessity that flows from the nature of concepts (conceptual, logical, "weak metaphysical," or analytic necessity), and (ii) the kind of necessity that flows from the immanent structures of things in the veridically apparent or manifestly real world, via essentially non-conceptual content (essentially non-conceptual, non-logical, "strong metaphysical," or synthetic necessity),and also that these in turn directly correspond to the two essentially different and basic kinds of mental content, namely, conceptual content and essentially non-conceptual content, and thus there are two essentially different kinds of necessary truth (= *content-and-rationality-based modal dualism*) (Hanna, 2015a: chs. 5-8). In the rest of this chapter, then, I'll carefully explicate and decisively criticize Quine's, Kripke's, Putnam's, and Kaplan's criticisms of the analytic-synthetic distinction. In turn, those thrilling adventures of the analytic-synthetic distinction will also add up to a thoroughgoing critique of the logical, semantic, epistemic, and metaphysical foundations of post-classical Analytic philosophy.

XVI.4 Quine's Critique of the Analytic-Synthetic Distinction, and a Meta-Critique

For the purposes of the rest of this chapter, for convenience's sake, I'm going to stipulate that the notions of *proposition, statement, meaningful indicative sentence, sentence-on-an-interpretation, sentence-on-a-reading,* and *sentence-according-to-a-constative-use,* and as all mutually necessarily equivalent, unless otherwise noted. Finer distinctions could be made between each term in the multiple equivalence, if needed. But at a suitable level of generality, it seems clear that they all convey the same basic notion: *that which expresses a complete and true-or-false belief, judgment, or thought.* So nothing special should turn on this stipulation. At the same time, however, I also want to re-emphasize a classical distinction between (i) *sentences,* i.e., grammatically and syntactically well-formed indicative complete-and-true/false-belief/judgment/thought-expressing units of some natural language L, and (ii) *statements,* i.e., logically structured, linguistically-expressed, intersubjectively-shareable semantic contents with respect to *L* that are also inherently truth-or-falsity bearers with respect to *L*.[7] It follows directly from this classical distinction, together with the semantic theory that I'm proposing, that one and the same sentence will always be able to express two or more distinct statements. More precisely, the semantic theory I am proposing is a systematic *dual-content* semantics (Hanna, 2015a). But this is intended to be smoothly consistent with the stipulation I made at the beginning of this section. Thus the following six notions are also all mutually necessarily equivalent: and (i) two or more distinct propositions expressed by the same sentence, (ii) two or more distinct statements made with the same sentence, (iii) two or more distinct meanings of the same indicative sentence, (iv) two or more distinct interpretations of the same sentence, (v) two or more distinct readings of the same sentence, and (vi) two or more distinct constative uses of the same sentence.

Foregrounded against that theoretical backdrop, here are Quine's working definitions of logical truth and analyticity, formulated in his favored terminology of "statements":

> A statement S is a logical truth if and only if S is true under every distinct uniform assignment of values to the non-logical constants of S (Quine, 1961b: p. 22, 1976c: p. 81).

> A statement S is a logical truth if and only if S is true and only logical constants occur essentially in S (Quine, 1976b: p. 110, 1976c: p. 81).

> A statement S is analytic if and only if S is true by virtue of meaning, independently of fact (Quine, 1961b: p. 20).

> A statement S is analytic if and only if S is either (i) true by virtue of (monadic) elementary logic, or (ii) translatable into a truth of (monadic) elementary logic by replacing synonyms by synonyms (Quine, 1961b: pp. 22-23)

---

[7] By saying that statements are inherently truth-or-falsity bearers, I mean that statements are inherently the sort of things that *can be* assigned truth-values, not that they are *always* assigned truth-values. For there can be statements that are not assigned truth-values under some interpretations, i.e., truth-value *gaps.*

A statement S is analytic if and only if S is necessary (Quine, 1961b: pp. 29-30)

A statement S is analytic if and only if S is a priori (Quine, 1961b: pp. 41-43).

Correspondingly, in view of those working definitions, here are what I take to be the six basic Quinean arguments against the analytic-synthetic distinction, and also eighteen critical replies to the six basic Quinean arguments.

1. The Carnap-Schlick-Ayer arguments against the synthetic a priori, assumed by Quine, even if not explicitly defended by him (Ayer, 1952: chs. I and IV; Carnap, 1935: pp. 9-38, 1959; Schlick, 1949).

Carnap-Schlick-Ayer(-Quine)'s Argument 1.1: A statement S is meaningful if and only if S is either analytic or empirically verifiable (= The Verifiability Principle). But synthetic a priori statements are neither analytic nor empirically verifiable. So synthetic a priori statements are meaningless.

Carnap-Schlick-Ayer(-Quine)'s Argument 1.2: Synthetic a priori statements presuppose transcendental idealism. But transcendental idealism is either analytically false or meaningless. So it's impossible for synthetic a priori statements to exist.

Three Critical Replies

Critical Reply #1: The Verifiability Principle is itself neither analytic nor empirically verifiable; hence The Verifiability Principle is deemed meaningless by The Verifiability Principle itself. Of course, this is a classical objection to Verificationism (Ayer, 1952: p. 16). One equally classical Verificationist reply is to claim that The Verifiability Principle is a meta-linguistic principle, not a first-order statement, and that The Verifiability Principle is intended to apply to all and only first-order statements, and not to itself (Hempel, 1959: pp. 123-126). But obviously, that still leaves open the following worry: What is the precise semantic status of *meta-linguistic principles*? Verificationists have never been able to answer this question satisfactorily, and thus have never been able to rule out the possibility that The Verifiability Principle is *itself* synthetic a priori. But if The Verifiability Principle itself is or at least might be synthetic a priori, then it cannot coherently be used in order to rule out the meaningfulness (or for that matter, the truth) of synthetic a priori statements.

Critical Reply #2: All forms of transcendental idealism hold that the world we directly perceive must conform to the non-empirical structures of our innately-specified cognitive capacities, in some or another substantive sense of "must conform." The Carnap-Schlick-Ayer argument against the synthetic a priori assumes that every Kantian theory of the synthetic a priori is committed to *strong transcendental idealism*. In turn, strong transcendental idealism makes the following three basic claims: (i) things-in-themselves aka "noumena" in the positive sense, or Really Real things, i.e., things as they could exist in a "lonely" way, altogether independently of rational human minds or anything else, by virtue of their intrinsic non-relational properties) really exist and cause our perceptions, although rational human cognizers only ever perceive mere appearances or subjective phenomena, (ii) rational human cognizers actually impose the non-empirical structures of their innate cognitive capacities onto the veridically apparent or manifestly real world they cognize, i.e., necessarily, all the essential forms or structures of the proper objects of human cognition are literally type-identical to the a priori forms or structures that are non-empirically generated by our innately specified spontaneous cognitive capacities, and (iii) necessarily, if all rational human cognizers went out of existence, then so would the manifestly real world they cognize. But the Carnap-Schlick-Ayer assumption is false. At least some contemporary Kantian theories of the synthetic a priori—for example, the one I defended in *Cognition, Content, and A Priori* and that I'm also asserting to be true here in this book (see, for example, section XV.1 above)—are committed instead just to weak or counterfactual transcendental idealism, which makes the following four claims: (i) things-in-themselves are logically possible, but at the same time it's a priori knowably unknowable and unprovable whether things-in-themselves/noumena exist or not, hence for the purposes of an adequate anthropocentric or "human-faced" metaphysics, epistemology, and ethics, they can be ignored (radical agnosticism and methodological eliminativism about things-in-themselves/noumena) (Hanna, 2017c), (ii) necessarily, all the proper objects of rational human cognition have the same forms or structures as—i.e., they are isomorphic to—the forms or structures that are non-empirically generated by our innately-specified spontaneous cognitive capacities, but at the same time those veridically apparent or manifestly real worldly forms or structures are not literally type-identical to those a priori cognitive forms or structures (the isomorphism-without-type-identity thesis), (iii) it's a necessary condition of the existence of the veridically apparent or manifestly real world that if some rational human animals were to exist in that world, then they would veridically cognize that world, via either essentially non-conceptual content or conceptual content, at least to some extent (the counterfactual cognizability thesis), (iv) the veridically apparent or manifestly real world has at some earlier times existed without rational human minded animals, or any other minded beings, to cognize it veridically, and could exist even if no rational human minded animals, or any other minded beings, ever existed to cognize it veridically, even though some rational human animals now actually exist in that world—for example, I (R.H.) now actually exist in the manifestly real world—who do in fact cognize it veridically, at least to some extent (the existential thesis). So even if it were correct that strong transcendental idealism is either analytically false or meaningless, it would nevertheless be a serious *non sequitur* to extend this to weak or counterfactual transcendental idealism without further substantive justification.

Critical Reply #3: After the fall of classical logicism and in the light of Gödel's incompleteness theorems, Tarski's semantic conception of truth, Kripke's modal essentialism, and Fine's non-modal essentialism, it's clear that there are some consistently deniable, non-logical, essentially non-conceptual, "strongly metaphysical," or synthetic necessities that are also knowable a priori, for example, mathematical truths. So it's clear that there are at least some synthetic a priori truths in that sense. Hence, at the very least, it's not impossible for synthetic a priori statements to exist, since clearly some synthetic a priori statements in that sense do indeed exist. Now it's true that Gödel himself held that the undecidable, unprovable mathematical truths whose existence is entailed by his first incompleteness theorem are consistently deniable, non-logical, and a priori, yet still analytic or conceptual truths (Hanna, 2009b). Nevertheless, that of course doesn't show that the Gödel sentences *aren't* synthetic a priori statements, but rather only that they can be called "analytic" according to a notion of "so-called analyticity" that deviates significantly from all the classical conceptions of analyticity. The problem here is partly historical, and partly terminological. If a philosopher belongs to the logical empiricist/positivist tradition or one of its immediate successors, then if any non-logically, essentially non-conceptually, or strongly metaphysically necessary truths are held to exist, they must nevertheless be called "analytic" or "conceptual" truths. That's because, according to that tradition and its immediate successors there simply cannot be synthetic a priori statements. Hence they'll be called "analytic" or "conceptual" truths according to the vacuous line of reasoning which question-beggingly assumes that all a priori necessity is analytic or conceptual necessity. Then any statements that are discovered to be a priori and necessary "must be" analytic or conceptual necessities, even if they do not fit any classical profile of analytically or conceptually true statements, and even if in fact they also satisfy the classical criteria of synthetic apriority (Juhl and Loomis, 2010: chs. 1, 3, 5). But such statements are "analytic" or "conceptual" truths only in a misnomer-based, Pickwickian, or so-called sense, simply because they deviate importantly from all the classical conceptions of analyticity and conceptual truth, and because they also satisfy the classical criteria for synthetic a priority. Strictly speaking, then, they should be called "synthetic a priori statements," although it would perhaps be even more accurate to call them "schmanalytic" statements. I'll come back again to this issue about so-called analyticity, so-called conceptual truth, or *schmanalyticity*, in section XVI.5 below.

2. Quine's logical regress argument against the conventionalist theory of the analytic-synthetc distinction in either 2(i*) the epistemic version or 2(ii*) the metaphysical version.

According to conventionalism, a meaningful sentence S is logically necessarily true by convention if and only if we stipulate that S is logically necessary within some logical system L, and also assert S to be true, come what may. Then according to the conventionalist theory of analyticity, a meaningful sentence S is analytic if and only S is true by convention. In criticizing conventionalism, Quine famously says that

> [i]n a word, the difficulty is that if logic is to proceed *mediately* from conventions, logic is needed for inferring logic from the conventions. Alternatively, the difficulty which appears thus as a self-presupposition of doctrine can be framed as turning upon a self-presupposition of primitives. It is supposed that the *if*-idiom, the *not*-idiom, the *every*-idiom, and so on, mean nothing to us initially, and that we adopt the conventions … by way of circumscribing their meaning; and the difficulty is that communication of [the conventions] themselves depends on free use of those very idioms which we are attempting to circumscribe, and can succeed only if we are already conversant with the idioms. (Quine, 1976c: p. 104)

Quine's argument here is clearly intimately related to our old friend, *The Logocentric Predicament*:

> Logic cannot be explained or justified without presupposing and using logic. So logic is both unjustifiable and inexplicable, i.e., rationally groundless (Sheffer, 1926; Hanna, 2006c: ch. 3).

Now, The Predicament can be construed either (i) epistemically, as a puzzle about justifying logical beliefs, or (ii) metaphysically, as a puzzle about the nature of logic. Correspondingly, Quine's critique of Conventionalism can be naturally read in these two distinct ways, either (i*) as an epistemic argument against conventionalism, or (ii*) as a metaphysical argument against conventionalism. I'll present both versions of Quine's argument directly below, and then proceed to criticize each of them.

Quine's Argument 2(i):* In order to justify our belief in meaningful sentences that are logically necessary or analytic by convention, we must presuppose and use non-conventional classical logical truths and logical notions. So not all our beliefs in logical or analytic truths are conventionalistically-justified beliefs. Therefore, conventionalism cannot support an intelligible or defensible analytic-synthetic distinction.

Quine's Argument 2(ii):* In order to explain the existence and specific character of meaningful sentences that are logically necessary or analytic by convention, we must presuppose and use non-conventional classical logical truths and logical notions. So not all analytic truths are truths by convention. Therefore, conventionalism cannot support an intelligible or defensible analytic-synthetic distinction.

Two Critical Replies

Critical Reply #1: I fully concede to Quine that conventionalism can't support an intelligible or defensible analytic-synthetic distinction. From this, of course, it doesn't follow that there can't be an intelligible or defensible version of the analytic-synthetic distinction, period. Indeed, I've argued in *Cognition, Content, and the A Priori*, section 4.7, that there's at least one intelligible and defensible version of the analytic-synthetic distinction—namely, precisely that version which is provided by what I rather long-windedly but still accurately call *the content-and-rationality theory of the analytic-synthetic distinction and modal dualism*.

Critical Reply #2: The epistemic version of The Logocentric Predicament argument says that our belief in meaningful sentences that are logically necessary or analytic by convention cannot be justified without also believing in non-conventional classical logic. And the metaphysical version of The Logocentric Predicament argument says that in order to explain the existence and specific character of meaningful sentences that are logically necessary or analytic by convention, we must presuppose and use non-conventional classical logical truths and logical notions. But can Quine himself avoid The Logocentric Predicament? There are very good reasons to think *that he can't*.

In "Two Dogmas," Quine says that no statement is immune from revision, including the laws of logic, and correspondingly that no belief—no matter how firmly it is held to be true come what may (i.e., no matter how a priori it seems)—is infallible, including beliefs in logical truths and logical laws:

> No statement is immune from revision. Revision even of the logical law of excluded middle has been proposed as a means of simplifying quantum mechanics; and what difference is there in principle between such a shift and the shift whereby Kepler superseded Ptolemy, or Einstein Newton, or Darwin Aristotle? (Quine, 1961b: p. 43)

I'll call Quine's thesis that no statement or belief is immune from revision *The Universal Revisability Principle*. One clear implication of The Universal Revisability Principle is *that even the logical law of non-contradiction must be revisable*. But here's what Quine says in *Philosophy of Logic* about the revisability of the law of non-contradiction:

> [Deviant logic] is not just a change of demarcation, either, between what to call logical truth and what to call extra-logical truth. It is a question rather of outright rejection of part of our logic as not true at all. It would seem that such an idea of deviation in logic is absurd on the face of it. If sheer logic is not conclusive, what is? What higher tribunal could abrogate the logic of truth functions or of quantification?... Here, evidently, is the deviant logician's predicament: when he tries to deny the doctrine [of the law of non-contradiction] he only changes the subject. (Quine, 1986: pp. 80-81)

So according to Quine, the law of non-contradiction is unrevisable *because its acceptance partially constitutes the very idea of a logic*. A deviant logician's attempted rejection of the law of non-contradiction is then "absurd on the face of it," for "when he tries to deny the doctrine he only changes the subject," and thereby gives up doing logic altogether. But on the contrary, says Quine, the law of non-contradiction is "sheer logic," i.e., *essentially* logic, and if sheer logic isn't "conclusive," i.e., true and "obvious" (Quine, 1986: p. 82), then nothing ever is conclusive. I'll call this *The Sheer Logic Principle*. Obviously, The Universal Revisability Principle and The Sheer Logic Principle are flat-out mutually inconsistent. Given The Universal Revisability Principle, it follows that no statement is unrevisable, therefore the law of contradiction is revisable; whereas given The Sheer Logic Principle, it follows that the law of non-contradiction is unrevisable, therefore some statements are unrevisable. So, given The Universal Revisability Principle and The Sheer Logic Principle, no statements are unrevisable and yet some statements are unrevisable, and the law of non-contradiction is both revisable and unrevisable. I'll call this inconsistency *Quine's Predicament*. I want to emphasize that Quine's Predicament is not just an unfortunate but philosophically forgivable howler or merely verbal inconsistency—as it were, Quine forgivably nodding off occasionally, 30 years after "Two Dogmas." On the contrary, I think that Quine's Predicament goes like a dagger into the very heart of Quine's overall critique of the analytic-synthetic distinction.

More precisely, Quine's Predicament is about the deeply puzzling nature and status of logic itself. Quine's argument against conventionalism's theory of the analytic-synthetic distinction says that logic cannot be justified or explained without presupposing and using logic. So when Quine asserts The Sheer Logic Principle, since he's thereby telling us precisely how our belief in the law of non-contradiction is to be justified and also how the semantic status of the law of non-contradiction is to be explained, he must also be presupposing and using logic. But then when Quine asserts The Universal Revisability Principle, which contradicts The Sheer Logic Principle, not only is he contradicting himself, but also he's presupposing and using logic in order to doubt the justifiability of logical beliefs and to doubt the truth of logical principles. So, in effect, Quine's Predicament is Quine's committing cognitive suicide by logical self-stultification (Katz, 1998: pp. 72-74; Hanna, 2001: pp. 281-285). And that's very bad news indeed for Quine's overall critique of the analytic-synthetic distinction. But that also means that for us there's still more philosophical work to be done—we can't merely leave Quine hanging, hoisted, as it were, on his own sheer logical petard. We still need to face up to the deeply puzzling nature and status of logic. Correspondingly, for better or worse, I've work out an explicit solution to Quine's Predicament in *Cognition, Content, and the A Priori*, ch. 5.

3. Quine's circularity-of-synonymy argument against the analytic-synthetic distinction.

As we saw at the beginning of this chapter, right at the beginning of "Two Dogmas" Quine informally characterizes analyticity as truth "grounded in meanings independently of matters of fact." But then a little later in "Two Dogmas" he also more carefully defines analyticity in two steps, by first identifying two distinct classes of analytic truths, and then secondly basing analytic truths of the second class on analytic truths of the first class. Or to be more precise, first, he says that at least some truths of elementary logic are analytic (the first class), and then, second, he says that all the other analytic truths result from the analytic truths of elementary logic by replacing synonyms by synonyms (the second class):

> [Analytic statements] fall into two classes. Those of the first class, which may be called *logically true*, are typified by:
>
> (1) No unmarried man is married.
>
> The relevant feature of this example is that it not merely is true as it stands, but remains true under any and all reinterpretations of "man" and "married." If we suppose a prior inventory of *logical* particles, comprising "no," "un-," "not," "if," "then," "and," etc., then in general a logical truth is a statement which is true and remains true under all reinterpretations of its components other than the logical particles. But there is a second class of analytic statements, typified by:
>
> (2) No bachelor is married.
>
> The characteristic of such a statement is that it can be turned into a logical truth by putting synonyms for synonyms; thus (2) can be turned into (1) by putting "unmarried man" for its synonym "bachelor." (Quine, 1961b: pp. 22-23)

Then he says, or at least he clearly implies, that although the first class of analytic truths is properly characterized, nevertheless the second class of analytic statements lacks a proper characterization:

> We still lack a proper characterization of this second class of analytic statements, and therewith of analyticity generally, inasmuch as we have had in the above description to lean on a notion of "synonymy" which is in no less need of clarification than analyticity itself. (Quine, 1961b: p. 23)

This lack of proper characterization stems from the fact that, in order to explicate analyticity in terms of replacing synonyms by synonyms, we must also explicate synonymy. But according to Quine, there are three and only three ways of explicating synonymy, namely, in terms of (i) definition, (ii) interchangeability *salva veritate* (i.e., "preserving truth"), or (iii) semantic rules. And each of these explications either presupposes or uses the notions of synonymy, necessity, or apriority. So the explanation of the second class of analytic statements in terms of synonymy is implicitly circular:

> Our argument is not flatly circular, but something like it. It has the form, figuratively speaking, of a closed curve in space. (Quine, 1961b: p. 30)

Therefore, there's no intelligible or defensible analytic-synthetic distinction.

Three Critical Replies

Critical Reply #1: Quine clearly assumes that at least some truths of elementary logic are properly characterized as analytic in order to define synonymy-based analyticity, then claim that synonymy-based analyticity is not properly characterized, and then attack the very idea of it. So even if the characterization of the second class of analytic statements is circular by way of synonymy, the characterization of the first class of analytic statements remains unchallenged by him. Therefore, it seems clear enough that by Quine's own admission, there's an intelligible and defensible analytic-synthetic distinction after all, namely, between (i) analytically true statements of *elementary logic*, and (ii) all other truths. Actually, it's arguable that for Quine not every truth of elementary logic is analytic in a properly characterized sense. Indeed, there's good reason to believe that Quine held that only the *monadic* truths of elementary logic are analytic in a properly characterized sense. Monadic logic is a restricted classical logic that includes sentential logic and the logic of quantification into one-place predicates. So the monadic truths of elementary logic include all the truth-functional tautologies, and all the logical truths involving one-place predicates and one-place quantifiers only. For more on these seemingly abstruse but in fact crucially important points, see *Cognition, Content, and the A Priori*, section 5.2. In any case, in a crucial footnote in *Word and Object*, Quine says:

> Those who talk confidently of analyticity have been known to disagree on the analyticity of the truths of arithmetic, but are about unanimous on that of the truths of logic. We who are less clear on the notion of analyticity may therefore seize upon

> the generally conceded analyticity of the truths of logic as a partial extensional clarification of analyticity; but to do this is not to embrace the analyticity of the truths of logic as an antecedently intelligible doctrine. I have been misunderstood on this score. (Quine, 1960: p. 65, n. 3)

It's easy enough to see why Quine had been "misunderstood on this score." What in Sam Hill is he actually saying here? One clear implication of the footnote is that he concedes "the generally conceded analyticity of the truths of logic." Therefore, he concedes that there is a generally conceded analytic-synthetic distinction between the analytic truths of elementary logic and all other truths. But "this is not to concede the analyticity of the truths of logic as an antecedently intelligible doctrine." That seems true enough on the face of it. But it doesn't follow from it that there's any reason whatsoever to believe that the analyticity of the analytic truths of elementary logic cannot be an *ultimately* intelligible doctrine. Indeed, Quine has offered no reason whatsoever to hold that the analyticity of analytic elementary logical truths isn't perfectly intelligible at the end of the day. On the contrary, as we have seen, he himself offers a beautifully clear and intelligible characterization of logical truth in "Truth by Convention" (Quine,; 1976c: p. 81; also in 1976b: p. 110). Moreover, as we've also seen, he holds in *Philosophy of Logic* that anyone who tries to deny the law of non-contradiction is merely changing the subject, and that if sheer logic is not conclusive, then nothing is. Therefore, Quine *ultimately* concedes both the intelligibility and also the defensibility of the analyticity of the analytic truths of elementary logic, even if he hasn't conceded this "antecedently," and thus he concedes that at the end of the logico-philosophical day there's at least one intelligible and defensible analytic-synthetic distinction.

Critical Reply #2: As many critics have noted, Quine's circularity-of-synonymy argument makes no attempt to exhaust the different possible explications of synonymy. More precisely, it's an argument by cases, and Quine makes no attempt to show that the logical space of possible cases has been exhausted.[8] Thus he hasn't ruled out the possibility of a non-circular explication of synonymy. And in this way, he hasn't even ruled out the possibility of an intelligible and defensible analytic-synthetic distinction between (i) the union of the first and *second* classes of analytic statements, and (ii) all other truths.

Critical Reply #3: In the first four sections of "Two Dogmas," Quine clearly assumes that only reductive explanations of analyticity will suffice for an adequate explication

---

[8] In September 1985, when I was still a graduate student at Yale, Jerrold Katz buttonholed me on a flight from New York to Pittsburgh, where we were both attending a conference (my very first), and vigorously pointed out to me, step by step, most of the major flaws in the argument of "Two Dogmas," including the argument-by-cases problem. As a recent matriculant of graduate school bootcamp, I'd pledged allegiance to the assumption that "Two Dogmas" was unchallengeable and written in stone: so I was utterly floored, and then the Quinean scales fell from my eyes. More precisely, and in all seriousness, this encounter changed my philosophical and professional academic life. It wasn't just that Quine's basic arguments and claims could and should be seriously challenged, criticized, and rejected, but also that the conventional wisdom of mainstream post-classical Analytic philosophy could and should receive the same treatment right across the board. Of course, Katz can't be held responsible for either the short-term or long-term consequences of my conversion on the road to Pittsburgh.

of it. But then he explicitly adopts both *semantic holism* for the contents of statements and also *confirmation holism* for the assertion of statements, in the last two sections:

> [O]ur statements about the external world face the tribunal of sense experience not individually but only as a corporate body.... The unit of empirical significance is the whole of science.... The totality of our so-called knowledge or beliefs, from the most casual matters of geography and history to the profoundest laws of atomic physics or even of pure mathematics and logic, is a man-made fabric which impinges on experience only along the edges. Or, to change the figure, total science is like a field of force whose boundary conditions are experience. A conflict with experience at the periphery occasions readjustments in the interior of the field. Truth values have to be redistributed over some of our statements. Reëvaluation of some statements entails reëvaluation of others, because of their logical interconnections—the logical laws being in turn simply certain further statements of the system, certain further statements of the field. Having reëvaluated one statement we must reëvaluate some others, which may be statements logically connected with the first or may be the statements of the logical connections themselves. But the total field is so undermined by its boundary conditions, experience, that there is much latitude of choice as to what statements to reëvaluate in the light of any single contrary experience. No particular experiences are linked with any particular statements in the interior of the field, except indirectly through consideration of equilibrium affected the field as a whole. (Quine, 1961b: pp. 42-43)

Now, it's obvious that any scientific or philosophical explanation of any fact or any phenomenon that could be offered by someone who is both a semantic holist and a confirmation holist, will be a holistic explication or explanation. So to the extent that Quine is committed to the acceptability of any explanation at all, he must at least be committed to the acceptability of holistic explanations. Therefore, as Grice and Strawson first pointed out in "In Defense of a Dogma," and as many others have also pointed out since then, Quine is thereby at least implicitly committed to the thesis that if a specifically holistic explanation of analyticity or more generally of the analytic-synthetic distinction can be given, then the analytic-synthetic distinction will be acceptable. For the record, I myself strongly doubt, as against Grice and Strawson, that there can be an adequate holistic explanation of either analyticity or the analytic-synthetic distinction—although I do also argue in *Cognition, Content, and the A Priori*, section 4.7, that one sub-type of analyticity depends on a special localized semantic holism with respect to the contents of certain concepts. But that's not the critical point I'm specifically concerned with here. The critical point I'm zeroing in on is about Quine's global holism with respect to meaning, confirmation, and explanation. And the point is just that since holism is inherently non-reductive, Quine's holding Frege, Carnap, or anyone else to the methodological standard of a strictly reductive explication or explanation of analyticity is rationally uncharitable at the best and rationally self-stultifying at worst. In the end, for my purposes, it's *non-reductive* philosophical explanations that really matter, not *holistic* explanations. Indeed, in *Cognition, Content, and the A Priori*, again in section 4.7, I offer a detailed non-reductive but also non-holistic—except for the special localized concept-holism I mentioned in passing just above—explanation of the analytic-synthetic distinction. But in any case, given Quine's global holism, certainly nothing he says in "Two Dogmas" can be used against non-reductive explanations per se, methodologically speaking.

4. *Quine's argument against the analytic-synthetic distinction from confirmation holism and universal revisability.*

In "Two Dogmas," the second Dogma of Empiricism is "the Verification Theory and Reductionism," hence *verificationist reductionism*, which says that truths are either analytic, hence unrevisable, or else semantically reducible to primitive observation sentences plus logical operations on them (compositional atomicity). And according to Quine, this is ultimately the same as the analytic-synthetic distinction: "[t]he two dogmas are, indeed, at root identical" (Quine, 1961b: p. 41). But contrariwise to these identical dogmas, all statements are necessarily related to one another via their contents (i.e., semantic holism), and all statements are confirmed collectively, not individually (i.e., confirmation holism). Furthermore, no statement is immune from revision (i.e., The Universal Revisability Principle). So verificationist reductionism is not only false, but also incoherent. Therefore, there is no intelligible or defensible analytic-synthetic distinction.

Four Critical Replies

Critical Reply#1: If The Universal Revisability Principle is true, then The Universal Revisability Principle is itself revisable. If The Universal Revisability Principle is itself revisable, then either (i) the denial of The Universal Revisability Principle is true (if The Universal Revisability Principle means that it is unrevisably true that every statement is revisable), or at the very least (ii) the denial of The Universal Revisability Principle is possibly true (if The Universal Revisability Principle means that it just so happens to be unrevisably true that every statement is revisable). So The Universal Revisability Principle either, on the one hand, deems the denial of itself to be true, which is flat-out paradoxical. Or, on the other hand, at the very least, The Universal Revisability Principle entails that it's possible that its own denial is true, which is virtually paradoxical. This is because there will then be some possible worlds accessible from the actual world—where, by hypothesis, The Universal Revisability Principle is strictly universally true—in which the denial of The Universal Revisability Principle is also true. This obvious "Liar"-paradox style objection is also, of course, of the same general form as the classical objection to The Verifiability Principle, and given Quine's keen interest in "the ways of paradox" (Quine, 1976d), it's hard to believe that Quine wasn't aware of it. Assuming charitably that he *was* aware of it, then he must have regarded The Universal Revisability Principle as a meta-statement and the rational result of an exercise in "semantic ascent" (Quine, 1960: pp. 270-276). But even so, The Universal Revisability Principle flat-out contradicts The Sheer Logic Principle. So the obvious "Liar"-paradox style objection to The Universal Revisability Principle also indirectly shows, again, just how philosophically dire Quine's Predicament is.

Critical Reply #2: Despite what Quine asserts, it's *not* true that verificationist reductionism and the analytic-synthetic distinction are "identical." It's clear that someone could deny verificationist reductionism, but also consistently assert the analytic-synthetic distinction. For example, semantic platonists like Katz can consistently hold that verificationist reductionism is false and that the analytic-synthetic distinction is both intelligible and defensible (Katz, 1981, 1990). Hence rejecting verificationist reductionism has no critical impact on semantic platonist approaches to the analytic-synthetic distinction. Now, the content-and-rationality theory of the analytic-synthetic distinction and modal dualism that I develop in *Cognition, Content, and the A Priori*, ch. 4, in fact rejects both verificationist reductionism and semantic platonism *alike*. Hence the most important philosophical moral of this story for my purposes here is that the analytic-synthetic distinction is logically independent of verificationist reductionism and not affected by the latter's falsity.

Critical Reply #3: It's quite true that both confirmation holism and The Universal Revisability Principle would be well-supported by the truth of the fusion of Dewey's pragmatism and C.I. Lewis's pragmatism (Lewis, 1923; White, 1950). So if Deweyan/Lewisian pragmatism were in fact true, then there's no intelligible or defensible analytic-synthetic distinction. But what is Quine's actual argument for accepting the truth of Deweyan/Lewisian pragmatism? And even more to the point: How can Deweyan/Lewisian pragmatism ever adequately explain the nature of logic and logical knowledge?

Critical Reply #4: This rhetorical leading question leads us right back into Quine's Predicament. In the famous text quoted a few paragraphs above, which spells out Quine's confirmation holism, he says:

> Reëvaluation of some statements entails reëvaluation of others, because of their logical interconnections—the logical laws being in turn simply certain further statements of the system, certain further statements of the field. Having reëvaluated one statement we must reëvaluate some others, which may be statements logically connected with the first or may be the statements of the logical connections themselves.

Deweyan/Lewisian pragmatism together with confirmation holism jointly entail The Universal Revisability Principle. The Universal Revisability Principle together with confirmation holism jointly entail the revisability of the law of non-contradiction. But then the revisability of the law of non-contradiction together with The Sheer Logic Principle jointly entail Quine's Predicament. Clearly, Quine must give up either Deweyan/Lewisian pragmatism, confirmation holism, The Universal Revisability Principle, or The Sheer Logic Principle, on pain of committing cognitive suicide by logical self-stultification. As long as this dire logical situation holds, and we still do not know which of the four theses Quine would actually give up, this means that any argument against the analytic-synthetic distinction that rests on one or more of them simply cannot be sound.

5. Quine's "flight from intensions" argument against the analytic-synthetic distinction.

Intensions or meanings, Fregean senses, and Kantian concepts are all nothing but Aristotelian essences fused to words, which, as obscure entities that mediate between the theory of synonymy and analyticity on the one hand, and the theory of reference on the other hand, should be eliminated:

> The Aristotelian notion of essence was the forerunner, no doubt, of the modern notion of intension or meaning.... Things had essences for Aristotle, but only linguistic forms have meanings. Meaning is what essence becomes when it is divorced from the object of reference and wedded to the word. For the theory of meaning a conspicuous question is the nature of its objects: what sort of things are meanings? A felt need for meant entities may derive from an earlier failure to appreciate that meaning and reference are distinct. Once the theory of meaning is sharply separated from the theory of reference, it is but a short step to recognizing as the primary business of the theory of meaning simply synonymy of linguistic forms and the analyticity of statements; meanings themselves, as obscure intermediary entities, may well be abandoned. (Quine, 1961b: p. 22)

It's true that, as Brentano and Chisholm argued, the notions of intentionality and intensionality are irreducible, interderivable, and mutually indispensable. But if one is personally inclined to believe that natural science limns the true and ultimate structure of reality, if one is a reductive physicalist, and if one is also a behaviorist, then one should also hold that intentionality and intensionality cannot be explained in scientific terms. So, again, one should eliminate intensions as well as intentionality:

> The Scholastic word "intentional" was revived by Brentano in connection with the verbs of propositional attitude and related verbs ... [such as] "hunt," "want," etc. The division between such idioms and the normally tractable ones is notable.... Moreover it is intimately related to the division between behaviorism and mentalism, between efficient cause and final cause, and between literal theory and dramatic portrayal.... [T]here remains a thesis of Brentano's, illuminatingly developed of late by Chisholm, that is directly relevant to our emerging doubts over the propositional attitudes and other intentional locutions. It is roughly that there is no breaking out of the intentional vocabulary by explaining its members in other terms. Our present reflections are favorable to this thesis.... Chisholm counts the semantical terms "meaning," "denote," "synonymous," and the like into the intentional vocabulary, and questions the extent to which such terms can be explained without the help of other semantical or intentional ones.... One may accept the Brentano thesis either as showing the indispensability of intentional idioms and the importance of an autonomous science of intention, or as showing the baselessness of intentional idioms and the emptiness of a science of intention. My attitude, unlike Brentano's, is the second.... Not that I would forswear daily use of intentional idioms, or maintain that they are practically dispensable. But

they call, I think, for bifurcation in canonical notation. Which turning to take depends on which of the various purposes of a canonical notation happens to be motivating us at the time. If we are limning the true and ultimate structure of reality, the canonical scheme for us is the austere scheme that knows no quotation but direct quotation and no propositional attitudes but only the physical constitution and behavior of organisms. (Quine, 1960: pp. 219-221)

Therefore, there's no intelligible or defensible analytic-synthetic distinction.

Four Critical Replies

Critical Reply #1: As Strawson very correctly pointed out, Quine's definition of a logical truth in "Truth by Convention"—a definition that Quine never renounced in later work, and in fact repeatedly cited—implicitly entails the existence of material concepts or material intensions, by way of its treatment of the semantic role of non-logical constants in logical truths (Strawson, 1957). But perhaps even more importantly, it's also the case that Quine's definition of a logical truth implicitly entails the existence of *formal* concepts or *formal* intensions, by way of its treatment of the logical constants in logical truths. More precisely, for Quine logical constants are expressions that have an "essential occurrence" in true statements, as opposed to non-logical constants, which have a merely vacuous occurrence (Quine, 1976c: p. 80). Otherwise put, in giving a proper characterization of a logical truth, *Quine helps himself to intensional essences*. Hence even if Quine officially rejects the existence of *material* intensions, he also always implicitly accepts the existence of *formal* intensions, and thus never completely eliminates all intensions from his semantics.

Critical Reply #2: When Quine explicitly rejects intensions or meanings, Fregean senses, and Kantian concepts by saying that they are nothing but Aristotelian essences "divorced from the object of reference and wedded to the word," he's just making a witty historico-philosophical remark, and as such, this obviously carries no special rational force as a philosophical criticism. But it also indicates a much more serious point, pointedly developed by Quine elsewhere. So, for example, in "Reference and Modality" (Quine, 1961c) and *Word and Object* (1960), section §41, Quine explicitly holds that Aristotelian essences, and correspondingly the kind of necessity that flows from the nature of things in the world, are both unintelligible and indefensible. But now, seventy years on, and after groundbreaking work by Kripke, Fine, and others (Chalmers, 1996: pp. 136-138; Fine, 1994, 1995, 2005b; Kripke, 1980, 1993), we know better. The doctrine of Aristotelian essentialism, and the doctrine that there exists a kind of necessity that is anchored in the nature of things in the world, are both at the very least intelligible, and I also think—at least, if one defends *manifest* realism and rejects *noumenal* realism—defensible doctrines. For one does not have to be a defender of *scientific* essentialism in order to hold this. Indeed, if I'm correct, then the doctrine of *manifest* essentialism is not only intelligible but also defensible (Hanna, 2006a: part 1).

Critical Reply #3: In *Word and Object*, Quine explicitly accepts the Brentano/Chisholm thesis that the notions of intentionality and intensionality are irreducible, interderivable, and mutually indispensable. But then he himself also explicitly *rejects* the Brentano/Chisholm thesis and counsels the elimination of intentionality and intensionality, by way of adopting scientific naturalism. The basic outline of Quine's argument is as follows.

1. Intentionality and intensionality are irreducible, interderivable, and indispensable.

2. But they're unscientific notions, and the scientific attitude should be preferred.

3. So given certain facts about contemporary human interests and purposes, it seems to Quine personally that science limns the true and ultimate structure of reality, that physicalism is true, and that behaviorism is the correct psychology.

4. Therefore, one should eliminate intensionality and intentionality.

5. Therefore, there's no real intensionality or intentionality.

6. Therefore, there's no intelligible or defensible analytic-synthetic distinction.

But this is clearly an unsound argument. In the first place, Quine offers no independent reasons for the theses that natural science limns the true and ultimate structure of reality, that reductive physicalism is true, and that behaviorism is true, but argues only that, from his own personal point of view, certain facts about contemporary human interests and purposes favor the ontological framework of natural science, reductive physicalism, and behaviorism. But second, and even more importantly, even if it *were* true that natural science limns the true and ultimate structure of reality, that reductive physicalism is true, and that behaviorism is the correct psychology, it still *wouldn't* follow that there is no intentionality or intensionality. At best, all that would follow is that Quine is justified in asserting that from his own personal point of view, together with certain facts about contemporary human interests and purposes, one should eliminate intentionality and intensionality. Nevertheless, the step from "For my money, i.e., given my personal commitments to reductive physicalism and behaviorism, and given certain facts about contemporary human interests and purposes, we should eliminate intentionality and intensionality" to "There is no intentionality or intensionality" is clearly a fallacious inference from a pragmatic *ought* to a factual *is*.

Critical Reply #4: Let's suppose for a moment, however, that Quine is correct, and that a thoroughgoing eliminativism about intentionality and intensionality is true. As I argued earlier in section XVI.1, it would follow directly from this semantic eliminativism that we'd also have to eliminate every fact or phenomenon that includes or presupposes the existence of semantic content. Thus we'd have to eliminate logical understanding, logical reasoning, conceptual understanding, conceptual reasoning, thinking, belief, cognition, knowledge and human rationality itself. In short, we'd have to assert the truth of postmodernist anti-rational nihilist skepticism, aka PARNS. But as I also pointed out earlier, PARNS is, in effect, cognitive suicide by means of logico-rational and moral self-stultification. And in any case, Quine's own acceptance of The Sheer Logic Principle is flat-out inconsistent with PARNS. So Quine's Predicament strikes again.

6. Quine's argument against the analytic-synthetic distinction from the radical indeterminacy of radical translation.

In appendix D of Meaning and Necessity, "Meaning and Synonymy in Natural Languages" (Carnap, 1956d) and in direct response to Quine's circularity-of-synonymy argument against the analytic-synthetic distinction in "Two Dogmas," Carnap worked out a pragmatic, behaviorist analysis of synonymy. Quine then replied to Carnap in Word and Object by developing his indeterminacy of translation argument against the analytic-synthetic distinction:

> Philosophical tradition hints of three nested categories of firm truths: the analytic, the *a priori*, and the necessary. Whether the first exhausts the second, and the second the third, are traditional matters of disagreement, though none of the three has traditionally been defined in terms of detectable features of verbal behavior. Pressed nowadays for such a clarification, some who are content to take the three as identical have responded in this vein: the analytic sentences are those that we are prepared to affirm come what may. This comes to naught unless we independently circumscribe the "what may." Thus one may object that that we would not adhere to "No bachelor is unmarried" if we found a married bachelor; and how are we to disallow his example without appealing to the very notion of analyticity we are trying to define? One way is to take "come what may" as "come what stimulation … may"; and this gives virtually the definition … of stimulus analyticity.

> We have had our linguist observing native utterances and their circumstances passively, to begin with, and then selectively querying native sentences for assent and dissent under varying circumstances. Let us sum up the possible yield of such methods.

> (1) Observation sentences can be translated. There is uncertainty, but the situation is the normal inductive one. (2) Truth functions can be translated. (3) Stimulus-analytic sentences can be recognized…. (4) Questions of intrasubjective stimulus synonymy of native occasion sentences even of a non-observational kind can be settled if raised, but the sentences cannot be translated.

> The indeterminacy I mean is … radical. It is that rival systems of analytical hypotheses can conform to all speech dispositions within each of the languages concerned and yet dictate, in countless cases, utterly disparate translations, not mere mutual paraphrases, but translations each of which would be excluded by the other system of translation.

Two such translations might even be patently contrary in truth value, provided there is no stimulation that would encourage assent to the other. (Quine, 1960: pp. 66, 68, 73-74)

Here's a rational reconstruction of that Quinean argument.

1. The existence of an intelligible and defensible analytic-synthetic distinction would entail that it is always possible, for any natural language L, for the speakers of L to distinguish sharply between the analytic/necessary/a priori sentences of L and the synthetic/contingent/a posteriori sentences of L.

2. This in turn presupposes that the intensions or meanings of most or all words can be fully individuated or determined—i.e., there would be no general or universal semantic indeterminacy.

3. But if we were linguistic anthropologists trying to figure what some tribe meant by "gavagai" by studying their uses of it, with no other relevant information about them other than that they are competent speakers of a natural language (i.e., the situation of "radical translation"), then there'd be no way of translating the unfamiliar word "gavagai" into our language that would rule out intensionally distinct interpretations of it.

4. That's because these interpretations would all be empirically equivalent in terms of the speech-behavioral and factual evidence in support of them.

5. For example, "gavagai" in the natives' language might mean the same in stimulus-terms as either "rabbit," or "a collection of undetached rabbit parts," or "rabbit-hood being instantiated now," in English.

6. But it's easy enough to see how in English we could assent to any one of the applications of any one of these labels to objects of experience, while dissenting from the others.

7. As linguistic anthropologists, we could then assert the existence of a "stimulus analyticity" or "stimulus synonymy" that's manifest in our use of such sentences as "Gavagai are rabbits," "Gavagai are collections of undetached rabbit parts," etc.

8. But this wouldn't entail the existence of the analytic-synthetic distinction, precisely because it would not entail semantic determinacy, or the individuation of meanings or intensions.

9. Hence it's generally or even universally the case that the intensions of words cannot be individuated or determined with certainty.

10. Therefore, there's no intelligible or defensible analytic-synthetic distinction.

Two Critical Replies

Critical Reply #1: In order to show that different empirically equivalent translations of "gavagai" are possible, it has to be possible to for us to discriminate sharply in English between the distinct intensions and distinct possible-worlds extensions of the different possible interpretations or translations of "gavagai." Otherwise, we'd have no reason for asserting that we could assent to the application of one term, and dissent from the other—since by hypothesis they're empirically equivalent. Hence radically indeterminate radical translations presuppose normal determinate non-radical interpretations or translations of words in English, which in turn fully supports the thesis of an intelligible and defensible analytic-synthetic distinction (Katz, 1990: ch. 5). So it's clearly a *non sequitur* for Quine to claim that the radical indeterminacy of radical translation entails the non-existence of an intelligible or defensible analytic-synthetic distinction.

Critical Reply #2: Quine explicitly asserts that his radical indeterminacy result doesn't hold for words that express the classical truth-functional logical constants.

Hence even if Quine's radical indeterminacy of radical translation argument were sound, it would not show that the truths of classical sentential logic are not all analytic. On the contrary, there would still be a proper characterization of them, according to Quine's definition of a logical truth, and thus a proper characterization of them as *analyticities of the first class*—see my *Critical Reply #1* to Quine's circularity-of-synonymy argument against the analytic-synthetic distinction (i.e., the third Quinean argument) above. Therefore, even if Quine's radical indeterminacy of radical translation argument were sound, there would still be a perfectly intelligible and defensible analytic-synthetic distinction holding between the truths of classical sentential logic and all other truths. Hence, again, it's clearly a non sequitur for Quine to claim that his argument entails that there is no intelligible or defensible analytic-synthetic distinction.

XVI.5 Three Dogmas of Post-Quineanism

In my critical examination of Quine's radical translation argument, I noted that he correctly pointed up an extremely important feature of the traditional conception of analyticity:

> Philosophical tradition hints of three nested categories of firm truths: the analytic, the *a priori*, and the necessary. Whether the first exhausts the second, and the second the third, are traditional matters of disagreement. (Quine, 1960: p. 66)

Indeed, for classical Kantians, the connection between apriority and necessity is even tighter than nesting: they analytically entail each other. (Hanna, 2001: section 5.2, pp. 245-255). Therefore, even if one were to accept my critique of Quine's critique, there would still be some reasons for rejecting the existence of an intelligible or defensible analytic-synthetic distinction, if it could be shown that analyticity, apriority, and necessity can be logically detached from one another. As is well-known, Kripke and early Putnam offer widely influential arguments for the detachability of the necessary and the a priori, in both directions, from the existence of necessary a posteriori statements and contingent a priori statements. And Kaplan also offers a slightly less well-known but equally challenging argument for the detachability of analyticity and necessity, from the existence of analytic contingent statements.

Importantly, however, Kripke did not himself think that his arguments for the existence of necessary a posteriori and contingent a priori statements actually undermine either the notion of analyticity or the analytic-synthetic distinction:

> I am presupposing that an analytic truth is one which depends on *meanings* in the strict sense and therefore is necessary as well as *a priori*. If statements whose a priori truth is known via the fixing of reference [e.g., "Stick S is one meter long at t_0,"] are counted as analytic, then some analytic truths are contingent; this possibility is excluded in the notion of analyticity adopted here…. I have not attempted to deal with the delicate problems regarding analyticity in these lectures, but I will say that some (though not all) of the cases often adduced to discredit the analytic-synthetic distinction, especially those involving natural phenomena and natural kinds, should be handled in terms of the apparatus of fixing a reference invoked here. (Kripke, 1980: n. 63, pp. 122-123.)

Moreover, the later Putnam explicitly rejects the necessity of "Water is H_2O" and also explicitly defends the existence of at least one analytic a priori necessary truth (Putnam, 1983, 1990).

I'll come back to those important facts later. Nevertheless, certainly most other post-Quinean and thus post-classical Analytic philosophers actually did and still do take Kripke's, early Putnam's, and Donnellan's arguments to show that the analytic-synthetic distinction is unintelligible or indefensible. So in order to understand and to criticize the post-Quinean, post-classical Analytic tradition, we must adopt the logical fiction of a conjoined philosopher called *Kripke-Putnam*, who, along with the real-life Donnellan and Kaplan, collectively hold that Kripke's, early Putnam's, Donnellan's, and Kaplan's arguments for the existence of the necessary a posteriori, the contingent a priori, and the analytic contingent, do indeed jointly undermine the intelligibility or defensibility of the analytic-synthetic distinction.

Now, one possible response to the Kripke-Putnam, Donnellan, and Kaplan arguments would be simply to concede the detachability of the "three nested categories" and then try to develop a theory of analyticity that is unaffected by the claims made by Kripke-Putnam, Donnellan, and Kaplan. And in fact, that's what the leading post-Quinean, post-classical Analytic defenders and theorists of the analytic-synthetic distinction have done. For example, impressed by arguments for the existence of necessary a posteriori statements, contingent a priori statements, and analytic contingent statements, Katz and Gillian Russell both explicitly concede that necessity does not entail apriority, that apriority does not entail necessity, and that analyticity does not entail necessity. Gillian Russell goes Katz even one better and claims that there are *analytic a posteriori statements*, for example, "Mohammed Ali is Cassius Clay" (Russell, 2008: pp. 67, 82-83, 200), although Katz always held the line on that one, and consistently asserted that analyticity entails apriority.

But it seems to me, however, that the concessive strategy has deep difficulties. According to *all* the classical theories of analyticity, including Kant's, Frege's, and Carnap's theories, no matter how much they may otherwise differ, nevertheless it's still the case that (i) analyticity generally entails necessity, (ii) analyticity generally entails a priori knowability, (iii) analyticity specifically entails either conceptually necessary truth or logically necessary truth, (iv) the properly conducted rational activity of either conceptual analysis or logical analysis entails knowledge of analytic a priori necessary truth, and (v) a correct theory of analyticity entails an adequate explanation of the nature and status of logic. *Only* entailment (ii) holds, according to Katz's theory of analyticity (Katz, 1997). By contrast, *none* of these entailments holds, according to Gillian Russell's theory of analyticity (Russell, 2008: pp. 1-3).

Similarly, *none* of these entailments holds, according to Boghossian's theory of analyticity, although for very different reasons, since he agrees with Quine and eliminates the very idea of a semantic (or what Boghossian calls "metaphysical") conception of analyticity in favor of an epistemic conception of analyticity, and more specifically in favor of the Quinean ersatz epistemic-pragmatic conception of analyticity, and thus simply replaces analyticity with epistemic-pragmatic apriority (Boghossian, 1996: pp. 363-368). As I mentioned in section XV.1 above, the Quinean ersatz epistemic-pragmatic version of the analytic-synthetic distinction that arises from this replacement runs as follows: (i) an asserted statement or belief *B* is analytic a priori if and only if *B* stubbornly resists recalcitrant experience and can be acquired without experiential evidence and inquiry (i.e., *B* is an "armchair belief"), and (ii) an asserted statements or belief *B* is synthetic a posteriori if and only if *B* is flexibly sensitive to recalcitrant experience and cannot be acquired without experiential evidence and inquiry (i.e., B is an "experimental belief"). But on the one hand, given this "armchair belief" criterion of analyticity, there's nothing that would intrinsically rule out the adoption of *highly contrarian* empirical-evidence-resistant scientific beliefs as analytic a priori, provided that they came to be sufficiently well-entrenched in the scientific community and the larger sociopolitical world. Take, for example, the following claims:

> The thought screen helmet scrambles telepathic communication between aliens and humans. Aliens cannot immobilize people wearing thought screens nor can they control their minds or communicate with them using their telepathy. When aliens can't communicate or control humans, they do not take them. (Menkin, 2021)[9]

---

[9] For the purposes of my example, it doesn't really matter whether Menkin's site is an elaborate parody, or intended seriously.

In the post-Trumpian, COVID-19 denialist, anti-vaxxer era, one can easily imagine a highly contrarian sociopolitical system, together with its own highly contrarian scientific community, that accepted these beliefs about alien-thought-screen-helmets as analytic a priori. In other words, my worry here is that, given the "armchair belief" criterion of analyticity, then there are no inherent constraints on the theoretical content of analyticity. But on the contrary, it seems to me self-evidently clear that there must be, at the very least, a set of minimal rational constraints on the theoretical content of analyticity, such that basic logical principles, basic mathematical principles, and basic natural-scientific principles are never arbitrarily flouted or violated. How else could an analytic statement ever plausibly purport to be rationally acceptable as such? And on the other hand, given this "experimental belief" criterion of synthetic aposteriority, beliefs in the truths of elementary arithmetic such as "7+5=12" would count as synthetic a posteriori and subject to empirical counterexample, if occasional failures of calculating this correctly were allowed by experimentalists to stand as falsifications, again provided that these highly contrarian falsifications of "7+5=12" again came to be sufficiently well-entrenched in the scientific community and the larger sociopolitical world.

In other words, my worry here is that, given the "experimental belief" criterion of synthetic aposteriority, there is nothing that would intrinsically rule out the completely crazy conversion of obviously necessary truths into contingent truths: hence my worry is that there are no inherent constraints on the theoretical content of synthetic aposteriority. On the contrary, it also seems to me self-evidently clear that there must be, at the very least, a set of minimal constraints on the theoretical content of synthetic aposteriority, such that basic logical principles, basic mathematical principles, and basic natural-scientific principles are never open to arbitrary conversion into contingent truths. So again, and now with appropriate changes for the shift in context, how else could a synthetic a posteriori statement ever plausibly purport to be rationally acceptable as such? Either way, then, the Quinean ersatz epistemic-pragmatic conception of the analytic-synthetic distinction is deeply problematic. To be sure, Boghossian's own account is rigorously-developed and subtly-detailed in many ways. So my objection isn't internal to Boghossian's own philosophically deft and highly interesting working-out of a Quinean ersatz epistemic-pragmatic conception of analyticity. Instead, it's an external objection to Quinean ersatz epistemic-pragmatic accounts generally, and Boghossian's account just happens to be one of these. Moreover, and in any case, there is an even more general objection I want to make to post-Quinean accounts of analyticity, applicable to Katz, Gillian Russell, Boghossian, and Juhl-and-Loomis alike, that I'll develop shortly.

Williamson, by contrast to Katz, Gillian Russell, and Boghossian, concludes from the same basic philosophical data—i.e., the Kripke-Putnam, Donnellan, and Kaplan arguments—that the very idea of analyticity, whether construed metaphysically or epistemically, is *largely philosophically uninteresting*, since it fails to meet any of the basic aims specified by the Fregean or Carnapian theories of analyticity (Williamson, 2007: chs. 3-4). Williamson's conclusion, I think, nicely captures the philosophical rationale lying behind the empirical data reported in the 2009 Bourget-and-Chalmers *PhilPap*ers survey that I mentioned in sections 1.1 and XVI.1. Moreover, I'm also in complete agreement with Williamson that *if* we start with the Frege-Carnap conception of the analytic-synthetic distinction as basic, and *if* we accept some or all of the Quinean, Kripke-Putnamian, Donnellanian, and Kaplanian arguments against the analytic-synthetic distinction, *then* the very idea of analyticity, whether construed metaphysically or epistemically, is indeed largely philosophically uninteresting. But ultimately I want to reject both antecedents of this conditional. I think that the Kantian conception of the analytic-synthetic distinction, not the Frege-Carnap conception, is basic; and I think that Quinean, Kripke-Putnamian, Donnellanian, and Kaplanian arguments are unsound.

Finally, Juhl and Loomis take Quine's critical arguments, as refined and reformulated by Gilbert Harman (Harman, 1967a, 1967b, 1996), to constitute a set of serious objections to all the classical conceptions of analyticity, as well as conceding the force of Williamson's reasonable worries about the philosophical uninterestingness of the very idea of analyticity. But in the face of all that, Juhl and Loomis also propose a significantly different conception of analyticity, which they call "analyticity*," based on the notion of *stipulation*, that apparently avoids several of the philosophically unhappy implications of the Quinean/Harmanian, Kripke-Putnamian, Donnellanian, and Kaplanian arguments, while also conceding the critical force of these arguments against the classical conceptions (Juhl and Loomis, 2010: esp. chs. 4-6).

Correspondingly, I have three objections to the stipulationist theory of analyticity*.

First, merely having a rational warrant for calling some statement "true" or "necessarily true" according to some individually or intersubjectively agreed-upon rule for the use of the terms "true" and "necessarily true" does not thereby make those statements true, much less necessarily true. Rule-justification is *all about us*; but truth and necessary truth are all about relations between statements and the way the world is. For example, in my highly contrarian community, we can adopt a rule according to which everything that is said sincerely about alien-thought-screen-helmets by alien-thought-screen-helmet-experts is not only called "true" but also "necessarily true." But the alien-thought-screen-helmet-experts' claims about alien-thought-screen-helmets are still false. So stipulationism does not adequately connect the concept of analyticity* with the classical Tarskian concept of truth.

Second, the very idea of stipulation presupposes and uses the unreduced notion of intentionality: to stipulate is *just to to resolve that statements be taken in a certain way*. Yet every *resolution* necessarily includes an intention. So it's very unclear whether appealing to stipulation in order to explain analyticity*, in the end, is any more explanatory than simply appealing to intentionality in order to explain analyticity*. But then Juhl and Loomis must *either* provide a good argument against Quine's reductive physicalist rejection of Brentano's thesis *or else* concede that the non-reductive metaphysics of of intentionality is more basic than stipulationism.

Third, and now harking back to my worries about the Quinean ersatz epistemic-pragmatic conception of the analytic-synthetic distinction, taken together with my first worry about stipulationism, it seems to me that the stipulationist theory will have essentially the same problem that Quinean ersatz epistemic-pragmatic conception of the analytic-synthetic distinction has. More precisely, I cannot see how stipulationism will be able to prevent either completely crazy stipulated statements counting as analytic* or the completely crazy conversion of obviously necessary truths into contingent truths. In other words, it seems to me that stipulationism introduces neither inherent constraints on the theoretical content of analyticity* nor inherent constraints on the theoretical content of synthetic aposteriority. But that's not rationally defensible.

I hasten to add that I certainly have no objection to the development of various conceptions of analyticity that are "akin" to the classical Fregean and Carnapian conceptions (Juhl and Loomis, 2010: p. 212), but deviate from them in other ways, in order to concede the force of standard objections to the classical Frege-Carnap conception of analyticity. *Let a hundred or even a thousand philosophical flowers bloom*, I say. My comprehensive critical question for all of these recent and contemporary defences and theories of analyticity is simply this: "How many classical criteria of analyticity can be denied by them, without actually changing the philosophical subject?" What I mean, is that it seems to me that an adequate theory of the analytic-synthetic distinction must defend *all* of (i) through (v) above—i.e., that (i) analyticity generally entails necessity, (ii) analyticity generally entails a priori knowability, (iii) analyticity specifically entails either logically necessary truth or conceptually necessary truth, (iv) the properly conducted rational activity of either logical analysis or conceptual analysis entails knowledge of analytic a priori necessary truth, and (v) a correct theory of analyticity entails an adequate explanation of the nature and status of logic—for otherwise, one is failing to keep rational faith with the basic aims and standards of the classical theories of analyticity from Kant to Frege and Carnap. Moreover, as far as I can tell, both Kripke himself and the later Putnam himself would actually agree with me. Therefore, at the end of the day, it seems to me self-evidently clear that Gillian Russell's, Katz's, Boghossian's, and Juhl's-and-Loomis's theories of analyticity are merely theories of *schmanalyticity*, not theories of analyticity.

Juhl and Loomis do explicitly consider this objection, and respond to it as follows:

> It is true that our notion of analyticity* does not solve all of the epistemic problems that beset the logical empiricists who thought that a single notion of analyticity could be deployed for mathematics, logic, many theoretical principles such as F = ma, and various seemingly a priori bits of knowledge such as color exclusion principles. We remain agnostic as to whether some accounts that generalize the notion of analyticity* can be adapted to illuminate a wider range of apparently a priori knowledge. We are hopeful on this front, but we are not in a position to provide accounts of logic, and some difficult examples of a priori knowledge such as color exclusion, in particular. Thus our defense of analyticity* might be thought of as a defense of one variety of analyticity, rather than of analyticity in general. (Juhl and Loomis, 2010: pp. 237-238).

Fair enough: but analyticity* is *still* schmanalyticity, *not* analyticity. So my overarching objection to the post-Quinean, post-classical Analytic accounts of analyticity is that Gillian Russell, Katz, Boghossian, and Juhl and Loomis, for all their philosophical ingenuity, insight, and rigor, *have simply changed the subject*. And for the reasons I gave in sections XV.2 and XV.3 above, I think that all Analytic philosophers, whether classical or post-classical, should be deeply committed to defending some or another version of the classical analytic-synthetic distinction in the Kant-Frege-Carnap tradition, and not—or at least not primarily—concerned about defending some post-classical or even post-modern *schmanalytic*-synthetic distinction. This, again, is just because, otherwise, without an intelligible and defensible analytiic-synthetic distinction, the very idea of a semantic content will go down, and correspondingly the very ideas of belief, cognition, thought, understanding, justification, knowledge, intentionality, and human rationality more generally will all go down too, since all these inherently involve the notion of semantic content.

If I'm correct in pursuing this line of criticism, then of course it shifts the burden of proof back onto the defender of an intelligible and defensible classically-oriented analytic-synthetic distinction in the Kant-Frege-Carnap tradition, and therefore, in particular, it shifts the burden of proof onto me. I then have to show, in addition to refuting all the Quinean criticisms, as well as directly addressing the deep problem of the nature and status of logic (see, for example, *Rationality and Logic*, and also *Cognition, and the A Priori*, ch. 5), under the rubric of what I have been calling "Quine's Predicament," not only that all the arguments offered for the existence of necessary a posteriori statements, contingent a priori statements, and analytic contingent statements are all unsound, but also that that there are really no such things as the necessary a posteriori, the contingent a priori, and the analytic contingent. All three of these pseudo-concepts must be eliminated. I'll freely and fully admit that this anti-post-classical-Analytic, Kantian eliminativist project in particular is a very strenuous task, given the canonical—indeed, almost biblical—status of the fictional conjoined philosopher Kripke-Putnam's writings in post-Quinean, post-classical Analytic philosophy, and especially Analytic metaphysics (Soames, 2003).[10] But if they're wrong, then they're wrong!, and *somebody* needs to point out that the Emperor Kripke-Putnam is actually wearing no clothes. So it might as well be me.

7. The Kripke-Putnam argument against the analytic-synthetic distinction from the existence of the necessary a posteriori.

It can be shown that if an identity statement S between directly referential terms (for example, natural kind terms or proper names) is true at all, then S is necessarily true, even if S is not known a priori:

> An argument like the following can be given against the possibility of contingent identity statements: First, the law of the substitutivity of identity says that, for any objects x and y, if x is identical to y, then if x has a certain property F, then so does y:

---
[10] See, e.g., Soames, *Philosophical Analysis in the Twentieth Century*.

(1) $(x)(y)[(x=y) \supset (Fx \supset Fy)]$

On the other hand, every object surely is necessarily self-identical:

(2) $(x)\Box(x=x)$

But

(3) $(x)(y)(x=y) \supset [\Box(x=x) \supset \Box(x=y)]$

is a substitution-instance of (1), the substitutivity law. From (2) and (3), we can conclude that, for every x and y, if x equals y, then, it is necessary that x equals y:

(4) $(x)(y)((x=y) \supset \Box(x=y))$

This is because the clause $\Box(x=x)$ of the conditional drops out because it is known to be true. (Kripke, 1993: pp. 162-163)

We have concluded that an identity statement between names, when true at all, is necessarily true, even though one may not know it *a priori*. (Kripke, 1980: p. 108)

For example, the statements

(WH) Water is H_2O

and

(GE) Gold is the element with atomic number 79

and many other similar statements expressing true essential identities between natural kind terms, are necessary but also a posteriori because they are believed (or known) to be true empirically, through contemporary microphysics and chemistry. Also, the statements

(CT) Cicero is Tully

(HP) Hesperus is Phosphorus

are necessary and a posteriori, because it's possible to believe (or know) that Cicero is Cicero or that Hesperus is Hesperus but not believe (or know) that Cicero is Tully or that Hesperus is Phosphorus. Therefore, necessity does not entail apriority. But according to the classical conception of the "three nested categories," analyticity, necessity, and apriority all entail one another. Therefore, there's no intelligible or defensible analytic-synthetic distinction.

Four Critical Replies

Critical Reply #1: In the first *Critique*, Kant says that

> Although all our cognition commences **with** experience, yet it does not on that account all arise **from** experience. (*CPR* B1, boldfacing in the original)

I think that this remark expresses a deep insight. In what follows, by *empirical facts* I mean inner or outer sensory experiences and/or contingent natural objects or facts. Now let's take it as a given for the purposes of argument that necessarily, all human cognition begins in causally-triggered, direct, essentially non-conceptual, non-inferential sense perception of contingent natural objects or facts—and for an argument to that effect, see *Cognition, Content, and the A Priori*, chapters 2-3. Then Kant's deep insight is that apriority is in fact *the necessary and constitutive underdetermination* of the semantic content, truth, or justification of a statement S by any and all empirical facts, or what is the same thing, that the semantic content, truth, and/or justification of S is neither strongly supervenient[11] on nor grounded by any and all empirical facts. This isn't the *exclusion* of empirical facts by the content, truth, or justifiability of S. Correspondingly, to say that a statement S is a posteriori is to say that the semantic content, truth, or justifiability of S is *necessarily or constitutively determined* by any or all empirical facts, or what is the same thing, that the semantic content, truth, and/or justification of S is strongly supervenient on or grounded by any or all empirical facts. So aposteriority does not mean that S's content must bear a relation to empirical facts, that the truth of S must be learned or confirmed by means of empirical facts, or that S's justification must be supported by empirical facts. To be sure, these are all fully consistent with and normally associated with S's aposteriority. But the crucial point is that S can still be a priori even if S's content must bear a relation to empirical facts, even if the truth of S must be learned or confirmed by means of empirical facts, and even if S's justification must be supported by empirical facts.

Otherwise put, Kant's deep insight is that there is no such thing as semantic content, truth, or knowledge (sufficiently justified belief) that altogether excludes empirical facts. But that it does not follow from this that either classical Lockean/ Humean empiricism or radical Quinean empiricism is true—i.e., it does not follow that semantic content, truth, and justifiability are either necessarily or constitutively determined by or (even more radically) reducible to any or all empirical facts. That's clearly, distinctly, and simply a *non sequitur*. Lining up with Kant's deep insight, then, here are three important empiricist fallacies: (i) *the fallacy of empirical content*: the semantic content of statement S necessarily includes a relation to empirical facts, therefore the content of S is necessarily or constitutively determined by empirical facts and is a posteriori, (ii) *the fallacy of empirical confirmation*: the truth of statement S must be confirmed or learned by means of sense experiences of empirical facts, therefore the truth of S is necessarily or constitutively determined by empirical facts and is a posteriori, and (iii) *the fallacy of empirical justifica-*

---
[11] For explicit definitions of strong supervenience, logical strong supervenience, and natural or nomological strong supervenience, see sub-section XVII.8.2 below.

tion: justified belief in statement S must be supported by empirical evidence, therefore the justification of belief in S is is necessarily or constitutively determined by empirical facts and is a posteriori. More specifically, as I indicated just above, not every necessary truth with significant empirical content, or every statement that must be learned or confirmed by means of sense experiences of empirical facts, or every statement, belief in which must be supported by empirical evidence, is a posteriori.

And here's an argument for that claim, which in turn shows that the three fallacies I just formulated are indeed fallacies. Following the classical semantic tradition, I'll call terms that have both intension or meaning and also extension or reference, *categorematic* terms. Now consider these two statements:

(KB) If Kant is a bachelor, then Kant is unmarried

and

($S+F=T_{beer\ bottles}$) Seven beer bottles plus five beer bottles equals twelve beer bottles.

Everyone will grant, I think, that the statements "If Kant is a bachelor, then Kant is unmarried" and "Seven beer bottles plus five beer bottles equals twelve beer bottles" are not only necessarily true but also (i) such that their semantic contents must bear a relation to empirical facts, via the categorematic terms *Kant, bachelor, beer*, and *bottles*, (ii) such that they must be confirmed and learned by means of sense experience of empirical facts, and (iii) such that justified belief in them must be supported by empirical evidence. Yet both statements "If Kant is a bachelor, then Kant is unmarried" and "Seven beer bottles plus five beer bottles equals twelve beer bottles" are obviously a priori. That's because the real presence of empirical facticity in those statements is inessential to their semantic, epistemic, and modal a priori status. Or otherwise put, what matters for apriority *is simply that their collective semantic, epistemic, and modal status isn't necessarily or constitutively determined by the real presence of empirical facticity*. Similarly, it's obviously correct that the following two statements, namely,

(WH) Water is H_2O

and

(GE) Gold is the element with atomic number 79

are (i) such that their semantic contents must bear a relation to empirical facts, via the categorematic terms *water, H_2O, gold*, and *element with atomic number 79*, (ii) such that they must be confirmed and learned by means of sense experience of empirical facts, and (iii) such that justified belief in them must be supported by empirical evidence. Yet the inference from *that* to the conclusion that the statements "Water is H_2O" and "Gold is the element with atomic number 79" are a posteriori remains fallacious, for the same reason that obtained in the cases of the statements "If Kant is a bachelor, then Kant is married" and "Seven beer bottles plus five beer bottles equals twelve beer bottles." Now, apriority is a statement's failed necessary or constitutive determination by any or all empirical facts. Then it's clear that the statements "If Kant is a bachelor, then Kant is married" and "Seven beer bottles plus five beer bottles equals twelve beer bottles" are both a priori, according to the following three-step test.

> 1. Suppose that the categorematic terms "Kant," "bachelor," "unmarried," "beer," and "bottles" retain their original actual-world reference, so that the necessary-or-constitutive-determination-base of content, truth, and justification is held fixed.

> 2. Then consider other possible worlds in which the actual-world referents of the caregorematic terms terms "Kant," "bachelor," "unmarried," "beer," and "bottles" either (2a) fail to exist, or (2b) radically change their empirical specific character, or (2c) radically change their essence or nature, whether this is a natural essence or only a social-functional essence. For example, consider possible worlds in which Kant never was born, or in which Kant and all the other actual-world bachelors are married and have large families, or which beer tastes like orange juice, or in which bottles are porous and do not retain liquid.

> 3. In those worlds, nevertheless, the statements "If Kant is a bachelor, then Kant is married" and "Seven beer bottles plus five beer bottles equals twelve beer bottles" are necessarily true, and known or believed with sufficient justification.

In this way, the semantic, alethic, and epistemic character of the actual-world-anchored categorematic terms terms "Kant," "bachelor," "unmarried," "beer," and "bottles" in the statements "If Kant is a bachelor, then Kant is married" and "Seven beer bottles plus five beer bottles equals twelve beer bottles" is what I'll call *robustly persistent with respect to changes in empirical facts*. Their maximal semantic, alethic, and epistemic character emerges in all other worlds beyond the actual world, even while "letting the empirical chips fall as they may" in those worlds. Or in other words, the very fact that confers maximal meaningfulness, truth, or justifiability on the statements "If Kant is a bachelor, then Kant is married" and "Seven beer bottles plus five beer bottles equals twelve beer bottles" in the actual world, also semantically, alethically, and epistemically robustly persists even in possible worlds in which the actual-world referents of their categorematic terms fail to exist, radically change their empirical specific character, or radically change their natural or social-functional essence or nature.

Here's a relevant side-comment in this connection. Strictly speaking, it's possible for a semantic, alethic, or epistemic feature to be what I will call *relatively but non-robustly persistent with respect to changes in empirical facts*. For example, mere conventions, decisions, or stipulations with respect to meaning, truth, belief, or knowledge are relatively but non-robustly persistent with respect to changes in empirical facts. You or your community can opt to take any statement to be meaningful, true, believable, or knowable "come what may." But this isn't robust persistence, because it's inherently subject to the variable idiosyncrasies, interests, or whims of the individual or community that carries out the convention, decision, or stipulation. Relative persistence with respect to changes in empirical facts but without robustness is the mark of what I will call the *voluntaristic a priori* that's defended by the logical empiricists/positivists and C.I. Lewis (Lewis, 1923), which, in turn, is clearly the ancestral origin of Quine's deflationary, ersatz epistemic-pragmatic conception of the a priori.

The crucial point here is that in order to establish the aposteriority of a statement S, what needs to be shown is that *the very fact* which confers meaningfulness, truth, or justifiability on S *is nothing but an empirical fact*, or that *the fact is solely and wholly empirical*. In other words, the rational criterion of aposteriority for any statement is the failure of semantic, alethic, or epistemic robust persistence in possible worlds in which the actual world referents of its categorematic terms either fail to exist, radically change their empirical specific character, or radically change their natural or social-functional essence or nature. In worlds that are importantly empirically different from the actual world, then the semantic, alethic, or epistemic characters of a posteriori statements change. Their semantic, alethic, and epistemic characters, like the wind, "bloweth where it listeth." This demonstrates that the statement's semantic, alethic, and epistemic character is necessarily or constitutively determined by its existential, specific empirical, or essential profile in the actual manifest world, and that it is semantically, alethically, and epistemically non-robust and non-persistent with respect to changes in empirical facts. Therefore the statement is a posteriori. For example, the very facts that are the meaningfulness-makers, truth-makers, and justification-makers for the true statements

(KP) Kant is a philosopher

and

(PM) All philosophers are mortal

are nothing but empirical facts. Hence the statements "Kant is a philosopher" and "All philosophers are mortal" are a posteriori. And this can be proved by using the same three-step test as described above.

1. Assume that the categorematic terms "Kant," "philosopher," and "mortal" all retain their original actual world reference.

2. Now consider possible worlds in which those actual-world referents either

(2a) do not exist, or (2b) radically change their empirical specific character, or (2c) radically change their natural or social-functional essence or nature. For example, consider worlds in which Kant never was born, or in which Kant is an insurance salesman, or in which philosophers live forever.

3. In those worlds, the statements "Kant is a philosopher" and "All philosophers are mortal" are either meaningless (due to local reference-failure in that world), false, or unjustified, hence the statements "Kant is a philosopher" and "All philosophers are mortal" are semantically, alethically, and epistemically non-robust and non-persistent with respect to changes in empirical facts, and therefore, the statements "Kant is a philosopher" and "All philosophers are mortal" are both a posteriori.

Now, what about the statements "Water is H_2O" and "Gold is the element with atomic number 79"? As before, let's assume that all their categorematic terms retain their original actual-world reference. Then, consider other possible worlds in which the actual-world referents of "water," "H_2O," "gold," and "element with atomic number 79" either do not exist, radically change their empirical specific character, or radically change their natural or social-functional essence or nature. Does that change the meaningfulness, truth, or justifiability of either "Water is H_2O" and "Gold is the element with atomic number 79"? By Kripke's own admission, the answer is definitively "no." Since the categorematic terms of "water," "H_2O," "gold," and "element with atomic number 79" are all stipulated to be cases of the special class of directly referential terms that Kripke calls "rigid designators," they refer to the very same actual-world stuff in every world in which that stuff exists, and never refer to anything else otherwise (Kripke, 1980: pp. 3-15, 48-49, and 55-60). Suppose that H_2O in that world looked and felt like sand does in the actual manifestly real world. Or suppose that the element with atomic number 79 in that world looked blue instead of looking yellow, the way it does in the actual manifestly real world. Or suppose that the element with atomic number 79 in that world wasn't a metal—instead of being metallic, the way it is in the actual manifestly real world. Nevertheless, both the statements "Water is H_2O" and "Gold is the element with atomic number 79" would still be fully meaningful and necessarily true (or at least, would never be false[12]), and would be believed with sufficient justification. In this way, the statements "Water is H_2O" and "Gold is the element with atomic number 79" are both robustly persistent with respect to changes in empirical facts, and therefore they are both a priori.

Critical Reply #2: Something that's thoroughly ambiguous in the texts in which Kripke argues for the aposteriority of some statement *S* or another, is whether he is saying that it is merely the *belief* in *S* that is being taken to be a posteriori, or instead *knowledge* of *S*. This may seem trivial. But in fact it is crucial, however, for the following reason. It's very plausible to hold that to know a statement *S* entails knowing the very fact that confers upon *S* its specific modal status as necessary or contingent. Now let's suppose that we know both statements "Water is H_2O" and "Gold is the element with atomic number 79," and that this entails knowing the very facts which confer not only meaning and truth but also necessity

---

[12] Let's consider possible worlds in which the essence or nature of, e.g., the actual-world stuff called "gold," changes due to a constitutive dependence on, e.g., natural laws. And let's call that stuff "schmold." Then the relevant statement expressed at that world, e.g., "Gold is the element with atomic number 79," refers to schmold and is a *truth-value gap*, and provides no counter-model to the synthetic a priori truth "Gold is the element with atomic number 79." For more details on the cognitive semantics of necessity in my modal dualist framework, see (Hanna, 2015a: section 8.4).

on these two true identity statements. This is the same as knowing essential facts, namely, the essential identity of water and its chemical microstructure, and the essential identity of gold and its chemical microstructure. But it seems clear that knowing the essential identity of a natural kind and its chemical microstructure is knowing something over and above knowing facts that merely confer truth on the two statements "Water is H_2O" "Gold is the element with atomic number 79." That's because, obviously, an empirical fact can confer truth on a given statement, without also conferring necessary truth on that statement. And all that it takes to know such a fact is a posteriori perceptual knowledge. It also seems clear, moreover, as of course it also seemed clear to Kant, that knowing the very fact which confers necessary truth on a given statement is a priori knowledge, not a posteriori knowledge. Furthermore, Kripke himself also explicitly points out that the knowledge of either of the statements "Water is H_2O" or "Gold is the element with atomic number 79," at the very least, requires analytic a priori knowledge of the fact that *if* an identity statement is true, *then* it is necessarily true:

> Certain statements—and the identity statement is a paradigm of such a statement on my view—if true at all must be necessarily true. One does know *a priori*, by philosophical analysis, that *if* such an identity statement is true, then it's necessarily true. (Kripke, 1980: p. 109)

In other words, the complete epistemic reason that sufficiently justifies belief in either of the statements "Water is H_2O" or "Gold is the element with atomic number 79" is thoroughly a priori. So it's clear that knowing the very fact that confers both truth and necessary truth on the two statements "Water is H_2O" and "Gold is the element with atomic number 79"— namely, the essential identity of a natural kind and its chemical microstructure—when it's also seamlessly combined with the background analytic fact that identity statements are necessarily true if true at all, must be a priori knowledge, not a posteriori knowledge.

Similarly, knowing the very fact that confers not merely meaning and truth, but also necessity on the two statements

(CT) Cicero is Tully

and

(HP) Hesperus is Phosphorus

is the same as knowing an essential fact, namely the *classical identity* of a thing with itself. And when this essential fact is seamlessly combined together with the background analytic fact that classical identity statements are necessarily true if true at all, then again this knowledge must be a priori knowledge, not a posteriori knowledge. By "classical identity" I mean the relation of necessary numerical or "token" identity, including the properties of symmetry, transitivity, and reflexivity, plus satisfaction of Leibniz's Laws for all non-modal, non-normative, and more generally non-intensional properties. Now, according to the three empiricist fallacies of content, confirmation, and justification, it would obviously be a mistake to think that from the mere facts that the two statements

(CC) Cicero is Cicero

and

(HH) Hesperus is Hesperus

are (i) such their semantic contents must bear a relation to empirical facts, via the categorematic terms *Cicero* and *Hesperus*, (ii) such that they must be confirmed and learned by means of sense experiences of empirical facts, and (iii) such that justified belief in them must be supported by empirical evidence, it thereby follows that they are a posteriori. On the contrary, it's obvious that "Cicero is Cicero" and "Hesperus is Hesperus" are a priori. This is shown by the fact that in natural deduction systems of classical first-order polyadic predicate logic with identity, any statement that's a substitution-instance of the "free" or quantifier-unbound formula "$x=x$" can be written on any line of a proof as following directly from the empty set of premises, hence the two statements "Cicero is Cicero" and "Hesperus is Hesperus" would be instances of elementary logical truths. But by the same reasoning, the very same point holds for the statements "Cicero is Tully" and "Hesperus is Phosphorus" alike. They're both a priori, precisely because knowing the very fact that confers not just truth but also necessity upon them, i.e., the classical identity fact, is a priori knowledge.

This might seem like a shocking claim. So someone might well object in this way:

"How could the statements 'Cicero is Tully' and 'Hesperus is Phosphorus' possibly be a priori? Didn't Frege show us, once and for all, that 'Hesperus is Phosphorus' is an informative identity statement?"

And I'd reply as follows. Yes of course, I concede that Frege was absolutely correct that "Hesperus is Phosphorus" is an informative identity statement, precisely because its two categorematic terms have the same reference but different senses (Frege, 1984b). Nevertheless, the fact that it's informative to know that Cicero is Tully or that Hesperus is Phosphorus does *not*, by itself, confer aposteriority on either "Cicero is Tully" or "Hesperus is Phosphorus." The informativeness of a statement is one thing, and its aposteriority is quite another thing. Suppose that Goldbach's Conjecture—which says that every even number greater than 2 is the sum of two primes—is true and provable. Everyone admits that *if* Goldbach's Conjecture is true, *then* it's necessarily true and also a priori. So anyone who comes to know that every even number greater than 2 is the sum of two primes by actually proving it, will also gain some very important new information, namely, a knowledge of the very fact which confers truth, necessity, and apriority upon Goldbach's Conjecture. So informativeness alone does not entail aposteriority. The statements "Cicero is Tully" and "Hesperus is Phosphorus," just like Goldbach's Conjecture—assuming that it really is true and knowable by proof—are both a priori.

Critical Reply #3: As we've seen, the thesis that *if* a true identity statement between rigid designators is true, *then* it's necessarily true, is a necessary a priori truth of philosophical analysis. So even if the necessary a posteriori exists, it presupposes that at least some statements are analytic, necessary, and a priori. Therefore, even if the necessary a posteriori *did* exist, its existence could not be consistently used to cast universal doubt on the analytic-synthetic distinction. Indeed, as we also saw above, Kripke himself argued for the existence of the necessary a posteriori and also holds a classical view about the relationship between analyticity, necessity, and apriority.

Critical Reply #4: Some post-Quinean, post-classical Analytic philosophers other than Kripke himself might find the Kripke-Putnam argument for the necessary a posteriori status of "Water is H_2O" and "Gold is the element with atomic number 79" to be highly compelling with respect to its undermining the analytic-synthetic distinction, even if they have also accepted the argument I gave in *Critical Reply #2* for the necessary a priori status of "Cicero is Tully" and "Hesperus is Phosphorus." This is because the argument for the necessary aposteriority of "Water is H_2O" and "Gold is the element with atomic number 79" presupposes the truth of *scientific essentialism*, and it may well be that the compellingness of the thesis of the necessary aposteriority of these two statements is largely based on the assumption that scientific essentialism is true. Scientific essentialism says that there exist necessary a posteriori truths about theoretical identities, based on microphysical essences of natural kinds, that are discovered via the contemporary natural sciences. And many or even most post-classical Analytic philosophers who are scientific realists are also scientific essentialists.

Nevertheless, I think that scientific essentialism is independently questionable (Hanna, 2006a: ch. 4). Indeed, even Putnam himself later rejected scientific essentialism in "Is Water Necessarily H_2O?" (Putnam, 1990). Later Putnam's basic criticism of scientific essentialism is this. The truth of the statement "Water is H_2O" depends on a special set of causal laws that all obtain in the actual world, and which jointly determine the microstructure of physical matter in that world. But this special set of laws does not hold in every logically possible world. Hence in worlds in which the causal laws are very different, and therefore in which the microstructure of physical matter is also very different, then the statement "Water is H_2O" can be false. And the same goes for the statement "Gold is the element with atomic number 79." Therefore, the statements "Water is H_2O" and "Gold is the element with atomic number 79" aren't true in every logically possible world in which the stuff that's identical to H_2O and the stuff that's identical to the element with atomic number 79 in the actual manifestly real world, also exist. But according to the doctrine of necessary truth held by defenders of the necessary a posteriori, if an identity statement *S* between rigidly-designating natural kind terms fails to obtain in every world in which the stuff designated by those terms exists, then *S* is not necessary. So according to the doctrine of necessity held by defenders of the necessary a posteriori, neither the statement "Water is H_2O" nor the statement "Gold is the element with atomic number 79" is necessary, and thus by the very standards held by defenders of the necessary a posteriori, the statements "Water is H_2O" and "Gold is the element with atomic number 79" don't qualify as genuine counterexamples to the classical thesis that necessity entails apriority. That line of criticism seems to me wholly cogent. Consequently, even despite its overwhelming philosophical popularity in post-classical Analytic philosophy, scientific essentialism is false.

8. The Kripke-Putnam argument against the analytic-synthetic distinction from the existence of the contingent a priori.

According to Donnellan, Kripke, and Putnam, these statements are all a priori but also contingent:

(SM) Stick S is one meter long at t_0 [According to Kripke.]

(WL) Water is a liquid [According to Putnam, but not Kripke.]

(CA) Cats are animals [According to Putnam, but not Kripke.]

and

(WM) Whales are mammals [According to Donnellan, but not Kripke.].

This can be shown in the following way. If stick S is the standard meter bar in Paris, then stick S is stipulated by someone to be one meter long because it is the paradigm of a meter, hence it's known a priori to be one meter long by the person who makes the stipulation. Nevertheless, it's conceivable and logically possible that stick S could have been longer or shorter than a meter at t_0. In the case of the other three examples, as Kant held, the predicate concept is intensionally contained in the subject concept. So anyone possessing the concept WATER, CAT, or WHALE is also able to infer a priori that water is a liquid, that cats are animals, and that whales are mammals. Nevertheless it's conceivable and logically possible that water is dry, that cats are robots, and that whales are non-mammals, in possible worlds in which the causal laws of nature are different and in which matter has a very different physical microstructure from that of the actual world. Therefore, apriority does not entail necessity. But according to Kant's conception of the analytic--synthetic distinction, necessity and apriority entail each other. And even according to the classical logical empiricist/positivist conception of the "three nested categories," analyticity entails apriority, and apriority entails necessity. Therefore, there is no intelligible or defensible analytic-synthetic distinction.

Two Critical Replies

Critical Reply #1: It's plausibly arguable that the *statement* "Stick S is one meter long at t_0," is analytic, necessary, and a priori, precisely because it captures at least one natural interpretation or reading of the *sentence* "Stick S is one meter long at t_0," that's analytic, necessary, and a priori. This can be seen in the following four-step way.

First, as I noted above, we must distinguish carefully between (i) *sentences*, i.e., grammatically and syntactically well-formed indicative complete-thought-expressing units of some natural language L, and (ii) *statements*, i.e., logically structured, linguistically-expressed, intersubjectively-shareable, semantic contents with respect to L that are also inherently truth-bearers with respect to L, such that the one and the same sentence will, as a trivial, internal consequence of the systematic dual-content semantics I'm proposing, always be able to express two or more distinct statements. At the same time, we must also remember that I am treating the notions of *proposition, meaningful indicative sentence, sentence-on-an-interpretation, sentence-on-a-reading,* and *sentence-according-to-a-constative-use* as all mutually necessarily equivalent with one another, and that as a consequence, these six notions are also all mutually necessarily equivalent:

(i) two or more distinct propositions expressed by the same sentence, (ii) two or more distinct statements made with the same sentence, (iii) two or more distinct meanings of the same indicative sentence, (iv) two or more distinct interpretations of the same sentence, (v) two or more distinct readings of the same sentence, and (v) two or more distinct constative uses of the same sentence.

Second, as Kripke explains, the statement "Stick S is one meter long at t_0" means the same as the following statement:

(SM*) The stick now stipulated by someone to be the standard meter bar is one meter in length at t_0.

But the statement "The stick now stipulated by someone to be the standard meter bar is one meter in length at t_0" has the same overall logico-semantic structure—i.e., "The F is (a) G"—as the following statements:

(PP) The current president of the USA is a president

and

(RR) The runner is a runner.

Now, each of *the sentences* used to express *these two statements* has at least one natural interpretation or reading that makes the corresponding statement expressed by that sentence analytically true and a priori. This can be seen if one appends to each of the above sentences another clause that simply forcibly induces the natural analytic reading:

(PP$_{analytic}$) The current president of the USA is a president, *because it's utterly obvious that every president is a president—what else would a president be?*

and

(RR$_{analytic}$) The runner is a runner, *because it's utterly obvious that every runner is a runner—what else would a runner be and do?*

Correspondingly, appending the same sort of "forcible inducing clause" to the sentence "The stick now stipulated by someone to be the standard meter bar is one meter in length at t_0," yields the following analytic a priori statement:

(SM$_{analytic}$) The stick now stipulated by someone to be the standard meter bar is one meter in length at t_0, *because it's utterly obvious that every standard meter bar is a bar that's one meter in length—what other length would a standard meter bar be?*

Therefore, *the sentence* "Stick S is one meter long at t_0," which expresses *the statement* "Stick S is one meter in length at t_0," has at least one natural reading that's analytic

a priori, i.e., the forcibly induced reading that's represented by

(SM$_{analytic}$) The stick now stipulated by someone to be the standard meter bar is one meter in length at t_0, *because it's utterly obvious that every standard meter bar is a bar that's one meter in length—what other length would a standard meter bar be?*

But then *the statement* "Stick S is one meter long at t_0," is also necessary, precisely because it's analytic, just as Kripke says:

I am presupposing that an analytic truth is one which depends on *meanings* in the strict sense and therefore is necessary as well as *a priori*. (Kripke, 1980: n. 63, pp. 122-123)

Third, it's true, as Kripke also says, that there's *another* natural reading of *the sentence* "Stick S is one meter long at t_0," which expresses a contingent statement. According to such a reading, the referring phrase "Stick S" is interpreted to express a rigid designator. One paradigm of a rigid designator is a proper name. So let's arbitrarily choose a proper name, for example, "Zaphod." Then the contingent *statement* which expresses the rigid designator reading of *the sentence* "Stick S is one meter long at t_0," can be represented by:

(SM$_{rigid\ designator:\ 'stick\ S' = 'Zaphod'}$) Zaphod is one meter in length at t_0.

Similarly, the referring phrases "The current president" and "The runner" might have been read so as to express rigidly designating definite descriptions, so that *the sentences* "The current president of the USA is a president" and "The runner is a runner" then are used to express different and contingent *statements*. Or, alternatively, those referring phrases could have been read so as to express plain old definite descriptions, and again express different and contingent statements. But that *doesn't* justify us in holding that *the statements* "The

265

current president of the USA is a president" and "The runner is a runner" are anything other than analytic, necessary, and a priori, which is made obvious when we forcibly induce the natural analytic readings of *the sentences* "The current president of the USA is a president" and "The runner is a runner," as represented by

>(PP$_{analytic}$) The current president of the USA is a president, *because it's utterly obvious that every president is a president—what else would a president be?*

and

>(RR$_{analytic}$) The runner is a runner, *because it's utterly obvious that every runner is a runner—what else would a runner be and do?*

Similarly, the contingent *statement* that would be expressed by using the referring phrase "Stick S" as a rigid designator, namely, the *statement*

>(SM$_{rigid\ designator:\ 'stick\ S'\ =\ 'Zaphod'}$) Zaphod is one meter in length at t_0

self-evidently isn't the same *statement* as

>(SM$_{analytic}$) The stick now stipulated by someone to be the standard meter bar is one meter in length at t_0, *because it's utterly obvious that every standard meter bar is a bar that is one meter in length—what other length would a standard meter bar be?*

Fourth and finally, it follows from the preceding three points that we have no sufficient reason to believe that there is any single *statement* whatsoever that is both contingent and also a priori. Indeed, by very much the same sort of argument I just used, Kripke concludes that we have no sufficient reason to believe that there is any single *statement* whatsoever that is both analytic and also contingent:

>If statements whose a priori truth is known via the fixing of reference [e.g., "Stick S is one meter long at t_0"] are counted as analytic, then some analytic truths are contingent; this possibility is excluded in the notion of analyticity adopted here. (Kripke, 1980: n. 63, pp. 122-123)

Therefore, if, like Kripke, our conception of analyticity is classical, then there's no sufficient reason for us to believe that the *statement* "Stick S is one meter long at t_0" is contingent a priori. If the statement "Stick S is one meter long at t_0" is counted as a priori, then it simply has to be analytic and necessary.

Critical Reply #2: The same four-part argument strategy I used in the last few paragraphs can also be used to argue for a precisely analogous conclusion in the other putative cases of the contingent a priori, namely, the statements

(WL) Water is a liquid

(CA) Cats are animals

and

(WM) Whales are mammals.

Now, let's see how that argument will go.

First, we distinguish carefully again between sentences and the statements (meanings, interpretations, readings, constative uses, propositions) expressed by means of those sentences, and recall that according to my systematic dual-content semantics, one and the same sentence will always be able to express two or more distinct statements.

Second, the sentences used to express *the statements* "Water is a liquid," "Cats are animals," and "Whales are mammals"—namely, *the sentences* "Water is a liquid," "Cats are animals," and "Whales are mammals"—each have a natural reading according to which the statement expressed by that sentence is analytic, necessary, and a priori. This can easily be shown by the method of appending the appropriate forcibly-inducing sentences in order to yield the natural analytic readings, as follows:

(WL$_{analytic}$) Water is a liquid, *because it's utterly obvious that water is one of the many specific kinds of things that are liquids—how else is water supposed to be identified?*

(CA$_{analytic}$) Cats are animals, *because it's utterly obvious that cats are one of the many specific kinds of things that are animals—how else are cats supposed to be identified?*

and

(WM$_{analytic}$) Whales are mammals, *because it's utterly obvious that whales are one of the many specific kinds of things that are mammals—how else are whales supposed to be identified?*

Third, the sentences used to express *the statements* "Water is a liquid," "Cats are animals," and "Whales are mammals"—namely, *the sentences* "Water is a liquid," "Cats are animals," and "Whales are mammals"—also each have a distinct natural rigid-designator reading according to which the statement expressed by that sentence is contingent. The other paradigm of a rigid designator is a natural kind term, and each natural kind term has the same meaning as an arbitrary demonstrative complex mass-term-cum-predicate "that kind of stuff (or: creatures of that kind), normally identified as being such-and-such." So we can represent the rigid-designator readings of the sentences "Water is a liquid," "Cats are

The Fate of Analysis

animals," and "Whales are mammals," that express *the statements* "Water is a liquid," "Cats are animals," and "Whales are mammals," as follows:

(WL$_{\text{rigid designator: "water" = "that kind of stuff, normally identified as being a wet, drinkable, etc., liquid"}}$) That kind of stuff, normally identified as being a wet, drinkable, etc., liquid, is a liquid.

(CA$_{\text{rigid designator: "cats" = "creatures of that kind, normally identified as being small soft-furred four-legged domesticated animals of the species Felis catus"}}$) Creatures of that kind, normally identified as being small soft-furred four-legged domesticated animals of the species *Felis catus*, are animals.

and

(WM$_{\text{rigid designator: "whales" = "creatures of that kind, normally identified as being any of the larger marine mammals of the order Cetacea, having streamlined body and horizontal tail, and breathing through a blowhole on the head"}}$) Creatures of that kind, normally identified as being any of the larger marine mammals of the order Cetacea, having streamlined body and horizontal tail, and breathing through a blowhole on the head, are mammals.

Fourth and finally, according to these two different natural readings—the analytic reading and the rigid-designator reading—the statements expressed in each case are obviously different, hence there is never any single statement whatsoever such that it is both contingent and also a priori.

9. Kaplan's argument against the analytic-synthetic distinction from contingent analyticity in the logic of indexicals.

The interpreted sentences "I am here now" and "I am, I exist" are analytic truths of the logic of indexicals. This is because every speech context in which the first-person singular indexical word "I" is assigned a referent according to the semantic rule for the use of that word—its "indexical character" or semantic role (Kaplan, 1989: pp. 505-507, 520-521, 523-524, 597-599; Perry, 1979), which can be made explicit as *whoever is here now and using this token of the word-type "I"*—is also such that it automatically delivers that referent in the very same place and time. Similarly, every speech context in which "I" is assigned a referent according to the character of "I" is also such that it automatically delivers an existing referent. But although it's actually true that, for example, R.H. is in Boulder, Colorado, USA on Monday 18 January 2021, in the second year of the 2020-2021 COVID-19 pandemic, this is also obviously not necessarily the case. Instead, somewhat distressingly, R.H. could have been in freezing, snowy Winnipeg, Manitoba, Canada on that very same mid-winter pandemicky (to quasi-rhyme with "panicky") day. Or, perhaps even more distressingly (for me), R.H. might not have existed on that very same mid-winter pandemic-y day. Nevertheless, on both of these days, just in virtue of the logic of indexicals, R.H. says "I am here now" and this comes out true. So even though the statements

(KAP) I am here now

and

(EXISTO) I am, I exist

are both *analytic truths* of the logic of indexicals, they're also *contingent* truths. But according to Kant, necessity and apriority entail each other. And according to the classical logical empiricist/positivist conception of the "three nested categories," analyticity entails apriority, and apriority entails necessity. Therefore, there's no intelligible or defensible analytic-synthetic distinction.

Two Critical Replies

Critical Reply #1: Indexicals are directly referential terms, and so too are reference-fixing rigid designators. For this reason, I can directly appeal to the authority of Kripke himself for an argument against the very idea of analytic contingent statements. As we saw above, Kripke disallows the semantic category of analytic contingent statements (i) because he accepts the classical conception of analyticity, and (ii) because he also sharply distinguishes between analytic statements and statements that express rigid-designator readings of referring words in the sentences that express those statements:

> I am presupposing that an analytic truth is one which depends on *meanings* in the strict sense and therefore is necessary as well as *a priori*. If statements whose a priori truth is known via the fixing of reference are counted as analytic, then some analytic truths are contingent; this possibility is excluded in the notion of analyticity adopted here.... I have not attempted to deal with the delicate problems regarding analyticity in these lectures, but I will say that some (though not all) of the cases often adduced to discredit the analytic-synthetic distinction, especially those involving natural phenomena and natural kinds, should be handled in terms of the apparatus of fixing a reference invoked here. (Kripke, 1980: n. 63, pp. 122-123).

In a precisely analogous way, I hold that no sentence that's used so as to include an *indexical* interpretation or reading of one of its referring words can possibly ever express an analytic statement. Therefore, there can't be any analytic contingent statements.

Critical Reply #2: I can also smoothly extend my argument-strategy in the two critical replies under argument 8. *The Kripke-Putnam argument against the analytic-synthetic distinction from the existence of the contingent a priori*, to the case of Kaplan's argument from analytic contingent statements. Here's how that extension will go.

First, we distinguish carefully again between *sentences* and the *statements* (meanings, interpretations, readings, constative uses, propositions) expressed by means of those sentences, and we also recall that according to my systematic dual-content semantics, one and the same sentence will always be able to express two or more distinct statements. Relatedly, we must also distinguish carefully between indexical *words* and indexical *terms*.

A word is a sub-sentential, sub-phrasal grammatical and syntactical unit in a natural language, and an indexical word is a word that at least sometimes plays an indexical role in the language. An indexical term, by contrast, is what results from a directly referential interpretation or reading of a given indexical word, and the same indexical word can always receive two or more distinct interpretations or readings; hence there can always be two or more distinct indexical terms associated with the same indexical word.

Second, each of *the sentences* used to express *the statements* "I am here now" and "I am, I exist"—namely, *the sentences* "I am here now" and "I am, I exist"—has a natural interpretation or reading according to which the statement expressed by that sentence is analytic, necessary, and a priori. This can again be shown by the method of appending appropriate forcibly-inducing sentences to those sentences in order to yield the natural analytic readings. The only difference in the case of natural analytic readings of sentences containing indexical words is that the appropriate forcibly-inducing sentence is also directly derivable from the indexical character or semantic role of the first-person singular indexical word. So here they are:

($KAP_{analytic}$) I am here now, *because it's utterly obvious that whoever is here now and is using a token of the word-type "I" is at the very same place and time—where else and when else would the user of that token be?*

and

($EXISTO_{analytic}$) I am, I exist, *because it's utterly obvious that whoever is here now and is using a token of the word-type "I" also exists—how else could that token have a user?*

Third, each of *the sentences* used to express *the statements* "I am here now" and "I am, I exist"—namely, *the sentences* "I am here now" and "I am, I exist"—also has a distinct natural indexical reading according to which the statement expressed by that sentence is contingent. As before, the character of the first person singular indexical provides a semantic guide. In order to represent the indexical reading of the word-type "I," we need only substitute the proper name of the relevant user of the relevant token of that word-type in the relevant speech-context, and also make the appropriate grammatical adjustments, as follows:

($KAP_{indexical}$) R.H. is here now

and

($EXISTO_{indexical}$) R.H. is, R.H. exists.

Fourth and again finally, according to these two different natural readings—the analytic reading and the indexical reading—the statements expressed in each case are obviously different, hence there is never any single statement whatsoever such that it is both analytic and also contingent. Kaplan's basic mistake was to assert the following false claim about the meaning of indexicals, with the false-making bit underlined:

> "I" is, <u>in each of its utterances,</u> directly referential. (Kaplan, 1989: p. 520, underlining added)

It's true that "I" is, in some of its utterances, directly referential. Indeed, this may even be mostly the case. But only in *some* of its utterances, and *not in each and every one of its utterances*. On the contrary, as I've shown, in at least some of its utterances, the first-person singular indexical word "I" instead expresses an indexical term that means the same thing as its indexical character or semantic role, which is included in a natural analytic reading of the whole sentence in which it occurs, and thus does not mean the referent of the directly referential use of "I."

XVI.6 So Much For Quine's Critique and The Three Dogmas

That completes my logical, semantic, epistemic, and metaphysical critique of Quine's critique of the analytic-sytnhetic distinction, and also of the three post-Quinean, post-classical Analytic dogmas: namely, (i) that there are necessary a posteriori statements, (ii) that there are contingent a priori statements, and (iii) that there are analytic contingent statements. In fact, there is not only a perfectly intelligible and defensible analytic-synthetic distinction, but also no such things as the necessary a posteriori, the contingent a priori, and the analytic contingent. Or in other words, to play two short ironic riffs—the riffs are indicated in italics—on Quine's purported dismissal of the analytic-synthetic distinction:

> For all its a priori reasonableness, a gap between *analytic, necessary, and a priori* statements simply has not been established. That there is such a gap to be established at all is an unsupported dogma of *post-Quinean, post-classical Analytic followers of the fictional conjoined philosopher Kripke-Putnam and/or the real-life philosophers Donnellan and Kaplan*, a metaphysical article of faith.

XVII. Crisis Management: Husserl's *Crisis*, Post-Classical Analytic Philosophy, and The Ash-Heap of History

XVII.1 Husserl's *Crisis* and Our Crisis

XVII.1.1 Introduction

In this chapter, I turn from the minutely-argued, nitty-gritty critical details of the logical, semantic, epistemic, and metaphysical adventures of the analytic-synthetic distinction in post-classical Analytic philosophy, to a more edgily-argued, general, and sociopolitically-oriented critique of the post-classical Analytic tradition. I'll start that critique by backtracking to Husserl, whose philosophical work, as we saw in sections II.10 and III.3 above, also runs in important comparative and contrastive parallel tracks to classical Analytic philosophy. Dermot Moran's book, *Husserl's Crisis of the European Sciences and Transcendental Phenomenology: An Introduction* (Moran, 2012)—henceforth, *Introduction* for short—is particularly important and timely, more than a decade after its original publication. This is for two reasons. **First**, it's a thoroughly excellent piece of historical-philosophical scholarship in its own right. And **second**, it also indirectly but powerfully indicates a radical Husserlian (and, by its intellectual provenance, also a broadly and radically Kantian) way of critically and constructively thinking about recent and contemporary professional academic post-classical Analytic philosophy, in the larger context of European and worldwide culture since the Enlightenment, and also in the largest context of the contemporary rational human condition itself.

In section II.10, I looked at Husserl's highly influential early-period views on pure logic and his critique of logical psychologism; and in section III.3, I looked at his equally influential early and middle-period views on phenomenology and intentionality. Husserl's unfinished *Crisis of European Sciences and Transcendental Phenomenology* (written in 1936, published in 1954), which was his last and in many ways most important work, is at once a devastating critique of the intellectual crisis brought on by "objectivism" and "naturalism" in the philosophical foundations of the exact sciences (i.e., the fundamental natural sciences—physics, chemistry, and biology—plus mathematics), an Existentialism-inflected defense of transcendental phenomenology, and also in effect a Husserlian re-writing of Kant's "What is Enlightenment?" Moreover, even despite its being unfinished, the *Crisis* is written with all the laser-beam focus, seriousness, and urgency of a great 20th century rationalist philosopher who was a victim of anti-semitic racism in the dangerous, frightening, oppressive period during the rise-to-power of Hitler and the Nazis, and at the same time approaching the natural end of his life.[1]

As Moran puts it:

---
[1] Husserl was born in 1859, and died of natural causes in 1938. In 1933, he was banned from teaching and publishing in Germany because he was Jewish, and then in 1935, for the same reason, he had his German citizenship revoked by the anti-non-aryan Nuremberg Laws.

In the *Crisis* .... Husserl makes a number of bold and interrelated claims:

1. There is a crisis of foundations in [the] exact sciences.

2. There is a crisis brought on by the positivity of the sciences.

3. There is a crisis in the human sciences, since they model themselves on the exact sciences.

4. There is an explicit crisis in psychology, the supposed science of the human spirit.

5. There is a crisis in contemporary culture ("a radical life-crisis of European humanity").

6. There is a crisis in philosophy (traditionally understood as the discipline which addresses the crisis in the sciences and in life). (*Introduction*, p. 7)

The overall crisis, for Husserl, then, is the failure of European rationality, despite the enormous advances of the sciences in the technological domination of the world and in the technical organization of society, to have supplied a cure for the social and psychic illness of the time, because of the crucial neglect of the subjective contribution to the experience of the world. Thus, in his 1935 "Vienna Lecture," he contrasts folk medicine with scientific medicine and wonders why there has been no scientific equivalent of medicine for cultural ailments. [Transcendental] phenomenology will provide that cultural medicine for our time. (*Introduction*, p. 9)

Clearly, lying behind Husserl's conception of "crisis" (*Krisis*) is Kant's conception of "critique" (*Kritik*), and, in many ways the *Crisis* is Husserl's response to Kant (*Introduction*, p. 36). So in these ways, Moran's *Introduction* made and makes it possible for the recent or contemporary reader to appreciate the multi-faceted philosophical significance of the *Crisis* in a larger historical and sociopolitical context that fully includes Kant, the post-Kantian European and worldwide cultural tradition, and *us*, contemporary philosophers, *especially* those in the post-classical Analytic tradition.

XVII.1.2 The Thematic Structure of the *Crisis*

Although it's unfinished, and in certain respects remains a patchwork quilt of closely related but not fully integrated manuscripts, nevertheless the *Crisis* has an overall four-part basic thematic shape or structure that's accurately and smoothly mirrored by the basic thematic structure of Moran's *Introduction*:

> **theme 1:** *a Husserlian critique of science*, including sub-critiques of the exact sciences (especially physics and geometry), the human sciences (especially psychology), and "scientific philosophy" (Reichenbach, 1951),

theme 2: *a teleological interpretation of European culture since the 17th century, focused on the history of modern philosophy*, interestingly reminiscent of Kant's "Idea for a Universal History with a Cosmopolitan Aim,"

theme 3: *the core notion of the "life-world"* (*Lebenswelt*), as a primitive starting-point for philosophical explanation, and

theme 4: *transcendental phenomenology*, as the realization of the proper end or *telos* of philosophy in particular and human rationality more generally, and as the solution to "the crisis of the European sciences."

In Moran's *Introduction*, chapters 3-4 correspond to theme 1, chapter 4 corresponds to theme 2, chapter 6 corresponds to theme 3, and chapter 7 corresponds to theme 4.

Chapter 1 provides a sketch of Husserl's life and works, and chapter 2 provides a preliminary outline of the four basic themes of the *Crisis*. Finally, chapter 8 discusses the philosophical impact and larger implications of the *Crisis*. In the rest of this section, **first**, I'll sketch the key points of Moran's treatment of the four basic themes, and then **second**, I'll work out some further Kantian and Husserlian critical thoughts inspired by Moran's treatment, and apply those thoughts to post-classical Analytic philosophy.

XVII.1.3 Theme 1: A Husserlian Critique of Science

As Moran rightly says, the very idea of "critique" in the context of the *Crisis* has a Kantian motivation. Now, for Kant, a critique of X is a specifically philosophical inquiry into the origins, scope, and limits of X, where X is some human cognitive or practical capacity, along with a set of characteristic mental representations, beliefs, claims, choices, or actions flowing from the use of that capacity. As such, a Kantian critique of X proceeds in two phases, (i) by showing how X can or does fall into self-undermining errors, fallacies, or paradoxes by failing to understand its own origins, scope, and limits, and (ii) by showing how a properly self-conscious, realistic, and restricted conception of its own origins, scope, and limits provides a means of adequately vindicating X's characteristic representations, beliefs, claims, choices, or actions, although in a radical way that, from the initial misguided standpoint of X, would seem cognitively inconceivable or practically impossible. Let's call the the first phase of Kantian critique, *the deconstructive phase*, and the second phase of Kantian critique, *the reconstructive phase*.

Correspondingly, Husserl's critique of science in the *Crisis* also has two phases, a deconstructive phase and a reconstructive phase.

In turn, the deconstructive phase has two parts.

The **first** part is a philosophical interpretation of Galileo's revolutionary physics and Galilean scientific method, as paradigmatic of the philosophical ideology of the exact sciences. Here, as Moran nicely spells it out, Husserl argues that the fundamental features of Galilean physics are its treatment of the natural world as an *idealized* infinite material whole inherently governed by causal relations and causal laws, and as a *formalized* domain that's inherently mathematically describable. This in turn presupposes that something more basic has been idealized and formalized, and this is the *life-world,* here understood as the rational human animal's pre-reflective, pre-predicative, non-conceptual, pre-theoretical, subjective-experiential encounter with the intuitively-given apparent or manifest world. The life-world in this subjective-experiential sense is the primitive starting place for philosophical explanation, precisely because it immediately reveals itself as expressing the fundamental structure of objective reality, namely the necessary and a priori "intentional correlation" between human consciousness and the multi-modal capacity for intentionality on the one hand (the intentional subject), and the basic structures of the apparent or manifest world on the other hand (the intentional object). This "intentional correlation" structure is of course none other than Husserl's version of Kant's landmark thesis of the necessary conformity of the world of appearances or phenomena to the rational human mind, rather than the converse—Kant's "Copernican revolution." But Husserl has added to Kant's account the crucial further idea that, as the primitive ground of objective reality, the life-world is epistemically and metaphysically *prior to* the natural world as representationally determined by the exact sciences. Formulated in Kantian language, Husserl's brilliantly original idea is that the world of appearances or phenomena, as representationally determined by empirical concepts, judgments, the schematized Categories, and the Principles of Pure Understanding, is essentially an *abstraction from and constitutively dependent on* the life-world. Husserl also works out a parallel life-world-grounded account of Euclidean geometry in "The Origins of Geometry," later critically studied by Jacques Derrida. The key idea shared by the accounts of Galilean physics and Euclidean geometry is that the exact sciences arise, each in its own way, via a process of *rationalizing abstractive intentional transformation,* whereby what is originally and intuitively given to experiencing subjects in the primitive subjective-experiential life-world is conceptually, judgmentally, and more generally theoretically determined, and indeed theoretically *over*determined, by representationally converting various high-level concepts and propositions into an *abstract overlay* of the primitive life-world. The tragic epistemic and metaphysical mistake of the hegemonic philosophical ideology of the exact sciences, the human sciences, and "scientific philosophy," is then to treat the abstract overlay as if *it* were "the real thing," that is, as if *it* were the epistemically and metaphysically primitive starting-place for philosophical explanation. In the mid-1920s, Whitehead had called the same tragic epistemic and metaphysical mistake "the fallacy of misplaced concreteness" (Whitehead, 1971: pp. 64, 72). In any case, in this connection the philosophical influences on Husserl of Kant's pre-Critical "Directions in Space" essay, as well as the Transcendental Aesthetic and Transcendental Analytic sections of the *Critique of Pure Reason,* and also the "existential analytic" of Heidegger's *Being and Time,* are all obvious.

The **second** part of the deconstructive phase of Husserl's critique of science is an analysis of empirical or scientific psychology, as paradigmatic of the philosophical ideology of the modern human sciences. Here Husserl's critique of *logical psychologism* in the *Prolegomena to Pure Logic,* the first volume of the *Logical Investigations* (see also sections II.10 to II.13 above), and also his critique of *objectivism* and *naturalism* in *Ideas 1* (Hanna, 2015b), lead the way. Logical psychologism for Husserl is the epistemic and metaphysical thesis that the a priori laws and truths of logic can be explanatorily and ontologically reduced to the a posteriori causal laws and truths of empirical or scientific psychology. Objectivism for Husserl, by contrast, is the epistemic and metaphysical thesis that human beings and the natural world are essentially *non-apparent* objectively entities or facts in-themselves (i.e., noumena), hidden behind the humanly subjective "veil of appearances" (for example, Lockean secondary qualities, Humean impressions, Russellian/Moorean or Carnapian sense data, etc.), and knowable only by the exact sciences or by "scientific philosophy." And finally, naturalism for Husserl is the epistemic and metaphysical thesis that everything whatsoever in the human or natural world, especially including organismic life, consciousness or subjective experience, intentionality (aka "consciousness-of," or "aboutness"), rationality (including cognitive/theoretical rationality and practical/moral rationality), meaning, truth (including mathematical truth and logical truth), necessity and modality (including essence and possibility), universals and ideality (including sets, structures, types, and infinity), and normativity (including non-instrumental or categorical principles, reasons, and values), is explanatorily and ontologically reducible to contingent facts knowable only by the natural sciences, especially physics, chemistry, and biology. Now psychologism is clearly a sub-species of naturalism, and objectivism is clearly Husserl's generalization of Kant's notion of noumenal realism. In turn, the conjunction of objectivism and naturalism is *scientism*. The fundamental problem with scientism, fully grasped by Husserl and also correctly identified by Moran, is that it's rationally self-refuting and self-stultifying, precisely because it *presupposes and uses* both pre-formal-and-natural-scientific human rationality (i.e., the proto-rationality of the life-world) and trans-formal-and-natural-scientific human rationality (i.e., logical rationality and non-instrumental practical rationality) in attempting to show that *only* the entities and facts known by natural science are primitively objectively real. But this cannot possibly be true, since the basic *natural sciences*, as rational human cognitive achievements, and also *natural scientists* themselves, as fully engaging in pre-formal-and-natural-scientific and trans-formal-and-natural-scientific human rationality at every moment of their conscious and self-conscious lives, are necessarily *ir*reducible to the physical facts known by those very sciences and those very scientists. Indeed, natural science cannot reductively explain either *mathematics* or *logic* without self-contradiction,[2] so how could it reductively explain *natural science*, which presupposes and uses mathematics and logic alike? Thus scientism both presupposes and uses, and yet also explicitly denies, the primitive objective reality of pre-formal-and-natural-scientific and trans-formal-and-natural-scientific human rationality. Hence the paradoxically false thesis that scientism is true, or even could be true, leads directly to skepticism and nihilism about human rationality itself. And in this way, for Husserl, the fundamental crisis of the European sciences is the skeptical, nihilist condition that scientism induces and produces. Otherwise put, *scientism is how naïve Enlightenment rationality commits cognitive suicide.*

---

[2] The case of mathematics, as Husserl clearly sees, is crucial, since it occupies a rational mid-point between natural science and logic. See (Hanna, 2015a: chs. 5 and 7, and 2015b).

It's extremely important to note here that rejecting *scientism* does *not* entail rejecting *the formal and natural sciences*.³ Indeed, Husserl is very clear and explicit that either skeptically rejecting the justified knowledge-claims and truths of the formal and natural sciences or failing to take them sufficiently seriously (for example, creationism, flat-earthism, superstitious magic, the theory of alien-thought-control-screen helmets, etc.), is "irrationalist," and every bit as rationally incoherent as scientism. The point of the phenomenological life-world analyses of Galilean physics and Euclidean geometry is to explain the exact sciences in terms of pre-formal-and-natural-scientific rationality and trans-formal-and-natural-scientific rationality, without appealing to either objectivism or naturalism, and therefore to *explain the exact sciences non-reductively* and *non-self-defeatingly*.

The reconstructive phase of Husserl's critique of science also has two parts, which segue respectively into **theme 2** and **theme 3**.

XVII.1.4 Theme 2: A Teleological Interpretation of European Culture Since the 17th Century, Focused on the History of Modern Philosophy

The *Crisis* is especially notable for its being Husserl's most sustained (and first published) discussion of the philosophy of history. What sets the frame of the discussion is Husserl's deconstructive critique of science. But once this deconstructive critique has been brought to self-consciousness, then the reconstructive phase of critique has already begun.

What I mean by that is this. According to Husserl, in the very process of critically deconstructing the philosophical ideology of the exact sciences, the human sciences, and "scientific philosophy," and then re-grounding them in the life-world, the philosopher is required to look back at the history of philosophy as a unified developing process, and thereby becomes historically and critically self-conscious. This philosophical achievement of historical self-consciousness, in turn, reveals that *the history of the crisis of the European sciences* is the same as *the history of modern philosophy*, which in turn is the same as *the history of Enlightenment human rationality*, and also reveals to the historically and critically self-conscious philosopher that the only possible solution to the crisis is *an affirmation of transcendental-phenomenological rationality*. Moran nicely summarizes Husserl's line of thinking here:

> Life, in Husserl's language, is always life in tradition; there is a constant gathering-up and passing-on (as well as forgetting) of what went before. The paradigm for considering historical processes is, as it was for Hegel, the history of philosophy. For Husserl, present philosophy encompasses all previous philosophy within

---

3 Contrapositively, *taking the formal and natural sciences seriously* does not entail accepting *scientism*, and *taking physics seriously* does not entail accepting *physicalism*. It's hard to overestimate the popularity of the fallacy of arguing directly from taking the formal and natural sciences and especially physics seriously (especially when this taking-seriously is inflated to secular reverence or worship: logic worship, mathematics-worship, and physics-worship), to scientism and physicalism.

its horizon, in his "living present".... The task of each philosopher is to renew and re-animate the tradition of philosophy, appropriating it and accommodating it into new horizons and new meanings. Husserl also emphasizes the responsibility of the philosopher charged with the task of creating the future through a re-animation of the past. Using the exemplary pattern of the history of philosophy enlivened and mediated by living philosophers. Husserl conceives of human history as a unified teleological structure, which is in a way supported by the living present, by contemporary actors in the social and communal world. History, as the movement of peoples in time, makes sense because it is appropriated and understood by the present generation who are the living agents in reconstituting the historical past as *their own time*.... To live is to live historically. Indeed, in a late manuscript from the summer of 1937, Husserl sees the exploration of what he had in *Ideas 1* called "the natural concept of the world" and later the "life-world" as precisely the exploration of the "historical world." (*Introduction*, p. 177)

XVII.1.5 Theme 3: The Core Notion of the Life-World

Moran rightly notes that despite (or perhaps because of) its being the core philosophical notion in the *Crisis*, the notion of the life-world is nevertheless a "problematical concept" (*Introduction*, p. 178). We already know that, at the very least, the concept of the life-world is the concept of the primitive ground of objective reality and of the necessary a priori "intentional correlation" between intentional subjects and intentional objects. But at the same time, the concept of the life-world is also drafted by Husserl into performing many other philosophical roles, including its being "the 'pre-scientific' intuitive world of naïve belief" (*Introduction*, pp. 185-186), but "also permeated with scientific and technological determinations" (p. 188), "essentially subjective and not objectifiable" (pp. 189-192), "historical and the cradle of tradition" (pp. 192-193), a "universal horizon" (pp. 193-195), "fundament," "ground," and "underground" (pp. 195-198), "the intersubjective, communal world" (pp. 198-201), "a region of evidences" (pp. 203-204), the "correlate of the natural attitude" (pp. 205-208), as "one world but also [allowing for] relativity of life-worlds" (pp. 208-211), as "home world" but also allowing for "alien worlds" (pp. 211-213), and as capturing "the truth of the pre-Copernican world" (pp. 213-214).

Given all these different characterizations, it may seem that Husserl's concept of the life-world is at best protean, and at worst hopelessly confused and ambiguous. If so, that would be devastating for the central argument of the *Crisis*. But I don't think—and I don't think that Moran thinks—that things are ultimately in such bad shape. Indeed, on the contrary, I do think that the "problematical" multivocity of Husserl's notion of the life-world can be substantially sorted out if we carefully distinguish between two essentially different conceptions of "the natural attitude" and the "life-world": (i) the natural attitude as the pre-reflective, pre-predicative, non-conceptual, pre-theoretical, proto-rational, pre-Enlightenment, pre-modern-state, *pre-scientific* attitude and its primitively objectively real *subjective-experiential life-world*, and (ii) the natural attitude as the *naturalistic* attitude and its *science-determined life-world*, i.e., human attitudes and social-cultural conditions in the life-world *after* their abstractive determination (and indeed over-determination) by higher-order reflection, concepts, judgment, logic, practical rationality, the Enlightenment, the modern state, and above all by the exact sciences and their hegemonic philosophical ideology. The pre-scientific attitude and its subjective-experiential life-world correspond closely to Sellars's *manifest image* of human-beings-in-the-world, and in turn the naturalistic attitude and its science-determined life-world correspond closely to Sellars's *scientific image* of human-beings-in-the-world. (Sellars, 1963c, and also section XVII.4 below). Strikingly, however, Sellars himself, as a scientific naturalist, *failed* to achieve Husserl's deeper critical insight that philosophers should provide not merely a naïve or Whiggish historical description of the naturalistic attitude and the science-determined life-world, but also a thoroughgoing *critique* of it, in relation to the pre-scientific attitude and its subjective-experiential life-world.

The vivid contrast between Husserl and Sellars here is highly instructive. One might have expected Sellars, as a brilliant, Kant-influenced philosopher who was sufficiently politically radical as to be a socialist soap-box speaker during the 1932 presidential elections, and who also seriously studied Husserl's writings with Marvin Farber at SUNY Buffalo in the mid-1930s (Sellars, 1975), to have come on his own to Husserl's deeper critical insight. But my own reading of the intellectual and cultural situation is that by the 1950s, Sellars, just like the other leading post-classical philosophers (especially including the exiled Vienna Circle logical empiricists/positivists, many of whom by then had comfortable professorial chairs at top universities in the USA), was in effect *lured or nudged into the sleep of reason* by the peculiarly triumphalist, moralistic, guilt-free, self-confidently anti-Fascist, and anxiously anti-Communist American vision of the post-World War II world. I'll come back to the political implications of scientism again in the last sub-section of this section.

XVII.1.6 Theme 4: Transcendental Phenomenology

As we know from section III.3 above, Husserl was a phenomenologist before he was a transcendental philosopher, and indeed in the first edition of *Logical Investigations* (1901), his view is clearly *anti*-idealist and *anti*-transcendentalist, a philosophical fact that Russell fully appreciated during his time in prison in 1918, when he read the second or 1913 edition (see section IV.1 above). But ironically enough, by the time of *Ideas 1* in 1913, Husserl had already explicitly become a transcendental phenomenologist, and he remained fully committed to transcendental phenomenology for the rest of his philosophical life.

Husserl's transcendental phenomenology is a species of Kantian transcendental idealism, and indeed in the *Crisis* Husserl claims that transcendental phenomenology is the "final form" of transcendental idealism (*Introduction*, p. 219). As we also know from section III.3, transcendental phenomenology is the conjunction and fusion of phenomenology and Kantian transcendental idealism. Phenomenology is the systematic philosophical description of the acts, contents, and objects of *conscious intentionality* (aka "consciousness-of"), broadly construed so as to include first-order consciousness (aka "lived experience" or

Erlebnis) and self-consciousness, interpersonal or intersubjective awareness, sense perception, judgment, belief, knowledge, memory, imagination, emotion, feeling, desire, act-intentionality and agency, and so-on. In turn, as I've pointed out in section XV.1, Kantian transcendental idealism says (i) that the proper objects of rational human cognition are always humanly sense-perceivable veridical appearances or manifestly real things, never things-in-themselves (cognitive idealism), (ii) that the innate capacities of the rational human mind, when triggered by the given inputs of human sensibility, actively contribute non-empirical forms and structures to the contents of cognition (representational transcendentalism), and (iii) that necessarily, the basic forms and structures of the veridically apparent or manifestly real world conform to the non-empirical forms and structures contributed to the contents of cognition by the rational human mind, and not the converse (transcendental idealism, aka Kant's "Copernican revolution").

Unfortunately and notoriously, as we *also* also know from earlier chapters of this book, Kant isn't perfectly clear about the precise nature of transcendental idealism, and correspondingly there are strong and weak versions of it. According to the strong or "identity" version, the apparent objects of human cognition are *token-identical to* the well-formed or well-structured contents of rational human cognition, and the essential forms and structures of the objects are *type-identical* to the forms and structures contributed to cognition by the rational human mind. This entails that the veridically apparent or manifestly real world is nothing more and nothing less than a complex nexus of humanly-created, humanly-significant meanings; as a consequence, the apparent or manifest world could not have existed if rational human minds had never existed, and necessarily it goes out of existence if and whenever rational human minds go out of existence. By contrast, according to the weak or "counterfactual" version of transcendental idealism, the apparent or manifest objects of human cognition are mind-independently "empirically real," in the sense that they exist even if rational human minds had never existed or do not currently exist. Nevertheless, the empirically real, veridically apparent, or manifestly real world is still inherently "mind-friendly": the apparent or manifest objects still do necessarily conform, at least isomorphically if not also type-identically, to the cognitive forms or structures of the rational human mind, and necessarily *would be* cognizable if and whenever rational human minds *were* to exist.

For Husserl, the *intentional subject* component of the necessary a priori "intentional correlation" structure (sometimes called the "noesis") is identical to the *transcendental ego* of Kantian transcendental idealism, and the *intentional object* component (sometimes called the "noema") is identical to the *world of appearances or phenomena*. Hence Husserl's transcendental phenomenology is not only a strong or "identity" version of Kantian transcendental idealism, but also a *super*-strong or *solipsist-subjectivist* version, similar to Wittgenstein's Schopenhauer-inspired solipsistic idealism in the *Tractatus*, since Husserl identifies what Kant calls "the original synthetic unity of apperception," or the spontaneous, self-conscious, unifying representational activities of rational human cognition, with the conscious intentionality of a *single universal* transcendental ego, sometimes called the "primal ego" (*Introduction*, pp. 237-255). The spontaneous, self-conscious, unifying representational activities of this single universal transcendental primal ego, the non-empirical subject of conscious intentionality, is what Husserl calls "constitution." For Husserl, even *intersubjectivity*, or the existence and social interconnection of other minds, is constituted by the transcendental ego. By contrast, according to weak or "counterfactual" versions of transcendental idealism, Kant's original synthetic unity of apperception is only a *mentalistic-type-structure* implemented or realized by many distinct rational human animal cognizers in an empirically real natural world, and other minds, as minded animals or embodied minds, are equally empirically real.

There are two other characteristically Husserlian features of transcendental phenomenology: (i) the *epochē* or bracketing, together with the transcendental-phenomenological "reduction," which involves a philosophical shift in attention from minds and objects considered *naturalistically*, to minds and objects considered instead *in terms of the necessary a priori "intentional correlation" structure and the subjective-experiential life-world*, and (ii) the thesis that the target domain of transcendental philosophy is not just "experience" or *Erfahrung* in Kant's narrow sense of the totality of objects known or knowable by the natural sciences, but in fact *life*, including all conscious life as embodied lived experience or *Erlebnis*, all biological and especially animal life, and the subjective-experiential life-world itself. As Moran puts it,

> In his mature writings, especially after *Ideas 1*, Husserl always insists that phenomenology is possible only *as transcendental philosophy*, and that the correct understanding of the *epochē* and the reduction are essential for understanding the move to the transcendental required by any genuine, ultimately grounded "first philosophy".... Husserl considers the domain of transcendental subjectivity not just to be a set of formal conditions for [scientific] knowledge (as in Kant), but to be a domain of *life*, of *living* (*Leben*), of genuine experience (*Erfahrung*), a domain that has never before been examined in philosophy. Husserl further insists that the *epochē* and reduction are necessary gateways to this transcendental "field" (*Feld*), which is a field of *experience*, a field of direct *intuition*, and, moreover, one of unlimited extent. The transcendental domain is a domain of conscious experiences, albeit a domain of experience which cannot be entered from the natural[istic] attitude. There is a genuine experience of worldly consciousness, of the sense of the past, the future, horizons of possibility, impossibility, and so on. In this regard, it is also important to realize that the "life-world" ... is actually a *transcendental* concept. (*Introduction*, pp. 218-219)

How will transcendental phenomenology, as the "final form" of transcendental philosophy, solve the crisis of the European sciences? The basic keys to answering to this question, I think, are provided by these insightful Husserlian thoughts, as aptly rendered by Moran:

> Husserl believes that recognizing the world as an accomplishment of subjectivity, of the "life of achievement" (*Leistungsleben*), is a hugely transformative insight.

> Naturalism, positivism, and objectivism, are, properly understood all forms of loss or distortion of subjectivity. (*Introduction*, p. 237)

> Perhaps above all else, Husserl offers in the *Crisis* a new way of thinking about reason and rationality. Human beings—and philosophers especially who are asked by Husserl to be custodians of culture or "functionaries of mankind"—have the duty to promote and protect reason and to oppose all forms of irrationalism. (*Introduction*, p. 299)

> Husserl ... is a critic of narrow versions of rationalism that have been pursued since the Enlightenment. The main problem facing the "renewal" (*Erneuerung*) of reason is that in the modern period reason has become construed in a one-sided manner, due to the successes of the mathematical [i.e., exact] sciences. In other words, Husserl—like Heidegger, who made similar criticisms in his essays of the 1930s, and later Herbert Marcuse—is criticizing the *one-dimensionality* of the framework of technologically-organized, calculative reasoning. Today's rationalism is in the grip of *objectivism* and *naturalism*, and it is transcendental phenomenological reflection (*Besinnung*), especially on the genesis of these meaning-formations, that will lead our concept of reason to a new form of "groundedness of existence" .... Husserl's critique of one-dimensional, technized reason needs to be understood alongside the better-known positions of Heidegger, Marcuse ..., and the Frankfurt School. (*Introduction*, pp. 300-301)

So for Husserl in the *Crisis*, transcendental phenomenology reveals that human reason is not only *world-constituting*, but also radically *autonomous* and radically *responsible*. It also reveals that naïve Enlightenment rationalism, via scientism, has undermined this rich, robust conception of human rationality, and in so doing has not only turned contemporary professional academic philosophy into a self-defeating enterprise, but also symbiotically relates to 20th and 21st century cultural and political practices and structures that are inherently alienating, inauthentic, and destructive. In the next sub-section, I'll push Moran's insightful Husserlian thoughts even further, indeed, radically further.

XVII.1.7 Crisis? What Crisis?

One of most depressing and also most striking things about recent and contemporary professional academic philosophy is its fragmentation, and correspondingly, the mutual isolation of philosophers as individuals and also as members of philosophical groups. It seems that, paradoxically, the more easily philosophers are able to communicate with one another, the less they actually do so for real philosophical purposes, and the less they actually share as thinkers and moral agents who are supposedly personally and collectively committed to philosophy as a way of life, or life-project, and not just a "job." Indeed, sometimes even philosophers working on exactly the same topics are essentially isolated from one another.

A perfect example is *phenomenology*, as initiated by Brentano, foundationally developed by Husserl (see sections III.2 and III.3 above), and then played out in importantly different variations by Meinong (see section III.4), Heidegger, Sartre, Merleau-Ponty, and other existential phenomenologists.[4] It's a sad but true fact that on the one hand, contemporary professional academic philosophers working on phenomenological topics from the standpoint of the Brentano-Husserl-Meinong-Heidegger-Sartre-Merleau-Ponty tradition, and on the other hand, contemporary professional academic post-classical Analytic philosophers working on "sensory phenomenology," "cognitive phenomenology," "agentive phenomenology," "phenomenal intentionality" (for example, Bayne and Montague, 2011; Kriegel, 2013), etc., have virtually nothing to do with one another: but why? One might think that this divisive situation is simply an unhappy consequence of the by-now almost complete dominance of academic professionalization and specialization in contemporary philosophy, combined with natural "in-crowd" and "out-crowd" effects of social clustering and social exclusion. And to some extent, it's precisely those things. But I think that there's also a deeper reason for the widespread state of fragmentation and mutual isolation in contemporary professional philosophy—to be sure, papered over by many academic administrative and careerist happy faces, as people grind their way through the graduate-school-PhD-job-tenure-and-promotion system—that Husserl was able to identify and address in the *Crisis*, and one that we should be equally worried about today. And, in turn, I think that this deeper reason pointedly exemplifies the deepest and most synoptic reason, also identified and addressed by Husserl in the *Crisis*, for being similarly worried about not just European but also world-culture from the 17th to the 21stth centuries and the rational human condition in the 21st century.

Both Kant (as per Hanna, 2006a) and Husserl (and also Wittgenstein, both early and late—see sections VIII.9 and XV.5 above) clearly and distinctly recognized that it's philosophically necessary "to deny [scientific] **knowledge** (*Wissen*) in order to make room for [moral] **faith** (*Glauben*)" (*Critique of Pure Reason* Bxxx, boldfacing in the original), in view of what they regard as the two fundamental philosophical mistakes of philosophy as they knew it in the 18th and 20th centuries respectively: namely, objectivism (noumenal realism) and naturalism (including anti-supernaturalism, classical or radical empiricist epistemology, and materialism/physicalism, whether all-out natural-scientific reductionism or non-reductive materialism/physicalism). As we've seen earlier in this section, these two fundamental philosophical mistakes, in turn, jointly constitute scientism. Now from our own 21st century point of view, it's easy to see that objectivism, naturalism, and scientism are the pervasive default assumptions of Logical Empiricist/Positivist and then mainstream post-Quinean, post-classical Analytic philosophy, from 1929, when The Vienna Circle published their revolutionary manifesto, "The Scientific Conception of the World" (Vienna Circle, 1996)[5] right through post-World War II Anglo-American philosophy and the rest of the 20th century and the first two decades of the 21st century, until this morning at 6am.

---

4 The most important "other existential phenomenologists" include Adoph Reinach, Max Scheler, Edith Stein, Hans-Georg Gadamer, Hannah Arendt, Simone De Beauvoir, Emmanuel Levinas, and Paul Ricoeur.

5 The manifesto was co-written by Carnap, Hans Hahn, and Otto Neurath on behalf of the other members of The Circle.

Husserl saw this more clearly than any other 20th century philosopher, in part because Husserlian and Heideggerian phenomenology were primary critical targets of the Circle, but also more fundamentally because Husserl fully recognized that scientism and transcendental phenomenology are directly opposed to one another, and indeed are strict contraries: if objectivism (as anti-phenomenological) and naturalism (as anti-transcendental) are true, then transcendental phenomenology is false, and conversely. Correspondingly, the pervasive scientistic default assumptions also account for the pervasive fragmentation and mutual isolation in contemporary philosophy, insofar as they have determined not only the longstanding and all-too-familiar "Great Divide" between historically- and phenomenologically-oriented philosophers in the post-Kantian European tradition, on the one hand, and post-classical Analytic philosophers on the other, but also a less noticed, yet perhaps even more insidious and invidious *Survivalist Divide*.

More precisely, it's simply a sad fact that if you want to *survive* in contemporary professional academic philosophy, then you do *not* challenge the post-classical Analytic mainstream by challenging objectivism, naturalism, or scientism, but instead you must implicitly or explicitly acknowledge its dominance, by either quietly retreating into your own little sphere of historical specialists, or even more effectively, by actually joining forces with the post-classical Analytic mainstream under the non-threatening, accommodationist flag of a specialization in some sub-area of "value theory." The point is, that as long as you never directly challenge the philosophical hegemonic ideology or institutional power of the post-classical Analytic mainstream, then you're in good shape professionally. But at the same time, the entire situation produces pervasive intellectual and emotional alienation, anomie, and inauthenticity, from anxious would-be graduate students obsessively reading the philosophy blogs to find out what they should be thinking and doing, all the way to cynical, embittered full professors merely putting in time and punching the clock until their pension-funds permit them to retire without risking old-age poverty. For more on this unhappy situation, see sections XVII.6 to XVII.7, and chapter XVIII below.

Moreover Husserl saw, at least prefiguratively, what I'll call *the fundamental problem of the modern era*, namely that scientism and its two fundamental errors of objectivism and naturalism *also* seep like poison gas (the doomsday weapon of World War I) and explode like an atomic bomb (the doomsday weapon of World War II) *into the larger cultural and practical world*, especially into the authoritarian politics of the modern state, and jointly produce the science-determined life-world of not just contemporary European culture, but also of world-culture and of contemporary rational human life. From our 21st century point of view, and with Husserl's critical help, then we can clearly see that *scientism* and *statism* play essentially the same functional role in their respective cultural domains, and that they also mutually support one another, indeed are symbiotic, each taking in the other's conceptual and practical laundry, and each making the other's existence and survival possible. On the one hand, scientism tells us that we are nothing but deterministic or indeterministic decision-theoretic "moist robots," to borrow a phrase from the aggressively naturalistic philosopher Daniel Dennett (Schuessler, 2013), itself borrowed by Dennett from the comic strip *Dilbert*. And on the other hand, statism tells us that we are obligated to obey the coercive commands of governments—powered by sophisticated exact science and its advanced technology, finance, and industry—no matter how absurd or immoral these commands might actually be, without ever daring to think or act or live for ourselves, lest we fall back into the chaotic, evil, pre-scientific, pre-statist Hobbesian "war of all against all" in the "state of nature,"[6] and lose the marvellous egoistic or collectivist benefits of life as decision-theoretic moist robots. Let's call this tightly-circular, dyadic, and symbiotic conceptual and practical system that governs the science-determined life-world, *scientistic statism*.

Earlier in this section, I noted Husserl's deep insight that scientism is how naïve Enlightenment rationalism commits cognitive suicide. But even more frighteningly and importantly, scientistic statism is the real-world manifestation of Francisco Goya's all-too-true observation and warning in the *Los caprichos* (1797-1799) that "the sleep of reason breeds monsters" (*el sueño de la razón produce monstruos*). Correspondingly, Hitler's totalitarian Nazi German state and Stalin's totalitarian Communist Russian state are, to be sure, scientistic statism's most brutal, destructive, and horrific instantiations. Nevertheless, throughout the 20th and early 21st centuries, the very same symbiotic system of scientistic statism has been and is fully at work worldwide, not merely in countries with blatantly authoritarian or totalitarian regimes, but also in neoliberal democratic societies, including the most scientifically-sophisticated and technologically-advanced, financially rich, and industrially powerful ones. Indeed, the richest and most powerful scientistic statist neoliberal democracy in the world, the so-called "Land of Liberty," dropped two atomic bombs on hundreds of thousands of Japanese non-combatants, co-authored the Cold War nuclear weapons build-up, social-institutionally entenches and sustains (i) capital punishment, (ii) widespread police brutality and the mass incarceration of Black and Brown people, and (iv) the private possession of lethal weapons, has one of the biggest economic-welfare gaps in the world between the richest and the poorest people, no universal system of free healthcare, and regularly invades other countries, all without rational or moral justification, and *also* claims, backed up by coercive violence or the threat of coercive violence, that its citizens must mechanically obey its political authority over all these and many other rationally unjustified acts, decisions, and laws. Scientistic statism is how naïve Enlightenment rationalism commits cognitive suicide and *then* turns into a killer-zombie.

Now as Moran notes, Husserl holds that philosophers are "functionaries of humankind" (*Funktionäre der Menschheit*) (*Introduction*, pp. 8, 299). In my opinion, Husserl is both right and wrong about this. He's *right* in the sense that real philosophy is inherently a committed way of life, a full-time, life-time calling, hence a life-project, and not just a "job," and that the life-project of philosophy is inherently rationalist, humanist, universalist, and cosmopolitan. But Husserl is also wrong, in the sense that the bureaucratic, mechanistic connotations of "functionary" are seriously misleading. They suggest thoughtless, robotic obedience to some external *political* authority. It would also be a serious mistake of misleadingness, although a different one, to speak or think of philosophy as a *vocation*, because the

---

[6] Here it's not irrelevant to remember that Hobbes was Galileo's friend, and later Francis Bacon's private secretary. So the symbiotic connection between scientism and statism was present at the very origins of the Enlightenment.

priestly connotations of "vocation" suggest dogmatic, genuflective obedience to an external *divine* authority. In my opinion, as personally and collectively commited to rationality and humanity, philosophers should be *neither* bureaucrats *nor* priests. The rational humanist commitment of philosophy is fully free-thinking, autonomous or self-legislating, radically responsible, ethical, critical, and self-critical. Properly speaking, then, philosophers should be *rational rebels for humanity*.

As Husserl clearly saw, or at least as he presciently anticipated, it's a highly ironic and also highly paradoxical fact that although scientistic statism is the cognitively-suicidal zombie monster that naïve Enlightenment rationalism released into the world, only a *transcendental-phenomenological radicalization of Enlightenment rationality* can slay the monster and liberate us. That is, only an anti-scientistic, anti-statist, freely-chosen and autonomous or self-legislating, humanist, universalist, cosmopolitan, ethical, critical, self-critical, and in effect existentialist re-affirmation of our own capacities for pre-formal-and-natural-scientific rationality and trans-formal-and-natural-scientific (and especially non-instrumental practical) rationality can awaken us from the sleep of reason. As real philosophers, then, we must actually become what we already potentially are—rational rebels for humanity. This is why, at the end of the day, it's the Kant-inspired Husserlian critique not merely of *scientism* but above all of *scientistic statism*, that I think is the truly important and truly radical message of the *Crisis*.

XVII.2 Formal and Natural Science After 1945, and the Rise of Natural Mechanism

Husserl's *Crisis* was a philosophical *cri de couer* from the mid-1930s, as the lights went out again all over Europe. By the end of World War II, physicists working on the USA-funded Manhattan Project had produced the atomic bomb, and thereby helped to kill hundreds of thousands of Japanese civilians in two cruel blows directed at Hiroshima and Nagasaki, and to create the Cold War atomic weapons build-up, thereby threatening humanity with extinction. At the same time, technological advances flowing from World War II and the US-Russian Space Race during the 1950s and 1960s, helped to cement a widespread cultural attitude that can be best described as *the scientistic mindset* (Haack, 2017b; Hanna, 2021c). Just as early Analytic philosophers and the logical empiricist/ positivist philosophers of The Vienna Circle placed their faith in logicism, i.e., the explanatory and ontological reduction of mathematics to logic, or at the very least in logic-driven philosophy, so too non-philosophers placed their faith in the idea of endless economic and sociopolitical progress driven by the formal and natural sciences-driven application of technology to humanity's problems.

Correspondingly, *mechanism* triumphed in physics, biology, and chemistry, as well as in the formal sciences that subserve those natural sciences, yielding the development of the earliest versions of real-world Turing machines (i.e., digital computers) decision-theoretic economics, and "cybernetics," i.e., artificial intelligence, aka *AI*. When you add the doctrine of *formal mechanism* about the computability/ decidability of truth and proof in logic, mathematics, and other formal sciences—which in fact, as we saw in chapter X, was already decisively refuted by Gödel's incompleteness theorems plus Tarski's semantic conception of truth in formalized languages —to the doctrine of mechanism in physics, biology, and chemistry, then what results is what I call the doctrine of *natural mechanism*. More specifically, natural mechanism says that all the causal powers of everything whatsoever in the natural world are ultimately fixed by what can be digitally computed on a universal deterministic or indeterministic real-world Turing machine, provided that the following three plausible "causal orderliness" and "decompositionality" assumptions are all satisfied: (i) its causal powers are necessarily determined by the general deterministic or indeterministic causal natural laws, especially including the Conservation Laws, together with all the settled quantity-of-matter-and/or-energy facts about the past, especially including The Big Bang, (ii) the causal powers of the real-world Turing machine are held fixed under our general causal laws of nature, and (iii) the "digits" over which the real-world Turing machine computes constitute a complete denumerable set of spatiotemporally discrete physical objects. So, if natural mechanism is true, then all organisms and everything else that exists are *nothing but more-or-less complex automata*, or "survival machines" (Dawkins, 2006), all of whose operations and quantitative properties can be calculated on an ideal digital computer. And in this way, natural mechanism resurrects Laplace's Demon in a digital format: just as Laplace could imagine a demon that predicted all possible events and their consequences, so too would computing provide the tools for mastering the inherently predictable realm of nature.

Mirroring an unbridled confidence in the dual doctrines of logically-driven mathematization, aka formal mechanism—see, for example, the work of John von Neumann, Norbert Wiener, John Nash, and the MIT/Princeton research axis—and natural mechanism, massive government and private funding for universities and computer scientists, decision-theoretic economics, and cybernetics/AI gradually turned Eisenhower's "military-industrial complex" into what I call *the military-industrial-university-digital complex*. This alarming development is perhaps best exemplified, for example, by the activities of The RAND Corporation (Isaac, 2013; McCumber, 2016: chs. 3-4), but in any case, it has been brilliantly criticized in Lutz Dammbeck's 2003 film, *The Net: The Unabomber, LSD, and the Internet* (aka *Das Netz*).

XVII.3 The Emergence of Post-Classical Analytic Philosophy

By the end of World War II, the early Cold War, and the period of the sociopolitical triumph of advanced capitalism and technocracy in the USA, classical Analytic philosophy had triumphed in a social-institutional sense; Whiteheadian organicist philosophy had virtually disappeared except in a vestigial form, as an aspect of American pragmatism; and existential phenomenology and all other kinds of non-Analytic philosophy, under the convenient and pejorative catch-all label, "Continental philosophy," gradually became the all-purpose social-institutional Other and professional academic slave of Analytic philosophy (Akehurst, 2008, 2011; Bloor, 2017; Katzav, 2018; Katzav and Vaesen, 2017; McCumber, 2001, 2016; Rorty, 1982b; Vrahimis, 2012, 2015, forthcoming; Wilshire, 2002).

Indeed, the post-classical Analytic tradition and so-called "Continental philosophy" came into existence simultaneously. Correspondingly, some have interpreted this social-institutional fact as *the creation of Analytic philosophy itself*. For example, Christoph Schuringa argues that

> [i]f there is a decisive moment of birth [of Analytic philosophy], it is the publication in 1949 of *Readings in Philosophical Analysis*, whose editors, Herbert Feigl and Wilfrid Sellars, consciously set out to shape the teaching of philosophy in the United States in an 'analytic' mould. This publication, and others such as Arthur Pap's *Elements of Analytic Philosophy* (also published in 1949), helped crystallize the idea of "analytic philosophy," in which a number of different approaches to philosophy were combined: the "logico-analytical method" of Russell, the commonsense/realist "analysis" of Moore, the logical positivism of the Vienna Circle, the logic of the Lwów-Warsaw school, and American approaches flowing from the pragmatist and realist traditions. By 1958 a group of curious French philosophers could invite leading Anglophone philosophers to a conference at Royaumont under the title *La philosophie analytique*, to see what all the fuss was about. In the very same period, however, the death knell was already being sounded for analytic philosophy in various quarters. In 1956 the Oxford philosopher J.O. Urmson published a history of analytic philosophy, *Philosophical Analysis*, which ends in an obituary for what he calls "the old analysis." The obituary notices have kept coming. In his book *Philosophy and the Mirror of Nature* (1979), the apogee of a sustained self-critique of analytic philosophy that had begun with the publication of W. V. Quine's "Two Dogmas of Empiricism" in 1951, Richard Rorty wrote: "I do not think that there any longer exists anything identifiable as 'analytic philosophy', except in some [...] stylistic or sociological way."... The claim that analytic philosophy was born after 1945 will seem startling to many. Wasn't there widespread talk of "analytic philosophy" (or "analytical philosophy") before that? The answer is no, at least if what is said in print is our guide. This by itself doesn't settle whether analytic philosophy *existed*—perhaps it wasn't necessary to use the phrase. But it is striking that philosophers felt the need to self-apply the label only after 1945. This Google Ngram (showing the incidence of the phrases "analytic philosophy" and "analytical philosophy" in books published over the period 1900–2010) illustrates the point well:

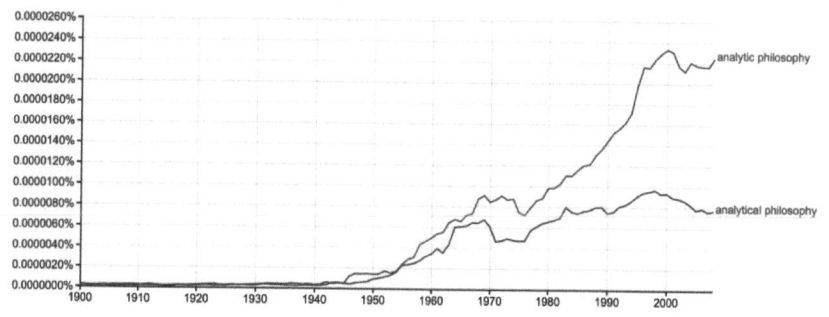

The term "analysis" was, certainly, much used by both Russell and Moore (even if they meant different things by it), and the founding of the journal *Analysis* in 1933 was a significant event (not least since the question of how to do philosophical "analysis" was much discussed in its pages). But the phrase 'analytic philosophy' is in no way commonplace until after 1945. In the first appearances in print of the phrase "analytic philosophy," the authors use it to express a critical attitude to the approaches they see as falling under it (R. G. Collingwood in *An Essay on Philosophical Method* and W. P. Montague in "Philosophy as Vision," both published in 1933) — although John Wisdom had written with approval of "analytic philosophers" (in a book on Jeremy Bentham) in 1931. There seems to be nothing earlier than this, other than a lone use of "the analytical philosophy" in an anonymously authored report of a meeting of the Aristotelian Society in 1915, where the phrase appears in a description of a point made by Russell in the discussion session. (Schuringa, 2020)

Nevertheless, Schuringa's conclusion from all this interesting and relevant information, namely, that

> [t]he idea that there was one thing that philosophers were doing prior to 1945 that could be called "analytic philosophy" is, then, a retrospective interpretation (Schuringa, 2020),

is too strong, and arises from the failure to distinguish sharply between (i) classical Analytic philosophy (roughly 1880 to 1950) and (ii) post-classical Analytic philosophy (roughly 1950 to the present). Moreover, as Schuringa himself notes, it's not a necessary condition of there being a set of philosophers who fully belong to a genuine philosophical tradition that's later accurately dubbed "X-ian philosophy," that at that time they typically or even ever call themselves "X-ian philosophers." For example, obviously the Pre-Socratic philosophers never called themselves "the Pre-Socratic philosophers"—since Socrates hadn't been immortalized by Plato's dialogues yet—nevertheless, they were genuinely Pre-Socratic philosophers just the same. Analogously, the classical Analytic philosophers didn't typically call themselves "Analytic philosophers," but they were genuinely Analytic philosophers just the same, for all the reasons I've provided in earlier chapters of this book. Still, Schuringa's overly-strong conclusion *does* also highlight a crucial point: namely, that post-classical Analytic philosophers were the first Analytic philosophers to entrench Analytic philosophy inside the professional academy, in part by officially labelling themselves "Analytic philosophers," and in part by simultaneously creating their own philosophical Enemy of the People, so-called "Continental philosophy."

In conformity with that, the first use of the term "Continental philosophy" seems to have been in 1945, in Russell's *History of Western Philosophy*, where he talks about "two schools of philosophy, which may be broadly distinguished as the Continental and the British respectively" (Russell, 1945: p. 643). But the term didn't come into general use in its recent and contemporary sense until roughly 1980, as Andreas Keller points out:

> An Ngram of the term "Continental Philosophy" shows that it took off around 1980[7] shortly after the smash-hit appearances of Richard Rorty's two highly controversial books, *Philos-*

---

[7] Google, available online at URL =<https://books.google.com/ngrams/graph?content=continental+philosophy&year_start=1800&year_end=2000&corpus=15&smoothing=3&share=&direct_url=t1%3B%2Ccontinental%20philosophy%3B%2Cc0>.

ophy and the Mirror of Nature in 1979, and *Consequences of Pragmatism* in 1982. It seems that before that time, many instances of the term were meant just in a geographic sense, not implying a contrast with "Analytic philosophy." This hints at an invention, or at least popularization, of the term in its current meaning around 1980. Perhaps there was not merely a temporal succession, but also some sort of causal connection, between the publication of Rorty's books and the later Anglo-American entrenchment of the term. (Keller, 2018)

Schuringa's Ngram of uses of the terms "analytic philosophy" and "analytical philosophy," which also spikes sharply upwards in the 1980s, smoothly conforms to Keller's suggestion that there's an important connection between the appearance and impact of Rorty's books *Philosophy and the Mirror of Nature* (1979) and *Consequences of Pragmatism* (1982), and the entrenchment of the term "Continental philosophy." Post-classical Analytic philosophy emerged and became social-institutionally *dominant* after 1950, but it didn't fully achieve a decisive social-institutional hegemonic *victory*—in part via the creation of its own social-institutional Other, so-called "Continental philosophy"—until the late 1970s and early 1980s, when Rorty explicitly and famously (or notoriously) pointed out these facts.

In any case, by 1950, Quine's devastating critique of the analytic-synthetic distinction in "Truth by Convention" (Quine, 1976c), "Two Dogmas of Empiricism" (Quine, 1961b) "Carnap and Logical Truth" (Quine, 1976b), and *Word and Object* (Quine, 1960) effectively ended the research program of classical Analytic philosophy and initiated post-classical Analytic philosophy. In the early-to mid-1950s, post-classical Analytic philosophy produced a Wittgenstein-inspired language-driven alternative to Vienna Circle logical empiricism/positivism, *ordinary language philosophy*. In the late 1950s and 1960s, powered by the work of H. P. Grice and Peter Strawson, ordinary language philosophy became *conceptual analysis* (Hanna, 1998a; and also section II.4 above). In turn, during that same period, Strawson created a new "connective"—that is, holistic—version of conceptual analysis, that also constituted a "descriptive metaphysics" (Strawson, 1959, 1992). In the 1970s, 1980s, and early 1990s, Strawson's connective version of conceptual analysis gradually fused with Donald Davidson's non-reductive naturalism about language, mind, and action (sometimes rather misleadingly called *semantics of natural language*), John Rawls's holistic method of "reflective equilibrium," and Noam Chomsky's psycholinguistic appeals to intuitions-as-evidence, and ultimately became what can be called *The Standard Model* of mainstream post-classical Analytic philosophical methodology, by the end of the 20th century (Jackson, 1998). In the late 1990s and first two decades of the 21st century, a domestic critical reaction to The Standard Model, combining *direct reference theory*, *scientific essentialism* and *modal metaphysics* (as per chapter XVI above), yielded recent and contemporary *Analytic metaphysics*.[8] In contemporary mainstream post-classical Analytic philosophy, co-existing and cohabiting with The Standard Model and Analytic metaphysics, is also the classical Lockean idea that philosophy should be an "underlaborer" for the natural sciences, especially as this idea was developed in the second half of the 20th century by Quine and Sellars, and their students, as the materialist or physicalist (whether eliminativist, reductive, or non-reductive) and scientistic doctrine of *scientific naturalism*, and again in the early 21st century, in even more sophisticated versions, as *experimental philosophy*, aka "X-Phi," and the doctrine of *second philosophy* (Sellars, 1963; Quine, 1969b, Maddy, 2007; Knobe and Nichols, 2008; Alexander, 2012; Horvath and Grundmann, 2012).

---

[8] The leading figures of Analytic metaphysics include David Lewis, David Chalmers, Kit Fine, John Hawthorne, Theodore Sider, and Timothy Williamson; and some of its canonical texts are (Lewis, 1986; Sider, 2011; Chalmers, 2012; and Williamson, 2013).

More precisely, scientific naturalism includes four basic theses: (i) *anti-mentalism and anti-supernaturalism*, which says that we should reject any sort of explanatory appeal to non-physical or non-spatiotemporal entities or causal powers, (ii) *scientism* (Haack, 2017b; Hanna, 2021c), which says that the formal and natural sciences, and especially the exact sciences, are the paradigms of reasoning and rationality, as regards their content and their methodology alike, (iii) *materialist or physicalist metaphysics*, which says that all facts in the world, including all mental facts and social facts, are either reducible to (whether identical to or logically strongly supervenient[9] on) or else strictly dependent on, according to natural laws (i.e., naturally or nomologically strongly supervenient on) *fundamental physical facts*, which in turn are *naturally mechanistic, microphysical facts*, and (iv) *radical empiricist epistemology*, which says that all knowledge and truths are a posteriori. The direct implication of the conjunction of these four theses is that everything which does not fit the scientific image can be safely regarded as epiphenomenal, folkloristic, quaint, superstitious, a matter of taste, or else downright naïve. So, to summarize, scientific naturalism holds **first**, that the nature of knowledge and reality are ultimately disclosed by pure mathematics, fundamental physics, and whatever other reducible natural sciences there actually are or may turn out to be, **second**, that this is the *only* way of disclosing the ultimate nature of knowledge and reality, and **third**, that even if everything in the world, including ourselves and all things human (including language, mind, and action), cannot be strictly eliminated in favor of or reduced to fundamental physical facts, nevertheless everything in the world, including ourselves and all things human, is metaphysically grounded on and causally determined by fundamental physical facts. In these ways, scientific naturalism is committed to providing The Vienna Circle's value-neutral set of formulae, expressing the underlying structure of the natural universe, just as architectural high modernism promised to provide a value-neutral set of design principles that express the ultimate order of the human universe.

Generalizing now, the central topics, or obsessions, of the classical Analytic tradition prior to 1950 were *meaning* and *necessity*, with special emphases on (i) pure logic as the universal and necessary essence of thought, (ii) language as the basic means of expressing thoughts and describing the world, (iii) the sense (*Sinn*) vs. reference, aka Meaning (*Bedeutung*) distinction, (iv) the conceptual truth vs. factual truth distinction, (v) the necessary truth vs. contingent truth distinction, (vi) the a priori truth vs. a posteriori truth distinction, and (vii) the analytic vs. synthetic distinction. A common and profoundly embedded thread running through all of these sub-themes is the following rough-and-ready multiple identity (or at least necessary equivalence):

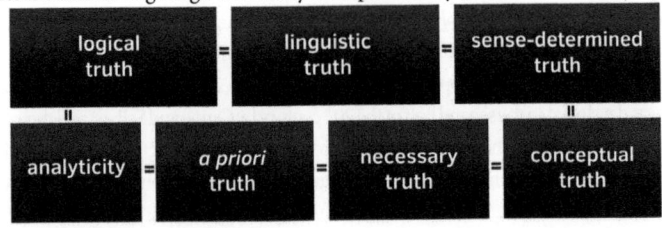

logical truth = linguistic truth = sense-determined truth
=
analyticity = *a priori* truth = necessary truth = conceptual truth

Figure 2. Seven necessarily equivalent notions in classical Analytic philosophy

---

[9] For explicit definitions of strong supervenience, logical strong supervenience, and natural or nomological strong supervenience, see sub-section XVII.8.2 below.

So, a very useful way of characterizing classical Analytic philosophy from late 19th century Frege to mid-20th-century Quine, is to say that it consisted essentially in *the rise and fall of the concept of analyticity*. By vivid contrast to classical Analytic philosophy, however, the central commitment, and indeed dogmatic obsession, of post-classical Analytic philosophy since 1950 until today at 6am, continues to be scientific naturalism.

This generalization is at least partially confirmed by some of the results of the Bourget-and-Chalmers 2009 *PhilPapers* survey of professional academic philosophers (Bourget and Chalmers, 2009, 2014):

Knowledge: empiricism or rationalism?

Other	346 / 931 (37.2%)
Accept or lean toward: empiricism	326 / 931 (35.0%)
Accept or lean toward: rationalism	259 / 931 (27.8%)

Metaphilosophy: naturalism or non-naturalism?

Accept or lean toward: naturalism	464 / 931 (49.8%)
Accept or lean toward: non-naturalism	241 / 931 (25.9%)
Other	226 / 931 (24.3%)

Mind: physicalism or non-physicalism?

Accept or lean toward: physicalism	526 / 931 (56.5%)
Accept or lean toward: non-physicalism	252 / 931 (27.1%)
Other	153 / 931 (16.4%)

Science: scientific realism or scientific anti-realism?

Accept or lean toward: scientific realism	699 / 931 (75.1%)
Other	124 / 931 (13.3%)
Accept or lean toward: scientific anti-realism	108 / 931 (11.6%)

The total survey population was 3226, and we'll remember from the Introduction that 81% of the respondents to that question—i.e., 2486 out of 3057 philosophers—explicitly self-identified as Analytic philosophers. So it seems to me very likely that had the survey directed these questions specifically to those 2486 philosophers *exclusively*, then the percentages of those who favored empiricism, naturalism, physicalism, and scientific realism, would have been even higher. Therefore, if scientific naturalism is false—as I strongly believe it is, precisely because its metaphysical foundation, *the mechanistic worldview*, is false (Hanna, 2020d, 2021b; Hanna and Paans, 2020)—then since at least the mid-1980s, post-classical Analytic philosophy has been powered essentially and indeed almost exclusively by the brute fact of its social-institutional domination of, and indeed hegemony over, professional academic philosophy, especially including its mythical Enemy of the People, so-called "Continental philosophy."

XVII.4 The Two Images Problem and its Consequences

In his 1951 book, *The Rise of Scientific Philosophy*—which, significantly, appeared in the same year that Quine published "Two Dogmas"—the logical empiricist/positivist and former Vienna Circle insider, Hans Reichenbach, sketched an influential and widely accepted history of the progress of modern philosophy that Whig-historically culminates with Analytic philosophy and merges it ineluctably with the progress of the logic and the exact sciences. Reichenbach's basic idea is that philosophy is legitimate only and precisely to the extent that (i) it's analysis, and (ii) it works on all and only foundational problems and conceptual puzzles arising from logic and the exact sciences. This is an exceptionally important metaphilosophical thesis, not only because it resuscitates Locke's seventeenth-century conception of philosophy as merely an underlaborer for the leading sciences of the Scientific Revolution, but also, and indeed primarily because, its unabashed scientism is the engine that has driven post-classical Analytic philosophy from the second half of the 20th century now into the third decade of the 21st century.

Correspondingly, it's plausibly arguable, and has indeed been compellingly argued by, for example, John McDowell and the later Putnam (McDowell, 1994; Putnam, 1990a, 1994, 1999), that the basic problem of both post-classical Analytic philosophy and phenomenology after 1950—and perhaps also *the* fundamental problem of modern philosophy—is how it is possible to reconcile two sharply different, seemingly incommensurable, and apparently even mutually exclusive global metaphysical conceptions, or world-pictures, of rational human animals and nature alike. On the one hand, there is the objective, non-phenomenal, perspectiveless, mechanistic, value-neutral, impersonal, and amoral metaphysical picture of the world delivered by logic, pure mathematics, and the fundamental natural sciences—the very ideal that animated The Vienna Circle. And on the other hand, there is the subjective, phenomenal, perspectival, teleological, value-laden, person-oriented, and moral metaphysical picture of the world yielded by the conscious experience of rational human beings. In 1963, Sellars aptly and evocatively dubbed these two sharply opposed world-conceptions "the scientific image" and "the manifest image" (Sellars, 1963c). So I'll call the profound difficulty raised by their mutual incommensurability and inconsistency *The Two Images Problem*.

In turn, scientific naturalism promises a possible complete solution to The Two Images Problem, by holding, according to Sellars's famous formulation, already quoted in section XV.6 above, that

> [i]n the dimension of describing and explaining the world, science is the measure of all things, of what is that it is, and of what is not that it is not. (Sellars, 1963b: p. 173)

Here, Sellars's term-of-art "science" clearly refers to the formal and natural sciences, alike, including logic, mathematics, physics, astronomy, and chemistry, with a special emphasis on physics, but *not* to biology—except to the extent that it's explanatorily and ontologically reducible to physics and chemistry. Correspondingly, according to the standard construal of *scientific theory-reduction*, astronomy, biology, and chemistry have a fully mathematically describable and microphysical basis in fundamental physical entities, properties, facts, and processes, and therefore they are all fully grounded in a fundamental, naturally mechanistic physics.

Nevertheless, it's critically essential, and indeed also both morally and mortally essential, to recognize that if scientific naturalism *were* true, then not only would (i) philosophy as a form of inquiry, as a practice, and as a social institution, be superseded by the exact sciences, which directly entails *the death-by-redundancy* of philosophy itself (Mabaquiao, 2021), but also, (ii) because our consciousness, intentionality, free agency, normative principles, truth, ideals-&-values, etc., are all either (iia) mere eliminable myths, or (iib) fully reducible to fundamentally physical facts, or, at the very least, (iic) strictly dependent on fundamentally physical facts and thus *epiphenomenal*, with no causal powers of their own, then it follows that (iii) we are nothing but biological machines with a built-in strong tendency to deceive ourselves by falsely believing in the irreducible and causally efficacious nature of our own consciousness, intentionality, free agency, normative principles, truth, ideals-&-values, etc. Hence (iv) by the same token, then we would be *just as likely to be self-deceived about the truth of scientific naturalism itself, as not*, so it follows that we are *not* rationally justified in believing it, all of which directly entails (v) the *death-by-self-stultification* of post-classical Analytic philosophy itself.

Therefore, at the foundational level, since 1950 and especially over at least the last thirty-five years, *the Analytic tradition has been living on borrowed time* and *running on fumes*, powered only by the combined inertia of its self-stultifying yet hegemonic philosophical ideology and its social-institutional domination in the professional academy: a philosophical *behemoth on wheels* that is built, like Hobbes's Leviathan—the early modern liberal State—solely and wholly out of the compliant, contract-bound, wage-enslaved, "captive," "disciplined" minds (Milosz, 1955; Schmidt, 2000) of post-classical Analytic philosophers, spiralling down into the ash-heap of history.

XVII.5 The Rise, Fall, and Normalization of Post-Modern Philosophy

By the early 1980s, the philosophical Great Divide between post-classical Analytic philosophy and so-called "Continental philosophy" was fully in place; and Richard Rorty and others more or less systematically fused post-structuralism, deconstructionism, and what was left of Deweyan pragmatism (Rorty, 1982; Hanna, 1983, 2020a) into philosophical *post-modernism* (Rorty, 1983), aka Po-Mo, which also began to dominate in the applied and fine arts, and in Comparative Literature and Humanities Departments at colleges and universities worldwide, by vigorously rejecting and replacing modernism in all its forms, but especially high modernism. Po-Mo also gradually fused with what was left of 1970s

New Left and emerging identity politics in the USA, thereby creating, inside the American professional academy, the social-institutional powerhouse of *identitarian multiculturalism* by the mid-90s (Rorty, 1994). More precisely, identitarian multiculturalism is the ideological patchwork composed of PARNS (i.e., postmodernist anti-rational nihilist skepticism), social justice activism, post-colonialism, Foucauldianism, critical race theory, neo-neo-Marxism, and posthumanism. Most importantly, it had become a juggernaut by the turn of the millennium, finally achieving a social-institutional domination and hegemony of its own by the end of first two decades of the 21st century, especially inside the professionl academy (Mann, 2019). By 1950, existential phenomenology had been discredited by Heidegger's association with the Nazis (Sluga, 1993), together with Sartre's and Merleau-Ponty's association with Marxism; and during the early Cold War and McCarthy era from the early 1950s into the early 60s, the professional academy was gradually purged of any remaining "Continental philosophers" who might have been brave enough to challenge the hegemony of the post-classical Analytic mainstream (McCumber, 2001, 2016). So by the 1980s—mainly in order to hold onto their comfortable tenured jobs, upper middle-class lifestyles, and professional academic social-status—like tragically unfortunate house-slaves who have fully "internalized the oppressor" (Gare, 2021), the remaining so-called "Continental philosophers" inside the professional academy gave up their trouble-making ways, gradually outsourced leftist Existentialism to writers, artists, and literary critics outside the professional academy, replacing their erstwhile neo-Marxism or anarcho-socialism with a politically harmless "life-style" radicalism in the post-1968 French academic mode, while also jumping on the French-driven theoretical bandwagons of post-structuralism, deconstructionism, Po-Mo, and posthumanism.

In 1996, all these bandwagons ran headlong into *The Sokal Hoax*. Alan Sokal, a physics professor at NYU, submitted a deliberately nonsensical article to the cultural studies journal *Social Text*, which was then accepted and duly published (Sokal, 1996). The article "argued" that quantum gravity was a linguistic and social construct. Three weeks later, Sokal revealed that the article was a hoax, and that the entire setup was to test the intellectual integrity and rigor of the emerging postmodernist elite. Professional academic "Continental philosophers" were, thereby, publicly shamed and scandalized by The Hoax. An anticipation of this public shaming and scandalizing had already been delivered in the 1970s and 80s by the post-classical Analytic philosopher John Searle, via his extended vituperative debate with Jacques Derrida in the pages of various journals and books.

Leaving aside its, at times, risible, impenetrable jargon and rhetoric, however, in a deeper sense and indeed fundamentally, Po-Mo is alienating, anti-humanistic, anti-rationalistic, and culturally nihilistic (Paans, 2020). Its program can best be described as "diversified modernism" (Jencks, 2010), or alternatively as "a philosophy of suspicion." Just as humanity was not the center of the universe after Galileo's discovery, and just as Darwin had dethroned the human species from the top of the animal hierarchy, so too Freud had argued that hidden, unconscious drives steer and direct the supposedly rational human being, and so too Nietzsche had declared a war on a universal, God-guaranteed morality. Po-Mo's final steps in dismantling the modernist world-picture were intended to stress that all grand societal visions are nothing more than grand narratives or *grand récits* (Lyotard, 1984), that meaning is endlessly postponed in the play of signs (Derrida, 1998, 2001), or that reality is inaccessible and merely a hyperreality (Baudrillard, 1991, 1994), or, alternatively, by demonstrating that every social institution is nothing but an instrument for coercively forming individuals according to covert, oppressive, preconceived ideals (Foucault, 1991, 2001, 2002a, 2002b).

As a consequence of The Sokal Hoax together with the fundamental alienation/anti-rationalism/cultural nihilism of Po-Mo itself, from the turn of the new millennium forwards, in another twist of "internalizing the oppressor," leading "Continental philosophers" began to compete with, and mirror, Analytic metaphysics and scientific naturalism by developing doctrines such as Alain Badiou's mathematics-driven metaphysics, Ray Brassier's and Quentin Meillasoux's versions of "Speculative Realism," "Trans-Humanism," and "NeuroHumanities" (Badiou, 2009, 2013; Brassier, 2007; Hanna, 2016a; Meillassoux, 2009). Nevertheless, on the side of their oppressors and social-institutional slave masters, from the mid-90s and especially since the mid-00s, post-classical Analytic philosophers have *also* had to share social-institutional power with, and even cede social-institutional power to, the professional academic identitarian multiculturalists, who by then were fully aligned with *normalized* Po-Mo thinking. Normalized Po-Mo-driven identitarian multiculturalism flexed its social-institutional muscles during the 2010s, in campus protests led by students but also supported by many faculty members, who demanded emotional comfort and safety, restrictions of all speech actually or potentially offensive to their cultural sensibilities, and the radical diversification of the philosophical canon (Lukianoff and Haidt, 2015). Whatever the specific issue involved, the basic idea is to assert the newly-acquired coercive social-institutional power and extended rights of group members rigidly adhering to a normalized Po-Mo-driven, identitarian multiculturalist, view of society, politics, and the world in general.

XVII.6 Why Hasn't Post-Classical Analytic Philosophy Produced Any Important Ideas Since 1985?

In chapter III.1 above, alongside my discussion of G.E. Moore's contribution to the classical Analytic tradition, I defined the term "an important philosopher." Here I'll apply the same line of thought to the term "an important philosophical idea." By *a brilliant philosophical idea*, I mean a philosophical idea that manifests great intellectual creativity, insight, and originality, opens up a new way of looking at a large domain of concepts, facts, phenomena, theories, and/or other information, and *would* have significant impact and influence *if it were to be* widely disseminated and adopted. And by *an important philosophical idea*, I mean a brilliant philosophical idea *that's actually widely disseminated and adopted*, that is, a brilliant philosophical idea with *actual significant impact and influence*.

This section has two basic theses: **first**, that there have been no important philosophical ideas produced by post-classical Analytic philosophers since 1985, especially including recent and contemporary Analytic metaphysics, and **second**, the most obvious and plausible explanation for this disturbing fact is that (i) that the hegemonic philosophical ideology of leading trends in post-classical Analytic philosophy, especially scientific naturalism, (ii) that the hyper-disciplined, rigidified institutional structures of professional academic philosophical education, and (iii) that the entrenched practices of professional academic philosophical research-and-publishing from 1985 to the present—or, at the *very* least, since the turn of the millennium—have systematically discouraged, ignored, overlooked, and/or suppressed brilliant philosophical ideas, whether produced inside or outside the professional academy.

Here's a working list of the generally-acknowledged nineteen most important ideas in post-classical Analytic philosophy, including the name of the philosophers who first produced them, the titles of the break-out/seminal publications in which they first presented and/or published those ideas, and their presentation and/or publication-dates:

1. Semantics for Modal Logic

R. Carnap, *Meaning and Necessity* (1953)

R. Barcan Marcus, "Modalities and Intensional Languages" (1962/1963)

S. Kripke, "Semantical Considerations on Modal Logic" (1971)

2. Direct Reference Theory/Externalism

S. Kripke, "Identity and Necessity" (1971)

S. Kripke, *Naming and Necessity* (1972)

H. Putnam, "Meaning and Reference" (1973), expanded as "The Meaning of 'Meaning'" (1975)

D. Kaplan, "Demonstratives: An Essay on the Semantics, Logic, Metaphysics and Epistemology of Demonstratives and Other Indexicals" (1971/1977)

G. Evans, *Varieties of Reference* (1982)

3. Scientific Naturalism and Scientific Essentialism

W. Sellars, *Science, Perception, and Reality* (1963)

S. Kripke, *Naming and Necessity* (1972)

4. Reductive or "Type-Type Identity" Materialism/Physicalism about the Mind-Body Relation

U.T. Place, "Is Consciousness a Brain Process?" (1956)

J.J.C. Smart, "Sensations and Brain Processes" (1959)

5. Functionalism about the Mind

H. Putnam, "Psychological Predicates," aka "The Nature of Mental States" (1973)

6. Non-Reductive or "Token-Token Identity" Materialism/Physicalism about the Mind-Body Relation

D. Davidson, "Mental Events" (1970)

7. Non-Reductive Non-Physicalism about the Mind-Body Relation

T. Nagel, "What is It Like to Be a Bat?" (1974)

8. Hard and Soft Determinism about the Free Will Problem

P. Edwards, "Hard and Soft Determinism" (1958)

9. The Denial of the Requirement of Alternate Possibilities for Reponsibility/Free Will, Responsibility's/Free Will's Compatibility with Determinism, and Free Will/Personhood as a Desire-Structure of the Will

H. Frankfurt, "Alternate Possibilities and Responsibility" (1969)

H. Frankfurt, "Freedom of the Will and the Concept of a Person" (1971)

10. Agent-Causal Libertarianism about Free Will

R. Chisholm, "Freedom and Action" (1966)

R. Chisholm, "He Could Have Done Otherwise" (1967)

R. Chisholm, "Reflections on Human Agency" (1971)

R. Chisholm, "The Agent as Cause" (1976)

11. Critiques of the Analytic-Synthetic and A Priori-A Posteriori Distinctions, and Ontological Relativity

W.V.O. Quine, "Two Dogmas of Empiricism" (1951)

W.V.O. Quine, "Carnap and Logical Truth" (1954/1963)

W.V.O. Quine, *Word and Object* (1960)

W.V.O. Quine, "Ontological Relativity" (1969)

S. Kripke, *Naming and Necessity* (1972)

12. Knowledge is Not (Merely) Justified True Belief

E. Gettier, "Is Justified True Belief Knowledge?" (1963)

13. Naturalized Epistemology

W.V.O.Quine, "Epistemology Naturalized" 1969.

14. New Virtue Ethics

E. Anscombe, "Modern Moral Philosophy" (1958)

P. Foot, *Virtues and Vices* (A collection of essays originally published between 1957 and 1977)

15. Contractarian Liberal Political Theory and Ethics: Justice As Fairness, The Original Position, The Veil of Ignorance, Reflective Equilibrium, Maximin Principle, Etc.

J. Rawls, *A Theory of Justice* (1971)

16. Applied or Problems-Driven Moral Theorizing and Non-Kantian Non-Consequentialism

J. Thomson, "A Defense of Abortion" (1971)

P. Singer, "Famine, Affluence, and Morality" (1972)

B. Williams, "A Critique of Utilitarianism" (1973)

J. Thomson, "Killing, Letting-Die, and the Trolley Problem" (1976)

17. Neo-Humean or Skeptical Theory of Personhood and Personal Identity

D. Parfit, *Reasons and Persons* (1984)

18. Artworks as Intentional Objects in Social-Institutional Contexts

A. Danto, *Transfiguration of the Commonplace* (1981)

19. Radical Philosophy of Science and Radical Metaphilosophy

T. Kuhn, *The Structure of Scientific Revolutions* (1970)

R. Rorty, *Philosophy and the Mirror of Nature* (1979)

R. Rorty, *Consequences of Pragmatism* (1982)

Note especially that *nothing on this list was presented or published by as late as 1985*. Therefore, no important philosophical ideas have been produced by post-classical Analytic philosophers since 1985. As a micro-study by way of supporting that claim, I'll briefly critically consider recent and contemporary Analytic metaphysics.

XVII.6.1 Analytic Metaphysics as a Copernican Devolution in Philosophy

Human reason has this peculiar fate in one species of its cognitions that it is burdened with questions which it cannot dismiss, since they are given to it as problems by the nature of reason itself, but which it also cannot answer, since they transcend every capacity of human reason. Reason falls into this perplexity through no fault of its own. It begins from principles whose use is unavoidable in the course of experience and at the same time sufficiently warranted by it. With these principles it rises (as its nature also requires) ever higher, to more remote conditions. But since it becomes aware in this way that its business must always remain incomplete because the questions never cease, reason sees itself necessitated to take refuge in principles that overstep all possible use in experience, and yet seem so unsuspicious that even ordinary common sense agrees with them. But it thereby falls into obscurity and contradictions, from which it can indeed surmise that it must somewhere be proceeding on the ground of hidden errors; but it cannot discover them, for the principles on which it is proceeding, since they surpass the bounds of all experience, no longer recognize any touchstone of experience. The battlefield of these endless controversies is called **metaphysics**. (*CPR* Avii-viii, boldfacing in the original)

The central theme of [*Writing the Book of the World*] is: realism about structure. The world has a distinguished structure, a privileged description. For a representation to be fully successful, truth is not enough; the representation must

> also use the right concepts, so that its conceptual structure matches reality's structure. There is an objectively correct way to "write the book of the world." ... I connect structure to fundamentality. The joint-carving notions are the fundamental notions; a fact is fundamental when it is stated in joint-carving terms. A central task of metaphysics has always been to discern the ultimate or fundamental reality underlying the appearances. I think of this task as the investigation of reality's structure. (Sider, 2011: p. vii)

It's an ironic fact that philosophers who fail to take the history of philosophy sufficiently seriously, are doomed to repeat its errors. As a striking case-in-point, let's consider recent and contemporary Analytic metaphysics, which, for all its logico-technical brilliance and its philosophical rigor, essentially amounts to what I'll call *a Copernican Devolution in philosophy* (Hanna, 2017b), retrograde philosophical epicycle within post-classica; Analytic philosophy that brings us back, full-circle, to naive, pre-Kantian, pre-critical conceptions of mind, knowledge, and world that are essentially Baconian, Cartesian, Spinozist, and especially Leibnizian-Wolffian in nature. As I mentioned in passing in section XVI.2 above, the leading figures of Analytic metaphysics include Saul Kripke, David Lewis, David Chalmers, Kit Fine, John Hawthorne, Theodore Sider, and Timothy Williamson; and some of its canonical texts are Kripke's *Naming and Necessity* (1980), Lewis's *On the Plurality of Worlds* (1986), Sider's *Writing the Book of the World* (2011), Chalmers's *Constructing the World* (2012), and Williamson's *Modal Logic as Metaphysics* (2013). Characteristic of this recent and contemporary philosophical backsliding are commitments to noumenal realism in ontology, to conceptualism about the nature of mental representation (see also sections XVII.8 and XVII.9 below), to a heavy reliance on modal logic as providing direct insight into the ultimate structure of noumenal reality, and to a dogmatic scientific naturalism (usually) combined with scientific essentialism.

Analytic metaphysics's Copernican Devolution is, in fact, a disastrously regressive turn in philosophy. More specifically, recent and contemporary Analytic metaphysicians really and truly need to learn Kant's eighteenth-century lessons (i) about the inherent limits of human cognition and knowledge, (ii) about the unsoundness of all possible ontological arguments from logical or analytic necessity to actual or real existence, (iii) about the essential cognitive-semantic difference between (iiia) mere logical, analytic (aka, "weak metaphysical") possibility and (iiib) real, synthetic (aka, "strong metaphysical") possibility, and (iv) about the essential ontological difference between noumena and phenomena. For without these insights, they have been, are, and forever will be inevitably led into the very same "obscurity and contradictions" that beset classical metaphysics prior to Kant (*CPR* Avii).

But as they say, *it's an ill wind that blows nobody any good*; that is, few misfortunes are so bad that they don't have some unintended good side effects for somebody or another. Hence, seeing Analytic metaphysics's Copernican Devolution for what it really is, i.e., a philosophically disastrous regression, makes it possible for us to provide a well-focused re-characterization of Kant's metaphysics in a contemporary context. In this light, Kant's or broadly Kantian critical metaphysics is decisively what I'll call a "real" (or, alternatively, "human-faced") metaphysics, and correspondingly it can be illuminatingly presented in terms that specially emphasize what I call Kant's "proto-critical" period in the late 1760s and early 1770s and also his "post-critical" period in the late 1780s and 1790s, both of which are somewhat neglected or undervalued, even by contemporary Kantians. Looked at this way, Kant's or broadly Kantian real or human-faced metaphysics consists, fundamentally, of the following six commitments: (i) a strict evidential appeal to human experience, which I call *the criterion of phenomenological adequacy for metaphysical theories*, (ii) a radical epistemic agnosticism about both the nature and existence of noumenal reality (see section XV.1 above), (iii) a thoroughgoing diagnostic critique of deep confusions in "ontological argument"-style (and more generally, noumenal-metaphysical) reasoning that's driven by modal logic, (iv) a maximally strong version of non-conceptualism in the theory of mental representation, and correspondingly, a direct argument for transcendental idealism from the nature of human sensibility together with strong non-conceptualism, that's essentially in place by the time of Kant's famous letter to Marcus Herz in 1772 (*C* 10:129-35), (v) modal dualism and apriorism (according to which there are two essentially distinct types of necessity, both of which are irreducibly a priori, combined with a strong commitment to the "necessity if and only if apriority" thesis), and finally, (vi) a theory of synthetic a priori truth and knowledge, grounded directly on strong non-conceptualism.

In freely going back and forth between Kant's philosophy and recent/ contemporary philosophy, I'm applying the following strong metaphilosophical principle that I call *The No-Deep-Difference Thesis*:

There's no fundamental difference in philosophical content between the history of philosophy and recent/contemporary philosophy. (Hanna, 2009a)

In other words, in doing recent/contemporary philosophy one is thereby directly engaging with the history of philosophy, and in doing the history of philosophy one is thereby directly engaging with recent/contemporary philosophy. There is no serious distinction to be drawn between the two.

In the B preface of the first *Critique*, Kant says that "there is no doubt that up to now the procedure of metaphysics has been a mere groping, and what is the worst, a groping among mere concepts [*bloßen Begriffen*]" (*CPR* Bxv). A "mere concept" is the same as an *empty* (*leer*) concept or *noumenal* concept, which in turn is a concept that is minimally well-formed in both a formal-syntactical and sortal sense, and also logically self-consistent, but essentially disconnected from human sensibility and actual or possible sensory intuition and all its apparent or manifestly real natural objects, hence a concept that does not have *objective validity* (*objective Gültigkeit*). In a way that's smoothly compatible with this Kantian critical line of thinking, in the mid-2010s, Peter Unger titled his bang-on-target critique of the Analytic tradition *Empty Ideas* (Unger, 2014). But according to Kant's and to broadly Kantian philosophy, real metaphysics must be evidentially grounded on human experience. Or otherwise put, real metaphysics reverse-engineers its basic metaphysical (including ontological) theses and explanations in order to conform strictly to all and only what is *phenomenologically self-evident* in human experience. By "phenomenologically self-evident" I mean this:

> A claim C is phenomenologically self-evident for a rational human subject S if and only if (i) S's belief in C relies on directly-given conscious or self-conscious manifest evidence about human experience, and (ii) C's denial is either logically or conceptually self-contradictory (i.e., a Kantian analytic self-contradiction), really metaphysically impossible (i.e., it is a Kantian synthetic *a priori* impossibility), or pragmatically self-stultifying for S (i.e., it is what Kant calls "a contradiction in willing" in the *Groundwork*).

In turn, this leads directly to what I call *the criterion of phenomenological adequacy for metaphysical theories*:

> A metaphysical theory MT is phenomenologically adequate if and only if MT is evidentially grounded on all and only phenomenologically self-evident theses.

By this criterion, post-classical Analytic metaphysics is clearly phenomenologically *inadequate*, and so is classical metaphysics more generally, whereas by sharp contrast, Kant's real metaphysics of transcendental idealism is, arguably, fully phenomenologically adequate.

According to Kant, both the origins and limits of human cognition or *Erkenntnis* are determined by the nature of our specifically human sensibility or *Sinnlichkeit* (CPR B1, A19-49/B33-73). In particular, there is an inherent cognitive-semantic constraint on all fully or "thickly" meaningful cognition: a cognition is "objectively valid," i.e., fully or "thickly" meaningful, if and only if it presupposes actual or possible externally-triggered sensory intuitions or *Anschauungen* of empirical objects (CPR A238-42/B298-300, A289/B345), presented within the global, framing structures of egocentrically-centered, orientable (i.e., it contains intrinsic enantiomorphic directions determined by a subject embedded in the space or time) phenomenal space and time. Empirical objects in this specific, anthropocentric sense are *appearances* (*Erscheinungen*) or *phenomena*; by sharp contrast, objects of cognition which, if they existed, would fall outside the scope of human sensibility, are mere "entities of the understanding [*Verstandeswesen*]" or *noumena* (CPR A235-60/B294-315, esp. B306). In short, a noumenon, if it were to exist, would be a non-sensory, non-empirical, non-spatiotemporal, trans-human object, a *supersensible object* (CPR A254-55/B355). If, in addition to being a noumenon in this supersensible-object sense (aka "a noumenon in the negative sense"), any noumenal object which, if it were to exist, would *also* be an individual Cartesian/Leibnizian substance, whose nature is completely determined by intrinsic non-relational properties, would be a "thing-in-itself [*Ding an sich*]" (aka, "a noumenon in the positive sense") (CPR B306-7).

Now, I'm being fairly careful about my formulations here, in two ways.

First, I'm distinguishing between *negative* noumena ("supersensible" objects in the minimal sense of *non-sensory* objects) and *positive* noumena (things in themselves). Why? Because I think it's arguable that Kant held that there are perfectly legitimate negative noumena, or supersensible/non-sensory objects (for example, abstract objects in the formal sciences, especially mathematical objects like numbers), that *aren't* positive noumena or things in themselves (for example, God, immortal souls, etc.), and indeed are at least partially constituted by (by being in necessary conformity with) the forms of our sensible intuition, and hence they are thoroughly as-it-were *phenoumenal*.

Second, I'm framing the concepts of a noumenon and of a thing-in-itself counterfactually, hence I'm *not* committing Kant to the claim that things in themselves really exist. Why? Because I think that we should not automatically assume that Kant believes that noumena or things in themselves really exist. This of course is one of the great controversies in Kant-interpretation. And my own view is that Kant is in fact a "methodological eliminativist" about things in themselves (CPR A30/B45, A255/B310, A286-87/B343). But at the very least, we need to remain open-minded and not be dogmatic about Kant's supposed commitment to the real existence of things in themselves, especially given Kant's own deep and fully explicit insight about the basic ontological distinction between (i) logically or analytically defined objects (merely thinkable objects), and (ii) actually or really existing objects (experienceable, knowable objects).

Back now to Kant's and broadly Kantian cognitive semantics. For Kant himself and broadly Kantian cognitive semanticists, a cognition is fully meaningful if and only if it is *empirically meaningful from the human standpoint*. Failing this, a cognition is "empty [*Leer*]" (CPR A51/B75), and therefore it not only (i) lacks a directly referential, empirical-intuitional grounding in actually existing empirical objects, but also (ii) lacks a truth-value (hence it is a "truth-value gap") (CPR A58/B83). Incidentally, element (i) is a crucial feature of Kant's famous critique of ontological arguments for God's existence: all such arguments lack a directly referential, empirical-intuitional grounding in actually existing empirical objects; hence the predicate "exists," as deployed in such arguments, is merely a "logical" predicate, and not a "real" or "determining" predicate.

Now, it's important to recognize that, for Kant himself and for broadly Kantian cognitive semanticists, "empty" cognition *need not necessarily be wholly meaningless, or nonsense*: it *can* be partially or "thinly" meaningful if (and only if) it is logically well-formed according to the logical forms of judgment/categories, and also conceptually and/or logically consistent (CPR Bxxvi n., A239/B298). This is what Kant calls mere "thinking [*Denken*]," according to concepts (*Begriffen*). In turn recognizing our natural capacity for mere thinking is *meta-philosophically* important because mere thinking is characteristic of classical metaphysics, and consequently also of recent/contemporary post-classical Analytic metaphysics.

Thinking about X establishes the *logical* or *analytic* possibility of X. But it *doesn't* establish the *real* or *synthetic* possibility of X. Hence a crucial mistake in classical metaphysics, and correspondingly a crucial mistake in recent/contemporary Analytic metaphysics, is to confuse logical or analytic possibility/necessity with real or synthetic possibility/necessity. This metaphysical confusion leads directly to deep "obscurity and contradictions" (*CPR* Aviii). In other words, Kripke, David Lewis, Fine, Chalmers, Hawthorne, Sider, and Williamson, for all their logico-technical brilliance and their philosophical rigor, and even despite their high-powered professional academic status, are every bit as confused and wrongheaded as Christian Wolff was. They make all the same old mistakes, just as if they'd never been made before. For example, when Sider asserts, without any doubt, hesitation, or irony whatsoever, just as if the previous 230 years of European philosophy (i.e., from 1781 to 2011) had never happened, that "[t]he world has a distinguished structure, a privileged description," that "[f]or a representation to be fully successful, truth is not enough; the representation must also use the right concepts, so that its conceptual structure matches reality's structure," and that "there is an objectively correct way to 'write the book of the world'" (Sider, 2011: p. vii) it simply takes your broadly and radically Kantian breath away. Amazing. That's really and truly a Copernican Devolution. On the contrary, broadly and radically Kantian philosophy holds that real metaphysics is based fundamentally on reasoning with real or synthetic possibilities/necessities, *not* on reasoning with logical or analytic possibilities/ necessities.

In any case, the cognitive-semantic determination of the full meaningfulness of a cognition by sensibility, in turn, sharply constrains the scope of knowledge in the strict sense of "[scientific] knowledge [*Wissen*]": objectively convincing true belief with certainty (*CPR* A820-22/B848-50). Since strict or scientific knowledge requires truth, but truth-valuedness requires objective validity or empirical meaningfulness, then if a cognition is not objectively valid/empirically meaningful, then it *cannot be either true or false*, and therefore *it cannot be strict or scientific knowledge*. In particular, it directly follows from this point that in the strict or scientific sense of "knowledge," *we cannot know things in themselves*, either *by knowing their nature*, or by *knowing whether they exist or do not exist*. In other words, we know *a priori*, by reflection on the cognitive semantics of human cognition, that we cannot have strict or scientific knowledge of things in themselves. This, as per section XV.1 above, is what I call *radical agnosticism* (Hanna, 2017c)—"radical," because unlike ordinary agnosticism (epistemic open-mindedness or doxic neutrality about some claim C), it's strict or scientific *a priori* knowledge about our necessary ignorance of things in themselves, and about our necessary inability to know or prove whether things-in-themselves (for example, God) exist or do not exist.

Given the truth of radical agnosticism, it directly follows that neither classical Rationalist metaphysics nor post-classical Analytic metaphysics, since they're based on mere thinking alone, and reasoning from mere logical or analytic possibilities, is capable of having strict or scientific knowledge, despite all their highly technically sophisticated, rigorous-sounding, dogmatic claims about knowledge of things in themselves. Moreover, it also directly follows from radical agnosticism that any claim in *speculative natural science* that violates the cognitive-semantic constraints on strict or scientific knowledge (for example, any natural-scientific claim about positive noumenal entities belonging to microphysical essences, for example, molecules, atoms, quarks, neutrinos, etc., etc.), is a truth-value gap. Hence *any form of metaphysical noumenal realism in natural science* is deeply mistaken (Hanna, 2006a: chs. 3-4).

So again, I conclude that no important philosophical ideas have been produced by post-classical Analytic philosophers since 1985.

XVII.6.2 A Reply to a Possible Objection

Now suppose, by way of an objection to what I've been arguing, someone said:

> "Well, all the evidence that you've provided actually shows, is that there was a burst of important philosophical ideas produced by post-classical Analytic philosophers between the early 1950s and the early 1980s, roughly thirty years. But it's also not implausible to think that it would take another roughly twenty-five years for other post-classical Analytic philosophers to absorb, ruminate on, and critically respond to these important ideas, and then move on to creating, presenting, and/or publishing some new ones."

Then I'd say in reply:

> "OK, fair enough. And looking back into the history of modern philosophy, it's true that it took roughly twenty-five years to get from Descartes's *Meditations* to Spinoza's *Ethics*; roughly another twenty-five years to get from Spinoza's *Ethics* to Locke's *Essay Concerning Human Understanding*; twenty-one years to get from Locke's *Essay* to Berkeley's *Principles of Human Knowledge*; twenty-nine years to get from Berkeley's *Principles* to Hume's *Treatise of Human Nature*; twenty-five years to get from the first edition of Kant's *Critique of Pure Reason* to Hegel's *Phenomenology of Spirit;* and roughly twenty-five years to get from Husserl's *Logical Investigations* to Heidegger's *Being and Time*. Perhaps, then, important philosophical ideas occur in roughly twenty-five year cycles."

So let's suppose that to be true, for purposes of argument. This means that by 2010 *at the very latest*, post-classical Analytic philosophers should have been creating, presenting, and publishing new important ideas.

Now, since 2000 there have been *only three dominant trends* in post-classical Analytic philosophy: (i) Analytic metaphysics, (ii) experimental philosophy, aka X-Phi, and (iii) Analytic feminism. But these three dominant trends *have produced no important philosophical ideas of their own*: on the contrary, they've merely cleverly re-cycled important ideas that already existed in the history of philosophy many years or even centuries before them. As I argued in the immediately preceding sub-section, recent and contemporary Analytic metaphysics is essentially a recurrence to classical pre-Kantian metaphysics in the Leibniz-Wolff tradition, plus modal logic and logical empiricism/positivism, together with the professional influence of Kripke in the late 20th century, and especially of David Lewis along with his Australian, New-York-ian, Oxonian, and Princetonian followers, in the late 1990s and first three decades of the 21st century. To be sure, Lewis was a *brilliant dialectician.* But can you honestly name one idea of his that doesn't already belong to classical pre-Kantian metaphysics or to logical empiricism/positivism, or that's not already on my pre-1985 list of important ideas? In turn, X-Phi is essentially a recurrence to various forms of empiricism, including Humean empiricism, Millian empiricism, logical empiricism/positivism, Quinean radical empiricism, and scientific naturalism more generally, together with cognitive neuroscience. And correspondingly, here's what Ann Garry says about Analytic feminism:

> Analytic feminists are philosophers who believe that both philosophy and feminism are well served by using some of the concepts, theories, and methods of analytic philosophy modified by feminist values and insights. By using "analytic feminist" to characterize their style of feminist philosophizing, these philosophers acknowledge their dual feminist and analytic roots and their intention to participate in the ongoing conversations within both traditions. In addition, the use of "analytic feminist" attempts to rebut two frequently made presumptions: that feminist philosophy is entirely postmodern and that analytic philosophy is irredeemably male-biased. Thus by naming themselves analytic feminists, these philosophers affirm the existence and political value of their work. (Garry, 2018)

In other words, Analytic feminists are post-classical Analytic philosophers who also just happen to be feminists. Feminism, in turn, says that "female ways of thinking yield insights that have been missed in male-dominated areas" (Rachels and Rachels, 2015). But this is an idea that has been around at least since Virginia Woolf and the early 20th century, if not since Mary Wollstonecraft in the 18th century, or at least since George Eliot, Harriet Martineau, and the suffragette movement in the 19th century. Therefore, even despite their popularity and social-institutional dominance and cultural hegemony, these three dominant trends in post-classical Analytic philosophy have produced *no important philosophical ideas.* Indeed, on the contrary, it seems very likely that the cultural hegemony of precisely *these* social-institutionally dominant trends since 2000, has itself contributed substantially to the "awful truth" and "plain fact" that post-classical Analytic philosophy has produced no important philosophical ideas in the last thirty-six years. Correspondingly, as I mentioned in the last sub-section, Peter Unger aptly entitled his bang-on-target critique of the tradition of Analytic philosophy *Empty Ideas.* Post-classical Analytic philosophy since 1985 has always been, and still is, *running on fumes,* i.e., *running on empty (ideas).*

Even granting that, and on the other hand, however, it also seems to me extremely unlikely that no *brilliant* philosophical ideas have been produced during the last thirty-five years by philosophers working either inside or outside mainstream professional academic post-classical Analytic philosophy. Indeed, and on the contrary, *surely,* quite a few *brilliant* philosophical ideas *must* have actually been produced by *somebody, somewhere* since 1985, or at the very least since 2010, if we adopt the twenty-five-year cycle hypothesis. Indeed, here are two cases in point.

First, there's Susan Haack's book *Evidence and Inquiry*, a brilliant reworking of the basic concepts of epistemology, from a pragmatist point of view (Haack, 1993). Haack's book has been consistently ignored by the leading post-classical Analytic epistemologists ever since its publication. And **second**, there's Thomas Nagel's *Mind and Cosmos*, an equally brilliant book in metaphysics and the philosophy of science, in which Nagel proposes to explain the nature and existence of the minds of conscious, rational animals in a physical world, by holding that "rational intelligibility is at the root of the natural order," and that biological life and the minds of conscious, rational animals are metaphysically continuous with one another:

> Nature is such as to give rise to conscious beings with minds; and it is such as to be intelligible to such beings. Ultimately, therefore, such beings should be intelligible to themselves. And these are fundamental features of the universe, not byproducts of contingent developments whose true explanation is given in terms that do not make reference to mind. (Nagel, 2012: p. 17)

> [My] teleological hypothesis is that … [there is] a cosmic predisposition to the formation of life, consciousness, and the value that is inseparable from them. (Nagel, 2012: p. 123)

Nagel's book hasn't been merely consistently ignored by the leading post-classical Analytic metaphysicians and philosophers of science: in fact, it was *angrily derided* by them at the time of its publication (Hanna, 2013c), and *then* consistently ignored by them ever since.

So, where are all those brilliant ideas *now*? Why haven't they become *important* ideas? Why is no one in contemporary post-classical Analytic philosophy *paying any attention whatsoever to those brilliant ideas*? To put not too fine a point on it, it seems to me that the most obvious and most plausible explanation for this "disconnect" between the actual production of brilliant philosophical ideas since 1985, or at the very least since 2010, and their dissemination and adoption by recent/contemporary mainstream post-classical Analytic philosophers, is threefold: **first**, the domination and indeed hegemony of the social-institutional triple-whammy consisting of Analytic metaphysics + X-Phi + Analytic feminism, since 2000, **second**, the steady increase of hyper-disciplined, rigidified practices of undergraduate and graduate training for all professional academic philosophers, but especially including those working in post-classical Analytic philosophy, since 1985, and last but by no means least, **third**, the gradual and now seemingly permanent entrenchment, since 1985, of a professional academic research-and-publication system that, like the mill of God, *grinds slow and exceeding small,* by which I mean that (i) it's highly adversarial and careerist, (ii) it's highly subject to fads and domination by professional academic status-networks, and (iii) it rigidly reinforces the "normal science" of insular, hyper-specialized, and ultimately irrelevant Scholastic philosophical debate, research, and publication (Haack, 2017a, 2020).

In short, since 1985, and especially since 2000, mainstream professional academic post-classical Analytic philosophy has been more-or-less systematically, but in any case relentlessly, killing real—or in Haack terminology, "serious" (Haack, 2016)—philosophy, and profoundly alienating many of post-classical Analytic philosophy's own practitioners. As a case-in-point, I'll now turn to a micro-study of that process of alienation.

XVII.7 The Ballad of Donald Kalish and Angela Davis: A Micro-Study

> I'd just like to say that I like being called sister much more than professor and I've continually said that if my job—if keeping my job means that I have to make any compromises in the liberation struggle in this country, then I'll gladly leave my job. This is my position. (Davis, 2009)

XVII.7.1 Introduction

What I regard as a very positive trend in recent and contemporary metaphilosophy is a steady flow of critical-historical studies of 20th century professional academic philosophy—especially post-classical Analytic philosophy—with a special emphasis on deeper and larger sociopolitical themes (Akehurst, 2008, 2011; Bloor, 2017; Katzav, 2018; Katzav and Vaesen, 2017; McCumber, 2001, 2016; Reisch, 2005; Vrahimis, 2012, 2015, forthcoming; Wilshire, 2002). These studies follow in the footsteps of Bruce Kuklick's classic 1977 *Rise of American Philosophy* (Kuklick, 1977), but with an edgier and, broadly speaking, Frankfurt-School-new-leftist/neo-Marxist-style philosophical sensibility, as per, for example, John McCumber's broad-focus 2000 study, *Time in the Ditch: American Philosophy and the McCarthy Era*, and his narrow-focus 2016 study *The Philosophy Scare: The Politics of Reason in the Early Cold War*, zoomed in on the UCLA Department of Philosophy. In the same metaphilosophical, critical-historical sociopolitical spirit, in this micro-study, I want to elaborate and extend some of the themes of *The Philosophy Scare*, by zooming in even more concentratedly on the UCLA-based professional academic philosophical careers—careers that were, respectively, very long and very short—of Donald Kalish and Angela Davis.

XVII.7.2 Stage-Setting

For purposes of stage-setting, here are two potted biographies of Kalish and Davis respectively (Davis, 1974; New York Times Staff, 2000; Davis and Wiener, 2020).

First, Donald Kalish, who was born in 1919 and died in 2020, was an American professional academic post-classical Analytic philosopher and a well-known anti-war activist. He earned his BA and MA degrees in psychology, and his doctorate in philosophy at the University of California, Berkeley. After teaching at Swarthmore College and UC Berkeley, he joined the faculty of UCLA in 1949. Kalish was perhaps best known for his outspoken opposition to the war in Vietnam and later, his opposition to U.S. military involvement in Nicaragua and Grenada. As chairman of the UCLA Philosophy Department, Kalish hired Marxist political activist Angela Davis, an act that was highly controversial at the time. Correspondingly, Kalish was a founder of the Concerned Faculty of UCLA, and also served as a member of the University Committee on Vietnam, and as Vice-Chairman of Peace

Action Council, Los Angeles. In that capacity, Kalish led the Peace Action Council in an infamous 1967 protest at the Century Plaza Hotel in Los Angeles, against President Lyndon Johnson's Vietnam policies, which brought out 10,000 people and triggered shocking police brutality. Indeed, Mike Davis and Jon Wiener aptly dub it "The Century City Police Riot" (Davis and Wiener, 2020: 299-314). Kalish was also an organizer of the 1967 March on the Pentagon to protest the Vietnam War and those activities were prominently chronicled in Norman Mailer's *The Armies of the Night* (1968). In 1967, Kalish signed a letter declaring his intention to refuse to pay taxes in protest against the U.S. war against Vietnam, and urging others to do the same. As a philosopher, Kalish specialized in logic and set theory, and co-authored the well-known and much-used 1964 text, *Logic: Techniques of Formal Reasoning*, with Richard Montague.

Reportedly, Kalish was a also first-rate and devoted teacher, who taught with compassion, enthusiasm, and precision, and had the rare ability of being able to make even the most complex and arcane concepts readily comprehensible to his students; and he regularly gave his students his home phone number with the instruction that if they ever wanted to discuss an assignment, to call him any time, day or night. Nevertheless, in his logic and set theory classes, over the course of his entire career, Kalish said nothing about his political opinions.

Second, Angela Davis, who was born in 1944, is an American political activist, philosopher, and professional academic. She's the author of more than ten books on class, feminism, race, and the U.S. prison system. As of 2021, she's a professor emerita at the University of California, Santa Cruz. Politically, Davis is a neo-Marxist, a longtime member of the Communist Party USA (CPUSA), and a founding member of the Committees of Correspondence for Democracy and Socialism (CCDS). Born to an African American family in Birmingham, Alabama, Davis studied French at Brandeis University and philosophy at the University of Frankfurt in West Germany, working with Herbert Marcuse, a leading figure in Frankfurt School critical theory. Returning to the United States, Davis did graduate work in philosophy at the University of California, San Diego, before moving to East Germany, where she completed a doctorate in philosophy at the Humboldt University of Berlin. After her return to the USA, Davis was heavily involved in radical Leftist politics, including activism for the CPUSA, the second-wave feminist movement, the Black Panther Party, and the campaign against the Vietnam War. In 1969, Davis was hired as an acting assistant professor in the UCLA philosophy department, and taught several heavily-attended, controversial courses. In 1949, the University of California had initiated a policy against hiring Communists. At their 19 September 1969 meeting, with strong support from California Governor Ronald Reagan, the UC Board of Regents fired Davis from her $10,000-a-year post because of her membership in the Communist Party, urged on by. Judge Jerry Pacht ruled the Regents could not fire Davis solely because of her affiliation with the Communist Party, and she resumed her post. The Regents fired Davis again on 20 June 1970, for the "inflammatory language" she had used in four different speeches. The report stated:

> We deem particularly offensive such utterances as her statement that the regents "killed, brutalized (and) murdered" the People's Park demonstrators, and her repeated characterizations of the police as "pigs."

The American Association of University Professors censured the Board for this action. Even more notoriously, in 1970, guns owned by Davis were used in an armed takeover of a courtroom in Marin County, California, in which four people were killed. Prosecuted for three capital felonies, including conspiracy to murder, and held in jail for over a year, Davis was finally acquitted of all charges in 1972. She visited Eastern Bloc countries in the 1970s, and during the 1980s was twice the Communist Party's candidate for Vice President; at this time, she also held the position of professor of ethnic studies at San Francisco State University. Much of her work focused on the abolition of prisons, and in 1997 she co-founded Critical Resistance, an organization working to abolish the prison–industrial complex. In 1991, in the aftermath of the dissolution of the Soviet Union, she helped start the CCDS, a platform initially operating inside the CPUSA seeking to reorient the party's ideology away from orthodox communism. When the majority of party members voted against CCDS proposals, along with CCDS colleagues, she left the CPUSA. Also in 1991, she joined the Feminist Studies department at the University of California, Santa Cruz, where she became department director before retiring in 2008. Since then she has continued to write and remained active in movements such as Occupy and the Boycott, Divestment, and Sanctions campaign.

Now, for further stage-setting, building on sections XVII.1 and XVII.2, I'll also postulate that the most celebrated works of post-classical Analytic philosophy since 1985—say, Lewis's *On the Plurality of Worlds* (1986), Chalmers's *The Conscious Mind* (1996), Williamson's *Knowledge and its Limits* (2000) and *Modal Logic as Metaphysics* 2013)—as clever, ingenious, and influential as they are, are nevertheless perfect examples of what Jeff Schmidt has aptly called "playpen creativity" and "playpen critical thinking" (Schmidt, 2000: pp. 40-41) and furthermore they are nothing but the works of what Axel Honneth, himself a contemporary Frankfurt-School New Leftist/neo-Marxist, aptly calls "normalized intellectuals" (Honneth, 2009) who have compliantly adjusted and whittled down the powers and scope of their own intellects, emotions, and practical activity to the professional academic and political status quo, in (one or another, or both, of) two fundamental ways. **First**, they never critically challenge or resisting the liberal (and nowadays, neoliberal or neoconservative) democratic advanced capitalist political status quo *outside* the academy. And **second**, they always smoothly conform their work to the identitarian multiculturalist philosophy *inside* what Rorty, with his usual bang-on-target critical acumen, but uncharacteristically employing a misnomer, called "the unpatriotic academy" (Rorty, 1994). It should have been *the identitarian academy*.

In other words, the most celebrated post-classical Analytic philosophers have consistently failed to criticize and resist the highly mind-manacled and hegemonic sociopolitical and professional ideologies and norms governing the coercive authoritarian social institutions that have so richly rewarded and supported them. Rewarded them, that is, not so much in economic terms that compare well to those of truly rich people in the USA and elsewhere, aka *the billionaires*, but then at least in social status terms, that certainly compare very well to those of leading intellectual elites in the USA and elsewhere around the world, aka *the new mandarins*. Hence these playpen- superstar, normalized post-classical Analytic philosophers are paradigm cases of what Schmidt, in fundamental elective affinity with Honneth's and Rorty's critiques, has called *ideologically disciplined minds* (Schmidt, 2000).

XVII.7.3 The Ballad

Now back to the story—or if you will, the ballad—of Donald Kalish and Angela Davis.

In 1949 when Kalish was an untenured faculty member teaching in the UCLA Philosophy Department, he very bravely refused to sign the notorious *California Oath*, a statewide anti-communist loyalty oath (Davis and Wiener, 2020: pp. 472-473). But in 1950, the year he was tenured at UCLA, Kalish signed the "Allen Formula" faculty resolution and loyalty oath, which actually had wider scope than the earlier California Oath by refusing employment to "anyone who is disloyal or who will not live up to the University's standards of impartial scholarship and teaching" (McCumber, 2016: pp. 152-153). In other words, the resolution that Kalish signed in 1950 *banned not only communists from the University, but also banned anyone else deemed disloyal for any other reason*; and if that weren't enough, the University could also use as a "justification" for dismissal or exclusion that such people were not living up to the University's (presumptively high) standards of *impartial* research and teaching, i.e., they could summarily fire or exclude anyone for holding or disseminating beliefs or opinions deemed biased or partisan (i.e., dangerous) by the University administration.

Then 15 years went by. According to Kalish's *New York Times* obituary:

"For 18 years [i.e., from 1947 to 1965], I was an ivory-towered academic," he told the *Christian Science Monitor* in 1969. "Sure, I was a liberal Democrat. I backed Stevenson and even Johnson against Goldwater. "But in 1965, my intense feelings about the Vietnam War pushed me toward issue politics."

Dr. Kalish also publicized the idea of reducing one's income tax payment by 25 percent—the share he calculated that was being used to support the military effort.

As vice chairman of the Peace Action Council, Dr. Kalish helped organize a tremendous demonstration in front of the Century Plaza Hotel in Los Angeles on June 23, 1967.

About 80 antiwar groups mustered almost 10,000 protesters to gather outside the hotel while President Lyndon B. Johnson was speaking there. (*New York*

Times Staff, 2000)[10]

So, after 1965, Kalish was a committed political activist in the New Leftist/neo-Marxist tradition. Then in the late 1960s, Kalish hired and publicly defended and supported Angela Davis, a young Frankfurt School New Leftist/neo-Marxist, Black power advocate, and radical feminist, who was dismissed in 1970. Granted, Kalish taught logic, not ethics or political philosophy; and yet, reportedly, throughout his career *he never mentioned his political beliefs in class*. Moreover, and according to my search of the *PhilPapers* archives, he published nothing except the co-authored book with Montague; so presumably, as a philosopher (although not as a logic teacher, at which he excelled), Kalish was basically just punching the post-classical Analytic professional academic clock for thirty-three years, from 1964 to 1997, when he retired.

To summarize. **First**, Kalish was (i) bravely non-compliant with, and actively resistant to the McCathyite/HUAC forces in 1949 as an untenured professional academic, but (ii) not-so-bravely compliant, and somewhat normalized in 1950, just as he was being tenured. And then **second**, fifteen years later, Kalish was a highly progressive, New Leftist/neo-Marxist political activist in the mid- to late-1960s—not only, as Chair of the UCLA Philosophy Department, hiring and publicly supporting someone, Angela Davis, *who clearly fell under both the disloyalty and non-impartiality disjuncts of the faculty resolution that he himself had signed in 1950*, and, I abductively infer,[11] was actually used to fire Davis in 1969 and again in 1970, but also, by his own autobiographical account of the emergence and evolution of his political beliefs in the mid-60s, as recounted during his interview with the *Christian Science Monitor* in 1969, outside the University, starting as early as 1965. And yet, reportedly, for thirty-three years, Kalish *never* mentioned his political beliefs in class. On the face of it, that's amazingly inconsistent life-conduct for someone who spend virtually his entire adult life as a professional logician.

So I conclude that this is all very strange, and also that Kalish's adult life as a professional academic post-classical Analytic philosopher is a paradigm example of what I've elsewhere called *the double life problem*:

How is it humanly possible, whether psychologically, prudentially, or existentially, to be at once *not only* a critical activist philosopher, *but also* a professional academic philosopher, and still survive? (Hanna, 2020a: p. 50, 2020b)

---
10 See also (Davis and Wiener, 2020: pp. 306-308, ch. 18). The march turned into what Davis and Wiener accurately call "The Century City Police Riot," and was a catastrophe. This must have also been a personal tragedy for Kalish, who, as a co-organizer of the march, and knowing the voilent coercive authoritarian history and reputation of the LAPD, altogether failed to anticipate the very real possibility of police brutality.

11 Abductive inference is *inference to the best explanation*. I don't have explicit factual evidence that in 1969-1970 the UCLA Regents used precisely the same "Allen Formula" faculty resolution and loyalty oath that Kalish had signed in 1950. But I do think that the evidence I've presented from McCumber's (2016), together with the public statements of the UCLA Regents in their purported justification of Davis's suspension and dismissal in 1969 and 1970, plausibly support this inference.

In my opinion, and based on my own thirty years' experience in professional academic philosophy, it's only by experiencing long-term cognitive, emotional, and practical incoherence and dissonance, aka compartmentalization, and thereby risking serious mental health issues, that such a double life can be survived and sustained. And perhaps, just perhaps, Kalish's refusal to publish anything from 1964 until he retired in 1997, was not only a practical manifestation of his psychological-existential predicament of compartmentalization, but also a silent protest against the highly restrictive ideologically-disciplined norms of professional academic post-classical Analytic philosophy. The other obvious possible way for someone to deal with the double-life problem is *careerist hypocrisy*, but in my opinion, this simply *cannot* have applied in Kalish's case. From all the available evidence, Kalish was the very antithesis of a careerist hypocrite. Moreover, surely, there must have been, and still must be, *a great many* non-careerist-non-hypocritical post-classical Analytic philosophers who have struggled and are struggling with essentially the same issues that Kalish struggled with, although less publicly, living professional academic philosophical lives of quiet desperation.

And now, what about Angela Davis? She was and is, famously and indeed notoriously, a critically- and independently-minded, outspoken, and courageous New Leftist/neo-Marxist, Black power, and radical feminist activist political philosopher in the 1960s and early 70s. And as a consequence, she was fired by UCLA. Shortly after her dismissal, she was unjustly imprisoned for two years; after her release from prison, she continued her radical activist political work through the 1980s; eventually, during the 1980s, she returned to the professional academy as a professor of ethnic studies at San Francisco State; and by 1991 she had switched over permanently to feminist studies with another professorship at UC Santa Cruz, where she has remained for thirty years, as an exceptionally productive scholar and writer, and as of 2021, a professor emerita. Most importantly for my purposes in this section, even despite having very high-powered professional academic credentials, *she's never held a permanent position in a philosophy department*. Indeed, in 1969 she was more than willing to give up her untenured professional academic philosophy position at UCLA—"if keeping my job means that I have to make any compromises in the liberation struggle in this country, then I'll gladly leave my job"(Davis, 2009). Moreover, in my opinion, and in any case, she would have *hated* being in a professional academic philosophy department *with a passion*, especially in the context of post-classical Analytic philosophy, as it was and is paradigmatically practiced in the UCLA Department of Philosophy in the 1970s and beyond, by Kalish's professional colleagues and their successors, through the turn of the millennium and the next two decades and beyond, right up to 6am this morning.

XVII.7.4 The Double Life Problem, and The Options

The double life problem of Donald Kalish, writ large, is what every professional academic post-classical Analytic philosopher, who, in their heart-of-hearts, and, when looking into the bathroom mirror or tossing uneasily in bed in the middle of the night, *dares to think for themselves*, and then seriously contemplates disseminating and enacting those dangerous thoughts via their professional interactions with academic colleagues, teaching, and/or publications—*but never actually does*. There are, of course, the careerist hypocrites. But, leaving them aside, as I've said, then surely there must have been and must still be *a great many* non-careerist-non-hypocritical professional academic post-classical Analytic philosophers, who, for their own good, and in order to flourish as persons, quietly and desperately struggle with, and try to face up to, this duality-problem. Their options clearly and distinctly are: either (i) to exit professional academic post-classical Analytic philosophy, before it's too late, and to change their philosophical, personal, and sociopolitical lives for the better, or (ii) to experience long-term cognitive, emotional, and practical incoherence and dissonance—the psychological-existential predicament of compartmentalization—and thus the risk of serious mental health issues. To be sure, given our natural and often unfortunate tendency to identify ourselves with our careers, the process of exiting-and-escaping itself, thereby leaping into a career-less or even homeless abyss—shades of Diogenes exiled from Sinope, living as a beggar on the streets and sleeping in a large recycled ceramic jar (*pithos*) in Athens, and later kidnapped and sold into slavery by pirates—can be emotionally and socially bumpy, disruptive, and stressful, or even worse. Nevertheless, and even despite all that, *I'm strongly recommending option (i)*.

XVII.8 Zero for Conduct at The Pittsburgh School: Three Dogmas and Three Radical Kantian Alternatives

> I am more interested in what separates concept-users from non-concept-users than in what unites them. (Brandom, 2000: p. 3, quotation edited slightly by substituting "non-concept-users" for "non-concept users")

Monsieur le professeur, je vous dis merde![12]

XVII.8.1 Introduction

As we've seen in chapters II to X above, from the 1880s up through the 1930s, Frege's *Foundations of Arithmetic*, Moore's "Refutation of Idealism" and "The Nature of Judgment," together with Russell's "On Denoting" and *Basic Problems of Philosophy*, early Wittgenstein's *Tractatus Logico-Philosophicus*, Carnap's "Elimination of Metaphysics through Logical Analysis of Language," and Ayer's *Language, Truth, and Logic* collectively ended and transcended the classical neo-Kantian and British neo-Hegelian traditions, and established classical Analytic philosophy. And as we've also seen in chapters XI to XVII, after World War II and up through the first two decades of the 21st century, Quine's "Three Dogmas of Empiricism," together with later Wittgenstein's *Philosophical Investigations*, Cold War politics, and the hegemony of scientistic/ technocratic neoliberalism, collectively ended and transcended classical Analytic philosophy, and institutionally entrenched *post*-classical Analytic philosophy. By *The Pittsburgh School of Philosophy*, following Chauncey Maher's history of The Pittsburgh School (Maher, 2012), I mean a more-or-less tightly bundled or unified set of doctrines and methods presented and defended in the 20th and/or 21st century philosophical work of Wilfrid Sellars, John McDowell, and Robert Brandom. The Pittsburgh

---
12 As blurted out rebelliously, and repeatedly, by the schoolboy Tabard (Gérard de Bédarieux), in Jean Vigo's 1933 film, *Zero de Conduit*, aka *Zero for Conduct*.

School of Philosophy represents an important and indeed unique last-ditch attempt *from within* the advanced phases of post-classical Analytic philosophy, to overcome its inherent flaws and limitations before it finally crashes,burns, and goes down into the ash-heap of history—or to switch metaphors for a moment, having hit an immense Quinean iceberg seventy years ago, before it finally sinks into the cold, grey sea of history—by reconnecting the Analytic tradition with the neo-Kantian and neo-Hegelian idealist traditions. But ultimately, as I'll argue in what follows in this section, The Pittsburgh School is a failed attempt: not only because of some basic philosophical problems internal to the doctrines of The School, but also because in a social-institutional sense it's essentially too conservative and unradical, leaving post-classical Analytic philosophy fundamentally unrevolutionized and untranscended. Hence, at best, the impact and legacy of The Pittsburgh School of Philosophy currently is, and always will be, the philosophical equivalent of rearranging deck-chairs on the *Titanic*

In his brilliant 1933 movie, *Zéro de Conduite*, aka *Zero for Conduct*, Jean Vigo presented a radical and indeed anarchist critique of contemporary French society by means of a deliriously comic visual fantasy about a student revolt at a boarding school (Reddebrek, 2016). Correspondingly, in this section, I want to repurpose at least the spirit of Vigo's cinematic *tour de force* by, **first**, spelling out and then criticizing three Analytic neo-Kantian and/or Analytic neo-Hegelian dogmas of The Pittsburgh School of Philosophy, namely, (i) *conceptualism*, (ii) *inferentialism*, and (iii) *metaphysical quietism*, and juxtaposed to those, **second**, presenting and defending three radical Kantian alternatives, namely, (i*) *strong non-conceptualism*, (ii*) *cognitive-semantics-&-human-knowledge-only-within-The-Grip-of-The-Given* and (iii*) *weak transcendental idealism*. Therefore, my intention in this section is nothing more and nothing less than to end and transcend The Pittsburgh School —*Monsieur le professeur, je vous dis merde!*—and, along with it, thereby also to transcend the bitter dregs of post-classical Analytic philosophy, by creating what, riffing on the subtitle of Nietzsche's *Beyond Good and Evil*, I'll call *a radical Kantian philosophy of the future*.

XVII.8.2 PS-Conceptualism and PS-Inferentialism *versus* Strong Non-Conceptualism and Cognitive-Semantics-&-Human-Knowledge-Only-Within-The-Grip-of-The-Given

By *PS-conceptualism*, I mean the doctrine of *conceptualism* as it has been presented and defended by The Pittsburgh School. And by *PS-inferentialism*, I mean the doctrine of inferentialism as it has been implicitly or explicitly presented by Sellars and especially by Brandom. PS-conceptualism and PS-inferentialism, in turn, jointly consititute the core of the curriculum in The Pittsburgh School; or to switch metaphors, it's the double-strand twine that ties together the entire more-or-less tightly bundled/unified set of doctrines and methods professed by The School. In particular, this means that if PS-conceptualism and PS-inferentialism are false, then the more-or-less bundled/unified set of doctrines and methods professed by The Pittsburgh School simply falls apart.

Where do PS-conceptualism and PS-inferentialism come from? Distally, they come from Kant and Hegel (Hanna, 2013a). But proximally, and most importantly, they come from C.I. Lewis. In 1929, Lewis published an important treatise in neo-Kantian epistemology, *Mind and the World Order*. Indeed, in 1936, *Mind and the World Order* was the first contemporary philosophical text ever to be taught at Oxford, in a seminar run by J.L. Austin and Isaiah Berlin (Hacker, 1996: p. 94). Wilfrid Sellars attended this Oxford seminar, started a D.Phil. dissertation on Kant with T.D. Weldon the same year, and later transferred to Harvard to work with Lewis (Sellars, 1975). Chapter II of *Mind and World* is called "The Given Element in Experience," and chapters III and IV are called, respectively, "The Pure Concept" and "Common Concepts and Our Common World." By and after 1950, in the new sociopolitical world order established by the victorious Anglo-American nations of World War II, especially the USA, decisively aligned against the Soviet Union, as Joseph McCarthy, HUAC, and other fanatical anti-communists terrorized Hollywood socialists and other artists, intellectuals, and scholars, and as the post-classical Analytic tradition decisively took over professional academic philosophy in the USA both ideologically and in a social-institutional sense (Katzav and Vaesen, 2017), then *Mind and the World Order* was almost entirely philosophically forgotten and neglected: good-bye and good riddance to the old-school Oxonian and Harvardian neo-Kantians! But Sellars was steeped-&-stewed in their work; and McDowell (also an Oxonian, steeped-&-stewed in P.F. Strawson's version of neo-Kantianism, and in later-Wittgensteinian and Dummettian philosophy of language[13]) and Brandom (a Princetonian, steeped-&-stewed in Richard Rorty's version of Deweyan pragmatism and in David Lewis's early work on conventionalism), in apostolic succession, were both subsequently steeped-&-stewed in Sellars's work at Pittsburgh. Thus PS-conceptualism and PS-inferentialism, boiled down to their nubs, are essentially (i) a thoroughgoing rejection of Lewis's neo-Kantian conception of The Given, which entails a purely causal, non-normative, and sense-datum-driven foundation for empirical knowledge, together with (ii) an equally thoroughgoing but dialectically-flipped development and totalization of Lewis's neo-Kantian conception of concepts and conceptual content, as a systematic semantics, epistemology, philosophy of language, and philosophy of logic, in a broadly neo-Hegelian, Deweyan pragmatist, and later-Wittgensteinian, Dummettian, and Davidsonian framework, in the larger context of post-classical Analytic philosophy.

The absolutely essential point that follows directly from this brief excavation in the mostly-forgotten history of early 20th century Oxonian-Harvardian-Princetonian-Pittsburghian Analytic philosophy, is that *not every* conception of The Given must be equivalent to Lewis's neo-Kantian conception of The Given. Correspondingly, I call the false assumption, characteristic of PS-conceptualism and PS-inferentialism alike, that *every* conception of The Given must be equivalent to Lewis's conception of The Given and thereby

---

[13] McDowell was *also* heavily influenced by the work of the brilliant yet—sadly—shortlived Gareth Evans, and in fact edited Evans's posthumous masterwork, *Varieties of Reference* (Evans, 1982). But Michael Dummett later excommunicated Evans from the Analytic tradition in *Origins of Analytical Philosophy* (Dummett, 1993: pp. 4) for repeatedly committing the sins of cognitive semantics and non-conceptualism in the face of language-driven neo-Fregeanism and and Davidsonian holism, and that also seems to have strongly influenced McDowell's turn from Evansian semantics and epistemology to Sellarsian semantics and epistemology in *Mind and World*. Interestingly, McDowell has retained a vestigial Evans-like commitment to cognitive semantics, and, correspondingly, a critical resistance to inferentialism; see, e.g., (McDowell, 2013); and (Maher, 2012: pp. 75-77).

entails a purely causal, non-normative, and sense-datum-driven foundation for empirical knowledge, *The Myth of The Myth of The Given* (Hanna, 2011a).

The strongest version of PS-conceptualism, defended by Sellars, early McDowell, and Brandom alike, says (i) that human conceptual (aka discursive) and linguistic capacities necessarily, sufficiently, and solely determine human intentionality and intentional content, and (ii) that all non-discursive, non-linguistic animals lack intentionality and intentional content (Sellars, 1963b; Brandom, 2000; Maher, 2012: ch 1). In later work, McDowell has moved over to a weaker version of PS-conceptualism, which says (i*) that conceptual capacities necessarily and sufficiently but not solely determine human intentionality and intentional content, because an input, priming, and/or triggering contribution of our non-conceptual capacities is also required, and (ii*) that *strictly speaking* all non-discursive, non-linguistic human or non-human animals *lack* not only the capacity for intentionality but also mental acts, processes, or states with intentional content, nevertheless, at least some non-discursive, non-linguistic human or non-human animals can be *ascribed* a *proto*-intentionality and *proto*-intentional content that's *parasitic* on the intentionality and intentional content of discursive and linguistic human animals (McDowell, 2009b).

It's crucial to recognize that PS-inferentialism requires PS-conceptualism; hence if PS-conceptualism is false, then PS-inferentialism is already false, no matter what other reasons might be offered in favor of it. In any case, here's how Brandom characterizes PS-inferentialism:

> The later Wittgenstein, Quine, and Sellars (as well as Dummett and Davidson) are linguistic pragmatists, whose strategy of coming at the meaning of expressions by considering their use provides a counterbalance to the Frege-Russell-Carnap-Tarski platonistic model-theoretic approach to meaning.... The master concept of Enlightenment epistmology and semantics, at least since Descartes, was *representation*. Awareness was understood in representational terms—whether taking the form of direct awareness of representings or of indirect awareness of representeds via representations of them. Typically, specifically conceptual representations were taken to be just one kind of representation of which and by means of which we can be aware.... This representational paradigm of what mindedness consists in is sufficiently ubiquitous that it is perhaps not easy to think of alternatives of similar generality and promise. One prominent countertradition, however, looks to the notion of expression, rather than representation, for the genus within which distinctively conceptual activity can become intelligible as a species. To the Enlightenment picture of mind as mirror, Romanticism opposed an image of mind as lamp. Broadly cognitive activity was to be seen not as a kind of passive reflection but as a kind of active revelation.... The master idea that animates and orients this [i.e., Brandom's] enterprise is that what distinguishes specifically *discursive* practices from the doings of non-concept-using creatures is their *inferential* articulation. To talk about concepts is to talk about their roles in reasoning. The original Romantic expressivists were (like the pragmatists, both classical and

contemporary) *assimilationists* about the conceptual. My [i.e., Brandom's] way of working out an expressivist approach is a *rationalist* pragmatism, in giving pride of place to practices of giving and asking for reasons, understanding them as conferring conceptual content on performances, expressions, and states suitably caught up in those practices.... And it is a rationalist expressivism in that it understands *expressing* something, making it *explicit*, putting it in a form in which it can serve as and stand in need of *reasons*: a form in which it can serve as both premise and conclusion in *inferences*. Saying or thinking *that* things are thus-and-so is undertaking a distinctive kind of *inferentially* articulated commitment: putting it forward as a fit premise for further inferences, that is, *authorizing* its use as such a premise, and undertaking *responsibility* to entitle oneself to that commitment, to vindicate one's authority, under suitable circumstances, paradigmatically by exhibiting it as the conclusion of an inference from other such commitments to which one is or can become entitled. Grasping the *concept* that is applied in such a making explicit is mastering its *inferential* use: knowing (in the practical sense of being able to distinguish, a kind of knowing *how*) what else one would be committing oneself to by applying the concept, what would entitle one to do so, and what would preclude such entitlement. (Brandom, 2000: pp. 6-7, 10-11)

Now, by a sharp and indeed diametric contrast to *either* strong PS-conceptualism *or* later McDowell's weaker version of PS-conceptualism, *strong non-conceptualism* (aka *Kantian non-conceptualism*, aka *essentialist content non-conceptualism*), as I've presented and defended it, says (i***) that human conceptual (i.e., discursive and linguistic) capacities *neither* necessarily, *nor* sufficiently, *nor* solely determine human intentionality and its content, and (ii***) that all minded non-discursive, non-linguistic animals *inherently possess* not only the capacity for intentionality but also mental acts, processes, or states with intentional content, both of which are universally shared with rational human animals (Hanna, 2005, 2008a, 2011a, 2015a: ch. 2, 2021b). The two basic arguments for PS-conceptualism and PS-inferentialism are these:

> (PS1) that non-conceptuality, whose putative cognitive and epistemic function it is to provide direct reference to the manifestly real world for the purposes of picking out and tracking individuals, properties, and kinds, and also truth-as-correspondence, and to stop any justificatory regress of inferential reasons by providing veridical, normative, and non-inferential pre-reflectively conscious evidental grounds for belief and knowledge (aka *The Given*), is in fact purely causal, non-normative, and sense-datum-driven, hence it cannot provide grounds for belief or knowledge (aka *The Myth of the Given*, aka *Foundationalism*), because only conceptuality can provide these in the form of self-conscious, inferential reasons (which may, however, be activated non-self-consciously by engaging "blindly," but still competently, in linguistic practices), and

> (PS2) that non-conceptuality is neither normative nor contentual because only conceptuality is normative and contentual, which is self-evident.

Argument (PS2), although surprisingly popular, is clearly question-begging, so it can be discounted right off the bat. Most importantly, however, argument (PS1) *also* fails, *provided that* it can be shown that according to at least one theory of non-conceptuality, non-conceptuality is *neither* purely causal *nor* non-normative *nor* sense-datum-driven, and on the contrary that it has essentially non-conceptual intentionality and inherently normative intentional content, and can also provide essentially non-conceptual directly referential, irreducibly normative, inherently non-inferential, pre-reflectively conscious grounds for picking out and tracking individuals, properties, and kinds in the manifestly real world, for truth-as-correspondence, for belief, and for knowledge (i.e. sufficiently justified true belief), independently of any self-conscious, inferential, or linguistically-mediated reasons there might also be. This is what I call *cognitive-semantics-&-human-knowledge-only-within-The Grip-of-The-Given*. Therefore, if strong non-conceptualism and cognitive-semantics-&-human-knowledge-only-within-The Grip-of-The-Given are both true, then not only are PS-conceptualism and PS-inferentialism both false, but also argument (PS1) fails, because it's clearly and distinctly grounded on a false assumption, The Myth of The Myth of The Given.

Again, with gusto: The knock-down problem for PS-conceptualism and PS-inferentialism is that they cannot provide direct cognitive access to individuals, properties, or kinds in the manifestly real world, to truth-as-correspondence, or to pre-reflectively conscious evidential facts that stop the regress of self-conscious inferential reasons for justification. In short, *PS-conceptualism and PS-inferentialism cannot provide a pre-reflectively conscious evidential veridicality-relation to the manifestly real world*. The assumption that nonconceptuality cannot provide a pre-reflectively conscious evidential veridicality-relation to the manifestly real world, because every theory of nonconceptuality is necessarily equivalent to C.I. Lewis's conception of The Given, is The Myth of The Myth of The Given; and it's false. But on the contrary, strong non-conceptualism together with cognitive-semantics-&-human-knowledge-only-within-The Grip-of-The-Given not only can and but also do provide a pre-reflectively conscious evidential veridicality-relation to the manifestly real world.

What arguments do I have for asserting the truth of strong non-conceptualism and cognitive-semantics-&-human-knowledge-only-within-The Grip-of-The-Given, and therefore for rejecting PS-conceptualism, PS-inferentialism, and argument (PS1) alike? I've presented and defended them in detail and at length in *Cognition, Content, and the A Priori*. So for my purposes here, I'll present and defend only short-&-sweet versions of those arguments.

According to a classical view in the philosophy of mind, both human and non-human minded animals inherently or innately possess a capacity to produce mental representations of objects (whether those objects are actual or merely possible, existing or non-existing), locations, events, actions or performances, other minded animals, and themselves. This classical view runs from the "faculty psychology" of the early 18th century up through Kant's "transcendental psychology," and then forward again through the phenomenological, introspectivist, Gestalt, and Chomskyan/cognitivist movements in 19th and 20th century psychology, and right into mainstream contemporary cognitive science and philosophical psychology. Whatever its particular incarnation, the classical view holds that minded animals inherently or innately possess a capacity to be *directed* to targets of all kinds; that is, they have the capacity for *intentionality*. In turn, mental representations have mental content, also known as "intentional content," where such content is (i) the cognitive or practical information that is internally carried by or contained in a mental representation, (ii) what individuates the mental act, process, or state, that has this content, and (iii) what normatively guides this mental act, state, or process by providing its accuracy-of-reference conditions, its truth-conditions, and its intentional performance success-conditions.

Mental or intentional content is shareable across minded animals, but also directly grasped on particular occasions and in particular contexts by individual minded animals. So, at least implicitly, according to the classical view, mental contents are *mental representation-types*. This means they are information-structures tokened in space and time with the following qualities: they are multiply realizable or repeatable (for example, the same information structure "my favorite blue coffee cup" is repeated each time I represent some real-world item as such, say in sense-perception, memory, or imagination), consciously-accessible, individuating, and normatively-guiding (for example, I represent various real-world items correctly or incorrectly as my favorite blue coffee cup, and track it more or less accurately in space and time under varying contextual conditions as I reach out for it). Correspondingly, the inherent psychological function of mental contents, insofar as they occur as *mental representation-tokens* directly grasped by individual minded animals on particular occasions and in particular contexts, is to individuate the very mental acts, states, or processes in which those tokens occur, to provide normative guidance for the cognition and practical agency that occurs via those self-same mental acts, processes, or states, and to provide the information that mediates their directedness to their intentional targets.

In turn, there are two fundamentally different, basic kinds of mental contents: (i) *concepts*, and (ii) *essentially non-conceptual contents*. Concepts are the inherently *descriptive, general, contextless, veridical or non-veridical* meanings of predicative or many-place relational terms in natural language (for example, "cat(s)," "mat(s)," "moon(s)," "x is sitting on y," etc.), that also inherently belong to two different kinds of larger meaning-complexes: (iii) "propositions" or "thoughts," whether simple or compound, built up out of concepts and various kinds of logical operators (for example, the "is" of predication, the "is" of identity, the "is" of assertion, "the/one and only one," "all/every," "some/at least one," the "not" of propositional/thought negation, the "non-" of predicate negation, "and," "either … or," "if … then," etc.), that either correspond to actual facts in the world and are true (for example, "Some cat is sitting on a mat") or fail to do so and are false "Some cat is sitting on the moon"), and (iv) arguments or inferences, which are chains or sequences of thoughts/propositions governed by laws of logical validity and soundness (for example, "Every cat is are sitting on some mat or another. Therefore some cat is sitting on some mat"). Essentially non-conceptual contents, by sharp contrast to concepts, are inherently *non-de-*

scriptive, *non*-general, *context-sensitive, veridical* meanings of (v) indexical terms in natural language, especially those involving spatial or temporal location or direction (for example, "this," "that," "here," "there," "up," "down," "right," "left," "now," "then," "before," "after," etc.), (vi) singular terms in natural language (for example, "John," "Jane," "Los Angeles, CA" "20 December 2019," etc), and (iii) personal pronouns (for example, "I," "me," "you," "he," "him," "she," "her," "they," "them," "we," "us," etc).

Another crucial difference between concepts and essentially non-conceptual contents is that whereas concepts are always and necessarily applied or deployed, at least potentially, by means of self-conscious cognition (say, in making statements, carrying out logical inferences, or constructing theories), essentially non-conceptual contents need *not* be so applied or deployed, and can on the contrary be applied or deployed in a fully *pre*-reflective or *non*-self-consciously conscious way (for example, while playing sports, walking, dancing, "spacing out," etc.). The basic cognitive function of a concept is to form a more-or-less general or universal, veridical or non-veridical notion of oneself, other people or animals, and things of all kinds, from an inherently *allocentric*, and more-or-less context-less, detached point of view, for the purposes of having a theoretical grasp of the world, whether that grasp be true or false. By sharp contrast, the basic function of an essentially non-conceptual content is veridically to locate and track oneself, other people or animals, and things of all kinds, from an inherently *egocentric*, contextual, embedded, spatially- and temporally-framed point of view, for the purposes of practical know-how and pre-reflective intentional bodily action.

It's crucial to note, before proceeding further, that although concepts and essentially non-conceptual contents are essentially *distinct* from one another, in that they cannot be reduced to one other and are logically independent of one another in the sense that at least one of them can occur without the other, nevertheless they are also fully *compatible* with one another in that they can coherently occur in the *same* proposition or thought (for example, "I'm here in Los Angeles now, sitting on this mat beside that cat"), and it might also be true that at least one of them *presupposes* the other, perhaps asymmetrically (for example, it might be that all concepts presuppose essentially non-conceptual contents, but not conversely).

Now the general thesis of *non-conceptualism* about mental content, especially including my thesis of *strong* non-conceptualism, says that *not all* mental contents in the intentional or representational acts, processes, or states of minded animals are necessarily, sufficiently, or solely mediated-and-determined by their conceptual capacities and their concepts, and also that *at least some* mental contents are necessarily, sufficiently, and solely mediated-and-determined by their non-conceptual capacities and their non-conceptual mental representations. Non-conceptualism is sometimes, but not always, combined with the further thesis that non-conceptual capacities and contents can be shared by rational human animals, non-rational human minded animals (and in particular, infants), and non-human minded animals alike, but in any case, that second thesis is *also* asserted by strong non-conceptualism. All in all, non-conceptualism is directly and indeed diametrically opposed to the general thesis of *conceptualism* about mental content, which says that all mental contents are necessarily, sufficiently, and/or solely determined by minded animals' conceptual capacities—and, as we've seen, all of those are asserted by the strongest version of PS-conceptualism. Conceptualism in general is also sometimes, but not always, combined with the further thesis that the psychological acts or states of infants and non-human minded animals lack mental content, but again, as we've seen it's also asserted the strongest version of PS-conceptualism.

So in a nutshell, strong non-conceptualism says that our cognitive access to the targets of our intentionality is *neither* necessarily, *nor* sufficiently, *nor* solely mediated-or-determined by concepts, and therefore that our cognitive access to the targets of our intentionality is sometimes wholly *un*mediated and *un*determined by concepts, i.e., it's altogether concept-free, which is the *autonomy* of non-conceptual content. By sharp contrast, PS-conceptualism says that our cognitive access to the targets of our intentionality is necessarily, sufficiently, and solely mediated-and-determined by our conceptual capacities and our concepts. The cognitive capacities generating and supporting non-conceptual content are pre-reflectively or non-self-consciousness-based, perceptual, imaginational, and more generally characteristic of human *sensibility*. On the other hand, the cognitive capacities generating and supporting conceptual content are self-consciousness-based, judgmental or propositional, logical, and more generally characteristic of human *discursivity* (i.e., human linguistic and thoughtful activity).

Here, then, is the fundamental philosophical question that's being asked in the so-called "debate about non-conceptual content," insofar as it's between PS-conceptualism and strong non-conceptualism:

> Can we, do we, and must we, at least sometimes, and in a minimally basic way, cognitively encounter other things and ourselves directly and non-discursively, hence non-intellectually or sensibly (strong non-conceptualism), or must we always cognitively encounter them only within the framework of discursive rationality, hence only intellectually or discursively (PS-conceptualism)?

Again, are we, as rational human animals, essentially different from other kinds of animals (PS-conceptualism), or do we share at least some minimally basic mental capacities with all minded animals (strong non-conceptualism)? Or even more simply put: Is a thoroughly *intellectualist* and *discursivity first* view of the rational human animal (PS-conceptualism) correct; or by sharp contrast is a thoroughly *non-intellectualist* and *sensibility first* view of the rational human animal (strong non-conceptualism) correct?

Of course, I'm asserting that the "sensibility first" view is the correct one (Hanna, 2021h), hence I'm a *card-carrying strong non-conceptualist*. —Card-carrying, yes, but *neither* dogmatic *nor* uncritical, since I do have in hand at least nine arguments for strong non-conceptualism, including two that I regard as philosophically decisive *as a pair*.

In the relevant "philosophical literature," as they say, there are at least seven arguments for non-conceptualism, all of which I endorse:

(I) *The argument from phenomenological richness*: Our normal human perceptual experience is so replete with phenomenal characters and qualities that we could not possibly possess a conceptual repertoire extensive enough to capture them. Therefore, normal human perceptual experience is always to some extent non-conceptual and has non-conceptual content.

(II) *The argument from perceptual discrimination*: It's possible for normal human cognizers to be capable of perceptual discriminations without also being capable of re-identifying the objects discriminated. But re-identification is a necessary condition of concept-possession. Therefore, normal human cognizers are capable of non-conceptual cognitions with non-conceptual content.

(III) *The argument from the distinction between perception (or experience) and judgment (or thought)*: It's possible for normal human cognizers to perceive something without also making a judgment about it. But non-judgmental cognition is non-conceptual. Therefore, normal human cognizers are capable of non-conceptual perceptions with non-conceptual content.

(IV) *The argument from the knowing-how vs. knowing-that (or knowing-what) distinction*: It's possible for normal human subjects to know *how* to do something without being able to know *that* one is doing it and also without knowing precisely *what* it is one is doing. But cognition which lacks knowing-that and knowing-what is non-conceptual. Therefore, normal human subjects are capable of non-conceptual knowledge-how with non-conceptual content.

(V) *The argument from the theory of concept-acquisition*: The best overall theory of concept-acquisition includes the thesis that simple concepts are acquired by normal human cognizers on the basis of non-conceptual perceptions of the objects falling under these concepts. Therefore, normal human cognizers are capable of non-conceptual perception with non-conceptual content.

(VI) *The argument from the theory of demonstratives*: The best overall theory of the demonstratives "this" and "that" includes the thesis that demonstrative reference is fixed perceptually, essentially indexically, and therefore non-descriptively by normal human speakers. But essentially indexical, non-descriptive perception is non-conceptual. Therefore normal human speakers are capable of non-conceptual perception with non-conceptual content.

(VII) *The argument from the "cognitive impenetrability" of subpersonal or subdoxastic representations*: Some representational states, for example, early vision, are not only subpersonal or sub-doxastic, but also "cognitively impenetrable," in the sense that the information represented by these states is not available to conscious or self-conscious mental processing. But nonconscious or non-self-conscious mental representation is non-conceptual. Therefore, normal human cognizers are capable of non-conceptual perception with non-conceptual content.

And here are the two arguments that I regard as philosophically decisive, as a pair:

(VIII) *The argument from babes-and-beasts:* Some normal human animals (for example, normal human infants), and many normal non-human animals (for example, normal cats) are capable of cognizing themselves, other animals, and the world, yet *lack* any capacity for conceptualization. And when normal human infants mature and acquire a capacity for conceptualization, they retain the capacity for cognition that they share with non-human animals. Therefore, human cognition is really possible *without* any concepts whatsoever: that is, concepts are *not generally necessary* for human (or for that matter, non-human) cognition.

(IX) *The argument from enantiomorphy:* Consider any object whatsoever, and *all* the concepts that correctly describe it. By hypothesis, we have a *complete* conceptual account of that object. Now consider that very object's *mirror-reflected counterpart* (aka its "enantiomorph"). By hypothesis, concepts alone cannot differentiate between the object and its mirror-reflected counterpart, hence no human cognizer *using concepts alone* could discriminate between the object and its enantiomorph. Then consider a conscious human subject embedded within an orientable space (that is, a space with intrinsic directions, for example, up-down, right-left, back-front, inside-outside, north-south-east-west, etc.) *exactly between the two counterparts, occupying the position of the mirror.* Thus one of the counterparts is on the subject's right-hand side, and one of the counterparts is on the subject's left-hand side. Therefore, the conscious human subject can tell the counterparts apart by essentially non-conceptual spatial representation, but by hypothesis, concepts alone are insufficient to do this: that is, concepts are *not generally sufficient for human cognition*.

To be sure, there are many attempts by conceptualists, including of course the PS-conceptualists, to answer and resist these arguments, to offer independent arguments for conceptualism, including of course for PS-conceptualism, and to finesse the impact of the pro-strong-non-conceptualist arguments by forming philosophical alliances with etiolated, weaker forms of non-nonceptualism. But rather than boring you senseless with all the moves in *that* dialectical game, I'll simply point you to *Cognition, Content, and the A Priori*, chapter 2, where I have dealt with all those moves in loving critical detail.

I'll conclude this first part of my argument, then, by claiming that strong non-conceptualism is true, whereas PS-conceptualism is false; and correspondingly, that the non-intellectualist and "sensibility first" view of the rational human animal is correct, whereas PS-conceptualism's thoroughly intellectualist and "discursivity first" view of the rational human animal is incorrect. This intermediate conclusion has many profound implications; but I think that the following pair of critical insights are paramount.

First, PS-conceptualism and intellectualism systematically *occlude* the two most important things about us, namely (i) that as rational "human, all-too-human" animals, we're *essentially embodied minds* (Hanna, 2011b; Hanna and Maiese, 2009) who are, thereby, directly connected to the world, to ourselves, and to each other by veridical, pre-reflectively conscious, essentially non-conceptual cognition, and (ii) that our "human, all-too-human," essentially embodied capacity for rationality grows right on top of and out of this dynamic and organismic cognitive, affective, and practical essentially non-conceptual foundation, without in any way being reducible to it, which is what I call *cognitive organicism* (Hanna, 2019).

Second, this PS-conceptualist and intellectualist systematic occlusion of the essentially embodied and essentially non-conceptual dimension of rational human animal nature carries an *existential punch*, namely that in hiding this fundamental dimension of our lives from ourselves, we are in effect *tragically refusing to face up to our own humanity*.

Assuming that strong non-conceptualism is true, it follows also that PS-inferentialism is false. So I'm now in a position to provide a general theory of the structure, specific character, and cognitive/epistemic function of essentially non-conceptual human intentionality and intentional content, which entails that they have direct referentiality and inherent non-discursive normativity, and provide inherently non-inferential grounds for picking out and tracking individuals, properties, and kinds in the menifestly real world, for truth-as-correspondence, for belief, and for knowledge, independently of any self-conscious, inferential, or linguistically-mediated reasons there might also be, via a pre-reflectively conscious evidential veridicality-relation to the manifestly real world. As I mentioned above, I call this doctrine *cognitive-semantics-&-human-knowledge-only-within-The-Grip-of-The-Given*. This is also the same as what I call *categorical epistemology*.

Cognitive-semantics-&-human-knowledge-only-within-The-Grip-of-The-Given, aka categorical epistemology, presupposes strong non-conceptualism, together with what I call *categorical normativity*. I believe that the primitive fact of categorical normativity inheres in all rational human intentionality whatsoever—including all essentially embodied rational human consciousness, mental content, belief, and knowledge. What is this primitive fact? Normativity, as I am understanding it, consists in the fact that all minded animals, whether merely sentient (conscious minimal agents) or also sapient (self-consciously conscious, rational agents), have desires, aims, commitments, ends, goals, ideals, and/or values. Now insofar as sapient or rational minded animals naturally treat these aims, commitments, ends, goals, ideals, and/or values as rules or principles for guiding theoretical inquiry and practical enterprises, as reasons for justifying beliefs and intentional actions, and also as standards for critical evaluation and judgment, then at least some of those rules, principles, reasons, and standards are non-instrumental, unconditional, desired for their own sake as an end-in-themselves, non-pragmatic, non-prudential, and obtain no-matter-what-the-consequences. These are *categorical norms*, and my claim is that they necessarily inhere in all rational human *caring*. Categorical norms are perfectly consistent with norms that are instrumental, conditional, desired for the sake of other ends, pragmatic, prudential, or obtain only in virtue of good consequences. Nevertheless, categorical norms are necessarily underdetermined by all other sorts of norms—that is, categorical norms do not strongly supervene on any other sorts of norms—and therefore they cannot be assimilated to or replaced by those other sorts of norms. Correspondingly, categorical norms provide overriding reasons for belief and intentional action.

In order to make my next point, I'll have to pause briefly for some slightly technical terminology and definitions. *Strong supervenience* is a necessary determination-relation between sets of properties or states of different ontological "levels," a relation that is weaker than strict property/state-identity, and is usually taken to be asymmetric, although two-way or bilateral strong supervenience is also possible (Horgan, 1993; Kim, 1993: esp. part 1; Chalmers, 1996: chs. 1-3). But assuming for the purposes of simpler exposition that strong supervenience is asymmetric, then, more precisely, B-properties/states (= the higher level properties/ states) strongly supervene on A-properties/states (= the lower-level properties/states) if and only if (i) for any property/state F among the A-properties/states had by something X, F necessitates X's also having property/state G among the B-properties/states (upwards necessitation), and (ii) there cannot be a change in any of X's B-properties/states without a corresponding change in X's A-properties/ states (necessary co-variation). It follows from strong supervenience that any two things X and Y share all their A-properties/states in common only if they share all their B-properties/states in common (indiscriminability). For example, if heat strongly supervenes on mean molecular motion, then two things have the same kinetic molecular properties in common only if they have the same temperature properties in common. Facts are just actual or possible instantiations of properties. Hence strong supervenience for properties entails strong supervenience for facts, and failures of strong supervenience for properties correspondingly entails failures of strong supervenience for facts. In turn, *logical* supervenience is a super-strong version of strong supervenience which says that the necessitation relations between the B-properties/states and the A-properties/states are *logical* and *a priori*. Or more simply put: The B-properties/states are "nothing more than" and "nothing over and above" the A-properties/states. If logical supervenience holds, then if there were such a being as an all-powerful and all-knowing creator God, and if They were to create and/or know all the A-properties/states, then They would have nothing more to do in order to create and/or know all the B-properties/states. The strict "downwards identity" of higher-level properties with corresponding lower-level properties entails logical strong supervenience; but logical strong supervenience is also consistent with the multiple instantiability or realizability of the same higher-level properties across different lower-level properties, hence consistent with "downwards non-identity." For example, even if human body heat logically strongly supervenes on mean molecular motion inside the human body, it remains conceivable and possible that the very same temperature properties are instantiated or realized in humanoids made out of quite different kinds of stuff that nevertheless plays the same mean-molecular-motion role—for example, the "replicants" imagined in Philip K. Dick's classic science fiction novel, *Do Androids Dream of Electric Sheep?* and in Ridley Scott's equally classic sci-fi movie, *Blade Runner*. Hence logical strong supervenience is the most inclusive reductive metaphysical relation. By contrast to logical strong supervenience, *natural or nomological* strong supervenience is a modally weaker notion which says that the the necessitation relations between the *B*-properties/states and the *A*-properties/states are determined by laws of nature, and hold in all and only the worlds in which those natural laws obtain. It's crucial to recognize that no matter what its level of modal strength, strong supervenience specifies at best a set of *extrinsic modal properties and relations* (namely, upwards necessitation, necessary co-variation, and indiscriminability) between a thing's *A*-properties/states and its *B*-properties/states, or between any two things' *A*-properties/states and *B*-properties/ states. If relations of strong supervenience hold for a thing or things, as such, then there's no further implication that these are relations of *constitution, essence*, or *efficacious causal power*, such that a thing's or things' immanent structural characteristics—and in particular, if the thing or things are natural or physical, their efficacious causal powers—depend on these relations. Conversely, if relations of constitution, essence, or causal efficacy hold for a thing or things, then there is no further implication that strong supervenience holds for them. In short, the metaphysics of strong supervenience is modally *shallow*, not modally *deep*, unlike the *real* metaphysics of manifestly real constitution, essence, or causality (see also sub-section XVII.6.1 above).

Here's the point I want to make by using the notion of logical strong supervenience. If a norm really is categorical, then it cannot be reduced to contingent physical facts or natural causal laws by means of logical strong supervenience. This is shown by the following *reductio* argument:

> 1. Suppose that categorical norms are reducible to contingent physical facts or natural causal laws.
>
> 2. Contingent physical facts and natural causal laws are inherently conditioned by, and conditional upon, the actual spatiotemporal locations of those facts and the actual constitution and distribution of matter and forces in the physical world, whereas categorical norms are inherently unconditioned and unconditional.
>
> 3. But the explanatory reduction of *X* to *Y* entails showing that *X* is, at the very least, logically strongly supervenient on *Y*,
>
> 4. So by the initial supposition made in 1., categorical norms would then be logically strongly supervenient on inherently conditioned, conditional facts.
>
> 5. But then categorical norms are both inherently unconditioned and unconditional and also strictly dependent on what is inherently conditioned and conditional, which is a contradiction.
>
> 6. Therefore, categorical norms cannot be reduced to contingent physical facts or natural causal laws, by *reductio ad absurdum* as applied to the initial supposition made in 1.[14]

---

[14] For an analogous argument against the very idea of scientific naturalism and reductive physicalism as applied to logic (aka *logical psychologism*—see section II.10 above), see (Hanna, 2006c: ch. 1).

In what follows in the rest of this sub-section, by *a conscious-evidence-based reason*, I mean a reason that is based on evidence provided by a conscious act, state, or process. And by *a conscious act, state, or process* I mean a subjectively-experienced, intentionally-directed mental act, state, or process. Thus reasons that are based on our capacities for sense perception, memory, imagination, apperception or self-consciousness, judgment (including the reception of testimony), deductive inference, inductive inference, abductive inference, mathematical intuition, logical intuition, or philosophical intuition, are all conscious-evidence-based reasons.

My account of the nature of knowledge, cognitive-semantics-&-human-knowledge-only-within-The-Grip-of-The-Given/categorical epistemology, is robustly normative in character, and it also flows naturally from the widely-known and almost universally-accepted "Gettier counterexamples" to the classical analysis of knowledge, according to which knowledge is the same as justified true belief (Gettier, 1963; Shope, 1983; Ichikawa and Steup, 2018). Duncan Pritchard and others have correctly pointed out that the Gettier cases show that the classical analysis of knowledge leaves justified true belief open to *luck*, that is, to merely accidental or contingent connections between justifying evidence and the truth-makers of beliefs. Hence, in addition to justified true belief, authentic knowledge further requires the satisfaction of an *anti-luck*, or *externalist*, condition. Pritchard and others have also correctly pointed out that the classical analysis of knowledge fails to require that cognitive subjects acquire their justifying evidence via properly-functioning cognitive capacities or mechanisms. Hence authentic knowledge also requires the satisfaction of a *cognitive virtues*, or *virtue epistemology*, condition (Pritchard, 2012). What I'll call *High-Bar knowledge* includes maximally strong versions of both the anti-luck condition and the cognitive virtues condition alike, as well as requiring the satisfaction of an *evidential-phenomenological*, or *internalist*, condition, and in this way it also rules out global or radical skepticism.

Here's what I mean by all that. The simplest kind of Gettier counterexample goes like this. I look at my iPhone, and it says that it is 7:00 am. And I know by experience that my iPhone has been working fine for months. So I have a conscious-evidence-based reason for asserting that it is 7:00 am. And, as it happens, it really is 7:00 am. But, unbeknownst to me, my iPhone has been broken since 7:00 pm last evening, when, by a malfunction of the digital mechanism, it started reading 7:00 am and froze at that setting; and I have not looked at it since then. So even though I have a conscious-evidence-based reason for asserting that it is 7:00 am, and it is true that it is 7:00 am, and I believe that it is 7:00 am, I do not know that it is 7:00 am. So, it would seem that knowledge is not justified true belief.

How should we understand this result? My own (non-standard) take on the Gettier counterexamples is that although knowledge really is justified true belief, the counterexamples initially suggest the opposite, by trading on a special internal normative feature of the concepts and facts of epistemic justification and knowledge: epistemic justification and knowledge are *normatively two-dimensional*, in the sense that by their very nature they are either *Low-Bar* or *High-Bar*. Let me now, in turn, explain what I mean by this.

Low-Bar. The "Low-Bar" dimension of epistemic justification allows for justification to be more or less detached from truth, and means: "whatever provides a conscious-evidence-based reason for the believer to assert her belief-claim, even if that belief turns out false," in which case that belief obviously is not knowledge in the normatively highest sense. But most importantly for the Gettier counterexamples, what I will call *Low-Bar justification* is also consistent with cases (like the broken iPhone case) in which the believer's claim is actually true, yet that actual truth is neither inherently or intrinsically connected to the believer's conscious-evidence-based reason for asserting her belief-claim, nor even in a context-sensitive way, causally reliably connected to the believer's conscious-evidence-based reason for asserting her belief-claim. Otherwise put, the truth of the claim in these cases is only accidentally or contingently connected to the believer's conscious-evidence-based reason for asserting her belief-claim. That's Low-Bar justification.

Now, this clearly and distinctly points up the fact that knowledge in the normatively highest sense, or what I will call *High-Bar knowledge*, requires an inherent or intrinsic connection—i.e., a non-accidental or necessary connection—between the truth of a believer's belief-claim and a believer's sufficient conscious-evidence-based reason for asserting her belief-claim, as delivered by her properly-functioning cognitive capacities or mechanisms. That is, it requires what I call *High-Bar justified true belief*. This is because in the cases in which there is only an accidental or contingent connection, the believer's belief-claim could just as easily have been false with no change whatsoever in the believer's conscious-evidence-based reason for asserting her belief-claim. So knowledge in the normatively highest sense, that is, High-Bar justified true belief, is *not* the same as Low-Bar knowledge, which involves justified true belief in the Low-Bar sense only. In that sense, High-Bar knowledge is not Low-Bar justified true belief, although High-Bar knowledge still is and always will be High-Bar justified true belief. Correspondingly, Low-Bar knowledge still is and always will be Low-Bar justified true belief. Hence, provided that we keep our bar-levels straight, knowledge really is justified true belief.

High-Bar. By sharp contrast, then, the "High-Bar" dimension of knowledge and justification requires that belief be inherently or intrinsically connected to truth, via the properly-functioning cognitive capacities or mechanisms of the cognitive subject, and means: "whatever provides a sufficient conscious-evidence-based reason for the believer to assert her belief-claim, via her properly-functioning cognitive capacities or mechanisms, and also is inherently or intrinsically connected to the truth of that belief-claim." Otherwise put, High-Bar knowledge has the following three fundamental features. **First**, belief is self-evident, i.e., intrinsically compelling, thereby satisfying an evidential-phenomenological or internalist condition on authentic knowledge. **Second**, this self-evidence is informationally delivered to belief by a properly-functioning cognitive capacity or mechanism, thereby satisfying a cognitive virtues condition on authentic knowledge. And **third**, belief provides a non-accidental or necessary tie to the truth-makers of belief, thereby satisfying an anti-luck or externalist condition on authentic knowledge.

An example of High-Bar knowledge would be a case that is radically different from any sort of Gettier case, and also radically different from any other sort of "bad" epistemic case involving falsity or failed justification. In this all-around good epistemic case, as a paradigm, and indefinitely many others relevantly like it, I objectively know, via basic authoritative a priori objectively necessarily true mathematical rational intuition, that

3+4=7, i.e., ||| + |||| = |||||||

and thereby achieve High Bar a priori knowledge. Now, by *an essentially reliable cognitive capacity or mechanism*, I mean a cognitive capacity or mechanism that tracks truth counterfactually and in a context-sensitive way across all relevantly similar metaphysically possible worlds. So High-Bar justified true belief is the same as High-Bar knowledge, precisely because justification occurs by means of an essentially reliable cognitive capacity or mechanism, in this case, basic authoritative mathematical rational intuition.

This paradigmatically good epistemic case should also be distinguished from another variant case in which my iPhone says it is 7:00 am, and my iPhone is still working fine, and it is actually 7:00 am, and I believe that it is 7:00 am, and it is also the case that (i) whenever, in relevantly similar cases, it were to be such-and-such a time, call it T, and I looked at my my iPhone and it read "T," then I would believe that it is T, and (ii) whenever, in relevantly similar cases, it were, by some salient difference, not to be T and I looked at my iPhone, yet my iPhone still read "T," then I would not believe that it is T and would instead believe that my iPhone was malfunctioning. So I know that it is 7:00 am, because my conscious evidence for asserting my belief is connected to the truth of that belief-claim with context-sensitive causal reliability. Now by *a context-sensitive causally reliable cognitive capacity or mechanism* I mean a cognitive capacity or mechanism that tracks truth in the actual world, and also counterfactually and in a context-sensitive way across all relevantly similar nomologically possible worlds. In this "pretty good" case, then, the context-sensitive causally reliable cognitive capacity or mechanism is my capacity for veridical, direct sense perception, together with a further online—that is, currently properly functioning—capacity of mine for detecting salient breakdowns of my iPhone whenever they occur.

But context-sensitive causally reliable knowledge, "pretty good" though it is, is not the normatively best or highest kind of knowledge, precisely because the connection between my conscious-evidence-based reason and the truth-maker of my belief is not inherent or intrinsic. On the one hand, context-sensitive causally reliable knowledge is open to global skeptical worries: in at least some introspectively indistinguishable, conceivably possible worlds containing the very same conscious-evidence-based reason, that belief is instead connected to a falsity-maker, not a truth-maker: this conceivable possibility in effect globalizes Gettier-style worries about justification (Cohen, 1984).[15] And on the other hand, even given context-sensitive causally reliable knowledge, it is not as if my capacity

---
15 This is also called "new evil demon" skepticism, in order to distinguish it from classical Cartesian evil demon skepticism, which postulates the conceivable possibility of falsity-makers in *the actual world* for any and all seemingly true beliefs.

for veridical, direct sense perception, together with my capacity to detect salient iPhone breakdowns, completely convincingly, intrinsically compellingly, or self-evidently "locks onto" the context-sensitive causal sequence that ties my well-functioning iPhone to the US standard atomic clock (or whatever) that grounds it. That is, even given context-sensitive causally reliable knowledge, it is not as if I have *rational insight* into the underlying structure of what connects my conscious-evidence-based reason for believing to the truthmaker of my belief. Indeed, my conscious-evidence-based reason for believing could be epistemically flawed in various ways, including greater or lesser irrelevance to the situation at hand, greater or lesser superficiality, greater or lesser triviality, or more or less obvious formal inconsistency with other beliefs I hold.

This point is also brought out clearly, although in a sense unintentionally, by Keith Lehrer's well-known "Truetemp" thought-experiment, whose explicit aim is to show that context-sensitive causally reliable true belief is not the same as knowledge (Lehrer, 1990: pp. 163-164). Lehrer's thought-experiment describes a context-sensitive causally reliable temperature-reading device connected (unbeknownst to Mr. Truetemp himself) to Mr. Truetemp's brain, that together with his brain yields a context-sensitive causally reliable cognitive capacity or mechanism for his beliefs about temperature. This example, in turn, is supposed to trigger our judgment that Mr. Truetemp's context-sensitive causally reliable true beliefs about temperature are *not* knowledge. But in fact, what the Truetemp case shows, just like my iPhone case, is simply that context-sensitive, causally reliable Low-Bar knowledge, even though it is pretty good, is *not* the same as High-Bar knowledge. Otherwise put, my context-sensitive causally reliable perceptual knowledge that it is 7:00am by looking at my iPhone is not *essentially reliable*, as it is in the paradigmatically good epistemic case where I know that

$$3+4=7, \text{ i.e., } ||| + |||| = |||||||$$

via basic authoritative mathematical rational intuition.

In this way, what the Gettier counterexamples and their variant cases show us are four distinct synthetic a priori philosophical truths about knowledge. **First**, High-Bar knowledge is not the same as Low-Bar knowledge, that is, High-Bar knowledge is not the same as Low-Bar justified true belief. **Second**, High-Bar knowledge is also not the same as context-sensitive causally reliable Low-Bar knowledge, that is, High-Bar knowledge is not the same as context-sensitive causally reliable Low-Bar justified true belief, which in turn is distinct from mere Low-Bar knowledge, or Low-Bar justified true belief. **Third**, High-Bar knowledge is the same as High-Bar justified true belief, or essentially reliable justified true belief. **Fourth** and finally, Low-Bar knowledge is the same as Low-Bar justified true belief; context-sensitive causally reliable Low-Bar knowledge is the same as context-sensitive causally reliable true belief; and High-Bar knowledge is the same as High-Bar justified true belief. Therefore, provided we keep our bar-levels straight, knowledge really is justified true belief.

The leading notion of cognitive-semantics-&-human-knowledge-only-within-The-Grip-of-The-Given/categorical epistemology is what I'm calling *High-Bar knowledge*. Any theory of knowledge that adequately establishes an inherent or intrinsic connection between the sufficient conscious-evidence-based reason for a believer's assertion of her belief-claim, via her properly-functioning cognitive capacities or mechanisms, and the truth of her belief, also shows that this is an essentially reliable belief. This theory thereby constitutes an adequate philosophical explanation of the highest kind of knowledge, which in turn counts as the highest good, or *summum bonum*, of epistemology. And that's High-Bar knowledge.

Furthermore, the cognitive-semantics-&-human-knowledge-only-within-The-Grip-of-The-Given/categorical epistemology-driven conception of a philosophical explanation of the normatively best and highest kind of knowledge—that it adequately establishes an inherent or intrinsic connection between the sufficient conscious-evidence-based reason for a believer's assertion of her belief-claim, via her properly-functioning cognitive capacities or mechanisms, and the truth of her belief—is (perhaps surprisingly) largely compatible with Williamson's highly plausible "knowledge first" approach to epistemology in *Knowledge and its Limits* (Williamson, 2000: p. v). There are three reasons for large measure of compatibility, all of which flow directly from cognitive-semantics-&-human-knowledge-only-within-The-Grip-of-The-Given/categorical epistemology.

First, High-Bar knowledge—i.e., intrinsically compelling, cognitively virtuous, essentially reliable justified true belief—which is the normatively highest kind of knowledge, is the primitive, non-analyzable, irreducible, immanently structured, and categorically normative highest good and ideal standard of rational human cognition with which epistemology is fundamentally concerned. **Second**, High-Bar justification contains the three basic elements of (i) intrinsically compelling, cognitively virtuous, essentially reliable justification, (ii) truth, and (iii) belief, and these are the metaphysically non-detachable, essentially-related elements of High-Bar Knowledge. And **third**, a priori knowledge via basic authoritative objectively necessarily true rational intuition is the perfection of our capacities for rational human cognition, and therefore counts as the normative paradigm of High-Bar Knowledge.

Or in other words, cognitive-semantics-&-human-knowledge-only-within-The-Grip-of-The-Given/categorical epistemology is a perfectionist Kantian morality of essentially embodied rational human cognition. No doubt, Williamson would sharply disagree with me about the robust rational normativity of authentic a priori knowledge. But at the same time, we do both hold that knowledge as such is a primitive, non-analyzable, irreducible cognitive phenomenon with which all serious explanatory epistemology must begin, even though I would contend, contra Williamson, that the non-analyzability of the proper parts of the cognitive phenomenon of knowledge is explained by their being connected *synthetically a priori*. Furthermore, we do agree that knowledge is inherently mentalistic and factive. So there's significant philosophical common ground shared between us, alongside some important differences. Leaving aside those differences, however, I strongly believe that the defensible core of Williamson's "knowledge first" approach to epistemology can in fact be traced back directly to Kant (Hanna, 2006a: ch. 7).

More generally, in any case, cognitive-semantics-&-human-knowledge-only-within-The-Grip-of-The-Given/categorical epistemology is both non-trivially similar to and also non-trivially dissimilar to other recent and contemporary approaches to epistemology. On the one hand, cognitive-semantics-&-human-knowledge-only-within-The-Grip-of-The-Given/categorical epistemology shares with virtue epistemology (Brady and Pritchard, 2003; Fairweather and Zagzebski, 2001; Sosa, 2007) and other recent or contemporary practically-oriented approaches to epistemology (for example, Stanley, 2005) the basic idea that both the ascription and also the actual occurrence of human knowledge have the following characteristics: they are inherently sensitive to our properly-functioning cognitive capacities or mechanisms; inherently motivated by rational human interests; inherently governed by rational human ideals, values, and reasons (i.e., norms); and ultimately grounded on the real fact of (or in at least the non-eliminable conception of ourselves as having) free agency. But on the other hand, cognitive-semantics-&-human-knowledge-only-within-The-Grip-of-The-Given/categorical epistemology sharply differs from other practically-oriented approaches to human knowledge in the following respect. According to cognitive-semantics-&-human-knowledge-only-within-The-Grip-of-The-Given/categorical epistemology, the principles of rational human animal knowledge are grounded on categorically normative principles, which in turn are all ultimately subsumable under the Categorical Imperative. Hence the governing norms of knowledge are explicitly and irreducibly categorical—i.e., unconditional, strictly universal, non-instrumental, and a priori—and also ultimately constrained by the Categorical Imperative.

Correspondingly, it should also be fully noted that the fundamental distinction in cognitive-semantics-&-human-knowledge-only-within-The-Grip-of-The-Given/categorical epistemology between High-Bar justification and knowledge, and Low-Bar justification and knowledge, is itself only a specification of a more general and necessary structure of human rationality, which I call *Two-Dimensional rational normativity*. Two-Dimensional rational normativity is the fact that the conditions on normative evaluations of rationality fall into two importantly different kinds:

(1) **Low-Bar rational normativity:** the necessary and sufficient conditions for minimal or nonideal rationality, which include the possession of online, uncompromised versions of all the cognitive and practical capacities constitutive of intentional agency, and

(2) **High-Bar rational normativity:** the necessary and sufficient conditions for maximal or ideal rationality, which include all the necessary and sufficient conditions for Low-Bar rational normativity as individually necessary but not jointly sufficient conditions, and also include the perfection, or correct and full self-realization, of all the cognitive and practical capacities constitutive of intentional agency, as individually necessary and jointly sufficient conditions.

Non-satisfaction of the conditions for *Low*-Bar rational normativity entails non-rationality and non-agency. As we'll see below, in a certain special range of cases of the non-satisfaction of the conditions for Low-Bar knowledge, Low-Bar rational normativity further allows for the possibility of what, following Frank Hofmann (2014),[16] I will call *Non-Conceptual Knowledge*, in non-human animals such as cats or horses, and also in non-rational human animals such as infants or unfortunate adult victims of various pathological cognitive conditions. Nevertheless, by sharp contrast, it is not the case that non-satisfaction of the conditions of *High*-Bar rational normativity entails either non-rationality or non-agency.

This point, in turn, makes it possible to see very clearly the fundamental flaw in *One-Dimensional* theories of rational normativity, no matter how plausible and sophisticated these theories might otherwise be (for example, Korsgaard, 2009). According to a One-Dimensional theory, any failure to meet the ideal standards of rational normativity entails non-rationality, non-agency, and non-responsibility. To be sure, on a sophisticated One-Dimensional theory, there can be a continuum of degrees of rationality with a variety of significant thresholds along the way. But the basic fact remains that in a One-Dimensional framework, any degree of rationality short of the ideal standards is to that extent *non*-rational. Or in other words, if you are not ideally or perfectly rational, then you are a rationally defective or irrational animal, and off the hook. For example, if you fail to know in the highest sense (i.e., if you fail to have High-Bar justified true belief), then you are not in any sense a rational or responsible cognitive agent, although you may approach that epistemically blessed state to a greater or lesser degree. Or if you fail to act in the practically or morally highest way (i.e., if you fail to have a *good will* in Kant's sense), then you are not in any sense a rational or responsible practical or moral agent, although you may approach that morally blessed state to a greater or lesser degree.

Disastrously, these results of One-Dimensionalism play directly into the hands of radical cognitive, practical, and moral skeptics, since as a matter of fact no actual rational human animal ever manages to meet *all* or even *most* of the High-Bar standards of rational normativity, but instead is doing extremely well indeed if she ever manages to meet *some* of them—for example, successfully performing some basic authoritative a priori objectively necessarily true rational intuitions in mathematics, logic, or philosophy. How convenient for the radical skeptic, then, that most or all of us, most or all of the time, turn out to be irrational animals. Perhaps even more disastrously, these results also play directly into the hands of "human, all too human" intentional agents looking for a fast track out of their everyday cognitive and practical difficulties in a thoroughly nonideal actual natural world. How convenient for them that falling short of rational perfection should entail the suspension of responsibility: If rationality—like God—is dead, then everything is permitted, and they can take the nihilist's way out, like the pathetically wicked character Smerdyakov in *The Brothers Karamazov*:

---

16 Hofmann compellingly argues that non-conceptual perception not only is regularly called "knowledge" by cognitive scientists, and furthermore satisfies four basic conditions on any cognitive activity that plays the "knowledge role," but also grounds conceptual/doxastic perceptual knowledge and justification *by putting the cognitive subject in a position to have them.*

> "Take that money away with you, sir," Smerdyakov said with a sigh.
>
> "Of course, I'll take it! But why are you giving it to me if you committed a murder to get it?" Ivan asked, looking at him with intense surprise.
>
> "I don't want it at all," Smerdyakov said in a shaking voice, with a wave of the hand. "I did have an idea of starting a new life in Moscow, but that was just a dream, sir, and mostly because 'everything is permitted'. This you did teach me, sir, for you talked to me a lot about such things: for if there's no everlasting God, there's no such thing as virtue, and there's no need of it at all.
>
> Yes, sir, you were right about that. That's the way I reasoned." (Dostoyevsky, 1958: vol. 2, p. 74)

For these reasons, then, it's clear that One-Dimensional theories of rational normativity are false.

In The Two-Dimensional theory, however, things are very different. Satisfaction of the conditions for Low-Bar rational normativity is a necessary and sufficient condition of the cognitive, practical, and moral *responsibility* of intentional agents, but it does not guarantee that any of the further conditions of High-Bar rational normativity are actually satisfied. In other words, it is fully possible for an intentional agent to be minimally and nonideally rational, but in a bad or wrong way, to any degree of badness or wrongness, all the way down to the lowest limiting case of cognitive or practical monstrosity within its kind. For example, at any point short of the limiting case of an utter disregard for, and a complete inability to heed, any and all canons of reasonable belief, truth, and validity/consistency in logical reasoning—at any point short of sheer madness—the intentional agent remains cognitively responsible to some degree. So too at any point short of the limiting case of an utter disregard for, and a complete inability to heed, any and all moral principles grounded on the dignity of persons, and any and all canons of validity/consistency in practical reasoning—at any point short of sheer sociopathy or the complete disintegration of agentive coherence—the intentional agent remains morally and practically responsible to some degree.

Correspondingly, it's also fully possible for an intentional agent to be minimally and nonideally rational in a good or right way, to any degree of goodness or rightness, all the way up to the highest limiting case of cognitive or practical perfection within its kind—for example, successfully performing some basic authoritative a priori objectively necessarily true rational intuitions in mathematics, logic, or philosophy—for all of which, again, the intentional agent is also fully cognitively and practically responsible.

As my discussion so far implies, explicitly situating cognitive-semantics-&-human-knowledge-only-within-The-Grip-of-The-Given/categorical epistemology within the framework of Two-Dimensional rational normativity yields a fourfold classification of different, basic, normatively-graded kinds of cognition. This fourfold classification comes clearly into view when we recognize the notion of context-sensitive causal reliability, together with the fact that certain kinds of cognitive acts or states in non-human animals, and in non-rational human animals, fall short of Low Bar knowledge, yet still include essentially non-conceptual content and what I call *direct sense perception* (Hanna, 2015a: chs. 1-2) and also a context-sensitive, causally reliable, cognitive mechanism for evidentially connecting sense perception with its worldly objects. So non-human animals, non-rational human animals, and rational human animals share the minimally basic epistemic capacities, and by exercising those capacities well, they thereby can all achieve Non-Conceptual Knowledge.

In a nutshell, my rationale for this claim is grounded on the following three points. **First**, direct sense perception based on essentially non-conceptual content is perceptual knowledge by acquaintance. **Second**, perceptual knowledge by acquaintance is genuine *knowledge* in at least three important senses, namely (i) that it guarantees an essentially reliable, non-accidental connection between cognition and the world, (ii) that it involves the successful exercise of the minimally basic epistemic capacities, and (iii) that its cognitive phenomenology is maximally evidential in that context. **Third**, therefore direct sense perception based on essentially non-conceptual content is also genuine knowledge in at least three important senses, even though it fails the belief condition and the truth-condition on Low Bar knowledge and High Bar Knowledge.

More explicitly, then, the larger Two-Dimensional framework that comprehends categorical epistemology provides for a non-conceptual, non-doxastic, non-alethic, and distinctively different fourth kind of minimally basic epistemic activity, namely Non-Conceptual Knowledge, to go along with mere Low-Bar knowledge, with context-sensitive causally reliable Low-Bar knowledge, and with High-Bar knowledge.

Non-Conceptual Knowledge is similar in several important ways to what Ernest Sosa calls "animal knowledge" (Sosa, 2001) but with two crucial additions: **first**, Non-Conceptual Knowledge is cognitively driven by essentially non-conceptual content, and **second**, it both occurs and also makes sense only within the larger, four-levelled, Two-Dimensional explanatory framework of categorical epistemology, whereas Sosa's explanatory framework utilizes a more compact binary contrast between animal knowledge and *reflective* knowledge (Sosa, 2009). As such, some classes of cases of Sosa's animal knowledge fall under Non-Conceptual Knowledge, and some of them fall under one or another of the kinds of Low-Bar knowledge. Correspondingly, some classes of cases of Sosa's reflective knowledge fall under the more Internalistically-sophisticated kinds of Low-Bar knowledge, and some of them fall under High-Bar knowledge. All things considered, I do think that Sosa's "virtue reliabilist" account is in many ways fundamentally correct, but also that the more complex structure of cognitive-semantics-&-human-knowledge-only-within-The-Grip-of-The-Given/categorical epistemology, embedded within a cognitive-semantic theory of essentially non-conceptual content and conceptual content, ultimately does more explanatory work, and also characterizes the highest kind of knowledge more completely.

In what follows in this sub-section, by *a contingently reliable cognitive capacity or mechanism* I mean a cognitive capacity or mechanism that tracks truth in the actual world. The notion of a contingently reliable cognitive capacity or mechanism can then be put alongside the two notions of a context-sensitive causally reliable cognitive capacity or mechanism and an essentially reliable cognitive capacity or mechanism, that I previously formulated.

Granting all that, then here are contextual-definition-style formulations of the four basic kinds of knowledge recognized by categorical epistemology:

(i) Non-Conceptual Knowledge: Perception P in an animal subject S is Non-Conceptual Knowledge if and only if (ia) P is based on essentially non-conceptual content, and (ib) S possesses a properly-functioning and context-sensitive causally reliable cognitive capacity or mechanism that yields S's conscious evidence E for P.

(ii) Low-Bar Knowledge: Belief B in an animal subject S is Low-Bar Knowledge if and only if (iia) B is true, (iib) S possesses a properly-functioning and at least contingently reliable cognitive capacity or mechanism that yields S's conscious evidence E for B, and (iic) S has a reason for asserting B based on E, i.e., S has a Low-Bar justification for B.

(iii) Context-Sensitive Causally Reliable Low-Bar Knowledge: Belief B in an animal subject S is context-sensitive causally reliable Low-Bar Knowledge if and only if (iiia) B is true, (iiib) S possesses a properly-functioning and context-sensitive causally reliable cognitive capacity or mechanism that yields S's conscious evidence E for B, and (iiic) S has a reason for asserting B based on E, i.e., S has a Low-Bar justification for B.

(iv) High-Bar Knowledge: Belief B in an animal subject S is High-Bar Knowledge if and only if (iva) B is true, (ivb) S possesses a properly-functioning and essentially reliable cognitive capacity or mechanism that yields S's intrinsically compelling conscious evidence E for B, and (ivc) S has a sufficient reason for asserting B based on E, i.e., S has a High-Bar justification for B.

This fourfold classification of kinds of cognition combines elements of epistemic internalism, epistemic externalism, virtue epistemology, and contextualism (Steup and Neta, 2020) within the progressively larger frameworks of categorical epistemology and Two-Dimensional rational normativity, while also sustaining the classical thesis that (conceptual, doxastic, rational) knowledge is justified true belief. In this connection, it should be specifically noted that although Non-Conceptual Knowledge is not in any way subject to Gettier considerations—that is, not subject to the possibility of a *merely* accidental or contingent connection between conscious evidence and the world—nevertheless Non-Conceptual Knowledge is not conceptual and not doxastic, and therefore not "in the logical space of reasons" (Sellars, 1963a: p. 169,

§17, §36) or directly subject to the constraints of of even Low-Bar rational normativity. So Non-Conceptual Knowledge flows from the successful exercise of minimally basic epistemic capacities, and is knowledge in a genuine sense—namely, the sense in which "knowledge by acquaintance" is genuine knowledge. Moroever, Non-Conceptual Knowledge constitutes a kind of essentially and also context-sensitively causally reliable animal cognition that grounds all the other kinds of knowledge. Furthermore, Non-Conceptual Knowledge anticipates some of the necessary features of rational human knowledge in the normatively highest sense. Nevertheless, Non-Conceptual Knowledge is at most pre-rational and proto-rational. Therefore, strictly speaking, it's neither Low-Bar knowledge nor High-Bar knowledge.

At the same time, however, although Low-Bar Knowledge is indeed "in the logical space of reasons," and thereby subject to the constraints of rational normativity, it's open both to Gettier considerations and also to global skeptical worries. More specifically, in some introspectively indistinguishable conceivably possible worlds the very same conscious-evidence-based reason for S's belief is connected to a falsity-maker, not a truth-maker, as per new evil demon skepticism (Cohen, 1984).

Thus Low-Bar Knowledge falls well short of knowledge in the normatively highest sense. By sharp contrast to both Non-Conceptual Knowledge and Low-Bar Knowledge, however, High-Bar Knowledge is not only "in the logical space of reasons," and thereby subject to the constraints of rational normativity, and both contingently and causally reliable. It is also essentially reliable, as well as sufficiently justified by a conscious-evidence-based reason, via a properly-functioning cognitive capacity or mechanism. High Bar Knowledge is thereby impervious to Gettier worries and to global or radical skepticism alike. Hence, again, High-Bar Knowledge is the highest good or *summum bonum* of epistemology.

Now, what about context-sensitive causally reliable Low-Bar knowledge? If S possesses knowledge in this sense, then S possesses context-sensitive causally reliable Low-Bar *a posteriori knowledge*, which is a pretty good kind of knowledge to have—say, via trustworthy testimony—but at the same time context-sensitive causally reliable Low-Bar knowledge is without complete conviction, intrinsic compellingness, or self-evidence, and also without essential reliability. For one thing, just as with Low-Bar Knowledge, so too with context-sensitive causally reliable Low-Bar knowledge, in some introspectively indistinguishable conceivably possible worlds the very same conscious-evidence-based reason for S's belief is connected to a falsity-maker, not a truth-maker. This possibility leaves context-sensitive causally reliable Low-Bar knowledge wide open to radical or global skepticism. And for another thing, as I pointed out earlier in this sub-section, because context-sensitive causally reliable Low-Bar knowledge does not necessarily include rational insight into the underlying structure of what connects S's conscious-evidence-based reason for believing to the truthmaker of her belief, her conscious-evidence-based reason for believing could be epistemically flawed in various ways, including greater or lesser irrelevance to the situation at hand, greater or lesser superficiality, greater or less triviality, or more or less obvious formal inconsistency with other beliefs she holds. However, by sharp contrast, when I look carefully at this sequence of strokes—

|||||||

—and thereby come to believe that there are seven strokes on the page, then I possess *High-Bar a posteriori knowledge*. This is because my evidence-based reason for believing that there are seven strokes on the page is inherently or intrinsically connected to the truth-maker for that belief, via veridical, direct sense perception. This in turn constitutes an epistemically appropriate, properly-functioning cognitive capacity or mechanism. And the cognitive phenomenology—i.e., the subjectively-experiential specific characters (Bayne and Montague, 2011; Smithies, 2013a, 2013b; and also sections III.2 and III.3 above)—of my perceptual belief is also intrinsically compelling or self-evident.

By another important contrast, when a normal, healthy, minimally linguistically competent 3-year old child comes to believe that 3+4=7 by counting aloud on her fingers, which for her is at best a semi-reliable cognitive process and clearly not mathematical rational intuition, then she possesses *Low-Bar a priori knowledge*.

And by a final important contrast, in the now-familiar case in which I know that

3+4=7, i.e., ||| + |||| = |||||||

via mathematical authoritative rational intuition, then I possess *High-Bar a priori knowledge*, which is the very best and highest of all kinds of knowledge, even better than High-Bar a posteriori knowledge. In so doing, I have thereby achieved membership in the indefinitely large class of cases of knowing that collectively constitute the jewel in the crown of the *summum bonum* of epistemology.

XVII.8.3 PS-Metaphysical-Quietism *versus* Weak Transcendental Idealism

In an important sense, all the philosophical heavy lifting for my argument against The Pittsburgh School has already been done: I've argued that PS-conceptualism is false, that PS-inferentialism is false, and also that the only prima facie strong argument in favor of PS-conceptualism and PS-inferentialism, from The Myth of the Given, has been shown to be unsound because it makes a false assumption, The Myth of The Myth of The Given. So now it remains for me only to criticize the third dogma of The Pittsburgh School, namely, the dogma of metaphysical quietism (Macarthur, 2017; and also section XVII.8 above), which re-activates an idea that Wittgenstein formulated in the *Tractatus* and later re-formulated in the *Investigations*.

Does The Pittsburgh School do metaphysics? The answer is: yes, sort-of, and no.

Yes: Sellars advocates a *scientific naturalist* metaphysics of *materialism*, aka *physicalism*, as per the famous remark that I've quoted several times already:

> [i]n the dimension of describing and explaining the world, science is the measure of all things, of what is that it is, and of what is not that it is not. (Sellars, 1963b: p. 173)

Materialism/physicalism says that everything in the world either logically or nomologically strongly supervenes on fundamentally physical entities, properties, and facts. If everything logically strongly supervenes, then that's *reductive* materialism/ physicalism. If everything nomologically strongly supervenes but doesn't logically supervene, then that's *non-reductive* materialism/physicalism. If a few things—say, conscious states, or rational conceptual states—only non-reductively nomologically strongly supervene, but everything else reductively logically strongly supervenes, then that's reductive materialism/physicalism "or something near enough" (Kim, 2005). Given Sellars's doctrine of The Manifest Image and The Scientific Image, and his view that The Scientific Image is inherently more fundamental than The Manifest Image (Sellars, 1963c), then that "or something near enough" version of reductive materialism/physicalism clearly is Sellars's version of scientific naturalist metaphysics.

Sort-of: On the one hand, from an inferentialist point of view, Brandom rejects any metaphysics that's based on representationalism, and also any scientific naturalist metaphysics of meaning, intentionality, belief, knowledge, and/or logic (Brandom, 2000). But on the other hand, Brandom's inferentialism is a systematic, "full-blooded"[17] theory of meaning, intentionality, belief, knowledge, and logic, and to that extent inferentialism is *somewhat* like a metaphysics.

No: Metaphysical quietism, as explicitly defended by McDowell, aka *PS-metaphysical-quietism*, says this:

> McDowell thinks that a typical philosophical problem has a certain shape: some important feature of ordinary existence (such as the meaningfulness of our words) is made to look impossible (in this case, because of the regress); the task is then to explain how this thing is nevertheless possible and, indeed, real (our words really are meaningful, despite the regress); typically, however, the explanations don't work ….; they leave the important feature of ordinary [rational human] existence looking questionable. For McDowell, good philosophy helps expose these putative problems as only apparent problems by showing that they rest on questionable and optional assumptions. Instead of accepting those problems as real, and then seeking an adequate answer to them (which typically fails), the goal is to reject the problem by explaining what faulty assumptions it rests on. Thereby, we restore the important feature of ordinary [rational human] existence that had been made to seem impossible. This outlook is often called quietism," for it advises us to remain quiet—to resist developing philosophical theories—once faulty and optional assumptions have been indentified and rejected. (Maher, 2012: p. 58)

---

17 This is McDowell's term: see (Maher, 2012: pp. 75-77; McDowell, 2009c).

Otherwise put, McDowell's PS-metaphysical-quietism says that all metaphysical theories should be eschewed by philosophy in favor of (i) a negative critique of metaphysics, followed by (ii) the restorative policy of leaving the manifestly real world of "ordinary [rational human] existence" alone. And the primary argument for PS-metaphysical-quietism is that metaphysics—whether *classical Rationalist* metaphysics as per Descartes, Spinoza, or Leibniz, *classical Idealist* metaphysics as per Berkeley, scientific naturalist materialist/physicalist metaphysics as per Sellars, or "full-blooded" systematic theorizing about meaning, etc., as per Brandom—inevitably leads to confusion, contradiction, and paradox.

Because I've already argued against the logical strong supervenience of categorical normativity on contingent physical facts or natural causal laws, hence on anything that can be explained by natural science, thereby rejecting Sellars's scientific naturalist materialist/physicalist metaphysics, and because I've already criticized Brandom's sort-of metaphysics of inferentialism, I'm going to focus for the rest of this sub-section on replying to McDowell's PS-metaphysical-quietism.

On the contrary to PS-metaphysical-quietism, in section XV.1 above I've presented and defended an alternative, radical-Kantian metaphysical view I call *weak transcendental idealism*, aka WTI, that emphatically and explicitly *isn't* either classical Rationalist metaphysics, classical Idealist metaphysics, scientific naturalist materialist/physicalist metaphysics, or "full-blooded" systematic theorizing about meaning, etc., and indeed explicitly *rejects* all those disastrously wrongheaded versions of metaphysics. Positively formulated, WTI is *a metaphysics of the rational human condition* (Hanna, 2015a: chs. 6-8, 2018a, 2018b, 2021d). So I'm saying, in direct reply to McDowell, that instead of "leaving 'ordinary [rational human] existence' alone," *we should try to explain it*, and thereby have a priori rational human insight into our own nature, scope, and limits, hence satisfying the classical Socratic injunction to "know thyself."

More specifically, WTI is my interpretation and philosophical updating of a doctrine that Kant presented and defended in the *Critique of Pure Reason* in order to explain the real possibility of *a priori* or non-empirical analytic and synthetic necessary truth and knowledge in logic, mathematics, metaphysics, and natural science, as well as the real possibility of *a posteriori* or empirical/ observational contingent truth and knowledge in natural science. According to Kant, a mental representation is *transcendental* when it's either part of, or derived from, our non-empirical (hence a priori) innately specified spontaneous cognitive capacities (*CPR* A11/B25, *Prol* 4: 373n.). Then, as I argued in section XV.1 above, transcendental idealism can be stated as a two-part philosophical equation, namely, **transcendental idealism = representational transcendentalism + cognitive idealism**, as per the following definitions:

> **(i) Representational Transcendentalism**: necessarily, all the forms or structures of rational human cognition are generated a priori by the empirically-triggered, yet stimulus-underdetermined, activities of our innately specified spontaneous cognitive capacities, i.e., cognitive competences, cognitive faculties, or cognitive powers.

> **(ii) Cognitive Idealism:** necessarily, all the proper objects of rational human cognition are nothing but sensory appearances or phenomena, i.e., mind-dependent, spatiotemporal, directly perceivable, manifestly real objects, and never things-in-themselves or noumena, i.e., mind-independent, non-sensible, non-spatiotemporal, real essences constituted by intrinsic non-relational properties. (*CPR* A369 and *Prol* 4: 293-294, 375)

Now (i) + (ii) also = Kant's "Copernican revolution" in metaphysics:

> Up to now it has been assumed that all our cognition must conform to the objects; but all attempts to find out something about them *a priori* through concepts that would extend our cognition have, on this presupposition, come to nothing. Hence let us once try whether we do not get farther with the problems of metaphysics by assuming that the objects must conform to our cognition, which would agree better with the requested possibility of an *a priori* cognition of them, which is to establish something about objects before they are given to us. This would be just like the first thoughts of Copernicus.... (*CPR* Bxvi),

which I rationally reconstruct as **The Conformity Thesis**:

> It's not the case that rational human minds passively conform to the objects they cognize, as in classical Rationalism and classical Empiricism. On the contrary, necessarily, all the proper objects of rational human cognition conform to—i.e., they have the same form or structure as, or are isomorphic to—the forms or structures that are non-empirically generated by our innately specified spontaneous cognitive capacities. So necessarily, the essential forms or structures of the manifestly real world we cognize are mind-dependent.

In this way, all versions of transcendental idealism hold that the manifestly real world we directly perceive conforms to the non-empirical forms or structures of our innately specified cognitive capacities in some modally robust sense.

I also argued in section XV.1 above that orthodox Kantians are also committed to *Strong Transcendental Idealism*, aka STI, which says: (i) things-in-themselves (aka "noumena," or Really Real things, i.e., things as they could exist in a "lonely" way, altogether independently of rational human minds or anything else, by virtue of their intrinsic non-relational properties) really exist and cause our perceptions, although rational human cognizers only ever perceive mere appearances or subjective phenomena, (ii) rational human cognizers actually impose the non-empirical structures of their innate cognitive capacities onto the manifestly real world they cognize, i.e., necessarily, all the essential forms or structures of the proper objects of human cognition are literally type-identical to the a priori forms or structures that are non-empirically generated by our innately specified spontaneous cognitive capacities, and (iii) necessarily, if either all rational human cognizers went out of existence or all minded beings of any kind went out of existence, then so would the manifestly real world they cognize, and if either no rational human cognizers had ever existed or no minded beings of any kind had ever existed, then the manifestly real world would never have existed.But, again, as I argued in section XV.1, I think that STI is clearly objectively false. More specifically now, I think that it's clearly objectively false that if either all actual human minds, including mine, or all other kinds of minds, went out of existence, then the manifestly real world would necessarily go out of existence too. I think that it is clearly false that, for example, the actual existence of Pike's Peak (a 14,000 foot mountain near Colorado Springs, CO, USA, with a cog railway that runs right to the summit) strictly depends on the actual existence of human minds, including mine, or on the actual existence of any other kinds of minds. Clearly, I think, Pike's Peak can exist even if everyone, and every minded being, including myself, does not actually exist, and in fact I think that Pike's Peak actually existed millions of years before any conscious minds of any kind existed, including of course the conscious minds of all rational human animals, obviously including mine. In this way, clearly, a great many things, including mountains like Pike's Peak, exist objectively—for example, shoes, ships, sealing wax, cabbages, kings, seas that do not boil, and pigs without wings. They are, all of them, neither subjective (i.e., strictly dependent on individual minds of any kind) nor relative (i.e., strictly dependent on cultures or societies of any kind). It's clear that they are all objectively manifestly real, and to that extent, mind-independent. So STI is clearly objectively false. QED.

On the contrary to STI, I think that WTI is clearly objectively true. WTI says: (i) that things-in-themselves/noumena are logically possible, but at the same time it is knowably unknowable and unprovable whether things-in-themselves or noumena exist or not, hence for the purposes of an adequate anthropocentric or "human-faced" metaphysics, epistemology, and ethics, they can be ignored (**radical agnosticism and methodological eliminativism about things-in-themselves/noumena**), (ii) that necessarily, all the proper objects of rational human cognition have the same forms or structures as—i.e., they are isomorphic to—the forms or structures that are non-empirically generated by our innately-specified spontaneous cognitive capacities, but at the same time those manifestly real worldly forms or structures are not literally type-identical to those a priori cognitive forms or structures (**the isomorphism-without-type-identity thesis**), (iii) that it's a necessary condition of the existence of the manifestly real world that if some rational human animals *were* to exist in that world, then they *would* know that world *a priori* and also *a posteriori*, at least to some extent (**the counterfactual knowability thesis**), and (iv) that the manifestly real world has at some earlier times existed without rational human minded animals, or any other minded beings, to know it, and could exist even if no rational human minded animals, or any other minded beings, ever existed to know it, even though some rational human animals now actually exist in that manifestly real world (for example, I [R.H.]), who do in fact know it *a priori* (for example, by my knowing some simple necessary truths of logic and mathematics, and also by my knowing that necessarily, if I'm thinking, then I actually exist) and also *a posteriori*, at least to some extent (**the existential thesis**).

Here's a slightly more precise formulation of WTI's crucial thesis (iii), the counterfactual knowability thesis:

$$Ap \Box \ (\forall x)\ (\exists y)\ [MRWx \rightarrow \{(RHAy\ \&\ MRWy)\ \Box \rightarrow Kyx\}]$$

Definitions:

Ap □ = a priori necessarily

P □ → Q = If P were the case, then Q would be the case

MRWx = x belongs to the manifestly real world

MRWy = y belongs to the manifestly real world

RHAy = y is a rational human animal

Kyx = y knows x *a priori* and also *a posteriori*, at least to some extent

Natural Language Translation:

A priori necessarily, anything that belongs to the manifestly real world is such that if some rational human animals were to exist in that world, then they would know that thing and that world *a priori* and also *a posteriori*, at least to some extent.

And here are two crucial implications of this thesis. **First**, the counterfactual knowability thesis holds even if *no* rational human minded animals, or any other minded beings, *actually exist, or ever actually existed*.[18] **Second**, if anything is such that rational human minded animals are *unable to know it, at least to some extent*—for example, things-in-themselves or noumena—then that thing does *not* belong to the manifestly real world.

The first crucial implication conveys the weak mind-independence and ontic integrity of the manifestly real world. The manifestly real world is what it is, even if no minds actually exist or ever actually existed. And the second crucial implication conveys the weak mind-dependence and inherent knowability of the manifestly real world. The manifestly real world is what it is, *only in relation to actual or possible rational "human, all-too-human" animal minds like ours*. The single upshot of the two crucial implications is that the manifestly real world is as real as anything can ever possibly be, on the reasonable assumption that some *epistemic-luck-resistant, global-new-evil-demon-skepticism-resistant* rational human knowledge of that world is actual or really possible. Or more precisely, and perhaps most surprisingly of all for anti-Kantians: any epistemically tenable realism—that is, any realism that's truly capable of avoiding *epistemic luck*, i.e., the merely accidental

---

18 It's generally believed by orthodox Kantians and anti-Kantians alike, that all Kantians must accept STI. For example, in his (1998: p. 9), Katz claims that "however Kant's transcendental idealism is understood, it locates the ground of [real] facts within ourselves in at least the minimal sense that it entails that such facts could not have existed if we (or other intelligent beings) had not existed" (underlining added). But in fact that's not correct: although this claim is true of STI, it's false of WTI.

connection between truth and conscious belief, and *new evil demon skepticism*, i.e., the globalized Gettier-style worry that in a nearby possible world we'd have the very same beliefs and the same apparent evidence for holding those beliefs, but they'd all be false, hence we aren't rationally justified in holding those beliefs in the actual world (Cohen, 1984)—requires WTI.

XVII.8.4 Concluding UnPittsburghian Prelude to a Radical Kantian Philosophy of the Future

In sub-sections XVII.8.2 and XVII.8.3, I've provided a slew of negative arguments *against* The Pittsburgh School and their heroic attempt to save the post-classical Analytic tradition from its fate—thereby scoring *a big red zero for conduct* at The Pittsburgh School—and also a corresponding slew of positive arguments *for* a radical Kantian alternative. Moreover, insofar as The Pittsburgh School is itself explicitly a brand of post-classical Analytic philosophy, then my contra-Pittsburghian and pro-radical-Kantian arguments significantly contribute to a more general argument *against* post-classical Analytic philosophy and *for* a broadly and radically Kantian philosophy of the future. More pointedly and precisely, this philosophy of the future shouldn't be *a Pittsburghian owl of Minerva*, fully embedded within the social institution of professional academic philosophy—hence fully caged by and under the control of the hegemonic ideology and coercive authoritarian norms of the neoliberal professional academy—stretching its wings only with the dying of the light, and always only interpreting the world and never changing it (Hegel, 1952: pp. 12-13; Marx, 1964: p. 69). On the contrary and instead, this philosophy of the future should be *a radical Kantian phoenix* that's a life-changing, world-changing metaphysics of the rational human condition (Hanna, 2017e), liberated from the controlling ideology and norms of the professional academy, stretching its wings only with the sunburst of a new dawn, that can arise from the ashes of the 140-year Analytic tradition, over the next two decades. Only that would be fully worthy of Vigo's legacy:

> [In *Zéro de Conduite*] there are also reminders of the life of Vigo's father [Miguel Almereyda] and the experience of the Children's Prison of La Petite Rocquette, which Almereyda had described in … *L'Assiette au Beurre*. And when the persecuted boy Tabard turns and bursts out "Monsieur le professeur, je vous dis merde!" he echoes a famous challenge addressed to the government which Almereyda had published in *La Guerre Sociale*, headed in large type, JE VOUS DIS MERDE. (Reddbrek, 2016)

XVIII. Epilogue: The New Poverty of Philosophy and Its Second Copernican Revolution

> Now, the power to judge autonomously—that is, freely (according to principles of thought in general)—is called reason. So the philosophy faculty, because it must answer for the truth of the teachings it is to adopt, or even allow, must be conceived as free and subject only to laws given by reason, not by the government. (*CF* 7: 27)

> The civil (*bürgerliche*) status of a contradiction, or its status in civil life: there is the philosophical problem. (*PI* §125)

> What is your aim in philosophy? —To show the fly the way out of the fly-bottle. (*PI* §309, translation slightly modified)

> The task [of understanding free will and agency] requires some reflection on the organizational principles of living creatures, for it is only through such reflection … that we can start to understand where the difference really lies between, on the one hand those things that are true agents, and, on the other, mere machines, entities that nothing will ever be up to, however impressive they may be…. I am exceedingly hopeful that the next few years will see the beginnings of a revolution in our conception of the human person, as philosophical and everyday conceptions of the scientific picture of the world are freed from outdated Newtonian ideas and begin to take more note, both of the complexities of science as it really is and of the undeniable fact of our animal nature. (Steward, 2012: pp. 198-199)

XVIII.1 Introduction

Karl Marx's 1847 book, *The Poverty of Philosophy*, a scathing attack on the economic and political ideas of the French anarchist Pierre-Joseph Proudhon, is notable primarily for wickedly witty title, which brilliantly flips the title of Proudhon's 1846 book, *The Philosophy of Poverty*. In a 1956 review of an English-language edition of Marx's book, the economist Joan Robinson wrote:

> The entertainment value…is not great. There is no wit in *The Poverty of Philosophy* apart from its title; Proudhon's ideas were confused enough to begin with, and Marx's presentation of them makes them totally unseizable, so that there is little sport to be got out of following the argument. (Robinson, 1956: pp. 334-335)

So much for Marx for the purposes of this concluding chapter, or more properly speaking, epilogue—except for one passing reference in section XVIII.5. In this epilogue, I want only *to re-cycle Marx's excellent title* in order to formulate and defend two theses. The **first** thesis is I what I call *The New Poverty of Philosophy*, which says this:

1. So-called "hard" problems in recent and contemporary philosophy are actually *institutional artifacts* of Analytic philosophy since 1912—the year in which Russell's immensely influential book, *The Problems of Philosophy* first appeared—and more specifically, they're institutional artifacts of the ideologically disciplined social-institutional structure of mainstream Anglo-American professional academic post-classical Analytic philosophy since the end of World War II, and especially since 1985.

And the **second** thesis is what I call *Philosophy's Second Copernican Revolution*, which says this:

2. In order to end and reverse The New Poverty of Philosophy, two fundamental paradigm shifts are required: **first**, *a radical Kantian metaphilosophical paradigm shift*: instead of uncritically assuming that philosophy is really possible only *inside* the professional academy, we critically postulate that philosophy is really possible only *outside* the professional academy, and **second**, *a radical Kantian metaphysical paradigm shift*: instead uncritically assuming a *natural mechanist* conception of the world, we critically postulate a *Kantian neo-organicist* conception of the world.

My conception of "The New Poverty of Philosophy" is a way of reinterpreting and updating Wittgenstein's deep insight that philosophy as he knew it by 1950—that is, Analytic philosophy on the cusp of the transition from classical Analysis to post-classical Analysis—is, in a cognitive, emotional, moral, and political sense, just like a fly buzzing around and around, forever trapped inside a fly-bottle. Correspondingly, my conception of "ending and reversing the new poverty of philosophy" is also a way of reinterpreting and updating Wittgenstein's deep insight that

> the clarity that we are aiming at is indeed *complete* clarity. But that simply means that the [hard] philosophical problems [as per, especially, Russell's *The Problems of Philosophy*] should *completely* disappear. The real discovery is one that makes me capable of stopping doing philosophy when I want to. —The one that gives philosophy peace, so that it is no longer tormented by questions which bring *itself* into question. (*PI* §133)

And finally, as I've indicated, my conception of "Philosophy's Second Copernican Revolution" not only embeds those reinterpreted and updated Wittgensteinian metaphilosophical ideas within the framework of a radically Kantian philosophical context, but also adumbrates *a philosophy of the future*—Kantian neo-organicism—that can and should emerge over the next forty years of the 21st century.

XVIII.2 Wittgenstein's Philosophy of Philosophy Revisited

In the *Tractatus*, early Wittgenstein wrote:

The general form of propositions is: Such-and-such is the case. (*TLP* 4.5)

And in the *Philosophical Investigations*, later Wittgenstein wrote:

> (*Tractatus Logico-Philosophicus*, 4.5): "The general form of propositions is: Such-and-such is the case." —That is the kind of proposition that one repeats to oneself countless times. One thinks that one is tracing the outline of the thing's nature over and over again, and one is merely tracing around the frame through which we look at it. A *picture* held us captive. And we could not get outside it, for it lay in our language and language seemed to repeat it to us inexorably. (*PI* §§114-115, translation slightly modified)

This cognitively enslaving philosophical "picture," in turn, is essentially bound up with *the sublimity of logic*, that is, the idea that philosophically-driven mathematical logic is a *super-science* yielding a priori certainty and noumenal ontological implications:

> In what sense is logic something sublime? For there seemed to pertain to logic a peculiar depth—a universal significance. Logic lay, it seemed, at the bottom of all the sciences and is not meant to concern itself whether what actually happens is this or that. —It takes its rise, not from an interest in the facts of nature, nor from a need to understand causal connections: but from an urge to understand the basis, the essence, of everything empirical. (*PI* §89)

> Thought is surrounded by a halo. —Its essence, logic, presents an order, in fact, the a priori order of the world: that is, the order of *possibilities*, which must be common to both world and thought. But this order, it seems, must be *utterly simple*. It is *prior* to all experience, must run through all experience; no empirical cloudiness or uncertainty can be allowed to affect it—It must rather be of the purest crystal. But this crystal does not appear as an abstraction; but as something concrete, indeed, as the most concrete, as it were the *hardest* thing there is (*Tractatus Logico-Philosophicus*, No. 5.5563). (*PI* §97)

Philosophy conceived as *logical analysis*, in the tradition of Frege, early Russell, and the author of the *Tractatus*, outright asserts or in any case presupposes the sublimity of logic.

Correspondingly, as we saw in chapters V to VII above, according to Wittgenstein's own highly original *Tractarian* version of philosophy, (i) philosophy is the activity (not the theory) of the logical clarification of thoughts, consisting essentially of analytic elucidations, without predetermining the completion of analysis (*TLP* 4.112), and (ii) all philosophy is "critique of language" in that it displays the senselessness of most propositions and questions that have been written about philosophical matters (*TLP* 4.003), and asserts only the propositions of natural science, then recognizes its own propositions as senseless and ends in mystical silence, thereby ending philosophy and at the same time radically transforming one's own life (*TLP* 6.54-7). Importantly, Wittgenstein's conception of logical analysis as having this basic structure, namely—

> logically clarifying activity → critique of language → ending philosophy → radically transforming one's own life

—also has the theoretical virtue of being able to avoid *the paradox of analysis*. According to the paradox of analysis, if an analysis is true then it must be uninformative because merely definitional, hence trivial; but if an analysis is non-trivial and informative, then it must be non-definitional, hence false; so analysis is either trivial or false. But if analysis is essentially a logico-philosophical *process* and not a logico-philosophical *product*, like a proposition or theory, then strictly speaking it's never true or false, so the paradox is avoided.

Nevertheless, if—as we also saw in chapters XI to XIV above—the later Wittgenstein's argument against the sublimity of logic and its intimately associated mind-manacling "pictures" of logic, language, mind, and thought, is sound, then philosophy as logical analysis, whether Fregean/early Russellian *or* early Wittgensteinian, is impossible. So what, according to the later Wittgenstein, does philosophy become *after* the collapse of logical analysis? In fact, as I noted in section IX.4, the later Wittgenstein's conception of philosophy in the *Investigations* has essentially the same basic structure, namely—

> logically clarifying activity → critique of language → ending philosophy → radically transforming one's own life

—as in the *Tractatus*, but now *without the sublimity of logic*. Here, again, are some of the most important texts that spell this out:

> Philosophy is a battle against the bewitchment of our intelligence by means of language. (*PI* §109)

> The results of philosophy are the uncovering of one or another piece of plain nonsense and of bumps that the understanding has got by running its head up against the limits of language. (*PI* §119)

> A philosophical problem has the form: "I don't know my way about." (*PI* §123)

> Philosophy may in no way interfere with the actual use of language; it can in the end only describe it. For it cannot give it any foundation either. It leaves everything as it is. (*PI* §124)

> It is the business of philosophy, not to resolve a contradiction by means of a mathematical or logico-mathematical discovery, but to make it possible for us to get a clear view of the state of mathematics that troubles us: the state of affairs *before* the contradiction I resolved. (And this does not mean that one is sidestepping a difficulty.)

XVIII. Epilogue: The New Poverty of Philosophy and Its Second Copernican Revolution

The fundamental fact here is that we lay down rules, a technique, for a game, and that when we follow the rules, things do not turn out as we had assumed, That we are therefore as it were entangled in our own rules. This entanglement in our rules is what we want to understand (i.e., get a clear view of). It throws light on our concept of *meaning* something. For in those cases things turn out otherwise than we had meant, foreseen. That is just what we say when, for example, a contradiction appears: "I didn't mean I like that."

The civil (*bürgerliche*) status of a contradiction, or its status in civil life: there is the philosophical problem. (*PI* §125)

Philosophy simply puts everything before us, and neither explains nor deduces anything. —Since everything lies open to view, there is nothing to explain. For what is hidden, for example, is of no interest to us. One might give the name 'philosophy' to what is possible *before* all new discoveries and inventions. (*PI* §126)

The work of the philosopher consists in assembling reminders for a particular purpose. (*PI* §127)

If one tried to advance *theses* in philosophy, it would never be possible to question them, because everyone would agree to them. (*PI* §128)

It is not our aim to refine or complete the system of rules for the use of words in unheard-of ways. For the clarity that we are aiming at is indeed *complete* clarity. But that simply means that the philosophical problems should *completely* disappear. The real discovery is one that makes me capable of stopping doing philosophy when I want to. -The one that gives philosophy peace, so that it is no longer tormented by questions which bring *itself* into question.... There is not *a* philosophical method, though there are indeed methods, like different therapies. (*PI* §133)

What is your aim in philosophy? —To show the fly the way out of the fly-bottle. (*PI* §309)

In philosophy we do not draw conclusions. "But it must be like this!" is not a philosophical proposition. Philosophy only states what everyone admits. (*PI* §599)

To summarize, for the later Wittgenstein, here's what philosophers do after they have rejected and transcended the method of logical analysis—they: (i) display and diagnose the dialectical structure of existing "hard" problems, especially including the cognitively enslaving pictures that hold philosophers captive, (ii) which are themselves *social-institutional* problems, each one displaying "the civil (*bürgerliche*) status of a contradiction," then (iii) describe, unpack, compare, and contrast the concepts implicit in our various ordinary uses of language and states various truisms about them, and then, (iv) having thereby purged themselves of bad, cognitively enslaving pictures, thus "show[ing] the fly the way out of the fly-bottle," finally (v) they stop doing (professional academic classical Analytic) philosophy and at the same time radically transform their own own lives. But for my purposes here, the essential thing about Wittgenstein's philosophy of philosophy—whether in the *Tractatus* or in the *Investigations*, but especially in the *Investigations*—is that according to this conception, *real* (as opposed to professional academic Analytic, whether classical or post-classical) philosophical analysis is emphatically *not* any kind of super-powered natural or formal science, and especially *not* a super-powered kind of mathematical logic, *nor* is it any kind of intellectual appendage or underlaborer to the formal or natural sciences, but instead it is *fundamentally emotive, practical, and existential (aka "non-cognitive), and social-institutional.*

XVIII.3 The New Poverty of Philosophy

In this section, using later Wittgenstein's emotive, practical, existential, and social-institutional conception of philosophical analysis as a jumping-off point, I'm going to reinterpret it by generalizing it and also update it by placing it in a larger historical context. In effect, this amounts to my inserting some provocative qualifiers into three of the texts I've already quoted in section XVIII.2 above, as follows:

> The civil (*bürgerliche*) status of a contradiction, or its status in [professional academic Analytic philosophical] life: there is the philosophical problem. (*PI* §125)

> [T]he clarity that we are aiming at is indeed *complete* clarity. But that simply means that the philosophical problems [characteristic of professional academic Analytic philosophy] should *completely* disappear. The real discovery is one that makes me capable of stopping doing [professional academic Analytic] philosophy when I want to. –The one that gives [real] philosophy peace, so that it is no longer tormented by questions which bring *itself* into question. (*PI* § 133)

> What is your aim in [real] philosophy? —To show the fly the way out of the [professional academic Analytic philosophical] fly-bottle. (*PI* §309)

In this reinterpretative generalization, a classical or typical "hard" philosophical problem, epitomized by the sort of problem discussed in Russell's immensely influential 1912 book, *The Problems of Philosophy*, has a three-part structure. **First**, there's an *explanatory gap* between some set of basic facts and another set of basic facts. For example, in the classical mind-body problem: "how is consciousness or subjective experience, which is fundamentally mental, possible in a fundamentally physical world?" The first set of basic facts are subjective, non-mechanical facts about consciousness (the mind), and the second set of basic facts are objective, mechanical facts about physical processes (the body). So there is an explanatory gap between mind-facts and body-facts. **Second**, there's a *conceptual knot*, or theoretical puzzle, that needs to be untangled before there can be any significant progress in philosophical understanding. For example, in the classical mind-body problem, it seems impossible to understand how something that is fundamentally mental could ever arise through fundamentally physical processes. This conceptual knot is also known as "Cartesian conceptual dualism." **Third**, there's a *philosophical picture*, that is, a critically-unexamined presupposition, or set of critically-unexamined presuppositions, being made by all participants in the existing debate. For example, in the classical mind-body problem, it is being uncritically presupposed by all philosophical participants in the existing debate that mental facts are inherently non-physical and essentially exclude physical facts, and also that physical facts are inherently non-mental and essentially exclude mental facts.

Significant progress on a "hard problem" can be made only by identifying the explanatory gaps, conceptual knots, and philosophical pictures, critically questioning the unexamined presuppositions, and then proposing a new, "outside-the-fly-bottle" way of conceptualizing the basic facts. For example, in the classical mind-body problem, it's possible to reject the philosophical picture/critically-unexamined presupposition of Cartesian conceptual dualism, and propose that that mental facts and physical facts are *not* mutually exclusive, and that in fact both mental facts and physical facts arise from *a single third domain of more basic facts that are neither fundamentally mental nor fundamentally physical*. So far, however, we've only gotten as far as *neutral monism*, which, to the extent that it usually has physicalist motivations–say, as per Spinoza or Russell–is still trapped inside the fly-bottle of Cartesian conceptual dualism. But a radically different third domain would be primitive facts about immanently-structured non-equilibrium complex thermodynamic systems–flows of actual and potential energy, and/or matter–especially including organismic living systems. This genuinely new, truly "outside-the-fly-bottle" way of conceptualizing the basic facts about the mind-body relation is particularized in later Wittgenstein's linguistic phenomenology of human mindedness in the *Investigations* (see chapters XIII and XIV above), and more generally elaborated and extended to its full scope in what I call *humanistic neo- organicism*, about which I'll have more to say in section XVIII.6 below. But for the moment and historically speaking, I'll call it *whiteheading the russell*, in view of A.N. Whitehead's breakthrough, brilliant 1929 organicist treatise, *Process and Reality*, much neglected by classical and post-classical Analytic philosophers alike. Exploring the Kantian neo-organicist option, therefore, involves truly "thinking outside the fly-bottle" of Cartesian conceptual dualism. Nevertheless, the great majority of contemporary post-classical Analytic philosophers cannot even *see* the Kantian neo-organicist option; or if they were exposed to it, they would instantly reject it as "crazy," thereby dismissing anyone who seriously holds it, shut their eyes, put plugs in their ears, take another Tylenol PM, roll over, and fall back into Francisco Goya's "sleep of reason" (as per the caption on his famous engraving: "*el sueña de la razon produce monstruos*/the sleep of reason breeds monsters") again. And the very same three-part structure and associated pattern of philosophical cognitive pathology can be found in the other so-called "hard problems": free will problem, the problem of knowledge, the realism/idealism problem, the personal identity problem, the problem of moral skepticism, the problem of God's existence or non-existence, the problem of political authority, and so-on.

What's my evidence for this? In an important 2017 article that I've already mentioned several times, Joel Katzav and Krist Vaesen argue compellingly that the mid-20th century emergence of post-classical Analytic philosophy in the USA consisted in an institutional take-over of leading philosophy departments and leading journals by Analytic philosophers immediately after World War II, that was consolidated by roughly 1948-1950 (Katzav and Vaesen, 2017). At the same time, leading post-classical Analytic philosophers engaged in a systematic professional exclusion of alternatives to Analytic philosophy, especially including existential phenomenology, speculative philosophy, and the earlier American pragmatic tradition, on the way towards the systematic professional exclusion of post-classical Analytic philosophy's all-purpose Other, so-called "Continental philosophy," by the 1980s. Katzav and Vaesen are fairly guarded about the political dimension of this story, and say there's no empirical evidence for a direct causal connection between McCarthyism and the institutional take-over of, for example, *The Philosophical Review*, by post-classical Analytic philosophers between 1948 and 1950. But that's not terribly surprising.

> "Dear Readers of *The Philosophical Review*,
>
> We just wanted to inform you that we're institutionally taking over and professionally pushing post-classical Analytic philosophy down your throats now, because we're scared—*really, really* scared—by The House Committee on UnAmerican Activities, aka HUAC, and by McCarthyism in America.
>
> And this works out *really, really well for US*, even if *not for YOU*, because post-classical Analytic philosophy is not only inherently politically conformist, given its commitment to the fact-value dichotomy and its methodological value-neutrality, its Scholastic formalism and logic-worship, and its scientism, but also fully complicit in the post-World War II military-industrial complex.
>
> Yours calculatingly,
>
> The New Editors"

Obviously, nothing like this would ever happen, except in a *Monty Python's Flying Circus* world.

Nevertheless, in the very next paragraph and in the concluding paragraphs of the paper, Katzav and Vaesen also say explicitly that their argument is smoothly consistent with John McCumber's critically edgy thesis, worked out in his books *Time in the Ditch: American Philosophy and the McCarthy Era* and *The Philosophy Scare: The Politics of Reason in the Early Cold War* (McCumber, 2001, 2016) that I approvingly mentioned in section XVII.7 above, to the same effect, namely, (i) there's an elective affinity between McCarthyism and the fact-value dichotomy and value-neutrality, Scholastic formalism and logic-worship, and scientism of Analytic philosophy, such that (ii) McCarthyism and post-classical Analytic philosophy in mid-20th century America, together, did indeed actually produce a style of professional academic philosophy that's not only inherently politically conformist but also fully complicit in the post-World War II military-industrial complex. Not only that, but in order for McCarthyism and Analytic philosophy to do this together, leading Analytic philosophers had to carry out the systematic exclusion of American pragmatism and also Heidegger-inspired, Sartre-inspired, and Merleau-Ponty-inspired existential phenomenology, insofar as (i) earlier pragmatists like Dewey had been explicitly *socialists*, (ii) pre-War Heidegger had been a *Nazi*, and (iii) post-War Sartre was a *communist*, and Merleau-Ponty at least a *neo-Marxist*. I think that McCumber is absolutely correct; and I also think that Katzav's and Vaesen's argument is smoothly consistent with McCumber's thesis.

Now, what about recent and contemporary post-classical Analytic philosophy? The central line of argument in Jeff Schmidt's compelling, radical 2000 book, *Disciplined Minds*, says that through various subtle and not-so-subtle means, most members of the professional academy are selected for their tendency *to obey*, by conforming to the ideological discipline of their professional academic field:

> Just as professionals engage in playpen creativity, innovating within the safe confines of an assigned ideology, so too they engage in playpen critical thinking. Their work involves judging whether or not the ideas of others are in line with the favored outlook, but does not involve developing their own, independent point of view. Hence professionals tend to be what might be called "book review" critical, which is intellectually and politically safe because it doesn't involve developing or taking a stand for an independent outlook. Professionals generally avoid the risk inherent in real critical thinking and cannot properly be called critical thinkers. They are simply ideologically disciplined thinkers. Real critical thinking means uncovering and questioning social, political and moral assumptions; applying and refining a personally developed worldview; and calling for action that advances a personally created agenda. An approach that backs away from any of these three components lacks the critical spirit. Ideologically disciplined thinkers, especially the more gung-ho ones, often give the *appearance* of being critical thinkers as they go around deftly applying the official ideology and confidently reporting their judgments. (Schmidt, 2000: pp. 40-41)

Evidence for Schmidt's thesis includes subtleties like biases in tests like the Graduate Record Exam, aka the GRE , which emphasize the ability for rule-following and disciplined memorization over deeper critical thinking, less-subtle selection methods like graduate school comprehensive exams, which again emphasize disciplined study/memorization over independent thinking, and even less-subtle selection methods like hiring practices that are clearly ideologically/politically driven by departmental politics, profession-wide politics, higher-administrative university politics, and straight-up local, state-level, or national-level governmental politics. It's been empirically shown, for example, that those who become professional academic post-classical Analytic philosophers do extremely well on the GRE. Only engineers, mathematicians, and physicists do better on the quantitative part, but those who are headed for a career in professional academic Analytic philosophy do best overall, when the analytical-reasoning and verbal-comprehension parts are taken into account.

Question: Why specifically *these* types of gates-of-entry to the professional world? *Answer*: Because it's exactly what the bosses/masters/administrators/rulers want to see in their employees/wage-slaves/administrees/subjects. This includes employees/wage-slaves/administrees/subjects like professional academics, including of course recent and contemporary professional academic Analytic philosophers. Schmidt's best-documented case for this involves his own Ph.D. field, physics, a field driven by its corporate and military applications, therefore driven by its connections to the unelected national and global power elite that runs the US government and every other neoliberal State, namely, what I call *the military-industrial-university-digital complex*, aka The Hyper-State. More explicitly, by *The Hyper-State* I mean an essentially coercive and authoritarian State-like national, international, and indeed global social institution, whose members belong to a highly networked power elite that includes military leaders, leading corporate capitalists, leading professional academics, and leading figures in the creation, dissemination, and control of all forms of media, especially digital media (Hanna, 2021g; Herman and Chomsky, 1988; Mills, 1956). It's a "Hyper-State" not only because it *operates above* first-order or ordinary neoliberal nation-states, but also because it combines and expresses state-like power structures in a uniquely *higher-order* and *hypertrophied* format. Just like post-1950s professional academic physics, post-1950s professional academic post-classical Analytic philosophy also lives, moves, and has its being, by buzzing around and around, forever trapped inside essentially the same kind of Hyper-State-controlled fly-bottle. For example, the scientism that afflicts and infects post-classical Analytic philosophy, via its dogmatic, obsessive commitment to *scientific naturalism*, as we've seen in chapter XVII, does so in ways that are completely out of proportion to the at-most moderate influence that formal and natural formal science *ought* to have on philosophical practice.

The multi-leveled problem of obedient specialization in post-classical Analytic philosophy is fundamentally what later Wittgenstein calls a "civil" problem, that is, a *social-institutional* problem, and indeed a *political* problem, because endemic, obedient, forced early-specialization, and hyper-specialization flow naturally from the deep but all-too-often unacknowledged influence of larger sociocultural and political mechanisms of scientism, global corporate capitalism, and statism on post-classical Analysis. So the role played by *language* and *civil society* in later Wittgenstein's conception of philosophy can be updated and replaced by *social institutions more generally, especially political ones*. And this updating and substitution is entirely natural, since language itself, according to the later Wittgenstein's own conception of it, *just is* a social institution, since social institutions are collective human actions under shared norms, and since language for later Wittgenstein *just is* a fundamental form of collective human action under shared norms, as we've seen in chapters XI to XV.

Now by a *bad philosophical picture* I mean a set of interlinked unarticulated, unargued presuppositions that consistently yields significant conceptual blindness/blinkeredness and conceptual confusion in philosophy. And by a *disastrously bad philosophical picture* I mean a bad philosophical picture that is so gripping and so severely mistaken it that covertly drives philosophy into a conceptual cul de sac or vicious loop, consisting of endless insoluble antinomies and/or radical skepticism, in effect killing real philosophy, and then generating from its death throes only arid, narrow, pointless, busy-busy-busy bee philosophical scholasticism and sophistry. —In other words, a philosophical *fly-bottle*. You know, the very sort of thing that the *Critique of Pure Reason* and the *Philosophical Investigations* were written to diagnose, undermine, and overcome? Sadly, there are all-too-many examples of how endemic, forced early-specialization and hyper-specialization, in the context of ideological discipline and obedient culture in post-classical Analytic philosophy, especially since 1985, covertly induces or outright produces new fly-bottles, disastrously bad philosophical pictures, for example, the fly-bottle of Cartesian conceptual dualism. In other words, then, all the fly-bottles, or disastrously bad philosophical pictures, that grip and haunt post-classical Analysis, especially since 1985, are covertly induced or outright produced by (i) the GRE-driven pre-selection of obedient, formally adept, rule-implementing people by PhD programs in philosophy, especially in the most highly-ranked departments, and (ii) endemic, forced early-specialization and hyper-specialization. Hence the reason that recent and contemporary post-classical Analytic philosophers typically cannot think outside their disastrously bad philosophical pictures, their fly-bottles, is that powerful mechanisms of ideological discipline induce or produce in them an ideologically-manipulated, obedient state of cognitive blindness/blinkeredness about the genuine space of conceptual options actually open to them. In short, the so-called "hard problems" in post-classical Analytic philosophy are actually *social-institutional artifacts* tracing their origins back to professional academic *classical* Analytic philosophy at least as far back as 1912, and above all and even more specifically, they're social-institutional artifacts of the ideologically disciplined professional academy that has captured, enclosed, and mind-man-acled post-classical Analytic philosophy since 1950 and especially since 1985.

The great philosophers of the past, up through the end of the 19th century and the first decade of the 20th century, prior to the publication of Russell's *Problems of Philosophy* in 1912, never formulated or understood these "hard" problems in just this way. Of course, those earlier philosophers were engaging and struggling with some or all of the same basic facts, explanatory gaps, conceptual knots, and bad philosophical pictures: but the bad pictures hadn't yet *hardened* into fly-bottles in the way they did after early Russell, and especially after 1950, and *extra*-especially after 1985. No wonder, then, that early Wittgenstein was so intensely annoyed and enervated by early Russell and his logico-philosophical work up to the beginning of World War I (Monk, 1990: sep. chs. 3-4) and no wonder that Wittgenstein's critical metaphilosophy unfolded as it did. –And it's also no accident, as far as his philosophical *organicism* is concerned, that even though he did teach in the Harvard Philosophy Department from 1924-1937, Whitehead *wasn't* trained as a professional academic philosopher, and therefore *wasn't* social-institutionally "disciplined" as a professional academic philosopher, hence he always felt himself to be a philosophical outsider during his Harvard career (Lowe, 1985/1990: esp. vol. 2, chs. V-X).

Of course, it wasn't really *all* Russell's fault. Indeed, Russell had his own Close Encounter with the coercive moralism of the professional academy, higher university administration, and government during World War I, being jailed for pacifist, social-anarchist activism, then having his Trinity fellowship rescinded (plus, the fellowship ouster also had something to do with Russell's "scandalous" personal life), and it all radically changed his philosophical and political life after World War I and into the 1920s (Monk, 1996: esp. chs. 8-21) and beyond. It was just that by the end of World War I and into the 1920s, the juggernaut of mainstream Anglo-American professional academic philosophy *per se* was already well on the move—indeed, the original stirrings of this juggernaut, aptly symbolized as a giant octopus sea-monster, were already critically witnessed, for example, by William James early in the 20th century (James, 1903)—and by 1950, it had pretty much conquered 20th century professional academic philosophy, and by now the first two decades of 21st century professional academic philosophy, as a whole, by means of the social-institutional triumph of Russell's more-or-less unintentionally created Dr Frankenstein's monster, *classical Analytic philosophy*. (In the soon-to-be released-to-streaming movie version of the history of early 20th century classical Analytic philosophy, based on the uncensored 1931 movie version of *Frankenstein*, directed by James Whale, G.E. Moore plays Fritz/Dwight Frye to Russell's Dr Frankenstein/Colin Clive. Russell in 1912 to Moore: "It's alive! It's alive! In the name of God! Now I know what it feels like to *be* God!")

By the time of the publication of the *Philosophical Investigations* in 1953, at the height of the McCarthy era, the hegemonic ideological and social-institutional structure of professional academic philosophy, by virtue of the triumph of Russell's more or less unintentional Frankensteinian creation, classical Analytic philosophy, on the cusp of turning into post-classical Analytic philosophy, The Son of Frankenstein, was not merely a leviathan and a juggernaut, and not merely a Frankenstein's monster, *it was a Frankenstein's-monster-leviathan-megamachine*. This is especially true in the USA, where professional academic post-classical Analytic philosophy was a sub-part of the larger post-World War II military-industrial-*university* complex; and from the end of the Cold War, it was also a sub-part of the *neoliberal* military-industrial-university complex; and nowadays, professional academic post-classical Analytic philosophy is also a sub-part of the neoliberal military-industrial-university-*digital* complex, aka The Hyper-State. In other words, and to mix and stack my metaphors even more wantonly, the social-institutional structure of recent and contemporary post-classical Analytic philosophy is nothing more and nothing less than the all-inclusive early Russellian fly-bottle that's the otherwise empty skull-box of the juggernaut that's the Frankenstein's-monster-leviathan-megamachine-military-industrial-university-digital-aka-Hyper-State *philosophical Terminator*. And *all that* is what I mean by *The New Poverty of Philosophy*.

XVIII.4 How is Philosophy Really Possible Inside the Professional Academy? A Global Metaphilosophical Problem

In the face of the new poverty of philosophy, recent and contemporary post-classical Analytic and non-Analytic philosophers all over the world are struggling with the following fundamental metaphilosophical problem:

How is philosophy really possible inside *the professional academy*, aka *the university*?

Here, for example, are fourteen recent articles that provide six different national perspectives on the problem: American, British, German, Japanese, Japanese/Latin-American, and Latin American:

1. An American Perspective

Robert Frodeman and Adam Briggle, "Socrates Tenured: The Argument in a Nutshell" (Frodeman and Briggle, 2016).

2. A British Perspective

Alexis Papazoglou, "Philosophy, Its Pitfalls, Some Rescue Plans and Their Complications" (Papazoglou, 2012).

3. A German Perspective

Wolfram Eilenberger, "Die deutschsprachige Philosophie ist in einem desolaten Zustand. Woran liegt das?" (Eilenberger, 2018).

4. Japanese Perspectives

Jeremiah Alberg, "Being on the Ground: Philosophy, Reading and Difficulty"

Wolfgang Ertl, "Home of the Owl? Kantian Reflections on Philosophy at University" (Alberg, 2017).

Yasuhira Yahei Kanayama, "The Birth of Philosophy as 哲學 (Tetsugaku) in Japan" (Kanayama, 2017).

Yasushi Kato, "The Crisis of the Humanities and Social Sciences in the Age of 'Innovation': Philosophy as a Critical Facilitator toward a 'Civic Turn' of the University" (Kato, 2017) .

Yuko Murakami, "Philosophy and Higher Education in Japan" (Murakami, 2017).

Yuji Nishiyama, "What Remains of Philosophers' Reflections on University?" (Nishiyamai, 2017).

5. A Japanese/Latin American Perspective

Hirotaka Nakano, "Is There Japanese/Latin American Philosophy? : A Reflection on Philosophy in University" (Nakano, 2017).

6. Latin American Perspectives

Marcelo D. Boeri, "The Presence of Philosophy in Latin American Universities" (Boeri, 2017)

SK, "An Insider's View of the Brazilian Philosophical World, Or, How to Build a Really Totalitarian System" (SK, 2016).

Manuel Vargas, "On the Value of Philosophy: The Latin American Case" (Vargas, 2010).

Manuel Vargas, "Real Philosophy, Metaphilosophy, and Metametaphilosophy: On the Plight of Latin American Philosophy" (2007).

I won't stop to summarize these articles: the interested reader can read them themselves; my point here is simply to demonstrate that I'm far from being the *only* contemporary philosopher who is grappling with this fundamental metaphilosophical problem. Without further ado, then, what I want to do in the next two sub-sections is to present and defend a radical Kantian response to the problem of The New Poverty of Philosophy, namely what I call *Philosophy's Second Copernican Revolution*, in two parts.

XVIII.5 Philosophy's Second Copernican Revolution, Part 1: The Radical Kantian *Metaphilosophical* Paradigm Shift to Anarcho- or Borderless Philosophy

Now *back to Kant*. (Haven't we heard that somewhere before?) In social, cultural, or intellectual history, a "Copernican Revolution" is a fundamental conceptual, emotional, or practical *Gestalt* shift: a change of worldview. In *The Structure of Scientific Revolutions*, Kuhn aptly likens such changes of worldview to our subjective experience of classic, multi-stable visual perceptual figures like the classic Jastrow duck-rabbit (Kuhn, 1970: ch. X). As I noted in section XIV.2 above, Wittgenstein also transcribed this figure into the *Investigations* (*PI* p. 194ᵉ), in the context of his discussion of direct seeing vs. interpretive seeing.

The first Copernican Revolution *in modern philosophy* was Kant's, in the *Critique of Pure Reason*. Kant said: Instead of assuming that our minds conform to the world-in-itself, we should postulate that the world as it appears to us conforms to the non-empirical structure of our minds (*CPR* Bxvi-xviii). In this way, the ducks of classical rationalism and classical empiricism became the rabbit of transcendental idealism. But at the same time, Kant also more or less unintentionally initiated professional academic philosophy. As Schopenhauer pointed out in his exceptionally edgy essay, "On University Philosophy," Kant was the first—and according to Schopenhauer, the *last* and indeed the *only*—professional academic who was also a truly great philosopher:

> [N]ormally a teacher of philosophy would be the last person to whom it would occur that philosophy could in effect be dead earnest, just as the most irreligious

Christian is usually the Pope. Hence it is among the rarest cases that a genuine philosopher is at the same time a lecturer in philosophy…. I have already discussed the fact that *Kant* represented this exceptional case, together with the grounds and consequences of this. (Schopenhauer, 2014: p. 127)

I wrote a few sentences above, that Kant "more or less unintentionally" initiated professional academic philosophy. This is because he actually formulated two extremely important, fateful, metaphilosophical claims about professional academic philosophy, in the "Transcendental Doctrine of Method" in the first *Critique*—right at the back of the book, the part that almost nobody ever reads, not even most Kantians–and in *The Conflict of the Faculties*, another book that almost nobody ever reads. Perhaps Kant should have also foreseen the dire consequences of these claims as likely side-effects, in view of the fact that he was the most famous and important philosopher in the world: but he didn't, and that's really too bad. Or if he *did* actually recognize these likely side-effects, he didn't explicitly point them out, which is even worse, because then he was being disingenuous on top of indirectly creating dire consequences for philosophy.

In any case, Kant's first metaphilosophical claim is that *real philosophy*, that is, authentic, serious philosophy by means of autonomous reasoning from a priori principles, is one thing, and *School philosophy* is another thing altogether, and that to confuse the two is an intellectual disaster. Indeed, he explicitly says that the School philosopher is someone who "has grasped and preserved well, i.e., he has learned [a system of philosophy]," but he is not someone who does real philosophy "from reason" and is in fact is nothing but "a plaster cast of a living human being" (*CPR* A836/B864). You can easily see Kant's prima facie good intention here: he wanted to liberate real philosophy from the inauthentic, superficial, dogmatic, hegemonic, Leibnizian-Wolffian Scholastic philosophy of his day. But the unintended dire consequence of this was to stigmatize the history of philosophy and alienate philosophy from its own past.

Kant's second metaphilosophical claim is that the philosophy faculty, as a social institution inside a university, must have critical autonomy from the other faculties—law, medicine, and especially theology—and also from the government. Again you can easily see Kant's prima facie good intention: he wanted to liberate philosophy from the coercive dogmatism and hegemony of the theology faculty, who were acting as mouthpieces for the authoritarian, religiously conservative political regime of his day, commanded by Frederick William II. But by focusing exclusively on philosophy's critical autonomy from theology, Kant also implicitly enslaved philosophy to the dogmatism and hegemony of the formal and natural sciences.

Moreover, and sadly, Kant's claim that the philosophy faculty is critically autonomous from the government is, in fact, bullshit. This is because Kant also explicitly says, both in *The Conflict of the Faculties* and in "What is Enlightenment?," that anyone who has either been officially appointed by the government or *de facto* is in a position to speak out in public from behind some sort of pulpit or lectern, falls directly under the jurisdiction of the government—so if he publicly argues against the government or is taken by the government to be teaching dangerous things, then "he would be inciting the people to rebellion" (*CF* 7: 29) and thereby subject to censorship, reprimand, loss of his appointment or position, or prison. The *most* he can do, as Kant famously puts in "What is Enlightenment?," citing the benevolent despot Frederick the Great's idea of free speech, is *to argue as much as he likes about whatever he likes, but obey*. But all university professors, including all philosophy professors, are either appointed by the government, or at the very least, as lecturers in a public or private university, they're in a position to speak out in public from behind a lectern, hence they fall under the direct jurisdiction of the government. Therefore, no matter what and how much university philosophy professors argue, if they publicly argue against the government or are taken by the government to be teaching dangerous things, then they are not only inciting the people to rebellion, and thereby subject to censorship, reprimand, loss of their appointments or positions, or prison, but also must ultimately obey. Thus an even more dire unintended consequence of Kant's second metaphilosophical claim was to entrench philosophy as a faculty or department within the university, and thereby cognitively and practically enslave philosophy to the coercive dogmatism and ideological hegemony of the university and its administrators, and of the state and its government, alike.

This terrible trifecta of fateful Kantian oversights—(i) stigmatizing the history of philosophy and alienating philosophy from its own past, (ii) cognitively enslaving philosophy to the natural and formal sciences, and (iii) entrenching philosophy as a department within a university, thereby cognitively enslaving philosophy to the university and its administrators, and to the state and its government—has manifested itself in three corresponding ways in 20th and 21st century post-classical Analytic philosophy: (iv) scientific naturalism, especially its scientism, (v) ideologically-disciplined academic professionalism, and (vi) statism in contemporary neoliberal nations. Now taking scientific naturalism/scientism, ideologically-disciplined academic professionalism, and statism in contemporary neoliberal nations together, more generally, we get the neoliberal military-industrial-university-digital complex, aka The Hyper-State. Then, applying these to philosophy specifically, and specifically including the stigmatization of the history of philosophy and the alienation of philosophy from its own past, we now have the following completely messed-up situation in the early decades of the 21st century: professional academic post-classical Analytic philosophy, especially as it is practiced at the leading universities and in the leading departments, and especially since 1985, is nothing but the most alienated, abstract, and abstruse intellectual arm of The Hyper-State. In other words, welcome to The New Poverty of Philosophy.

That being so, what is to be done? My proposal, as I've said, is *Philosophy's Second Copernican Revolution*:

> In order to end and reverse The New Poverty of Philosophy, two fundamental paradigm shifts are required: **first**, a *radical Kantian metaphilosophical* paradigm shift: instead of uncritically assuming that philosophy is really possible only *inside* the professional academy, we critically postulate that philosophy is really possible only *outside* the professional academy, and **second**, a *radical Kantian metaphysical*

paradigm shift: instead uncritically assuming a *natural mechanist* conception of the world, we critically postulate a *Kantian neo-organicist* conception of the world.

Only in this way can philosophy re-connect with its own past, be critically autonomous from The Hyper-State, and become *real (*that is, authentic, serious) philosophy again.

As regards the **first** paradigm shift, in concrete, practical terms, this means (i) that we must engage in a serious critique of professional academic philosophy, especially including recent and contemporary post-classical Analytic philosophy—for example, the project *Against Professional Philosophy* (Z, 2013-2021). (2) that we must exit university departments of philosophy, and, if it is also humanly and practically possible, also exit universities, *altogether,* (3) that we must engage in a serious critique of the military-industrial-university-digital complex, aka The Hyper-State (Hanna, 2021g; Herman and Chomsky, 1988; Mills, 1956), and (4) that *il faut cultiver notre jardin*: that is, we must cultivate our garden as real philosophers (Z, 2017a), that is, we must create and sustain a new social institutional framework for the radical Kantian philosophy of the future—*anarcho-* or *borderless philosophy* (Hanna, 2020a).

But here's an amazingly difficult problem. Seriously pursuing (1), (2), and (3) are extremely likely to make you unemployed, and, if not literally homeless, like Diogenes, then at least a complete outsider to the contemporary intellectual Establishment, aka the intelligentsia, which, of course, is relentlessly dominated and jealously protected by professional academics. So if you're unemployed and either literally homeless or at least a complete intellectual outsider, then how can you ever make (4) happen? In *The Conflict of the Faculties,* Kant says:

> In addition to … *incorporated* scholars [i.e., professional academics], there can also be scholars *at large,* who do not belong to the university but simply work on part of the great content of learning, either forming independent organizations, like various workshops (called *academies* or *scientific societies*), or living, so to speak, in a state of nature as far as learning is concerned, each working by himself, as an *amateur* and without public precepts or rules, at extending and propagating [his field of] learning. (CF 7: 18)

Translated out of Kant's quaint terminology, "scholars at large" are nothing more and nothing less than anarcho-scholars aka borderless scholars, i.e., truly independent scholars, and, as philosophers, anarcho-philosophers aka borderless philosophers, i.e., truly independent philosophers. Therefore, the most important and urgent task of contemporary philosophy, precisely because the fate of the real, radical Kantian philosophy of the future depends on it, is to figure out how to make anarcho- or borderless philosophy really possible.

Admittedly, what I've argued so far in this chapter is pretty provocative and somewhat telegraphic: hence some natural objections or worries about my two core theses and their justification might naturally arise. So here are some follow-up thoughts, by way of further elaboration.

First, the parallel philosophical and metaphilosophical trajectories I'm tracing in the work of the later Wittgenstein and Kant, in support of *The New Poverty of Philosophy* thesis, obviously need more elaboration and defense than I can provide in this particular section—but see chapter XIV above for an extended attempt to do that.

Second, the parallel between what I'm arguing in support of my *Philosophy's Second Copernican Revolution* thesis, and Kuhn's ideas about "Copernican revolutions" in *The Structure of Scientific Revolutions*, is also extremely important. Put in Kuhnian terminology, I think that the largely implicit, unselfconscious, and pre-reflective guiding presupposition or *paradigm* that has dominated philosophy since the late 18th century, which says that philosophy is really possible only inside the professional academy, has finally played itself out, and is now in a fatal *crisis* phase. Therefore, it's not that I disqualify and reject everything that has been done or is being done inside recent and contemporary professional academic post-classical Analytic philosophy, or consider the best of that work to be in any way unintelligent or less than extremely clever or sometimes even brilliant—just as, from the Copernican or Newtonian standpoint, looking back at pre-Copernican or pre-Newtonian physics, or from the relativity/quantum standpoint, looking back at Copernican or Newtonian physics, one wouldn't in any way disqualify and reject everything that was done inside earlier scientific paradigms or consider the best of that work to be in any way unintelligent or less than extremely clever or sometimes even brilliant. Far from it. "Normal science" inside the Newtonian scientific paradigm, for example, clearly is often extremely clever, sometimes even brilliant. So too, "normal philosophy" inside the post-classical Analytic paradigm *clearly* is often extremely clever, sometimes brilliant, and sometimes even important, as witnessed by the nineteen important philosophical ideas that I listed in section XVII.6.

Moreover, I do think that Kuhn, or at least early Kuhn, *over*emphasized the sharpness of the breaks created by revolutionary scientific paradigm shifts and also the supposed rational incommensurability (whether metaphysical, semantic, epistemic, emotional, moral, or political) between the different scientific paradigms or worldviews. On the contrary, there's a significant background of conceptual and non-conceptual continuity, and many shared higher-level assumptions, even across genuinely revolutionary shifts between scientific paradigms or worldviews. Correspondingly, there's a significant background of conceptual and non-conceptual continuity, and many shared higher-level assumptions, across the first revolutionary philosophical paradigm-shift from pre-Kantian to Kantian philosophy; and the same is the case with the revolutionary paradigm-shift I'm proposing from professional academic post-classical Analytic philosophy to a radical Kantian extra-professional-academic, non-Analytic, non-so-called "Continental," anarcho- or borderless philosophy. Nevertheless, Copernican paradigm-shifts in natural science are still genuinely revolutionary, and so is Part 1 of the second Copernican paradigm-shift I'm proposing in philosophy. As in our subjective experience of the *Gestalt* shift between the duck-profile and the rabbit-profile in the multistable duck-rabbit figure, the *duck* of professional academic post-classical Analytic philosophy, becomes the *rabbit* of anarcho- or borderless philosophy.

Third, both *The New Poverty of Philosophy* thesis and *Philosophy's Second Copernican Revolution, Part 1*, even allowing for their importantly later-Wittgensteinian provenance, are really and truly *radical Kantian* theses, in that they rely heavily for inspiration on Kant's ideas about critical, autonomous rationality. As I argued in *Kant and the Foundations of Analytic Philosophy* and in *Kant, Science and Human Nature*, Kant more or less unintentionally made what we now know as Analytic philosophy really possible, and in fact, more than that, Kant's philosophy causally triggered its emergence and existence via the neo-Kantian tradition to which all the leading early classical Analytic philosophers belonged. But I also think that there were some serious oversights in Kant's own views about the role of the professional academy in relation to philosophy, that have in fact eventually proved fatal for real philosophy inside the professional academic classical or post-classical Analytic paradigm, namely: the stigmatization of the history of philosophy and the alienation of philosophy from its own past; cognitive heteronomy under scientific naturalism/scientism; cognitive, emotional, moral and political heteronomy under professional academic ideological discipline; and cognitive, emotional, moral, and political heteronomy under the government in contemporary neoliberal nation-states. In a word, then, this is The New Poverty of Philosophy: post-classical Analytic philosophy's alienation from its own history, and its cognitive, emotional, moral, and sociopolitical slavery under the neoliberal military-industrial-university-digital complex, aka The Hyper-State; and Kant himself is partially to blame.

Moreover, it's not that I think that there *aren't* all sorts of bullshit, alienation, and cognitive, emotional, moral, and sociopolitical slavery *outside* the professional academy, and that philosophy couldn't be heteronymous in relation to *those*, if it weren't constantly raising critically autonomous questions and worries, and daring to think, feel, and act for itself. It's just that I think that the "peculiar institution" of the professional academy in neoliberal states under advanced capitalism, and especially the "peculiar institution" of post-classical Analytic philosophy since 1985, is actually killing real philosophy (that's the bad news); and that radical Kantian philosophy can help us end and reverse this crisis (that's the good news).

Fourth, like Kant's first Copernican Revolution hypothesis in the *Critique of Pure Reason*, what I'm calling *Philosophy's Second Copernican Revolution, Part 1* is another philosophical *hypothesis*, not a dogmatic pronouncement. I'm saying: since the professional academic paradigm in post-classical Analytic philosophy has now played itself out and is in fatal crisis phase, going down into the ash-heap of history, then we should try a radical change in worldview about the nature of philosophy, and see what happens.

Fifth, nothing I've said fundamentally contradicts Kant's first Copernican Revolution. Indeed, I think that we're still fully within the scope of *that* philosophical revolution. It's just that we haven't yet realized its full potential for real philosophy, not by a long shot, for example, the neo-organicist conception of the world (Hanna, 2020d, 2021c), including what I call *rational anthropology* (Hanna, 2017e), or some other Promethean attempt to do *philosophy unbound* (Z, 2017b). And as to *Philosophy's Second Copernican Revolution, Part 1*–well, Marx famously *turned Hegel on his head*, so I'm saying:

> *Let's turn Kant sharply to the left* by liberating Kantianism from the self-alienated cognitive, emotional, moral, and sociopolitical *Ivory bunker* that's professional academic post-classical Analytic philosophy, especially since 1985.

Sixth, all in all then, what I'm saying is that the way forward in philosophy beyond the professional academic post-classical Analytic philosophy paradigm, now in fatal crisis mode, is a radical Kantian philosophy—whether one calls it *Left Kantianism* (Hanna, 2017a), or anarcho- or borderless philosophy—that envisions a new historically-sensitive, anti-scientistic, extra-professional-academic, radical Kantian metaphilosophical paradigm for the philosophy of the future. Or, as a philosophical call-to-arms: *Forward and leftward to Kant!*

The one amazingly difficult problem that remains, as I noted above, is to figure out how to implement anarcho- or borderless philosophy in the face of likely unemployment and banishment by the contemporary intellectual Establishment, aka the intelligentsia, which, of course, is so relentlessly and jealously controlled by professional academics. One real-world attempt at a solution to this seemingly insoluble problem is a mega-project called *Philosophy Without Borders* (Hanna, 2017-2021), which, four years into its existence, is (as of August 2021) being supported by 24 generous, visionary patrons, to the tune of a fabulous USD $129.00 per month, no strings attached. Leaving aside for a moment the generosity and vision of these patrons, and looking sideways at the military-industrial-university-digital complex in all its leviathan-Frankenstein-megamachine monster glory, it's a laughably, pathetically small number of supporters and dollars for undertaking the first part of a philosophical revolution. But thinking realistically and also optimistically, it's a start.

XVIII.6 Philosophy's Second Copernican Revolution, Part 2: The Radical Kantian *Metaphysical* Paradigm Shift to Kantian Neo-Organicism

As regards Philosophy's Second Copernican Revolution, Part 2, namely its radical Kantian metaphysical paradigm shift to Kantian neo-organicism, in order to understand it we must first look very briefly at *first-wave organicism*. During the period from 1900 to the end of second World War, in parallel with classical Analytic philosophy, there was an emerging *organicist* movement, drawing on earlier British and German Romanticism (Beiser, 2005: ch. 4), expressing itself in philosophy, the applied and fine arts, and the formal and natural sciences alike, including, in philosophy specifically, Henri Bergson's *Matter and Memory* in 1896, *Creative Evolution* in 1907, Samuel Alexander's *Space, Time, and Deity* in 1920, John Dewey's *Experience and Nature* in 1925, and especially Whitehead's "philosophy of organism" in *Process and Reality* in 1929; in the applied and fine arts, the architecture of Frank Lloyd Wright and the other members of the Prairie School, the "golden period of Scandinavian design" in Norway, Sweden, Denmark, Finland, and Iceland, and the poetry of T.S. Eliot, Robert Frost, and Wallace Stevens; and, in the formal and natural sciences, C. Lloyd Morgan's *Emergent Evolution* in 1923, and Erwin Schrödinger's *What is Life? The Physical Aspect of the Living Cell* in 1944. Schrödinger's break-through book initiated *non-equilibrium thermodynamics* and *complex systems dynamics*, as developed by Ilya Prigogine and his associates (Nicolis and Prigogine, 1977; Prigogine and Stengers, 1984; and Prigogine, 1997), and by J.D. Bernal, in the second half of the 20th century; and alongside and inspired by this work, it also primed *the autopoietic approach to organismic biology* worked out by Francisco Varela and his associates during the 1970s (Varela, Maturana, and Uribe, 1974; Varela, 1979).

Here's an important caveat. It is essential *not* to confuse the first wave of organicism in philosophy, the applied and fine arts, and the formal and natural sciences, on the one hand, with *organic nationalism*, aka *organic romanticism*, in the arts, science, and sociopolitics, as it occurred during the rise of fascism and militarism in Germany, Italy, and Japan—for example, in Nazi architecture and visual art—on the other. Organic nationalism is authoritarian up to and including totalitarianism, anti-dignitarian, anti-democratic in its focus on the *Führerprinzip* and/or Strong Man dictator or emperor, and pervasively historically backward-looking, insular, reactionary, and regressive. Sharply on the contrary, first wave organicism is essentially intertwined **first**, with the anti-authoritarian, anti-totalitarian, dignitarian, and democratic versions of *socialism*, and **second**, with the search for a humane modernity that would avoid the excesses of the Industrial Revolution and extreme urbanization.

Jumping forward now to the end of the second decade of the 21st century, if I'm correct, then we are—or at least we ought to be—currently in the earliest stages of *the second wave of organicist philosophy*, aka Kantian neo-organicism, which will finally bring to completion what the most brilliant and radical philosophy and formal-and-natural science of the early 20th century—first wave organicism—initiated, before fascism, World War II, the Cold War, and post-classical Analytic philosophy all disruptively intervened.

The worldview of Kantian neo-organicism per se can be briefly defined in six words:

Everything flows, grows, reposes, and repurposes.

It's essential to recognize that this definition is *not* merely an updated version of Heraclitus's famous dictum *panta rhei*, "everything flows." Heraclitus is saying that the world is nothing but an undifferentiated "becoming" that never really "is": a river you cannot really step into *even once*, much less twice. On the contrary, according to new wave organicism, "flows" means that everything belongs to a complex system of causally efficacious dynamic, natural processes; "grows" means that everything has a mode of activation, actualization, and kinetic energy; "reposes" means that everything has another mode of relative rest, power-in-reserve, and potential energy; and "repurposes" means that everything also has a further mode of "messy" creativity when it is temporarily dismantling some existing causal mechanism or mechanisms, in order to reconfigure it or them for new causal functions and operations.

So in its appeal not only to the metaphysics of *process*, but also to the metaphysics of causally efficacious *actuality* (aligned with activating immanent form or structure), *potentiality* (aligned with activated-or-able-to-be-activated matter or stuffing), and what Kant called *natural purposes*, i.e., living organisms (Weber and Varela, 2002), especially including *minded animals like us*, it's essentially a Kantian *continuation of* and *variation on* the first wave organicism that briefly appeared between 1900 and 1940 as an alternative to the natural mechanist aberrations of high modernism and scientism (Hanna and Paans, 2020).

Kantian neo-organicism is a direct rejection of the scientistic mindset, that by a diametric contrast consists in a *liberally naturalistic* and *pro-scientific*, but also *anti-mechanistic* and *anti-scientistic* conception of the world, including ourselves (Hanna, 2020d; Hanna and Paans, 2020). Kantian neo-organicism in the formal and natural sciences can be found, for example, in new applications of intuitionist mathematics to modeling "time's arrow," i.e., its asymmetrically forward flow from the past to the future (Wolchover, 2020); in new work towards the unification of biology and physics (Torday, Miller Jr, and Hanna, 2020); and by contemporary "processual" approaches to biology (Nicholson and Dupré, 2018).

Above all, however, Kantian neo-organicism is committed to the metaphysical doctrine of *liberal naturalism*. Liberal naturalism says that the irreducible but also non-dualistic mental properties of rational minded animals are as basic in nature as biological properties, and metaphysically continuous with them. More precisely, according to liberal naturalism, rational human free agency is an immanent structure of essentially embodied conscious, intentional, emotional human animal mind; essentially embodied conscious, intentional, emotional human animal mind is an immanent structure of organismic life; and organismic life is an immanent structure of spatiotemporally asymmetric, non-equilibrium matter and/or energy flows. Each more complex structure is metaphysically continuous with, and embeds, all of the less complex structures (Hanna and Maiese, 2009; Hanna, 2018b, 2021c).

Again, according to Kantian neo-organicism and its liberal naturalism, human freedom is dynamically inherent in and dynamically emerges from essentially embodied conscious, intentional, caring human animal mind. And essentially embodied conscious, intentional, caring human animal mind is dynamically inherent in and dynamically emerges from life. Therefore, human freedom is dynamically inherent in and dynamically emerges from life. Moreover, life is dynamically inherent in and dynamically emerges from spatiotemporally asymmetric, non-equilibrium matter and/or energy flows. Therefore, human freedom, human mind, and life are all dynamically inherent in and dynamically emerge from spatiotemporally asymmetric, non-equilibrium matter and/or energy flows.

In view of Kantian neo-organicism and its liberal naturalism, to borrow an apt phrase from later Wittgenstein in the *Investigations*, our rational human free agency is just our own "form of life," and free agency, as such, naturally grows and evolves in certain minded animal species or life-forms. Correspondingly, freedom naturally grows and evolves in certain species of minded animals, including the human species, precisely because *minds like ours* naturally grow and evolve in certain species of animals, including the human species (Thompson, 2007).

By way of a quick summary, here is a diagram of the basic metaphysical continuities and structural embeddings according to the liberal naturalist conception:

[Diagram: concentric circles showing, from outermost to innermost: "free agency"; "minded animality (incl. human rational mind)"; "organismic life"; "asymmetric non-equilibrium matter/energy flows"]

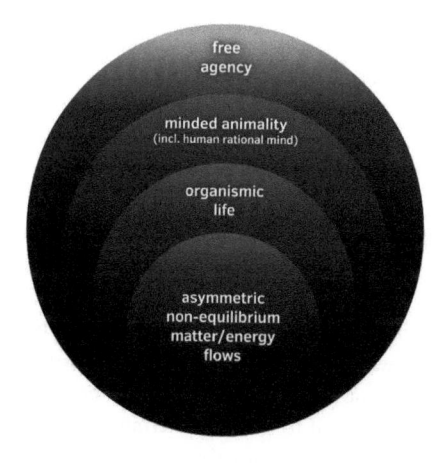

Figure 3. Liberal Naturalism: Basic Metaphysical Continuities and Structural Embeddings

Another name for liberal naturalism is *weak transcendental idealism* (Hanna, 2021a; and also section XVII.8.3 above). Weak transcendental idealism is sharply distinct both from *subjective idealism*, which says that the world is nothing a phenomenal mental construction of an individual cognizer (defended in interestingly different ways, for example, by Berkeley, the neo-Kantians, early Carnap, C.I. Lewis, and Nelson Goodman) and also from *absolute idealism*, which says that the world is nothing but a giant mind, its thought-forms, and its thought-processes (defended in interestingly different ways, for example, by Fichte, Schelling, and Hegel[1]). As opposed to either subjective idealism or absolute idealism, liberal naturalism, i.e., weak transcendental idealism, says that rational human mindedness *naturally grows and evolves* in the manifestly real physical world, in organisms whose lives have an appropriately high level of non-mechanical thermodynamic complexity and self-organization. The manifestly real natural physical world necessarily includes our real possibility and is immanently structured for the dynamic emergence of lives like ours and conscious rational minds like ours. Or in Thomas Nagel's

---

[1] Leaving aside their absolute idealism, however, there are also some significant organicist themes in Schelling's and Hegel's works that provide a philosophical bridge between Kant's third *Critique* and early 20th century *process metaphysics*, i.e., in my terminology, *first wave organicist philosophy*. See, e.g., (Gare, 2011, 2017, 2019). Indeed, there are many overlaps and similarities between what I'm calling "Kantian neo-organicism" and what Gare calls "speculative naturalism" (Gare, 2017).

apt, crisp formulation: "rational intelligibility is at the root of the natural order" (Nagel, 2012: p. 17).

By now, it should be self-evidently clear that Kantian neo-organicism's liberal naturalism is directly opposed to the doctrine of natural mechanism. The doctrine of natural mechanism, as I've spelled it out in section XVII.2, says that all the causal powers of everything whatsoever in the natural world are ultimately fixed by what can be digitally computed on a universal deterministic or indeterministic real-world Turing machine, provided that the following three plausible "causal orderliness" and "decompositionality" assumptions are all satisfied: (i) its causal powers are necessarily determined by the general deterministic or indeterministic causal natural laws, especially including the Conservation Laws, together with all the settled quantity-of-matter-and/or-energy facts about the past, especially including The Big Bang, (ii) the causal powers of the real-world Turing machine are held fixed under our general causal laws of nature, and (iii) the "digits" over which the real-world Turing machine computes constitute a complete denumerable set of spatiotemporally discrete physical objects. In direct opposition to natural mechanism, however, the Kantian neo-organicist philosophy's liberal naturalism says that the causal powers of biological life (and in particular, the causal powers of living organisms, including all minded animals, especially including rational human animals) are neither fixed by, identical with, nor otherwise reducible to the Conservation-Law-determined, Big-Bang-caused, real-world-Turing-computable causal powers of thermodynamic systems, whether these causal powers are governed by general deterministic laws or general probabilistic/Statistical laws. So if humanistic new wave organicism's liberal naturalism is true, then anti-mechanism is true and natural mechanism is false.

It's essential to recognize that Kantian neo-organicism's liberal naturalism does *not* postulate any supernatural, extra-spatiotemporal or sub-spatiotemporal, and essentially mysterious, aether-like and/or external divine causal force that somehow creates, designs, and guides the natural universe. On the contrary, Kantian neo-organicism's liberal naturalism is *radically agnostic* in the radical Kantian sense (see section XV.1 above), and also committed to the doctrines of (i) *formal piety*, as per chapter X above, and as paradigmatically exemplified by Cantor, Gödel, and Tarski, and (ii) what the early 20th century British process philosopher Samuel Alexander—following the Romantic poet Wordsworth—called *natural piety*. According to Alexander:

> I do not mean by natural piety exactly what Wordsworth meant by it–the reverent joy in nature, by which he wished that his days might be bound to each other–though there is enough connection with his interpretation to justify me in using his phrase. The natural piety I am going to speak of is that of the scientific investigator, by which he accepts with loyalty the [phenomena] which he cannot explain in nature and has no right to try to explain. I may describe it as the habit of knowing when to stop in asking questions of nature.

> [T]hat organization which is alive is not merely physico-chemical, though

completely resoluble into such terms, but has the new quality of life. No appeal is needed, so far as I can see, to a vital force or even an *élan vital*. It is enough to note the emergence of the quality, and try to describe what is involved in its conditions.... The living body is also physical and chemical. It surrenders no claim to be considered a part of the physical world. But the new quality of life is neither chemical nor mechanical, but something new.

We may and must observe with care our of what previous conditions these new creations arise. We cannot tell why they should assume these qualities. We can but accept them as we find them, and this acceptance is natural piety. (Alexander, 1939: pp. 299, 306, 310-311)

According to natural piety, *neither* are you alienated from nature (a Cartesian ghost-in-a-machine) *nor* are you a "lord and master" of nature (a Baconian/Cartesian technocrat). To believe both of these at once was Victor Frankenstein's tragic mistake, repeated endlessly and magnified infinitely in the adoption of deeply misguided epistemic and metaphysical doctrines, combined with the scientistic-technocratic ideology of natural mechanism:

Learn from me, if not by my precepts, at least by my example, how dangerous is the acquirement of [naturally mechanistic] knowledge, and how much happier that man is who believes his native town to be the world, than he who aspires to become greater than his nature will allow. (Shelley, 1818: vol. 1, ch. 3)

In a closely-related way, Kantian neo-organicism and its liberal naturalism fully conform to contemporary physics and in particular to non-equilibrium thermodynamics, under the non-deterministic interpretation of it offered, for example, by Prigogine, who also wrote this sharp, Shelley-like criticism of natural mechanism:

The attempt to understand nature remains one of the basic objectives of Western thought. It should not, however, be identified with the idea of control. The master who believes he understands his slaves because they obey his orders would be blind. When we turn to physics, our expectations are obviously different, but here as well, Vladimir Nabokov's conviction rings true: "What can be controlled is never completely real; what is real can never be completely controlled." The [natural mechanist] classical ideal of science, a world without time, memory, and history, recalls the totalitarian nightmares described by Aldous Huxley, Milan Kundera, and George Orwell. (Prigogine, 1997: pp. 153-154)

Correspondingly, as I've already mentioned, Kantian neo-organicism and its liberal naturalism fully conform to contemporary attempts to unify physics and biology, and to processual approaches to biology, as well as to processual approaches to chemistry and cognitive neuroscience, insofar as these are all construed in terms of the non-deterministic interpretation of non-equilibrium thermodynamics. In other words, Kantian neo-organicism and its liberal naturalism take natural science seriously *precisely because* they reject natural mechanism. It is the outdated model of *natural mechanism* that can no longer serve as a workable paradigm for scientific activity. To be a Kantian neo-organicist philosopher and a liberal naturalist, is to integrate physics and processual approaches to biology—especially including organismic biology and ecosystemic biology—and chemistry, and finally, cognitive neuroscience, in an essentially *anti*-mechanistic manner.

So, I'm hereby directly challenging the natural mechanist approach to science: why must all the basic sciences be interpreted in accordance with natural mechanism? After all, Alonzo Church and Alan Turing show us that logical truth in every system at least as rich as classical first-order polyadic quantified predicate logic with identity, aka "elementary logic," cannot be decided or determined by Turing-computable algorithms, and therefore cannot be naturally mechanized (Boolos and Jeffrey, 1989); Gödel's incompleteness theorems show us that every logico-mathematical system at least as rich as Peano arithmetic contains uncomputable, undecidable, unprovable truths, that no such system can demonstrate its own consistency, and that more generally, truth-in-a-mathematical-system cannot be determined by Turing-computable algorithms or by formal proof, nor can it be determined internally to that system, and therefore mathematical truth cannot be naturally mechanized; and Tarski's semantic conception of truth in formalized languages show us that truth of any kind on the one hand, and formal proof/decidability of any kind on the other, are essentially distinct. Yet no one regards *elementary logic*, *Gödel-incompleteness*, *Peano arithmetic*, and *Tarski's semantic conception of truth* as less than seriously scientific. So, if *formal* piety about logic and mathematics is intelligible and defensible, as it surely is, then by the same token, so too is *natural* piety about physics, biology, chemistry, and cognitive neuroscience.

Therefore, if one can be fully serious about logic and mathematics without reducing them to natural mechanist models, then it follows that in order to be fully serious about physics, biology, chemistry, and cognitive neuroscience, then one must do away with the natural mechanist models on which they have hitherto been based, since all of the natural sciences presuppose logic and mathematics. And in particular, if all logico-mathematical systems at least as rich as Peano arithmetic are formally incomplete, *then so are the natural sciences that presuppose these logico-mathematical systems* (Hanna, 2021i). More generally, if the non-deterministic interpretation of non-equilibrium thermodynamics, together with Church's and Turing's discoveries about logic, together with Gödel's incompleteness theorems, together with Tarski's semantic conception of truth, are all true, then natural mechanism is false even about *physics itself* and yet we can still be fully serious about logic, mathematics, physics, and the other exact sciences. Kantian neo-organicism and its liberal naturalism, together with the doctrines of formal piety and natural piety, clearly collectively meet this theoretical high standard of formal and exact-scientific full seriousness.

For all these reasons, Kantian neo-organicism can *also* be the source of a range of new and productive philosophical analogies and metaphors that override and supersede those of natural mechanism, and can guide us cognitively, affectively, and practically into the future. In 1874, roughly sixty years before Turing's breakthrough paper (Turing, 1936), here is how the ultra-Darwinian biologist Thomas Huxley analogized and compared human and other minded animals to natural automata:

> The consciousness of brutes would appear to be related to the mechanism of their body simply as a collateral product of its working, and to be completely without any power of modifying that working as the steam-whistle which accompanies the work of a locomotive engine is without influence on its machinery. Their volition, if they have any, is an emotion indicative of physical changes, not a cause of such changes… It is quite true that, to the best of my judgment, the argumentation which applies to brutes holds equally good of men; and, therefore, that all states of consciousness in us, as in them, are immediately caused by molecular changes in the brain substance. It seems to me that in men, as in brutes, there is no proof that any state of consciousness is the cause of change in the motion of the matter of the organism. If these positions are well based, it follows that our mental conditions are simply the symbols in consciousness of the changes which take place automatically in the organism; and that, to take an extreme illustration, the feeling that we call volition is not the cause of a voluntary act, but the symbol of that state of the brain which is the immediate cause of that act. We are conscious automata, endowed with free will in the only intelligible sense of that much-abused term—inasmuch as in many respects we are able to do as we like—but nonetheless parts of the great series of causes and effects which, in its unbroken continuity, composes that which is, and has been, and shall be—the sum of existence. (Huxley, 2002: pp. 29-30)

Radically in opposition to Huxley's naturally mechanistic world-picture, according to Kantian neo-organicism and its liberal naturalism, human and other minded animals are *not* nothing but highly complicated locomotive engines, steam whistles, and Turing-machines, belonging to "the great series of causes and effects": radically on the contrary, we and other minded animals are nothing less than complex living organisms, ineluctably and irreducibly embedded in, complementary to, and in an endlessly delicate homeostatic balance with, our microphysical, ecological, geophysical, and cosmological environments, whose minds, freedom, and social activities are all and only forms of life. As per the fifth epigraph at the head of this chapter, Helen Steward has remarked that

> [t]he task [of understanding free will and agency] requires some reflection on the organizational principles of living creatures, for it is only through such reflection … that we can start to understand where the difference really lies between, on the one hand those things that are true agents, and, on the other, mere machines, entities that nothing will ever be up to, however impressive they may be…. I am exceedingly hopeful that the next few years will see the beginnings of a revolution in our conception of the human person, as philosophical and everyday conceptions of the scientific picture of the world are freed from outdated Newtonian ideas and begin to take more note, both of the complexities of science as it really is and of the undeniable fact of our animal nature. (Steward, 2012: pp. 198-199)

In full solidarity with Steward, I'm "exceedingly hopeful" that we're at the beginning of a Kantian neo-organicist revolution in metaphysics that's fully comparable to the metaphysical part of Kant's "Copernican Revolution" in philosophy. Kant's Copernican Revolution, we will remember, says that in order to explain rational human cognition and authentic a priori knowledge, we must hold that necessarily, the manifestly real world structurally conforms to our minds, rather than the converse. The Kantian neo-organicist metaphysical revolution, in turn, says that the real possibility of human consciousness, cognition, caring, rationality, and free agency, and *therefore also the "Copernican" necessary structural conformity of world-to-conscious-and-rational-human-minds, provided that we actually do exist*, is built essentially into the non-equilibrium thermodynamics of organismic life (Hanna, 2021a) and *necessarily underdetermined* by any and all naturally-mechanical processes and facts. Hence the Kantian neo-organicist revolution in philosophy, the fine and applied arts, the formal and natural sciences, the human sciences, the social sciences and society, politics, and civilization itself, would not only *includes* Kant's Copernican Revolution, but also go one full revolutionary cycle *beyond* it.

Since the 17th century, philosophical revolutions have happened roughly every one hundred years, and each revolution takes roughly twenty years to unfold: (i) the late 17th and early 18th century anti-Scholastic Rationalist revolution—Descartes, Spinoza, and Leibniz, but also including Newtonian scientific mechanism, followed by an Empiricist reaction, (ii) the late 18th and early 19th century anti-Rationalist, anti-Empiricist Kantian Copernican Revolution and absolute idealism—Kant, Fichte, Schelling, and Hegel, followed by an anti-Hegelian reaction, including Kierkegaard and neo-Kantianism, then by Brentano, Husserl, Heidegger, Sartre, Merleau-Ponty and phenomenology (especially existential phenomenology) more generally, (iii) the late 19th and early 20th century anti-idealist Analytic philosophy revolution that I've been critically studying in this book—Frege, Russell, Moore, and early Wittgenstein, followed by Vienna Circle logical empiricism/positivism, then by Quinean and Sellarsian scientific naturalism, alongside the later Wittgenstein's work and ordinary language philosophy, then by Strawsonian conceptual analysis, direct reference theory and scientific essentialism, and currently, Analytic metaphysics, X-Phi, and Analytic feminism. Now it has been almost exactly one hundred years since the neo-Kantian and British neo-Hegelian traditions went down into the ash-heap of history and were superseded by classical Analytic philosophy, in the late 1920s and 30s. So if the historical pattern persists, then we are actually at the beginning of another philosophical revolution, over the next twenty years, and fully into the heart and soul of the 21st century, although it may be difficult to see its precise shape because we do not have the benefit of historical hindsight or an adequate emotional and reflective distance from actual historical processes, and because we are naturally distracted by our own everyday affairs, domestic and international politics, and global crises like the 2020-2021 COVID-19 pandemic. But in any case, we can be certain that when professional academic post-classical Analytic philosophy goes down into the ash-heap of history, then its all-purpose dialectical Other, social-institutional slave, and Enemy of the People, so-called "Continental philosophy," will *also* disappear along with it—to borrow Marx's famous phrase, it will "melt into air," just like everything that seems eternally solid and permanent, yet in reality is merely a social-institutional structure produced by a hegemonic ideology.

Therefore, if I'm correct, then there's still a serious metaphysical alternative to the natural mechanist metaphysics of mainstream Anglo-American professional academic post-classical Analytic philosophy: namely, Kantian neo-organicism, powered by weak transcendental idealism, drawing directly for philosophical inspiration on the ill-fated first wave of organicism. Once again, the Kantian neo-organicist part says that everything flows, grows, reposes, and repurposes; and the weak transcendental idealist part says that this essentially processual, purposive, and self-organizing world necessarily structurally conforms to conscious, rational "human, all-too-human" animal minds, provided that they/we do actually exist. So according to this comprehensive radical Kantian neo-organicist metaphysics of humanity, nature, and the cosmos, the world is endlessly in a dynamic process of beginning, unfolding, resting, and then beginning again, and this processual, purposive, and self-organizing world necessarily structurally includes the real possibility of conscious, rational humanity.

XVIII.7 Conclusion: Analytic Philosophy, The Owl of Minerva, and The Radical Kantian Phoenix of Future Philosophy

Beyond the philosophically chequered yet social-institutionally dominant 140-year tradition of Analytic philosophy, then, lies the alternative of the Philosophy's Second Copernican Revolution, including equally its Part 1 (the radical Kantian metaphilosophical paradigm shift): anarcho- or borderless philosophy, and its Part 2 (the radical Kantian metaphysical paradigm shift): Kantian neo-organicism. Correspondingly, my proposal for a real philosophy of the future, bounded in a nutshell, is that we not only *can* but most urgently *should* enact this double paradigm shift over the next two decades of the 21st century, so that real philosophy is again reborn, like a radical Kantian phoenix, from the ash-heap into which the 140-year tradition of Analytic philosophy has driven it. According to Hegel's famous trope in the final paragraph of his Preface to *The Philosophy of Right*, philosophy is the owl of Minerva that "spreads its wings only with the falling of the dusk":

> One more word about giving instruction as to what the world ought to be. Philosophy ... always comes on the scene too late to give it. As the thought of the world, it appears only when actuality is already there cut and dried after its process of formation has been completed.... When philosophy paints its grey-on-grey, then has a shape of the world grown old. By philosophy's grey-on-grey it cannot be rejuvenated but only understood. The owl of Minerva spreads its wings only with the falling of the dusk. (Hegel, 1952: pp. 12-13, translation slightly modified)

So Hegel is claiming that philosophy is inherently *quietist*. But sharply contrariwise, I'm claiming that philosophy is inherently *activist*, both individually and social-institutionally (Hanna, 2017e, 2020b), and to repeat what I said in sub-section XVII.8.4, with gusto, I'm also claiming that the radical Kantian phoenix of future real philosophy can and should arise in the blazing sunburst of a new dawn, over the next twenty years.

BIBLIOGRAPHY

(Akehurst, 2008). Akehurst, T. "The Nazi Tradition: The Analytic Critique of Continental Philosophy in Mid-Century Britain." History of European Ideas, 34: 548-557.

(Akehurst, 2011). Akehurst, T. The Cultural Politics of Analytic Philosophy: Britishness and the Spectre of Europe. London, Bloomsbury.

(Alberg, 2017). Alberg, J. "Being on the Ground: Philosophy, Reading and Difficulty." Tetsugaku, 1: Philosophy and the University. Available online at URL = <http://philosophy-japan.org/tetugaku/volume-1-2017-philosophy-and-the-university/>.

(Alexander, 2012). Alexander, Joshua. Experimental Philosophy: An Introduction. Cambridge: Polity Press.

(Alexander, 1939). Alexander, Samuel. "Natural Piety." In S. Alexander, Philosophical and Literary Pieces. London: Macmillan. Pp. 299-315.

(Appiah, 2008). Appiah, K.A. Experiments in Ethics. Cambridge, MA: Harvard Univ. Press.

(Augustine, 1961). Augustine. Confessions. Trans. R. Pine-Coffin. Harmondsworth, Middlesex: Penguin.

(Austin, 1962). Austin, J.L. How to Do Things with Words. Cambridge, MA: Harvard Univ. Press.

(Ayer, 1952). Ayer, A.J. Language, Truth, and Logic. 2nd edn., New York: Dover.

(Ayer, 1959). Ayer, A.J. (ed.), Logical Positivism. New York: Free Press.

(Badiou, 2009). Badiou, A. Logics of Worlds. Trans. A. Toscano. London: Bloomsbury.

(Badiou, 2013). Badiou, A. Being and Event. Trans. O. Feltham. London: Bloomsbury.

(Baghramian and Marchetti, 2019). Baghramian, M. and Marchetti, S. "Philosophy in the Twentieth Century: The Mingled Story of Three Revolutions." In M. Baghramian and S. Marchetti, (eds.), Pragmatism and the European Traditions: Encounters with Analytic Philosophy and Phenomenology Before the Great Divide. London: Routledge. Pp. 1-19.

(Baldwin, 1990). Baldwin, T. G.E. Moore. London: Routledge.

(Baldwin, 2020). Baldwin, T. "G.E. Moore: A Great Philosopher?" TLS (October 2020). Available online at URL = <https://www.the-tls.co.uk/articles/g-e-moore-a-great-philosopher/>.

(Barnes, 1959). Barnes, H. Humanistic Existentialism: The Literature of Possibility. Lincoln, NE: Univ. of Nebraska Press.

(Baudrillard, 1991). Baudrillard, J. The Gulf War Did Not Take Place. Trans. P. Patton Bloomington, IN: Indiana Univ. Press.

(Baudrillard, 1994). Baudrillard, J. Simulacra and Simulation. Trans. S.F. Glaser. Ann Arbor, MI: Univ. of Michigan Press.

(Bayne and Montague, 2011). Bayne, T. and Montague, M. Cognitive Phenomenology. Oxford: Oxford Univ. Press.

(Beaney, 2013). Beaney, M. (ed.) The Oxford Handbook of the History of Analytic Philosophy. Oxford: Oxford University Press.

(Beaney, 2018). Beaney, M. "Analysis." In E.N. Zalta (ed.), The Stanford Encyclopedia of Philosophy (Summer 2018 Edition). Available online at URL = <https://plato.stanford.edu/archives/sum2018/entries/analysis/>.

(Bearn, 1997). Bearn, G. Waking to Wonder: Wittgenstein's Existential Investigations. Albany, NY: SUNY Press.

(Beiser, 2005). Beiser, F. Hegel. New York: Routledge.

(Beiser, 2014). Beiser, F. The Genesis of Neo-Kantianism, 1796–1880. Oxford: Oxford Univ. Press.

(Bell and Cooper, 1990). Bell, D. and Cooper, N. (eds.) The Analytic Tradition. Oxford: Blackwell.

(Benacerraf, 1973). Benacerraf, P. "Mathematical Truth." Journal of Philosophy 70: 661-680.

(Benacerraf, 1981). Benacerraf, P. "Frege: The Last Logicist." In (French et al., 1981). Pp. 17–35.

BIBLIOGRAPHY

(Bermúdez and Cahen, 2020). Bermúdez, J. and Cahen, A. "Nonconceptual Mental Content." In E.N. Zalta (ed.), The Stanford Encyclopedia of Philosophy (Summer 2020 Edition). Available online at URL = <https://plato.stanford.edu/archives/sum2020/entries/content-nonconceptual/>.

(Block, 1980). Block, N. "Behaviorism." In N. Block (ed.), Readings in the Philosophy of Psychology. 2 vols., Cambridge, MA: Harvard Univ. Press. Vol. 1. Part 1. Pp. 11-63.

(Bloor, 2017). Bloor, S. "The Divide Between Philosophy and Enthusiasm: The Effect of the World Wars on British Attitudes Towards Continental Philosophies." In M. Sharpe et al. (eds.), 100 Years of European Philosophy Since the Great War. Cham, CH: Springer. Pp. 201-213.

(Boeri, 2017). Boeri, M. "The Presence of Philosophy in Latin American Universities." Tetsugaku, 1: Philosophy and the University (2017). Available online at URL = <http://philosophy-japan.org/tetugaku/volume-1-2017-philosophy-and-the-university/>.

(Boghossian, 1996). Boghossian, P. "Analyticity Reconsidered." Noûs 30: 360-391.

(Bolzano, 1972). Bolzano, B. Theory of Science. Trans. R. George. Berkeley & Los Angeles, CA: Univ. of California Press.

(Bonjour, 1998). BonJour, L. In Defense of Pure Reason. Cambridge: Cambridge Univ. Press.

(Boolos and Jeffrey, 1989). Boolos, G. and Jeffrey, R. Computability and Logic. 3rd edn., Cambridge, Cambridge Univ. Press.

(Bourget, 2020). Bourget, D. "The 2020 PhilPapers Survey is Here." PhilPapers (15 October 2020). Available online at URL = <https://philpapers.org/post/27014>.

(Bourget and Chalmers, 2009). Bourget, D. and Chalmers, D. "Philosophical Papers Survey 2009." PhilPapers (2009). Available online at URL = <https://philpapers.org/surveys/results.pl>.

(Bourget and Chalmers, 2014). Bourget, D. and Chalmers, D. "What Do Philosophers Believe?" Philosophical Studies 170: 465-500.

(Braddon-Mitchell and Nola, 2008). Braddon-Mitchell, D. and Nola, R. Conceptual Analysis and Philosophical Naturalism. Cambridge, MA: MIT Press.

(Brady and Pritchard, 2003). Brady, M. and Pritchard, D. (eds.) Moral and Epistemic Virtues. Oxford: Blackwell.

(Brandom, 2000). Brandom, R. *Articulating Reasons: An Introduction to Inferentialism*. Cambridge, MA: Harvard Univ. Press.

(Brassier, 2007). Brassier, R. *Nihil Unbound: Enlightenment and Extinction*. Basingstoke, UK: Palgrave Macmillan.

(Brentano, 1995). Brentano, F. *Psychology from an Empirical Standpoint*. Trans. A. Rancurello et al. London: Routledge.

(Brentano, 2002). Brentano, F. "Descriptive Psychology or Descriptive Phenomenology." In D. Moran and T. Mooney (eds.), *The Phenomenology Reader*. London: Routledge. Pp. 51-54.

(Brockhaus, 1991). Brockhaus, R. *Pulling Up the Ladder: The Metaphysical Roots of Wittgenstein's Tractatus Logico- Philosophicus*. La Salle, IL: Open Court.

(Burge, 1992). Burge, T. "Philosophy of Language and Mind: 1950-1990." *Philosophical Review* 101: 3-51.

(Cantor, 1891). Cantor, G. "Ueber eine elementare Frage der Mannigfaltigkeitslehre." *Jahresbericht der Deutschen Mathematiker-Vereinigung* 1: 75–78. Also available—ironically enough—in an English machine-translation, as "On an Elementary Question of the Theory of Manifolds," at URL = <https://cs.maryvillecollege.edu/wiki/images/c/cb/Cantor_UeberEineElementare_Trans_v1.pdf>.

(Carnap, 1935). Carnap, R. *Philosophy and Logical Syntax*. London: Routledge & Kegan Paul.

(Carnap, 1937). Carnap, R. *The Logical Syntax of Language*. Trans. A Smeaton. London: Routledge & Kegan Paul.

(Carnap, 1956a). Carnap, R. *Meaning and Necessity*. 2nd edn., Chicago, IL: Univ. of Chicago Press.

(Carnap, 1956b). Carnap, R. "Empiricism, Semantics, and Ontology." In (Carnap, 1956a). Pp. 205-221.

(Carnap, 1956c). Carnap, R. "Meaning Postulates." In (Carnap, 1956a). Pp. 222-229.

(Carnap, 1956d). Carnap, R. "Meaning and Synonymy in Natural Languages." In (Carnap, 1956a). Pp. 233-247.

(Carnap, 1959). Carnap, R. "The Elimination of Metaphysics through the Logical Analysis of Language." In (Ayer, 1959). Pp. 60-81.

(Carnap, 1963). Carnap, R. "Intellectual Autobiography." In (Schilpp, 1963). Pp. 3-84.

(Carnap, 1967a). Carnap, R. The Logical Structure of the World. Trans. R. George. Berkeley & Los Angeles, CA: Univ. of California Press.

(Carnap, 1967b). Carnap, R. Pseudoproblems in Philosophy. Trans. R. George. Berkeley & Los Angeles, CA: Univ. of California Press.

(Carroll, 1895). Carroll, L. "What the Tortoise Said to Achilles." Mind 4: 278-280.

(Carroll, 1988). Carroll, L. Through the Looking-Glass. New York: Dial.

(Cassirer, 1967). Cassirer, E. "Kant and the Problem of Metaphysics: Remarks on Heidegger's Interpretation of Kant." In M. Gram (ed.), Kant: Disputed Questions. Chicago: Quadrangle. Pp. 131-157.

(Cassirer, 1981). Cassirer, E. Kant's Life and Thought. Trans. J. Haden. New Haven, CT: Yale Univ. Press.

(Cavell, 1979). Cavell, S. The Claim of Reason: Wittgenstein, Skepticism, Morality, and Tragedy. Oxford: Oxford Univ. Press.

(Chalmers, 1996). Chalmers, D. The Conscious Mind: In Search of a Fundamental Theory. New York: Oxford Univ. Press.

(Chalmers, 2002). Chalmers, D. (ed.) Philosophy of Mind: Classical and Contemporary Readings. New York, Oxford Univ. Press.

(Chalmers, 2004). Chalmers, D. "Foundations of Two-Dimensional Semantics." In M. Garcia-Carpentero and J. Macia (eds.), Two Dimensional Semantics: Foundations and Applications. New York: Oxford Univ. Press. Pp. 55-140.

(Chalmers, 2012). Chalmers, D. Constructing the World. Oxford: Oxford Univ. Press.

(Chalmers and Jackson, 2001). Chalmers, D. and Jackson, F. "Conceptual Analysis and Reductive Explanation," Philosophical Review 110: 315-360.

(Chignell, 2013). Chignell, A. "Rational Hope, Moral Order, and the Revolution of the Will." In E. Watkins (ed.), Divine Order, Human Order, and the Order of Nature. Oxford: Oxford Univ. Press. Pp. 197-218.

(Chignell, 2015). Chignell, A. What May I Hope? London: Routledge.

(Chomsky, 1965). Chomsky, N. Aspects of the Theory of Syntax. Cambridge, MA: MIT Press.

(Chomsky, 1966). Chomsky, N. Cartesian Linguistics. New York: Harper and Row.

(Chomsky, 1986). Chomsky, N. Knowledge of Language. Westport, CT: Praeger.

(Clarke, 1972). Clarke, T. "The Legacy of Skepticism." Journal of Philosophy 69: 754-769.

(Clarke, 2019). Clarke, E. "Neo-Kantianism: The Marburg and Southwest Schools." In J. Shand (ed.), The Blackwell Encyclopedia of 19th Century Philosophy. Oxford: Blackwell. Pp. 389-417.

(Cohen, 1984). Cohen, S. "Justification and Truth." Philosophical Studies 46: 279–295.

(Coffa, 1991). Coffa, A. The Semantic Tradition from Kant to Carnap. Cambridge: Cambridge Univ. Press.

(Conant, 1991). Conant, J. "The Search for Logically Alien Thought: Descartes, Kant, Frege, and the Tractatus." Philosophical Topics 20: 115-180.

(Crowell, 2012). Crowell, S. (ed.) The Cambridge Companion to Existentialism. Cambridge: Cambridge Univ. Press.

(Crowell, 2017). Crowell, S. "Neo-Kantianism." In S. Critchley and W. Schroeder (eds.), The Blackwell Companion to Continental Philosophy. Oxford: Blackwell. Pp. 185-197.

(Davidson, 1963). Davidson, D. "Actions, Reasons, and Causes." Journal of Philosophy 60: 685-700.

(Davidson, 1984). Davidson, D. Inquiries into Truth and Interpretation. Oxford: Clarendon/Oxford Univ. Press.

(Davidson, 1999). Davidson, D. "Intellectual Autobiography." In L. Hahn (ed.), The Philosophy of Donald Davidson, Library of Living Philosophers. Volume XXVII. Chicago: Open Court. Pp. 3-79.

(Davis, 1974). Davis, A. Angela Davis: An Autobiography. New York: International Publishers.

(Davis, 2009). Davis, A. "The Liberation of Our People: Transcript of a Speech Delivered by Angela Y. Davis at a Black Panther Rally in Bobby Hutton Park (aka DeFremery Park), Oakland, CA on Nov. 12, 1969." East Bay History (15 April 2009). Available online at URL = <https://www.indybay.org/newsitems/2009/04/15/18589458.php>.

(Davis and Wiener, 2020) Davis, M. and Wiener, J. Set the Night on Fire: L.A. in the Sixties. London: Verso.

(Dawkins, 2006). Dawkins, R. The Selfish Gene. Oxford: Oxford Univ. Press.

(Dennett, 2002). Dennett, D. "Quining Qualia." In (Chalmers, 2002). Pp. 226-246.

(Derrida, 1998). Derrida, J. Of Grammatology. Trans. G.C. Spivak. Baltimore, MD: The Johns Hopkins Univ. Press.

(Derrida, 2001). Derrida, J. Writing and Difference. Trans. A. Bass. London: Routledge.

(Descartes, 1984). Descartes, R. "Meditations on First Philosophy." In R. Descartes, Philosophical Writings of Descartes. Trans. R. Cottingham et al. 3 vols., Cambridge: Cambridge Univ. Press. Vol. II. Pp. 3-62.

(Dretske, 1969). Dretske, F. Seeing and Knowing. Chicago, IL: Univ. of Chicago Press.

(Diamond, 1991). Diamond, C. The Realistic Spirit: Wittgenstein, Philosophy, and the Mind. Cambridge: MIT Press.

(Donnellan, 1962). Donnellan, K. "Necessity and Criteria." Journal of Philosophy 59: 647-658.

(Donnellan, 1966). Donnellan, K. "Reference and Definite Descriptions." Philosophical Review 75: 281-304.

(Dostoyevsky, 1958). Dostoyevsky, F. The Brothers Karamazov. Trans. D. Magarshack. 2 vols., Harmondsworth, Middlesex: Penguin Books.

(Dummett, 1993). Dummett, M. Origins of Analytical Philosophy. Cambridge, MA: Harvard Univ. Press.

(Eames, 1992). Eames, E.R. "Introduction." In (Russell, 1992). Pp. vii-xxxvii.

(Edmonds, 2020). Edmonds, D. The Murder of Professor Schlick: The Rise and Fall of The Vienna Circle. Princeton, NJ: Princeton Univ. Press.

(Eilenberger, 2018). Eilenberger, W. "Die deutschsprachige Philosophie ist in einem desolaten Zustand. Woran liegt das?" Die Zeit (28 February 2018). Available online at URL = <https://www.zeit.de/2018/10/philosophie-deutschland-universitaeten-wissenschaft-konformismus>.

(Ertl, 2017). Ertl, W. "Home of the Owl? Kantian Reflections on Philosophy at University." Tetsugaku, 1: Philosophy and the University (2017). Available online at URL = <http://philosophy-japan.org/tetugaku/volume-1-2017-philosophy-and-the-university/>.

(Evans, 1982). Evans, G. Varieties of Reference. Oxford: Clarendon/Oxford Univ. Press.

(Fairweather and Zagzebski, 2001). Fairweather, A. and Zagzebski, L. (eds.) Virtue Epistemology. Oxford: Oxford Univ. Press.

(Feferman, 2006). Feferman, S. "The Nature and Significance of Gödel's Incompleteness Theorems." Unpublished MS, 2006. Available online at URL = <https://www.academia.edu/160391/The_nature_and_significance_of_G%C3%B6dels_incompleteness_theorems>.

(Field, 1972). Field, H., "Tarski's Theory of Truth." Journal of Philosophy, 69: 347–375.

(Fine, 1994). Fine, K. "Essence and Modality." Philosophers' Annual 17: 151-166.

(Fine, 1995). Fine, K. "Senses of Essence." In W. Sinnott-Armstrong (ed.), Modality, Morality, and Belief. Cambridge: Cambridge Univ. Press. Pp. 53-73.

(Fine, 2005a). Fine, K. Modality and Tense: Philosophical Papers. Oxford: Oxford Univ. Press.

(Fine, 2005b). Fine, K. "The Varieties of Necessity." In (Fine, 2005a). Pp. 235-260.

(Fodor, 1975). Fodor, J. The Language of Thought. Cambridge, MA: Harvard Univ. Press.

(Foucault, 1991). Foucault, M. Discipline and Punish: The Birth of the Prison. Trans. A. Sheridan. London: Penguin.

(Foucault, 2001). Foucault, M. Madness and Civilization. Trans. R. Howard. London: Routledge.

(Foucault, 2002a). Foucault, M. The Order of Things: An Archaeology of the Human Sciences. London, Routledge.

(Foucault, 2002b). Foucault, M. The Archaeology of Knowledge. Trans. A. Sheridan. London: Routledge.

(Frege, 1953). Frege, G. The Foundations of Arithmetic. Trans. J. L. Austin, 2nd edn., Evanston, IL: Northwestern Univ. Press.

(Frege, 1964). Frege, G. The Basic Laws of Arithmetic. Trans. M. Furth. Berkeley and Los Angeles, CA: Univ. of California Press.

(Frege, 1971). Frege, G. "On the Foundations of Geometry." In G. Frege, On the Foundations of Geometry and Formal Theories of Arithmetic. Trans. E.-H. Kluge. New Haven, CT: Yale Univ. Press. Pp. 22–37 and 49–112.

(Frege, 1972). Frege, G. Conceptual Notation and Related Articles. Trans. T. W. Bynum. Oxford: Oxford Univ. Press.

(Frege, 1979). Frege, G. "Logic [1897]." In G. Frege, Posthumous Writings. Trans. P. Long et al. Chicago, IL: Univ. of Chicago Press, 1979. Pp. 127-151.

(Frege, 1984a). Frege, G. Collected Papers on Mathematics, Logic, and Philosophy. Trans. M. Black et al. Oxford: Blackwell.

(Frege, 1984b). Frege, G. "On Sense and Meaning." In (Frege, 1984a). Pp. 157–77.

(Frege, 1984c). Frege, G. "Review of E. G. Husserl, Philosophie der Arithmetik I." In Frege, 1984a). Pp. 195-209.

(Frege, 1984d). Frege, G. "Thoughts." In (Frege, 1984a). Pp. 351–372.

(French, 1981). French, P. et al. (eds.), The Foundations of Analytic Philosophy. Midwest Studies in Philosophy 6. Minneapolis, MN: Univ. of Minnesota Press.

(Friedman, 1999). Friedman, M. Reconsidering Logical Positivism. Cambridge: Cambridge Univ. Press.

(Friedman, 2000). Friedman, M. *A Parting of the Ways: Carnap, Cassirer, and Heidegger*. La Salle, IL: Open Court.

(Frodeman and Briggle, 2016). Frodeman, R. and Briggle, A. "Socrates Tenured: The Argument in a Nutshell." *Against Professional Philosophy* (25 August 2016). Available online at URL = <https://againstprofphil.org/2016/08/25/socrates-tenured/>.

(Galison, 1990). Galison, P. "Aufbau/Bauhaus: Logical Positivism and Architectural Modernism." *Critical Inquiry* 16: 709-752.

(Gare, 2011). Gare, A. "From Kant to Schelling to Process Metaphysics: On the Way to Ecological Civilization." *Cosmos and History* 7: 26-69.

(Gare, 2017). Gare, A. "The Case for Speculative Naturalism." In A. Gare and W. Hudson (eds.), *For a New Naturalism*. Candor NY: Telos Press. Pp. 9-32.

(Gare, 2019). Gare, A. "Consciousness, Mind and Spirit." *Cosmos and History* 15: 236-264.

(Gare, 2021). Gare, A. "Against Posthumanism: Posthumanism as the World Vision of House-Slaves." *Borderless Philosophy* 4: 1-56.

(Garry, 2018). Garry, A. "Analytic Feminism." In E.N. Zalta (ed.), *The Stanford Encyclopedia of Philosophy* (Fall 2018 Edition). Available online at URL = <https://plato.stanford.edu/archives/fall2018/entries/femapproach-analytic/>.

(Gefter, 2015). Gefter, A. "The Man Who Tried to Redeem the World With Logic." *Nautilus* (5 February 2015). Available online at URL = <https://getpocket.com/explore/item/the-man-who-tried-to-redeem-the-world-with-logic-835536698>.

(Gentzen, 1969). Gentzen, G. "Investigations into Logical Deduction." In G. Gentzen, *The Collected Papers of Gerhard Gentzen*. Trans. M. Szabo. Amsterdam: North Holland. Pp. 68-131.

(Gettier, 1963). Gettier, E. "Is Justified True Belief Knowledge?" *Analysis* 23: 121-123.

(Gewarth, 2016). Gewarth, R. *The Vanquished: Why the First World War Failed to End*. New York: Farrar, Strauss, and Giroux.

(Gödel, 1967). Gödel, K. "On Formally Undecidable Propositions of Principia Mathematica and Related Systems." In J. Van Heijenoort (ed.), *From Frege to Gödel*. Cambridge, MA: Harvard Univ. Press. Pp. 596-617.

(Goodman, 1983). Goodman, N. "The New Riddle of Induction." In N. Goodman, Fact, Fiction, and Forecast. 4th edn., Cambridge, MA: Harvard Univ. Press. Pp. 59-83.

(Grice and Strawson, 1956). Grice, H.P. and Strawson, P.F. "In Defense of a Dogma." Philosophical Review 65: 141-158.

(Griffin, 1991). Griffin, N. Russell's Idealist Apprenticeship. Oxford: Clarendon/Oxford Univ. Press.

(Gunther, 2003). Gunther, Y. (ed.) Essays on Non-Conceptual Content. Cambridge MA: MIT Press, 2003.

(Haack, 1993). Haack, S. Evidence and Inquiry: A Pragmatist Reconstruction of Epistemology. Amherst, NY: Prometheus Books.

(Haack, 1996). Haack, S. Deviant Logic, Fuzzy Logic. Chicago, IL: Univ. of Chicago Press.

(Haack, 2016). Haack, S. "Serious Philosophy." Against Professional Philosophy (28 July 2016). Available online at URL = <https://againstprofphil.org/2016/07/28/serious-philosophy-2/>.

(Haack, 2017a). Haack, S. "The Real Question: Can Philosophy Be Saved?" Free Inquiry (October/November 2017): 40-43.

(Haack, 2017b). Haack, S. Science and its Discontents. (Rounded Globe, 2017). Available online at URL = <https://roundedglobe.com/books/038f7053-e376-4fc3-87c5-096de820966d/Scientism%20and%20its%20Discontents/>.

(Haack, 2020), Haack, S. "Not One of the Boys: Memoirs of an Academic Misfit." Against Professional Philosophy (3 August 2020). Available online at IRL = <https://againstprofphil.org/2020/08/03/susan-haacks-not-one-of-the-boys-memoir-of-an-academic-misfit/>.

(Hacker, 1972). Hacker, P. Insight and Illusion: Wittgenstein on Philosophy and the Metaphysics of Experience. Oxford: Oxford Univ. Press, 1972.

(Hacker, 1986). Hacker, P. Insight and Illusion: Themes in the Philosophy of Wittgenstein. 2nd edn., Oxford: Clarendon/Oxford Univ. Press, 1986.

(Hacker, 1996). Hacker, P. Wittgenstein's Place in Twentieth-Century Analytic Philosophy. Oxford: Blackwell.

(Hacking, 1975). Hacking, I. *Why Does Language Matter to Philosophy?* Cambridge: Cambridge Univ. Press.

(Hallett, 1984). Hallett, M. *Cantorian Set Theory and Limitation of Size.* Oxford: Oxford Univ. Press.

(Hanna, 1983). Hanna, R. "Review of R. Rorty, The Consequences of Pragmatism." *Review of Metaphysics* 37: 140-143.

(Hanna, 1984). Hanna, R. "The Relation of Form and 'Stuff' in Husserl's Grammar of Pure Logic." *Philosophy and Phenomenological Research* 44 (1984): 323-341.

(Hanna, 1993a). Hanna, R. "Direct Reference, Direct Perception, and the Cognitive Theory of Demonstratives." *Pacific Philosophical Quarterly* 74: 96-117.

(Hanna, 1993b). Hanna, R. "Logical Cognition: Husserl's Prolegomena and the Truth in Psychologism." *Philosophy and Phenomenological Research* 53 (1993); 251-275.

(Hanna, 1997). Hanna, R. "Extending Direct Reference." *ProtoSociology: Special Volume on Cognitive Semantics I.* 10: 134-154.

(Hanna, 1998a). Hanna, R. "Conceptual Analysis." In E. Craig (ed.), *Routledge Encyclopedia of Philosophy.* 10 vols., London: Routledge. Vol. 2. Pp. 518-522.

(Hanna, 1998b). Hanna, R. "A Kantian Critique of Scientific Essentialism." *Philosophy and Phenomenological Research* 58 (1998): 497-528.

(Hanna, 2000). Hanna, R. "Why Gold is Necessarily a Yellow Metal." *Kantian Review* 4: 1-47.

(Hanna, 2001). Hanna, R. *Kant and the Foundations of Analytic Philosophy.* Oxford: Clarendon/Oxford Univ. Press.

(Hanna, 2005). Hanna, R. "Kant and Nonconceptual Content." *European Journal of Philosophy* 13: 247-290.

(Hanna, 2006a). Hanna, R. *Kant, Science, and Human Nature.* Oxford: Clarendon/Oxford Univ. Press.

(Hanna, 2006b). Hanna, R. "Rationality and the Ethics of Logic." *Journal of Philosophy* 103: 67-100.

(Hanna, 2006c). Hanna, R. *Rationality and Logic.* Cambridge: MIT Press.

(Hanna, 2007). Hanna, R. "Kant, Wittgenstein, and the Fate of Analysis." In M. Beaney (ed.), The Analytic Turn. London: Routledge. Pp. 145-167.

(Hanna, 2008a). Hanna, R. "Kantian Non-Conceptualism." Philosophical Studies 137: 41-64.

(Hanna, 2008b). Hanna, R. "Kant in the Twentieth Century." In D. Moran (ed.), Routledge Companion to Twentieth-Century Philosophy. London: Routledge. Pp. 149-203.

(Hanna, 2009a). Hanna, R. "Back to Kant: Teaching the First Critique as Contemporary Philosophy." APA Newsletter on Teaching Philosophy 8: 2-6. Available online at URL = <http://c.ymcdn.com/sites/www.apaonline.org/resource/collection/808CBF9D-D8E6-44A7-AE13-41A70645A525/v08n2Teaching.pdf>.

(Hanna, 2009b). Hanna, R. "Logic, Mathematics, and the Mind: A Critical Study of Richard Tiezen's Phenomenology, Logic, and the Philosophy of Mathematics." Notre Dame Journal of Formal Logic 50 (2009): 339-361.

(Hanna, 2011a). Hanna, R. "Beyond the Myth of the Myth: A Kantian Theory of Non-Conceptual Content." International Journal of Philosophical Studies 19: 321–396.

(Hanna, 2011b). Hanna, R. "Minding the Body." Philosophical Topics 39: 15-40.

(Hanna, 2011c). Hanna, R. "What is a 'Representation-in-Itself'? Kant, Bolzano, and Anti-Psychologism." Unpublished MS. Available online at URL = <https://www.academia.edu/13452551/What_is_a_Representation-in-Itself_Kant_Bolzano_and_Anti-Psychologism>.

(Hanna, 2013-2021). Against Professional Philosophy. Available online at URL = <https://againstprofphil.org/>.

(Hanna, 2013a). Hanna, R. "Kant, Hegel, and the Fate of Non-Conceptual Content." Hegel Society of Great Britain Bulletin 34: 1-32.

(Hanna, 2013b). Hanna, R. "Transcendental Idealism, Phenomenology, and the Metaphysics of Intentionality." In K. Ameriks and N. Boyle (eds.), The Impact of Idealism. 4 vols., Cambridge: Cambridge Univ. Press. Vol. I. Pp. 191-224.

(Hanna, 2013c). Hanna, R. "Nagel and Me: Beyond the Scientific Conception of the World." Unpublished MS, 2013. Available online at URL = <https://www.academia.edu/4348336/Nagel_and_Me_Beyond_the_Scientific_Conception_of_the_World>.

(Hanna, 2014a). Hanna, R. "If God's Existence is Unprovable, Then is Everything Permitted? Kant, Radical Agnosticism, and Morality." DIAMETROS 39: 26-69.

(Hanna, 2014b). Hanna, R. "What is the Nature of Inference?" In V. Hösle (ed.), Forms of Truth. Notre Dame, IN: Univ. of Notre Dame Press, 2014. Pp. 89-101.

(Hanna, 2015a). Hanna, R. Cognition, Content, and the A Priori: A Study in the Philosophy of Mind and Knowledge. THE RATIONAL HUMAN CONDITION, Vol. 5. Oxford: Oxford Univ. Press.

(Hanna, 2015b). Hanna, R. "Transcendental Normativity and the Avatars of Psychologism." In A. Stati (ed.), Husserl's Ideas I: New Commentaries and Interpretations. Berlin: De Gruyter. Pp. 51-67.

(Hanna, 2016a). Hanna, R., aka Z. "How the 'Continentals' Internalized Their Oppressors." Against Professional Philosophy (5 June 2016). Available online at URL = <https://againstprofphil.org/2016/06/05/how-the-continentals-internalized-their-oppressors/>.

(Hanna, 2016b). Hanna, R. "Kantian Madness: Blind Intuitions, Essentially Rogue Objects, Nomological Deviance, and Categorial Anarchy." Contemporary Studies in Kantian Philosophy 1 (2016): 44-64. Available online at URL = <http://www.cckp.space/#!Kantian-Madness-Blind-Intuitions-Essentially-Rogue-Objects-Nomological-Deviance-and-Categorial-Anarchy/cmbz/576018190cf2c6c572641509>.

(Hanna, 2017-2021). Hanna, R. Philosophy Without Borders. Available online at URL = <https://www.patreon.com/philosophywithoutborders>.

(Hanna, 2017a). Hanna, R. "Kant, Adorno, and Autonomy." Critique (2017). Available online in preview at URL = <https://www.academia.edu/44881739/Kant_Adorno_and_Autonomy_On_Martin_Shusters_Autonomy_After_Auschwitz_Critique_2017_>.

(Hanna, 2017b). Hanna, R. "Kant, the Copernican Devolution, and Real Metaphysics." In M. Altman (ed.), Kant Handbook. London: Palgrave Macmillan. Pp. 761-789.

(Hanna, 2017c). Hanna, R. "Kant, Radical Agnosticism, and Methodological Eliminativism about Things-in-Themselves." Contemporary Studies in Kantian Philosophy 2. Available online at URL = <https://www.cckp.space/single-post/2017/05/10/Kant-Radical-Agnosticism-and-Methodological-Eliminativism-about-Things-in-Themselves>.

(Hanna, 2017d). Hanna, R. "Kant's Theory of Judgment." In E.N. Zalta (ed.), The Stanford Encyclopedia of Philosophy (Winter 2017 Edition). Available online at URL = <https://plato.stanford.edu/archives/win2017/entries/kant-judgment/>.

(Hanna, 2017e). Hanna, R. "Life-Changing Metaphysics: Rational Anthropology and its Kantian Methodology." In G. D'Oro and S. Overgaard (eds.), The Cambridge Companion to Philosophical Methodology. Cambridge: Cambridge Univ. Press. Pp. 201-226.

(Hanna, 2018a). Hanna, R. Preface and General Introduction, Supplementary Essays, and General Bibliography. THE RATIONAL HUMAN CONDITION, Vol. 1. New York: Nova Science.

(Hanna, 2018b). Hanna, R. Deep Freedom and Real Persons: A Study in Metaphysics. THE RATIONAL HUMAN CONDITION, Vol. 2. New York: Nova Science.

(Hanna, 2018c). Hanna, R. Kantian Ethics and Human Existence. THE RATIONAL HUMAN CONDITION, Vol. 3. New York: Nova Science.

(Hanna, 2018d). Hanna, R. Kant, Agnosticism, and Anarchism: A Theological-Political Treatise. THE RATIONAL HUMAN CONDITION, Vol. 4. New York: Nova Science.

(Hanna, 2019). Hanna, R. "Kant's B Deduction, Cognitive Organicism, the Limits of Natural Science, and the Autonomy of Consciousness." Contemporary Studies in Kantian Philosophy 4: 29-46. Available online at URL = <https://www.cckp.spacesingle-post/2019/06/17/CSKP4-2019-Kant%E2%80%99s-B-Deduction-Cognitive-Organicism-the-Limits-of-Natural-Science-and-the-Autonomy-of-Consciousness>.

(Hanna, 2020a). Hanna, R. "Consequences of Consequences: Against Professional Philosophy, Anarcho- or Borderless Philosophy, and Rorty's Role." Borderless Philosophy 3: 39-84. Available online at URL = <https://www.cckp.space/single-post/2020/06/04/BP3-2020-Consequences-of-Consequences-Against-Professional-Philosophy-Anarcho--or-Borderless-Philosophy-and-Rorty%E2%80%99s-Role-pp-39-84>.

(Hanna, 2020b). Hanna, R. "How to Philosophize with a Hammer and a Blue Guitar: Quietism, Activism, and The Mind-Body Politic." Borderless Philosophy 3: 85-122. Available online at URL = <https://www.cckp.space/single-post/2020/06/04/BP3-2020-How-to-Philosophize-with-a-Hammer-and-a-Blue-Guitar-Quietism-Activism-and-The-Mind-Body-Politic-pp-85-122>.

(Hanna, 2020c). Hanna, R. "The Kant Wars and The Three Faces of Kant." Contemporary Studies in Kantian Philosophy 5: 73-94.

(Hanna, 2020d). Hanna, R. "The Organicist Conception of the World: A Manifesto." Unpublished MS.

(Hanna, 2021a). Hanna, R. "Can Physics Explain Physics? Anthropic Principles and Transcendental Idealism." In L. Caranti (ed.), Kant and The Problem of Knowledge in the Contemporary World. London: Routledge. Forthcoming. Also available online in preview at URL = <https://www.academia.edu/45586285/Can_Physics_Explain_Physics_Anthropic_Principles_and_Transcendental_Idealism_Final_draft_version_March_2021_>.

(Hanna, 2021b). Hanna, R. "The Debate About Non-Conceptual Content Revisited: On Corijn van Mazijk's Perception and Reality in Kant, Husserl, and McDowell." International Journal of Philosophical Studies 29: 90-115. Available online at URL = <https://www.tandfonline.com/doi/abs/10.1080/09672559.2021.1873543>.

(Hanna, 2021c). Hanna, R. THE END OF MECHANISM: An Apocalyptic Philosophy of Science. Unpublished MS. Available online at URL = <https://www.academia.edu/44630033/THE_END_OF_MECHANISM_An_Apocalyptic_Philosophy_of_Science_With_contributions_by_Michael_Cifone_Emre_Kazim_Andreas_Keller_and_Otto_Paans_January_2021_version_>.

(Hanna, 2021d). Hanna, R. FROM COSMOLOGY TO DIGNITY: A Theory of Life, the Universe, and Everything. Unpublished MS. Available online at URL = <https://www.academia.edu/45217233/FROM_COSMOLOGY_TO_DIGNITY_A_Theory_of_Life_the_Universe_and_Everything_Final_draft_version_March_2021_>.

(Hanna, 2021e). Hanna, R. "How to Complete Quantum Mechanics, Or, What It's Like To Be A Naturally Creative Bohmian Beable." Unpublished MS. Available online at URL = <https://www.academia.edu/49285300/How_to_Complete_Quantum_Mechanics_Or_What_Its_Like_To_Be_A_Naturally_Creative_Bohmian_Beable_July_2021_version_>.

(Hanna, 2021f). Hanna, R. "Jäsche Logic." In J. Wuerth (ed.), Cambridge Kant Lexicon. Cambridge: Cambridge Univ. Press, 2021. Pp. 707-711.

(Hanna, 2021g). Hanna, R. "The New Conflict of the Faculties: Kant, Radical Enlightenment, The Hyper-State, and How to Philosophize During a Pandemic." Con-Textos Kantianos 11: forthcoming. Also available online in preview at URL = <https://www.academia.edu/42632182/The_New_Conflict_of_the_Faculties_Kant_Radical_Enlightenment_The_Hyper_State_and_How_to_Philosophize_During_a_Pandemic_Final_draft_version_February_2021_>.

(Hanna, 2021h). Hanna, R. "Sensibility First: How to Interpret Kant's Theoretical and Practical Philosophy," Estudos Kantianos 9 (2021): 97-120. Available online at URL = <https://revistas.marilia.unesp.br/index.php/ek/article/view/12288>,

(Hanna, 2021i). Hanna, R. "The Incompleteness of Logic, the Incompleteness of Physics, and the Primitive Sourcehood of Rational Human Animals." Unpublished MS. Available online at URL = <https://www.academia.edu/49232541/The_Incompleteness_of_Logic_the_Incompleteness_of_Physics_and_the_Primitive_Sourcehood_of_Rational_Human_Animals_June_2021_version_>.

(Hanna and Maiese, 2009). Hanna, R. and Maiese, M. Embodied Minds in Action. Oxford: Oxford Univ. Press.

(Hanna and Paans, 2020). Hanna, R. and Paans, O. "This is the Way the World Ends: A Philosophy of Civilization Since 1900, and A Philosophy of the Future." Cosmos and History 16, 2: 1-58. Available online at URL = <http://cosmosandhistory.org/index.php/journal/article/viewFile/865/1510>.

(Hanna and Paans, 2021). Hanna, R. and Paans, O. "Thought-Shapers." Cosmos and History 17, 1: 1-72. Available online at URL = <http://cosmosandhistory.org/index.php/journal/article/view/923>.

(Harman, 1967a). Harman, G. "Quine on Meaning and Existence I." Review of Metaphysics 21: 124-151.

(Harman, 1967b). Harman, G. "Quine on Meaning and Existence II." Review of Metaphysics 21: 343-367.

(Harman, 1996). Harman, G. "Analyticity Regained?" Noûs 30: 392-400.

(Hegel, 1952). Hegel, G.W.F. Philosophy of Right. Trans. T.M. Knox. Oxford: Clarendon/Oxford Univ. Press.

(Heidegger, 1962). Heidegger, M. Being and Time. Trans. J. Macquarrie and E. Robinson. New York: Harper & Row.

(Heidegger, 1977). Heidegger, M. "What is Metaphysics?" In M. Heidegger, Martin Heidegger: Basic Writings. Trans. D.F. Krell. New York: Harper & Row. Pp. 95-112.

(Heidegger, 1984). Heidegger, M. The Metaphysical Foundations of Logic. Trans. M. Heim. Bloomington: Indiana Univ. Press.

(Heidegger, 1990). Heidegger, M. Kant and the Problem of Metaphysics. Trans. R. Taft. 4th edn., Bloomington, IN: Indiana Univ. Press.

(Heidemann, 2013). Heidemann, D. (ed.) Kant and Nonconceptual Content. London: Routledge.

(Heis, 2018). Heis, J. "Neo-Kantianism." In E.N. Zalta (ed.), The Stanford Encyclopedia of Philosophy (Summer 2018 Edition). Available online at URL = <https://plato.stanford.edu/archives/sum2018/entries/neo-kantianism/>.

(Hempel, 1959). Hempel, C. "The Empiricist Criterion of Meaning." In (Ayer, 1959). Pp. 108-129.

(Herman and Chomsky, 1988). Herman, E. and Chomsky, N. Manufacturing Consent: The Political Economy of the Mass Media. 2nd edn., New York: Pantheon.

(Hofmann, 2014). Hofmann, F. "Non-Conceptual Knowledge." Philosophical Issues 24: 184-208.

(Honneth, 2009). Honneth, A. "Idiosyncrasy As a Tool of Knowledge: Social Criticism in the Age of the Normalized Intellectual." In A. Honneth, Pathologies of Reason: On the Legacy of Critical Theory. Trans. J. Ingram et al. New York: Columbia Univ. Press. Pp. 179-192.

(Horgan, 1993). Horgan, T. "From Supervenience to Superdupervenience: Meeting the Demands of a Material World." Mind 102: 555-586.

(Horvath and Grundmann, 2012). Horvath, J. and Grundmann, T. (eds.), Experimental Philosophy and its Critics. London: Routledge.

(Hume, 1977). Hume, D. Enquiry Concerning Human Understanding. Indianapolis, IN: Hackett.

(Husserl, 1970a). Husserl, E. Logical Investigations. Trans. J.N. Findlay. 2 vols., London: Routledge & Kegan Paul.

(Husserl, 1970b). Husserl, E. The Crisis of European Sciences and Transcendental Phenomenology. Trans. D. Carr. Evanston, IL: Northwestern Univ. Press.

(Huxley, 2002). Huxley, T. "On the Hypothesis That Animals are Automata, and Its History." In (Chalmers, 2002). Pp. 24-30.

(Hylton, 1990). Hylton, P. Russell, Idealism, and the Emergence of Analytic Philosophy. Oxford: Clarendon/Oxford Univ. Press, 1990.

(Hylton, 2007). Hylton, P. Quine. London: Routledge.

(Ichikawa and Steup, 2018). Ichikawa, J. and Steup, M. "The Analysis of Knowledge." In E.N. Zalta (ed.), The Stanford Encyclopedia of Philosophy (Summer 2018 Edition). Available online at URL = <https://plato.stanford.edu/archives/sum2018/entries/knowledge-analysis/>.

(Isaac, 2013). Isaac, J. "Donald Davidson and the Analytic Revolution in American Philosophy, 1940-1970." Historical Journal 56: 757-779.

(Isaac, 2019). Isaac, J. "The Many Faces of Analytic Philosophy." In W. Breckman and P. Gordon (eds.), The Cambridge History of Modern European Thought. Cambridge: Cambridge Univ. Press. Pp. 176-199.

(Jackson, 1998). Jackson, F. From Metaphysics to Ethics: A Defense of Conceptual Analysis. Oxford: Oxford Univ. Press.

(James, 1903). James, W. "The Ph.D. Octopus." The Harvard Monthly Magazine (March 1903). Available online at URL = <https://www.uky.edu/~eushe2/Pajares/octopus.html>.

(James, 1950). James, W. Principles of Psychology. 2 vols., New York: Dover.

(Janik and Toulmin, 1973). Janik, A. and Toulmin, S. Wittgenstein's Vienna. New York: Simon & Schuster.

(Jencks, 2010). Jencks, C. "What then is Post-Modernism?" In C. Jencks (ed.), The Post-Modern Reader. Hoboken, NJ: John Wiley and Sons. Pp. 14–37.

(Judt, 1992). Judt, T. Past Imperfect: French Intellectuals 1944-1956. Berkeley & Los Angeles, CA: Univ. of California Press.

(Juhl and Loomis, 2010). Juhl, C. and Loomis, E. Analyticity. London: Routledge.

(Kanayama, 2017). Kanayama, Y. "The Birth of Philosophy as 哲學 (Tetsugaku) in Japan." Tetsugaku, 1: Philosophy and the University (2017). Available online at URL = <http://philosophy-japan.org/tetugaku/volume-1-2017-philosophy-and-the-university/>.

(Kaplan, 1978). Kaplan, D. "Dthat." In P. Cole (ed.), Syntax and Semantics 9: Pragmatics. New York: Academic Press. Pp. 221-223.

(Kaplan, 1989). Kaplan, D. "Demonstratives: An Essay on the Semantics, Logic, and Epistemology of Demonstratives and Other Indexicals." In J. Almog et al. (eds.), Themes from Kaplan. New York: Oxford Univ. Press. Pp. 481-614.

(Kato, 2017). Kato, Y. "The Crisis of the Humanities and Social Sciences in the Age of 'Innovation': Philosophy as a Critical Facilitator toward a 'Civic Turn' of the University." Tetsugaku, 1: Philosophy and the University (2017). Available online at URL = <http://philosophy-japan.org/tetugaku/volume-1-2017-philosophy-and-the-university/>.

(Katz, 1967). Katz, J. "Some Remarks on Quine on Analyticity." Journal of Philosophy 64: 36-52.

(Katz, 1981). Katz, J. Language and Other Abstract Objects. Totawa, NJ: Rowman & Littlefield.

(Katz, 1986). Katz, J. Cogitations. New York: Oxford Univ. Press.

(Katz, 1990). Katz, J. The Metaphysics of Meaning. Cambridge, MA: MIT Press.

(Katz, 1997). Katz, J. "Analyticity, Necessity, and the Epistemology of Semantics." Philosophy and Phenomenological Research 57: 1-28.

(Katz, 1998). Katz, J. Realistic Rationalism. Cambridge, MA: MIT Press. Pp. 72-74.

(Katzav, 2018). Katzav, J. "Analytic Philosophy, 1925-1969: Emergence, Management and Nature." British Journal for the History of Philosophy 26: 1197-1221.

(Katzav and Vaesen, 2017). Katzav, J. and Vaesen, K. "On the Emergence of American Analytic Philosophy." British Journal for the History of Philosophy 25: 772-798.

(Keller, 2018). Keller, A. "On the Use of the Term 'Continental Philosophy.'" Against Professional Philosophy (13 April 2018). Available online at URL = <https://againstprofphil.org/2018/04/13/on-the-use-of-the-term-continental-philosophy/>.

(Kent, 2013). Kent, S. (ed.) The Influenza Pandemic of 1918-1919: A Brief History with Documents. Boston, MA: Bedford/St. Martin's.

(Keynes, 1949). Keynes, J.M. "My Early Beliefs." In J.M. Keynes, Two Memoirs. London: R. Hart-Davis. Pp. 78-103.

(Kim, 1993). Kim, J. Supervenience and Mind. Cambridge MA: Cambridge Univ. Press.

(Kim, 1998). Kim, J. Philosophy of Mind. Boulder, CO: Westview.

(Kim, 2005). Kim, J. Physicalism, or Something Near Enough. Princeton, NJ: Princeton Univ. Press.

(Knobe and Nichols, 2008). Knobe, J. and Nichols, S. (eds.), Experimental Philosophy. Oxford: Oxford Univ. Press.

(Köhnke, 1991). Köhnke, K. The Rise of Neo-Kantianism. Trans. R. Hollingdale. Cambridge: Cambridge Univ. Press.

(Kolakowski, 1987). Kolakowski, L. Husserl and the Search for Certitude. Chicago, IL: Univ. of Chicago Press.

(Korsgaard, 2009). Korsgaard, C. Self-Constitution: Agency, Identity, and Integrity. Oxford: Oxford Univ. Press.

(Kriegel, 2013). Kriegel, U. (ed.) Phenomenal Intentionality. Oxford: Oxford Univ. Press.

(Kripke, 1980). Kripke, S. Naming and Necessity. 2nd edn, Cambridge, MA: Harvard Univ. Press.

(Kripke, 1982). Kripke, S. Wittgenstein on Rules and Private Language. Cambridge, MA: Harvard Univ. Press.

(Kripke, 1993). Kripke, S. "Identity and Necessity." In A. Moore (ed.), Meaning and Reference. Oxford: Oxford Univ. Press. Pp. 162-191.

(Kuhn, 1970). Kuhn, T. The Structure of Scientific Revolutions. 2nd edn., Chicago, IL: Univ. of Chicago Press.

(Kuklick, 1977). Kuklick, B. The Rise of American Philosophy. New Haven, CT: Yale Univ. Press.

(Kumar, 2010). Kumar, M. Quantum: Einstein, Bohr, and the Great Debate about the Nature of Reality. New York: W.W. Norton & Co.

(Kusch, 1995). Kusch, M. Psychologism. London: Routledge & Kegan Paul.

(Langford, 1952). Langford, C.H. "The Notion of Analysis in Moore's Philosophy." In (Schilpp, 1952). Pp. 321-342.

(Lear, 1982). Lear, J. "Leaving the World Alone." Journal of Philosophy 79: 382-403.

(Lear, 1986). Lear, J. "Transcendental Anthropology." In J. McDowell and P. Pettit (eds.), Subject, Context, and Thought. Oxford: Oxford Univ. Press. Pp. 267-298.

(Lear and Stroud, 1984). Lear, J. and Stroud, B. "The Disappearing 'We'." Proceedings of the Aristotelian Society, Supplementary Vol. 58: 219-258.

(Lehrer, 1990). Lehrer, K. Theory of Knowledge. London: Routledge.

(Levy, 1980). Levy, P. Moore: G.E. Moore and the Cambridge Apostles. New York: Holt, Rinehart and Winston.

(Lewis, 1918). Lewis, C.I. Survey of Symbolic Logic. Berkeley & Los Angeles: Univ. of California Press.

(Lewis, 1923). Lewis, C.I. "A Pragmatic Conception of the A Priori." Journal of Philosophy 20: 169-177.

(Lewis, 1956). Lewis, C.I. Mind and the World Order: Outline of a Theory of Knowledge. New York: Dover.

(Lewis, 1986). Lewis, D. On the Plurality of Worlds. Oxford: Blackwell.

(Lotze, 1888). Lotze, H. Logic. Trans. B. Bosanquet. 2nd edn., 2 vols., Oxford: Clarendon/Oxford Univ. Press.

(Lowe, 1985/1990). Lowe, V. Alfred North Whitehead: The Man and His Work. 2 vols., Baltimore, MD: Johns Hopkins Univ. Press.

(Lucas, 1961). Lucas, J.R. "Minds, Machines, and Gödel." Philosophy 36: 112-127.

(Luft and Capeillères, 2010). Luft, S. and Capeillères, F. "Neo-Kantianism in Germany and France." In K. Ansell-Pearson and A. Schrift (eds.), The History of Continental Philosophy Volume 3: The New Century. Durham, UK: Acumen. Pp. 47-85.

(Lukianoff and Haidt, 2015). "The Coddling of the American Mind. The Atlantic (September 2015). Available online at URL = <https://www.theatlantic.com/magazine/archive/2015/09/the-coddling-of-the-american-mind/399356/>.

(Lyotard, 1984). Lyotard, J.F. The Postmodern Condition: A Report on Knowledge. Minneapolis, MN: Univ. of Minnesota Press.

(Mabaquiao, 2021). Mabaquiao, N. "The Death of Philosophy Through the Naturalization of the Mind." Unpublished MS, 2021. Available online at URL = <https://www.academia.edu/21801066/The_Death_of_Philosophy_Through_the_Naturalization_of_the_Mind>.

(Macarthur, 2017). Macarthur, D. "Metaphysical Quietism and Everyday Life." In G. D'Oro and S. Overgaard (eds.), The Cambridge Companion to Philosophical Methodology. Cambridge: Cambridge Univ. Press. Pp. 249-273.

(Maddy, 2007). Maddy, P. Second Philosophy: A Naturalistic Method. Oxford: Oxford Univ. Press.

(Maher, 2012). Maher, C. The Pittsburgh School of Philosophy: Sellars, McDowell, Brandom. London; Routledge.

(Maiese and Hanna, 2019). Maiese, M. and Hanna, R. The Mind-Body Politic. London: Palgrave Macmillan.

(Mann, 2019). Mann, D. "The New Inquisitors." Against Professional Philosophy (4 March 2019). Available online at URL = <https://againstprofphil.org/2019/03/04/the-new-inquisitors/>.

(Marcus, 1978). Marcus, R. "Modalities and Intensional Languages." In I. Copi and J.A. Gould (eds.), Contemporary Philosophical Logic. New York: St. Martin's Press. Pp. 257-272.

(Marx, 1964). Marx, K. Karl Marx: Selected Writings in Sociology & Social Philosophy. Trans. T.B. Bottomore. New York: McGraw-Hill.

(Mayr, 1985). Mayr, E. The Growth of Biological Thought: Diversity, Evolution, and Inheritance. Cambridge, MA: Harvard Univ. Press.

(McCumber, 2001). McCumber, J. Time in the Ditch: American Philosophy and the McCarthy Era. Evanston, IL: Northwestern Univ. Press.

(McCumber, 2016). McCumber, J. The Philosophy Scare: The Politics of Reason in the Early Cold War. Chicago, IL: Univ. of Chicago Press.

(McDowell, 1994). McDowell, J. Mind and World. Cambridge MA: Harvard Univ. Press.

(McDowell, 2009a). McDowell, J. Having the World in View. Cambridge, MA: Harvard Univ. Press.

(McDowell, 2009b). McDowell, J. "Avoiding the Myth of the Given." In (McDowell, 2009a). Pp. 256-272.

(McDowell, 2009c). McDowell, J. "Intentionality as a Relation." In (McDowell, 2009a). Pp. 44-65.

(McDowell, 2013). McDowell, J. "Perceptual Experience: Both Relational and Contentful." European Journal of Philosophy 21: 144-157.

(McGrath and Frank, 2018). McGrath, M. and Frank, D. "Propositions." In E.N. Zalta (ed.), The Stanford Encyclopedia of Philosophy (Spring 2018 Edition), available online at URL = <https://plato.stanford.edu/archives/spr2018/entries/propositions/>.

(Meillassoux, 2008). Meillassoux, Q. After Finitude: An Essay on the Necessity of Contingency. Trans. R. Brassier. London: Routledge.

(Meinong, 1960). Meinong, A. "The Theory of Objects." Trans. R. Chisholm. In R. Chisholm (ed.), Realism and the Background of Phenomenology. Glencoe, NJ: Free Press. Pp. 76-117.

(Meinong, 1983). Meinong, A. On Assumptions. Trans. J. Heanue. Berkeley and Los Angeles, CA: Univ. of California Press.

(Menkin, 2021). Menkin, M. "Stop Alien Abductions." Personal Blog. Available online at URL = <http://www.stopabductions.com/>.

(Methven, 2015). Methven, S. Frank Ramsey and the Realistic Spirit. London: Palgrave Macmillan.

(Mills, 1956). Mills, C.W. The Power Elite. New York: Oxford Univ. Press.

(Milosz, 1955). Milosz, C. The Captive Mind. Trans. J. Bielonsky. New York: Vintage.

(Misak, 2020). Misak, C. Frank Ramsey: A Sheer Excess of Powers. Oxford: Oxford Univ. Press.

(Monk, 1990). Monk, R. Ludwig Wittgenstein: The Duty of Genius. London: Jonathan Cape.

(Monk, 1996). Monk, R. Bertrand Russell: The Spirit of Solitude. London: Jonathan Cape.

(Moore, 1899). Moore, G.E. "Review of B.A.W. Russell, Essay on the Foundations of Geometry." Mind 8: 397-405.

(Moore, 1903). Moore, G.E. Principia Ethica. Cambridge: Cambridge Univ. Press.

(Moore, 1922). Moore, G.E. Philosophical Studies. London: Kegan Paul, Trench, & Trubner.

(Moore, 1952). Moore, G.E. "Analysis." In (Schilpp, 1952). Pp. 660-667.

(Moore, 1953). Moore, G.E. "Sense Data." In G.E. Moore, Some Main Problems of Philosophy. London: George Allen & Unwin. Pp. 28-40.

(Moore, 1993a). Moore, G.E. G.E. Moore: Selected Writings. London: Routledge.

(Moore, 1993b). Moore, G.E. "The Nature of Judgment." In (Moore, 1993a). Pp. 1-19.

(Moore, 1993c). Moore, G.E. "The Refutation of Idealism." In (Moore, 1993a). Pp. 23-44.

(Moran, 2012). Moran, D. Husserl's Crisis of the European Sciences and Transcendental Phenomenology: An Introduction. Cambridge: Cambridge Univ. Press.

(Murakami, 2017). Murakami, Y. "Philosophy and Higher Education in Japan."Tetsugaku, 1: Philosophy and the University (2017). Available online at URL = <http://philosophy-japan.org/tetugaku/volume-1-2017-philosophy-and-the-university/>.

(Nagel, 2012). Nagel, T. Mind and Cosmos. Oxford: Oxford Univ. Press.

(Nakano, 2017). Nakano, H. "Is There Japanese/Latin American Philosophy?" A Reflection on Philosophy in University." Tetsugaku, 1: Philosophy and the University (2017). Available online at URL = <http://philosophy-japan.org/tetugaku/volume-1-2017-philosophy-and-the-university/>.

(Natorp, 1977). Natorp, P. "On the Question of Logical Method in Relation to Edmund Husserl's Prolegomena to Pure Logic." In J.N. Mohanty (ed.), Readings on Edmund Husserl's Logical Investigations. The Hague: Martinus Nijhoff. P. 57.

(Nelson, 2018). Nelson, E. "Dilthey and Carnap: The Feeling of Life, the Scientific Worldview, and the Elimination of Metaphysics." In J. Feichtinger et al., The Worlds of Positivism: A Global Intellectual History. London: Palgrave Macmillan. Pp. 321-346.

(New York Times Staff, 2000). New York Times Staff. "Donald Kalish, 80, a Vietnam-Era Protest Leader [Dies]." The New York Times (18 June 2000). Available online at URL = <https://www.nytimes.com/2000/06/18/world/donald-kalish-80-a-vietnam-era-protest-leader.html>.

(Nicholson and Dupré, 2018). Nicholson, D.J. and Dupré, J. (eds.) Everything Flows: Towards a Processual Philosophy of Biology. Oxford, Oxford Univ. Press.

(Nicolis and Prigogine, 1977). Nicolis, G. and Prigogine, I. Self-Organization in Nonequilibrium Systems. New York: Wiley.

(Nishiyama, 2017). Nishiyama, Y. "What Remains of Philosophers' Reflections on University?" Tetsugaku, 1: Philosophy and the University (2017). Available online at URL = <http://philosophy-japan.org/tetugaku/volume-1-2017-philosophy-and-the-university/>.

(Numminen, 2021). Numminen, M.A. "Wovon man nicht sprechen kann, darüber muss man schweigen." You Tube. Available online at URL = <https://www.youtube.com/watch?v= 57PWqFowq-4>.

(O'Shea, 2019). O'Shea, J. "Review of Kantian Nonconceptualism." Notre Dame Philosophical Reviews (7 January 2019). Available online at URL = https://ndpr.nd.edu/news/kantian-nonconceptualism/>.

(Ostertag, 1998). Ostertag, G. (ed.) Definite Descriptions: A Reader. Cambridge, MA: MIT Press.

(Paans, 2020). Paans, O. "Postmodernity and the Politics of Fragmentation." Borderless Philosophy 3. Available online at URL = <https://www.cckp.space/single-post/2020/06/04/BP3-2020-Otto-Paans-%E2%80%9CPostmodernity-and-the-Politics-of-Fragmentation%E2%80%9D-264-310>.

(Pap, 1958). Pap, A. Semantics and Necessary Truth. New Haven, CT: Yale Univ. Press.

(Pap, 1972). Pap, A. Elements of Analytic Philosophy. 2nd edn., New York: Hafner.

(Papazoglou, 2012). Papazoglou, A. "Philosophy, Its Pitfalls, Some Rescue Plans and Their Complications." Metaphilosophy 43: 1-18.

(Passmore, 1967). Passmore, J. "Logical Positivism." In P. Edwards, (ed.), The Encyclopedia of Philosophy. 8 vols., New York: MacMillan. Vol. 5. Pp. 52-57.

(Pears, 1987). Pears, D. The False Prison: A Study of the Development of Wittgenstein's Philosophy. 2 vols., Oxford: Clarendon/Oxford Univ. Press.

(Penrose, 1990). Penrose, R. The Emperor's New Mind. Oxford: Oxford Univ. Press.

(Perry, 1979). Perry, J. "The Problem of the Essential Indexical," Noûs 13: 3-21.

(Potter, 1990). Potter, M. Sets: An Introduction. Oxford: Clarendon/Oxford Univ. Press.

(Potter, 2000). Potter, M. Reason's Nearest Kin: Philosophies of Arithmetic from Kant to Carnap. Oxford: Clarendon/Oxford Univ. Press.

(Potter, 2009). Potter, M. Wittgenstein's Notes on Logic. Oxford: Oxford Univ. Press.

(Potter, 2019). Potter, M. The Rise of Analytic Philosophy, 1879–1930: From Frege to Ramsey. London: Routledge.

(Priest, 1987). Priest, G. In Contradiction. Dordrecht: Martinus Nijhoff.

(Priest, 1998). Priest, G. "What Is So Bad About Contradictions?" Journal of Philosophy 95: 410-426.

(Priest, 2001). Priest, G. An Introduction to Non-Classical Logic. Cambridge: Cambridge Univ. Press.

(Priest, 2002). Priest, G. Beyond the Limits of Thought. 2nd edn., Oxford: Oxford Univ. Press.

(Prigogine, 1997). Prigogine, I. The End of Certainty: Time's Flow and the Laws of Nature. New York: The Free Press.

(Prigogine and Stengers, 1984). Prigogine, I. and Stengers, E. Order Out of Chaos. New York: Bantam.

(Pritchard, 2012). Pritchard, D. "Anti-Luck Virtue Epistemology." Journal of Philosophy 109: 247-279.

(Proust, 1989). Proust, J. Questions of Form: Logic and the Analytic Proposition from Kant to Carnap. Trans. A. Brenner. Minneapolis, MN: Univ. of Minnesota Press.

(Putnam, 1975a). Putnam, H. Mind, Language, and Reality: Philosophical Papers, Vol.2. Cambridge: Cambridge Univ. Press.

(Putnam, 1975b). Putnam, H. "The Analytic and the Synthetic." In (Putnam, 1975a). Pp. 33-69.

(Putnam, 1975c). Putnam, H. "Brains and Behavior." In (Putnam, 1975a). Cambridge: Cambridge Univ. Press, 1975. Pp. 325-341.

(Putnam, 1975d). Putnam, H. "The Meaning of 'Meaning.'" In (Putnam, 1975a). Pp. 215-271.

(Putnam, 1979). Putnam, H. "It Ain't Necessarily So." In H. Putnam, Mathematics, Matter, and Method: Philosophical Papers, Vol. 1. 2nd edn., Cambridge: Cambridge Univ. Press. Pp. 237-249.

(Putnam, 1983). Putnam, H. "There is at Least One A Priori Truth." In H. Putnam, Realism and Reason: Philosophical Papers, Vol. 3. Cambridge: Cambridge Univ. Press. Pp. 98-114.

(Putnam, 1990a). Putnam, H. Realism with a Human Face. Cambridge, MA: Harvard Univ. Press.

(Putnam, 1990b). Putnam, H. "Is Water Necessarily H2O?" In (Putnam, 1990a). Pp. 54-79.

(Putnam, 1996). Putnam, H. "Meaning and Reference." In A.P. Martinich (ed.), Philosophy of Language. 3rd edn., New York: Oxford Univ. Press. Pp. 284-291.

(Putnam, 1994). Putnam, H. Words and Life. Cambridge, MA: Harvard Univ. Press.

(Putnam 1999). Putnam, H. The Threefold Cord: Mind, Body, and World. New York: Columbia Univ. Press.

(Quine, 1960). Quine, W.V.O Word and Object. Cambridge: MIT Press.

(Quine, 1961a). W.V.O. Quine, From a Logical Point of View. 2nd edn., New York: Harper & Row.

(Quine, 1961b). Quine, W.V.O. "Two Dogmas of Empiricism." In (Quine, 1961a). Pp. 20-46.

(Quine, 1961c). "Reference and Modality." In (Quine, 1961a). Pp. 139-159.

(Quine, 1969a). Quine, W.V.O. Ontological Relativity. New York: Columbia Univ. Press.

(Quine, 1969b). W.V.O. "Epistemology Naturalized." In (Quine, 1969a). Pp. 69-90.

(Quine, 1969c). Quine, W.V.O. "Ontological Relativity." In (Quine, 1969a). Pp. 26-68.

(Quine, 1976a). Quine, W.V.O. The Ways of Paradox. 2nd edn., Cambridge, MA: MIT Press.

(Quine, 1976b). Quine, W.V.O. "Carnap and Logical Truth." In (Quine, 1976a). Pp. 107-132.

(Quine, 1976c). Quine, W.V.O. "Truth by Convention." In (Quine, 1976a). Pp. 77-106.

(Quine, 1976d). Quine, W.V.O. "The Ways of Paradox." In (Quine, 1976a). Pp. 1-18.

(Quine, 1986). Quine, W.V.O. Philosophy of Logic. 2nd edn., Cambridge, MA: Harvard Univ. Press.

(Rachels and Rachels, 2015). Rachels, J. and Rachels, S. The Elements of Moral Philosophy. 8th edn., New York: McGraw-Hill.

(Reddebrek, 2016). Reddebrek. "The Anarchism of Jean Vigo." Anarchy: A Journal of Anarchist Ideas 6 (4 June 2016). Available online at URL = <https://libcom.org/library/anarchism-jean-vigo>.

(Reichenbach, 1951). Reichenbach, H. The Rise of Scientific Philosophy. Berkeley & Los Angeles, CA: Univ. of California Press.

(Reisch, 2005). Reisch, G. How the Cold War Transformed Philosophy of Science: To the Icy Slopes of Logic. Cambridge: Cambridge Univ. Press.

(Richardson, 1998). Richardson, A. Carnap and the Construction of the World. Cambridge: Cambridge Univ. Press.

(Robinson, 1956). Robinson, J. "Review of The Poverty of Philosophy, by Karl Marx." Economic Journal 66: 334–335.

(Rorty, 1967a). Rorty, R. (ed.), The Linguistic Turn. Chicago, IL: Univ. of Chicago Press.

(Rorty, 1967b). Rorty. R. "Introduction: Metaphilosophical Difficulties of Linguistic Philosophy." In (Rorty, 1967a). Pp. 1-39.

(Rorty, 1979). Rorty, R. Philosophy and the Mirror of Nature. Princeton, NJ: Princeton Univ. Press.

(Rorty, 1982a). Rorty, R. Consequences of Pragmatism. Minneapolis, MN: Univ. of Minnesota Press.

(Rorty, 1982b). Rorty, R. "Philosophy in America Today." In (Rorty, 1982a). Pp. 211-230.

(Rorty, 1983). Rorty, R. "Postmodernist Bourgeois Liberalism." Journal of Philosophy 80: 583-589.

(Rorty, 1994). Rorty, R. "The Unpatriotic Academy." The New York Times (13 February 1994). Available online at URL = <https://www.nytimes.com/1994/02/13/opinion/the-unpatriotic-academy.html>.

(Royce, 1970). Royce, R. The Letters of Josiah Royce. Chicago, IL: Univ. of Chicago Press.

(Russell, 1914.) Russell, B. Our Knowledge of the External World. London: Allen & Unwin.

(Russell, 1945). Russell, B. A History of Western Philosophy. New York: Simon & Schuster.

(Russell, 1959). Russell, B. My Philosophical Development. London: Allen and Unwin.

(Russell, 1971a). Russell, B. Logic and Knowledge. New York: G.P. Putnam's Sons.

(Russell, 1971b). Russell, B. "On Denoting." In B. Russell, Logic and Knowledge. New York: G. P. Putnam's Sons, 1971. Pp. 41–56.

Russell, 1971c). Russell, B. "Mathematical Logic as Based on the Theory of Types." In Russell, Logic and Knowledge, pp. 59-102.

(Russell, 1971c). Russell, B. "The Philosophy of Logical Atomism." In Russell, Logic and Knowledge, pp. 177-281.

(Russell, 1973a). Russell, B. Essays in Analysis. New York: George Braziller.

(Russell, 1973b) Russell, B. "Meinong's Theory of Complexes and Assumptions." In (Russell, 1973a). Pp. 21-76.

(Russell, 1973c). Russell, B. "On the Nature of Truth and Falsehood." In (Russell, 1973a). Pp. 147-159.

(Russell, 1975). Russell, B. Autobiography. London: Unwin.

(Russell, 1981). Russell, B. "Knowledge by Acquaintance and Knowledge by Description." In B. Russell, Mysticism and Logic. Totowa, NJ: Barnes and Noble. Pp. 152-167.

(Russell, 1992). Russell, B. Theory of Knowledge: The 1913 Manuscript. London: Routledge.

(Russell, 1993). Russell, B. Introduction to Mathematical Philosophy. London: Routledge.

(Russell, 1995). Russell, B. The Problems of Philosophy. Indianapolis, IN: Hackett.

(Russell, 1996). Russell, B. Principles of Mathematics. 2nd edn., New York: W.W. Norton.

(Russell, 2008). Russell, Gillian. Truth in Virtue of Meaning. Oxford: Oxford Univ. Press.

(Ryle, 1963). Ryle, G. The Concept of Mind. Harmondsworth, UK: Penguin.

(Schilpp, 1952). Schilpp, P. (ed.) The Philosophy of G.E. Moore The Philosophy of G.E. Moore. 2nd edn., New York: Tudor.

(Schilpp, 1963). Schilpp, P. (ed.), The Philosophy of Rudolf Carnap. La Salle, IL: Open Court.

(Schlick, 1949). Schlick, M. "Is There a Factual A Priori?" In H. Feigl and W. Sellars (eds.), Readings in Philosophical Analysis. New York: Appleton-Century Crofts. Pp. 277-285.

(Schmidt, 2000). Schmidt, J. Disciplined Minds: A Critical Look at Salaried Professionals and the Soul-Battering System that Shapes their Lives. New York: Rowman & Littlefield.

(Schopenhauer, 2014). Schopenhauer, A. "On University Philosophy." Trans. S. Roehr and C. Janaway. In A. Schopenhauer, Parerga and Paralipomena: Short Philosophical Essays. Cambridge: Cambridge Univ. Press. Pp. 125-176.

(Schuessler, 2013). Schuessler, J. "Philosophy That Stirs the Waters." The New York Times (29 April 2013). Available online at URL = <http://www.nytimes.com/2013/04/30/books/daniel-dennett-author-of-intuition-pumps-and-other-tools-for-thinking.html?emc=eta1&_r=0>.

(Schulting, 2016). Schulting, D. (ed.) Kantian Nonconceptualism. London: Palgrave-Macmillan.

(Schuringa, 2020). Schuringa, C. "The Never-Ending Death of Analytic Philosophy." Noteworthy: The Journal-Blog (28 May 2020). Available online at URL = <https://blog.usejournal.com/the-never-ending-death-of-analytic-philosophy-1507c4207f93>.

(Scott, 1998). Scott, J.C. Seeing Like a State: How Certain Schemes to Improve the Human Condition Have Failed. New Haven CT, Yale Univ. Press.

(Searle, 1969). Searle, J. Speech Acts. Cambridge: Cambridge Univ. Press.

(Sellars, 1963a). Sellars, W. Science, Perception, and Reality. London: Routledge & Kegan Paul.

(Sellars, 1963b). Sellars, W. "Empiricism and the Philosophy of Mind." In (Sellars, 1963a). Pp.127-196.

(Sellars, 1963c). Sellars, W. "Philosophy and the Scientific Image of Man." Pp. 1-40.

(Sellars, 1975). Sellars, W. "Autobiographical Reflections." In H-N. Castañeda (ed.), Action, Knowledge, and Reality: Critical Studies in Honor of Wilfrid Sellars. Indianapolis, IN: The Bobbs-Merrill Company, Inc., 1975.

(Sheffer, 1926). Sheffer, H.M. "Review of Principia Mathematica, Volume I, second edition." Isis 8: 226-231.

(Shelley, 1818). Shelley, M. Frankenstein; Or, the Modern Prometheus. Available online at URL = <http://www.rc.umd.edu/editions/frankenstein>.

(Shope, 1983). Shope, R. The Analysis of Knowing: A Decade of Research. Princeton, NJ: Princeton Univ. Press.

(Sider, 2011). Sider, T. Writing the Book of the World. Oxford: Oxford Univ. Press.

(Simons, 2010). Simons, P. "The Origins and Evitability of the Analytic-Continental Rift." International Journal of Philosophical Studies 9: 295-311.

(SK, 2016). SK. "An Insider's View of the Brazilian Philosophical World, Or, How to Build a Really Totalitarian System." Against Professional Philosophy (7 April 2016). Available online at URL = <http://againstprofphil.org/an-insiders-view-of-the-brazilian-philosophical-world-or-how-to-build-a-really-totalitarian-system/>.

(Sluga, 1980). Sluga, H. Gottlob Frege. London: Routledge & Kegan Paul.

(Sluga, 1993). Sluga, H. Heidegger's Crisis: Philosophy and Politics in Nazi Germany, Cambridge MA, Harvard Univ. Press.

(Smithies, 2013a). Smithies, D. "The Nature of Cognitive Phenomenology." Philosophy Compass 8: 744-754.

(Smithies, 2013b). Smithies, D. "The Significance of Cognitive Phenomenology." Philosophy Compass 8: 731-743.

(Soames, 2003). Soames, S. Philosophical Analysis in the Twentieth Century. 2 vols., Princeton, NJ: Princeton Univ. Press.

(Solomon, 1974). Solomon, R. (ed.) Existentialism. New York: The Modern Library/McGraw-Hill.

(Sosa, 2001). Sosa, E. "Human Knowledge, Animal and Reflective." Philosophical Studies 106: 193-196.

(Sosa, 2007). Sosa, E. A Virtue Epistemology. Oxford: Oxford Univ. Press.

(Sosa, 2009). Sosa, E. Reflective Knowledge. Oxford: Oxford Univ. Press.

(Speaks, 2005). Speaks, J. "Is There a Problem about Nonconceptual Content?" Philosophical Review 114: 359-398.

(Stanley, 2005). Stanley, J. Knowledge and Practical Interests. Oxford: Clarendon/Oxford Univ. Press.

(Stern, 2019). Stern, R. "Transcendental Arguments." In E.N. Zalta (ed.), The Stanford Encyclopedia of Philosophy (Summer 2019 Edition). Available online at URL = <https://plato.stanford.edu/archives/sum2019/entries/transcendental-arguments/>.

(Steup and Neta, 2020). Steup, M. and Neta, R. "Epistemology." In E.N. Zalta (ed.) The Stanford Encyclopedia of Philosophy (Fall 2020 Edition). Available online at URL = <https://plato.stanford.edu/archives/fall2020/entries/epistemology/>.

(Steward, 2012). Steward, H. A Metaphysics for Freedom. Oxford: Oxford Univ. Press.

(Strachan, 2005). Strachan, H. The First World War. London: Penguin.

(Strawson, 1957). Strawson, P.F. "Propositions, Concepts, and Logical Truths." Philosophical Quarterly 7: 15-25.

(Strawson, 1959). Strawson, P.F. Individuals: An Essay in Descriptive Metaphysics. London: Methuen.

(Strawson, 1966). Strawson, P.F. The Bounds of Sense. London: Methuen.

(Strawson, 1992). Strawson, P.F. Analysis and Metaphysics: An Introduction to Philosophy. Oxford: Oxford Univ. Press.

(Stroud, 1968). Stroud, B. "Transcendental Arguments." Journal of Philosophy 65: 241-256.

(Stroud, 1984). Stroud, B. The Significance of Philosophical Skepticism. Oxford: Clarendon/Oxford Univ. Press.

(Tait, 2010). Tait, W. "Gödel on Intuition and Hilbert's Finitism." In S. Feferman, C. Parsons, and S. Simpson, (eds.), Kurt Gödel: Essays for His Centennial. Cambridge: Association For Symbolic Logic, Lecture Notes in Logic. Vol. 33. Pp. 88-108.

(Tarski, 1943). Tarski, A. "The Semantic Conception of Truth and the Foundations of Semantics." Philosophy and Phenomenological Research 4: 342–360.

(Tarski, 1956). Tarski, A. "The Concept of Truth in Formalized Languages." In A. Tarski, Logic, Semantics, and Metamathematics. Oxford: Oxford University Press. Pp. 152–278.

(Thompson, 2007). Thompson, E. Mind in Life. Cambridge MA: Harvard Univ. Press.

(Torday, Miller Jr, and Hanna, 2020). Torday, J.S., Miller Jr, W.B., and Hanna, R. "Singularity, Life, and Mind: New Wave Organicism." In J.S. Torday and W.B. Miller Jr, The Singularity of Nature: A Convergence of Biology, Chemistry and Physics. Cambridge: Royal Society of Chemistry. Ch. 20. Pp. 206-246.

(Tugendhat, 1982). Tugendhat, E. Traditional and Analytical Philosophy. Trans. P.A. Gorner. Cambridge: Cambridge Univ. Press.

(Turing, 1936). Turing, A. "On Computable Numbers, with an Application to the Entscheidungsproblem." Proceedings of the London Mathematical Society, series 2, 42: 230-265, with corrections in 43: 644-546.

(Turing, 1950). Turing, A. "Computing Machinery and Intelligence." Mind 59: 433–460.

(Turner, 2019). Turner, S. "Beyond the Academic Ethic." In F. Cannizzo and N. Osbaldston (eds.), The Social Structures of Global Academia. London/New York: Routledge. Pp. 35-52.

(Unamuno, 2005). Unamuno, M. The Tragic Sense of Life. Available online at URL = <http://www.gutenberg.org/files/14636/14636-h/14636-h.htm>.

(Unger, 2014). Unger, P. Empty Ideas: A Critique of Analytic Philosophy. Oxford: Oxford University Press.

(Urmson, 1956). Urmson, J.O. Philosophical Analysis: Its Development between the Two World Wars. Oxford: Oxford Univ. Press.

(Van Cleve, 1999). Van Cleve, J. Problems from Kant. Oxford: Oxford Univ. Press.

(Varela, 1979). Varela, F. Principles of Biological Autonomy. New York: Elsevier/North Holland.

(Varela, Maturana, and Uribe, 1974). Varela, F., Maturana, H., and Uribe, R. "Autopoiesis: the Organization of Living Systems, its Characterization and a Model." Currents in Modern Biology 5: 187-196.

(Vargas, 2007). Vargas, M. "Real Philosophy, Metaphilosophy, and Metametaphilosophy: On the Plight of Latin American Philosophy." CR: The New Centennial Review 7: 51-78.

(Vargas, 2010). Vargas, M. "On the Value of Philosophy: The Latin American Case," Comparative Philosophy 1: 33-52.

(Veisdal, 2020). Veisdal, J. "Cantor's Diagonal Argument." Medium (6 July 2020). Available online at URL = <https://medium.com/cantors-paradise/cantors-diagonal-argument-c594eb1cf68f>.

(Vienna Circle, 1996). Vienna Circle, The. "The Scientific Conception of the World." In S. Sarkar (ed.), The Emergence of Logical Empiricism: From 1900 to The Vienna Circle. New York: Garland Publishing. Pp. 321–340.

(Von Wright, 1984). Von Wright, G.H. "Biographical Sketch of Wittgenstein." In N. Malcolm, Ludwig Wittgenstein: A Memoir, with a Biographical Sketch by G.H. Von Wright. Oxford: Oxford Univ. Press. Pp. 3-20.

(Vrahimis, 2012). Vrahimis, A. "Modernism and The Vienna Circle's Critique of Heidegger." Critical Quarterly 54: 61-83.

(Vrahimis, 2015). Vrahimis, A. "Legacies of German Idealism: From The Great War to the Analytic/Continental Divide." Parrhesia 24: 83-106.

(Vrahamis, 2019). Vrahimis, A. "The 'Analytic'/'Continental' Divide and the Question of Philosophy's Relation to Literature." Philosophy and Literature 43: 253-269.

(Vrahimis, forthcoming). Vrahimis, A. "Russell Reads Bergson." In M. Sinclair and Y. Wolf (eds.), The Bergsonian Mind. London, Routledge. Also available online in preview at URL = <https://www.academia.edu/41702088/Russell_Reads_Bergson>.

(Waismann, 1979). Waismann, F. Wittgenstein and The Vienna Circle. Trans. J. Schulte and B. McGuinness. New York: Harper and Row.

(Ward, 1911). Ward, J. "Psychology." In Encyclopedia Britannica. 11th edn., 29 vols., New York: Encyclopedia Britannica Co. Vol. xxii. Pp. 547-604.

(Weber and Varela, 2002). Weber, A. and Varela, F. "Life After Kant: Natural Purposes and the Autopoietic Foundations of Biological Individuality." Phenomenology and the Cognitive Sciences 1: 97-125.

(Weinberg, 2005). Weinberg, G. A World at Arms: A Global History of World War II. 2nd edn., Cambridge, Cambridge Univ. Press.

(White, 1950). White, M. "The Analytic and the Synthetic: An Untenable Dualism." In S. Hook (ed.), John Dewey: Philosopher of Science and Freedom. New York: Dial Press. Pp. 316-330.

(Whitehead, 1971). Whitehead, A.N. Science and the Modern World. Cambridge: Cambridge Univ. Press.

(Whitehead, 1978). Whitehead, A.N. Process and Reality: An Essay in Cosmology. Corrected edn., Cambridge: Cambridge University Press.

(Whitehead and Russell, 1962). Whitehead, A.N. and Russell, B. Principia Mathematica to *56. 2nd edn., Cambridge: Cambridge Univ. Press.

(Willey, 1978). Willey, T. Back to Kant: The Revival of Kantianism in German Social and Historical Thought, 1860-1914. Detroit, MI: Wayne State Univ. Press.

(Williams, 1981). Williams, B. "Wittgenstein and Idealism." In B. Williams, Moral Luck: Philosophical Papers 1973-1980. Cambridge: Cambridge Univ. Press. Pp. 144-163.

(Williamson, 2000). Williamson, T. Knowledge and its Limits. Oxford: Oxford Univ. Press.

(Williamson, 2007). Williamson, T. The Philosophy of Philosophy. Oxford: Blackwell.

(Williamson, 2013). Williamson, T. Modal Logic as Metaphysics. Oxford: Oxford Univ. Press.

(Wilshire, 2002). Wilshire, B. Fashionable Nihilism: A Critique of Analytic Philosophy. Albany, NY: SUNY Press, 2002.

(Wittgenstein, 1953). Wittgenstein, L. Philosophical Investigations. Trans. G.E.M. Anscombe. New York: Macmillan.

(Wittgenstein, 1972). Wittgenstein, L. On Certainty. Trans. D. Paul and G.E.M. Anscombe. New York: Harper and Row.

(Wittgenstein, 1978). Wittgenstein, L. "On Heidegger on Being and Dread." In M. Murray (ed.), Heidegger and Modern Philosophy. New Haven, CT: Yale Univ. Press. Pp. 80-81.

(Wittgenstein, 1979a). Wittgenstein, L. Notebooks 1914-1916. Trans. G.E.M. Anscombe. 2nd edn., Chicago, IL: Univ. of Chicago Press.

(Wittgenstein, 1979b). Wittgenstein, L. "Notes on Logic." In (Wittgenstein, 1979a). Appendix I. Pp. 93-107.

(Wittgenstein, 1980). Wittgenstein, L. Culture and Value. Trans. P. Winch. Chicago, IL: Univ. of Chicago Press.

(Wittgenstein, 1981). Wittgenstein, L. Tractatus Logico-Philosophicus. Trans. C.K. Ogden. London: Routledge & Kegan Paul.

(Wolchover, 2020). Wolchover, N. "Does Time Really Flow? New Clues Come From a Century-Old Approach to Math." Quanta (7 April 2020). Available online at URL = <https://www.quantamagazine.org/does-time-really-flow-new-clues-come-from-a-century-old-approach-to-math-20200407/>.

(Z, 2013-2021). Z (aka R. Hanna). Against Professional Philosophy. Available online at URL = <https://againstprofphil.org/>.

(Z, 2017a). Z (aka R. Hanna). "Il Faut Cultiver Notre Jardin." Against Professional Philosophy. (20 February 2017). Available online at URL = <https://againstprofphil.org/2017/02/20/il-faut-cultiver-notre-jardin/>.

(Z, 2017b). Z (aka R. Hanna). "Philosophy Unbound." Against Professional Philosophy (2 July 2017). Available online at URL = <https://againstprofphil.org/2017/07/02/philosophy-unbound/>.

Born and raised in Canada, Robert Hanna received his PhD from Yale University USA in 1989 and has held international research or teaching positions at the University of Cambridge UK, Yale USA, the University of Luxembourg LU, PUC-PR BR, and York University CA.

Currently, Hanna is an independent philosopher, Co-Director of the online philosophy mega-project, Philosophy Without Borders, and Director of The Contemporary Kantian Philosophy Project.

Outside of his philosophical interests, Hanna is a cinephile, obsessive (re)reader of nineteenth century fiction and history, and long-distance walker, walking two-hours every day alongside mountains or oceans.

Contact the author or read the full bio on thmaduco.org:

For any related live events or collaborations, please contact The Mad Duck Coalition through its contact form.

Author Recommendations

Rutger Bregman
Humankind: A Hopeful History

David Edmonds
The Murder of Professor Schlick: The Rise and Fall of The Vienna Circle

Arran Gare
Philosophical Foundations of Ecological Civilization: A Manifesto for the Future

John McCumber
Time in the Ditch: American Philosophy and the McCarthy Era
&
The Philosophy Scare: The Politics of Reason in the Early Cold War

Thomas Nagel
Mind and Cosmos

Jeff Schmidt
Disciplined Minds: A Critical Look at Salaried Professionals and the Soul-Battering System that Shapes their Lives

And the special works of his fellow mad ducks.

Concluding Note

Thank you so much for purchasing this work! Your support allows us to continue to avoid resorting to anti-consumer DRM practices and encourages our authors, not just this one, to continue following their passions and producing intellectually stimulating works. It also enables us to provide special programs for supporters like you!

One of our programs is a special discount for reviews, positive and negative! We believe that even negative feedback is vital feedback, so you should say what you really think. For more information about our review program, contact us through our contact form and select the appropriate category. In short, if the thought of supporting the authors and our jolly little coalition isn't enough to move you, we offer 5% off your next order for each review you post, with limitations obviously. So send us a message!

Information about our other programs and offers can be found on our website, including but not limited to: complimentary copies, contests, and collaborations.

Please reach out for further information. If you couldn't tell, we like to...*quack!!!*

The Mad Duck Coalition

The Mad Duck Coalition publishing house is a group of innovative intellectuals who want to publish what they are passionate about without compromising themselves or their work solely in the hopes of being published.

As such, The MDC publishes quality works that intellectually stimulate the mind, not necessarily the pockets. We wholeheartedly believe that quality and commerciality are two different things and that quality is far more important.

Check us out at thmaduco.org: